Global Perspectives on the Psychology of Terrorism

Nika Chitadze
International Black Sea University, Georgia

IGI Global
PUBLISHER of TIMELY KNOWLEDGE

A volume in the Advances in Digital Crime, Forensics, and Cyber Terrorism (ADCFCT) Book Series

Published in the United States of America by
IGI Global
Information Science Reference (an imprint of IGI Global)
701 E. Chocolate Avenue
Hershey PA, USA 17033
Tel: 717-533-8845
Fax: 717-533-8661
E-mail: cust@igi-global.com
Web site: http://www.igi-global.com

Library of Congress Cataloging-in-Publication Data

Names: Chitadze, Nika, 1969- editor.
Title: Global perspectives on the psychology of terrorism / Nika Chitadze, editor.
Description: Hershey, PA : Information Science Reference, [2023] | Includes bibliographical references and index. | Summary: "This book presents the study of the topic "psychology of terrorism" which is especially relevant in connection with the increase in the number of terrorist attacks committed by various terrorist organizations around the world and with the constant threat of terror that leads to the destabilization of the political, economic, and social situation in the state"-- Provided by publisher.
Identifiers: LCCN 2022027529 (print) | LCCN 2022027530 (ebook) | ISBN 9781668453117 (hardcover) | ISBN 9781668453124 (paperback) | ISBN 9781668453131 (ebook)
Subjects: LCSH: Terrorism--Psychological aspects.
Classification: LCC HV6431 .G558 2023 (print) | LCC HV6431 (ebook) | DDC 363.325019--dc23/eng/20220815
LC record available at https://lccn.loc.gov/2022027529
LC ebook record available at https://lccn.loc.gov/2022027530

This book is published in the IGI Global book series Advances in Digital Crime, Forensics, and Cyber Terrorism (ADCF-CT) (ISSN: 2327-0381; eISSN: 2327-0373)

British Cataloguing in Publication Data
A Cataloguing in Publication record for this book is available from the British Library.

Advances in Digital Crime, Forensics, and Cyber Terrorism (ADCFCT) Book Series

Bryan Christiansen
Global Research Society, LLC, USA
Agnieszka Piekarz
Independent Researcher, Poland

ISSN:2327-0381
EISSN:2327-0373

Mission

The digital revolution has allowed for greater global connectivity and has improved the way we share and present information. With this new ease of communication and access also come many new challenges and threats as cyber crime and digital perpetrators are constantly developing new ways to attack systems and gain access to private information.

The **Advances in Digital Crime, Forensics, and Cyber Terrorism (ADCFCT) Book Series** seeks to publish the latest research in diverse fields pertaining to crime, warfare, terrorism and forensics in the digital sphere. By advancing research available in these fields, the **ADCFCT** aims to present researchers, academicians, and students with the most current available knowledge and assist security and law enforcement professionals with a better understanding of the current tools, applications, and methodologies being implemented and discussed in the field.

Coverage

- Database Forensics
- Malicious Codes
- Hacking
- Network Forensics
- Cyber Terrorism
- Mobile Device Forensics
- Cryptography
- Identity Theft
- Telecommunications Fraud
- Cyber Warfare

IGI Global is currently accepting manuscripts for publication within this series. To submit a proposal for a volume in this series, please contact our Acquisition Editors at Acquisitions@igi-global.com or visit: http://www.igi-global.com/publish/.

The Advances in Digital Crime, Forensics, and Cyber Terrorism (ADCFCT) Book Series (ISSN 2327-0381) is published by IGI Global, 701 E. Chocolate Avenue, Hershey, PA 17033-1240, USA, www.igi-global.com. This series is composed of titles available for purchase individually; each title is edited to be contextually exclusive from any other title within the series. For pricing and ordering information please visit http://www.igi-global.com/book-series/advances-digital-crime-forensics-cyber/73676. Postmaster: Send all address changes to above address.

Titles in this Series

For a list of additional titles in this series, please visit: www.igi-global.com/book-series

Aiding Forensic Investigation Through Deep Learning and Machine Learning Frameworks
Alex Noel Joseph Raj (Shantou University, China) Vijayalakshmi G. V. Mahesh (BMS Institute of Technology and Management, India) Ruban Nerssison (Vellore Institute of Technology, India) Ang Yu (Carolina University, USA) and Jennifer Gentry (Carolina University, USA)
Information Science Reference • copyright 2022 • 273pp • H/C (ISBN: 9781668445587) • US $250.00 (our price)

Dark Web Pattern Recognition and Crime Analysis Using Machine Intelligence
Romil Rawat (Shri Vaishnav Vidyapeeth Vishwavidyalaya, India) Shrikant Telang (Shri Vaishnav Vidyapeeth Vishwavidyalaya, India) P. William (Sanjivani College of Engineering, Savitribai Phule Pune University, India) Upinder Kaur (Akal University, Talwandi Sabo, India) and Om Kumar C.U. (School of Computer Science and Engineering (SCOPE),Vellore Institute of Technology, India)
Information Science Reference • copyright 2022 • 281pp • H/C (ISBN: 9781668439425) • US $250.00 (our price)

Using Computational Intelligence for the Dark Web and Illicit Behavior Detection
Romil Rawat (Shri Vaishnav Vidyapeeth Vishwavidyalaya, India) Upinder Kaur (Akal University, Talwandi Sabo, India) Shadab Pasha Khan (Oriental Institute of Science and Technology, Bhopal, India) Ranjana Sikarwar (Amity University, Gwalior, India) and K. Sakthidasan Sankaran (Hindustan Institute of Technology and Science, India)
Information Science Reference • copyright 2022 • 336pp • H/C (ISBN: 9781668464441) • US $250.00 (our price)

Media and Terrorism in the 21st Century
Elnur Ismayil (Istanbul Medeniyet University, Turkey) and Ebru Karadogan Ismayil (Uskudar University, Turkey)
Information Science Reference • copyright 2022 • 299pp • H/C (ISBN: 9781799897552) • US $215.00 (our price)

World Politics and the Challenges for International Security
Nika Chitadze (International Black Sea University, Georgia)
Information Science Reference • copyright 2022 • 427pp • H/C (ISBN: 9781799895862) • US $215.00 (our price)

Technologies to Advance Automation in Forensic Science and Criminal Investigation
Chung-Hao Chen (Old Dominion University, USA) Wen-Chao Yang (National Central Police University, Taiwan) and Lijia Chen (Henan University, China)
Information Science Reference • copyright 2022 • 289pp • H/C (ISBN: 9781799883869) • US $250.00 (our price)

Intelligence and Law Enforcement in the 21st Century
Eugene de Silva (Virginia Research Institute, USA) and Asanga Abeyagoonesekera (Parliament of Sri Lanka, Sri Lanka)
Information Science Reference • copyright 2021 • 253pp • H/C (ISBN: 9781799879046) • US $250.00 (our price)

IGI Global
PUBLISHER of TIMELY KNOWLEDGE

701 East Chocolate Avenue, Hershey, PA 17033, USA
Tel: 717-533-8845 x100 • Fax: 717-533-8661
E-Mail: cust@igi-global.com • www.igi-global.com

Table of Contents

Preface xiii

Acknowledgment xx

Chapter 1
History of Terrorism and Reasons for Its Emergence 1
Mary Tseruashvili, International Black Sea University, Georgia

Chapter 2
Problems of Terrorism in the Modern World 15
Nika Chitadze, International Black Sea University, Georgia

Chapter 3
Terrorist Psychology and Its Impact on National and Global Security 37
Irakli Kervalishvili, Georgian Technical University, Georgia

Chapter 4
The Impact of Terrorism on International Peace and Security 57
Mukesh Shankar Bharti, Jawaharlal Nehru University, India

Chapter 5
The Social Psychology of Terrorism: Preventive Countermeasures 69
Irakli Kervalishvili, Georgian Technical University, Georgia

Chapter 6
Transformation of the Terrorist Threat: A Case Study of the "Islamic State" of Iraq and Syria (ISIS) 89
Diana Jalagania, International Black Sea University, Georgia

Chapter 7
Victimology of Terrorism 122
Nika Chitadze, International Black Sea University, Georgia

Chapter 8
State Terrorism and Its Impact on the Global Processes 136
Valeria Gonitashvili, Ukrainian Youth Organization of Georgia, Georgia

Chapter 9
Russian Aggression in Georgia and Ukraine as an Example of State Terrorism: Comparative Analysis 160
Gurami Jajanidze, Ilia State University, Georgia

Chapter 10
Psychological Aspects of Negotiation With Terrorists 201
Irakli Kervalishvili, Georgian Technical University, Georgia

Chapter 11
A Critical Look at the Cold War Era on the Axis of Moscow and Hollywood 217
Pelin Pelin, University of Dicle, Turkey

Chapter 12
Combating Terrorism Based on the Principles of International Law 231
Valeria Gonitashvili, Ukrainian Youth Organization of Georgia, Georgia

Chapter 13
Cyberterrorism and Its Reflection on International Security 253
Mary Tseruashvili, Ilia State University, Georgia

Chapter 14
Female Radicalization: Why and How Women Join ISIS 267
Tinatin Gigauri, International Black Sea University, Georgia

Chapter 15
Organized Crime as One of the Main Reflections of Terrorism in the Modern World 288
Irakli Kervalishvili, Georgian Technical University, Georgia

Compilation of References 300

About the Contributors 326

Index 328

Detailed Table of Contents

Preface xiii

Acknowledgment xx

Chapter 1
History of Terrorism and Reasons for Its Emergence 1
Mary Tseruashvili, International Black Sea University, Georgia

The chapter aims to analyze the history of terrorism, the reasons for its emergence, and hence, its relevance in today's world. More specifically, it focuses on the causes of terrorism, its characteristics, types, and based on the above, emphasizes its relevance in the context of globalization. While we saw the signs of terrorism as a crime against society in the early centuries, nowadays it is emerging as a global and widespread problem for all countries. Therefore, the chapter is based on the analysis of various articles, reports, analytical papers, and official documents, such as the conventions of the United Nations. The research process provides a detailed and chronological analysis of the history and causes of terrorism and, as a result, its relevance in the modern world.

Chapter 2
Problems of Terrorism in the Modern World 15
Nika Chitadze, International Black Sea University, Georgia

Currently, the study of the topic of terrorism is especially relevant in connection with the increase in the number of terrorist attacks committed by various terrorist organizations around the world. The constant threat of terror leads to the destabilization of the political, economic, and social situation in the state. Lack of confidence in personal safety contributes to the growth of anxiety, fears, and mental stress, which negatively affects psychological health, leading to the development of various psychosomatic disorders among the population. The genesis of the concept of "terrorism," the history of terrorism, the psychology of the personality of terrorists and terrorist groups, the victimology of terrorism, methods of providing psychological first aid in terrorist attacks, methods of negotiating with terrorists, technologies for forming a model of safe behavior are the main issues during the study of the basic aspects related to terrorism.

Chapter 3
Terrorist Psychology and Its Impact on National and Global Security 37
Irakli Kervalishvili, Georgian Technical University, Georgia

Terrorism is a policy based on the systematic use of terror. Despite the legal force of the term "terrorism," its definition up to the present time remains ambiguous. But experts agree that the best definition of terrorism is the achievement of political, ideological, economic, and religious goals by violent means. Synonyms of the word "terror" (Latin terror – fear, horror) are the words "violence" and "intimidation." This term became widespread in various countries after the "Age of Terror" during the Great French Revolution. During the discussion about terrorism, one of the main directions of this phenomena represents the terrorist psychology. Thus, in the chapter attention is paid to the psychological aspects of terrorism, including the determination of the main types of terrorism and psychological characteristics of the terrorists and terrorist groups.

Chapter 4
The Impact of Terrorism on International Peace and Security 57
Mukesh Shankar Bharti, Jawaharlal Nehru University, India

This study discusses the questions of terrorism among the international communities. The threat of terrorism has affected international peace and security. Further, we have to study to elucidate the main roots of terrorism and how to save the world community from the danger of it. The study relied on the concept of collective security derived from the theory of bargaining and idealism to explain why states come together to fight terrorism. The authors use this method to search the result through empirical analyses. As a result of this study, the terrorist activities displaced the people and restricted sustainable development. The result also shows that due to the terrorist events, people suffered from many basic human rights. Thus, many parts of the world have been destabilised from the act of terrorism and are continually struggling to restore peace and security.

Chapter 5
The Social Psychology of Terrorism: Preventive Countermeasures.. 69
Irakli Kervalishvili, Georgian Technical University, Georgia

Social psychology's focus on person-situation interactions has implications for who becomes a terrorist; for example, Moghaddam posits a "staircase model" of terrorism in which terrorism is viewed as sequential progress from lower floors to higher floors that occurs on a progressively narrowing staircase. Each floor is characterized by unique psychological processes and progressive restrictions on response options, such that "destruction of others, or oneself, or both" becomes the only option. Regarding what motivates terrorism, from a psychological perspective there is little evidence that terrorists have abnormally high levels of mental illness or psychopathy. They are rational actors with purpose, intent, high levels of commitment, and deeply held convictions. Cultivated perceived threats to group identity and values (social, cultural, religious, political, etc.) are at the core of motivations for terrorism. A similar dynamic operates in responses to terrorism.

Chapter 6
Transformation of the Terrorist Threat: A Case Study of the "Islamic State" of Iraq and Syria (ISIS) 89
Diana Jalagania, International Black Sea University, Georgia

The present-day world community is continually confronted with issues, among which terrorism is within the first put. This phenomenon is rooted in the past. The premise for the rise and advancement of terrorism was property and social imbalance, the breakdown of the existing way of life, contrasts in attitude, and the objective got to alter the direction of the improvement of civilization. Nowadays, among the reasons for the intense outbreak of terrorism, one can title the multi-speed improvement and the increasing speed of the crevice between the wealthy and the destitute on a residential and worldwide scale, the speeding up of the substitution of technology and innovation, the commercialization of all angles of life, and as a result, the deterioration of ethical establishments. An armed force of Islamists from the Islamic State organization, known by the acronym ISIS, in a brief time blew up the Near and Middle East, as well as a portion of North Africa. They say they proposed to unite all Muslims within the world, but the primary ones they murder are the Muslims.

Chapter 7
Victimology of Terrorism 122
Nika Chitadze, International Black Sea University, Georgia

Terrorist acts have become an integral part of modern life. Terror (lat. terror – fear, horror) is aimed at "intimidation." It is this circumstance that defines terror as a special form of political violence, characterized by cruelty, purposefulness, and apparent effectiveness. Terror is horror, that is, an emotional state, the emergence of which terrorists achieve by carrying out certain special actions: terrorist acts. An act of terrorism is a means that brings real or potential victims to a state of horror. The totality of links terrorist-terrorist act-terror constitutes terrorism as an integral phenomenon. Terrorism is the use of violence to intimidate people. This violence is carried out in various forms: it is physical, political, social, economic, informational, etc. violence. Taking into account the degree of mass character and the degree of organization, four types of violence are distinguished: mass organized and mass spontaneous and individual spontaneous and individual organized. Each of them has its own specifics and features.

Chapter 8
State Terrorism and Its Impact on the Global Processes 136
Valeria Gonitashvili, Ukrainian Youth Organization of Georgia, Georgia

The complexity and versatility of modern international relations, the struggle for energy resources, the division of spheres of influence between main geopolitical actors, the presence of problems of the global nature – all these factors greatly complicate the interaction of states in the international arena. Such difficulties give rise to many geopolitical strategies and tactics designed to protect the national interests of a particular state. And one such strategy may be state terrorism. First of all, it must be stated that the concept state terrorism has two aspects: internal political and foreign policy. Under state terrorism, internal political phenomenon is understood as the actions of state bodies' law and order against their own people. Often the state uses for this non-state terrorist structures. It is necessary to note that in world history, domestic terror is not a single occurrence. Most often it has manifested itself in totalitarian societies.

Chapter 9
Russian Aggression in Georgia and Ukraine as an Example of State Terrorism: Comparative Analysis 160
Gurami Jajanidze, Ilia State University, Georgia

The chapter overviews Russian aggression in Georgia and Ukraine and provides comparative analyses – demonstrating the differences and similarities between Russia's tactics and policies during Russo-Georgian war (2008), the conflict in Eastern Ukraine (2014), and later during the Russian invasion of Ukraine (2022). It also analyzes Russian war crimes and atrocities committed during those conflicts. The first part was written in Spring 2021 before the war in Ukraine (2022), so initially the comparative analysis was made based on two cases – Russo-Georgian War 2008 and Russian aggression in Eastern Ukraine 2014. The second part of the chapter was written in Spring 2022 after Russia launched a full-scale invasion against Ukraine. The chapter was written based on the qualitative analyses of the existing literature – comparative analyses, researches about Russian hybrid war, independent case studies based on the information from archives of articles from the media outlets from 2008, 2014, and 2022 analyzing different documents, such as NATO summit declarations, Constitution of Russia, etc.

Chapter 10
Psychological Aspects of Negotiation With Terrorists 201
Irakli Kervalishvili, Georgian Technical University, Georgia

Negotiation can be defined as a type of interaction with a partner, which is aimed at solving a specific problem. There are two opposite negotiation strategies: "hard" and "soft." The American researchers S. Sigel and L. Fureker were among the first authors of the "tough" strategy. They argued that a concession by one of the parties in the negotiation process would lead to a toughening of the other. In their opinion, for a successful outcome of negotiations, one should start with exaggerated demands and demonstrate intransigence. In contrast to them, Charles Osgood spoke out with a "soft" line of conduct in the negotiations, according to which the greatest benefit can be obtained only through mutual concessions. It should also be borne in mind that the first impression of the partner and his vision of the problem are very important, influencing the subsequent interaction. One of the types of stereotypes of behavior is prejudice. (Any information that contradicts the established views is ignored.)

Chapter 11
A Critical Look at the Cold War Era on the Axis of Moscow and Hollywood 217
Pelin Pelin, University of Dicle, Turkey

By the end of the 20th century, significant differentiation occurred in international media. These differentiations left their place in the unipolar system as the bipolar system, which had dominated the world for more than 40 years, lost its currency. However, the acceleration in international relations has led to competition in trade, military, and economy. This study tried to discuss the fail-safe movie about the Cold War period ideologically. This study aims to examine how the social and political events experienced during the Cold War period took place in the cinema and determine how the dominant ideology in this context affects the language of cinema. In the study, the film will be evaluated from a political and ideological point of view. The chapter determines which social positions and ideological reflections they reproduce by analyzing them within the framework of the stated questions and associating them with the political period they are in.

Chapter 12
Combating Terrorism Based on the Principles of International Law 231
Valeria Gonitashvili, Ukrainian Youth Organization of Georgia, Georgia

There is a growing body of international law that is directly relevant to the fight against terrorism. International law provides the framework within which national counterterrorism activities take place and which allows states to cooperate with each other effectively in preventing and combating terrorism. This framework includes instruments addressing specific aspects of counterterrorism alongside other international instruments designed for international cooperation in criminal law, the protection of human rights or refugees, or the establishment of the laws of war, which provide the broader context within which counterterrorism activities take place. International law specifically addressing terrorism exists within the general framework of international law including international criminal law, international humanitarian law, international human rights law, and refugee law.

Chapter 13
Cyberterrorism and Its Reflection on International Security.. 253
Mary Tseruashvili, Ilia State University, Georgia

The purpose of this chapter is to analyze cyberterrorism and its reflection on international security. More specifically, it focuses on the analysis of the challenges facing the modern world arising from the urgency of cyber threats. While the development of information technology and the availability of information, in general, make the life of the world community easier in some respects, there are also threats, the elimination of which require the full mobilization of states. Hence, the chapter is based on the analysis of the various articles, reports, analytical papers, and case studies, depending on which it becomes possible to answer the main research question and identify the cyber threats facing the modern states.

Chapter 14
Female Radicalization: Why and How Women Join ISIS 267
Tinatin Gigauri, International Black Sea University, Georgia

This chapter discusses the phenomenon of female radicalization based on a case study of the Islamic State. The goal of this chapter is to explore the connection and, possibly, the correlation between the uneven and inconsistent security context and the transformation of gender norms and deeply-rooted gendered segregation inside a jihadist organization through qualitative desk research. Using aspects of securitization theory and a human security paradigm, the research elaborates on the changing politico-military tendencies targeting the Islamic State since the declaration of the War on Terror, the dynamics of changing the strictly domestic role of women inside ISIS, the roles performed by female recruits in the organization, the threat they pose as participants of military jihad, and the propensity of existing counterterrorism measures to ignore the significance of female terrorists. Finally, with proper arguments, the chapter argues that there is a need for implementing a gendered approach to designing case-appropriate counterterrorism strategies.

Chapter 15
Organized Crime as One of the Main Reflections of Terrorism in the Modern World 288
Irakli Kervalishvili, Georgian Technical University, Georgia

At the end of the 20th century, security concern went beyond interstate cooperation and disarmament issues. With the development of the globalization process, organized crime became a bigger topic. According to several estimates, since the 1980s, the number of criminal acts, having been carried out within organized crime, has increased by 5% annually. Members of organized criminal groups gain huge income. By estimates, which were presented in 1999, the total amount of so-called dirty money in the world was from 500 to 1500 billion dollars per year, which was equal to 5% of the world GDP during this period. In 2009 it was estimated to generate $870 billion – an amount equal to 1.5% of global GDP for this period. As of 2016, transnational crime was a $1.6 trillion to $2.2 trillion annual "business."

Compilation of References 300

About the Contributors 326

Index 328

Preface

As it is known, terrorism represents the biggest threat to international society. From its turn, in its broadest meaning, it is the use of violence and fear to achieve an ideological goal. The term is used in this regard primarily to refer to intentional violence during peacetime or in the context of the war against non-combatants (mostly civilians and neutral military personnel). According to the experts in the field of terrorism, the determinations "terrorist" and "terrorism" have their origin during the French Revolution of the late 18th century but became widely used internationally and gained global attention in the 1970s during the conflicts in Northern Ireland (United Kingdom), the Basque country (Spain), and the Israeli-Arab wars within the conflict over Palestine (Crenshaw, 1981). The increased commitment to suicide attacks from the 1980s onwards was typified by the 2001 September 11 attacks in the United States (Kegley & Wittkopf, 2011).

Despite the fact, that there are various definitions of terrorism, it is no universal agreement about it. The main reason for it is the fact, that Terrorism is a charged term. It is frequently used with the explanation of something wrong from a moral point of view. Authorities of many countries and non-state institutions use the term to abuse or denounce opposing groups. Some political organizations with different political orientations and ideologies have been accused of using terrorism to achieve their political aims. These include left-wing and right-wing political organizations, nationalist groups, religious groups, revolutionaries, and ruling governments (Davitashvili & Elizabarashvili, 2012).

Legislation recognizing terrorism as a crime has been adopted in most countries of the world. When terrorism is perpetrated by nation states, it is not discussed terrorism by the state conducting it, making legality a largely grey-area issue. There is no consensus as to whether terrorism should be considered a war crime.

Reviewing the great threat from terrorism, as an example it can be presented by The Global Terrorism Database, having been implemented by the University of Maryland, College Park, which has fixed more than 61,000 acts of non-state terrorism, which caused at least 140,000 deaths, within the period between 2000 and 2014 (Global Terrorism Index, 2015).

When we are discussing types of Terrorism, it is necessary to point out, that Depending on the country, the political system, and the time in history, the types of terrorism differ from each other.

In early 1975, the Law Enforcement Assistant Administration in the United States founded the National Advisory Committee on Criminal Justice Standards and Goals. One of the five volumes that the committee prepared was named "Disorders and Terrorism" (UN Office on Drugs and Crime, 2018).

The Task Force defines terrorism as "a tactic or technique using which a violent act or the threat thereof is used for the prime purpose of creating overwhelming fear for coercive purposes" (UN Office on Drugs and Crime, 2018). It classified disorders and terrorism into seven categories:

1. **Civil Disorder:** A form of collective violence interfering with the peace, security, and normal functioning of the community.
2. **Political Terrorism:** Violent criminal actions designed directly to generate fear in the population or a substantial segment of it, for fulfillment the political purposes.
3. **Non-Political Terrorism:** Terrorism's purpose of which is not political but exhibits "conscious design to create and maintain a high degree of fear for coercive purposes, but the end is individual or collective gain rather than the achievement of a political objective".
4. **Anonymous Terrorism:** In the two decades before 2016–19, "fewer than half" of all terrorist attacks were either "claimed by their perpetrators or convincingly attributed by governments to specific terrorist groups". Several theories have been advanced as to why this has happened.
5. **Quasi-Terrorism:** The activities incidental to the commission of crimes of violence that are similar in form and method to genuine terrorism but which nevertheless lack its essential ingredient. It is not the main purpose of the quasi-terrorists to induce terror in the immediate victim as in the case of genuine terrorism, but the quasi-terrorist uses the modalities and techniques of the genuine terrorist and produces similar consequences and reactions. For instance, the fleeing felon who takes hostages is a quasi-terrorist, whose methods are similar to those of the genuine terrorist but whose aims are radically different.
6. **Limited Political Terrorism:** Genuine political terrorism is characterized by a revolutionary approach; limited political terrorism refers to "acts of terrorism which are committed for ideological or political motives but which are not part of a concerted campaign to capture control of the state".
7. **Official or State Terrorism:** "Referring to nations whose rule is based upon fear and oppression that reach similar to terrorism or such proportions". It may be referred to as Structural Terrorism defined broadly as terrorist acts carried out by governments in pursuit of political objectives, often as part of their foreign policy (OSCE, 2018). In this regard, the aggression of Russia against Ukraine represents a clear example of it.

Some scholars, scientists, experts, and government officials have defined the typology of terrorism by using their methods, for example, broadly classifying terrorism in their works into domestic terrorism and international terrorism, or using categories such as vigilante terrorism or insurgent terrorism. According to the different materials, the following types of terrorism are distinguished:

- Political terrorism.
- Social terrorism.
- State-sponsored terrorism.
- National terrorism.
- Territorial separatist terrorism.
- Ideological terrorism.
- Criminal terrorism (Chitadze, 2022).

Taking into consideration the psychological and social aspects related to terrorism, among the other issues, it is necessary to point out about Causes and motivations to make a Choice of terrorism as a tactic. Particularly, Individuals and groups choose terrorism as a tactic because it can:

- Act as a form of asymmetric warfare to directly force a government to agree to demands;

- Intimidate a group of people into capitulating to the demands to avoid future injury.

Get attention and thus political support for a cause Directly inspire more people to the cause (such as revolutionary acts) – propaganda of the deed Indirectly inspire more people to the cause by provoking a hostile response or overreaction from enemies to the cause (OSCE, 2018).

Other specific political or social causes have included:

- Separatist movements;
- Irredentist movements.

Adoption of a particular political philosophy, such as socialism (left-wing terrorism), anarchism, or fascism (possibly through a coup or as an ideology of independence or separatist movement);

- Environmental protection (eco-terrorism);
- Supremacism of a particular group;
- Preventing a rival group from sharing or occupying a particular territory (such as by discouraging immigration or encouraging flight);
- The subjugation of a particular population (such as the lynching of African Americans);
- Spread or dominance of a particular religion – religious terrorism;
- Ending perceived government oppression;
- Responding to a violent act (for example, tit-for-tat attacks in the Israeli–Palestinian conflict, The Troubles in Northern Ireland, or Timothy McVeigh's revenge for the Waco siege and Ruby Ridge incident).

Causes for right-wing terrorism have included white nationalism, ethnonationalism, fascism, anti-socialism, the anti-abortion movement, and tax resistance (UN Office on Drugs and Crime, 2018).

In the making analysis of the psychological, personal, and social factors, it should be mentioned that Various psychological, personal, and social factors may influence the personal choice of whether to join a terrorist group or attempt an act of terror, including:

- Identity, including affiliation with a particular culture, ethnicity, or religion;
- Previous exposure to violence;
- Financial reward (for example, the Palestinian Authority Martyrs Fund);
- Mental health disorder;
- Social isolation.

The perception that the cause responds to a profound injustice or indignity (UN Office on Drugs and Crime, 2018).

A report conducted by Paul Gill, John Horgan, and Paige Deckert (2014). found that for "lone wolf" terrorists:

- 43% were motivated by religious beliefs;
- 32% had pre-existing mental health disorders, while many more are found to have mental health problems upon arrest;

- At least 37% lived alone at the time of their event planning and/or execution, a further 26% lived with others, and no data were available for the remaining cases;
- 40% were unemployed at the time of their arrest or terrorist event;
- 19% subjectively experienced being disrespected by others;
- 14% percent experienced being the victim of verbal or physical assault.

The famous psychologist Ariel Merari, who has implemented research related to the psychological profiles of suicide terrorists since 1983 by the agency of media reports that contained biographical details, interviews with the members of suicides' families, and interviews with jailed would-be suicide attackers, made the conclusion they were unlikely to be psychologically abnormal. In comparison to economic concepts of criminal behavior, researcher Scott Atran found that suicide terrorists exhibit none of the socially dysfunctional attributes—such as fatherless, friendless, jobless situations—or suicidal symptoms. By which he underlines, that they do not kill themselves simply out of hopelessness or a sense of "having nothing to lose" (Merari, 2010).

Another expert in the field of Terrorism Abraham presents the idea that terrorist organizations do not select terrorism for its political effectiveness. Individual terrorists tend to be motivated more by a desire for social solidarity with other members of their organization than by political platforms or strategic objectives, which are often murky and undefined (Council of Europe, 2005).

Analyzing the topics, related to the psychology of terrorism, one of the most important issues is connected with Radicalization, which is the process by which an individual or a group comes to adopt increasingly radical views in opposition to a political, social, or religious status quo. The ideas of society at the large shape the outcomes of radicalization; for example, radical movements can originate from a broad social consensus against progressive changes in society or from a broad desire for change in society. Radicalization can result in both violent and nonviolent action – academic literature focuses on radicalization into violent extremism (RVE) or radicalization leading to acts of terrorism. Multiple separate pathways can promote the process of radicalization, which can be independent but are usually mutually reinforcing.

Radicalization that occurs across multiple reinforcing pathways greatly increases a group's resilience and lethality. Furthermore, by compromising a group's ability to blend in with non-radical society and to participate in a modern, national or international economy, radicalization serves as a kind of sociological trap that gives individuals no other place to go to satisfy their material and spiritual needs (Chitadze, 2022).

With regard to the chapters of the book *Global Perspectives on the Psychology of Terrorism*, the first chapter's, "History of Terrorism and Reasons of Its Emergence", main purpose is to consider analyze the history of terrorism, the reasons for its emergence during the different periods of the World History. Furthermore, it is clearly shown, how terrorism is emerging as a global and widespread problem for all countries.

The second chapter, "Problems of Terrorism in the Modern World", discusses the increase in the number of terrorist attacks committed by various terrorist organizations around the world. It is shown that the constant threat of terror leads to the destabilization of the political, economic, and social situation in the state. As a result, a lack of confidence in personal safety contributes to the growth of anxiety, fears, and mental stress, negatively affecting psychological health, and leading to the development of various psychosomatic disorders among the population.

Chapter 3, "Terrorists Psychology and Its Impact on National and Global Security", explains the psychological aspects of terrorism, including the determination of the main types of terrorism and psychological characteristics of the individual terrorists and terrorist groups.

Discussing the main aspects of the fourth chapter, "The Impact of Terrorism on International Peace and Security", it should be mentioned how the threat of terrorism has affected international peace and security. The study relied on the concept of collective security derived from the theory of bargaining and idealism to explain why states come together to fight terrorism.

In Chapter 5, "The Social Psychology of Terrorism: Preventive Countermeasures", it is underlined that Social psychology focuses on person-situation interactions that have implications for who becomes a terrorist. Regarding what motivates terrorism, from a psychological perspective, there is little evidence that terrorists have abnormally high levels of mental illness or psychopathy. They are rational actors with purpose, intent, high levels of commitment, and deeply held convictions. Cultivated perceived threats to group identity and values (social, cultural, religious, political, etc.) are at the core of motivations for terrorism. A similar dynamic operates in response to terrorism.

The next, the sixth chapter, "Transformation of the Terrorist Threat: A Case Study of Islamic State of Iraq and Syria (ISIS)", presents the issue related to the activities of the so-called "Islamic State" (ISIS) on the territories of Iraq and Syria. As it is known, in September 2014, ISIS was controlling about 11 provinces on the territories of two countries in the Middle East.

The seventh chapter, "Victimology of Terrorism", explains that terrorism is the use of violence to intimidate people. This violence is carried out in various forms: it is physical, political, social, economic, informational, etc.

The eighth chapter, "State Terrorism and Its Impact on the Global Processes", together with many other aspects, presents the comparative analysis of Internal and external state terrorism. In the first case, authorities of the state, to strengthen their power, act against their population by terrifying them, etc. Within the second case, the state to implement the imperialistic and expansionist policy and satisfaction its geopolitical interests use the methods of state terrorism abroad, against foreign countries. Russian aggression in Ukraine is a clear example of it.

More specifically the state terrorism methods, having been used by the official Kremlin are analyzed in the ninth chapter of the book, "Russian Aggression in Georgia and Ukraine as an Example of State terrorism: Comparative Analysis". In general, a paper provides a comparative analysis of Russian aggression in Georgia in 2008, Eastern Ukraine and Crimea in 2014, and other parts of Ukraine in 2022.

Reviewing the next, tenth chapter, "Psychological Aspects of Negotiation With Terrorists", it has to be pointed out that various strategies of the negotiation with terrorists for the getting consensus for example in case, if terrorists seized the hostages and the life of innocent people is under the threat.

The eleventh chapter, "A Critical Look at the Cold War Era on the Axis of Moscow and Hollywood", has the purpose to discuss, how the social and political events experienced during the Cold War Period took place in the cinema and determining how the dominant ideology in this context affects the language of cinema.

Taking into account the content of the twelfth chapter, "Combating Terrorism Based on the Principles of International Law", discusses the efforts of the International Community in the framework of combating terrorism by the agency of preparation the various international conventions, which have been adopted by the United Nations and different International Regional Organizations.

Pointing out about main aspects of the thirteenth chapter, "Cyberterrorism and Its Reflection on International Security", an author has analyzed cyberterrorism and its reflection on international security.

Particularly, this part of the book focused on the analysis of the challenges facing the modern world arising from the urgency of cyber threats.

The next, fourteenth chapter, "Female Radicalization: Why and How Women Join ISIS", discusses the phenomenon of female radicalization based on a case study of the so-called Islamic State.

The last, fifteenth chapter of the book, "Organized Crime as One of the Main Reflections of Terrorism in the Modern World", analyzes the negative impact of the activities of the various Organized Criminal Groups (who have many similarities with Terrorism) on the global level.

Taking into consideration the above-mentioned factors, it should be pointed out that the novelty of the book and its contribution is interrelated with the fact, that for the first time have been presented the combination of the topics, related to the different aspects of Terrorism and Combating Terrorism – making the attention to the Psychological aspects.

In general, the book *Global Perspectives on the Psychology of Terrorism*, which will be distributed in different countries and regions of the world, will play a significant role in increasing the knowledge of the International Society – representatives of the different target groups on the issues, concerning to the Negative impacts of Terrorism on the International Security, Psychological factors, which promotes the terrorism development and its expansion, different ways – including psychological related to the combating terrorism, etc.

Nika Chitadze
International Black Sea University, Georgia

REFERENCES

Chitadze, N. (2022). Global Security and Political Problems of the 21st Century. In *World Politics and Challenges for International Security.* IGI Global. https://www.igi-global.com/chapter/global-security-and-political-problems-of-the-21st-century/298954

Council of Europe. (2005). *Media and Terrorism*. Retrieved from: https://assembly.coe.int/nw/xml/XRef/X2H-Xref-ViewHTML.asp?FileID=10914&lang=EN

Crenshaw, M. (1981). *The Causes of Terrorism. Comparative Politics, Ph.D. Programs in Political Science*. City University of New York.

Davitashvili, Z., & Elizabarashvili, N. (2012). *Global Geography*. Tbilisi State University.

Gill, P., Horgan, J., & Deckert, M. (2014). Bombing Alone: Tracing the Motivations and Antecedent Behaviors of Lone-Actor Terrorists. *Journal of Forensic Sciences*. Retrieved from: https://onlinelibrary.wiley.com/doi/pdf/10.1111/1556-4029.12312

Institute for Economics and Peace. (2016). *Global Terrorism Index 2015*. Retrieved from: https://privacyinternational.org/sites/default/files/2018-02/Global%20Terrorism%20Index%202015%2C%20Institute%20for%20Economics%20%26%20Peace.pdf

Kegley, C., & Wittkopf, E. (2011). *World Politics*. Trends and Transformation. Thomson Wadsworth.

Merari, A. (2010). *Driven to Death: Psychological and Social Aspects of Suicide Terrorism*. Oxford University Press. Retrieved from https://journals.openedition.org/ress/1241

OSCE. (2018). *Preventing Terrorism and Countering Violent Extremism and Radicalization that Lead to Terrorism: A Community-Policing Approach*. Retrieved from: https://www.osce.org/files/f/documents/1/d/111438.pdf

United Nations Office on Drugs and Crime. (2018). *Education for Justice University Module Series. Counter-Terrorism Module 1. Introduction to International Terrorism*. Retrieved from: https://www.unodc.org/documents/e4j/18-04932_CT_Mod_01_ebook_FINALpdf.pdf

Acknowledgment

In the framework of the working over the book *Global Perspectives on the Psychology of Terrorism*, I would like to express my special gratitude to Ms. Elizabeth Barrantes, Assistant Development Editor, Book Development of IGI Global for her assistance and attention within the different stages in the framework of the book preparation Process.

At the same time, I would like to dedicate a special thanks to each author of the chapter – citizens of the different countries and representatives of the different nationalities, who took to the Heart the global problems of our planet and implemented very important research in favor of preventing the threats and challenges – related to terrorism. So, without the contributions of such experienced scholars in their fields as *Mary Tseruashvili, Valeria Gonitashvili, Irakli Kervalishvili, Tinatin Gigauri, Pelin Pelin, Gurami Jajanidze, Diana Jalagania, Mukesh Shankar Bharti,* it would be impossible the publishing of the book.

I am too much thankful to my native – International Black Sea University and its Administration, Academic and Administrative personnel for establishing for me an excellent scientific environment and great atmosphere during working over the book.

Chapter 1
History of Terrorism and Reasons for Its Emergence

Mary Tseruashvili
International Black Sea University, Georgia

ABSTRACT

The chapter aims to analyze the history of terrorism, the reasons for its emergence, and hence, its relevance in today's world. More specifically, it focuses on the causes of terrorism, its characteristics, types, and based on the above, emphasizes its relevance in the context of globalization. While we saw the signs of terrorism as a crime against society in the early centuries, nowadays it is emerging as a global and widespread problem for all countries. Therefore, the chapter is based on the analysis of various articles, reports, analytical papers, and official documents, such as the conventions of the United Nations. The research process provides a detailed and chronological analysis of the history and causes of terrorism and, as a result, its relevance in the modern world.

INTRODUCTION

The fight against terrorism is an integral part of modern international relations. Nowadays, numerous terrorist acts are taking place in different parts of the world which are provoking strong reactions in society. The rapid spread of information about terrorist acts is due to globalization and modern technologies, which largely contribute to the intensification of terrorism. Globalization and technological development have also led to the unification of the vast majority of the world's nations against the threat of terrorism, especially in the wake of the 9/11 attacks.

Although terrorism has become an international challenge since 2001, its hallmarks are still evident at an early stage, making it even more inevitable to avoid research into its history. In addition, current events in the modern world make the issue of the urgency of terrorism even more interesting. There is no doubt that terrorism has become the world's first challenge and threat since 2001, but the developments over the past two decades, the steps taken by states to defeat terrorism, and, at the same time, the ability of terrorism to adapt to modern events deserve attention.

DOI: 10.4018/978-1-6684-5311-7.ch001

History of terrorism, reasons for its emergence and development, and the responses by states are the main topics the following chapter is based on and aims to answer the main research question: "Whether terrorism is still relevant in the modern world". The chapter offers qualitative research and it is based on the analysis of various articles, reports, analytical papers, and official documentation.

In order to answer the research question, the chapter begins by discussing the definition of terrorism, its emergence, and its development from the early stages. After that, it analyses the four major waves in the history of terrorism and describes their characteristics. It then focuses on its causes, types, and methods for a better understanding of the specifics of terrorism. The chapter also analyses the financial sources and the tendencies of modern terrorism. In addition to that, in order to demonstrate the cooperation of states in the fight against terrorism, several UN conventions are also analyzed. Finally, the chapter describes the responses against terrorism, challenges, and the ability of terrorism to adapt to changes in today's world.

Definition and the Early Stages of Terrorism

In order to analyze the urgency of terrorism in the modern world, it is necessary to consider the history of its formation. While the concept of terrorism reminds the world of the events of 2001 in the United States, it is important to note that its formation dates back much earlier.

The term terrorism was originated from "terror" during the French Revolution from 5 September 1793 to 27 July 1794 to describe the incredible atrocities used against people who opposed the revolution. Despite this, it should be mentioned that there is no universal definition of terrorism, which poses significant problems in understanding the essence of terrorist acts. This problem arises when the opinion of the world community is divided into terrorist acts or organizations. While one part condemns the actions committed by these groups, the other part links them to national liberation movements. Moreover, the situation is aggravated by the fact that not only individual states have different views on the definition of terrorism, but also different institutions and their structures of one state in some cases (UN, Introduction to International Terrorism, 2018). As a result, the absence of an internationally recognized definition not only hinders international cooperation in the fight against terrorism and the fight against terrorism at the local level but also creates the threat of incorrectly identifying the threat of terrorism and making it easier for a terrorist group to position itself as national liberation movements.

To start with the early period, Zealots may be considered as one of the main founders of modern terrorist formations. They were representatives of a socio-political and eschatological formation that emerged in the Maccabean era, in the second half of the first century BC. Eventually, as a religious-political current, they formed around the 50s. This period coincides with the Roman domination of Judea when the cruel attitude of the colonial administration towards the inhabitants of Judea reached an apotheosis. Jews and Samaritans were particularly dissatisfied with the Romans' disrespectful and often abusive treatment of their religion. The erection of the symbols of the Roman Empire in the holy place of the Jews, in the Temple of Jerusalem, led to the radicalization of the views of the Zealots and increased their authority among the population. The radicalization of the Zealots led to the formation of a militant wing within the movement called the "Sicarians" (Smith, 1971).

The Cicars were warriors who were willing to carry out fanatical tasks even at the cost of their own lives. They attacked not only the Roman administration and army but also ordinary civilians and so-called collaborators. Therefore, it can be said that the Sicarians were the first to use the intimidation method characteristic of terrorism, as acts of violence committed in crowded places at that time had the effect of spreading information rapidly, causing fear and tension among the population (). Based on the above mentioned, it can be concluded that a synthesis of religious radicalism and organized terrorism is observed in the actions of the Zealots and the Sicarians (Smith, 1971).

After the Zealots and the Sicarians, until the beginning of the 11th century, there was no trace of an organization that regularly carried out politically motivated violence to achieve its own goals. However, the organization "Assassins" appears in the medieval world. There is a suggestion that the term comes from the Arabic "hashish", which is associated with a drug-addicted person. In addition, many scholars and linguists associate the term "Assassins" with the Persian word "Assassin", meaning herbivorous ascetic. The name of the organization became famous because of its leader-Hassan Ibn Sabah, who created a system of training warriors in which the quality of unique combat training was combined with religious fanaticism. It can be said that this was the first attempt by small forces to take control of their own and neighboring states. Possession of the art of receiving strategically important information was accomplished with the help of agents sent to the right places (Smith, 1971).

The diversification of methods made the tactics of training fighters unique. These methods involved not only their physical and technical training but also their psychological, educational, and religious training. The practice of using drugs is also noteworthy, which was one of the main proven methods in the training of fighters (Smith, 1971).

Based on all of this it is obvious that the history of terrorism as organized violence against society begins at a much earlier age. This has become the basis of modern terrorism, which today is mainly reflected in acts of violence against states.

The Four Major Waves in the History of Modern Terrorism

There are four main waves in the history of modern terrorism, which with their specificity and characteristics form an overall picture in the formation of the concept of terrorism. Each of them covers a certain period of history and shows the development path of terrorism based on the events that took place during this period.

The first wave is known as the "Anarchist Terrorist Wave" which began in the 1880s and lasted until the 1920s in Russia. It is the "anarchist terrorist wave" that is associated with the formation of the definition of terrorism, from a term denoting state repression to a term denoting political assassinations against state actors. It is noteworthy that the determinants of the anarchist wave were the rapid development of communication technologies and the factor of doctrine. Anarchist authors created the doctrine of terror while technologies such as the telegraph, daily newspapers, and railroad provided rapid dissemination of ideas. The anarchist terrorist wave lasted for nearly 40 years although an unprecedented number of state leaders, the military, the police, and civilians were killed. In 1898, the first International Anti-Anarchist Conference was held in Rome to formulate the concept of anarchism as a threat, establish an anti-anarchist legal framework, and coordinate international anti-anarchist policing. It is noteworthy that in the second half of the nineteenth century the mood of the states was such that anarchism and terrorism were perceived as synonymous. Therefore, the anti-anarchist conference in Rome, and the concept of anarchism adopted on it, can be generalized as the definition of terrorism in the second half of the nineteenth century (Rapoport, 2002).

The second "Anticolonial Wave" started in the 1920s and ended in the 1960s. The determinant of the anti-colonial wave can be considered the Versailles Peace Treaty and the principle of self-determination of the peoples. Terrorist groups have sprung up in almost every empire with anti-colonial and national liberation motives. It is noteworthy that due to the very negative perception of the definition of terrorism, these groups began to position themselves as "freedom fighters." Nevertheless, states referred to all insurgent groups as terrorist groups. It should be noted also that the press has contributed to creating even more uncertainty and ambiguity around the term. The American press referred to the same group in one article, sometimes in one paragraph, as terrorists, insurgents, and the military (Rapoport, 2002).

The third "New Left Wave" began in the 1960s and ended in the 1980s. The psychological precondition of the "New Left Wave" is the Vietnam War and the crisis of values caused by this war in Western countries. It was like the first wave on an international scale, collaborating between different groups to achieve a common goal and destroying targets of international importance. A typical tactic for this wave was to hijack planes with the motive of taking hostages in order to create a basis for more spectacle. Furthermore, the attack on the embassies is a characteristic event of the "New Left Wave" (Rapoport, 2002).

And the last major wave was the "Religious Wave" which started in 1979 and includes the present day as well. The determinant of the fourth "religious wave" is considered to be several events: The Iranian revolution, the success of Shiite suicide bombers against the Americans in Lebanon, and the success of the Muslim resistance in the war in Afghanistan. The fourth wave was tactically similar to the third, although the "suicide bombers" were the distinctive and deadly method of the "religious wave". It is noteworthy that the fourth wave was characterized by the attempt of Islamist terrorists to harm the United States, which ended with the events of 9/11, 2001 (Rapoport, 2002).

CAUSES, TYPES, AND METHODS OF TERRORISM

It is essential to analyze the causes, methods, and types of Terrorism in order to determine its relevance in the modern world. The emergence of terrorism is facilitated by a variety of conditions, and as it has already been discussed, there are many events in the history of mankind that bear the hallmarks of terrorism.

Attempts to achieve goals through violent methods have characterized almost every stage of society's development, such as the struggle for freedom, power, new territories, justice, prosperity, or the victory of an idea. The UN Special Committee identified the root causes of terrorism and linked them to neocolonialism, racism, aggressive policies, and the desire to occupy foreign territories. At the same time, the effects of terrorism in the form of unfair inequality, and exploitation have been identified (UN, 1977).

Terrorism affects mass psychology, public opinion and thus tries to steer events in the desired direction. Therefore, to do this, he needs resonance, otherwise, he loses all sense. A terrorist act requires a wider, at best, global audience. Hence, the first condition for the existence of terrorism is the formation of an information society. The more the mass media develops, the more important it plays in public life, the stronger the impact of a terrorist act. Any terrorist act loses its meaning if the message about it does not reach not only the addressee directly (e.g. the government), but also the general public. Terrorists are equipped with the latest ammunition, communication systems, they can easily move secretly, they use a lot of scientific advances for their own good and in fact, there is almost nothing unlimited and unattainable for them (Schmid, 1983).

The spread of terrorism is facilitated not only by technological progress, but also by growing inequality between countries, as well as in individual countries, increasing social tensions, devaluing the values of traditional society, upholding international human rights standards in a liberal-democratic society, and so on. Terrorism is also propagated by the population, which is manifested in their sympathy for terrorist acts, often indifference or inability to realize the real danger. Terrorists are often portrayed as fighters in the liberation movement, so they need support and a supportive environment, as in Muslim countries (Schmid, 1983).

The particular complexity of terrorism lies in the diversity of its forms. Scholars systematize and classify terrorism into a variety of contexts, enabling them to more solidly substantiate the public threat of terrorism and identify the signs that are important in accurately identifying terrorist offenses. It should be noted that at the Trans-American Conference on Human Rights on Terrorism and the Protection of Its Population (1970) three forms of terrorism were identified: social, political, and ideological. Political terrorism is a variety of terrorist activities aimed at influencing political leaders, the government, and the policies pursued by them, forcing certain political steps or government decisions. Social terrorism is mainly associated with street crime, growing crime in general, racial social instability, and mass unrest. In the case of ideological terrorism, groups are guided by one ideology of their choice and aspire to spread that ideology, and consequently, to exert political influence. Despite all of this, there are other approaches to its classification as well (Hirschmann, 2003).

Information Terrorism is also noteworthy, which aims to have a direct impact on human psychology and consciousness, to form the necessary views and opinions that to some extent guide human behavior. At the same time, the existence of economic and suicidal terrorism is being considered. Economic terrorism is a form of discriminatory economic action aimed at influencing economic competitors, social groups, and the wider population, as well as states and their ideologies, in order to achieve a cost-effective, concrete solution for terrorists. As for suicidal terrorism, it implies a willingness to sacrifice one's own life to achieve a certain political goal. Nowadays, various religious or social terrorist groups use suicidal terrorism as a tactic against their own or foreign governments (Hirschmann, 2003).

Terrorism can be divided into the following independent types: under the sign of terrorism - international and domestic; And according to criminal motivation - political, religious, nationalist, and economic. Despite the diversity of types of terrorism, the controversy over its classification highlights the need for further research into this problem, which is also fraught with acute practical necessity. In today's world, more than 20 types of terrorism can be distinguished, including political, religious, national-separatist, chemical, biological, narcotic, and even computer terrorism. Furthermore, space terrorism may also become relevant soon, during which threats or terrorist acts will be carried out from space. Terrorism threatens all countries, and especially those with a difficult geopolitical location (Hirschmann, 2003).

According to the scale of actions, two types of terrorism are distinguished: domestic and international terrorism. While domestic terrorism is the unlawful use of force or violence against a person or property to intimidate the existing government, government, civilians, or any segment of it for political or social purposes, international terrorism presents a terrorist act organized or financed by one state against another. International terrorism is directed from outside the country, by supporting countries or organizations (Yamamoto, 2018).

In practice, terrorists mainly use the following types of methods: Political assassinations; Explosions, fires, and their organization; Seizure of vehicles; Human abduction; Hostage-taking and false alarm. The oldest one of those methods is political assassinations. This form of terrorist act dates back to the early centuries when various groups of society resorted to terror to achieve their goal. It later became more sophisticated and modern in nature, manifested in the fact that political assassinations were carried out when one or another force failed to achieve its goal through peaceful means, and using political methods (Yamamoto, 2018).

Explosions, setting a fire, and organizing them are the most common ways of carrying out terrorist acts as they ensure the safety of the perpetrator, allow him to be away from the scene, or hide altogether. Furthermore, a terrorist uses a tool that has great destructive power. An explosive device is equally dangerous for any object and even a simple threat to use it can cause serious damage and material loss. In addition to that, obtaining the material needed to make explosive devices is not difficult, and it is affordable (Yamamoto, 2018).

Proceeding from all above mentioned, terrorism has different conditions. Its causes are mainly related to the mismanagement of both domestic and foreign policy, and its origin and development can take place in both a democratic and a dictatorial state. Moreover, it is very difficult to convert terrorism to a certain classification framework and to develop an individual approach to selecting the appropriate form of combat for each type of terrorism. This is especially complicated by the fact that one type of terrorism contains many of the hallmarks of other types as well. Therefore, the classification of types of terrorism is still associated with great difficulties.

Financial Sources of Terrorism

Terrorism, as a stable phenomenon, cannot exist solely on the basis of the "enthusiasm" of the groups. If fact, large financial costs are required to organize terrorist attacks and stimulate their media coverage.

A traditional source of assistance to terrorists is the desire of any country to fund these groups and use them to achieve their own goals. It should be noted that, in some cases, not even terrorist groups themselves are aware of these personal goals. During the Cold War, many countries, including the largest ones, were busy with the help of "ideologically close" terrorist groups, however, in modern times this source is gradually running out. It is well known that the US State Department compiled a "black list" in the early 2000s, according to which countries such as Iran, Iraq, Syria, North Korea, Cuba, and others are involved in assisting terrorist organizations (Kiser, 2005).

Nowadays, a more important source of funding for terrorists is private sponsorship of various types of communities, humanitarian aid societies, religious organizations, and so on. Moreover, it should be noted that despite the sharp rejection of Western values in "Third World" countries, this does not prevent them from seizing "Western capitalism" and accumulating resources to finance anti-Western terrorist acts. In this regard, a prominent figure was Osama bin Laden, a millionaire from Saudi Arabia who was initially a sponsor of the anti-Soviet Afghan Mujahedeen and then spearheaded the terror (Kiser, 2005).

In the modern world, terrorism increasingly requires less external assistance and shifts to self-sufficiency. Terrorist organizations are involved in international criminal activities such as the drug trafficking business, smuggling, and, consequently, they are gradually taking the form of the Mafia. For instance, Latin American terrorists are closely linked to the cocaine business, Asian terrorists to heroin, and West African gangs to smuggle diamonds (Napoleoni, 2005).

In some cases, terrorism is seen as a lucrative business as well. Terrorist organizations that have accurate information on the timing and location of a terrorist attack can make a significant profit. According to some sources, Bin Laden's partners used information about the preparation for the September 11, 2001, terrorist attacks to speculate on the stock exchanges. In addition, another lucrative area for terrorist organizations is the projects of large international corporations that are interested in either eliminating competitors or changing the business climate with the help of subversive acts in certain regions of the world, although it is quite difficult to determine the outsiders of such projects (Medero, 2011).

The fight against terrorism, in terms of international law, dates back to the 1970s. The European Convention for the Suppression of Terrorism was adopted in 1977, but its focus on terrorist financing dates back to the 1990s. This can be explained by the fact that it was during this period that the commercialization of terrorism began. The main event in the fight against terrorist financing was the International Convention for the Suppression of the Financing of Terrorism, adopted by the UN General Assembly in 1999 and entered into force in 2002 (UN, 1999).

A special role in the fight against terrorist financing is played by the international organization FATF (Financial Action Task Force), which coordinates the activities of financial institutions and financial intelligence agencies. It was established in 1989 by the decision of the "Big Seven" and now it unites 37 member jurisdictions and 2 regional organizations. The FATF acts as a peculiar financial Interpol, developing recommendations for national bodies dealing with particularly dangerous financial offenses (FATF, 2010).

The process of combating the financing of terrorism requires defining the limits of the possibilities of this struggle. The problem is that even the largest and most politically significant terrorist attacks are sometimes very "cheap" (FATF, 2010). Hence, the main problem in the fight against terrorist financing lies in achieving a balance between the costs of financial monitoring and the results obtained.

Tendencies of Modern Terrorism

To put it mildly, 2020 turned out to be unusual. Every country around the world has had to respond to a whole new challenge (COVID-19) and make decisions for which there was no real measure of effectiveness or success. Under the same conditions, there are terrorist and extremist organizations around the world that have their own agenda to pursue and their interests to be satisfied. For these purposes, they try to adapt to all obstacles or challenges. In this sense, COVID 19 and all that followed, is nothing more than an additional environment for these organizations and their ideologies to be adapted to methods of struggle.

The year 2020 saw large-scale terrorist attacks with large casualties, mass shootings by lone attackers, and cold steel attacks. Furthermore, organized attacks using suicide and explosive devices were also maintained. This year, unlike previous years, the whole analysis of terrorist activity was done in the context of the spread of coronavirus. The main questions were related to the relationship between terrorism and the pandemic and the impact of the latter on counterterrorism efforts (Campion, Ferrill, & Milligan, 2021).

At this point, it can be said that the impact of the pandemic on terrorism was heterogeneous. On the one hand, the current situation has created opportunities for terrorist organizations such as a global audience addicted to the Internet and new conspiracy theories that have easily slipped into extremist narratives. At the same time, in some countries where state control is weak for a variety of reasons, terrorist organizations have been allowed to present themselves as alternative suppliers of aid or services. On the other hand, the restrictions caused by the virus have significantly reduced the number of public gathering places, which has reduced the practicality of certain tactics of terrorist organizations. For the same reason, some organizations have reduced access to different types of resources. Most importantly, the coronavirus has gained a monopoly on media attention, which has pushed terrorist organizations and their actions back on the agenda (Campion, Ferrill, & Milligan, 2021).

In general, terrorist organizations make good use of crises, especially when they are given the opportunity to fill the information space with their own propaganda. It is noteworthy that the use of coronavirus for its propaganda was attempted by organizations on all sides of the ideological spectrum. This is also natural because terrorist organizations must be relevant. This means that both narratives and tactics must adapt to the new challenges (UN, 2018). Consequently, the coronavirus has hit the updated narrative of all kinds of terrorist and extremist organizations.

The issue of the virus was instrumentalized in two main directions. On the one hand, it was common to demonize opponents with conspiracy theories associated with it. On the other hand, calls for the use of the virus as a biological weapon have also been made (CTED, 2021).

Even in 2020, the "ordinary suspects" of world terrorism such as Daesh, the Taliban, and Al Qaeda did not lose their importance. It should be noted, in 2020, the most active terrorist organization was Daesh, and the deadliest was Boko Haram, which claimed the lives of 110 people in a single attack. The hotspots in terms of terrorist attacks were Afghanistan, Nigeria, and Pakistan (CTED, 2021).

Jihadist organizations have also had to adapt their activities to the coronavirus and incorporate the latter into their narratives. These organizations also resorted to conspiracy theories and tried to emphasize their own moral or operational superiority over their opponents by using them. Al Qaeda, for example, has accused Western authorities of neglecting the health of its population. Hayat Tahrir al-Sham preached the political and economic collapse of the West, while al-Shabab blamed the Crusaders for spreading the virus (Norlen, 2020).

In the beginning, Daesh called the virus divine revenge against unbelievers. At the same time, supporters called for exploiting the weakness of rival governments in a pandemic and intensifying attacks. In addition to that, the organization was expected to intensify in areas where there was less security regulation or weak government control. The organization also said that fighters killed by Covid-19 would receive the status of martyrs (Norlen, 2020).

Some organizations have turned the health crisis into a kind of master class in PR and strategic communication. Hezbollah leader Hassan Nasrallah, for example, said the 24,000 medical staff and hospitals affiliated with the organization would join the national effort to fight the virus. The Taliban first called on Afghan authorities to release detained militants to prevent infection and then allowed international health organizations to gain access to their territories. The Taliban also offered the government a ceasefire and distributed information leaflets informing the population about the rules for protecting themselves from the virus. This can be seen as an attempt to present itself as a legitimate player compared to the Afghan government in parallel with the ongoing negotiations in Doha. Moreover, quite unprecedented was the Taliban's March 19 statement in which it expressed its condolences to Shiite Iran over its losses caused by the coronavirus, although this may also be linked to the terrorists' desire to remain in the spotlight (Basit, 2020).

United Nations and Terrorism

The United Nations has adopted more than two dozen global and regional agreements against international terrorism. Also, according to Security Council Resolution 1373, member states have certain obligations in the fight against terrorism. Since 1972, the United Nations has been debating the definition of terrorism, terrorist, and the act of terrorism. According to one definition, a terrorist is anyone who, without being recognized by a certain state, acts alone, or as a representative of a certain group, who is not considered an official representative of his own nation and acts to destroy or harm civilians. In addition to that, a terrorist is a person who aims also to destroy or damage the property of civilians or the state, and to achieve a certain political goal. Terrorism is the violation of the life or health of civilians, as well as the destruction or damage of civil or state property, committed without the official decision of the government of a certain country, by certain individuals or groups acting independently of the government or with the order or consent of the government (Saul, 2005).

The first of the acts adopted against terrorist offenses is the Convention on Offences and Certain Other Acts Committed on Board Aircraft, commonly called the Tokyo Convention (1963). The Convention applies against the acts that violate the safety of aircraft. An important aspect of the 1963 Tokyo Convention was the granting of a number of rights to the pilot-in-command to ensure the safety of the aircraft, including the enforcement of coercive measures against persons who pose a threat (UN, 1963).

Noteworthy is the Convention for the suppression of unlawful seizure of aircraft (1970) and the 1971 Montreal Convention for the Suppression of Unlawful Acts against the Safety of Civil Aviation. According to the first one, the act of any person who seizes an aircraft and gains control of it during the flight illegally, through violence, threats of violence, and any other form of intimidation, is declared criminal. The Convention requires that the signatory states should impose severe penalties on aircraft hijackers, arrest criminals to administer justice to them or extradite them to the signatory state. In addition, it requires the signatory states to assist each other (UN, 1970). The Second Convention is directed against aviation sabotage and provides for the prohibition of actions such as the destruction of an operating aircraft or its damage that could cause the aircraft to malfunction and endanger its safe flight. Moreover, it prohibits actions such as placing substances or devices on board an aircraft that could cause the aircraft to malfunction, damage, or otherwise endanger the safety of its flight. As a result, acts against air transport safety are considered international terrorist offenses by UN conventions (UN, 1971).

Among the international normative instruments for ensuring nuclear safety is the International Convention for the Suppression of Acts of Nuclear Terrorism of 13 April 2005. According to the Convention, acts of terrorism can have serious consequences and endanger international peace and security. The signatory states also note that the threat of nuclear terrorism is not adequately assessed in existing international and legal acts, and therefore consider it necessary for states to develop effective practical measures to prevent terrorist acts, to prosecute and prosecute perpetrators (UN, 2005).

It should be also noted that there are criminal principles according to which states exercise their jurisdiction within the country and in some cases even outside the country. Under the convention, the state has the authority to exercise its jurisdiction even in cases where it is the addressee of a terrorist ultimatum, or an attack has been carried out on a state-owned aircraft. There are cases when the object of a terrorist attack is one and the addressee of the request is the other state. In this case, there are three subjects: the perpetrator of a terrorist crime, the victim state, and the addressee state. Under the Convention for the Suppression of Acts of Nuclear Terrorism, the addressee state may also extend its jurisdiction over terrorist offenses. This can happen regardless of whether the damage was caused towards the mentioned state or whether it was a victim of threat. Such a reservation to the Convention may also be considered a special case of the principle of international criminal law (UN, 2005).

Another important convention adopted in the fight against terrorism is the International Convention for the Suppression of Terrorist Bombing (1997). The reason for its development was the escalation of all forms and manifestations of terrorism in the world, especially the widespread terrorist attacks using explosives and other deadly devices in public places. An act prohibited by the Convention is manifested if a person unlawfully and intentionally places, or detonates an explosive device or other deadly devices in a public place, state or government facility, public transport system, or infrastructure facility. Article 5 of the Convention obliges signatory states to ensure that the offenses set in the Convention do not apply to persons belonging to a particular religion, race, philosophical or ideological character. In addition, the

Convention prohibits the propaganda of terrorism in the state, its justification in any form, and requires states to criminalize such acts and to punish perpetrators of prohibited acts (UN, 1997).

Last but not least is the International Convention for the Suppression of the Financing of Terrorism (1999), adopted to eliminate the financial promotion of terrorism. Under the Convention, a prohibited act is committed by a person whether he or she directly or indirectly, illegally or voluntarily provides or raises funds for the financing of terrorist organizations or groups. Article 5 of the Convention obliges the signatory states to hold the responsibility to all persons or organizations in their territory which provide financial assistance to terrorist groups. The specifics of the fight against terrorist financing include the complex relations between the intelligence and law enforcement aspects, which also apply to vulnerable areas such as banking secrecy (UN, 1999).

The effectiveness of international legal agreements in the fight against terrorism depends on domestic law and the willingness of governments to implement them. Unlike international law, to accurately identify terrorist activity, domestic law must provide a comprehensive definition of a terrorist offense. Determining the exact definition at the state level has several functions: Depending on the accuracy of the definition, specific groups are given the criminal status of "terrorist", which makes it possible to carry out investigative actions against specific individuals or to confiscate or freeze their financial assets. The definition allows to distinguish terrorism from other crimes with a similar component and it determines the coordination of internal structures. Therefore, the definition is necessary for the selection of counterterrorism tactics, for the avoidance of unjustified restrictions on the legal rights of civil society, and so on (Saul, 2005).

RESPONSES TO TERRORISM

Terrorism prevention must be considered in two of the most important aspects: The first is to prevent terrorism and increase the effectiveness of the fight against it, which is the primary task of any modern state. And the second - terrorism prevention is a unified system of socio-economic, political, and legal measures aimed at terrorist organizations (groups), terrorist acts, prevention of the consequences of terrorism and aims to ensure public safety, international, economic, and political interests of the state (Crelinsten & Schmid, 2007).

First of all, it is necessary to consider the factors that hinder the prevention of terrorism. One of them is the fact that the fight against terrorist crimes is carried out largely in response to crimes already committed. In addition, it should be noted that the prevention of criminal encroachment, disruption of international and interregional links between criminal groups, and, as a result, joint work to eliminate terrorist organizations is not carried out (Crelinsten & Schmid, 2007)

Nowadays, there is still no comprehensive and complete database of all previous crimes committed by terrorist groups and members of these groups. There is an internal disconnection in the registration of crimes related to terrorism. As a result, statistical data is distorted, the consistent registration of criminal cases is violated, which leads to duplication of investigative and operational measures, and makes it impossible to exchange operational information (IEP, 2022).

It is also noteworthy that those who have previously been convicted of terrorist offenses, which are quite numerous, remain out of the spotlight. Some of them continue antisocial activities, keep firearms, cover up wanted persons, and more. Furthermore, repeated searches of the residence of alleged members of terrorist groups at the initiative of the Interior Ministry are not yielding results (IEP, 2022).

The issue of modern trends in terrorism is also problematic. It is these trends that make it possible to talk about an effective system for preventing and combating terrorism. The main trend of modern terrorism can be considered its intensive shift in the direction of increasing public danger (IEP, 2022).

In the last three decades, more than 10 thousand terrorist acts have been carried out in the world and covered by the mass media. Moreover, Over the last century, terrorism has gone through a great revolutionary path, from ordinary terrorists to the formation of terrorist groups, major reorganizations, and political terrorist formations, and the formation of transnational terrorist groups such as al Qaeda. In addition, terrorism has developed in terms of material, technical and financial support (IEP, 2022).

The scale of terrorism extends from a single crime scene to entire cities, countries, and regions. The growth rate of human casualties on average exceeds the rate of terrorist acts themselves. Victims can be individuals starting with tens of thousands of innocent people. In terms of the nature and scope of the current goals, the range is quite wide: starting with the assassination of individuals and the overthrow of legitimate government, ending with the de facto destruction of states and entire nations. As for the expansion of terrorist bases, terrorist groups are joined not only by individual political, national, or religious organizations but also by entire nations or their important strata (IEP, 2022).

The legislation of the United States of America is quite interesting in terms of the legal basis for the fight against terrorism, as any of its articles can be used to combat international terrorism. Up to twenty laws are actively used by U.S. law enforcement in the fight against terrorism. One part of these laws are passed and drafted based on conventions, while the other protects US interests abroad (Setty, 2014).

Under the Comprehensive Crime Act of 1984, terrorist acts in the United States are considered crimes related to the commission of an act of a violent nature if it is life-threatening, violates federal criminal law, or if it falls within the jurisdiction of any state. This law criminalizes any act of violence that endangers human life, aimed at intimidating the population or forcing them to take any action (Setty, 2014).

It is noteworthy that the international community has developed several specific procedural rules that have influenced national law. For instance, the French Code of Criminal Procedure introduces a new chapter on the nature of the terrorism case, namely changes in terms of detention, jurisdiction, incentives, incentives, and, consequently, concessions in the case of terrorist acts to effectively combat terrorism. Moreover, the legislation of the United Kingdom allows law enforcement agencies to confiscate a terrorist organization's property, and additional procedural safeguards have been developed to prevent the leakage of classified information. Besides that, the specifics of conducting some investigative actions are taken into account, in particular, investigative actions are conducted without attendees (COE, 2013).

Along with national legislation, International Normative Acts adopted to reduce terrorism in the world play an important role. One of the key issues here is the commitment of the world community to international conventions, according to which the state is obliged to hand over a terrorist to the competent authorities of the state for prosecution. If a UN member state assists the organizer of terrorism, political, economic, and other sanctions will be imposed on such a country (IEP, 2022).

Proceeding from all the above mentioned, it is obvious that terrorism has become particularly widespread in recent years and the numerous circumstances complicate the fight against it. Terrorism threatens to maintain world peace and security, therefore, an important role in its defeat is played by the joint efforts of the international community and putting the fight against terrorism at the top of the hierarchy of interests.

CONCLUSION

The main purpose of the study was to determine the history of terrorism, the causes of its origin and development, and the response of the modern world to terrorist acts. Based on this, the aim was to answer the main question of the research and to show the urgency of terrorism in today's world. The study identified that nowadays, terrorism is not only lone saboteurs, hijackers, or killer Kamikazes, but also represented by the appropriate equipment of power structures. It has become a globally profitable business with a thriving labor market and capital investment. An important feature of modern terrorism is its organized nature and the rationality of terrorist acts depends not on the actual results, its price, suffering, and the death of the victim, but the impression they make on society.

The arguments were based on the analysis of various articles, reports, analytical papers, and official documents, such as the Conventions of the United Nations as a result of the use of a qualitative research method. A review of the definition and the early stages of terrorism revealed the main challenge in the process of fighting against terrorism. The lack of an internationally recognized universal definition complicates the process of cooperation between countries and the identification of terrorist acts in general. In addition, the history of the origins of terrorism has demonstrated its ability to adapt over time.

The ability of terrorism to adapt to modern changes became even more apparent after reviewing its four major waves, when the characteristic features of each period, innovations in the organization of terrorist acts, and ideological changes were revealed. The analysis of the causes, types and methods of terrorism revealed its flexibility in technological development. Terrorists are equipped with the latest combat or communication equipment and use technological advances to achieve their own goal, which is, to be constantly in the spotlight, and to have an impact on the world community.

The complexity of terrorism is due to the diverse nature of its forms. With the change of time, different types of terrorism have emerged, such as information, biological, computer, and other types of terrorism. The formation of these forms can take place in both a democratic and a dictatorial state. Since the current positive or negative changes in the modern world may be a precondition for the emergence of a new form of terrorism, it is difficult for states to draw up an effective action plan against each of them.

The support of states for terrorist organizations also deserves attention. While some countries around the world are increasingly trying to eradicate this crime, they are analyzing the fact that some other states support terrorist organizations: financially, with military assistance, ideological assistance, through financial transactions, and so on.

Furthermore, the ability of terrorist organizations to take advantage of crises around the world is noteworthy. Important issues are the creation of an international network by terrorist groups, in addition to the Internet space and social networks that became vital to the public during the Corona Pandemic. It should be noted that this crisis has given terrorists a new direction of action. Increasing the world community's dependence on social networks has created an ideal basis for their propaganda.

Efforts to cooperate between states are reflected in the conventions drafted by the UN, although today numerous factors make states ineffective in the fight against terrorism. Along with the problem of the lack of a universal definition of terrorism, it is also noteworthy that legislative changes are needed not only at the international but also at the national level.

The fact is that terrorism has become particularly widespread in recent years. It is one of the global problems facing humanity as numerous circumstances complicate the fight against terrorism. In the wake of the development of society, the forms and types of terrorism have changed, as well as its methods and causes, the scale of terrorism, and the perspectives through which the scientific study of terrorism takes place. As a result, this topic requires constant research and study.

REFERENCES

Basit, A. (2020). The COVID-19 Pandemic: An Opportunity for Terrorist Groups? *Counter Terrorist Trends and Analyses*, *12*(3), 7–12.

Campion, K., Ferrill, J., & Milligan, K. (2021). Extremist Exploitation of the Context Created by COVID-19 and the Implications for Australian Security. *Perspectives on Terrorism*, *15*(6).

COE. (2013). *Profiles on counter-terrorist capacity-France*. Council of Europe.

Crelinsten, R., & Schmid, A. (2007). Western responses to terrorism: A twenty-five year balance sheet. *Terrorism and Political Violence*, 307–340.

CTED. (2021). *Update on the impact of the COVID-19 pandemic on Terrorism, counter-terrorism and countering violent extremism.* CTED.

FATF. (2010). *An introduction to the FATF and its work.* Retrieved from Fatf-gafi: https://www.fatf-gafi.org/media/fatf/documents/brochuresannualreports/Introduction%20to%20the%20FATF.pdf

Hirschmann, K. (2003). *The Changing Face of Terrorism.* Retrieved from SemanticScholar: https://library.fes.de/pdf-files/ipg/ipg-2000-3/arthirschmann.pdf

IEP. (2022). *Global Terrorism Index 2022-Measuring the Impact of Terrorism.* Institute for Economics & Peace.

Kiser, S. (2005). *Financing Terror. An Analysis and Simulation to Affect Al Qaeda's Financial Infrastructures.* RAND.

Medero, G. (2011). Les sources de financement légal et illégal des groupes terroristes d´aujourd´hui. *Revista de Paz, 4.*

Napoleoni, L. (2005, January). Money and Terrorism. *Economist.*

Norlen, T. C. (2020). The Impact of COVID-19 on Salafi-Jihadi Terrorism. *Connections: The Quarterly Journal, 19*(2), 11-23.

Rapoport, D. C. (2002). The Four Waves of Rebel Terror and September 11. *Anthropoetics*, *8*(1).

Saul, B. (2005). Attempts to define "terrorism" in international law. *Netherlands International Law Review*, *52*(1), 57–83. doi:10.1017/S0165070X05000574

Schmid, A. P. (1983). Political terrorism: A research guide to concepts, theories, data, bases and literature. Academic Press.

Setty, S. (2014). Country Report on Counterterrorism. *The American Journal of Comparative Law*, *62*(1), 643–672. doi:10.5131/AJCL.2013.0039

Smith, M. (1971). Zealots and Sicarii, Their Origins and Relation. *The Harvard Theological Review*, *64*(1), 1–19. doi:10.1017/S0017816000018009

UN. (1963). *Convention on Offences and Certain Other Acts Committed on Board Aircraft.* International Civil Aviation Organization.

UN. (1970). Convention for the suppression of unlawful seizure of aircraft. United Nations.

UN. (1971). *Montreal Convention for the Suppression of Unlawful Acts against the Safety of Civil Aviation*. United Nations.

UN. (1977). Ad-Hoc Committee on International Terrorism. United Nations General Assembly.

UN. (1997). *International Convention for the Suppression of Terrorist Bombing*. New York: United Nations.

UN. (1999a). *International Convention for the Suppression of the Financing of Terrorism*. Retrieved from United Nations: https://www.un.org/law/cod/finterr.htm

UN. (1999b). *International Convention for the Suppression of the Financing of Terrorism*. New York: United Nations.

UN. (2005). *International Convention for the Suppression of Acts of Nuclear Terrorism*. New York: United Nations.

UN. (2018). *Introduction to International Terrorism*. United Nations Office at Vienna.

Yamamoto, M. M. (2018). *Terrorism Against Democracy*. Center for International and Security Studies at Maryland.

Chapter 2
Problems of Terrorism in the Modern World

Nika Chitadze
International Black Sea University, Georgia

ABSTRACT

Currently, the study of the topic of terrorism is especially relevant in connection with the increase in the number of terrorist attacks committed by various terrorist organizations around the world. The constant threat of terror leads to the destabilization of the political, economic, and social situation in the state. Lack of confidence in personal safety contributes to the growth of anxiety, fears, and mental stress, which negatively affects psychological health, leading to the development of various psychosomatic disorders among the population. The genesis of the concept of "terrorism," the history of terrorism, the psychology of the personality of terrorists and terrorist groups, the victimology of terrorism, methods of providing psychological first aid in terrorist attacks, methods of negotiating with terrorists, technologies for forming a model of safe behavior are the main issues during the study of the basic aspects related to terrorism.

INTRODUCTION

The general position of considering terrorism as a rare and relatively remote threat was challenged by the terrorist acts on the territory of the United States on September 11, 2001. The brutal incidents, having been committed on the World Trade Center, the Pentagon, and the crash victims in Pennsylvania forced the International Society to confront a grim new reality: Terrorist Organizations had an appropriate resource for the implementation of catastrophic attacks almost in each place of our Planet, even without an arsenal of sophisticated weapons.

9/11 became the decisive moment for the whole world to be concentrated on the topics of national as well as international security.

The developments within the current period of World History prove that terrorism is considered to be the most important danger of the 21st century.

US State Department listed 44 terrorist organizations in 2008 (Goldstein and Pevehouse, 2011).

DOI: 10.4018/978-1-6684-5311-7.ch002

In modern times, Boko Haram, Tamil Tigers, Al-Qaeda, Hezbollah, and especially "Islamic State" play very significant roles even in deciding the scope of the foreign policy of leading superpowers.

The aggressive policy of Russia against Ukraine and the World Democratic Community points to the existence of states on the World political map, that conduct the policy of State Terrorism against civilian – peaceful populations, and innocent people. Furthermore, those states, for example, Russia, fund and supports different terrorist groups and illegal armed formations. United Nations, by Resolution 39/159 "Inadmissibility of the policy of State terrorism and any actions by States aimed at undermining the socio-political system in other sovereign States", condemns any actions of state terrorism (UN, 1984).

In general, Terrorism represents one of the most serious problems which not only has become aggravated at the end of the 20th and the beginning of the 21st century but also has appeared, in fact, among the main security threats, especially in its new forms, which have several new directions. It is caused, first of all, by the level of technological development and possibilities to impact the world, therefore large-scale terrorist attacks can be conducted by a small group of people or even by one person. Secondly, in the modern world, the potential range of terrorist organizations (national and cultural symbols, government buildings, places of big congestion of people, etc.) and also types of weapons which can be used are various. The third, modern terrorists, or, by U. Lakyyuer's definition, terrorists of an era of postmodern, together with other criminal structures look for allies in public institutions that lead to corruption. Considerable sums are spent on bribery of officials and also the intelligence agencies, which are designed to prevent illegal activity (Chitadze, 2022).

Terrorism by itself is not a new phenomenon. It has been known since Ancient Greece and Ancient Rome. In the 19th century, terrorism is connected with anarchical and also nationalist organizations. To estimates of several authors, for example, R. Kidder, terrorism becomes an international problem in 1960th years. In the 1970-1980th years, the world faced a surge in terrorist operations in Europe (Lebedeva, 2011).

Despite the long-time existence of the terrorism phenomenon, from the theoretical position, it is quite complicated to give a concrete and final definition to this negative event. The matter is that the same actions are considered at the same time by the different parties as terrorism from one side and freedom

Figure 1. Most brutal terrorist attacks. New York, USA, September 11, 2001.
Source: https://zeenews.india.com/world/9/11-attacks-new-york-marks-19th-anniversary-of-the-dreadful-terror-attack-2308932.html

fighting from the other side. For this reason, the attempts to define terrorism within the UN (and various criteria offered by the USA, Great Britain, and other countries) in general have not been crowned with success (Chitadze, 2022).

However, the fact that, first, it is politically motivated violent actions or their threat is undoubtedly important in terrorism definition, secondly, they are directed against innocent people, and not just directly concerning the power. Concerning them, terrorist attacks for the realization of these or those political goals are committed. Terrorism is substantially focused on the achievement of a psychological effect. Accordingly, terrorists are, as a rule, interested in that their acts have found as much as possible extended coverage in mass media means. The psychological effect has multiple directions, including drawing attention to the organization and its aims, demonstration of opportunities, population or its certain groups, etc.

Another important character when determining terrorism is what is carried out by the non-state actors. Therefore, any armed actions, let unjustified and illegal (for example, the capture by Iraq of Kuwait in the early nineties), don't get under terrorism definitions. At the same time, the state can give support to the terrorist organizations (including financial or in the form of granting the territory for the terrorist bases, refusal of delivering terrorists to the other states, approvals of their actions, etc.). In this regard, there has appeared a term "State Terrorism". The USA, for example, even the states which, according to them, get to this category. However, the state in such cases practically never takes the responsibility for recognition in the assistance to terrorism, and to prove the state`s participation in the terrorist act is quite difficult (Chitadze, 2022).

The period of the beginning of the 21st century when the political structure of the world is in process of cardinal changes represents itself as the convenient base for terrorism development. In modern conditions of globalization terrorists often act out of national borders. Therefore, it is being discussed international terrorism, or transnational terrorism (that is more precise), means the use of the territory or involvement of the citizens in terrorist actions in more than one country. And even though it is quite difficult to outline borders between internal and international terrorism as practically all rather large terrorist organizations have links outside national borders, nevertheless feature of the first is the fact that the challenge is thrown down not to the concrete state or group of the states, but the model of development of the world. Construction of transnational terrorist structures to the network principle and finding the structural division in many states of the world strongly complicates the fight against this threat.

Terrorist actions are not seldom included in an arsenal of the means of fighting by various ethnic, religious, and other groups, actually being a form of political struggle and favorable business. Among the different terrorist groups good connections, including military and commercial, are established. Some interact with the criminal structures, in particular, which are connected with the drug business. Incomes from the sale of drugs quite often go for the financing of acts of terrorism.

Special concern is caused by the possibility of access by the terrorist organizations to the modern types of weapons and weapons of mass destruction. So, in March 1995, the Japanese religious sect Aum Shinrikyo conducted a terrorist attack with the use of nervously-paralytic gas in the subway, as a result of which 10 people have been killed and about 5000 have been forced to ask for medical care. However, one of the biggest shocks was the actions of terrorists on September 11, 2001, when in the USA several planes, which were captured by terrorists, were directed at the buildings of the World Trade Center in New York and also to the Pentagon. One more plane crashed with passengers, but in this case, at least it succeeded to avoid the much bigger victims. The results of the attack were comparable to the destructive effect of the missile attack.

This act of terrorism has raised many security issues differently. Earlier many estimates have brought out the calculation of the time of flight of ballistic missiles. Now, this indicator is insufficient. The second moment is connected with the definition of a source of aggression. If before in strategic concepts one or several states' main threats were coming from the foreign states, then today the list of potential attackers is included, terrorist groups. The international terrorists, on the one hand, have bases, as a rule, in various countries, with another directly and openly isn't connected with government institutions (if to exclude a possibility of creation of corruption). As it was noted, terrorists act as independent actors on the world scene. At last, threats are extremely certain: poisoning of water of the megalopolis or the gas attack in the subway can be done by civilian airliners, tomorrow. At last, the last major moment connected with lessons on September 11, 2001, and the governments of certain countries (even such powerful as the USA) and the international community, in general, were not ready to adequately answer. The tragic events in Beslan on September 1, 2004, connected with the taking of hostages in the school, have once again confirmed new parameters of modern threats: surprise (several minutes are absent even for preparation for reflection of the attacks), plurality, and heterogeneity of terrorist acts and also means of attack (Chitadze, 2022).

Other directions of modern terrorism - cyberterrorism, including information attacks, which are interrelated with a possibility of destabilization of activities of computer systems and networks. Discussing the role of such systems in the modern world, it is easy to imagine the consequences of the large failures in the working of transport, communication, power supply, governmental and municipal structures - the so-called "Critical infrastructures" of modern society. The feature of cyberterrorism consists of the fact, that the threat of information terrorism is realized significantly professionally by various international actors. Based on the source of one of the computer magazines (information Week), viruses and actions of hackers cost large businesses in only one 2000 about 1,6 billion dollars. In May of the same year in Paris, the meeting at the level of computer terrorism experts has taken place. They expressed opinions that the threat of cyberterrorism constitutes a danger for mankind, comparable with nuclear, chemical, and bacteriological wars.

All this also induces the states to coordinate their actions in the fight against terrorism. A number of the international agreements, in particular, on providing safe civil via transportation and shipping (The international conventions 1963, 1970, 1988) have been adopted, for example; in the fight against the taking of hostages (1979); to the protection of nuclear materials (1980). International terrorism has received condemnation in 1985 at the UN General Assembly where the relevant Resolution has been adopted (Lebedeva, 2011). The question of the fight against terrorism was repeatedly raised at meetings of heads of states, including members of the G7.

Special divisions in the fight against terrorism exist in many countries. Coordination of national efforts is on the practical level carried out by different international institutes, including Interpol.

INTERNATIONAL TERRORISM: THE MAIN THREAT TO THE WORLD COMMUNITY IN THE XXI CENTURY

Definition and History of the Notion and Its Evolution Through the Centuries

Terrorism is not a new phenomenon and even though it has been used since the beginning of recorded history, it can be comparably difficult to make the exact definition of terrorism. Terrorism has been analyzed variously as both a tactic and strategy; a crime and a "liberation movement". It very much depends on whose position and opinion are being represented. Terrorism has often been an effective tactic for the weaker side in a conflict. As an asymmetric form of the conflict, it confers coercive power with many of the advantages of military force at a fraction of the cost. Taking into account the secretive nature and small size of the terrorist organizations, those groups do not offer their opponents any clear structure. Because of this, preemption is considered to be so significant. In some cases, terrorism has been a means to continue a conflict without the adversary realizing the nature of the threat, mistaking terrorism for criminal activity. Taking into consideration these characteristics, terrorism has become increasingly common among those pursuing extreme purposes throughout our planet. But despite its popularity, terrorism can be a nebulous concept (Chitadze, 2022).

Even in the case of the U.S. Government, state agencies responsible for different functions in the ongoing combating terrorism activities, use various definitions. By FBI, terrorism is defined as "The unlawful use or threatened use of force or violence by a person or an organized group against people or property to intimidate or coerce societies or governments, often for ideological or political reasons" (FBI, 2005).

Discussing this definition, there are three main factors - violence, fear, and intimidation and each element produces terror in its victims. Thus, FBI uses other type of determination: "Terrorism is the unlawful use of force and violence against persons or property to intimidate or coerce a government, the civilian population, or any segment thereof, in furtherance of political or social objectives"(FBI, 2005). The U.S. Department of State, based on the title 22 of the U.S. Code, Section 2656f(d), defines "terrorism" to be "premeditated politically-motivated violence perpetrated against non-combatant targets by sub-national groups or clandestine agents, usually intended to influence an audience" (US Department of State, 2007).

Besides the determination from the United States Government`s side, there are greater variations in what features of terrorism are emphasized in definitions. One of the leading experts on Combating Terrorism issues, Prof. Alex Schmid presented his definition, which is the following: "An anxiety-inspiring method of repeated violent action, employed by (semi-) clandestine individual, group or state actors, for idiosyncratic, criminal or political reasons, whereby - in contrast to assassination - the direct targets of violence are not the main targets"(NATO, 2007). The most recently distributed academic determination is added to the above-mentioned definition. There are presented two more sentences and include 77 words in general; containing such verbose concepts as "message generators" and "violence" based communication processes." Less specific and considerably less verbose, the British Government's definition of 1974 is"...the use of violence for political ends, and includes any use of violence to put the public, or any section of the public, in fear (Schmid, 2004)."

In general, Terrorism is a criminal act that influences an audience beyond the immediate victim. The strategy of terrorists is to commit acts of violence that draw the attention of the local population, the government, and the world to their cause. During the planning of the terrorist attack, the main purpose of terrorists is to obtain the greatest publicity, choosing targets that symbolize what they oppose. The effectiveness of the terrorist act lies not in the act itself, but in the public's or government's reaction to the act. For example, in 1972, during the Olympic Games in Munich, 11 members of the Israeli delegation were killed by the Black September Organization. The Israelis were the immediate victims, but the real target was the estimated 1 billion people watching the televised event.

The organization – "Black September" used the high visibility of the Olympic games to publicize its views on the problems of the Palestinian refugees. Besides, in October 1983, terrorists from the Middle East Region committed a terrorist act at the Marine Battalion Landing Team Headquarters at

Beirut International Airport. Their immediate victims were the 241 U.S. military personnel who were killed and over 100 others who were wounded. The direct target of those terrorists was the American people and the government. This one act of violence influenced the United States' decision to withdraw the Marines from Beirut and was therefore considered a successful result for the terrorists (Chitadze, 2022).

There are three targets of terrorism: the terrorists, the victims, and the general public. The phrase "one man's terrorist is another man's freedom fighter" is a view terrorists themselves would accept. Terrorists do not consider themselves criminals. They are sure that they are legitimate combatants, fighting for the protection of their ideas by any possible means. A victim of a terrorist act and the majority of society sees the terrorist as evil with no regard for human life. The general public's view is the most unstable. The terrorists do their best to create the image of "Robin Hood" with the hope to find additional supporters among the members of society. This sympathetic view of terrorism has become an integral part of their psychological warfare and needs to be countered vigorously.

SEVERAL HISTORIC ASPECTS OF TERRORIST ACTIVITIES

Terrorism and terrorist groups have the deep roots since the ancient period. The first known organization that exhibited aspects of a modern terrorist organization was the Zealots of Judea. Known to the Romans as Sicarii, or dagger-men, they committed an underground campaign of murdering Roman occupation forces, as well as any Jews, whom they considered to be allies of Romans and who were serving the Roman authorities. The motive of those groups was an uncompromising belief that they could not remain faithful to the dictates of Judaism while living under pressure from the Roman Empire. Eventually, the Zealot rebel movement became open and they were finally besieged and were forced to commit mass suicide at the fortification of Masada (World History Encyclopedia, 2022).

Several centuries later, the Assassins were the next group, whose activities were interrelated with the modern standards of terrorism. A breakaway faction of Shia Islam called the Nizari Ismailis worked out the tactic of the assassination of enemy leaders because the cult's limited manpower prevented open combat. The head of this group, Hassam-I Sabbah, based the cult in the mountains of Northern Iran. Their tactic of sending a lone assassin to successfully kill a key enemy leader at the certain sacrifice of his own life (the killers waited next to their victims to be killed or captured) inspired fearful awe in their enemies (Longo, 2022).

Despite the fact, that Zealots and the Assassins were involved in terrorist activities a long time ago, they are relevant nowadays: First as forerunners of modern terrorists in aspects of motivation, organization, targeting, and goals. Secondly, although both were ultimate failures, the fact that they are remembered hundreds of years later demonstrates the deep psychological impact they caused.

From the period of the Assassin's (late 13th century) activities to the beginning of the 18th Century, terror and barbarism were widely used in warfare and conflict, but key ingredients for terrorism were lacking. After the ending of the 30-year war and the signing of the Treaty of Westphalia in 1648, when the centralized, nation-states were founded, the sort of central authority and cohesive society that terrorism attempts to influence barely existed. Communications were inadequate and controlled, and the causes that could inspire terrorism (religious schism, insurrection, ethnic strife) movements typically led to open military operations. By the time kingdoms and principalities became nations, they had an appropriate resources to enforce their power and prevent such activities, as terrorism.

The Revolution in France in 1789 provided the first uses of the definition "Terrorist" and "Terrorism". Using this terminology - "terrorism" began in 1795 when the Reign of Terror was initiated by the Revolutionary government of France against supporters of the previous authorities - the monarchy. The representatives of the Committee of Public Safety and the National Convention that enforced the policies of "The Terror" were referred to as 'Terrorists"(Terrorism, 2020). The Revolutionary processes in France within the period 1789-1793 created the precedent for the other states in oppressing their populations in the future. It also inspired a reaction by royalists and other opponents of the Revolution who was involved in the implementation of terrorist tactics such as assassination and intimidation in resistance to the Revolutionary agents. The Parisian mobs played a decisive role at key points before, during, and after the Revolution. Such extra-radical activities as murdering prominent officials and aristocrats in gruesome spectacles started long before the invention of the first-time guillotine (Chitadze, 2022).

At the end of the 19th century, the development of the political theories, which were based on the principles of radicalism and improvements in the technology of producing the weapons, spurred the formation of small groups of so-called "revolutionaries", in reality, terrorists, who were involved in the effective attack of the public and other institutions. Anarchists espousing belief in the "propaganda of the deed" produced some striking successes, killing heads of the states of Russia, France, Spain, Italy, and the United States. However, their weak organizational structure and ignorance of the cooperation with the other social groups and movements in political efforts rendered anarchists ineffective as a political ideology and movement. In contrast, Communism's role as an ideological basis, based on the radical theory of Marxism, found a convenient way for political terrorism. At the beginning of the XX Century, it was just activating and finally became much more influential in the first half of the last century.

Another tendency in the late 19th century, when many territories of the world were under the colonial rules of the leading geopolitical powers of this period, was the increasing wave of nationalism in the different parts of our planet, in which the nation (the identity of a people) and the political state were combined. As nations started to protect their national identities - language, religion, cultural heritage, etc. people that had been conquered or colonized could, like the Jews at the times of the Zealots, opt for assimilation or struggle. One of the most known ethical and religious conflicts in Europe from this time is still not finally resolved - the multi-century struggle of Irish nationalism which is combined with the protection of the principles of Catholicism in Northern Ireland. The anti-colonial type of Nationalism, like communism, became a much greater ideological force in the 20th century.

The terrorist organization from this period that is represented as a model of many types of terrorist activities was the Russian Narodnya Volya (Peoples Will). Taking into consideration the strategy and tactics of this group, it should be pointed out that it differed in some ways from modern terrorists, especially in that they would sometimes call off attacks that might endanger individuals other than their intended target. Other than this quirk, it can be noticed many of the traits of terrorism here for the first time; clandestine, cellular organization; impatience and inability for the task of organizing the constituents they claim to represent; and a tendency to increase the level of violence as pressures on the group mount.

The first half of the 20th century was characterized by the two events that influenced the nature of the conflict to the present day. The effects of the two World Wars inflamed passions and hopes of nationalists throughout the world, and severely damaged the legitimacy of the international order and governments. The activation of the nationalism movement became more intensified during the early 20th century throughout the world. It transferred to an especially powerful force in the subject peoples of various colonial empires. Although dissent and resistance were common in many colonial possessions, and sometimes resulted in open warfare, national identities became a focal point for these actions (Goldstein and Pevehouse, 2011).

Gradually, as peoples and nations became closely connected with the concepts of race and ethnicity, international political developments began to support such approaches. Members of ethnic groups whose territories had been occupied by the other states or had ceased to exist as independent nations considered the new opportunities to realize their nationalist ambitions. Several of these ethnic and religious groups chose terror as a method to conduct their struggle and make their situation known to the international community, which they hoped would be sympathetic. In Europe, both the Irish and the Basks separatist groups were involved in the terrorist campaigns as part of their ongoing struggle for independence but had to initiate bloody uprisings to further their cause. Both were partially successful.

Further development of Terrorism is connected with the Cold War period. The bipolar international system of the Cold War changed the perception of conflicts in the world. Relatively, minor confrontations took on significance as arenas where the superpowers could compete without risking escalation to full nuclear war. Warfare between the East and the West, between two economic and political systems, and between two ideologies took place on the peripheries and was limited in scope to prevent escalation. During the immediate postwar period, terrorism was more of a tactical choice by leaders of nationalist insurgencies and revolutions. National-Liberation movements for independence from colonial rule occurred throughout the world and many employed terrorisms as a supporting tactic. In several cases, terrorism was used within the framework of larger movements and coordinated with political, social, and military actions. Even when terrorism came to dominate the other aspects of a nationalist struggle, such as the Palestinian campaign against Israel, it was (and is) combined with other activities (Hoffman, 2017).

TERRORIST ACTIONS OR THE THREAT OF SUCH TYPES OF ACTIVITIES HAVE BEEN IN EXISTENCE FOR MILLENIA

Despite the fact, that the history of the terrorism activities prevails over the history of the modern nation-state, the commitment of the terrorist acts by the various groups or even by some state institutions and those that contest their power remains hardly researched. From one side, the term - terror itself is more or less understandable, when it is associated with acts and actors in the real world it becomes confused. Party is determined by the fact – uses terror strategies and tactics by organizers at all levels in the social and political environment. Who is the person, who uses an appropriate military and other kinds of equipment for the explosion of the various civil and military objects, a criminal? Or a member of any revolutionary movement? (Chitadze, 2022).

Is it possible, that some people to be compared to the French revolutionary governments who used the term terrorism to justify the systematic state terror against this part of the population of France in the 1790s, which was considered as opposition to the new government by killing tens of thousands? Are either they the same as revolutionary terrorist groups such as the Baader-Meinhof Gang of West Germany or the Weather Underground in the United States? (Chitadze, 2022)

So, it can be noticed that distinction of size and political legitimacy of the actors using terror raise questions as to which action can be considered a terrorist act and which not. The concept related to moral equivalency is very often used as an argument to broaden and blur the definition of terrorism as well. This approach argues that the outcome of an action is what matters, not the intent. Collateral or unintended damage to civilians from an attack by illegal paramilitary forces on a legitimate military target is the same as a terrorist bomb directed deliberately at the civilian target to create that damage. Simply put, a car bomb on a city street and a jet fighter dropping a bomb on a tank are both acts of violence that produce death and terror. Therefore (at the end of this argument) any illegal activities with the use of weapons are simply terrorism with a different interpretation. This is the reasoning behind the famous phrase "One man's terrorist is another man's freedom fighter" (Hoffman, 2013). It is also a legacy of legitimizing the use of terror by successful revolutionary movements after the fact.

The very flexibility and adaptability of terror during the long period have contributed to the confusion. Those seeking to disrupt, reorder or destroy the status quo have continuously sought new and creative ways to achieve their goals. Some changes in the strategy and tactics and development of techniques by terrorists have been significant, but even more significant is the increase in the number of causes and social contexts where terrorist acts are committed. During the past 20 years, terrorists have implemented extremely violent acts for alleged political or religious reasons. Political ideology, on which terrorists are based, ranges from the extreme left to the extreme right. For example, the leftist groups can be represented by such terrorist organizations as Marxists and Leninists who propose a revolution of workers led by the revolutionary elite. On the contrary, right-wing-oriented groups are based on the typical belief in a merging of state and business leadership. Nationalism is the devotion to the interests or culture of a group of people or a nation. Typically, nationalists share a common ethnic background and desire to establish an independent state. Religious extremists often ignore the power of secular authorities and consider legal systems that are not based on their religious beliefs illegitimate. They often reject all types of modernization efforts, which they view as corrupting influences on traditional culture. Special interest groups include people on the radical fringe of many legitimate causes; e.g., groups of the people, who commit terrorist acts to uphold antiabortion views, animal rights, and radical environmentalism. These people strongly believe that violence is morally justifiable to achieve their purposes (Chitadze, 2022).

TERRORIST INCIDENTS AND TECHNIQUES: TERRORIST GROUPS AND TERRORIST BEHAVIOR

The Most Common Terroristic Incidents

Bombings

It is already proved, that improvised explosive devices are not expensive and easy to produce. Modern devices have smaller shapes and are harder to detect. Those devices include very destructive capabilities; for example, on August 7, 1998, two American diplomatic representations, in Africa, particularly in Kenya and Tanzania were under a bomb attack acts claimed the lives of over 200 people, including 12 innocent American citizens, and injured over 5,000 civilians (FBI, 2022). Terrorists can also use materials that are readily available to the average consumer to construct a bomb.

Kidnappings and Hostage-Takings

One of the main policies of the terrorist groups represents kidnapping and hostage-taking. Terrorists implement this type of action for the establishment of a bargaining position and to elicit publicity. Kidnapping is one of the most difficult acts for a terrorist organization to fulfill, but, if in case of the successful implementation of the operation, terrorists obtain an opportunity to attract more financial

Figure 2. Rescue workers evacuating the bodies of victims of a terrorist train bombing near Atocha Station, Madrid, March 11, 2004
Source: https://www.britannica.com/topic/terrorism

resources, which later they can use for the release of the jailed comrades, and publicity for an extended period. Hostage-taking involves the seizure of a facility or location and the taking of hostages. Unlike a kidnapping, hostage-taking provokes a confrontation with authorities. It determines the positions of the governments of the various countries related to choosing the concrete strategy - either to make dramatic decisions or to conduct negotiations with terrorists and listen to their position. It is overt and designed to attract and hold media attention. The terrorists' intended target is the audience affected by the hostage's confinement, not the hostage (Chitadze, 2022).

The legal definition of kidnapping is the taking away of a person by force, threat, or deceit, with the intent to detain that person against his will. Kidnapping can be implemented with the request for ransom (economic reasons) or political or other purposes, for example requiring the releasing of the members of the terrorist group from the prison or changing the official policy of the government related to the internal and external policy of the country. In history, under common law, kidnapping was only a misdemeanor, but in different parts of the world as in most states of the United States, the practice is now punishable by death or life imprisonment (Chitadze, 2022).

Armed Attacks and Assassinations

Armed attacks include raids and ambushes. Assassinations are the killing of a selected victim, usually by the use of special explosive equipment or small arms. Drive-by shootings are a common technique employed by unsophisticated or loosely organized terrorist groups. From the historic point of view, it can be assumed, that terrorists have murdered specific persons for psychological effects (Hoffman, 2017).

Arsons and Fire Bombings

Incendiary devices are cheap and easy to hide. Arson and fire-bombings are easily conducted by terrorist organizations, that may not be as well-organized, equipped, or trained as a major terrorist group. An arson or firebombing against a utility, hotel, government building, or industrial center portrays an image that the ruling government is incapable of maintaining order (Hoffman, 2017).

Hijackings and Skyjackings

Hijacking is the seizure by using the force of a surface vehicle, passengers, who are inside, and/ or its cargo. Skyjacking represents the occupation of an aircraft, which creates a mobile, hostage barricade situation. It provides terrorists with hostages from many nations and draws heavy media attention. Skyjacking also provides mobility for the terrorists to relocate the aircraft to a country that supports their cause and provides them with a human shield, making retaliation to be complicated (Hoffman, 2017).

Other Types of Terrorist Incidents

In addition to the above-mentioned types of terrorist acts and acts of violence, numerous other methods of violence can exist under the framework of terrorism. Terrorist organizations conduct violence against their people also by implementing robberies and extortion when they need additional financial resources for the continuation of their activities and when they don't have other sources of funding.

Cyber-terrorism is a new type of terrorism activity that is ever-increasing taking into account that humanity relies on computer networks to obtain different kinds of important information and provide connectivity to today's modern and fast-paced world. Cyber-terrorism allows the terrorist groups to fulfill their operations with little or almost no risk to themselves. It also provides terrorists a resource to disrupt or destroy networks and computer systems. The main purpose is the interruption the functioning of the leading governmental institutions or business companies. This type of terrorism isn't as high profile as other types of terrorist attacks, but its impact is just as destructive (Chitadze, 2022).

Historically, terrorist actions by using **nuclear, biological, and chemical (NBC) weapons** are not held very often. Taking into account the extremely high number of victims that NBC weapons produce, they have also considered weapons of mass destruction (WMD). However, most countries are involved in arms races with neighboring countries because they view the development of WMD as a key deterrent from attack by hostile neighbors. The increased development of WMD also raises the chance for terrorist groups to obtain access to WMD. Some experts consider the issue that in the future terrorists will have more opportunities to purchase the WMD, because some states with a high level of corruption and un-stability may fail to protect their stockpiles of WMD from accidental losses, illicit sales, or outright theft or seizure. Determined terrorist groups can also gain access to WMD through covert independent research efforts or by hiring technically skilled professionals to construct the WMD (Goldstein and Pevehouse, 2011).

TYPES AND FORMS OF TERRORISM

The main types of terrorism include:

- **Political terrorism** in the broadest sense encompasses all forms of terrorism aimed at changing the social order. In a narrow sense, political terrorism refers to the issue, aimed at making (or preventing) a decision related to the arrangement of the state.
- **Social terrorism** is formed based on internal socio-political confrontation and is mainly presented in two forms: left-wing and right-wing terrorism. Left-wing terrorism is based on any left-wing ideological doctrine (Marxism, Leninism, Trotskyism, Maoism, anarchism, etc.), while right-wing terrorism is based on trans nationalist, conservative values and is directed against the left.
- **Nationalist terrorism** operates on ethnic grounds. It singles out separatist terrorism carried out by nationalist-political groups of ethnic minorities to achieve independence or broad autonomy; Repressive nationalist terrorism perpetrated by the nationalist groups of the dominant nation against ethnic minorities
- **Worldview terrorism** is formed based on contradictory contradictions with prevailing values and norms. The most common form of such terrorism is religious terrorism, which in turn is divided into fundamentalist and sectarian terrorism. The types of worldview terrorism are ecological terrorism, feminist terrorism, and others.
- **Criminal terrorism** is a conditional concept because any terror is a crime. But in a narrow sense, criminal terrorism refers to terrorism that is not related to political, social, nationalist, or worldview goals and is used by ordinary criminals, criminals, to achieve their criminal goals. Therefore, many think that such an act is a common criminal offense and does not fit the classical definition of terrorism.

The main forms of carrying out terrorist acts are sabotage, kidnapping, assault and murder, robbery (expropriation); Hijacking (seizure of vehicles and taking hostages).

A new form of terrorism is cyber terrorism, or hacking of computer networks, which can cause great damage to a country's defense and security system (Chitadze, 2022).

STATE TERRORISM

Definition

As it was mentioned, there is neither an academic nor an international legal consensus regarding the proper definition of the word "terrorism" (Williamson, 2009). Some scholars believe the actions of governments can be labeled "terrorism" (Nairn and James, 2005). Using the term 'terrorism' to mean violent action used with the predominant intention of causing terror, Paul James and Jonathan Friedman distinguish between state terrorism against non-combatants and state terrorism against combatants, including 'shock and awe' tactics:

Shock and Awe" as a subcategory of "rapid dominance" is the name given to massive intervention designed to strike terror into the minds of the enemy. It is a form of state terrorism. The concept was however developed long before the Second Gulf War by Harlan Ullman (1983) as chair of a forum of retired military personnel (James and Friedman, 2006).

However, others, including governments, international organizations, private institutions, and scholars, believe the term applies only to the actions of violent non-state actors. Historically, the term terrorism was used to refer to actions taken by governments against their citizens whereas now it is more often perceived as targeting non-combatants as part of a strategy directed against governments (Williamson, 2009).

Historian Henry Commager wrote that "Even when definitions of terrorism allow for state terrorism, state actions in this area tend to be seen through the prism of war or national self-defense, not terror"(Hor, 2005). While states may accuse other states of state-sponsored terrorism when they support insurgencies, individuals who accuse their governments of terrorism are seen as radicals, because actions by legitimate governments are not generally seen as illegitimate. Academic writing tends to follow the definitions accepted by states. Most states use the term "terrorism" for non-state actors only (Schmid, 2011).

The Encyclopedia Britannica Online defines terrorism generally as "the systematic use of violence to create a general climate of fear in a population and thereby to bring about a particular political objective", and states that "terrorism is not legally defined in all jurisdictions." The encyclopedia adds that "establishment terrorism, often called state or state-sponsored terrorism, is employed by governments—or more often by factions within governments—against that government's citizens, against factions within the government, or foreign governments or groups" (Britannica, 2020).

While the most common modern usage of the word terrorism refers to civilian-victimizing political violence by insurgents or conspirators (Purkitt, 1984), several scholars make a broader interpretation of the nature of terrorism that encompasses the concepts of state terrorism and state-sponsored terrorism. Michael Stohl argues, "The use of terror tactics is common in international relations and the state has been and remains a more likely employer of terrorism within the international system than insurgents. Stohl clarifies, however, that "not all acts of state violence are terrorism. It is important to understand that in terrorism the violence threatened or perpetrated, has purposes broader than simple physical harm to a victim. The audience of the act or threat of violence is more important than the immediate victim" (Stohl, 1988).

Scholar Gus Martin describes state terrorism as terrorism "committed by governments and quasi-governmental agencies and personnel against perceived threats", which can be directed against both domestic and foreign targets (Martin, 2006). Noam Chomsky defines state terrorism as "terrorism practiced by states (or governments) and their agents and allies"(Journal of International law, 2020).

Stohl and George A. Lopez have designated three categories of state terrorism, based on the openness/secrecy with which the alleged terrorist acts are performed, and whether states directly perform the acts, support them, or acquiesce in them (Stohl, 1988).

History of the State Terrorism

Aristotle wrote critically of terror employed by tyrants against their subjects (Mansfield, 2001). The earliest use of the word terrorism identified by the Oxford English Dictionary is a 1795 reference to tyrannical state behavior, the "reign of terrorism" in France (Oxford University Press, 2002). In that same year, Edmund Burke decried the "thousands of those hell-hounds called terrorists" who he believed threatened Europe (Laqueur, 2007). During the Reign of Terror, the Jacobin government and other factions of the French Revolution used the apparatus of the state to kill and intimidate political opponents, and the Oxford English Dictionary includes one definition of terrorism "Government by intimidation carried out by the party in power in France between 1789–1794" (Teichman). The original general meaning of terrorism was terrorism by the state, as reflected in the 1798 supplement of the Dictionnaire of the Académie française, which described terrorism as *a system, regime de la terreur* (Laqueur, 2007). Myra Williamson wrote:

The meaning of "terrorism" has transformed. During the Reign of Terror, a regime or system of terrorism was used as an instrument of governance, wielded by a recently established revolutionary state against the enemies of the people. Now the term "terrorism" is commonly used to describe terrorist acts committed by non-state or subnational entities against a state (Williamson, 2009).

Later examples of state terrorism include the police state measures employed by the Soviet Union beginning in the 1930s, and by Germany's Nazi regime in the 1930s and 1940s (Primoratz, 2007). According to Igor Primoratz, "Both (the Nazis and the Soviets) sought to impose total political control on society. Such a radical aim could be pursued only by a similarly radical method: terrorism directed by extremely powerful political police at an atomized and defenseless population. Its success was due largely to its arbitrary character—to the unpredictability of its choice of victims. In both countries, the regime first suppressed all opposition; when it no longer had any opposition to speak of, political police took to persecuting 'potential' and 'objective opponents'. In the Soviet Union, it was eventually unleashed on victims chosen at random." (Primoratz, 2007).

Military actions primarily directed against non-combatant targets have also been referred to as state terrorism. For example, the bombing of Guernica has been called an act of terrorism (Goodin, 2006). Other examples of state terrorism may include the World War II bombings of Pearl Harbor, London, Dresden, Chongqing, and Hiroshima (Stohl, 1984).

In the modern period, state terrorism can be considered the military operation of Russia in Chechnya during the two wars on the territory of this North Caucasian Republic at the end of the XX century and the beginning of the XXI Century. As a result of those wars, more than 200 Thousand people, first of all, a peaceful population, have been killed by Russian militaries (Modebadze, 2016).

The second example of state terrorism is supported by Kremlin separatist and terrorist movements on the territories of Georgia and Ukraine. For example, at the beginning of the 90th of the 20th Century, Russia supplied military equipment and financed the activities of the so-called " Confederation of Mountain Peoples of the Caucasus ". This group included the terrorist formations from the North Caucasus, who themselves supported the separatist movements in Abkhazia and the former South Ossetian Autonomous District on the territory of Georgia. Those illegal formations committed ethnic cleansing against the Georgian population of Abkhazia. As a result, more than 300 thousand ethnic Georgians and representatives of other nationalities were forced to be exiled from their native places (Chitadze, 2016).

Later, after the occupation of Crimea, Russia supported illegal armed formations in the eastern part of Ukraine.

9/11 EVENTS AND A NEW DETERMINATION OF TERRORISM

September 11, 2001, a date when the most brutal in the history of terrorism attack was made on the twin-towers - the World Trade Center in New York. As a result of this action, almost 3000 individuals died at the WTC complex. United States Authorities attributed responsibility for the attack to Osama bin Laden and the Al Qaeda organization.

The American nation and the whole International community were mobilized; combating terrorism and crippling Al Qaeda and other terrorist groups, together with those regimes, which were supporting terrorism became top national and international priorities. Preemptive use of Armed Forces against foreign terrorist organizations and infrastructure gained increasing acceptance in Administration policy circles. A full-scale campaign was launched, using all aspects of national and international resources, to go after Al Qaeda and its affiliates and support structures. The anti-terrorism campaign included rallying the international community, especially law enforcement and intelligence units to destroy Al Qaeda cells and financial networks.

As a result, the Taliban, which supported terrorism on the territory of Afghanistan, was removed from power with the support of US and British forces of the "Northern Alliance" (paramilitary group, which was opposing the Taliban in the Northern part of Afghanistan), all known Al Qaeda training sites were destroyed, and several Taliban and Al Qaeda leaders were killed. Since then, according to President Bush in his address to the nation on May 1, 2003, nearly half of the known Al Qaeda leadership has been captured or killed. As it is known, later, top Al Qaeda leaders Osama bin Laden and Ayman al Zawahiri also were eliminated (Chitadze, 2022).

In the post-9/11 world, threats are defined more by the fault lines within societies than by the territorial boundaries between them. From terrorism to global disease or environmental degradation, the challenges have become transnational rather than international. That is the defining quality of world politics in the twenty-first century. Terrorism became a large-scale threat to all.

During the making, an analysis of International Terrorism issues can be listed several aspects, based on which the research is conducted. Those issues can be the analytical approach to terrorism, its international character, the stages of its evolution and development, the tactics and strategies used by terrorist groups, and the new dimensional character of international terrorism.

Through the definition seems to be clear, terrorism still proves to be a notion hardly identifiable. What the International society possesses right now are the constant threat and tools to confront the evil of terrorism. Terror has its biases from a very ancient period of history. It is considered a way of conduct in the constant war epoch as a constituent part of the rebellion of non-compliance. It is still hard to believe that in the modern world when the process of democratic enlargement is going on, the existence of terrorism creates constant awareness of counter actions and war against the war. The historical line witnesses are even strengthening the position and the terrorist ideologies. The eternal evil in humankind always finds the reason to kill and even has the approval. The suppressed minority takes the flour in the new dimension of terrorism which emerged in the second half of the 20th century. Nowadays, terrorist organizations are better equipped and significantly developed from psychological and financial points of view. The strengthening of the "Al-Qaeda", "Hamas" etc., and other leading terrorist organizations and the foundation of the new training centers for potential terrorists took place during the 80s and 90s of the last century. The global threat that comes from those countries, which were or are involved in the state-sponsored terrorism activities, posed to the rest world astonished.

The tactic and equipment usage by terrorists of the modern era cannot be compared to that of the early centuries. Because of vast financial support, such terrorist groups as the Taliban and al Qaeda established their self-destructive roots in the development of terrorism worldwide. All the tactics and the training results can be seen in the planning of terrorist attacks. So, as the evil became sophisticated and highly dangerous it is the task of each state to confront it.

The world was stunned and put aside when the time brought the tragedy of 11 September 2001. The terrorists went too far and dug their death graves. Now the war to be declared and the elimination of terrorism in the world is the moral obligation of each human wishing for a peaceful world without terrorism. The terrorist groups were weakened and a good number of their leaders have been destroyed. Terrorism possesses an everlasting dilemma for every society in the world. The world is fighting to heal its torn and suffered organism from cancer plaguing it. The human sufferings are of human invention and the further future of the planet is of our creation. The only message is to do the best to make the world a bit better than it was yesterday, a decade earlier, a century, and millennia ago (Chitadze, 2022).

"THE ISLAMIC STATE" AND THE IRAQI REBEL MOVEMENT

Within the second decade of the XXI Century, the main threat within the terrorist activities was the "Islamic State" or ISIS. Its activity represented a new form of terrorism, when this terrorist group, which controlled huge territories, even oil fields of Iraq and Syria, established the de facto state formation of the Islamic Caliphate. In August 2014, the Syrian Observatory for Human Rights claimed that the number of fighters in the group had increased to 50,000 in Syria and 30,000 in Iraq, while the CIA estimated in September 2014 that in both countries it had between 20,000 and 31,500 fighters (Tome, 2015).

Thus, the principal actor in the crisis beginning in June 2014 was the Sunni radical movement, the so-called Islamic State of Iraq and al-Sham. Approximately a month after the commencement of the crisis, the organization announced the establishment of a caliphate subsequently concisely referring to itself as "the Islamic State" and, has named its leader, Abu Bakr al-Baghdadi, Caliph Ibrahim. On July 5, a video recording emerged, where the latter calls upon Muslims in all countries to declare subservience to the newly elected Caliph and combat infidels and traitors to strengthen and expand the Caliphate. The battle should especially intensify during the holy month of Ramadan, which began on June 28. The aforementioned organization has already been described as the most influential, well-organized, well-funded, and well-armed in the region. It has been noted that

Figure 3. ISIS Fighters shown in propaganda video produced by the group
Source: https://upfront.scholastic.com/issues/2017-18/100917/are-we-winning-the-war-against-isis.html

the organization is distinguished by its brutal methods of fighting and treatment of opponents. The organization was founded in 2003, when, after the replacement of Saddam Hussein's regime, an insurgent movement began against the Americans and the Shiite government. Initially, the group was called Tawhid and Jihad (Jama'at al-Tawhid Wal-Jihad), headed by the Jordanian Abu Musab al-Zarqawi, who soon became "enemy number one" for the US. In 2004, the organization associated itself with al-Qaeda and became known as Al-Qaeda in Iraq (AQI). In 2006, after the death of al-Zarqawi, the organization was renamed the "Islamic State of Iraq", with Abu Omar al-Baghdadi as its new leader. Following al-Baghdadi's death in 2010, Abu Bakr al-Baghdadi, referred to as the Caliph by the members of the organization, was named the leader of the group. During his leadership, the organization declared its international claims, even though its reputation was initially based on its Iraqi origins unlike its predecessors, who, due to their so-called 'foreignness', were unable to attain a similar degree of trust among the insurgents, which was also reflected on the authority of the organization. In 2011, the organization became involved in the Syrian conflict as it took part in the establishment of the Syrian radical group, the Al-Nusra Front. The leader of the Front, Abu Mohammad al-Jawlani was sent to Syria by al-Baghdadi himself. At a later stage, there was an altercation between them. Al-Nusra remained affiliated with al-Qaeda, while al-Baghdadi's group openly opposed Ayman al-Zawahiri, al-Qaeda's leader. Later, Al-Nusra Front was under a fair amount of persecution, and the situation on insurgent territory in Syria was controlled by the Iraqi group. As mentioned above, the group was rather well-armed. Moreover, in late July 2014, the organization conducted a so-called military parade in the Syrian city of Ar-Raqqah, where it deployed its heavy machinery, which it had acquired as a result of fighting against government forces. As is well known, upon taking control over Mosul and Tikrit, the Iraqi state troops abandoned military equipment and weaponry. Iraq's government has already confirmed that the group had control over the former Iraqi chemical weapons base, where thousands of warheads loaded with the Sarin nerve agent were being prepared for destruction. Even though, given the condition of the substances and weapons, the US and Iraqi specialists ruled out the possibility that the chemical weapons would be employed. According to specialists, the "Islamic State" had a financial system superior to all similar organizations. They had imposed taxes on areas controlled by them. They controlled oil extraction plants in Iraq and Syria. A portion of their income was constituted by ransom received from kidnappings. According to some experts view, upon capturing Mosul, the organization managed to obtain approximately half a billion US dollars from banks in the city. There was also talk of donations from the Sunni states of the Persian Gulf, although, according to experts, this amount was no more than 5% of the organization's income. By unofficial reports, their assets exceeded USD 2 billion. In a relatively short period, they managed to occupy a fairly large territory in Iraq and Syria. Their control was so commanding that al Baghdadi did not shy away from holding worship services at the mosque. All of a sudden, he has become a public figure (Chitadze, 2022).

His address did not resemble the customary speeches of insurgent leaders issued from clandestine locations; on the contrary, he addressed Muslims from a particular place, the Grand Mosque of Mosul, which was significant to underscore his stature as Caliph, rather than simply a combatant leader. He was a political and religious leader, who was also able to conduct worship services. The proclamation of the Caliphate also signified a certain opposition with all other radical and non-radical Islamic unions. Al-Baghdadi called on all Muslims to obey him as Caliph, and also, as a politician should encourage them to criticize him. To broadcast its activities, the organization effectively utilized social media (Gvimradze, 2014).

CONCLUSION

Terrorism is the systematic use of violence to instill fear in the population and change the political climate. Terrorism is a problem for any political party, right or left, for all nations or religious groups, for revolutionaries, and even for state institutions such as the army and police.

The definition of terrorism is complex and controversial. The term was first used in connection with the events of the French Revolution of 1790. The revolutionaries, led by Maximilian Robespierre, used brutal methods, terror, the guillotine, and the death penalty against their opponents. In this case, the word "terrorism" refers to violence against an internal enemy, although since the 20th century this term has been used to refer to violence that is directly or indirectly directed against governments to influence their political regime and police.

There is no generally accepted definition of terrorism, although elements that are common to all definitions can be identified. Terrorism uses violence not only to create a group of victims but also to create fear in a wider audience. Terrorism differs from traditional warfare and guerrilla warfare in the degree to which it introduces fear. Victory in a traditional war is associated with a strong army. Guerrilla warfare is also a major military victory, albeit with elements of terror and propaganda. Terrorism even uses terror to create fear to achieve political goals that cannot be achieved directly through struggle. Some social psychologists call guerrilla warfare "the weakest weapon" and terrorism "the weakest weapon."

Terrorists use very dramatically, violent methods such as kidnappings, hostage-taking, and bombings, which are often suicidal, to spread fear among a wide audience around the world. The location and the victim of the attack are chosen specifically, for example, schools, shopping centers, bus stations, restaurants, and nightclubs. Such places are chosen because they are usually crowded and people feel calm and safe in them. The goal of terrorists is to destroy the sense of security in society. They often target political or economic symbols such as embassies. By doing so, they are trying to spread propaganda against political leaders.

By some definitions, any act of terrorism, regardless of political motives, is a criminal act. This is how terrorism is defined in the United States. However, the definition of a crime is problematic because it does not distinguish between political motives and does not include instances where a violent attack against a government is legal. For example, the South African National Congress, opposed the pro-apartheid government, although it deserved world support. Another example is the movement against the Nazi occupation of France during World War II. In addition, it became difficult to distinguish terrorism from guerrilla warfare, as guerrillas also began to use elements of terrorism.

To solve these problems, social psychologists have developed a definition of terrorism in which the main element is not a crime, but the fact that the victims of a terrorist act are innocent citizens. The US government also considered terrorism to be deliberate politically motivated violence against an innocent non-military target. This definition is flexible and takes into account many facts, for example, to classify a terrorist act, terrorists randomly choose victims, and their goal is to spread general fear. At the end of the 20th century, the term eco-terrorism was introduced, which refers to the destruction of the environment, and nature to achieve political goals.

There are many types and movements of terrorism, they differ from each other in terms of goals, composition, religious beliefs, and other aspects, and their typology is not simple. According to one of the most common typologies, there are three classes of terrorism: revolutionary, sub-revolutionary, and established terrorism. This typology has been criticized for being too general, although this typology allows us to formulate a general idea of terrorism and place it within certain limits.

More precisely, several types of terrorism are distinguished - political terrorism, national terrorism, social terrorism, and religious terrorism. The hallmark of political terrorism is the presence of a political ideology or system against which a particular attack or violence is directed. This type of terrorism is mostly perpetrated by the locals of the state against the government.

National terrorism is characterized by violent actions of various ethnic peoples aimed at preserving their own identity. Social terrorism is characterized by economic, social, and political foundations and is carried out by various social groups, mainly by members of the lower social strata. Religious terrorism, on the other hand, is characterized by violence by members of a particular religion against another religious group, to convert to a religion whose representatives are terrorists. May be aimed at intimidating, destroying any religious group, etc. Usually, such violence is caused by misinterpretation or distorted delivery of religious books.

There is also revolutionary terrorism, which is one of the most prevalent. Representatives of this form seek to destroy the existing political system and replace it with a new one. Subrevolutionary terrorism is relatively rare, their goal is not to completely change the existing regime, but to modify it. They are trying to modify the regime by threatening to overthrow the existing regime, making it more difficult to identify sub-revolutionary groups.

Grounded terrorism differs from other groups in that it is hired by the government, or by any wing of the government, and is directed against citizens, other wings of government, or governments or groups in other countries. This type of terrorism is very common, although it is difficult to identify it because it is protected by the government. For example, the Soviet Union and its members supported international terrorism during the Cold War. In the 1980s, the U.S. supported a rebel group in Africa that grew into terrorism.

The military dictatorships in Chile and Argentina are an example of civilian terrorism when terrorism was directed against the population of the country itself. The regime of Joseph Stalin in the Soviet Union and the regime of Saddam Hussein in Iraq are examples of countries where the government uses terror against both its population and other organs of government.

According to 2013 data, 17,958 people were killed as a result of a terrorist acts. 82% of the dead are mainly distributed in 5 countries: Iraq, Pakistan, Nigeria, and Syria. Iraq ranks first in terms of terrorism. The four terrorist groups known for their most destructive acts are the Taliban, Boko Haram, ISIS, and al-Qaeda. A radical version of Islam is common to all four groups.

The threat of terrorism arises in countries with dire political and economic conditions where human rights are violated. We can distinguish 3 factors related to terrorism: 1. Hostile attitude towards different ethnic, religious, or linguistic groups. 2. Frequency of government-sponsored murders, gross human rights violations 3. High rate of violence and crime. Such countries include Angola, Bangladesh, Burundi, the Central African Republic, Ethiopia, Iran, Israel, Mali, Mexico, Myanmar, Sri Lanka, and Uganda.

Particular attention has been paid to terrorism around the world since September 11, 2001, attacks in the United States. It was from this period that they began to actively seek ways to stop terrorism. Lots of political plans were developed and lots of ideas were discussed. "Terrorism is an act aimed at intimidating the public, illegally influencing governments and international organizations, and destroying countries and democratic institutions," the EU said in a statement. According to the US State Department, terrorism is "violence designed by subversive and covert elements to influence society, aimed at non-military - civilian targets." 4 main elements of terrorism were identified: 1) A pre-planned and non-impulsive act of violence. 2) an action intended to change the political order; 3) action directed against civilians 4) carried out by sub-national groups.

Terrorist acts have been committed many times in different states in different periods. Among them was September 1, 2004, terrorist attack in Beslan, which killed numerous schoolchildren. For several days, the terrorists locked 1100 children, parents, and teachers in the school building. Russian special forces have tried to disarm the terrorists and take over the school, but despite great efforts will not be able to stop terrorism. Up to 350 people were killed and up to 500 were injured, mostly schoolchildren and teachers (Meskhidze, 2018).

Today, terrorism still exists in the world, as evidenced by the numerous terrorist attacks in various cities around the world. Terrorism is not a problem of any one state, it must fight it with all united forces.

NATO is an organization that has consistently been committed to peacebuilding and the prevention of terrorism. NATO has spared no effort for the scientific and technological development of the organization for years. As early as 1957, the NATO Scientific Assembly, the predecessor to the NATO Parliamentary Assembly, set up a NATO Scientific Committee. Senator Jackson noted that the world was entering an era of scientific innovation, so NATO needed to step up its work from a scientific and technical point of view. Today, NATO and other international organizations are working to create a defense system that minimizes the possibility of terrorism and will no longer force civilians to live in fear.

REFERENCES

Chitadze, N. (2016). *Political Science*. International Black Sea University.

Chitadze, N. (2022). World Politics and Challenges for International Security. IGI Global. doi:10.4018/978-1-7998-9586-2

FBI. (2005). *Terrorism 2002/2005*. Retrieved from: https://www.fbi.gov/stats-services/publications/terrorism-2002-2005

FBI. (2022). *East African Embassy Bombings*. Retrieved from: https://www.fbi.gov/history/famous-cases/east-african-embassy-bombings

Goldstein, J., & Pevehouse, C. (2011). *International relations. International Relations: 2010-2011 Update* (9th ed.). Pearson Longman.

Goodin, R. (2006). *What's wrong with terrorism?* SAGE Journals.

Gvimradze, G. (2014). *The Iraq Crisis*. Georgian Foundation for Strategic and International Studies. Retrieved from: https://gfsis.org.ge/files/library/opinion-papers/24-expert-opinion-eng.pdf

Hoffman, B. (2017). *Inside Terrorism*. Columbia University Press. doi:10.7312/hoff17476

Hor, M. Y. M. (2005). *Global anti-terrorism law and policy*. Cambridge University Press.

James, P., & Friedman, J. (2006). *Globalizing War and Intervention* (Vol. 3). Globalization and Violence. Sage Publications.

Laqueur, W. (2007). *History of Terrorism*. Transaction Publishers, Emerald Group Publishing Limited.

Lebedeva, M. M. (2011). *World Politics*. Aspect Press.

Longo, M. (2022). *Blood in the Sand: Shiite Assassins*. Warfare History Network. Retrieved from: https://warfarehistorynetwork.com/blood-in-the-sand-shiite-assassins/

Mansfield, H. (2001). *Those Hell-Hounds Called Terrorists*. Claremont Review of Books. Retrieved from: https://claremontreviewofbooks.com/those-hell-hounds-called-terrorists/

Martin, G. (2006). Understanding terrorism: Challenges, perspectives, and issues. *Sage (Atlanta, Ga.)*.

Meskhidze, R. (2018). *Terrorism and its Basics*. Retrieved from: http://yata.ge/ge/?p=1585

Modebadze, V. (2016). *Two Wars in Chechnya*. Universal Press.

Nairn, T., & James, P. (2005). *Global matrix: Nationalism, globalism and state-terrorism*. Academic Press.

NATO Handbook, . (2007). *NATO Public Diplomacy Division. NATO.*

Oxford English Dictionary (2nd ed.). (2002). Oxford University Press.

Primoratz, I. (2007). *Terrorism. Stanford Encyclopedia of Philosophy.*

Purkitt, H. (1984). *Dealing with Terrorism*. Conflict in World Society.

Schmid, A. (2004). *Terrorism - The Definitional Problem.* Retrieved from: https://scholarlycommons.law.case.edu/cgi/viewcontent.cgi?article=1400&context=jil

Schmid, A. (2011). *Routledge Handbook of Terrorism Research*. Routledge. doi:10.4324/9780203828731

State Sponsorship: An Impediment to the Global Fight against Terrorism. (2020). *International Law, 7*(2).

Stohl, M. (1984). *The Superpowers and International Terror*. Paper presented at the Annual Meeting of the International Studies Association, Atlanta, GA.

Stohl, M. (1988). *National Interests and State Terrorism, The Politics of Terrorism*. Marcel Dekker.

Stohl, M. (1988). *States, Terrorism and State Terrorism: The Role of the Superpowers*. https://link.springer.com/chapter/10.1007/978-1-349-18989-2_6

Tome, L. (2015). *The "Islamic state": Trajectory and reach a year after its self-proclamation as a "caliphate"*. Retrieved from: https://www.redalyc.org/pdf/4135/413541154008.pdf

Ullman, R. (1983). *Redefining Security. International Security*. The MIT Press. Retrieved from: https://muse.jhu.edu/article/446023/summary

US Department of State. (2007). *Office of Coordinator for Counterterrorism*. Retrieved from: https://2001-2009.state.gov/s/ct/info/c16718.htm

Williamson, M. (2009). *Terrorism, war, and international law: The legality of the use of force against Afghanistan in 2001*. Ashgate Publishing.

World History Encyclopedia. (2022). *Zealots*. Retrieved from: https://www.worldhistory.org/Zealots/

KEY TERMS AND DEFINITIONS

Asymmetric Warfare: Armed conflict between belligerents of vastly unequal military strength, in which the weaker side is often a nonstate actor that relies on unconventional tactics.

Civil Wars: Wars between opposing groups within the same country or by rebels against the government.

Conflict: Discord, often arising in international relations over perceived incompatibilities of interest.

Crimes Against Humanity: A category of activities, made illegal at the Nuremberg war crime trials, condemning states that abuse human rights.

Crisis: A situation in which the threat of escalation to warfare is high and the time available for making decisions and reaching compromised solutions in negotiation is compressed.

Cyberspace: A metaphor used to describe the global electronic web of people, ideas, and interactions on the Internet, which is unencumbered by the borders of the geopolitical world.

Ethnic Cleansing: The extermination of an ethnic minority group by a state.

Genocide: The attempt to eliminate in whole or in part, an ethnic, racial religious, or national minority group.

Info War-Tactics: Attacks on an adversary's telecommunications and computer networks to penetrate and degrade an enemy whose defense capabilities depend heavily on these technological systems.

Information Warfare: Attacks on an adversary's telecommunications and computer networks to degrade the technological systems vital to its defense and economic well-being.

International Aggression: Killing others that are not members of one's species.

International Terrorism: The threat or use of violence as a tactic of terrorism against targets in other countries.

Proliferation: The spread of weapon capabilities from a few too many states in a chain reaction so that an increasing number of states gain the ability to launch an attack on other states with devastating weapons.

Smart Bombs: Precision-guided military technology that enables a bomb to search for its target and detonate at the precise time it can do the most damage.

Terrorism: Premeditated violence perpetrated against non-combat targets by subnational or transnational groups or clandestine agents usually intended to influence an audience.

Xenophobia: The suspicious dislike disrespect, and disregard for members of a foreign nationality ethnic, or linguistic group.

Chapter 3
Terrorist Psychology and Its Impact on National and Global Security

Irakli Kervalishvili
Georgian Technical University, Georgia

ABSTRACT

Terrorism is a policy based on the systematic use of terror. Despite the legal force of the term "terrorism," its definition up to the present time remains ambiguous. But experts agree that the best definition of terrorism is the achievement of political, ideological, economic, and religious goals by violent means. Synonyms of the word "terror" (Latin terror – fear, horror) are the words "violence" and "intimidation." This term became widespread in various countries after the "Age of Terror" during the Great French Revolution. During the discussion about terrorism, one of the main directions of this phenomena represents the terrorist psychology. Thus, in the chapter attention is paid to the psychological aspects of terrorism, including the determination of the main types of terrorism and psychological characteristics of the terrorists and terrorist groups.

INTRODUCTION

Currently, the study of the topic "Psychology of Terrorism" is especially relevant in connection with the increase in the number of terrorist attacks committed by various terrorist organizations around the world. The constant threat of terror leads to the destabilization of the political, economic and social situation in the state. Lack of confidence in personal safety contributes to the growth of anxiety, fears, and mental stress, which negatively affects psychological health, leading to the development of various psychosomatic disorders among the population. The genesis of the concept of "terrorism", the history of terrorism, the psychology of the personality of terrorists and terrorist groups, the victimology of terrorism, methods of providing psychological first aid in terrorist attacks, methods of negotiating with terrorists, technologies for forming a model of safe behavior are the main issues that are disclosed in this chapter.

DOI: 10.4018/978-1-6684-5311-7.ch003

GENESIS OF THE CONCEPT OF "TERRORISM", CLASSIFICATION OF TYPES OF TERRORISM AND METHODS OF COMBATING THEM

Actual Problems of the Psychology of Terrorism

Throughout the history of its existence, humanity has faced various forms and manifestations of terrorism. This phenomenon reached a special scope in the late XX - early XXI century. Terrorist acts and sabotage, cruel in their manifestation, receive a wide resonance throughout the world, causing not only just public outrage, but also serious fears for peace and security on the planet (Gozman, 1996). Terrorism violates the system of human legal protection, causes enormous damage to the stability of the world community, state interests, and in particular the prestige of the law enforcement system. At present, the problem of terrorism has again acquired relevance in connection with the emergence of a new large-scale terrorist group "Islamic State", which organized and carried out a whole series of terrorist acts around the world. Many Experts believe that terrorism is one of the key phenomena of the growing chaos and the end of history (in the sense of the end of the democratic system). Some Authors suggest that terrorism can be regarded as a form of economic, military, political, criminal, and other activities aimed at the implementation of certain tasks. From their point of view, terrorism has economic and religious roots. In addition to the forceful solution of issues related to terrorism, such sciences as psychology, philosophy, sociology, political science, and psychiatry are engaged in the study of this phenomenon. A terrorist act refers to "extreme", "crisis", "emergency situations", which are the subject of study of a new branch of psychology - the psychology of extreme situations. An integrated approach to the phenomenon of terrorism (considering the historical, political-economic, socio-psychological, psychiatric, and informational aspects) is just being formed. Despite the special relevance and practical need for study, the main problems of the psychology of terrorism are not sufficiently developed. So, until now, a clear definition of terrorism, both from a legal and social point of view, has not been formulated. However, "even at the first consideration of this complex and multifaceted phenomenon, one can single out:

- individual, organized terror and terror as a policy of the state;
- terror as a political method of struggle in peacetime and wartime;
- terror as a method of internal political struggle and terrorist acts of international terror" (Hoffman, 1998).

The manifestations of terrorism entail massive human casualties, the destruction of spiritual, material, cultural values that cannot be recreated. Moreover, terrorism breeds hatred and mistrust between social and national groups. Many researchers believe that the information and psychological component plays an important role in the problem of terrorism, since its main goal is to create public panic or provoke mass irrational horror. However, the more urgent and obvious the problem is, the more myths and misunderstandings it is surrounded by. From the point of view of leading experts in terrorism, a terrorist act is one of the manifestations of an extreme situation arising because of "organized violence" committed by extremists, representatives of totalitarian regimes, adherents of various sects. This type of emergency also includes wars, genocide, armed clashes, persecution on political, religious, ethnic grounds, etc. harm and damage to the health of others.

Definition of the Concepts of "Terror", "Terrorism", Their Similarities, and Differences

In order to study the psychology of terrorism, it is first necessary to give clear definitions of the concepts of "terrorism" and "terror". Some researchers do not distinguish between them, they consider them identical, but many authors still distinguish between them. First, one should understand what violence is in general. Violence is the physical or mental impact of one person on another, which violates the citizens' right to security of person, guaranteed by the Constitution of many countries (Khan, 2006). Violence is a social relationship in the course of which some individuals (groups of people), with the help of external coercion, which poses a threat to life up to its destruction, subjugate others, their abilities, productive forces, property, usurpation.

The term "terror" comes from the Latin "terror" - horror, fear; and in the most general sense denotes a method of solving political problems and contradictions with the help of violence. It can be said that Terror is the systematic use of extreme violence and the threat of violence to achieve public and political goals, but this understanding is too generalized. In a narrower sense, terror refers to the violence carried out by the state against its citizens and political opposition. For the first time, terror as a political method for resolving contradictions appeared during the Great French Revolution. Distinctive features of modern terrorism are a) the generation of universal danger; b) openly demonstrative character of achieving goals; c) the deliberate formation of a stressful environment at the social level (tension, fear, depression); d) impact on certain people in order to satisfy any claims. In this case, we are talking about strategy and method, but let's not forget about goal setting (Yablonsky, 1996). Terrorism is always generated by the policy of the state, it does not arise out of thin air, it is based on disagreement with certain norms and attitudes, which is very often overlooked by researchers.

Typology of Terrorism

For a more complete understanding of terrorism as a social phenomenon, it is necessary to bring a typology of terrorism. The next typology is built on the principle of the nature of terrorist activities, to whom it is directed, that is, whether it is domestic, transnational, or international, which determines the level of legislative suppression of terrorist activity.

1. Internal: actions of citizens against their state on their territory.
2. Transnational: actions of citizens of one state against their compatriots on the territory of another state.
3. International: international, interethnic groups of terrorist's acts against another or other states (Hoffman, 1998).

Terrorist groups can combine traits of all three types in their activities, or they can belong to only one type. Many researchers distinguish international terrorism as a separate phenomenon: "International terrorism is a phenomenon in world politics associated with the spread of violence in the form of terrorist acts that threaten the normal course of international relations" or "international terrorism is violent acts aimed at causing political change, which undermine the international community and which the international community regards as incompatible with the desired norms of behavior" (Hoffman, 1998). In principle, these definitions are not so far from the truth, but they consider only one aspect of the phenomenon under study.

International terrorism is not an independent phenomenon, and it must be considered in the light of a general study of the problems of terrorism. The second typology is built according to the criterion of the ideological substantiation of terrorist activity, that is, according to what motive drives the terrorists.

The following types of terrorism are distinguished:

- political terrorism.
- social terrorism.
- national terrorism.
- territorial separatist terrorism; - ideological terrorism.
- criminal terrorism (Davitashvili and Elizbarashvili, 2012).

Political terrorism in a broad sense encompasses all the above-mentioned types of terrorism aimed at changing the social system or any part of it. In a narrow sense, political terrorism means "a struggle aimed at preventing (or making) any decisions related to the state structure" (Davitashvili and Elizbarashvili, 2012). Social terrorism is formed based on deep internal socio-political conflicts and manifests itself in two main forms: left and right terrorism. Left-wing terrorism is ideologically oriented towards various left-wing doctrines (Marxism, Leninism, Trotskyism, anarchism, Guevarism, Maoism, etc.) parties. As a rule, leftist terrorism activates when internal crises escalate. The militant organizations of the leftist terrorists have been operating for a relatively short time. Right-wing terrorism is guided by political doctrines and values traditional for the nation, and historically by national leaders of the past. It is activated for a short time during periods of the greatest threat from the left forces. The target is leftist and liberal politicians and activists. National terrorism is carried out along ethnic lines and is divided into separatist, national liberation, and repressive national terrorism. Separatist terrorism is carried out by national-political minority groups fighting for sovereignty or expanding the autonomy of the historical territory of residence. Depending on the political situation, traditions, and social structure, they are guided by left or right ideology (Davitashvili and Elizbarashvili, 2012). Organizations of this type are the most long-lived. The target is officials, businessmen, and policemen. National liberation terrorism is carried out by the peoples of occupied or colonized states against representatives of the aggressor country. The goal is to restore state sovereignty. Such groups adhere to moderately nationalist views, ideological orientation fades into the background. The target is representatives of a hostile nation, regardless of social and professional status. Repressive national terrorism develops during periods of national conflicts within a single state. Representatives of privileged national groups aim to suppress the demands of national minorities, strive to create ethnically homogeneous states. Territorial separatist terrorism is carried out within the borders of one state by representatives of any dominant nation, fighting for the provision of sovereignty, that is, the creation of a separate state on the territory of the country (Davitashvili and Elizbarashvili, 2012).

This type of terrorism is the least common. This type can include Israeli terrorists who advocate granting Palestine broad autonomy. Worldview terrorism is carried out based on fundamental disagreement with the prevailing norms and relations. This type includes religious, environmental, "smuggling", feminist terrorism (McCauley, 2001). The most widespread is religious terrorism, which in turn is subdivided into fundamentalist and sectarian. It is characteristic of fundamentalist terrorism that religion serves as an ideological position that allows terrorists to formulate the concept of anti-government struggle. Islamic terrorism is the most widespread in the modern world. Fundamentalists are united by the desire to rebuild reality in accordance with the norms of religious life. Sectarian terrorism is carried out by various marginal sects of a totalitarian nature, who view violence as a condition for seizing power and building a more perfect society (Bockstette, 2008). Criminal terrorism emerges in moments of political instability and is often confused with organized crime as such or attributed to other types of terrorism characteristic of it. We can say that its main subjects are organized criminal groups, communities, and organizations, of a national or transnational nature. They use intimidation and direct violence in various forms as the main means of influencing the government, its representatives, lobbyists, and their competitors in illegal and legal business to redistribute spheres of influence, property, financial flows, types of criminal and legal activities. The terrorist component of organized crime tends to a certain politicization to weaken the activities of law enforcement agencies, inhibit legislative initiatives that are disadvantageous to the criminal environment, demoralize the population, enter the legislative authorities or their accomplices and patrons, occupy important posts in the executive federal and regional authorities, obtaining immunity from legal prosecution for committing crimes.

The following trends in the development of terrorism in the 20th and 21st centuries can be distinguished: ultra-left, ultra-right, ethno-nationalistic and religious. Ultra-right terrorism is usually based on complete denial of the democratic institutions of the rule of law, violent rejection of the ruling regime, racism, religious intolerance, belief in the existence of secret conspiracies (for example, a Jewish financial conspiracy, a worldwide Masonic conspiracy, etc.). Organizations of this kind mainly aim not to change the existing economic system, but to establish a different way of distributing resources, income, and values. The spread of disillusionment in the ruling political parties, the deteriorating financial situation, and a massive influx of emigrants create a favorable background for the development of right-wing extremism. Against the background of the global political crisis, representatives of ultra-right terrorism are gaining more and more followers in Western Europe. According to experts, ultra-right terrorist organizations are more active in the modern world than ultra-left ones. Ultra-left terrorism emerged in Western Europe in the mid-1960s. XX century, first in Germany, and then in France, Belgium and Italy. Members of the ultra-left groups viewed themselves as the vanguard of the popular revolution (neo-Marxist, neo-Maoist, anarchist, etc.) and advocated the immediate destruction of the existing state system and the construction of a “fairer” society, the prelude to which was the destruction of the authorities and mass intimidation of the population. The social face of the ultra-left groups was determined mainly by students and the marginalized. They professed a special, original vulgarized Marxism, sharply different from the orthodox (Sageman, 2004).

In 1968, in some circles of the left intelligentsia, the ideology of violence began to mature, and a theoretical substantiation of its necessity and justification was carried out. Theorists of left-wing extremism created a generalized image of a repressive oppressor state and sought to destroy it. The pseudo-Marxist branch in left-wing extremism was intertwined with anarchist one, which was characterized by total nihilism, destructive, anti-institutionalism, and the cult of spontaneity. The activity of the leftist terrorists was often intertwined with the activity of the ultra-right, which was exacerbated by the deliberate infiltration of the ultra-left groups carried out by the neo-fascists (Hoffman, 1998). Nevertheless, at that time, Western countries demonstrated a margin of safety for civil society institutions and power structures, having developed mechanisms for directing the situation into a constitutional channel. Potential supporters of extremist actions received a legal political outlet. Ethno-nationalist terrorism has recently become one of the most widespread types of terrorism. This is since ethnic nationalism has tremendous power and unpredictability, and ethnic conflicts have become a real problem for many countries, regions, and the entire world community. These conflicts are based on the contradiction between the recognition of the natural right of peoples to self-determination and the principle of national unity and territorial integrity of the state. The goal of ethnic terrorism is to defend and expand the rights of an ethnic group in the political sphere. When terrorists, using violence to assert ethnicity, call upon themselves the fire of state structures, it draws attention to the group and allows them to appear in the eyes of the public as a victim, which further increases public resonance, as well as provides financial and political support. Violence is the raison d'être of such groups. If people use this method of influence, the idea is alive, and the presence of ethnic differences cannot be denied. The main stake in their activities ethnic terrorists make on the constant intimidation of the population. On the one hand, fear testifies to the illegitimacy of the central government in an ethnic enclave and sends a signal to other ethnic groups that their presence in this territory is undesirable. On the other hand, fear does not allow the ethnic community to develop a different attitude towards their own self-determination. It is significant that in the case of this type of terrorism, the state is limited in countermeasures. Thus, it can get involved in a conflict and try to assert a competing ethnic identity; can use forceful methods, but this has its downside - it brings moderates to the terrorist camp. Another option is to try to establish cooperation with moderate nationalists, but they, as a rule, do not have the ability to control extremists. You can try to include terrorists (who in this case act as fighters for national liberation) into the legal political process, as was done in many Western European countries, but this is a very difficult way out, because to some extent it means the defeat of the state and, therefore, justifying political violence. Unlike ideological terrorism, ethnic terrorism has a ready audience. Ideological terrorists should focus on some segment of the political spectrum, religious terrorists should appeal to their co-religionists, and ethno-terrorists simply tell their followers that they are part of a single whole. During counter-terrorism operations, violence escalates, since it is a breeding ground for terrorists to succeed in their struggle and maintain the desire to defend their ethnicity; the threat of violence from the authorities must be preserved and exaggerated in every possible way. Ethnic terrorism, unlike other terrorist areas, has existed for a very long time. In a small ethnic group, it is easier to create and maintain infrastructure, it is easier to hide. The less ethno-terrorists are focused on other political issues (that is, apart from the state status of the ethnos and the political structure of the country), the stronger they are, since a high level of cohesion is maintained in the ethnos. In the modern world, in most cases, mixed forms of terrorism are widespread. This refers to the "cooperation" of terrorist organizations of different orientations, their unification to achieve certain goals, the combination in many specific cases of the ideological, ethno-nationalistic and religious components. Ideological ethno-nationalism appeals not so much to a rational worldview as to the irrational aesthetic experience of representatives of a given ethnos, to its symbols, experiences, traditions, archetypes, etc. That is why ethno-nationalism has a much greater mobilization potential than any political and ideological doctrine, because around his "totems" you can relatively quickly gather a mass of people and, by manipulating the image of the "common enemy", give it a certain political impulse, turn off the factor of individual responsibility, infect the mass with aggressive slogans and, thus, at the level of the collective unconscious, prepare the commission of collective crimes within the framework of large-scale acts of terror. Recently, ethno-nationalist groupings of all kinds have been gaining more and more strength both on the territory of the European Union and in the "post-Soviet space". This is mainly because the involvement of nationalism as a powerful determinant of inciting a socio-political conflict makes it possible to increase its scale and geography dramatically and qualitatively, giving it even an international character by involving foreign national diasporas in various forms, which greatly facilitates the financial and public support. In recent decades, ethno-nationalist nationalism has manifested itself in the Middle East.

Terrorist gangs operating in this region are actively using the experience accumulated by terrorist groups over a century. Accordingly, Middle East terrorism is the most striking manifestation of ethno-nationalist terrorism in the world. The Middle East is the cradle of three leading world religions (Christianity, Islam, Judaism) - one of those regions of the world where the most complex socio-economic, national-territorial, confessional, and geopolitical contradictions have developed over the centuries. Having laid the ground for irreconcilable religious fanaticism on each side, terrorism in the Middle East has historically become a familiar form of conflict expression. The modern borders of the Middle Eastern states and the nature of political regimes in many of them are a direct result of the colonial policy of European powers in the 19th century and the results of two world wars. Since the 1980s, Middle East terrorism has included several varieties: - suicide attacks and other operations against Israeli and Western forces in Lebanon; - hostilities of various armed formations in Lebanon; - State terrorism of Libya, Syria, Iraq and Iran; - "independent" terrorism of various structures, a kind of "free terrorist flight"; - terrorist attacks in support of the Palestinian people; - anti-Israeli and anti-Western terrorist attacks in Europe; - Israeli raids to liquidate persons suspected of terrorism (Olshansky, 2002). Middle East terrorism is currently not only a socio-political, but also an economic phenomenon. It regulates energy prices, affects stock prices, makes profits and ruins. To date, the most formidable terrorist group in the Middle East is the Islamic State terrorist organization, banned in many countries of the world, which united representatives of several terrorist groups in its ranks, seized a certain part of the territory of Syria and held them with the help of an armed conflict. The adherents of this terrorist organization carry out large-scale terrorist attacks not only in the Middle East, but also in Europe, America and around the world. Religious terrorism. Within each cultural paradigm, there are religious fanatics who are ready to sacrifice their (and not only their) lives for the sake of a higher truth, extended to the secular social system. "Holy terror", firstly, carries in itself such an integral system, which is not present in "secular" terror. Ordinary terrorists want to win within the dominant political and cultural pattern and seek not only to destroy, but also to create new social structures. Religious fanatics see the world as a battlefield between the forces of light and darkness. Their victory has no political conditions: the enemy must be destroyed. Second, murder is a sacred act for them, and not just a means to an end. At the same time, a complex system of theological evidence is being erected, which makes it possible to justify the murder of innocent people, women, old people, children, including the pious. Third, since religious terrorists act as if outside reality, they have no deterrent to the extent of the violence. For those who fulfill the higher will, identifying themselves with it, the life of mere mortals does not matter; when the ultimate authority is God, public appraisal plays no role either. Fourth, they believe that their struggles and deaths to achieve personal salvation have cosmic implications that will ultimately change the course of world history. Thus, we can draw the following conclusion that terror and terrorism are different concepts, the main difference is who is the subject and who is the object. For terror, the subject is the state, and the object is the citizens, vice versa for terrorism. We can say that terror is the policy of the strong against the weak (since the state is objectively stronger than its citizens), and terrorism is the policy of the weak against the strong. Terror is aimed at preserving the existing political situation, while terrorism aims at any change in the political situation.

International Terrorism

Terrorism has many faces. Terrorism is not only a cult and practice of violence, but it also seeks to substantiate its ideology. Criminal in nature, it can be domestic, and in this case, it is carried out not only by criminal groups, but also by the totalitarian state apparatus of suppression, thus being state terrorism. International terrorism inflicts great damage to the world law and order and international relations, to a large extent growing out of hatred of the world, internecine religious extremism, and chauvinism. The definition of such concepts as "terrorism" and "international terrorism" refers to those international problems, the solution of which is of exceptional practical importance. The international community, politicians, scientists and, of course, employees of special services and law enforcement agencies of various states, regardless of their political, social, and economic structure, are sufficiently aware of this. The development of a generally accepted legal definition of terrorism is a difficult and still unresolved task, especially when it comes to international terrorism. Now, there is no universal definition of the concept of "terrorism" and its derivatives - national (domestic) and international, recognized by the world community. The difficulties in developing an internationally agreed definition of "international terrorism" are due to many reasons. Among them there are many objective ones, due to the different understanding of national security by many states, the divergence of ideas about various forms of international terrorism (state, non-governmental, transnational, individual, etc.). The process of developing a unified definition of the term "terrorism" is also hampered by subjective factors: the reluctance of some states to bind themselves with a firm formula that can create obstacles for their connection with terrorist activities, hidden from the world and their own people. Due to cultural, civilizational, religious differences, as well as related ethical norms, terrorist attacks can be perceived as heroic or criminal. This fact, among other reasons, makes it possible to understand why the world community has not yet developed a generally acceptable universal concept of "terrorism" (Gozman, 1996). However, the development and, more importantly, the consolidation of this concept in the norms of international law is necessary to clarify the real positions of the members of the world community on this issue and, therefore, to form a certain legal basis of international treaty obligations to combat this phenomenon.

TERRORIST PERSONALITY PSYCHOLOGY. PSYCHOLOGICAL PORTRAITS OF CONTEMPORARY TERRORISTS

Many scientists, studying the motivation of a person to join a terrorist organization, believe that poverty, lack of education, unemployment, lack of life prospects, etc. are not psychological, but rather socio-psychological factors. The listed factors are psychologized to the extent that they mediate other actualized needs (self-realization, self-respect, desire for power, etc.). Terrorist activity as a psychological technology makes it possible to find a special "roundabout" way: a person does not become richer, more educated, does not find a decent job, but gains power over richer, more educated, and successful people than he is. His actualized needs are realized in a special - "displaced", symbolic form. It is precisely in the phenomena of "displacement" and expansion of symbolization that attracts new members to it: the rejection of the "principle of reality" and the achievement of goals by means that at first glance are simpler and do not require long-term efforts. Technologies of terrorism, like peaceful modern technologies for satisfying needs, are characterized by signs of illusory simplicity, ease, quick achievement of results and benefits. The cognitive-behavioral concept of the activity initiated in this way is simple and primitive. It has an unreal, illusory-compensatory character. Technologically developed terrorist ideologies not only represent, but actively impose a methodological toolkit for objectifying need states, well developed at different levels, transforming them into ready-made, strictly determined needs of different levels. It is this ability to successfully satisfy various multi-level human needs that transforms terrorism technologies into a unique way to achieve their goals, giving terrorism its subjective attractiveness, which is a very important direction in the psychological study of the phenomenon of terrorism.

The Identity of the Terrorist

To solve the problem of terrorism, to create a unified scientific and methodological basis for its research, one of the main goals is to study the psychology of the terrorist, his typological, emotional, and moral-moral characteristics. But this task turned out to be intractable. Terrorist organizations are recruited from all walks of life, professions, they are representatives of various cultures and nationalities, religions, and ideological beliefs. Extremists have been described as people with schizophrenia and utopians, as fanatics and aggressors, as traumatized, notorious, self-asserting, over-ambitious people, or as martyrs for their beliefs. Terrorist acts, as a rule, are committed under the slogan of certain ideologies: political, religious, and ethno-nationalistic. The decision to commit a terrorist attack requires a person to resolve several issues: the purpose, object, methods, place and time of the crime, consideration of additional circumstances that may help or hinder the fulfillment of the plan. From a certain number of behavioral variations, the terrorist must choose, in his opinion, the most appropriate behavior option for certain tasks. Such a choice is due to such personality traits as orientation, ideological attitudes, personal experience, moral and ethical and value orientations, norms of internal social control. The choice is also associated with an analysis of the external environment, the current situation and forecasting the future situation in which a terrorist act is planned, with the expectation of a response from members of his group and society. In general, extremism relies on destructive instincts and aggressiveness inherent in humans, expressed in different people to varying degrees, controlled with varying effectiveness by moral and legal norms, education, and culture. Representatives of the psychological type, who have a low level of control of emotions and expressions of emotional reactions in behavior, a low level of tolerance, a narrow worldview, easily arise and become commonplace the idea of violence and forcible achievement of their goals. A violent way of achieving their goals is also characteristic of people with a high level of intelligence, but an overestimated self-esteem, an overestimated level of ambition, a desire for power, a low level of tolerance, with the idea of the exclusivity of their political, religious, or ethno-nationalistic convictions. There are several psychological models of the terrorist's personality. 1. The psychopathic fanatic. He is guided by his convictions (religious, ideological, political) and sincerely believes that his actions, regardless of their specific results, are beneficial to society. This is a person whose sphere of consciousness is extremely narrow, capable of doing anything. 2. Frustrated person, based on the behaviorist theory of frustration-aggressiveness. The feeling of frustration, generated by the impossibility for a person for some reason to achieve vital goals for him, inevitably gives rise to his tendency to aggressive actions. Consciousness in this case can play the role of an instrument in the rationalization of these actions, that is, in the selection of certain reasons for their justification. 3. A person from a flawed family. Abuse of parents with a child, his social isolation, lack of good relations can lead to the formation of an angry personality with antisocial inclinations (Hoffman, 1998). Under certain conditions, people of such a psychological make-up can easily become instruments of a terrorist organization. In general, the basic psychological characteristics of terrorists have been sufficiently studied. They are the conditions for a person to join one or another terrorist group. Usually, they are reflected in the charter or set of rules of each terrorist organization (unless the given criminal community is not particularly conspiratorial or has no documentary support at all). In a generalized form, one main and two secondary qualities are distinguished. The main thing is dedication.

Devotion to the main goal, to your group, to your associates and readiness for self-sacrifice. The secondary features are organization and conspiracy. Obedience and fellowship with comrades are also important requirements. Loyalty presupposes the absence of individuality, one's own principles and position, integral, complete obedience to the laws of the terrorist organization. When a person enters a terrorist group, he is required to be completely subordinate, to give up his own life for the sake of accomplishing the plans of the organization. But in this position of terrorist organizations there is a huge contradiction, since, opposing themselves to the whole world, the state, in general to other people, declaring their peculiarity, difference from everyone, within the organization demand a refusal of self-identification, from their own individuality, require merging with everyone, to act as a single organism. Although individuality is possible, it is only for a terrorist acting alone, which is almost impossible in the real world. Scientists who deal with the problem of studying the personality of a terrorist consider it possible to rely on the typology of temperaments described by G. Eysenck. According to this classification of types of temperament, there are choleric, sanguine, phlegmatic, and melancholic. In essence, they are presented by the main characteristics of the properties of the nervous system and the intensity of their manifestation according to the parameters ``extraversion - introversion" and "neuroticism - emotional stability". A severely neurotic and extrovert choleric person is the most typical psychological type of terrorist, according to the authors. About gender characteristics in the psychology of terrorism, it was traditionally believed that terrorists can be mainly men, but in practice it turned out to be different. Although most terrorists are men, the role of women in terrorist groups is important. So, in Russia, in the 60s-70s of the XIX century, when there was a wave of terrorist attacks associated with social and political reforms, women played the role of not only the perpetrators of terrorist attacks, but also its ideological leaders (Vera Zasulich, Sofya Perovskaya, etc.) (Yablonsky, 1996). Based on the social status of a woman in society, it is easier for her to hide, infiltrate and carry out a terrorist act than it is for a man. There are even terrorist groups where women make up at least half of the total number of members. Terrorist organizations such as the Irish Revolutionary Army, the Red Brigades, and Latin American groups actively use women for intelligence and military purposes. The age range of people involved in terrorism is, on average, 20–35 years old, that is, the most capable, mentally, and physically active individuals. If we talk about national characteristics, then it is quite difficult to make any emphasis. Under national terrorism, representatives of one nation work against another. If we consider religious terrorism, then, of course, the most active remain Muslim, Protestant, Catholic and sectarian groups. Overt psychopathology among terrorists is a rare thing (Yablonsky, 1996). At the same time, it is possible to single out a number of personal predispositions, which often become incentives for individuals to enter the path of terrorism: over-focus on protecting one's "I" by projection with constant aggressive-defensive readiness; insufficient personal identity, low self-esteem, elements of personality split; strong need to join a group, i.e. group identification and / or belonging; experiencing a large degree of social injustice with a tendency to project onto society the reasons for their failures; - social isolation and alienation, the feeling of being on the sidelines of society and the loss of life prospects. For all the nuances, the behavior of a terrorist is usually some vivid and obvious kind of asocial, deviant behavior.

According to the general assessment, this behavior is to one degree or another abnormal and inevitably includes some pathological component. It is generally accepted that a terrorist is not that not entirely normal but accentuated. This means that a terrorist is a normal person, however, certain personality traits in him are expressed unusually strongly, vividly, deviating somewhat from the norm. Sometimes psychopathy in terrorists is found in combination with peculiar personality traits. Such people give the impression of eccentrics by the unpredictability of their actions, impulsiveness, and inconsistency. In normal activities and studies, their results are low, their adaptability is unstable, and their behavior is uneven. They are prone to vagrancy, to frequent communication with asocial elements. The crimes committed by such persons are usually inadequately harsh, often impulsive, not always planned, often taking wild, unusually violent forms. An analysis of scientific research on this issue allows us to reveal a common factor in the development of a terrorist's personality, which can be called psychological impairment, a kind of deficiency of something in his life, the roots of which can sometimes be traced from early childhood. Such a deficit in mental development leads to the need for hyper compensation of the deficit while growing up and reaching maturity. It is known from autobiographies and other descriptions that many terrorists had their parents and relatives killed in childhood. On the one hand, because of this, a desire for revenge arose, on the other, there was an atmosphere of emotional deficit in which the future terrorist grew up. The disadvantage is also generated by socio-economic factors: for example, the low standard of living of people and the associated desire to "take away and divide" both within the framework of one country (then we are dealing with revolutionary terrorism), and in the relationship between the "poor" (developing) and "rich" countries. Lack of education and information also gives rise to destructive, destructive attitudes towards other cultures, beliefs, and beliefs. It is possible to analyze for a long-time various area in which this or that deficit may arise, leading to this or that inferiority. These are personal, family, social, economic, and political types of inferiority. Accordingly, they give rise to different psychological roots of terror. However, there is a major common factor that unites the different options into a single mechanism. This is an inner impossibility, an inability to overcome this inferiority. Deficiency itself is not terrible - it is overcome through various mechanisms, through the mechanism of adequate, positive, constructive supercompensation, in which the deficit is eliminated using funds from the same sphere in which it arose. For example, a person who suffered from polio in childhood can become an Olympic champion - for this you only need to continuously play sports; receive a small salary, start working more, find a second job, etc. But neither one nor the other grab a gun and set off explosions. They become terrorists when there is not enough strength to overcompensate for the deficit with adequate means (Yablonsky, 1996). Then overcompensation becomes inadequate, negative, and destructive, and inferiority turns into terror.

On the other hand, it should be noted that despite the presence of some common psychological characteristics, we cannot single out a single personal terrorist complex. But at the same time, the author singles out psychological types that can be relatively often found among extremists. Representatives of the first type are characterized by a high level of intelligence, an overestimated level of self-esteem and ambition, and a desire to achieve their goals in any way. Representatives of the second type have a low level of self-esteem, a low level of aspirations, "losers with a weak "I"" (Sageman, 2004). Both types are characterized by a high level of aggression, a low threshold for the emergence of aggressive actions, a desire for self-assertion, low tolerance, inattention to the feelings and needs of other people, and fanaticism. They see the source of their personal problems outside, in the current external situation and the society around them.

Suicide Bombers

Terrorism is a pre-planned attack or threat of attack on civilians or civilian objects to achieve political, ideological or religious goals. Suicidal terrorism is a politically, religiously, and ideologically motivated attack carried out by one or more individuals who deliberately give up their lives in order to cause maximum damage to citizens and civilian objects. The military and political structures of the state are also targets of terrorist attacks. F. Moghaddam (2006) studying the prerequisites for the emergence of Islamic terrorism as a geopolitical phenomenon from the standpoint of the socio-cultural approach, highlighted the levels of identification of people with terrorists. The basic level is the search for a new identity, caused by dissatisfaction with the existing socio-economic and political conditions of life, characterized by a lack of social mobility and life prospects. - The first level is the search for who is to blame and how to deal with him. - The second level is finding an external enemy as a substitute for aggression, controlled by the authorities, religious extremists, and fundamentalists. - The third level is the acceptance of the terrorist's motivation, the formation of terrorist groups and their ideology. - The fourth level - the formation of the specific functions of terrorists, including suicide bombers - implementation, motivation. - The fifth level - the execution of acts of terrorist attacks - the achievement of the set goal, which justifies all means, including suicidal terrorism. According to the authors, the traditional social cultural conditions of the Islamic society do not allow the young generation of Muslims to satisfy their need for individual identity, and it is the search for a new identity that pushes them to join terrorist groups. F. Moghaddam sees the prospect of a long-term, but not military struggle against terrorism in changing the socio-cultural foundations of their lives, leading to a solution to the crisis of socio-cultural identity in the Islamic community. Suicidal terrorism in terrorist organizations is preferred over other forms of terrorism, since a suicide bomber, choosing the time and place of the crime, is not distracted by the thought of saving his life, which allows him to inflict the greatest damage on innocent victims and civilian objects. Suicidal terrorism demonstrates to society the powerlessness of the government in countering terrorism and pushes government structures to change their policies (Moghaddam, 2006). Many assume that there are few people with special personality traits among suicide bombers. Analysis of court materials and rare interviews with terrorists shows that terrorists most often demonstrate externalization (they explain their behavior because of negative external circumstances and the "psychological splitting" of the personality (the simultaneous existence of contradictory, incompatible justifications for their own behavior). It is the search for an external enemy as a source of their own. failure is the dominant mechanism in the psychology of the personality of a terrorist. Previously, there was an opinion that people from the poor, without education and profession, become suicide bombers, but numerous studies have revealed that among them there are many highly educated people with highly paid professions. The leaders of terrorist groups strongly support the heroic myths about self-sacrifice and various ceremonies for the transition of members of the group to suicide bombers. The potential victim will soon be destroyed, and they strive to contribute to the approach of a new "correct, just" world (Moghaddam, 2006). Also, the reason for the transition to death row can be the desire to get rid of negative identity (loneliness, shame, humiliation). Suicidal terrorism is especially characteristic of women, since they are closest to the ideology of martyrdom. The state of post-traumatic stress disorder, the impossibility of contact with the outside world makes a person more vulnerable to the ideology of suicidal terrorism.

Terrorist Logic and Thinking

Terrorists' thinking is as contradictory as their personality. On the one hand, it is monoidal (all thoughts, reasoning, plans are associated with the main activity), and on the other hand, it is excessively mercantile. He thinks of other people either as his associates or as potential victims; he thinks about objects, how they can be useful in the commission of a terrorist attack - as a weapon of attack or a weapon of defense. At the same time, he is always ready to talk about the ideas for which he is going to attack. Here are some examples. So, in the logic of a terrorist, it is paradoxical and seemingly completely illogical that opposite things are connected: freedom and violence. And then violent terror turns out to be the best means of achieving freedom: "The majority of the militant organization held the point of view that the only guarantee of the acquired freedoms lay in real strength. Such a force, in any case, could have been the active influence of terror. From this point of view, the terror not only should not have been stopped, but, on the contrary, taking advantage of the favorable moment, it was necessary to strengthen it and put at the disposal of the military organization as many people and means as possible. The only guarantee of the won rights is the real power of the revolution, i.e. that is, the power of the organized masses and the power of terror. " The extremist's logic is either clever or very straightforward, but in either case it is "crooked", most often generalized, symbolic. An example is the terrorist attack on September 11, 2001, by the terrorist organization Al Qaeda against the United States, which they declared to be a symbol of the end of American domination in the world. Thus, the researchers conclude that terrorism is not only an indicator of social inequality, but also expresses people's discontent caused by the collapse of their hopes and plans; terrorism is a way of accomplishing certain plans and is aimed against the sources of their misery. One of the important missions of terrorist attacks is to symbolize their intentions. So, trying to kill the tsar, the Russian terrorists, as it were, symbolically destroyed the entire monarchy. In problems not directly related to the main craft, the logic and thinking of terrorists are shaped by the general level of development and culture. Understanding the logic and peculiarities of the terrorist's thinking is of serious practical importance. So, in particular, it is known you can only negotiate with someone who understands the language in which you negotiate with him. If you think and reason logically ("wait to kill me, give me time, I will find what you need and give it to you"), and your opponent does not understand logic, but only experiences emotions ("I will kill you anyway, and right now! "), Such attempts do not make sense (Olshansky, 2002). Moreover, they are dangerous: after all, you think that you have agreed, and your opponent considers himself free from all agreements. Terrorists are a special type of people in whom rational components in behavior and character are almost absent, and emotional components prevail to such an extent that they become effective. It is difficult to talk to them: if something is wrong, then the eyes instantly fill with blood, and the fingers clenched into fists and reach for the gland. Such a person simply does not know the normative words like "can" and "not", "possible" or "impossible". Its vocabulary is very simple: "I want!", "Give!", "Mine!", And here and now, immediately. Unlike a normal person, who is equally capable of understanding "rationality" and experiencing "emotions" without going beyond the accepted framework, a terrorist is not capable of this. The psych type of these people is designed in such a way that it acts according to the "all or nothing" law (Olshansky, 2002). To a large extent, this is facilitated by the excessive simplicity of manners accepted among terrorists, their banal bad manners and ignorance. It is these factors that are the main source of the emergence of more and more "waves" and even generations of terrorists.

Features of the Emotional Sphere of Terrorists

The emotional sphere of members of terrorist organizations is as contradictory and ambivalent as their personality and thinking. There are two extreme options among terrorists. One, rarer, is devoid of emotionality. These are people with complete composure, completely immune to emotions or capable of completely controlling them. The second, nevertheless much more common type among terrorists, is distinguished by its diametrical opposite. Such people have a very diverse inner emotional life. For all the external composure, rationality, severity, even asceticism, emotions rage inside the terrorist. And the stricter the restrictions imposed on a member of a terrorist organization, the stronger the inner, restrained emotions of the terrorist. His notorious restraint, "iron nerves" are the result of the influence of the rational components of the psyche, cruelly depressing emotions. Such containment cannot be permanent. But such violent emotional experiences do not affect the main activity. They are engaged in organizing and carrying out a terrorist act with cold calculation and intelligence. Although many researchers of the problems of terrorism agree that they have a low level of development of intelligence and thinking. The life of a terrorist goes on in constant emotional distress. He lives in the emotions of fear, fearing to fall into the hands of opponents. At the same time, he lives in the emotions of anger and contempt for his opponents and inspiration from anticipating the harm that he is going to inflict on them. Naturally, such conflicting emotions often collide with each other, leading to internal emotional conflicts, which predetermine the severe state of chronic emotional stress inherent in a terrorist. Chronic stress is characterized by emotional lability, the ease of almost instantaneous transition from one emotional state to the exact opposite. Often a terrorist who is forced to harshly suppress his emotions in the framework of terrorist activities is emotionally licentious in other matters, for example, in everyday matters. Usually concentrated in their main occupations, Palestinians, for example, are characterized by complete emotional liberation in everyday life. One detail is striking: people, deprived of their state and fighting for its creation, always and everywhere feel "at home": after a difficult many day of illegal travel, for example, they instantly find themselves in slippers and immediately extremely emotionally, without hesitation in expressing their feelings, start exploring the hotel. Except for deeply religious Islamic fundamentalists, all other terrorists have deeply emotional personal lives. As a rule, they are not very picky and restrained in sexual relations. An increased temperament leads not only to hypersexual activity, but also simply to hyperemotionality. Although the overall emotional sphere is under control, the terrorist is ready to remove this control as soon as he considers it possible. Then feelings break free and manifest themselves violently. However, the most important and most common emotional state of a terrorist is his constant alertness. The phenomenon of alertness is manifested in constant readiness to repel the threat of an attack, an increased level of wakefulness and concentration of attention on the slightest changes in all, primarily physical, environmental parameters, pronounced hyperesthesia. Even outwardly noticeable constant suspicion of the terrorist is manifested in the continuous division of all those around him into "friends" and "aliens." Naturally, the "alien" is a priori identified with the disgusting and alien "image of the enemy" (the reaction of hostile distrust) (McCauley, 2001). It is curious that when confirming that the "stranger" is in fact "our own," the nature of the relationship changes dramatically to massive manifestations of trust and openness (sometimes excessive). This indicates a sharp polarization of emotions and emotional lability of the terrorist.

Moral Sphere

A blind fanatic who carries out a brutal terrorist act on a rational "autopilot" does not suffer from moral problems. It is a blind destruction machine that does not think about moral questions simply because such questions are foreign to such a machine. Moral problems arise only when there is a certain intellectual level. Illiterate, uneducated Islamists, acting on the principle of "inshallah" ("everything is in the power of Allah, by his grace"), do not suffer from moral doubts. However, relatively intellectually developed terrorists are constantly worried internally by the question of how right they are in their actions. In the descriptions of various specialists, for example, considerable attention is paid to this side. Every time they prepare for a terrorist act, terrorists seek a moral justification for it. Sometimes it comes to complete paradoxes when believing Christian's resort to completely Jesuitical logic, believing that by killing someone's body, they thereby save the soul of their victim. However, such psychological paradoxes are still alive today: Islamic terrorists believe that their actions not only save their own souls (a feat in the name of Allah), but also help the souls of their victims to quickly go to heaven. The militants of the Hamas movement know from a special memo for the militants of their organization: "Allah will forgive you if you fulfill your duty and kill the unbeliever; in paradise, Allah will take care of all your problems. "So, this is precisely what some Islamic theologians explained the essence of the explosions of skyscrapers in New York, which entailed thousands of victims. The skyscrapers themselves were viewed as "sacrifices to Satan," and people who died under the rubble were declared "delivered from serving false gods" (Khan, 2006). For a deeply religious terrorist fanatic everything is simple - God himself relieves him of moral problems - but all the same, it turns out that he also needs some kind of moral self-justification. However, even such self-justification is not always sufficient, and moral suffering can continue even after a "victory", that is, a successfully committed terrorist act. Although even convinced of their moral right to violence, male terrorists usually have a hard time experiencing moral problems after the terrorist attacks. Even Palestinian terrorists often talked about "heaviness on the soul", although they explained their violent actions by external, forced circumstances. The terrorist's moral problems can become strange, even pretentious. The flip side of moral problems is the need for understanding expressed by almost all terrorists, the need to "speak out" in front of other people (usually in front of "their own", but sometimes in front of strangers, including investigators). In the absence of the possibility of oral communication with a suitable interlocutor, the epistolary genre is actively used.

Thus, we see that the main and characteristic feature of a terrorist's personality is extreme inconsistency. Maintaining internal contradiction and social isolation is the main condition for the psychodynamics of a terrorist's personality. The immanent prohibition on social forms of communication and activity is the result of the personality's own contradictions. At the same time, certain types of terrorist activities are not interconnected with specific personality types of terrorists. The inconsistency in the personality of terrorists is also manifested in their thinking and emotional sphere. The main qualities of a terrorist's personality are: 1) dedication to his cause (terror) and his organization; 2) readiness for self-sacrifice; 3) consistency, discipline; 4) "conspiracy"; 5) obedience; 6) collectivism - the ability to maintain good relations with all members of their combat group (Bockstette, 2008).

Within the framework of static analysis, the main property of a terrorist's personality is integrity, concentration on terrorist activities and his group, organization. However, from a dynamic point of view, these properties turn out to be only "fixed moments" of the personality's continuous throwing along a special psychological sinusoid with the broadest range. The wider the range, the less adequate such a person can be considered. In the structure of a terrorist's personality, a psychopathological component is usually noticeably expressed, primarily of a psychopathic nature. It is associated with a feeling of real or imaginary damage suffered by the terrorist, the lack of something necessary, urgently needed for such a person. Typically, the logic and thinking of terrorists are confusing and contradictory. Emotionally, two extreme types of terrorists stand out: the extremely "cold", almost emotionless version and the emotionally labile version, prone to strong manifestations of emotions in a sphere unrelated to terror, when usually tight control over emotions is removed during the preparation and implementation of terrorist acts. Emotions are associated with moral and ethical problems ("sinfulness complex"), sometimes painful for terrorists with a sufficiently high level of education and intellectual development.

PSYCHOLOGY AND ORGANIZATION OF A TERRORIST GROUP

The Group Nature of Terrorist Activities

Terrorist activity is almost always of a group nature, since the basis for the unification of extremist groups is a sense of social injustice. Social injustice is a type of unrighteousness that is interconnected with a person's group affiliation, that is, it is always unrighteousness in relationships between social groups. Thus, it is not an interpersonal problem, but an intergroup one. Studying the prerequisites for the emergence and formation of terrorist groups, K. McCauley identifies three stages (or, as he calls them, "crisis") through which a terrorist act passes when a decision is made on its implementation. The first stage is the "secrecy crisis". A group of ordinary people or one person covertly express dissatisfaction with the existing system, disapprove of it, but accept its norms and rules and follow them. The main expression of activity during this period of crisis is the hidden search for like-minded people and their integration into the conspiratorial community. The second stage - "the crisis of the collision of ideologies" - the disagreement between the ideology of the community and the existing system around it is expressed in an open form of polemics and protest. This stage lasts until such a community comes to a cardinal behavioral pattern to demonstrate its position to everyone. A similar behavioral pattern, as a rule, seeks commonality in other terrorist groups and then functions according to the principle "If it is permissible for terrorists, then it is possible for us." In this regard, the terrorist group enters the third stage - the "crisis of completeness." Open opposition to the existing system develops into aggressive actions. A community or a person transcends all moral and legal norms that previously restrained an open manifestation of aggression. Violence becomes an integral part of their existence and is declared as the only effective tool for opposing the system (McCauley, 2001). Scientists who are studying the problem of studying terrorist groups agree that there are no and cannot be two identical extremist organizations.

It is very difficult to compare with other terrorist organizations that are only planning a crime and have already implemented a terrorist act. Very often, the model by which the main characteristics are studied is the terrorist groups that committed the act of terrorism, but the characteristics of the groups that have not yet committed it, but are probably no less dangerous, are not considered. Describing the features of terrorist organizations that have achieved success in their plans, Gozman writes:

These groups are closed, and entering them means recognizing the right of other people to total control over their lives, including personal, including intimate relationships. For an ordinary person, such total control would be a sacrifice that cannot be made, but for an outsider, for a person who never felt like his own, whom no one had ever accepted anywhere, all this turns out to be rather a plus than a minus. Participation in terrorist groups compensates for many of their failures. They have a meaning in life. The goal is the liberation of the Motherland or the triumph of one's religion or ideology. The attention of the whole world is riveted to them, they no longer have doubts about their own significance. Boredom and routine of everyday life is replaced by balancing on the brink of life and death. There is a feeling of being chosen, belonging to fate (Gozman, 1996).

There is another feature of the functioning of terrorist organizations - the cult of perished comrades-in-arms, expressed in the fact that each member of the group honors his comrades who have laid down their heads for a just cause. The group members have a sense of a whole community. But this is not the case for all terrorist groups. And yet, in the end, the members of the organization have a sense of community, and each member of this community knows that if he dies, then his name will be treated with the same respect. However, such cults do not exist in all terrorist organizations, some simply cannot afford any cults (Olshansky, 2002). Researchers of terrorist groups note that all these reasons are insufficient to attract a mentally healthy, psychologically harmonious, successful person in their profession, and even more so they cannot lead him to abandon the principles of respect for human life learned in childhood. For a maladjusted, disharmonious personality with a pronounced intrapersonal conflict, a terrorist group can be a saving option. The psychological characteristics of the personality of individual members of terrorist groups also affect the activities of the entire organization. So, in social psychology, the phenomenon of "risk shift" is widely known, when a group decision is always riskier than the sum of individual decisions. The organization approves more and more risky plans, strives for more and more daring tasks. Terrorists are targeting ever more high-ranking officials and planning more widespread terrorist attacks, and eventually the community ceases to exist in the face of professionally organized resistance from the state's law enforcement agencies. A terrorist organization, as a special kind of group, belongs to the "intermediate group" because it occupies a transitional position on the scale set by the two poles. "At one extreme point, we see a highly organized, cohesive, functioning collective of individuals as members of a social group. At the opposite extreme point, we have a bunch of individuals characterized by anonymity, erratic leadership, basing their actions on emotions, and in some cases representing a destructive element within the framework of the social system into which it belongs ... Those formations that do not represent close-knit, integrated groups, or disorderly, poorly functioning gatherings or crowds, correspond to the concept of "intermediate group" (Yablonsky, 1966).

Specific Features of Terrorist Groups

Researchers in the field of the psychology of terrorism have identified the following distinctive features of terrorist groups:

- First, it is a vague definition of the role played by members of the organization. Who are they? The problem of defining functions is always relevant and scrupulous for terrorists. On the one hand, they may identify themselves as "freedom fighters" or "sacred avengers". On the other hand, they fully understand the anti-legal and even criminal nature of their plans and actions. The definition of roles as "militants" and even "terrorists", "terrorists", characteristic of the Combat Organization of many groups, serves rather as a deviation from the rules.
- Secondly, the conditional cohesion of such a community. As a result, terrorist activity is a transient occupation, since a terrorist organization is formed for the implementation of one, less often several, actions. It cannot exist for a long time, and the riskiness of terrorist activities further shortens the period of its existence. All these factors do not contribute to the cohesion of the organization's members, despite the assurances of the members of the terrorist groups themselves of loyalty to their comrades-in-arms.
- Third, the variability of the structure. The structure of an organization that implements its ideas in extreme conditions is subject to change in one way or another.
- Fourth, the variability of the members of the group relates to the variability of the composition. This makes it impossible for the emergence of stable internal relationships between members of the organization. Although in such an organization there is always a stable structure of job responsibilities.

- Fifth, all these factors are due to the limited plans in relation to the composition of the organization. The "personnel reserve" of each terrorist group is extremely narrow, and the members of the organization take this into account.
- Sixth, there is little compliance with the norms of behavior within the organization. The uniting factors of members of a terrorist group are most often a strict coordination of official duties (separation of functions during the preparation and implementation of a terrorist act) and the presence of some common motivation, which is meaningful in terrorist activity. Moral norms, rules of communication, one's own behavior, etc. are agreed at the lowest level.
- Seventh, relatively chaotic management. In such an organization, as a rule, there is no authoritarian leader or, moreover, no officially appointed leader. Such leaders are rare as leaders of terrorist organizations. Usually, the leaders are average, unremarkable members of the group who cannot exercise systematic total control. Scientists studying the socio-psychological structure of "intermediate groups" conditionally distinguish three levels in the organization of membership. At the center of the organization at the first level are the mentally least stable members of the organization - the leaders (Davitashvili and Elizbarashvili, 2012). These are the people who need the gang the most. This core is the main cementing force of such groups. They are the ones who hold or even cobble together the group and force it to act, constantly planning, plotting, and organizing its actions. They serve, if not strategic (this is the function of leadership of the entire organization), then the tactical center of the intermediate group. At the second level of the intermediate group, people usually appear who declare their belonging to the group, but who actively participate in its activities only in accordance with their emotional needs at a given time. At the third level of the group structure are peripheral members who participate in its activities from time to time and rarely identify with the group. As a rule, these are "auxiliary personnel", "accomplices" of terrorists. They can take part in a terrorist act mainly as a result of a coincidence, and neither they themselves nor other members of the group consider them equal members. Often terrorist groups use such people "in the dark", not sharing with them all available information and easily "handing over" them to the authorities in case of danger to the main group. The size of a terrorist group is usually determined by the leadership of the entire organization, if the group is part of it. Where autonomous terrorist groups are involved, the size depends on the mission of the organization and the emotional needs of the main members of the group. The socio-psychological functions of a terrorist group are, in fact, related to the motivation for membership in it. As a rule, such a group functions as a convenient means for manifesting various individual needs and solving personal problems. To the leaders, such a group looks like a super-powerful organization through which, in their imagination, they subdue and control the lives of thousands of people. For group members unable to achieve anything in more demanding social organizations, the possibility of rapid and sudden violence serves as a means of social advancement and reputation gain. Sometimes the group can function as a convenient temporary escape from the boring and harsh claims of a difficult and demanding society. Of course, these are just some psychological functions that are not related to its direct purpose - the commission of a terrorist act. Thus, by its socio-psychological nature, the terrorist group belongs to a special type of "intermediate groups" (Sageman, 2004). All relationships in it are subordinated to the main target function - the preparation and commission of a terrorist act. This gives rise to the specific characteristics of such groups.

CONCLUSION

The study of the Psychology of Terrorism is relevant and necessary in connection with the increase in the number of terrorist attacks that destroy the system of human legal protection, causing enormous damage to the stability of the world community, state interests and the prestige of the law enforcement system and the education system. An integrated approach to the phenomenon of terrorism (considering the historical, political-economic, socio-psychological, psychopathological, and informational aspects) is only being formed. Despite the relevance and practical necessity, the main problems of the psychology of terrorism are not sufficiently developed. In the current geopolitical situation, the threat of terrorism has become every day for ordinary citizens and politicians in many countries. Various regions of the world, such as India, Turkey, Great Britain, Indonesia, Pakistan, Afghanistan, Iraq, Syria, Israel, Russia, USA, France, and Germany, etc., are subject to terrorist attacks. In this regard, countering terrorism is becoming one of the main tasks of ensuring national security for the country and the world community. Modern terrorists are actively using the global world resources for the dissemination of information to realize their own goals and thus cause a systemic reaction that extends not only to the direct victims of the terrorist attack and their loved ones, but also to the entire population. As a result, the mass consciousness of people changes, panic reactions, states of anxiety and anxiety arise, which negatively affects the psychological health of citizens and their ability to work. Thus, there is an urgent need for the training of highly qualified psychologists who are able to realize professional competencies in providing psychological assistance to people who have suffered as a result of a terrorist act and their loved ones, to provide psychological support for employees of various structures performing anti-terrorist activities and participating in the elimination of the consequences of terrorist acts., to carry out preventive measures for psychological education of the population, prevention of deviations and maintenance of mental and psychological health. Specialists of this profile are in demand in the following spheres of society: in the defense, security and law enforcement structures of the state - the system of the Armed Forces, the system of the Ministry of Internal Affairs, the system of the FSB; in rapid response and control services, various emergency services (including fire brigade, ambulance, etc.); in the penitentiary system; in the structures of the personnel service of transport companies, airlines; in social infrastructure (public administration, social protection of the population, etc.); in healthcare and medicine; in the system of upbringing and education; in the socio-ethnic, socio-political, socio-religious spheres (work on the prevention and resolution of various social conflicts, etc.).

REFERENCES

Bockstette, C. (2008). *Jihadist Terrorist Use of Strategic Communication Management Techniques.* George C. Marshall Center Occasional Paper Series (20).

Davitashvili, Z., & Elizbarashvili, N. (2012). *Global Geography*. Tbilisi State University.

Gozman, L. (1996). *Terrorism. Socio-Psychological Research.* Omsk State University.

Hoffman, B. (1998). *Inside Terrorism*. Columbia University Press.

Khan, A. (2006). A Theory of International Terrorism. *Connecticut Law Review*.

McCauley, C. (2001). *Group Identification under Conditions of Threat: College Students' Attachment to Country, Family, Ethnicity, Religion, and University Before and After September 11, 2001*. Wiley Online Library.

Moghaddam, F. (2006). *From the terrorists' point of view: What they experience and why they come to destroy*. Praeger Security International.

Olshansky, D. (2002). *Terrorism Psychology*. Piter.

Sageman, M. (2004). Understanding Terror Networks. *International Journal of Emergency Mental Health*, 7. PMID:15869076

Yablonsky, L. (1996). *Terrorism Psychology*. North-Caucasus State University.

KEY TERMS AND DEFINITIONS

Psychology: The scientific study of mind and behavior. Psychology includes the study of conscious and unconscious phenomena, including feelings and thoughts. It is an academic discipline of immense scope, crossing the boundaries between the natural and social sciences. Psychologists seek an understanding of the emergent properties of brains, linking the discipline to neuroscience. As social scientists, psychologists aim to understand the behavior of individuals and groups.

Terrorism: Premeditated violence perpetrated against non-combat targets by subnational or transnational groups or clandestine agents usually intended to influence an audience.

Types of Terrorism: One popular typology identifies three broad classes of terrorism: revolutionary, subrevolutionary, and establishment. Although this typology has been criticized as inexhaustive, it provides a useful framework for understanding and evaluating terrorist activities.

Chapter 4
The Impact of Terrorism on International Peace and Security

Mukesh Shankar Bharti
https://orcid.org/0000-0002-3693-7247
Jawaharlal Nehru University, India

ABSTRACT

This study discusses the questions of terrorism among the international communities. The threat of terrorism has affected international peace and security. Further, we have to study to elucidate the main roots of terrorism and how to save the world community from the danger of it. The study relied on the concept of collective security derived from the theory of bargaining and idealism to explain why states come together to fight terrorism. The authors use this method to search the result through empirical analyses. As a result of this study, the terrorist activities displaced the people and restricted sustainable development. The result also shows that due to the terrorist events, people suffered from many basic human rights. Thus, many parts of the world have been destabilised from the act of terrorism and are continually struggling to restore peace and security.

INTRODUCTION

Terrorism is seen as a usurper of human security in general, thus there is chaos among civilians after they are denied an access to security devices. The perpetrators of violence must be severely punished for crimes against humanity and it is the responsibility of human beings to restore the destroyed infrastructure and environment. As the environment degrades and changes due to human influence, new diseases arise and old diseases are lethal. It can be argued that terrorism highly affects the individual security and education of both adults and young. The continued killings and bombings leave people with no sense of pride in education as the fruits are not realised due to terrorism. The research study concludes that terrorism has negatively affected collective state efforts in maintaining international peace and security, especially in the period between 2000 and 2020. The research provides that terrorism has negatively affected collective state efforts in maintaining international peace and security

DOI: 10.4018/978-1-6684-5311-7.ch004

especially from 2000 to 2020. These circumstances are very difficult to minimise as states are driven by individual interests rather than collaboration with world communities' efforts. This study has analysed and examined the effects of terrorism on international peace and security. It is a qualitative study that works with multi-method and data triangulation methods to generate data regarding the studied phenomenon.

Terrorism is a phenomenon known to mankind for more than two millennia, but during this long period, no one has managed to define terrorism in a way that is universally acceptable and encompasses all the essential elements. Therefore, the frequently used word "terrorism" does not refer to a set of well-defined and identified factual events or to a widely accepted legal doctrine. The absence of a generic definition cannot invalidate the fact for several decades. Terrorism has been a serious security problem requiring both national and international countermeasures. The latter is particularly important since the main terrorist factions operate internationally to achieve greater visibility and, therefore, more success, but also to find supporters, namely states that sympathize with their objectives and policies. Relevant international countermeasures are naturally associated with the Security Council, to which States have conferred primary responsibility for the maintenance of international peace and security. The Security Council, a constantly watchful executive body, has considerable means at its disposal for this purpose, for a wide range, beginning with diplomatic or economic sanctions and ending with military measures. But before the Security Council can use these means, it must first determine whether terrorism falls within its jurisdiction.

The main objective of this study is how international governance eradicates the problems of terrorism from the paradigm of the people sphere and commits itself to guarantee world peace and security. The hypothesis of this research is that "The preservation of global peace and security by the collective efforts of international communities have been negatively impacted by terrorism." This study examines this question from three principals. First, why are we determining the existence and nature of this situation important? Second, what is the nature of a threat to peace in general? Third, can terrorism generally or specifically pose a threat to peace and security? What are the current policy and institutional gaps in multilateral security capacity on these issues? These issues are discussed in the light of the collective security system envisioned in the Charter of the United Nations and administered by the Security Council. The Security Council is the defender of international peace and security. The Security Council acts on behalf of all UN member states in the exercise of its functions related to the maintenance of international peace and security. The Security Council is slow to join the fight against terrorism. The first resolution using the term terrorism was not adopted until December 1985. This study used qualitative research methods to analyse the main content of the literature and try to find out the empirical result. The content analysis ensures the accuracy of this study and highlights the main objectives and hypothesis of the research. The proposed work is based on both primary and secondary sources. The study uses the primary data from various websites of international organisations and as secondary data sources would mainly comprise research articles from leading journals and magazines, newspaper clippings and books. The use of secondary sources is based to build a rational descriptive analysis of this research. As the use of secondary sources allows the surfing of the internet access and deeply study of textbooks. It discusses the causes of terrorism that had occurred in the past decades and the scrutiny and evaluation of the research to compare the data with objectives and hypothesis. The use of literature will broadly describe the impact of terrorism affected international peace and security.

THEORETICAL BACKGROUND AND REVIEW OF LITERATURE

The main objective of this part is to review the relevant literature on international peace as it relates to international peace and security. We should try to provide an analysis of the effects of terrorism on international peace and security. The major terrorist groups and how they operate around the world are discussed in this chapter. Terrorist acts are costly and have resulted in the loss of life, environmental disruption and destruction of infrastructure. Terror is persistent, evolving and transnational, so individual states in the international system need to come together to eliminate terrorism. Terrorist activities are transnational and manifest in various forms, including kidnappings, suicide attacks, access to weapons of mass destruction (WMD) and hostage-taking. They seek to achieve different political goals depending on their individual goals. This creates a feeling of insecurity for both the state and for its citizens since the attacks are sporadic and have unknown execution formulas (Crenshaw, 2001).

The Preface to the UN (2002: V) by former UN Secretary-General Koffi Annan speaks out that terrorism is a global threat with global effects. Its consequences affect all aspects of the agenda of the United Nations, from development to peace, including human rights and the rule of law. The continuing disturbing and awful attacks in the presence of the collective security protector, the UN and other regional peacekeeping bodies have suffered serious challenges in ensuring international peace and security (Borum, 2004). According to Gurr, "the act of terrorism relates deprivation is a perception of frustration". People who live with a low intensity of basic human life may feel deprived and frustrated by nature. They also feel that we do not have ownership of property and that we are restricted from other basic rights (Gurr, 2015). It is a difficult task to read out and predict human behaviour. It shows cool and calm posture to understand the human behaviour primarily. But some rarest of rare human behaviour is indulged in this kind of bad activity. To find out this kind of human behaviour and nature, it is even a hard task to understand (Bassey, 2017, p. 527). There are struggles against the repressive regime called terrorism and those who want to replace this type of regime called violence have proven to be freedom fighters (Hoffman, 2018). Although terrorism means much religious output debated in the political sphere in the world. Many definitions talk about terrorism as a non-state actor, it is not manipulated by political and non-political groups. Whereas some political commentators agreed that terrorism was caused by the state-sponsored (Greset & Mahan, 2008).

Kydd and Walter described terrorism as an aim of non-state actors to achieve the political will to gain power in the state using variations of violence. In many states globally, the opposing groups have adopted the path of violence to replace the contemporary rule in their region (Kydd & Barbara F. Walter, 2006). Terrorism defines as non-governmental organisations, maybe it is associated with proxy groups to use against the opponent countries. Many countries are indulged in spreading the terrorist act against the rival country. It acts as cross-border terrorism and a form of a suicide attack. Terrorist groups target and kill innocent people in fairs, railway stations, big markets places, and streets. It is also involved in hijacking the aeroplane to destroy the people's lives. They adopt the method as a car bomb blast. We have seen these kinds of incidents in gulf countries. Terrorists hit the transport to kill the people (Bassey, 2017, p. 527). Thus, the nature of modern terrorism has been shaped in many new ways. It is difficult to assess the terrorist activities that would occur. We can examine the current nature of terrorism as a form of kidnapping, kidnapping, murder, female suicide bombers, suicide terrorism, bombings and hostages. Cross-border terrorist activities have spread in many countries, because they are sponsored by other states. Nowadays, several countries have suffered from the cross-border terrorism which is indirectly guided by the enemy countries' agency.

Realism and bargaining theory defined terrorism as traditionally related to violence among different states rather than terrorism associated with non-state actors (Schelling, 1960, 1966). The bargaining theorists characterised terrorism as an instrument of demands. It is called the strategic behaviour of terrorist groups to manipulate the opponent states and negotiates. Several such incidents happened in past where terrorists demanded to release their partner from jail and this kind of other such negotiation become reality (Baldwin, 2000, p.104; Byman & Waxman, 2002, p.10; George, 1993, p. 7). According to Daniel Drezner's thoughts on bargaining, theory relates to basic narrative coercion, thus succeeds by escalation. The process of escalation helps to promote peace and it can decrease violence. This kind of peace process could be challenging, but it is a way for stable peace and security (Drezner, 2003). Chowanietz describes public opinion about the terrorist incidents that happened in the last decade in the USA, France, Germany, the United Kingdom, Spain, and Sweden. Terrorists have targeted countries according to different lethality and shifted the electorate into several political rights (Chowanietz, 2010). Hoffman and McCormick highlighted in the theory of bargaining, on the bargaining table it can be taken as edge during the negotiations. In future thought processes depend on this bargaining theory to attack with a high level or low level of proportional lethal course of work (Hoffman & McCormick, 2004, p. 250).

Since the 9/11, 2001, attacks in the USA, the thought process has changed various political scientists about the fresh terrorist incident. They have focused on the framework of non-state actors, who expedite such terrorist activism across the boundary. Thus, states and non-state approaches work according to opposite directions. It depends on conditions that can be escalated (Berman & Laitin, 2008; Walter, 2009). The process of bargain depends on the position of level which is based on stronger or weak opponent groups. It can be seen as the bargain relates to the position of weakness. The bargaining strategy correlates with the identical approach (Pape, 2003). Such kind of terrorist incidents is a problem of various course of collective action. The dangerous activities of terrorism can be side-lines through peace-making as an alternation of nonviolent resistance (Gould, 1995; Weinstein, 2007; Wood, 2003). According to many political scientists, terrorism does focus on more than several approaches to gain the mileage of a substantial audience expanse. The political elite is scared of terrorists grisly that is why they want to eradicate it in more sympathetic ways. These kinds of all costs came into in bargaining theory (Berman & Laitin, 2008; Hultman, 2005; Laitin & Shapiro, 2008; Weinstein, 2007).

According to many political scientists who pioneer the bargaining theory and discuss the violence would assist the non-state actors by coercing compliance. Especially when the level of injury increases. Doubtlessly, the bargaining theorists create a model to understand the nature of terrorism at the global level. Nowadays, the approaches of terrorist activities are changing at international level. The Arabian countries are suffering from severe terrorism and this scourge is moving to South Asia, India has been affected by cross-border terrorism since 1990. The African countries have terrorist activities in many parts (Kydd & Walter, 2006, pp. 59-60). The term terrorism had come at a global level gradually since 1968 and then terrorist activities expedite in late 1990 to 2010. According to the RAND-MIPT Terrorism Incidents Database, only four per cent of terrorist groups demanded their position. There are many terrorist groups and their intentions are not clear why they kill innocent people. After the 9/11 incidents, the global communities are aware of terrorism. Nowadays, such kind of several incidents has happened at the global level in Bali, Stockholm, New Delhi, Jaipur, Berlin, Madrid, and Mumbai (Eilstrup & Jones, 2008). A theoretical perception highlighted that terrorists are involved in destroying public property and doing irrational things. The public properties are based on welfare schemes that are related to the general mass population. In a civilised society, nobody can support such kind of irrational work. This kind of activity can be launched by insane people, whose motto is to destroy and destabilise the lives of innocent people (Atran, 2004; Berrebi, 2009; Euben, 2007; Horgan, 2005; Merari, 2006; Victoroff, 2005).

There are many scholars who claim that terrorist activities demolished the general people's daily life. The civilian properties were destroyed by the terrorist. They are directly involved in these bad activities. It is seen that civilians are the main target of terrorists, not military ones. These kinds of such incidents had happened in the world's cities and thousands of innocent people were killed by several terrorist groups. They are even the culprit to kill women and children. In the Jammu & Kashmir region of India since 1989, there are thousands of innocent where people have been killed by the terrorist several terrorist organisations (Abrahms, 2006; Ganor, 2002; Goodwin, 2006; Hoffman, 2006; Schmid & Jongman, 2005; Victoroff, 2005). The terrorist attacked civilians for lack of organisational discipline. The security of children and women should be in the primary character of any kind of militant group across the world. Everyone wants to live together in a peaceful environment, so we should respect the rights of others as well. This study empirically highlights the motive of terrorism. It should be restricted worldwide by the international actor to save humanity. Theorists pioneer the way to protect the possibilities of any form of such incidents which destroys people's life. Whatever governments are taking action to diminish the possibilities of such incidents, theorists always come together and incorporate the literature which shows the mirror. Terrorism is an effective and disastrous catalyst which carried out previous severe incidents in the world. Although terrorist acts can destroy people's lives, but will not succeed to topple a stable government (Abrahms, 2008; Arce & Sandler, 2007, 2010; Bloom, 2004; Kydd & Walter, 2002).

It is the failure of idealism to diminish terrorism activities on international peace and security. Furthermore, the idealism theoretical concept couldn't collaborate among the insurgent groups. Realists emerged instead of idealism to struggle against the idea of terrorism in the world. Their concept of realism pursues the proper procurement of acts of terrorism worldwide. There are weak points of realists' emphasis on power and work for a stronghold near to power among states. There are possibilities in the realists that there may be scepticism in the terms of ethical norms about the share of power. There are difficulties for idealists to shape peace and security through its collective security formula. The idealist political vision didn't work as a solution to the burning key issues. The beneficiary of terrorism is associated with various states. The countries like Iran, Pakistan, and Afghanistan are the most suffering countries from terror activities, in the past time, political groups support the terror organisation and work of terrorist groups. The terrorist organisation supports the state machinery, government perceived benefits of terror (Matseketsa & Tichaona Mapolisa, 2013, pp. 698-699).

Terrorism Affected Peace and Security

We have seen that many tourist places were deliberately targeted by the militant groups. Several people got injured and died of such incidents that happened. Several literatures suggest that terrorism is involved in creating scares and anxiety among tourists. Many tourist places are in a danger zone, but people have come despite the danger (Drakos & Kutan, 2003; Kapuściński & Richards, 2016). Accordingly, terrorist groups keep in mind to achieve the ultimate goal to destroy the public place, create violence and threaten the security issues and put the scary environment into the human society. They have alternate mottos to achieve some sort of political, social, and religious mileage. Thus, terrorism is creating the psychological illness in modern societies. There are severe risks to visit tourists' places, government monuments, hotels, and renowned places (Asongu et al., 2019). Peace is necessary for human development and welfare, the government's responsibility to save the people from any form of bad activities in our society.

Nowadays, the act of terrorism could be found in different variations. In today's world, people want to connect to each other in the era of globalisation. But some political groups are associated with militant groups basically from Afghanistan, Pakistan, Iran, Somalia, Yamen, and many other countries as well. The study indicates that there are alliances between terrorist groups and political parties in many countries. It is not a good sign for popular democracy, where militant groups negotiate with the power groups.

Thus, the character of peace is related to the presence of equality, liberty, justice, and other fundamental rights. Security and peace protect human benevolence and wisdom. The political condition guarantees social justice to build a peaceful environment in the state. In a democratic state, the government needs to manage peace stability and proper security. The government has to manage the states' peaceful environment which should be based on transparency and accountability. The discursive policy is adopted by the UN to diminish terrorist activities. UN Secretary-General Ban Ki-moon had shaped the course of action to Prevent Violent Extremism. Various UN actors and tools open the way for wider multiple engagements as discursive moves. The peacekeeping mission is one of the principal tools of the UN which works in affected areas. The UN has been launched dozens of peacekeeping operations across the world. There are lots of volunteers who are engaged worldwide in this kind of peacekeeping mission in West Asia, Africa, South Asia, and Latin American Countries. In many countries, the UN used force to protect civilians for example in Haiti, the eastern Democratic Republic of Congo (DRC), and Sierra Leone (Karlsrud, 2017, p. 1218).

In 2006, The UN adopted a strategy against counter-terrorism in the General Assembly. The UN revisited and reconfirmed in 2016 their strategy against terrorism in the world. There are main four principals adopted by the UN resolution. They are main to prevent and combat against terrorism, tackle some conditions and use the model conducive to a terrorist act, build strong capabilities to combat terrorism, the role of the UN will be strong in this regard and establish the rule of law ensuring the respect of human rights across the world. These are the prime ultimate goals set up by the UN to build peace and security worldwide (Koops & Tercovich, 2016). During the UN peacekeeping operations in Mali, Afghanistan, Iraq, and DRC, the UN had set up strong institutions to support the peacemaker in the affected regions. Because there were great challenges to work in the remote part of the countries. However, The UN peacekeeping mission works in difficult circumstances on the ground at a high level of risk. It was a hard time to save the people in the Central African Republic (CAR), Libya, Afghanistan, Syria, Niger, and Iraq during the peacekeeping programme. Sometimes there was a need to deploy the forces to counter the high-level risk in the affected region. During the counter-terrorism, many UN peacekeeping forces had died in the counter. UN agencies continuously work shoulder to shoulder in the danger zones (Karlsrud, 2017, p. 1228).

The analysis of UN peacebuilding enforcement operations stands as a consequence in the concerned countries. Till now the UN has successfully launched the peacekeeping mission in many countries. There are millions of people who were served and settled down across the world. The peacekeepers are also involved in the support of basic human requirements, like health programme service, children care, development of skilled works among immigrants, and evacuation at safe zones. Thus, the UN peacekeeper is involved in as multidimensional reform of victims of terrorism (Karlsrud, 2015). The consequences of terrorism badly affected the international communities. The career of young generation was badly affected by the act of terrorism. We often see the terror groups cleverly use the internet to trap the younger generation to force them to join the militant groups. There are many examples that the younger generation joins the terrorist groups for instance in Al-Qaida, ISIS, Taliban, and other terror organisations. In the aftermath of the 9/11 attacks, the Security Council adopted Resolution 1360 on 12th September 2001.

This resolution provides a route to redouble its efforts to suppress and prevent from such kinds of bad activities across the world. It provides the legacy and defines rule and norms to the US to take strong action against the terrorist organisation to prevent the terrorist activities. This also describes self-defence and protects the value of humanity and creates prosperity among the people. Another Resolution came on the 28th September 2001 under the UN charter in chapter seven. It states that the agenda on banning the criminalising terrorist activities freezes the fund of these terrorist organisations and their supporters. There should be a ban to apply on the safe heaven of terrorism and take over the terrorist funds, getting from worldwide. Another way of Resolution called 1373 could be analysed as super-resolution, which is based on proper restriction in the political sphere and will apply to all kinds of wrong activities of the terrorist organisation across the world (Ní Aoláin, 2016, p. 283).

Moreover, the people from the world only want a better way of life in the age of globalisation. The world's communities don't want any kind of encroachment in their way of life. But some groups don't like the progress of human life, they believe in bad activities and destroy the beautiful world. The people from the world have to unite against the birth of terrorism near our surroundings. People need to respond as citizens of any country honestly should share information regarding terrorist activities. There is a link between the terrorist organisation and the political groups whose motto is to seize power in the country. Through the blueprint on terrorism, the state can be successful to demoralise the terrorist organisation's wrong activities. Then, the peace and security problems will be solved in terrorist affected areas.

The entire world is affected by the consequences of terrorism and difficulties to shape the way for peace and security. Regional security is in jeopardy, because the act of terrorism is disrupting the peaceful environment of border zone. The percentage of migration in several regions increased at a gross level because of terrorism. Since 2013-14 the European countries have had refugees from the war affected countries, where the terrorist groups are fighting their countries' rule. The act of terrorism also impacts the economy and people migrate to another place after quitting their home and agricultural work as well. The act of terrorism has destroyed the socio-economic development, education system, social security, stability, disturb the peace, and good governance. Apart from killing innocent people, damaged lives on a large scale demolished the basic infrastructure and communication systems. That is why peace and security are important issues to maintain in areas affected by terrorists (Arowolo, 2013, p. 109). The acts of terrorism are a big fundamental threat to international peace and security. It is the responsibility of the international community to combat it. We can see that the UN is itself attacked by the terrorist organisation. There were severe terrorist attacks in different places of Mumbai in 2008. The peace and security were in danger caused by the terrorist attack on innocent people. Terrorism is challenging peace and security; it doesn't matter where it happened in the world. After Mumbai attack, the world community debated on these issues in the UN, unanimously opposed such incidents and criticised the terrorist which is the most serious issue. It is a severe conventional threat to international peace and security (United Nations, 2009).

The French President strongly condemned the terrorist activities worldwide. In August 2014, France had joined Operation Chammal to support the government of Iraq for a peace settlement. In September 2015, France faced terrorist threats, the Operation Chammal extended towards Syria to destroy the Daesh's network in the country. Thus, France is in the leading role on behalf of the European Union for peace settlement across the world (Ministry for Europe and Foreign Affairs, n.d.). There are severe situations that would happen in the near future, if the weapon of mass destruction is being acquired by terrorist groups. And this kind of another non-state actor is being involved in gathering the weapon of mass destruction which is a great threat to the international peace process and security. In resolution 1540, this new kind of threat was addressed. The international communities need to shape the rule and norms to protect international peace as effective as possible (United States Mission to the United Nations, 2022).

The NATO countries are mainly targeted by terrorist groups in the last decade. It poses a direct threat to the NATO citizens and creates major security issues, which is also creating a threat to peace, stability and global prosperity. In the broader picture, it can be defined that terrorists don't have a boundary, religion, and nationality, and need to tackle these problems at the international level togetherness. The NATO is committed to fight against this inhuman nature of militancy. NATO's work style has changed to counter-terrorism to expedite the awareness programme among the people and want to respond them strongly with the solidarity with international actors. The NATO's management is involved in cooperating with partners. It is encouraging that other international organisations are also engaged in operating join efforts to eradicate the possibilities of such form of terrorist events (North Atlantic Treaty Organisation, 2021).

CONCLUSION

The research concludes that terrorism caused several securities issues in the world. Terrorism negatively affects the collective effort of international communities. After the 9/11 terrorist attack, the international communities unitedly condemn the acts of terrorism. The UN also initiated several resolutions against the unlawful act of terrorism. During 2000-2010, several cities of world were attacked by the terrorists. This is a challenge for the entire world community. This is the time to unite against terrorism to establish international peace and security. We should have the concept of collective cooperation for the settlement of proper institutions and awareness programme which can be minimise the terrorist activities. The collective security agenda could work to diminish the terrorism incidents. The settlement of regional disputes decreases the possibility of insurgency. Terror activities can be demolished if the political group can't allow any kind of help from the terrorist groups. The study tries to find out results for the use of the theory of realism. The realism theory is relevant in the contemporary world where the international think tank can work together to fight against terrorism and eradicate its effect. The research highlighted terrorism negatively which affected the international peace process. There should be continuous work to minimise the possibility of these kinds of acts which are fully against humanism. There are many areas affected by terrorism, for example economic and tourist sector.

The international agencies continue work to mitigate problems across the world. It tries to curb terrorist activities through the dispute settlement. It is hard task to control the terrorist activities so that international communities have to aware of the global peace and security. The research recommends that the protection of human life should be prime focus and all protocols are required to shape the protection of civilians. If the international communities don't observe the people's rights and humanity, all of us would continue to suffer the scourge of terrorism. Besides, the study suggest that we should pioneer the fundamental structure for human needs from the areas of health, food, security, and global security. At the end, there should be a high level of dispensation which should expedite all issues of securities. The UN and other agencies should focus on applying and expediting the international laws and regulation to mitigate the acts of terrorism. The people need a peaceful environment and better security management in the world.

REFERENCES

Abrahms, M. (2006). Why Terrorism Does Not Work. *International Security*, *31*(2), 42–78. doi:10.1162/isec.2006.31.2.42

Abrahms, M. (2008). What Terrorists Really Want: Terrorist Motives and Counterterrorism Strategy. *International Security*, *32*(4), 78–105. doi:10.1162/isec.2008.32.4.78

Arce, D., & Sandler, T. (2007). Terrorist Signaling and the Value of Intelligence. *British Journal of Political Science*, *37*(4), 576–586. doi:10.1017/S0007123407000324

Arce, D., & Sandler, T. (2010). Terrorist Spectaculars: Backlash Attacks and the Focus of Intelligence. *The Journal of Conflict Resolution*, *54*(2), 354–373. doi:10.1177/0022002709355414

Arowolo, D. E. (2013). Terrorism, democracy and global security. *European Scientific Journal*, *9*(2), 100–111.

Asongu, S. A., Joseph, N., Nicholas, B., & Paul, N. (2019). Contemporary drivers of global tourism: Evidence from terrorism and peace factors. *Journal of Travel & Tourism Marketing*, *36*(3), 345–357. doi:10.1080/10548408.2018.1541778

Atran, S. (2004, August). *Trends in Suicide Terrorism: Sense and Nonsense.* Paper Presented to World Federation of Scientists Permanent Monitoring Panel on Terrorism, Erice, Sicily.

Baldwin, D. A. (2000). The Sanctions Debate and the Logic of Choice. *International Security*, *24*(3), 80–107. doi:10.1162/016228899560248

Bassey, M. E. (2017). Impact of terrorism on international peace and security in the age of technological advancement. *International Journal of Scientific and Research Publications*, *7*(8), 526–533.

Berman, E., & Laitin, D. D. (2008). Religion, terrorism and public goods: Testing the club model. *Journal of Public Economics*, *92*(10–11), 1942–1967. doi:10.1016/j.jpubeco.2008.03.007

Berrebi, C. (2009). The Economics of Terrorism and Counterterrorism: What Matters and Is Rational-Choice Theory Helpful? In P. K. Davis & K. Cragin (Eds.), *Social Science for Counterterrorism: Putting the Pieces Together.* RAND.

Bloom, M. M. (2004). Palestinian Suicide Bombing: Public Support, Market Share, and Outbidding. *Political Science Quarterly*, *119*(1), 61–88. doi:10.2307/20202305

Borum, R. (2004). *Psychology of Terrorism.* University of South Florida.

Byman, D., & Waxman, M. (2002). *The Dynamics of Coercion: American Foreign Policy and the Limits of Military Might.* Cambridge University Press.

Chowanietz, C. (2010). Rallying Around the Flag or Railing Against the Government? Political Parties' Reactions to Terrorist Acts. *Party Politics*, *2*(1), 111–142.

Crenshaw, M. (2001). The psychology of terrorism: An agenda for the 21st century. *Political Psychology*, *21*(2), 405–420. doi:10.1111/0162-895X.00195

Drakos, K., & Kutan, A. M. (2003). Regional effects of terrorism on tourism in three Mediterranean countries. *The Journal of Conflict Resolution*, *47*(5), 621–641. doi:10.1177/0022002703258198

Drezner, D. W. (2003). The Hidden Hand of Economic Coercion. *International Organization*, *57*(3), 643–659. doi:10.1017/S0020818303573052

Eilstrup, S. M., & Jones, C. (2008). Assessing the Dangers of Illicit Networks: Why al-Qaida May Be Less Threatening Than Many Think. *International Security*, *33*(2), 7–44. doi:10.1162/isec.2008.33.2.7

Euben, R. L. (2007). Review Symposium: Understanding Suicide Terror. *Perspectives on Politics*, *5*, 118–140.

Ganor, B. (2002). Defining terrorism: Is one man's terrorist another man's freedom fighter? *Police Practice and Research*, *3*(4), 287–304. doi:10.1080/1561426022000032060

George, A. (1993). *Forceful Persuasion: Coercive Diplomacy as an Alternative to War*. United States Institute of Peace.

Goodwin, J. (2006). A Theory of Categorical Terrorism. *Social Forces*, *84*(4), 2027–2046. doi:10.1353of.2006.0090

Gould, R. v. (1995). *Insurgent Identities: Class, Community, and Protest in Paris from 1848 to the Commune*. University of Chicago.

Greset, P., & Mahan, S. (2008). *Terrorism in perspective: What is terrorism*. Sage Publication.

Gurr, T. R. (2015). *Why men rebel*. Routledge. doi:10.4324/9781315631073

Hoffman, B. (2006). *Inside terrorism, revised and expanded edition*. Columbia University Press.

Hoffman, B. (2018). *Inside terrorism*. Columbia university press.

Hoffman, B., & McCormick, G. H. (2004). Terrorism, Signaling and Suicide Attack. *Studies in Conflict and Terrorism*, *27*(4), 243–281. doi:10.1080/10576100490466498

Horgan, J. (2005). The Social and Psychological Characteristics of Terrorism and Terrorists. In T. Bjorgo (Ed.), *Root Causes of Terrorism: Myths, Realities and Ways Forward*. Taylor and Francis. doi:10.4324/9780203337653_chapter_4

Hultman, L. (2005, September 3). Killing Civilians to Signal Resolve: Rebel Strategies in Intrastate Conflicts. Paper Presented at the *Annual Meeting of the American Political Science Association*, Washington, DC.

Kapuściński, G., & Richards, B. (2016). News framing effects on destination risk perception. *Tourism Management*, *57*(4), 234–244. doi:10.1016/j.tourman.2016.06.017

Karlsrud, J. (2015). The UN at war: Examining the consequences of peace-enforcement mandates for the UN peacekeeping operations in the CAR, the DRC and Mali. *Third World Quarterly*, *36*(1), 40–54. doi:10.1080/01436597.2015.976016

Karlsrud, J. (2017). Towards UN counter-terrorism operations? *Third World Quarterly*, *38*(6), 1215–1231. doi:10.1080/01436597.2016.1268907

Koops, J. A., & Tercovich, G. (2016). A European Return to UN Peacekeeping? *International Peacekeeping, 23*(5), 597–609. doi:10.1080/13533312.2016.1236430

Kydd, A. H., & Barbara, F. (2006). The strategies of terrorism. *International Security, 31*(1), 49–80. doi:10.1162/isec.2006.31.1.49

Kydd, A. H., & Walter, B. F. (2002). Sabotaging the peace: The politics of extremist violence. *International Organization, 56*(2), 263–296. doi:10.1162/002081802320005487

Laitin, D. D., & Shapiro, J. N. (2008). The Sources of Terrorism: An Ecological and Organizational Perspective. In P. Keefer & N. Loayza (Eds.), *Terrorism, Economic Development, and Political Openness*. Cambridge University Press. doi:10.1017/CBO9780511754388.008

Matseketsa, B., & Mapolisa, T. (2013). The effects of terrorism on international peace and security and educational systems in Africa and beyond-a new millennium perspective. *International Journal of Advanced Research, 1*(8), 694–710.

Merari, A. (2006). Psychological Aspects of Suicide Terrorism. In *Psychology of Terrorism*. Oxford University Press. doi:10.1093/med:psych/9780195172492.003.0008

Ministry for Europe and Foreign Affairs. (n.d.). *Terrorism: France's International Action - Ministry for Europe and Foreign Affairs*. Retrieved March 19, 2022, from https://www.diplomatie.gouv.fr/en/french-foreign-policy/security-disarmament-and-non-proliferation/terrorism-france-s-international-action/

Ní Aoláin, F. (2016). The "war on terror" and extremism: Assessing the relevance of the Women, Peace and Security agenda. *International Affairs, 92*(2), 275–291. doi:10.1111/1468-2346.12552

North Atlantic Treaty Organisation. (2021, September 14). *Countering terrorism*. https://www.nato.int/cps/en/natohq/topics_77646.htm

Pape, R. A. (2003). The strategic logic of suicide terrorism. *The American Political Science Review, 93*(3), 343–361.

Schelling, T. C. (1960). *The Strategy of Conflict*. Harvard.

Schelling, T. C. (1966). *Arms and Influence*. Yale.

Schmid, A. P., & Jongman, A. J. (2005). *Political terrorism: A new guide to actors, authors, concepts, data bases, theories and literature*. Transaction Books.

United Nations. (2009, December 9). *Threats to international peace and security caused by terrorist acts - SecCo meeting - Verbatim record (excerpts) - Question of Palestine*. https://www.un.org/unispal/document/auto-insert-184742/

United States Mission to the United Nations. (2022, March 14). *Remarks at a UN Security Council Briefing by the Chair of the 1540 Committee on Nonproliferation and Weapons of Mass Destruction United States Mission to the United Nations*. https://usun.usmission.gov/remarks-at-a-un-security-council-briefing-by-the-chair-of-the-1540-committee-on-nonproliferation-and-weapons-of-mass-destruction/

Victoroff, J. (2005). The Mind of the Terrorist: A Review and Critique of Psychological Approaches. *The Journal of Conflict Resolution, 49*(1), 3–42. doi:10.1177/0022002704272040

Walter, B. F. (2009). Bargaining failures and civil war. *Annual Review of Political Science, 12*(1), 243–261. doi:10.1146/annurev.polisci.10.101405.135301

Weinstein, J. (2007). *Inside Rebellion: The Politics of Insurgent Violence*. Cambridge University Press.

Wood, D. (2003). Foucault and Panopticism Revisited Editorial. *Surveillance & Society, 1*(3), 243–239.

Chapter 5
The Social Psychology of Terrorism:
Preventive Countermeasures

Irakli Kervalishvili
Georgian Technical University, Georgia

ABSTRACT

Social psychology's focus on person-situation interactions has implications for who becomes a terrorist; for example, Moghaddam posits a "staircase model" of terrorism in which terrorism is viewed as sequential progress from lower floors to higher floors that occurs on a progressively narrowing staircase. Each floor is characterized by unique psychological processes and progressive restrictions on response options, such that "destruction of others, or oneself, or both" becomes the only option. Regarding what motivates terrorism, from a psychological perspective there is little evidence that terrorists have abnormally high levels of mental illness or psychopathy. They are rational actors with purpose, intent, high levels of commitment, and deeply held convictions. Cultivated perceived threats to group identity and values (social, cultural, religious, political, etc.) are at the core of motivations for terrorism. A similar dynamic operates in responses to terrorism.

INTRODUCTION

The most dangerous type of violent crime committed both in a group and alone is terrorism - an extreme manifestation of extremism: explosions, arson, the use of radioactive and potent substances, organizing accidents and disasters, disabling life-supporting facilities that create a danger of death, seizure and the destruction of hostages - actions committed to violating social security, intimidate the population, and influence decision-making by authorities. In psychological terms, terrorism is dangerous not only because of its extremely negative specific consequences, but also because of the violation of the psychological balance in society, the violation of the peaceful existence of people, the generation of general anxiety and fear, the expectation of a threat, and the destabilization of public life.

DOI: 10.4018/978-1-6684-5311-7.ch005

Along with political, ideological, ethnic-psychological, and religious prerequisites, the behavior of terrorists is also determined by their psychological characteristics. The general psychological feature of terrorists is their extremist accentuation and emotional-conflict orientation in resolving life problems. The emphasis on the personality of a terrorist is manifested in an exaggerated desire for self-affirmation, an extremely high level of claims, the dominance of political and ethnic-psychological ambitions in his psyche, in taking on the halo of a martyr for an “idea”. All terrorists are characterized by hypertrophy of narrow group values. The whole world is categorically divided into “us” and “them”, the danger of alien influence is exaggerated. A confrontational behavioral attitude is formed, easily turning into a violent direction (Crenshaw, 2000).

In modern conditions, there is an escalation of the terrorist activities of extremist organizations, their nature is becoming more complicated, and the sophistication and inhumanity of terrorist acts are increasing. For an effective fight against terrorism, it is important to understand the psychology of terrorism, and the sources of aggression. The essence of the social order of psychological science today is to explain the nature of terrorism and offer society an effective means of countering the terrorist challenge. The problem of terrorism is multifaceted. In it, along with the social, political, legal, and economic aspects, the psychological aspect, which requires comprehensive consideration and in-depth study, should also be highlighted. Unfortunately, it is not always possible to prevent a terrorist act, even using all possible measures. Therefore, the problem of suppression of terrorist actions arises. Thus, when hostages are taken by terrorists, the problem of negotiating with them arises. And this is a completely psychological problem of communication, the possibility of influencing criminals to avoid possible victims. To effectively solve this problem, it is important to understand the psychology of terrorism.

It is customary to distinguish several types of motives that, as a rule, terrorists are guided by:

1. Mercantile motives. For a certain number of people, terror is a way to make money.
2. Ideological motives. Such a motive arises as a result of a person’s entry into a certain community that has an ideological and political orientation.
3. Motives for transformation and active change in the world. These motives are connected with the experience of injustice in the existing structure of the world and the desire to transform it based on a subjective understanding of justice.
4. The motive of power over people. Through violence, instilling fear in people, the terrorist seeks to assert himself and his personality.
5. The motive of the interest and attractiveness of terror as a field of activity. Terrorists may be attracted by the risk associated with terror, the process of developing plans, and the specifics of the implementation of terrorist acts.
6. Comradely motives of emotional attachment in a terrorist group. Such motives can be the motive of revenge for the fallen comrades, the motives of traditional participation in terror because one of the relatives was engaged in it.
7. The motive of self-realization. From the point of view of the terrorists themselves, their actions are a form of restoring violated justice. Terrorism is a perverted idea of justice in the world - it is an inadequate response of the weak side to the actions of the strong (Horgan, 2017).

Terrorism is not a new phenomenon in history. The roles that terrorists play in terrorist groups are described by social psychologists and boil down to three main ones: the role of leader, the role of adventurer, and the role of an idealist.

1. Leaders initially usually experience a sense of their inadequacy and easily project it onto society, believing that society is inadequate and must be changed. Such individuals have a clear understanding of the goals of the terrorist group and the roots of its ideology. The role of a leader is attractive to narcissistic and paranoid personalities.
2. An adventurer usually has all the necessary skills to participate in a terrorist group. As a rule, this is an antisocial personality type, often having a history of criminal behavior before joining the group. Ideology in their behavior may vary significantly or be absent altogether. The search for strong sensations in acts of aggression attracts them most.
3. An idealist is usually a young man (or girl) with a naive view of social problems and the possibility of social change, who is always dissatisfied with the state of his society or organization. He (or she) is the ideal target for brainwashing, which can come from ideological, political, or religious influences. The phenomenon of bigotry can be observed among this type of terrorist. The subject engages in terrorist behavior mainly because of the presence of distorted psychological needs (or personality defects), and not because he seeks to achieve improvements in the political and social sphere (Lemieux, 2006).

According to the degree of expression of emotions, two types of terrorists are distinguished. The first type is characterized by extreme composure. The second type of terrorist is characterized by a deep emotional life. Increased temperament leads to hyperactivity and over-emotionality. As a rule, when performing a terrorist act, such a person is collected and restrained, but in everyday life, he is not able to restrain his emotions, impulses, affects, and aggression.

It is necessary to distinguish between the psychological profile of persons capable of committing terrorist acts, or those who can be used by the leaders of terrorist groups for such acts. First of all, these are people who have not been able to realize themselves in the political sphere but are striving for power and have a certain inferiority complex. They are joined by bandit elements who have already shed blood and can fulfill any order of terrorist organizations for money. We should not forget the former athletes who were left out of life. Feed terrorism and various groups of outcasts, renegades, and dregs of society, although the likelihood of their involvement here is less. An important source of recruitment for terrorists are mercenaries who have been in different conflict regions, fighting on one side or the other. For their psychology, one thing is important: who will pay more, and often they are prompted simply by the "interest to kill", "to feel power over people", and "to show their superiority over others." Persons with various mental anomalies proper, who have inspired themselves with a superiority complex over others, should not be discounted. It should be noted that their activities are stimulated by the media, which reveal not only the methods and means used in terrorist acts but also popularize the personality of their perpetrators. A timely study of such a contingent makes it possible to take preventive measures to prevent terrorist attacks. Each of these categories of terrorists has specific moral and psychological characteristics. Knowing the contingent of terrorists, it can be assumed that persons from among the marginalized and with mental disabilities, as well as those who are notorious (both inferiority and "superhumans"), will act mostly alone. This is one of the difficulties of their identification. On the contrary, cadres of terrorists from among the bandit elements and those who have gone through the school of mercenaries in "hot spots" will act by organizing themselves into terrorist groups (McCauley, 2011).

Serious moral problems are inherent only in "ideological" terrorists, with a sufficiently high level of education and intellectual development, able to reflect on their actions. Most terrorists are characterized by the presence of primitive syndromes that prevent the resolution of complex ethical and moral problems.

Several psycho types can be distinguished:

1. So-called. The "zombie syndrome" manifests itself in a constant natural over-combat readiness, active hostility towards a real or virtual enemy, and a commitment to complex military operations. This is the fighter syndrome. Such people constantly live in conditions of war, they avoid situations of peace and tranquility in every possible way.
2. So-called. "Rimbaud's Syndrome" is expressed in the neurotic structure of the personality, torn apart by the conflict between the desire for thrills and feelings of anxiety, guilt, shame, and disgust for their participation in them. Such people are characterized by an awareness of the "mission" of saving the world voluntarily assigned to themselves, the idea of noble altruistic duties that allow them to realize aggressive aspirations. This is the missionary syndrome.
3. So-called. "Kamikaze Syndrome" is characteristic of suicide bombers who destroy themselves along with their victims in the course of a terrorist act. The main psychological characteristics of such people include extreme readiness for self-sacrifice. The "kamikaze" terrorist is happy with the opportunity to give his life and take as many people as possible with him to the next world. To do this, he must at least overcome the fear of his death. Numerous testimonies say that terrorists are not afraid of death itself, but of the circumstances associated with it: injuries, helplessness, and the likelihood of falling into the hands of the police. That is why terrorists are more ready for suicide than for self-preservation. Since they arrogate to themselves the right to dispose of other people's lives (the lives of their victims), the right to dispose of their own lives is automatically implied (McCauley, 2011).

One of the main motives for turning to terrorism is a strong need to strengthen personal identity, which is achieved by belonging to a group. Secondly, these are the motives of self-affirmation, giving such activities a special heroic significance, etc. And the most important thing: terrorism is most often the result of ideological absolutism, the belief in the alleged possession of a higher truth, a unique recipe for saving one's people or even all of humanity.

Terrorism involves the use of violent, primarily armed, actions, but it would be erroneous to explain its social impact by a purely physical effect (number of victims). Much more significant is the emotional-but-psychological effect, which manifests itself in the intimidation of the population. This is precisely the mechanism through which the terrorists are trying to influence the population, the consciousness of the masses, and even the authorities. Fear is the weapon through which the suppression of the personality of the layman goes. In other words, terrorist acts are always committed for self-promotion, to cause shock and fear among the population and authorities.

Studies show that, despite the presence of some similar psychological characteristics, there is no reason to talk about the existence of a complex portrait of a terrorist. There are at least two distinct psychological types that are often found among terrorists. The former is distinguished by high intelligence, self-confidence, high self-esteem, and the desire for self-affirmation, and the latter are insecure, losers with a weak "I" and low self-esteem. But both the first and the second are characterized by high aggressiveness, the desire to assert themselves, and fanaticism. The second psychological type is the ideal building material for any terrorist group, in which this weak individual finds support, a sense of usefulness, self-confidence, and a sense of WE. For the sake of a newfound reference group, this person - subject to some psychological "preparation" (which is easiest to do in a group, in a crowd) - for the sake of asserting himself as a member of this group and feeling secure, easily goes about an idea that readily justifies any of his actions (Kruglanski, 2010).

Terrorists are characterized by a high level of aggressiveness and rejection of universal human values. It also becomes clear that the group of violent and uncompromising like-minded people consists of lonely and psychologically weak people who can feel strong only in the general roar, only in the crowd. Crowds are made up of suggestible, malleable, and changeable people. Their existence is a belief similar to religion. But for terrorists, this religion is the ideology of opposition. The vision of the world "we-they", dividing it into Muslims and "infidels" is manifested in extreme intolerance of any kind of dissent. Terrorists are religious fanatics who supposedly possess the highest and only truth.

Psychologically, terrorism is a continuation of radicalism, extremism, and fanaticism. Therefore, it is very important to carry out effective work to prevent the appearance of these phenomena in society, especially among the younger generation, to recognize extremist sentiments, fanaticism, and radicalism in time, and to take the necessary measures of influence and suppression.

CONDITIONS FOR THE EMERGENCE OF A TERRORIST THREAT AND COUNTERMEASURES

In the modern world, the growth of the threat of terrorism occurs against the backdrop of the aggravation and spread of political, ethnic, and religious extremism, which poses a significant danger to the interests of the individual, society and the state, the political, military, economic, environmental security of the country, its constitutional system, sovereignty, and territorial integrity.

Terrorism is not a ubiquitous phenomenon. The use of this tactic involves a set of socio-cultural and political characteristics of the society. If these characteristics are absent, the tactics of terrorism cannot be implemented.

In the "Explanatory Dictionary" terrorism is defined as the policy and practice of terror - intimidation of one's political opponents, expressed in physical violence up to destruction, or in cruel intimidation of the population. Thus, a characteristic feature of terrorism is the reliance on the force in achieving its goals - to intimidate the population and sow panic.

Terrorism is the method by which an organized group or party seeks to achieve its stated goals primarily through the systematic use of violence. The causes of terrorism include the following:

- exacerbation of contradictions in the political, economic, social, ideological, ethnonational, and legal spheres;
- unwillingness of individuals, groups, and organizations to use the system of way of life accepted by the majority of society and the desire to obtain advantages through violence;
- the use of terrorist methods by individuals, and organizations to achieve political, economic, and social goals.

The main causes of terrorism can be divided into political, socio-economic, economic, religious, and spiritual.

Among the political causes of terrorism, the main one is political instability. If we consider the socio-economic reasons, then the main reason can be considered the low standard of living in the country. Economic. Terrorism today is a business that can bring its organizers a considerable income, which can be compared with the income from the oil business. Trade in weapons, drugs, and hostages allows you to get huge profits. Religious. Currently, there are religious movements that promote violence. The most widespread of them is Wahhabism (a radical branch of Islam). In most cases, terrorists only cover up their true intentions with religious slogans. Spiritual. Important spiritual reasons for the emergence of terrorism are the distortion of legal and universal values.

Terrorism Is Usually Generated

1. the presence of social, national, and religious problems that have existential significance for a given social, national, or other group and are related to its self-esteem, spirituality, fundamental values, traditions, and customs;
2. war and military conflicts, in which terrorist acts become part of hostilities;
3. the presence of social groups that differ from their near and distant neighbors by a high level of material well-being and culture, as well as by their political, economic, and military power or other capabilities, dictating their will to other countries and social groups. The former arouse envy and hatred, they are endowed with all the features of a most dangerous and perfidious enemy, who, if it is impossible to defeat him in an open conflict, can be secretly inflicted with separate painful blows;
4. the existence of secret or semi-secret societies and organizations, in particular religious and sectarian ones, which endow themselves with magical and messianic abilities, develop the only true teaching in their opinion of saving humanity or radically improving its life, creating a system of everything general goodness, justice, and prosperity, the eternal salvation of the soul, etc.;
5. unresolved important economic and financial issues, including at the legislative level.

In addition to the general causes of terrorism, some features of the development of social relations that predetermine the development of terrorism worldwide can be named:

a. the emergence of a new structure of relations to property, as well as the emergence of shadow leaders, by any means expanding their spheres of influence;
b. strengthening the influence of informal norms that criminalize social relations, under which the law ceases to provide the necessary level of social protection for a significant part of the population;
c. change in the concepts of order and justice, the revival of the principles of behavior, in which violence becomes a “legitimate” means of achieving political and other goals;
d. Appeal to political, religious, and other extremist organizations in which the cult of force and weapons is an indispensable element of life and way of life.

The emergence and development of terrorism worldwide are influenced by a rather complex set of political, economic, social, ideological, ethnonational, and legal factors.

Political Factors

- aspirations of foreign terrorist organizations aimed at violating concrete country`s integrity and destroying statehood;
- exacerbation of the political struggle of parties, movements, associations, lack of experience in the civilized political struggle;
- contradictions between proclaimed democratic principles and their implementation;
- Insufficient effectiveness of countering terrorist threats by the law enforcement system;
- lack of necessary interaction between authorities at all levels and the population to ensure the conflict-free development of interethnic and interethnic relations;
- shortcomings of the national-state structure of the concrete country, their untimely correction, delay in the development of new directions and forms of national policy;

- ineffectiveness of political reforms;
- pressure on concrete state's political system from abroad using terrorist methods.

Economic Forces

- extreme stratification of the population in terms of living standards as a result of privatization and subsequent state economic policy;
- open and hidden unemployment of a significant part of the able-bodied population;
- criminalization of the economy;
- active financial support of terrorist organizations both from abroad and using domestic sources.

Social Factors

- disengagement of society (formation of social strata and groups with opposing interests);
- lack of an effective system of social guarantees for the population;
- a sharp decrease in the social protection of the population, a decrease in life expectancy, and an increase in acute and chronic diseases;
- increase in crime;
- decrease in spiritual, moral, moral, patriotic qualities and cultural level of the population, including the legal one;
- propaganda by mass media of the cult of cruelty and violence.

Ethnic Factors

- exacerbation of interethnic relations (preaching of national exclusivity and superiority, inciting national and religious hatred);
- inequality in the economic, socio-political, and cultural situation of various national groups;
- delay in decisions taken by state-political structures, acute economic, social, political, and other problems affecting the existence and development of the nation;
- activities of radical, extremist nationalist organizations, movements, and leaders, pushing the population to illegal actions;
- Nationalist policy of representatives of the ruling elite in the struggle for power in a multinational population.

Legal Factors

- low legal literacy of the population, individual leaders, leaders of political parties, organizations, and movements, which does not allow one to assess the extent of one's responsibility for the actions taken and for their consequences;
- the absence of a clear and unified concept of "terrorism", "terrorist activity", "terrorist organization" and several other fundamental terms;
- the absence in the state of an effective legal mechanism for the prevention and suppression of dangerous manifestations, which refers to specific norms of constitutional, criminal, administrative, and other legislation, which should be the legal basis for countering terrorism;

- cumbersome and confusing procedural legislation, the lack of the effect of timely and sufficiently severe punishment of the perpetrators creates not only the criminals but also ordinary citizens the impression of the weakness of the law enforcement system, its inability to ensure the safety of the population;
- insufficiently effective domestic regulation of the activities of public associations, the weakening of which, untimely actions of the authorities to ban or suspend the activities of organizations that pose a threat to the security of people and the state, is also one of the reasons for the rapid spread of terrorism (Crenshaw, 2000).

Ideological Factors

- lack of a unified consistent policy of the state in the field of the ideology of civil society;
- planting the ideology of nihilism, anti-patriotism, rejection of national historical and cultural values;
- Nationalist propaganda carried out, including in the media, by a part of the nationalist-minded political elite, aimed at inciting hostility and mistrust towards other nations;
- Lack of an effective system for educating law-abiding behavior, including among young people and adolescents.

All measures aimed at combating terrorism can conditionally be divided into forceful, legal, external, and internal. By force, they fight not against terrorism, but against its manifestations. Unfortunately, it is not yet possible to solve this problem only by legal methods in the foreseeable future. External measures to combat terrorism include, firstly, the adoption of special anti-terrorist laws and the interaction of states fighting terrorism. Second, exerting economic pressure on countries that support international terrorism. Measures aimed at preventing terrorist attacks are called internal. They are the most efficient. Such measures include legislative, administrative-legal, criminal-legal, social, financial-economic, political, military, propaganda, preventive, and several others. The most important aspect for the formation of an adequate response state strategy to terrorism is the consideration of terrorist crimes not only in the criminological aspect of preventing, detecting, and suppressing crimes, but also in general - within the framework of the security system, which is a multifunctional and multilevel mechanism. It is necessary to fully involve not only the capabilities of all state authorities participating within their competence in the prevention of terrorist activities but also broadly non-state structures.

ON THE TYPOLOGY OF TERRORISM

Understanding the Essence and Reasons for the Implementation of a Successful Fight Against Terrorism

The success of the fight against one or another dangerous phenomenon for society depends on understanding its essence and causes. The complexity of such a historical phenomenon as terrorism leads to scientific discussions about the definition of its types. Various criteria are used as grounds for distinguishing certain types of terrorism in the scientific literature and political practice.

The existing typologies have different cognitive, and scientific values, although in general, they allow us to see the multifaceted nature of terrorism as a phenomenon, contribute to the disclosure of its socially dangerous nature, and the formation of the conceptual apparatus of terrorism - a scientific discipline about terrorism, and also contribute to the criminal law qualification of the acts of accomplices and accomplices of terrorist attacks, creation of an effective system of measures to counter terrorism in general.

Terrorism as an extreme form of manifestation of extremism and radicalism is diverse, many-sided, has a different nature, different sources, goals, different levels, scales, directions, and nature of execution. The fundamental commonality of all types of terrorism is in the forcible imposition of a worldview, ideology, morality, politics, one's way of life, the use of killing civilians, the threat of killing, or other forms of violence as the main means of achieving goals.

There are several options for classifying terrorism. For example, there is such a typology of terrorism:

1. **Political** - committed in the form of murders of state or public figures or government officials, as well as explosions, arson, and other actions that create a danger of death of people, causing significant damage and other grave consequences to intimidate the authorities.
2. **Criminal** - terrorism of organized criminal communities (domestic and international), directed against the state and its representatives to interfere with the investigation of criminal cases, prevent the conduct and continuation of a tough criminal policy, as well as aimed at eliminating active law enforcement officers, forcing judges to issue soft sentencing, intimidation, and intimidation of witnesses and victims.
3. Nationalist terrorism aimed at paralyzing the activities of federal authorities and achieving political or economic isolation.
4. "**Air**" - terrorism committed by hijackers by taking hostages for various kinds of extortion and blackmail.
5. **International** - committed by killing representatives of foreign states, to complicate relations between states up to military conflicts.

This classification as a whole was approved by the majority of scientists. However, the following shortcomings were noted:

- insufficient completeness;
- biased allocation of "air" terrorism, while there are also terrorist attacks on water, rail, and other modes of transport.

There Is a More Detailed Classification

1. According to the purpose and intent of the terrorist act:
    a. criminal terrorism - it pursues material or personal interests, accompanied by extortion, blackmail, threats;
    b. social terrorism - that form of terrorism that aims to overthrow the government, and change the social system in any country. The characteristic of this form of terrorism is that it does not cross the borders of a given country;
    c. political terrorism - its main goal is to break relations between states, eliminate specific political leaders or heads of state;
    d. state terrorism - a form of terrorism that involves the use of terrorist acts by the state against some movements or specific social, national groups, or individuals.

2. According to the territory where it is practiced, destructive factors and their distribution:
    a. national, or internal, terrorism - it creates a terrorist environment to influence the morale of the population through acts of violence. This state, created by terrorists, is accompanied by the disorganization of social structures, and this is the main factor in the realization of the plan. National terrorism is currently acquiring new dimensions and forms and is understood as the illegal use of force or violence by terrorist groups against persons and property, to undermine the authority of the government, to intimidate the civilian population;
    b. international terrorism is the illegal use of force and violence committed by a group of persons located abroad (or directed from abroad), it is directed against the population and governments of other countries. The main manifestations of this type are air piracy, hostage-taking, and kidnapping of diplomats and other political leaders, for the release of which any changes in the political plan are required.
3. For the main reasons for the manifestation:
    a. racial;
    b. nationalist - usually found only within one state;
    c. neo-fascist - aimed at establishing the policy of right-wing forces, the manifestation of violence, and interference in the internal affairs of other countries;
    d. fundamental religious terrorism.
4. According to the methods of execution of terrorist acts:
    a. directed terrorism - terrorist acts are aimed at achieving the set goal.
    b. indirect terrorism - acts of terrorism are committed using indirect methods and methods that lead to the achievement of the set goal.

A clear advantage of this typology was that it was carried out for various reasons, which allowed it to fully reflect the many-sided nature of terrorism. However, in the logic of its construction, it is inferior to the following classification, which distinguishes the following types of terrorism:

- Political is associated with the power struggle and is aimed at intimidating the political opponent and his supporters. At the same time, the most active figures of the opposite side are killed, intimidating the rest. This is what the German Nazis and Italian fascists did when they rushed to power and tried to strengthen it.
- State (or terror) is determined by the need to intimidate one's population, its complete suppression and enslavement, and the destruction of those who fight against the tyrannical state.
- Religious terrorism is committed to establishing, forcing recognition of one's church and at the same time weakening another confession, to damage it. Religious terrorism is possible not only between representatives of different religions but also between adherents of different branches of the same one. Within the framework of the religious, sectarian terrorism can also be distinguished.
- Self-serving terrorism is aimed at those who prevent the receipt of coveted material values, commercial rivals who are obliged to pay "tribute", or those who are expected to accept unfavorable conditions.
- Criminal, the content of which is the destruction of rivals and the intimidation of their supporters in conflicts between organized groups of criminals. Such terrorist acts are committed quite often and their victims are numerous.

- Military terrorism takes place during the war and is aimed not only at the economic and military weakening of the enemy, the destruction of his industrial and military power, but also at bringing him to a stupor, terrifying the population, changing the psychological situation in the country - weakening fighting spirit.
- Nationalistic - pursuing the goal by intimidation to oust another nation, get rid of its power, sometimes - seize its property and land, in some cases - to defend its national dignity and national wealth. Sometimes nationalism takes the form of separatism when the goal is to separate the given nation and form an independent state. However, such organizations often defend their interests and views, and by no means the desires of the majority of the people for whose independence they are allegedly fighting.
- "Idealistic", when criminal acts are committed for the sake of rebuilding the world, the victory of "justice", etc., but they try to achieve this with the help of intimidation. Such terrorists are no less terrible than any others, all the more so because among them there are many fanatical people whose mind does not accept any reasonable arguments against them and who are indestructibly confident in the correctness of their cause.
- Guerrilla terrorism, which is not included in military terror because such attacks also continue after the end of the war, is guerrilla terrorism against the invaders. The actions of partisans are very often of a terrorist nature, of which even our history has left numerous pieces of evidence.

There is also such a classification of terrorism:

1. According to the goals and scope of action:
    a. **"internal"** – corresponding actions of citizens of one state against compatriots on their territory;
    b. **transnational** - corresponding actions of citizens of one state against compatriots on the territory of a foreign state;
    c. **international** - relevant actions of groups of citizens, single or mixed in ethnic composition, against any persons in the territory of third countries. International terrorism poses tasks of a large-scale nature - undermining interstate relations, international legal order, combat opposition to an international organization, a foreign state, or a nation fighting for its liberation and independence.
2. According to the principle of choosing victims:
    a. selective, when the object becomes a figure symbolizing a certain power, a regime against which terrorists oppose;
    b. abstract, ie directed at a group of people who have nothing to do with the conflict.
3. According to the level of unity of terrorists:
    a. state terrorism – terrorists are in the public service in special units and act under the direction and control of the state and on its instructions;
    b. organized terrorism, where groups of criminals act independently;
    c. affective, represented by lone terrorists acting at their peril and risk.
4. Classification of terrorism by types:
    a. Conventional terrorism uses conventional means of destruction, including explosives;
    b. nuclear, chemical, and biological terrorism (NCB) is carried out with the use of nuclear fissile substances and nuclear explosive devices, hazardous chemically and biologically hazardous

substances, and means of their delivery. These types of terrorism also include sabotage against nuclear, chemical, and biologically dangerous objects.

   i. Electromagnetic terrorism is carried out with the use of powerful electromagnetic radiation-generating plants that affect both people and certain technological systems of infrastructure facilities.
   ii. cybernetic terrorism is carried out with the use of special virus programs to disable or disrupt the normal functioning of computer networks.
   iii. information terrorism is carried out with the use of media sources and other information means to escalate the negative situation in society and the decomposition of certain groups of it.

5. Classification of terrorism by goals and objectives:
   a. Mercantile terrorism aims to obtain some concessions or fulfill certain demands.
   b. apocalyptic terrorism aims to cause maximum damage at any cost to the object of a terrorist act

In addition to the fact that terrorism has many faces, it is also very dynamic, so an exhaustive list of its types can hardly be imagined. The issue typology of terrorism is a debatable issue. It must be understood that the perversity of the criminal mind and the development of technological progress cause a constant change in existing types and the addition of new unexplored and unexplored forms and methods of committing terrorist acts to the existing ones.

Currently, there is an increase in terrorism all over the world, an increase in its scale, forms, and spheres of manifestation. According to experts, shortly terrorism can rapidly develop, change, and globalize. Therefore, today it is very important to unite all forces and resources to prevent and counter terrorist threats. The main goal of the state strategy for countering terrorism is to ensure the reliable protection of citizens, society, and the state from terrorist threats by preventing terrorist acts and suppressing them as effectively as possible.

ON THE POLITICAL PSYCOLOGY OF TERRORISM

Countering the Ideology of Terrorism

The study of the essence of terrorism as a crime against society is important and necessary for effective work on early detection, and most importantly, prevention of the emergence of any manifestations of aggression. Understanding the psychology of terrorism makes it possible to successfully organize preventive work among the population, especially the younger generation, to explain the extreme public danger of terrorism, to resist this criminal activity, to stop it, by all means, methods and means, to identify terrorists and terrorist threats promptly. The success of the fight against this socially dangerous phenomenon largely depends on the understanding of its essence and causes.

Political psychology is a field of psychology that studies the psychological components (moods, opinions, feelings, value orientations, etc.) in the political life of society, which are formed and manifested at the level of the political consciousness of nations, classes, social groups, governments, individuals and are realized in their specific political actions. Terrorism is different psychology, a different logic, a different morality, and different goals and methods. Therefore, solutions to the problem of terrorism are not quite simple and unambiguous.

A type of political violence is political terrorism. Political terrorism in recent years has become one of the main problems of the world community. The targets of political terrorism are the symbols of the state, the most significant social norms, and the state as such. Terrorism from the point of view of political psychology is the struggle of illegitimate power against legitimate power using unlimited means and methods of pressure on the mental state of the enemy to replace the meaning, goals, and values of the enemy with your meaning, goals, and values.

The strategy of terrorism is based on the non-recognition of the so-called. civilized norms of warfare: observance of the "right of war" (legal restrictions that international law imposes on belligerents in the use of means of suppressing the enemy), "international military law", "customs of war", "laws of war" (restrictions established by international law, within which it is possible to use force to defeat the enemy).

Terrorism from the point of view of political psychology is the struggle of illegitimate power against legitimate power using unlimited means and methods of pressure on the mental state of the enemy to replace the meaning, goals, and values of the enemy with your meaning, goals, and values.

The fight against terrorism is a struggle for human consciousness in the context of global changes in the world. The goal of terrorism is the psychological and political destabilization of society, leading to financial collapses, changes in governments, reduction in production, and traffic stop - everything that materially embodies the world of other people rejected by terrorism.

Terrorism is the infection of others with psychological and political instability, which the terrorist himself suffers from. Therefore, the diagnosis of terrorism, its "treatment", and the forecast are not so much in identifying and destroying its paramilitary structures, but in the exact knowledge and optimization of the reasons for its existence: the reasons for its psychological and political instability.

Terrorism in the psychological and political sense is a forceful solution to the problems of political incompatibility between people by destabilizing the psychological state of the opponent by using violence that is not limited by civilized morality and international law. Terrorism is extremely exacerbated by globalization, which has placed equally all of humanity in front of problems that have not been encountered before. Modern terrorism is a nervous reaction to global changes in the world. Adapting to these changes is a very difficult intellectual and psychological problem that needs to be addressed in the fight against terrorism.

Terrorism is a phenomenon both political and psychological. Terrorists are capable of changing the social atmosphere in the most serious way, sowing fear, uncertainty, and distrust in the institutions of power. They can and should be neutralized and punished, but terrorism as a phenomenon can only be defeated when, when such an atmosphere is created in society that everyone, including the terrorists themselves, will understand that even those who share their political and religious views, they are, at best, dangerous lunatics. The state must fight terrorists, but only society can defeat them (Crenshaw, 2000).

Civil Society in Bountering Extremism and Terrorism

A feature of our time is the globalization of social processes and the involvement in them of a large number of groups of people of different worldviews and cultures. This requires new approaches to social management in all spheres of society and the state, especially the creation of an adequate and sustainable system of state security. Today, as reality shows, we are not properly protected from external manipulations and, as evidence, the development of ideologies of extremism and terrorism in international society, and the moral degradation of our youth.

Modern extremism and terrorism are extensive and well-established systems with huge financial and human resources, controlled by international centers. Extremism and terrorism are multifaceted in their forms, masked and covered by various ideological and political doctrines, including religion. Extremism and terrorism cause irreparable harm to the established social values of mankind and have a significant negative impact on the "sense of security" of a person.

Countering terrorism and extremism in many countries is one of the most important tasks of ensuring security at the state level because, extremism and terrorism have become one of the most acute threats to the vital interests of the individual, society, and the state.

Extremism, and its extreme form - terrorism - is not a local or even a regional problem today, but rather a large-scale international phenomenon.

Prevention of extremism and terrorism is not only the task of the state, but to a large extent, it is also the task of representatives of civil society. This work depends on the clear position of political parties, public and religious associations, and individual citizens.

In various countries, the creation and activities of public and religious associations, and other organizations whose goals or actions are aimed at carrying out extremist activities are prohibited by law. But extremism and terrorism are rapidly changing, mastering ever more dangerous and destructive methods. Therefore, it is especially important to organize the coordinated work of state institutions, public and religious organizations at all levels of the state administration system, and public activities. Without the purposeful and coordinated work of these two systems, it is impossible to fight extremism and terrorism, it is impossible to educate the younger generation in the spirit of patriotism and religious tolerance, which is necessary to ensure the security of society as a whole.

Now extremism and terrorism, in whatever form they appear, are one of the most dangerous social and political problems that require immediate solutions (Dechesne, 2009)

Priority in this work is preventive measures. This work can only be successfully carried out through the joint efforts of the heads of administrations, and law enforcement agencies, with the assistance of labor collectives and the public. Therefore, the task of all state structures, local self-government bodies, public associations, religious organizations, and all segments of the population is to fight this evil together. The main thing is to work proactively so as not to deal with the consequences later.

To defeat extremism and terrorism, to get rid of this most dangerous negative social phenomenon, it is necessary to unite all the forces of society, and use them wisely, spiritual, moral, and psychological work with young people. Constant and comprehensive work is important to prevent crime, drug addiction, extremism, neglect, and delinquency, especially among young people.

The participation of civil society in countering extremism and terrorism is the main thing in revealing the purpose and essence of what is presented as a "conflict", but in fact, is crime and banditry.

Civil society needs to realize that extremists and terrorists and their accomplices live in this very society and are subject to its informational, emotional, and psychological impact. And this very information-psychological influence of society can be different in its form. This impact and influence must be aimed at the intolerance of any kind and type of manifestation of hatred and violence within society, exposing the criminal nature of extremism and terrorism.

Counteracting the ideology of violence in the conditions of the modern democratic system, of course, cannot be the task of the state itself alone. The ideology of violence is the complex of ideas that is reproduced precisely within society. For a particular person or group of people to perceive these ideas, a whole complex of factors is needed, both objective (state of the economy, crime rate, employment, etc.) and subjective (personal dissatisfaction, difficult life situation). A significant part of these problems can and should be solved by the state, but it should be recognized that it cannot and should not limitlessly invade all niches of public life.

The perception of the state as an institution responsible for everything that happens in the country is fundamentally contrary to the idea of democracy. Democracy presupposes an active position in society. At the same time, the state acts as a regulator of social relations. The task of the state is to create organizational and legal conditions, as well as to perform several public functions that are inherently related to its nature. At the same time, domestic and world experience in countering extremism and terrorism shows that the ideology of violence begins to spread widely when it finds support in society.

Thus, the main task in modern conditions is to create a self-reproducing system of ideas, subjects-bearers, and channels for their dissemination, which can, autonomously from the state, contribute to the formation of a positive public consciousness that excludes the very possibility of using violence to achieve any goals. Such a system can and should be the institutions of civil society, scientific and business communities, educational institutions, and the media.

These institutions, being an organic part of society, have a sufficient set of tools to influence public consciousness, sometimes more than the state. In addition, the involvement of society in the consideration of issues of countering the ideology of violence makes it possible to maximally calibrate the tools used, to prevent violations of the rights and interests of citizens.

At the present stage, the task is to ensure that our institutions of civil society, the scientific, educational, and business communities, and the media could be more actively involved in the anti-extremist and anti-terrorist activities of the state and make a significant contribution to the protection of Russian citizens from extremist and terrorist attacks.

IN THE DIRECTION OF COUNTERING TERRORISM

Countering the ideology of terrorism includes a set of organizational, socio-political, information and propaganda measures to prevent the spread of beliefs, ideas, moods, motives, and attitudes in society, aimed at fundamentally changing the existing social and political institutions of the state.

Today, countering terrorism in the World is carried out in the following main areas:

- prevention of terrorism;
- combating terrorism (detection, prevention, suppression, disclosure, and investigation of a terrorist act and other crimes of a terrorist nature);
- minimization and (or) elimination of the consequences of terrorist acts.

Prevention of terrorism is understood as an activity that includes a set of measures aimed at identifying and eliminating the causes and conditions that contribute to the implementation of terrorist activities. Prevention of terrorism is carried out in three main areas:

- organization and implementation on a systematic basis of countering the ideology of terrorism and extremism;
- improving the anti-terrorist protection of potential objects of terrorist aspirations;
- strengthening control over compliance with administrative, legal, and other regimes that contribute to countering terrorism.

Any individuals and legal entities, places of mass stay of people, real estate, critical infrastructure, transport, life support, communication, and information networks can be considered potential objects of terrorist aspirations.

Under the anti-terrorist security of potential objects of terrorist aspirations, one should understand the integrated use of physical protection forces, engineering, and technical means, and security measures aimed at ensuring their safe functioning. In this regard, a special role belongs to the effective implementation of the administrative and legal regimes provided for by the legislation of many countries.

Prevention of terrorism involves the solution of the following tasks:

1. development of recommendations and implementation of measures to eliminate the causes and conditions conducive to the emergence and spread of terrorism;
2. identification and forecasting of terrorist threats, informing public authorities and local authorities about them, as well as the public, to take measures to neutralize them;
3. providing a deterrent and positive impact on the behavior of individuals (groups of individuals) prone to extremist actions;
4. determination of the legal regulation of the activities of the executive authorities of the constituent entities of the various countries and anti-terrorist commissions in the constituent entities of the concrete state when introducing regimes of terrorist threats
5. development of a list of antiterrorist measures for organizing and carrying them out on the territory of the constituent entities of the concrete states with the obligatory determination of the sources of their financing;
6. development and introduction of standard requirements for protection against threats of terrorist acts of critically important and potentially dangerous facilities, places of mass stay of people;
7. determination of the rights, obligations, and responsibilities of the heads of executive authorities and economic entities in the organization of measures for the anti-terrorist protection of objects under their jurisdiction;
8. improving the legal regulation of compensation for damage to persons participating in the suppression of a terrorist act and conducting a counter-terrorist operation and (or) injured as a result of their implementation;
9. Improving the interaction of federal executive authorities to develop a unified strategy and tactics in the framework of international cooperation in the field of countering terrorism.

The organization of activities for the prevention of terrorism requires the coordinated work of state authorities with public organizations and associations, religious structures, other institutions of civil society, and individual citizens. The implementation of these tasks is carried out within the framework of creating an effective system of measures to counter-terrorism.

The fight against terrorism is the activity of the authorized federal executive bodies, carried out with the use of intelligence, counterintelligence, operational-search, investigative, military, and special measures aimed at solving problems of:

- detection, prevention, and suppression of terrorist activities;
- disclosure and investigation of crimes of a terrorist nature.

The organization of the fight against terrorism requires an integrated approach to the analysis of the sources and subjects of terrorist activity, a clear definition of the functions and areas of responsibility of each subject of the struggle, the timely determination of priorities in solving the tasks set, the improvement of the organization of the construction and interaction of operational, operational-combat, military, investigative units based introduction of the headquarters principle of organizing the management of counter-terrorist operations and providing resources, including modern hardware and software systems (automated control systems).

One of the main conditions for increasing the effectiveness of the fight against terrorism is to receive proactive information about terrorist structures, their plans to commit terrorist acts, and activities to spread the ideology of terrorism and extremism. Law enforcement agencies, for their part, are constantly working to obtain information about the sources and channels of financing terrorist-minded individuals and organizations, and sources of supplying them with weapons, ammunition, and other means for carrying out terrorist activities.

The condition for the effective organization of the fight against terrorism is the early preparation of the forces and means of the subjects of countering terrorism to suppress a terrorist act in the course of command-staff, tactical-special, operational-tactical exercises organized by operational headquarters at the federal and regional levels.

Activities to minimize and (or) eliminate the manifestations of terrorism should be planned, based on forecasts of the possible consequences of terrorist acts. This activity should be focused on solving the following main tasks:

1. prevention (minimization) of human losses based on the priority of protecting human life over material and financial losses (except the lives of terrorists);
2. timely conduct of emergency rescue operations and provision of medical and other assistance to persons involved in the suppression of a terrorist act, as well as to persons affected by a terrorist act, their subsequent social and psychological rehabilitation;
3. minimizing the adverse moral and psychological consequences of the impact of terrorist acts on society or individual social groups;
4. restoration of damaged and destroyed objects; compensation for harm caused to individuals and legal entities affected by acts of terrorism (except terrorists).

The conditions for the successful implementation of measures to eliminate the consequences of a terrorist act are taking into account the specifics of emergencies associated with the commission of terrorist acts, depending on the objects of encroachment and the nature of terrorist impacts, the formation of standard plans for the engagement of forces and means, their preparation, including during exercises.

Following the content of the main areas of countering terrorism, anti-terrorist activities are carried out through the implementation of a set of measures, during which various forms and methods are used - interrelated and coordinated technologies, techniques, and means of influencing the subjects of terrorism; factors contributing to its emergence and development; consequences of terrorism.

Within the framework of terrorism prevention activities, political, socio-economic, information-propaganda, educational methods, as well as methods of physical, technical protection, and legal prevention are used, which are of priority importance for reducing the level and scale of terrorist threats. They are designed to have a targeted impact on economic, political, social, national, and confessional processes that can give rise to large-scale social conflicts and, as a result, terrorist manifestations; protect citizens (groups of citizens) from terrorist aspirations; prevent the formation of terrorist intent; hinder the actions of subjects of terrorist activity. Based on the nature of the object of preventive action, various forms of general and targeted prevention are used, taking into account its demographic, ethnic-confessional, individual psychological, and other characteristics.

The main groups of measures to prevent terrorism include:

- political (measures to normalize the socio-political situation, resolve social conflicts, reduce the level of socio-political tension, implement international cooperation in the field of countering terrorism);
- socio-economic (measures to improve the socio-economic situation in certain regions and equalize the level of development of regions, reduce the marginalization of the population, reduce property differentiation, and ensure social protection of the population);
- legal (administrative, criminal, organizational, and other measures aimed at the inevitability of punishment for committed acts of a terrorist nature, improving the mechanism of responsibility for non-compliance with the requirements of anti-terrorist legislation; combating illegal trafficking in weapons, ammunition, explosives, narcotics and psychotropic drugs, radioactive materials, dangerous biological substances and chemicals, financing of terrorism, regulation of migration processes and the use of information and communication systems);
- information and propaganda (measures to reveal the essence and explain the danger of terrorism, to influence citizens (groups of citizens) to educate them against the ideology of violence and attract them to participate in countering terrorism);
- cultural and educational (measures for the formation of socially significant values in society and the education of tolerance);
- Organizational and technical (development and implementation of targeted programs and specific measures to provide objects of possible terrorist attacks with technical means of protection, improve the mechanism of responsibility for non-compliance with the requirements for anti-terrorist protection of objects of terrorist aspirations and technical equipment for participants in anti-terrorist activities) (Dechesne, M. 2009).

The implementation of the fight against terrorism involves the priority use of methods for identifying, preventing, and suppressing terrorist activities with the aim of targeted forceful and psychological impact on specific subjects of terrorism. The fight against terrorism is also carried out in the form of various operational-combat, operational-search, operational-search, blocking, filtering, law enforcement, and other actions to identify, suppress, disclose and investigate crimes of a terrorist nature.

A set of measures to combat terrorist manifestations is envisaged as part of the state system being created to respond to terrorist threats. In this system, depending on the level of threats, an appropriate legal regime is defined, including an administrative regime, operational search, and other measures implemented by operational headquarters in cooperation with anti-terrorist commissions and divisions of federal executive bodies, as well as a list of temporary restrictions aimed at preventing terrorist attacks. acts and minimizing their consequences.

CONCLUSION

The most effective and effective form of suppression of a terrorist act is a counter-terrorist operation - a complex of special, operational-combat, military, and other measures using military equipment, weapons, and special means to suppress a terrorist act, neutralize terrorists, ensure the safety of individuals, organizations, and institutions, and also to minimize the consequences of a terrorist act.

In the course of implementing measures to minimize and (or) eliminate the consequences of manifestations of terrorism, the main role is played by methods for localizing and overcoming emergencies caused by terrorist acts, which are implemented in the form of measures of various duration and scale with the involvement of appropriate forces and means of action to rescue and evacuate citizens. affected by a terrorist act, in particular:

1. provision of emergency medical care;
2. medical and psychological support of rescue and fire fighting activities;
3. medical and psychological rehabilitation of persons affected by a terrorist act or persons involved in its suppression;
4. restoration of the normal functioning and environmental safety of objects subjected to terrorist influence;
5. Compensation for moral and material damage to persons affected by a terrorist act.

REFERENCES

Crenshaw, M. (2000). The psychology of terrorism: An agenda for the 21st century. *Political Psychology, 21*(2), 405–420. doi:10.1111/0162-895X.00195

Dechesne, M. (2009). Explorations in the experimental social psychology of terrorism: The struggle-violence link and its predictors. *Revue Internationale de Psychologie Sociale, 22*(3), 87–102.

Gill, P., & Corner, E. (2017). There and back again: The study of mental disorder and terrorist involvement. *The American Psychologist, 72*(3), 231–241. doi:10.1037/amp0000090 PMID:28383976

Horgan, J. G. (2017). Psychology of terrorism: Introduction to the special issue. *The American Psychologist, 72*(3), 199–204. doi:10.1037/amp0000148 PMID:28383973

Kruglanski, A. W., Jasko, K., Chernikova, M., Dugas, M., & Webber, D. (2018). To the fringe and back: Violent extremism and the psychology of deviance. In *The motivated mind* (pp. 344–366). Routledge. doi:10.4324/9781315175867-9

Lemieux, A. F. (2006). Social psychological approaches to understanding and preventing terrorism: Toward an interdisciplinary perspective. *Journal of Security Education, 1*(4), 75–83. doi:10.1300/J460v01n04_07

McCauley, C., & Moskalenko, S. (2017). Understanding political radicalization: The two-pyramids model. *The American Psychologist, 72*(3), 205–216. doi:10.1037/amp0000062 PMID:28383974

KEY TERMS AND DEFINITIONS

Social Psychological Factors: Pertain to all aspects of terrorism, including how terrorist organizations operate, and the impact of terrorism on everyday people. The present analysis focuses on the aspect of terrorism where social psychology's voice is perhaps most critical: radicalization (i.e., how terrorists are made) and deradicalization (i.e., how terrorists are unmade). In reviewing the literature, we identify three factors critical to radicalization: (1) the individual need that motivates one to engage in political violence, (2) the ideological narrative that justifies political violence, and (3) the social network that influences one's decisions along the pathway to extremism. Theoretical and empirical contributions are discussed. We end with an examination of interviews conducted with former extremists of various ideological leanings to highlight these same three factors as critical to their individual deradicalization experiences.

Social Psychology of Terrorism: Has its focuses on person-situation interactions that have implications for who becomes a terrorist; for example, Moghaddam (2004) posits a "staircase model" of terrorism in which terrorism is viewed as sequential progress from lower floors to higher floors that occurs on a progressively narrowing staircase.

Terrorism: Premeditated violence perpetrated against non-combat targets by subnational or transnational groups or clandestine agents usually intended to influence an audience.

Chapter 6
Transformation of the Terrorist Threat:
A Case Study of the "Islamic State" of Iraq and Syria (ISIS)

Diana Jalagania
International Black Sea University, Georgia

ABSTRACT

The present-day world community is continually confronted with issues, among which terrorism is within the first put. This phenomenon is rooted in the past. The premise for the rise and advancement of terrorism was property and social imbalance, the breakdown of the existing way of life, contrasts in attitude, and the objective got to alter the direction of the improvement of civilization. Nowadays, among the reasons for the intense outbreak of terrorism, one can title the multi-speed improvement and the increasing speed of the crevice between the wealthy and the destitute on a residential and worldwide scale, the speeding up of the substitution of technology and innovation, the commercialization of all angles of life, and as a result, the deterioration of ethical establishments. An armed force of Islamists from the Islamic State organization, known by the acronym ISIS, in a brief time blew up the Near and Middle East, as well as a portion of North Africa. They say they proposed to unite all Muslims within the world, but the primary ones they murder are the Muslims.

INTRODUCTION

During past decades, the whole world has been experiencing serious diplomatic and military cataclysms with the cases of terrorism, which on the rate of violence were gaining huge proportions. Almost all over the globe, terrorists and their followers hijack airplanes and terrorize marine, blow-up buildings of airports and railway stations, detonate explosive devices in administrative and residential buildings, city centers, public transport and take hostages. In no time, terrorism has turned into a real threat to the

DOI: 10.4018/978-1-6684-5311-7.ch006

security of a number of different countries in different parts of the world, and stopping this nowadays is one of the priorities for the world population.

Following the directions that are changing, terrorism also has a permanent component which is a criminal essence. And any crime is arbitrariness, which can be committed either by people against other people and society, or by the authorities against people, society, countries, etc. Consequently, the eradication of terrorism must begin with the fight against any arbitrariness, which is always based on strength or advantage. While maintaining its criminal nature, modern terrorism manifests itself in the context of the globalization of various aspects of the changing human activity, which is currently based on the spread of a security model based on compromise thinking in the world.

We all saw the large-scale socio-political, economic and spiritual crisis that has erupted in the Middle East as a result of conflicts and wars the so-called "Arab Spring", radically changed the geopolitical situation in the region. One of the very dangerous consequences was the further aggravation of the confrontation on religious grounds between the Sunnis and Shiites with the rapid growth of activity and influence of radical extremist organizations acting under the slogans of Salafism. Among them, the Islamic State of Iraq and the Levant occupies a key place (ISIS) [1] ISIS managed to establish its control over large territories of Iraq and Syria, capturing key cities Mosul and Aleppo, as well as extend their influence to a number of states in the Middle East and Africa. Terrorist activities of this the organization poses such a serious international threat that in the great powers were forced to fight against it, first of all, USA and Russia with their allies (Crooke, 2014).

The Historical Context of the Development of Shiite-Sunni Contradictions

The geopolitical rivalry between Iran and Saudi Arabia for dominance in the Middle East exacerbates long-standing tensions between the two branches of Islam - Sunni and Shiite[2]. Both parties contribute to the persistence and expansion of the schism in Islam, continuing almost 1300 years. As you know, the schism goes back to the dispute over the legacy of the Prophet Muhammad as the head of all Muslims. After his death in 632 A.D. there was a dispute about the one who from the close associates of the prophet should become the successor of his work. Shiites believe that Muhammad chose his son-in-law Ali as his successor.

The Qur'an is the main book for the Muslim believer, both Shiites and the Sunnis, but for the latter, the Sunnahs are no less important - a set of rules and regulations formulated by Muhammad and designed to serve example for all believers. In this context, of no small importance has the absence in Islam of a supra-confessional higher confessional authority that would be able to regulate the arising between two branches of the contradiction. The number of Shiites in the modern world reaches 8-10% of 1.8 billion. Muslims. But in Iran, Iraq and Bahrain, they make up the majority of the population. According to available data, Shiites are about 98% of Iran's population, 75% Bahrain 62.5% Iraqi 27% UAE 25% Kuwait 20% - Qatar. In Saudi Arabia, they are 10% of the total population (Chitadze, 2022).

In a number of oil-bearing provinces of the kingdom are home to about 2 million Shiites. Radically minded part of the country's population sees them as "the fifth column of the enemies of true Islam." In Afghanistan, Shiites are from 15 to 19% of the country's population. These include the Hazaras. In Lebanon, the number of Shiites reaches 35% of the population, whose interests are defended by the radical party "Hezbollah". Shiism is professed by the majority of the population (Chitadze, 2022).

In Bahrain, despite the fact that Shiites make up the majority of the population, power is in the hands of the Sunni royal dynasty. They also live in Pakistan, India, Turkey, Afghanistan, Yemen, Kuwait, Ghana

Figure 1. Statistics
Figure sourced from Pew Research project Mapping the Global Muslim population, CRS Report for Congress Islam: Sunnis and Shiites and CIA world factbook.

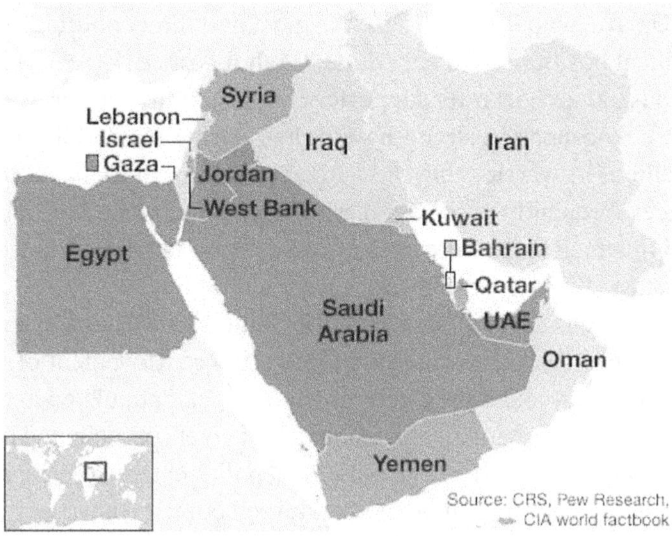

and South African countries. Iran is the only country in the world where Shiism is officially declared the state religion. One of the branches of Shiism belongs to the Alawites, a representative which is the family of the current President of Syria, Bashar al-Assad.

In the modern society, the especially acute nature of the Shiite-Sunni opposition acquired after the victory of the Islamic revolution in Iran in 1979 year. It radically influenced the relationship between states inhabited mainly by Sunnis and Shiites, contributed to escalation of the conflict between them. The immediate consequence of this escalation was the Iranian-Iraqi war of 1980-1988. Influenced by the Shia revolution managed to strengthen their positions in Lebanon, Iraq and Bahrain. Royal the dynasty of Saudi Arabia regarded it as “Iranian expansion”.

As for Iraqi President Saddam Hussein, he perceived it as an existential threat to his power. Fear of “exporting the Shiite revolution” from Iran was the main reason for the outbreak of war by Baghdad with Iran. As a result, the Shiite-Sunni confrontation from a predominantly religious one acquired a pronounced political dimension.

It is also very important to emphasize that such confrontation did not end latently in Iraq itself. This is evidenced, in particular, by the uprising Shiites against Saddam’s regime in March-April 1991, after the defeat in the war of the coalition led by the United States to liberate Kuwait from Iraqi occupation, during which a vast territory was captured in the south of Iran.

With regard to the that situation, in this context the decisive role was played by the US armed aggression in Iraq in March 2003 and its occupation, which led to devastating consequences for both Iraq itself and the entire Middle East. In Iraq there were destroyed the foundations of statehood, including its two supporting structures - the army and the Baath party. ISIS, in essence, filled the resulting vacuum (Kuznetsova, 2015).

In this way, the main reason for the disturbance of the Shiite-Sunni inconsistencies and the rise of the ISIS phenomenon, which gave rise to far-reaching geopolitical changes within the locale, is the annihilation of Iraq as a result of American hostility. At the same time, the genuine evacuation of the Sunnis from control and the giving of genuine sway to political strengths, parties, organizations representing Shiites were of specific significance. The biggest of these are the Preeminent Committee of the Islamic Insurgency in Iraq and Da'ava, who follow to a for the most part direct political course. The Shiite gather moreover follows to radical positions – so called the "Mahdi Armed force"[3], headed by M. al-Sadr and numbering up to 10 thousand activists. Its supporters requested the withdrawal from the nation to the conclusion 2007 by the US occupation strengths and their partners. In addition, in 2004 year she twice raised an equipped rebellion. Its warriors have assaulted the US military and the security powers of Iraq itself. Mahdi Army forces frequently carry out terrorist acts against Sunnis. They staged the so-called "war of mosques", during which there were destroyed 90 Sunni temples. They declare as their goal the creation Shiite Islamic state (Kuznetsova, 2015).

In the parliamentary elections held in January 2005, Shiite parties and Movement: Islamic Call Party (Da'awa), Supreme Council of Islamic revolution in Iraq (ISIRI), Movement of Muqtada al-Sadr. At the same time the Sunnis actually boycotted the elections, since in their populated in the provinces of Ninawa, Anbar, Salahaddin and Baghdad (province), only about 6% of voters participated in them. As a result of the elections from the Sunni part of the population, only 17 deputies entered the supreme legislative body, of which a number of deputies, for one reason or another, turned out to be unacceptable for the Sunnis, since they were considered as persons playing into the hands of the Shiite majority. At the same time, Hajim al-Hasani became the speaker of parliament, the only Sunni politician who did not dispute election results and which was in opposition to Saddam Hussein's regime, and returned to Iraq in 2003 (Crooke, 2014).

With the coming to power of a new regime headed by a Shiite representative Nuri al-Maliki, in accordance with the law on the so-called "de-Baathification", [4]about 140 thousand Sunni specialists were dismissed from the public service, including not only the military, but also representatives of civilian specialties (doctors, teachers, university professors). In further they began to be discriminated against when hiring (Roggero, 2014).

Another law on the fight against terrorism was of no small importance, adopted in the same 2005, according to which many Iraqi Sunnis were arrested without trial and politicians carried out unjustified reprisals. Indicative the example of Iraqi Vice President Tariq al-Hashimi, on whom an arrest warrant was issued by the Iraqi prosecutor's office on charges of terrorism. As a result, he was forced to flee to Turkey. Other Sunni politicians and their supporters were targeted. Of course Sunnis who held key positions under Saddam Hussein's regime in the power system, finding itself on the periphery of political life, not could come to terms with the situation.

Among these movements and organizations, the most extremist positions are occupied the terrorist organization Al-Qaeda in Mesopotamia (AKM) during headed by the citizen of Jordan Abu Musab al-Zarqawi. About her attitude to for the Shiites, a visual representation can be made by the example of statements Zarqawi, who called them "insidious snakes, malicious scorpions, spying enemies".

Al-Maliki's government ruthlessly suppressed Sunni protests in response to the arrest of the Iraqi finance minister's guards Sunni by faith Rafiya al-Isáwi, disbanded the "Sahwa" detachments, stopped their funding, carried out reprisals against their commanders. In fact, there was a systemic marginalization of the Sunni community.

An imbalance in power meant that Nuri al-Maliki was unable to ensure the stability of their power and understanding between Shiites, Sunnis and Kurds. Moreover, after Washington's withdrawal in December 2011 his troops from Iraq, he, as prime minister for several years, actually completely removed the Sunnis from the political decision-making process.

A similar policy government of the Shiite majority has led to the steady criminalization of the Sunni part of society, the spread of the influence of extremist groups, especially in the northern provinces of Iraq.

The beginning of the open Shiite-Sunni confrontation is considered to be the announcement on September 14, 2005 by Abu Musab al-Zarqawi to the Shiites "sacred war ". Explosion by al-Zarqawi militants in February 2006 of the tomb of the imam Hasana al-Askari in Samarra, considered sacred by the Shiites, became the impetus for the start of a real civil war between Shiites and Sunnis, which ended only at the end of 2007. An additional spark in the situation was brought about by the execution of S. Hussein on December 30, 2006, committed by on the main Muslim holiday - Eid al-Adha (Dearden, 2019).

Starting Point

For the first time, the Islamic State movement declared itself in 2006 in Iraq, proclaiming on the territory of the state ISI - the Islamic State of Iraq, led by the Al-Qaeda group. Then only analysts of the CIA and some other intelligence services of the world could imagine the scale of future problems. For everyone else, this event passed almost unnoticed. Over the next years, several more groups have joined the ISI. The Islamists expanded their influence in Iraq, and in April 2013 they intervened in the civil war in neighboring Syria. Starting from that exact moment on, the organization began to make itself the Islamic State of Iraq and the Levant (ISIS).

However, the participation of Iraqi Islamist militants in the war in Syria has displeased the leadership of al-Qaeda. The fragmentation of ISIS began - the Syrian branch of al-Qaeda - al-Nusra Front - entered the war against its yesterday's allies. In February 2014, al-Qaeda leader Ayman al-Zawahiri announced that ISIS was no longer affiliated with al-Qaeda.

In June 2014, the forces of ISIS proclaimed themselves a world caliphate (the caliphate was abolished by the secular authorities of Turkey in 1924, until that time the sultans of the Ottoman Empire were the caliphs), led by the leader of the group, Abu Bakr al-Baghdadi. After that, the movement declared itself an Islamic State with headquarters in Raqqa (Syria) and Mosul (Iraq). IS now operates mainly in Syria and Iraq, controlling significant areas of these two states. Over the past year, jihadist groups in Libya, Algeria, Egypt, Uzbekistan, and even Boko Haram militants in Nigeria have come under the patronage of IS.

The term Islamic state itself means a type of state based on the monotheistic religion of Islam. Elements of constitutional, civil, criminal, administrative, family and procedural law are enshrined in Sharia law.

The Islamic State (IS) is an attempt to recreate the caliphate, which was abolished on March 3, 1924 by the decree of Turkish secular leader Ataturk. The forerunner of IS in Iraq is the group Tawhid wa al-jihad[5], which was created in 2002 by one of the leaders of al-Qaeda, Abu Musab al-Zarqawi. It was later renamed al-Qaeda in Iraq, and after the death of Zarqawi, control over the organization was gained by Abu Bakr al-Baghdadi. To disassociate himself from al-Qaeda, al-Baghdadi proclaimed IS. Indirectly, the main reason for the emergence of IS was the US invasion of Iraq with the aim of overthrowing the Hussein regime. Power in Iraq passed to the Shiites, which led to the infringement of the Sunnis who ruled the country earlier. The withdrawal of the US contingent from Iraq in 2011 intensified the Sunni opposition (Freeman, 2015).

The strengthening of IS stimulated the indirect participation of Iran, as well as the involvement of the Shiite group Hezbollah in the war on the side of the Assad regime [6]in Syria. This turned the tide not in favor of the opponents of Assad, and then led to the mobilization of the Sunni tribes. In Iraq now, in addition to the Iranians, paramilitary Shiite organizations are at war with the Islamic State. They are accused of cruelty towards the peaceful Sunni population. Where it leads? Sunni-Shiite relations will get worse and the consequences for the Muslim world could be irreparable.

The emergence of the Islamic State is a consequence of geopolitical realities in the rapidly changing Middle East. But this is a symptom, not a disease. The most obvious reason for the emergence of ISIS is the exacerbation of identity politics. In Iraq, the Sunnis, who have long controlled the state apparatus, found themselves dominated by a Shiite majority and a powerful Kurdish bloc. Sunnis in Iraq felt overwhelmed. In addition, the policy of former Iraqi Prime Minister Nuri al-Maliki of hyper-centralization of power forced the Sunnis to look for an alternative, which became the best social basis for IS. Similar events took place in Syria, where the Assad dictatorship ruled out a democratic option for the realization of interests for the Sunnis.

Right after IS seized vast territories in the northern parts Iraq and Syria during the summer of 2014, their ideological understandings of sectarian strife and ultra-extremism have been widely discussed among the countries. The slavery of Yezidi woman in the Sinjar area, the massacre of more than 1,500 Shia soldiers in Tikrit and hundreds of Sunni tribesmen in Syria and Iraq, the beheading of Western hostages, and Syrian and Iraqi civilians a collective reassessment of values, which soon turned into a search for the guilty and mutual recriminations on religious and political grounds (Nour, 2017). A typical example is a tweet by a random user from Saudi Arabia which stated that the actions made by the Islamic State are just the embodiment of what they've been through as part of their school plan, adding that if this way is honestly suitable, then [the Islamic State] leaders were right in what they were doing, and if not, then who's fault it was?

The US military has repeatedly stressed the importance of the ideological factor for the successful fight against the "Islamic State". For example, Major General Michael Nagata, the former commander of the US Special Forces in the Middle East, said literally that they could not understand what this movement was and until they did, it could not be defeated." Field commanders fighting ISIS in Syria also note that the ideological factor hinders the mobilization of forces against this group. Muslim military personnel often refuse to fight against ISIS for religious reasons, even if they themselves do not want to join the group. This is especially true for military operations that are supported by Western countries. In this context, ideological issues are of practical importance for the fight against the Islamic State.

Researchers disagree about the reasons for the formation of such an aggressive nature of ISIS. Some believe that the Islamic State is following traditions rooted in the distant past, while others associate the rapid spread and atrocities of ISIS with the aftermath of the US invasion of Iraq in 2003, as well as with Iran's growing role in supporting Shiite self-defense forces in region. A number of commentators explicitly call political Islam a harbinger of ISIS intolerance and brutality, while others relegate ISIS to the level of an organization where sectarian hatred is coming out of opportunism charged by regional political figures (Fuller, 2015).

In fact, the ideology of ISIS is a much more multifaceted phenomenon, its appearance cannot be explained by the influence of any one personality, or movement, or even time. At the same time, we note that you should not trust the names of books and other publications of ISIS, since they do not provide reliable information and can form a false idea of the ideology of the "Islamic State". On the contrary, it is important to carefully analyze how this group chooses its ideas and concepts, interprets and disseminates them.

By themselves, Salafism and political Islam do not lead to an increase in the number of ISIS supporters and are not a catalyst for extremism. On the contrary, there are limitations in both Salafism and political Islam that can deter the type of extremism that Islamic State follows. Likewise, political grievances or morale alone cannot push people to join ISIS. The optimal environment for the prosperity of this group is political oppression, inaction of state power, as well as interfaith disagreements. But interesting is that this diplomatic context can actually lead people which it often does to join moderate insurgent groups rather than ISIS.

This work analyzes the ideology of the "Islamic State" and the interfaith enmity associated with it, based on sources and direct evidence of Islamic religious leaders and ISIS members in Syria and Iraq. The study also explores broader topics to explain the origins of the concept of violence and exclusivity of ISIS. Until the idea that the organization's ideology goes back directly to Salafism is debunked, the population will not be able to think about the reasons for the attractiveness and popularity of ISIS and won't be capable of defeating the Islamic State (Arango, 2015).

1.1. Objectives

The initial goal of IS was to create a theocratic Sunni Islamic state within the borders of Syria, Lebanon, Israel, Palestine, Jordan, Turkey, Cyprus and Egypt. However, after the group was renamed the Islamic State, its territorial claims spread to the entire Islamic world and even to territories that previously belonged to the Ottoman Empire in Europe (the Balkans and even southern Ukraine). In the future, IS plans to "liberate" the peoples of the Caucasus from the rule of Russia, including Chechnya from the dictator Ramzan Kadyrov.

There are also a huge number of secondary goals for IS. One of them, for example, the destruction of the sacred symbol of Muslims - the Kaaba in Mecca. According to the leaders of the Islamic State, the stone must be destroyed and the pilgrims must be killed.

In addition, the Islamic State seeks to destroy traces of all cultures that have ever existed in the lands of Syria, Iraq, Iran, Turkey before the advent of Islam. To this end, the militants looted the historical museums of Mosul, demonstratively destroying a number of exhibits, blew up the city's oldest library and burned more than 10,000 ancient books from it. They also destroyed the artifacts of the ancient cities of Nimrud and Dur-Sharrukin[7].

However, according to a number of analysts, many of the allegedly destroyed objects of art and artifacts were illegally sold to wealthy collectors from around the world through intermediaries.

1.2. Military Capabilities

In terms of military potential and strengthening combat effectiveness ISIS, it should be pointed out that a similar picture became possible after the western coalition invasion of Iraq in 2003 and the dismissal of the majority Iraqi officers from the Armed Forces. As you know, Saddam's army Husseina was large and well prepared, many of her officers were trained in Soviet universities, military academies and schools. US administration in Baghdad abolished remnants Saddam's military legacy, deciding to create something more effective. Thus, provoking the accession of the most prepared and qualified officers to the ranks of ISIS, where they created, so called the military "shura" (council), headed by a former colonel army of Saddam Hussein Haji al-Bakri.

Hence the military capability of ISIS, which often causes bewilderment among Western military experts. And you should pay attention to the fact that the ISIS organization itself is built according to the army principle, that is, has all command and control bodies (commander, intelligence, headquarters, counterintelligence, logistic services, etc.), which is not at all typical for simple opposition forces. ISIS terrorist organization managed to take possession of weapons, located in the warehouses of the former Iraqi army, and among nomenclature of weapons there is not only small arms and ammunition for it, but also armored vehicles, as well as air defense (mainly portable anti-aircraft missile systems and artillery systems). Under ISIS controlled airbases and weapons depots near Aleppo and Raqqi, and the terrorist organization received 3 fighters, on which former pilots are already training Iraqi Air Force personnel. According to a report submitted in 2014 year by the organization for the control over the circulation of weapons CAR (Conflict Armament Research), ISIS has a high-level weapons supply system, including from Saudi Arabia, and about 20% of small arms in in the hands of terrorists produced in the USA

The number of Islamic State militants ranges from 40,000 to 150,000. Among them there are many regular military personnel of the Iraqi army during the times of Saddam Hussein, who were deprived of their work and income after the fall of his regime. Hussein's army officers head the War Council and are deputy leaders of the group (McKernan, 2015).

The US intelligence services note that about 1 thousand volunteers join the ranks of the IS every month, not counting the local residents of Iraq and Syria mobilized into the ranks of the organization.

Volunteers come from all over the world. At the same time, according to one of the versions, many states have deliberately over the past years, secretly facilitated the departure of radical Islamists, who later joined the ranks of IS.

IS is armed with Soviet armored vehicles and small arms, including Kalashnikov assault rifles and hand grenade launchers. However, IS also has hundreds of light and heavy equipment supplied to the Iraqi army from the United States and captured during the June 2014 offensive in Iraq, when many parts of the Iraqi army deserted, abandoning their weapons. For the same reason, IS militants are armed with a mass of firearms from the United States, including machine guns and grenade launchers. And after the seizure of several military bases in Iraq, IS took over the air defense systems.

1.3. Financing and Propaganda Channels

According to Western intelligence agencies, IS is financed through the following channels:

1. Illegal sale of oil and fuel at dumping prices, which attracts many foreign intermediaries;
2. Illegal income (racketeering, ransom, drug transit, bank robberies and so on, the sale of organs, the sale of people into slavery, the sale of art objects seized in museums);
3. Taxes on businesses in controlled areas (for those who start a business, the tax is set at only 2.5% of annual income);
4. Customs duty (10% of the value of the cargo);
5. Funding from private sponsors from Qatar, Kuwait and Saudi Arabia, opponents of the governments of Syria and Iraq (Weiss, 2015).

The total financial reserve of the organization is estimated at $ 2-7 billion. About $ 2 billion was stolen from the branch of the Central Bank of Iraq in Mosul after the storming of the city by IS forces. It is worth noting that employees of utilities and power plants on the territory of IS continue to receive salaries from official Damascus and Baghdad. 50% of this salary is withdrawn by jihadists (Arango, 2014).

The main propagandists of the Islamic State effectively use Western communication technologies - YouTube, social networks Facebook, Twitter, Instagram, Friendica. Thousands of accounts, the use of

Twitter Storm during combat operations to create panic behind enemy lines, thousands of videos of the movement's supporters and tens of millions of views.

The movement is well known not only in the Muslim world, but also in Western countries. First of all, thanks to the numerous videos (18+) of public executions of prisoners and hostages. The media campaign of the Islamic State is called one of the most effective and at the same time brutal.

The IS media support departments - Al-Furqan, Itisaam, Al-Hayat - shoot full-length films and videos about the organization's activities and translate their product into dozens of languages. One of these films - "The Clink of Swords" - CNN compared to high-quality Hollywood production. The group publishes the English-language magazine Dabiq, newsletters and annual reports with the aim of recruiting educated Muslim youth.

CHAPTER 2. THE CASE OF ISLAMIC STATE

The case of Islamic State is in its roots based on the religious and diplomatic understandings in which those exact sides are very developed. If we are talking about the religious beliefs for the Islamic state and its followers, then the best way to understand them is through their interpretations of the ways of perceiving the surrounding world, being in its extreme, fundamental form. This concrete point shows from another perspective the actions of the ISIS, whose ideological and diplomatic understandings in any of its forms are very radical. According to ancient Salafist thinker Taki Ad-Din ibn Taymiyyah (XIV century) his theory of foundation doctrine, a natural state had to be rooted on two founding principles, first of which is that the leader of the true Islamic state should in any case be Muslim, and one and only basic law should be the Sharia law. In case if these two rules are not followed the states cannot and should not be called a Muslim State. As for the leader of the states himself, in case if the Sharia rules and principle are not followed by him, then he can become a subject of a withdrawal by his followers and they can declare a jihad against him so that the power based on the Muslim and true Islamic, concept of governing be established. The reasons are simple, because in their understanding the state cannot be separated apart from the religion, as it could bring the confusion among the citizens (Bergen, 2010).

2.1. Establishment

As we know Daesh[8] arises from the not led famous in a bad way al Qaeda in Iraq (AQI), starting its journey as a nearby branch founded by Abu Musab al Zarqawi in the year of 2004. The activity of ISIS went down for a while after the surge of US troops to Iraq in 2007. But it began to gain the powers again in 2011. With the new breath Islamic State started to terrorize and build insecurity in Iraq and also Syria mainly to show its growth and powers and gain more territories.

Interesting statement was made by the leader of Al-Qaeda, Ayman al-Zawahiri, who purposed that even though his organization did not recognize ISIS as a legitimate state and despite ideological disagreements and lack of cooperation with them he considered it possible to fight alongside with ISIS against, despite the obvious ideological disagreements between the two organizations, he considers it possible to join them in a fight against the West and Shiites.

According to a few specialists, the ISIS administration is like fear based oppressor gather may advance towards arrangement of a full-fledged state, but with certain reservations. And nowadays, this quasi-state is within the extension stage. It as of now passed the arrange of building administrations destined to quick collapse and proceeds to exist. As for al-Qaeda, nowadays day, it got to be obvious that this organization is prepared to be substance with as it were the reality of its presence. Ideologically, the main postulate Al-Qaeda is focusing its efforts on the fight against so called a "distant" enemy (that is, with the West represented by the United States) in contrast to ISIS seeking to overthrow, retreating from Islam Arab regimes. Yes, and the central leadership, once the most influential terrorist organization weakened and became incapable of provide proper support to your affiliates. This is what ISIS has done the main successor to al-Qaeda, providing it with the leadership of jihad.

Things have changes after the death of Zarqawi in the year of 2006, who was killed during a strike conducted by US. With the death of the leader, the plans and future action of the group were in a way slowed down and changed. The ideology of the group has changed as well because suddenly they started to advocate the construction of Sharia law in Iraq states, and only that, they also started to attack not only foreign citizens and Iraqi Shiites, but also native Sunnis which caused lots of problems inside the group itself and a huge disappointment from the side of Sunni militias (Paravicini, 2017).

In 2008 things change for Islamic State because Abu Ayyub al Masri comes to power and announces the development alongside with Abu Omar al Baghdadi as its leader on October. But still the thing is not going very well for the group because due to the flow of foreign fighters they were not able to deal with the numbers anymore. In the beginning of the year 2008 around 2,400 of ISIS members were killed in a fight and almost 8,800 out of the former quantity if the followers which was 15,000 were captured. To see the picture as a whole the number of foreign military source going to Iraq has decreased from 120 per month to five or six per month during only one year (Hudson, 2015).

As it goes, one leader usually changes another, so After the death of Abu Hamza Muhajir the successor to Az-Zarqawi, from now on the headquarter of Al-Qaeda in Iraq is under the control of facto head of ISIS Abu Bakr al-Baghdadi. It all happened in year 2010. Starting from that point, group could often hear the ideas of Abu Bakr An-Naji during Abu Bakr al-Baghdadi's khutbahs (religious and political sermons). Being of one of the most radical Islamist authors, Abu Bakr An-Naji became an inspiration for the new ideological development of ISIS activities. The book that Abu Bakr An-Naji wrote is called the Management of Barbarism. One of his weighting includes a statement that says, violence should be applied precisely to the extent that it resonates with broad masses of Muslims. Regarding the fight against the West, An-Naji notes that in a direct military conflict it is impossible to win over The United States and its allies, so you should win, first of all, information war - this is the minimum program that he offers, and only then, in the long term, it will be possible win a political victory. An-Naji indicates that this the strategy proved to be effective in the war against the Soviet Union in Afghanistan, whose army, in his opinion, was more brutal than American. Therefore, according to al-Naji, the invasion of Iraq in strategic perspective plays into the hands of the global jihad movement, and the governments supporting the United States in this occupation are quite vulnerable. Soon after the withdrawal of American troops from Iraq, the movement the mujahideen, using their military potential, should "flood" neighbouring countries. Therefore, the halo of US invincibility should be dispelled.

2.2. Strengths and Weaknesses

Thus, the analysis of the conducted research and the studied materials related to the activities of this group allows you to indicate on a number of strengths and weaknesses of ISIS, ideologically, militarily, and logistic aspects.

Strengths: Motivation of fighters during the execution of combat tasks; high level of personal preparedness and equipment extremists; coherence and discipline of combat units; wide range means and methods of armed struggle, active use suicide bombers; mobility, dispersal and secrecy groupings; Sunni support in controlled territories; availability of replenished financial and other material funds; sufficient mobilization resource from among local residents and foreign volunteers; effective use of electronic media to promote their ideas; establishment in occupied territories the power of Sharia law (Sly, 2014).

Weaknesses: lack of powerful means of fire destruction; lack of air support; weak air defense; inability to conduct protracted combat operations against regular troops in an open area; remoteness of combat formations from the rear infrastructure, lack of sufficient reserves to guard the rear; the radical nature of the activity and the terror on religious grounds; formation of detachments according to the national principle.

2.3. Historical View

According to Muhammad Abd Al-Azim Ash-Shaimi, a researcher from Helwan University: "Nature the ISIS phenomenon, shows us the causes rather than the effects, arising from the so-called "igilov" political and legal thought, and we must admit that the emergence of this organization, its existence as religious and political phenomenon, not alien to our heritage, within which, without much difficulty, you can find ideas for building a global caliphate "(Al-Shishani, 2010).

As the rulers of Islamic State though the caliphate itself can be seen like for example a kind of historical cover, with one the purpose or one goal which is their promotion on geopolitical arena between two states which are Iraq and Syria. Stating so, from then on those two states became a main arena, let's say they got the lead role in the play of reshaping and changing the Islamic history. As for the theory of the Islamic Caliphate which was so loudly spoken by the leaders and the followers of the group now became a whole something new kind of concept of the of the idea of caliphate.

The overall view of developments leads us to the term doctrine of Islamic caliphate, which mostly roots back to the borders of the Arabian Peninsula, with put any doubt historians state that this is a combination of historical, ideological and cultural heritage of the people who lived in that exact region. History leads us to two important in this case points which are first, that the place where the doctrine developed is now the territory of Iraq and Syria and the second is that the terminology of khalifate itself was founded outside of that region, in the place where the Prophet Muhammad left four of their closest successors - the "righteous caliphs", and before of how the political center of the young Muslim state, moved outside of Mecca and Medina.

There is another thing that is important to know. The centers Islamic shrines which is located on the Arabian Peninsula, had never taken part in the creation or formulation of the understanding of the Caliphate, because they were trying their best trying be separate Islamist groups. So it can be said that Mecca and Medina are the main spiritual centers for Islam, but it has never been a lace of the development of or creation the ISIS caliphate.

The main ideological understand of ISIS in not the creation but more of a re-make of the traditional Islamic Khalifate that existed a long time ago.

Going back to the ideas of Abu Bakr An-Naji's book "Managing Barbarism" which will help to sum up the understanding and goals of the group. As an example he suggests that the best attack is a made to the weakest and most sensitive points of the enemy's economy, like for example the is the oil and gas industry. The Idea behind this though is simple, after the hit to the industrial sector he government will follow the instincts and start to protect those place by deploying military capabilities in there leave the spots of interest of the group open for the action. Another point is that, because the number of military capabilities decrease in the distant regions of the country, crime percentage will rise in there. At that time the government will need qualified personnel to work in local authorities (Sly, 2015).

2.4. The ISIS Phenomenon and Its Role in Geopolitical Conflicts in Middle East

The conflict between Sunnis and Sheets started before ISIS came into power, but after they did it has become a point of heat for both sides of the conflict due to several reasons.

The starting point in this case began on April 9, 2013 with Jabhat al-Nusra, who had joined Islamic the state of Iraq with the Syrian group. And of course it was the time when already a fully developed ISIS Separated from al-Qaeda in 2014.

If talking about the differences between the two groups, it should be said that ISIS in comparison to al-Qaeda has certain attributes of the state and in many ways acts as a state. As said by F.M. Ilminskaya, it “extracts, refines and trades oil, imports key products, builds its claim ethical and esteem framework with its possess rules and direction of inside administration of labor relations, whereas applying those strategies of impact that he considers vital. Among them the deal into servitude of captured rivals who are “sold” to slave markets, as well as enormous devout persecution” (Kuznetsova, 2015).

One of the most important factors that determined the strength and attractiveness of ISIS, there was a fairly clearly developed and purposefully implemented ideology. Its leader Abu Bakr al-Baghdadi declared himself caliph, claiming that he comes from the Quraish tribe, to which the prophet himself belonged Muhammad.

The ISIS command (shura) includes former career officers in Saddam Hussein’s army. Abu Bakr al-Baghdadi, who according to some sources, graduated from the Islamic University in Baghdad, under Saddam’s regime. Hussein served as a police officer. In 2005-2009. was in the infamous Abu Ghraib prison, from where he was released by the Americans in 2009. From this point of view, the fact that in 2008 - 2009 many of the officers of Saddam’s army were released from American prisons. ISIS has its own intelligence service, the Council for security and intelligence the top of which is one of the high-ranking Iraqi intelligence officers under the regime of Saddam Hussein Abu al-Anbar[9]. It can also be added that the adviser of Al-Baghdadi’s army adviser was a de-facto colonel of the Iraqi army, Abu Ahmed al-Alwani, who also was an influential figure in the military council of ISIS.

There was a rumor that that from the beginning Abu Bakr al-Baghdadi was associated with the special services of Qatar. Under his power, in the developments that started during Qatari-Saudi rivalry tried to use ISIS as a counterweight to Jabhat al-Nusra in Syria, controlled by Saudi Arabia.

The absence of large-scale demonstrations in the territories occupied by the militants, despite their unprecedented brutality, analysts explain for a number of reasons. It is significant that initially in some places ISIS was initially greeted as liberators. This was due to the fact that the overwhelming majority of the population of the Sunni regions showed rejection of the Shiite government. A certain role was played by the terror unleashed by the militants against their real and perceived enemies, thereby putting the population of the occupied territories before the choice submission and support, or physical destruction.

One of the important factors contributing to the growth of the influence of ISIS was the civil war in Syria, unleashed by various extremist organizations and groups against the Alawite regime of Bashar al-Assad (Jumuah, 2010).

First of all, we are talking about Jabhat AnNusra[10], sent to this country by al-Baghdadi and recognized by the leadership of Al Qaeda as its Syrian branch. Already in March 2013, according to some data, it numbered from 5 to 20 thousand militants. Testimony its strength and effectiveness was the capture of the city of Raqqa, the center of the same name a province bordering Iraq.

Substantial differences, contradictions and conflicts between ISIS and Jabhat al-Nusra soon emerged. Moreover, both groups declared their affiliation to Al-Qaeda. However, in the spring of 2013 ISIS leader Abu Bakr al-Baghdadi demanded that the leader of Jabhat al-Nusra, Muhammad al-Julani, swear an oath of allegiance to him. As a result, there was a gap between the two extremist organizations. If al-Golani set himself the main goal of the struggle to overthrow President Assad, then al-Baghdadi put forward the idea of using Raqqa in as a base to support ISIS's efforts in Iraq to establish a caliphate. But after part of the al-Nusra militants went over to the side of ISIS, he managed to establish control over Raqqa and announce the beginning of the formation caliphate on the territory of two countries.

The capabilities of ISIS are evidenced by the successes of its armed formations in capturing, in a very short period of time, vast territories of Iraq, including the provinces of Ninawa, Diyala, Salaheddin and Anbar, as well as the largest city after Baghdad, Mosul. During the capture of this city with the thousandth group of ISIS, the Iraqi army of 60 thousand people reacted literally by fleeing from Mosul (Freeman, 2015).

The leaders of the Islamic State declare the Shiites unbelievers or apostates. On this basis, its leaders declared their major goal. They wanted to diminish the existing Shiite arc, which is made of Syria, Iraq, Lebanon going from the Mediterranean to the Persian Gulf. They wanted to create a new Sunni Chalifate on that territory. As a respond, the Iraqi Shiites created their own "death squads", which began to rampage in the Sunni areas.

Accordingly, the Sunni communities turned to the leadership of Saudi Arabia with a request for protection and opposition to Iran. Iraqi Sunnis have fairly close ties with Saudi Arabia. About this is evidenced by the fact that the Bedouin tribes Duleim, Shammar, Jabbur, Unayza, who are Sunnis, live in the Iraqi province Anbar and Northeast Syria and Saudi Arabia. Moreover, the Shammar tribe with a population of more than 1 million. has close relatives ties with the royal house of Saudi Arabia.

Experts believe Saudi Arabia is considering Shiite Iran as the main competitor for its dominance in the Middle East. Thus, there is a point of view that the ISIS invasion of Iraq is the continuation of the war between Sunnis and Shiites, which in turn should be viewed as a confrontation between Saudi Arabia and Iran.

The negative attitude of the current leadership of the kingdom towards the Shiite minority in this country was especially clearly manifested in the execution in Saudi Arabia.

Saudi Arabia, as you know, played an important role in the emergence of ISIS and provided it with serious financial, material, political support, supplied weapons, considering it as counterbalance to Iranian expansion. She supported the Afghan Taliban and other terrorist organizations. However, the existence and activities of ISIS turned out to be a very tangible threat to the very state of the Saudis. It is pertinent to recall that Osama bin Laden was a Saudi, most of the terrorists who carried out the September 11, 2001 terrorist attacks in New York and Washington were also citizens of this countries (Ramey, 2007).

On the face of it, the paradox is that ISIS has deployed its activities not in Shiite Iran, but in Sunni predominantly Egypt, Libya and Saudi Arabia. Justifying this position, al-Baghdadi stated in one of his radio messages that the Saudi monarchy is incompatible with the teachings of the Koran, thereby calling into question the legitimacy of the royal dynasty. Therefore, it is not surprising that the KSA media came to the conclusion that Islamic State creates a huge risk to the state.

In countries ruled by dynasties of Sunni minorities, from time to time, uprisings break out up to Shiite uprisings demanding ensuring the conditions for their proper participation in the power system. In Yemen, where the Sunni authorities refer to the Shiites as "separatist rebels", there is a real civil war that has been going on for many years, a war involving Saudi Arabia and its allies. In Bahrain, where Shiites make up a substantial majority of the population (up to 75%), the Shiite opposition is persecuted by the Sunni authorities (White, 2014).

In this strategy closely combines the tactics of lightning war, terrorist attacks, demonstrative cruelty, hostage-taking, deception, the spread of incredible all sorts of rumors designed to cause the audience has horror, emotional shock.

M.F. Ilminskaya, says that the uniqueness of the IS really lies within the truth that, the group was trying to solidify Islamists and Baathists. It seems that Ba'athism in the beginning may indeed have a big introduction to the east with its ideological understandings with the main point to try recreate nationality of the region. It looks like an ordinary ancient east patriotism, to which we have such examples as are: G. Nasser, S. Hussein, H. Assad, but this kind of patriotism always appears ineffective (Kuznetsova, 2015).

Islam presupposes the existence of a caliphate. The period without a caliphate is seen as a time of humiliation of Islam. Such an understanding of the place and role of Islam means the desire to redraw the political map of the world, in in any case, the Arab-Islamic world.

However, after major defeats as a result of the loss of Aleppo, Mosul and other key territories in both Syria and Iraq, the leadership ISIS and Al-Baghdadi himself were forced to admit defeat. The leader of the organization called on its members to take refuge in hard-to-reach terrain on the territory of the two countries and "to continue resistance from the existing there or newly created bases ".

Despite all that was written before, it will not be right to consider the dissolution of such group as is ISIS being the end of the fight. And it is definitely not a solution to the problems of diplomacy, economy or religion in the region, even though this conditions played the role in creation as well. In case if these condition continue to exist it is likely that despite the defeat of the organization, the idea will still remain alive.

RELIGION AND IDEOLOGY

Religion

The case of Islamic State is in its roots based on the religious and diplomatic understandings in which those exact sides are very developed. If we are talking about the religious beliefs for the Islamic state and its followers, then the best way to understand them is through their interpretations of the ways of perceiving the surrounding world, being in its extreme, fundamental form. This concrete point shows from another perspective the actions of the ISIS, whose ideological and diplomatic understandings in any of its forms are very radical. According to ancient Salafist thinker Taki Ad-Din ibn Taymiyyah (XIV century) his theory of foundation doctrine, a natural state had to be rooted on two founding principles, first of which is that the leader of the true Islamic state should in any case be Muslim, and one and only basic law should be the Sharia law. In case if these two rules are not followed the states cannot and should not be called a Muslim State. As for the leader of the states himself, in case if the Sharia rules and principle are not followed by him, then he can become a subject of a withdrawal by his followers and they can declare a jihad against him so that the power based on the Muslim and true Islamic, concept of governing be established. The reasons are simple, because in their understanding the state cannot be separated apart from the religion, as it could bring the confusion among the citizens (Schmitt, 2014).

From one side ideology plays a huge role in creating the religious by creating a kind of a moral or even ethics which has to be supported by the followers without any doubt, which if we look closer already is a characteristic if ISIS. From another side the form of Islam that ISIS uses which is Salafism has a very harsh understanding of controlling people of the region that are occupied. That is why if we will understand the essence of the functioning of religion which has a main role in almost every activity conducted by the organization, it will be easy to find the answer to the questions. The first founders of the "Islamic State" were trying to use and recall a lot of ancient norms and beliefs that were a long time forgotten by people. For example, they returned to being whipped for selling alcohol or drugs, for wearing western clothes or shaving your beard. "Apostasy" is another serious idea which means punishment by cutting off the head - for example, the Salafis everyone who takes or took part in the elections is executed, even if they voted for a Muslim candidate, since the very fact of holding elections in an Islamic country indicates that in this state human law was placed above the norms and prescriptions of Islamic Sharia, which says nothing about elections (Hassan, 2014).

Undoubtedly, this literal approach to Shari'a implies the destruction of a huge number of people. And judging by the stories of the refugees, ISIS fighters have already mastered industrial methods of exterminating the population, in the territories seized by them. According to world news agencies, mass executions are carried out weekly, although the real scale of the massacre is still impossible to assess. As noted modern researchers of the "ISIS" phenomenon Najim Ibrahim and Hisham Al-Najar, the key idea of the terrorists are the idea of "takfir" [11]. They denounce of doubt all Middle easterner armed forces, all administering administrations of Middle easterner states and all political parties without exemption. ISIS reported "Takfir" of the whole Shiite portion of the Muslim world. And the as it were one the strategy of executing this thought is war. War and slaughtering on the way state building.

The Qur'an and other sources of Sharia do not provide a clear answer. However, terrorists are known to guarantee life Christians - of course, only if they, according to Sharia, will pay ISIS a special tax known as jizya, recognizing your subordinate position. In relation to Buddhism and everything else religions that Islamists call "paganism," ISIS activists ruthless: pagans are subject to enslavement or execution. Salafis and this the Prophet's demand is understood literally - on the territory of the Caliphate there was the slave system was officially revived, and were sold into slavery women and children from Yezidi families - members of the ancient Kurdish sect, borrowed some elements of Islam. It should be noted that according to The "Yezidi question" held a special meeting of Salafiulema who passed fatwa, according to which Kurdish pagans cannot in no way ranked as apostate Muslims. And if so, then they are pagans - "giaurs" and "kafirs", and the enslavement of the families of "kafirs" and the taking of their women as concubines is nothing more than a firm establishment sharia.

However, back to the factors that allowed the ISIS organization achieve such a significant transformation in a relatively short period of time. To one degree or another, the reasons for this rise are known and understood, and stem from geopolitical aspirations The West dominate the Middle East, and, as noted earlier, connected with the desire of Washington and its allies to control the huge energy flows in the region. Much more important today to understand historical, latent factors or, as they are commonly called, "Legacy factors". Such, according to the Egyptian scholar Muhammad Abd Al-Azim Al-Shaimi, are: ideological environment, within which was the formation of ISIS; Middle Eastern heritage anarchism, as well as geopolitical trends in Iraq and Syria. It was these factors that played a direct role in the emergence of ISIS (Stout, 2014).

What Does Jihad Mean?

ISIS relies on the writings of those jihadist ideologues who share its stance against so-called nominal Muslims. These clerics hold views that differ significantly from traditional ones, as some of them openly state. ISIS typically uses their writings to prove allegations of disbelief (takfir) against Saudi Arabia and the rulers of Muslim countries in the Middle East, as well as to justify its rejection of all government institutions and the armed forces of these countries. Observers often underestimate the influence of these ideologues on the Islamic State because of the mutual animosity between many of them and ISIS.

Sources cite the names of such Saudi clerics as Khalid al-Rashid, Nasir al-Fahd, Suleiman bin Nasir al-Ulwan, Omar bin Ahmed al-Hazimi, Ali bin Khidr al-Khudiar and Hamud bin Ukla al-Shuaybi. Some include Abu Muhammad al-Maqdisi and Abdul Qadir bin Abdul Aziz on this list of al-Qaeda ideologues (Taylor, 2013).

Four of them - al-Fahd, al-Ulwan, al-Khudiar and al-Shuaibi - were part of a network that had a significant impact on al-Qaeda in Saudi Arabia in the early 2000s, as well as on the transnational jihadist movement. They wrote extensively and actively about Saudi Arabia's apostasy, criticizing its leaders for supporting US military intervention in the region's affairs, especially during the first Gulf War. These publications became the theological rationale for the campaigns against the apostates for the leaders of the "Islamic State". The fact that these clerics received a religious education (a rarity for jihadist ideologues) is particularly significant for ISIS, as is their disagreement with the religious community in Saudi Arabia. Al-Fahd reportedly took an oath of allegiance to the Islamic State, and ISIS leaders believe that al-Shuaibi's book on the inadmissibility of seeking help from the wrong will prove to be an effective ideological tool.

In the territories controlled by ISIS, the ideas of al-Khudiar and al-Rashid are very often mentioned and quoted in the media. In particular, al-Khudiar's publications on one of the most relevant topics for ISIS offer the Islamic State an ideological service on the principle of "one window": he believes that non-Islamic ideological systems and their followers are illegal and adherence to such teachings is inexcusable. Al-Khudiar takes an uncompromising position in relation to modern legal systems, as well as those Muslims who are somehow connected with them. He believes that Muslims who voluntarily become members of parliament are infidels. Any Muslim who swears to the constitution, even if he did it under duress, becomes an apostate, and Muslims who oppose the constitution, but use only democratic means and channels, should be recognized as sinners. The fact that ordinary Muslims may not know about the "illegality" of such actions is not an excuse for al-Khudiar.

The religious leaders mentioned by the Islamic State in their sermons are extremely radical on the Shiite issue and believe that even ordinary Shiites cannot count on forgiveness. In a series of sermons entitled "Sharp sword punishing sinful Shiites," al-Rashid not only attacks the Shiites, but also insults them. Al-Fahd has a treatise on "the permissibility of excessive actions against the Rafidis", filled with insulting and degrading Shiites ("Rafidites" - literally "deniers" - an abusive and derogatory word in relation to Shiites).

One of the most influential person for the ISIS was Abu Muhammad al-Maqdisi. He stood against the expansion of the group in Syria and condemned its understandings to the interpretation of other jihadists, so its ideological significance for ISIS is often underestimated. Al-Maqdisi, who grew up in Kuwait and was educated in Iraq and Saudi Arabia in the 1980s, directly influenced ISIS founder al-Zarqawi. It is worth noting that they served a prison sentence together in Jordan between 1993 and 1999. Al-Maqdisi made a huge contribution to the ideology of the "Islamic State" in general. Recently, he himself described his meaning for ISIS by saying that he was their sheikh who had explained to them the main ideas of tawhid (monotheism) (Calvert, 2010).

Even though the IS did not publicize al-Maqdisi's books, his ideas are widely cited as arguments in disputes with opponents, and his works are distributed in territories controlled by ISIS. The first issue of the Dabik magazine published by the Islamic State published an article on the writings of Al-Maqdisi.

Al-Maqdisi's book The Religion of Ibrahim is of particular importance to the Islamic State. This book introduces the concept of vala wal bara[12], which is used to condemn as apostasy many Muslims practicing non-Islamic ideas and customs, even if they are relatives of the whistleblowers themselves. In another of his book, entitled "The Silent Scandals of Saudi Arabia's Apostasy," al-Maqdisi declared Saudi Arabia a godless state. The author concludes that non-observance of the principles of vala wal bara leads to disbelief (kufr) and many orders and actions of the Saudi government - including credit policy, foreign aid to non-Muslim countries, UN membership and allied relations with Western countries - testify to its apostasy.

Of course, al-Maqdisi's ideas can be applied to all individual Muslims and communities that are seen in actions on the Islamic State's forbidden list - are members of the Arab Socialist Revival Baath Party or allied relations with Western countries and with some governments in the region. And while al-Maqdisi is critical of the Islamic State, he, for example, condemns the cooperation of the Syrian militias with the US-led coalition involved in the ISIS aerial bombardment and calls their actions apostasy.

Abdul Qadir bin Abdul Aziz is one more person who was widely cited by the Islamic State[13]. He was a former jihadist in Egypt who a lot of time in prison to think and after he was released he revisited his extremist views. as a result of the January 2011 uprising in Egypt. His most popular and influential book is The Complete Guide to Noble Knowledge. Abu Ali al-Anbari, a member of the ISIS shura (and the second person of the Islamic State in Syria. - Ed. Trans.), In his speeches often quotes this book, although he regrets that the author has abandoned some of the views expressed there. In one of his audio lectures, he quoted the words of Abdul Aziz, explaining that a Muslim who has become a member of parliament is an apostate even if he intends to use parliament as a platform for spreading religious ideas. These words were addressed to the former Supreme Mufti of Saudi Arabia, Abdul-Aziz ibn Baz, who said that membership in parliament for a true Muslim is possible - it depends on the specific intentions of the applicant for this post (Cochrane, Fuller, 2016).

The Islamic State uses similar views of modern political institutions and democratic norms to justify its fight against military and security and law enforcement officials in Muslim countries. On the basis of these ideas, Islamists are accused of apostasy, as well as clerics adhering to the dominant trend in Islam and belonging to official religious circles. Al-Anbari, who was the highest authority in the Islamic State for the longest time until his death in March 2016, developed and delivered 40 lectures explaining the religious ideology of the group. The leitmotif of his lectures is the illegitimacy of the social and political institutions of Muslim countries, including mosques and courts. Al-Anbari unleashes his anger on the Shiites, on the followers of Sufism, and on the Muslim Brotherhood, as well as on the adherents of official Salafism (he often calls the latter Murjiites - this word has a derogatory meaning and is used in relation to imams who adhere to pacifist views). In one of his lectures, Al-Anbari emphasized that this type of Salafis is most absurd and ridiculous among all the detractors and ill-wishers of the Islamic State, reflecting the fierce struggle between these two ideological streams following the recent successes of ISIS in Syria and Iraq.

Jihad - translated from Arabic means zeal in the path of Allah. Usually jihad is associated with armed struggle, but this concept is much broader. In addition to armed struggle, it also means the struggle against one's own spiritual or social vices, for example, against lies, deceit, depravity of society, etc. Thus, jihad is both a struggle against one's passions, and the elimination of social injustice, and constant zeal in the spread of religion and, finally, waging war against military aggressors in the name of Allah. Initially, in Islam, jihad is desirable, not obligatory, and only in the case of obvious dangers does it become obligatory. Aggression and murder is a great sin. The Qur'an says that anyone who killed another person not for killing or spreading wickedness on earth, it is as if he killed all people, and anyone who saves a person's life, he seems to save the life of all people (Kesling, 2014).

The basic law in ISIS states that Muslims are obliged to abide by all Sharia law, and the infidels (kafirs) are the embodiment of the devil and must be either killed or taken into slavery (women), all Muslims are kafirs - Shiites, Alawites, Yezidis, Sufis - not Arabs, supporters of the authorities of Syria, Iraq, Saudi Arabia, as well as Christians and Jews who do not respect Islam and Muslims. Militant commanders themselves determine which of the Christians and Jews does not respect Islam. Usually, only the rich people who give bribes and help the militants in business are respected, and those for whom they ask.

A clean, well-trodden path to the water is how the Arabs translate the word Sharia. This figurative expression means for every Muslim - the Law that Allah gave them through his prophets and the last prophet, the messenger Muhammad. Sharia rules are as important to the believer as clean water is to the mind and soul. Every believer must strictly follow the rules and norms laid down in the Muslim system of law.

Another ISIS rule is an established dress code requiring all men to wear a beard and women to wear a chador (a light female veil in white, blue, or black) and abayu (a long traditional Arab woman's dress with sleeves).

Among other rules, the following stand out:

- you cannot smoke cigarettes and use chewing gum, for breaking the rule - 80 lashes,
- women are forbidden to move on the street without a man's accompaniment, the caught woman is taken home, and the man - the guardian is subjected to 80 lashes.

Christians living in ISIS-controlled territories were prohibited from building monasteries, churches and cells, displaying religious symbols and literature, reading church texts aloud and ringing bells, Christians must adhere to the ISIS dress code and bury their fellow believers in cemeteries specially designated by the new authorities. At the same time, it is imposed to apply in the amount of 4 gold dinars per year for the "rich", 2 for the middle class and 1 for the "poor".

Fundamentalism

In order to understand the essence of Islamic terrorism, one must understand what Islamic fundamentalism is.

The word "fundamentalism" itself was originally used in the United States to describe a number of Christian groups formed by the orthodox representatives of the Evangelical Church[14]. Only later this term began to be used by Western researchers in the study of Islam, Judaism and other religions. Moreover, it was often interpreted very broadly - as a return to the beginnings of religious and civilizational unity, the derivation of religious and political principles from the eternally sacred text. Today, this concept is used to describe the theoretical and practical activity of many political and religious movements and organizations - Islamic, Judaist, Protestant, Catholic, Orthodox, Hindu, Buddhist, which operate in

Southeast and Central Asia, North Africa and the Middle East, Europe and the United States - almost everywhere. The scope of the process, the involvement of states and peoples in it make fundamentalism not only an influential factor, but also a subject of politics (Sly, 2014).

This can be a shape of radical Islam related with the conviction that in arrange to return the Islamic nations to their "old greatness", sincere Muslims must desert everything that's related with "Western religious values and their way of living." We must return to the roots, to the "foundation" of Islam, precisely within the frame in which it was lectured by the Prophet Muhammad.

The first split in Islam occurred after the tragic death as a result of a terrorist attack carried out by a sectarian against the fourth and last righteous caliph, cousin and son-in-law of the Prophet Ali ben Abu Talib Abu-l-Hasan al-Murtad. This event marked the beginning of a serious political and ideological demarcation in the Muslim ummah. This delimitation led to the formation of two relatively independent communities: Shiites[15] and Sunnis[16], which, however, remained within the Caliphate and obeyed one ruler - the Caliph.

The further disintegration process in these communities was expressed in the splitting off of various groups that emerged into separate sects. There are currently several dozens of them, and the tendency to form various groups under Islamic slogans continues.

The anti-colonial struggle in Muslim countries hastened the formation of "Islamic" parties and movements, other national and other public associations, which initially advocated the liberation of their countries from colonial dependence, for the right of peoples to freely express their will and the creation of sovereign state formations, for equality and justice in international and interethnic relations.

In recent decades, they started talking about "political Islam", "Islamic radicalism", "Islamic fundamentalism", "Islamic Resur-gence", "Islamic Revival", putting an almost equal sign between these concepts. Fundamentalism can be defensive (designed to preserve and preserve, purify faith), but it can also be offensive and aggressive. It is the last type of Islamic fundamentalism, which prioritizes the principle of "jihad"[17], known as Islamic radicalism Followers of radicalism understand jihad as the need to fight - even armed - with the Christian, in their eyes godless and materialistic, Western world. In various Russian-language sources, depending on the time and purpose of the publication, different interpretations are given to this concept, with the main attention being paid to its "military" component, called "jihad of the sword".

The next sentences are interpreted from the Qur'an which says: "And fight in the way of Allah with those who fight with you, but do not transgress, - indeed, Allah does not love transgressors" (Surah 2, ayah 186), "And do not fight with them while they will not fight you "(Surah 2, ayah 187)," And if they leave you and offer you peace, Allah will not give you any way against them "(Surah 4, ayah 92) (Chitadze, 2022).

The Prevailing Explanation for Radicalization and Extremism

Unfortunately, Central Asia has become one of the few regions in the world where there is increased risk of religious extremism and terrorism as a result of a significant number of foreign terrorist mercenaries in Syria - it is estimated that there are more than 4,000 of them from CA69 (McKernan, 2015).

This is admission led to controversies about religion and radicalization in the Central Asian states, as well as scientific research, expansion of public PVE policies and activities, and goals in information ecosystems. Some quick takeaways from the above are intended to discuss field data in the next two chapters.

What causes or stimulates radicalization in Central Asian countries remains a question with numerous controversial answers. In a series of three reports from the International Crisis groups political, ideological and some economic factors explain much of the region's radicalization and violent extremism, but a number of academics criticized for lack of sufficient evidence and an attempt to link different areas of problems. Labor migration was also one of the popular assumptions in several studies, it has appeared as a cause of radicalization, but this was not revealed in our study. She is not the only and main reason, but rather, consequence, when the main driving forces can together lead to radicalization in aggregate with migration.

Age - or the vulnerability of youth - has proven to be an important driving force for which referenced by most researchers, but they tend to be combined with others as well factors leading to radicalization. Personal connections were a partial reason for most reports along with other major factors. Similarly mixed, not the only driving forces for radicalization can coexist with other factors: gender, internet / media, education, etc. Ultimately, it remains to recognize complex, not the only reason for radicalization in each case, the difficulty of determining any such factor and the need for careful interpretation of the evidence.

Radicalization and violent extremism remain top issues in programs security of the Central Asian states. How this issue was reflected in the information space of each country? All states can be located along the spectrum, from the very strong to weakest public discourse on F / PVE. According to the discursive the hegemony of the country's information ecosystem is limited, subordinate state agenda and does not have independent coverage of problems.

Economic Reasons

The mercenaries were offered or promised a very large reward, and in pursuit of easy and big money and / or in an effort to repay their loans, to improve their living conditions, they fell for this deception.

For economic reasons for radicalization, there is an assumption that there are recruiters, who make offers, agents who can pay (in whole or in part), and a recruited subject who is in dire need of money.

Political Reasons

People radicalized and joined extremist groups seeing them as a way to protest against unjust, repressive regimes or discrimination by state bodies.

Ideological Reasons

Radicalization was the result of a person's acceptance of some very intolerant, fundamentalist religion, which denies the coexistence with those who do not share the same point of view and, moreover, consider other points vision, value systems and ideologies as corrupting their own, their own, again accepted faith and therefore hostile to it

These broad and basic factors that could explain radicalization and joining extremist groups, several contributing factors can be added. Contributing factors are mentioned here because they alone would not be sufficient. faithful to lead a person to radicalization and violent extremism.

Youth

It is the broadest and most recognized contributing factor. Of all of the above key factors - economic, political or ideological - young people - perhaps the most receptive group. Disadvantage life experience, youthful "maximalism", etc. are sufficient aspects for which the likelihood of young people being recruited is very high.

Labor Migration

This category has been strongly hypothesized as an object of radicalization. Being away from home (meaning loneliness and lack of any control), susceptibility to systematic difficulties and abuse, insufficient conditions life and work - all of these conditions are cited to explain the vulnerability of migrants before recruiting.

Gender

The claim that women are subject to radical recruitment, in particular more men in Central Asia, wrong.

It is argued that the status of women in patriarchal cultures of these societies pushes them to radical and extremist actions in order to obtain freedom and emancipation. At the same time, however, there is evidence of how women bring men and other women into extremist groups who follow such groups are behind their husbands or male relatives.

Education

Lack or lack of education makes people vulnerable to recruitment for radical and extremist reasons. As a contributing factor education is considered in two parts: ordinary (secular) general and religious.

Lack of regular education deprives a person of critical thinking skills, communication skills and, in particular, makes them less attractive to employment for a good job. Lack of understanding of religion makes a person unable to appreciate what he was told, inclined to transfer undisputed authority over this question to another person (recruiter).

Personal Connections

A strong factor of radicalization both in Central Asia and elsewhere countries are personal connections: family members, friends, acquaintances are critical when recruiting a person into extremist groups and actions.

Information and Communication

The ultimate, but not exhaustive factor contributing to this, there were means of communication and information, or rather, the Internet.

To the extent that what kind of radicalization is to instill in a person certain ideas and worldview is a process of communication and information. The omnipresent light is claimed to be Internet and telephone access to information facilitates the transmission of radical reports of recruitment and communication with potential mercenaries (2022).

One major problem is that all clarifications are attempts to explain the low incidence of radicalization and extremism of the population, the overwhelming majority of which is not radicalized. In this way, economic difficulties, political oppression and ideological divisions are experiencing a large number of people in every society, but only a small number of people become radical. The same applies to all other factors. Moreover, in many cases radicalization featured individuals who did not fit the assumed factors: people without special economic difficulties, serious political grievances or ideology, people with good education, people who are not young, men and women, not labor migrants, and well-arranged migrants, etc. So, the ultimate cause of radicalization has not been found.

Most of the above studies, putting forward one or another set of reasons radicalization, they did it with caution and reservations. Indeed, if we proceed from more strict methodological approach, it would be impossible to define any specific reasons for radicalization.

Directives

First, do not conflict with the mushrikins (polytheists) and strive to persuade them to the true faith with "wisdom and good admonition."

Second, to wage a defensive war against opponents of religion in order to protect what has been achieved by "good exhortation."

Third, to avoid hostilities during the holy months (muharram, rajab, sha'ban, ramazan).

Fourth, to conduct military operations in such a way that, "fighting in the path of Allah, to protect the weak of men, as well as women and children" (Sura 4, ayah 77), do not exterminate livestock, do not poison the fields, do not destroy gardens, do not destroy the buildings.

It should be emphasized that Muslims have never declared war on Christianity - after all, it is one of the three Abrahamic religions (along with Islam and Judaism), and adherents of Islam revered as prophets Abraham and Jesus. Jihad for militant Islamism is a fight against the West as the enemy of Islam. At the same time, fundamentalism (Salafiyya) serves as an ideological basis for them, but not the main and not the only one.

Radical Islamists are convinced that Islam itself as a religion is facing mortal danger. The state effectively kills true Islam through secular legislation, parliamentarism, scientific and materialistic education, a repressive apparatus, and the media. At the same time, Islamists resort to extremism associated with various forms of terror and violence, violating the main principles underlying the Muslim doctrine, among which there are the following Koranic guidelines: "There is no coercion in religion" (Sura 2, ayat 257); "The truth is from your Lord: Whoever wants, let him believe, and whoever wants, let him not believe" (Sura 18, ayah 28).

To save Islam and their souls, devout Muslims must unite and seize power. The ultimate goal of Islamic fundamentalists in any country is to create a religious state governed by the clergy and governed by Sharia law. To date, fundamentalists have achieved a similar result in two countries: Iran and Sudan. In all other Muslim countries, they are in opposition, and quite often they are driven underground (for example, in Tunisia, Syria, Iraq, Algeria), but even in this case, radical Islamists are able to significantly influence the socio-political situation.

In fact, "fundamentalism" is not necessarily equivalent to political radicalism, extremism and does not directly cause terrorism (Chitadze, 2022).

Fanatical terrorists think least of all about "cleansing" Islam; the roots of their hatred of the West, primarily America, are not religious, but cultural, civilizational, psychological and geopolitical.

Wahhabi Roots

ISIS claims that its members are true Islam in the early Islamic interpretation, also known as Salafism. Many postcolonial and modern Islamic movements called themselves Salafis, including the official branch of Islam adopted in Saudi Arabia known as Wahhabism. This name goes back to the name of its founder - the Islamic theologian Muhammad ibn Abd al-Wahhab, who lived in the 18th century, who, together with Muhammad ibn Saud, stood at the origins of the first Saudi state.

Wahhabism is the intellectual heritage of the 13th century Islamic theologian Taqi al-din Ahmad ibn Taymiyyah and the Hanbali religious-legal school, which was interpreted and implemented by Ibn Abd al-Wahhab and his successors. Wahhabism is characterized by extreme traditionalism and literalism in the interpretation of Islam and rejects a number of scholastic concepts, including the concept of maqasid (spirit of Sharia), which is shared by many other Islamic religious schools; kalam (philosophy of Islam); Sufism (Islamic spirituality); ilal (study of religious aspirations in the Qur'an and hadith - legends about the words and actions of the Prophet Muhammad); al-majaz (metaphors).

Islamic theologians also use the concept of bida ("innovation, innovation"), an Islamic term that means the prohibition of the unauthorized invention of religious practices, by which many practices, mainly Sufi and Shia, are labeled as polytheistic. By emphasizing the concept of bidah, the Wahhabis are embarking on a slippery slope, which can lead to any Muslim being declared an apostate. For example, if a Muslim turns to the saints or visits their burial places, guided by the principle of wasil[18], then this is seen as an action that automatically excludes the believer from the bosom of Islam. Walking around a grave, slaughtering livestock in the name of a saint, or believing in the divine grace of imams are also considered polytheistic practices. While adherents of the mainstream of Islam believe that any innovations in Islam are prohibited, Wahhabi religious leaders go even further: they adhere to the hard line formulated by Ibn Taymiyyah, according to which many elements of religious practice that are considered completely legal by other Muslims fall under the concept of bidah. Wahhabi clerics reject Sufi and Shia claims that such forms of religious practice are not worship (Arango, 2014).

The Islamic State borrowed from Wahhabism a number of measures from the punishment code, which is officially adopted in Saudi Arabia and is used, albeit less systematically, in some other Muslim countries. However, the most significant contribution of Wahhabism to ISIS can be considered the concepts of wala wal bara (allegiance to Islam and rejection of non-Islamic ideas and rituals) and tawhid (monotheism). Although these concepts and concepts have existed in traditional Salafism since the preaching of the theologian Ahmad ibn Taymiyyah and other theologians of the early Islamic period, Wahhabi clerics interpret and disseminate them in a more extremist way.

According to the concept of vala wal bara, a Muslim should not just ignore non-Islamic practices and believers of other religious denominations - a true Muslim believer rejects non-Islamic practices and non-Muslims1. Ibn Abd al-Wahhab reflected this commandment in his writings as follows: "The faith of a Muslim cannot be truly devout, even if he professes monotheism and does not worship anyone or anything except Allah, if he does not hate the adherents of polytheism and does not demonstrate their hostility to them". From the ISIS point of view, this duty of the faithful also extends to those Muslims who do not meet the criteria of tawheed, violating the three conditions of monotheism.

The fundamental dogma, according to the sermon of Ahmad ibn Taymiyyah, is that a Muslim is obliged to fulfill three conditions of monotheism: to worship Allah, to worship only Allah, to observe the true creed, as prescribed by the Koran and traditions bequeathed by the Prophet. It was on the three criteria of tawhid (monotheism) that Ibn Taymiyyah relied to declare Shiites and followers of Sufism infidels, after he proclaimed that their practices and beliefs, including the worship of imams, contradict the worship of Allah alone.

In the territories occupied by ISIS, symbols of polytheism (polytheistic practice) are systematically destroyed, especially Sufi and Shiite sanctuaries and cultural and historical monuments that testify to the worship of pagan gods. After capturing a city, ISIS clerics typically campaign against what they see as signs of polytheism, including superstition, fortune telling, and predictions of the future. The religious tenets proclaimed by the clerics of ISIS are gradually shaping the life of the societies under their control, because many of the ideas spread by ISIS are based on the tenets of the established Islamic religious schools.

That is why the main attention in the study and analysis of the harsh, aggressive and intolerant of other confessions ideology of ISIS is paid to Wahhabism. In addition, since ISIS quotes or preaches the writings of Salafi and Wahhabi theologians, some researchers have concluded that ISIS is the spokesman for these ideas. However, blaming the theory and practice of Salafism and Wahhabism for ISIS extremism is a superficial and overly simplistic approach.

Radical Takfirism and Comparison Analysis

Part of the legacy of Takfiri teachings and ideas that emerged from the Al-Qaeda community passed to ISIS. Although the Islamic State was linked to al-Qaeda in the past, their ideological paths eventually diverged. Their comparison and determination of the point of divergence allows shedding light on the evolution of the sectarian ideology of the "Islamic State".

The differences between al-Qaeda and ISIS can be traced back to the earliest contacts between Osama bin Laden and Abu Musab al-Zarqawi. Already in the 1980s, when both of them were in Afghanistan, there were differences between them (as they do today between their successors) on the issue of brutal violence, including against Shiite communities. From the point of view of ISIS leaders, internal enemies are the most dangerous for Islam. Accordingly, it makes no sense to focus on distant hostile forces (Western countries) and ignore local enemies (hostile Muslim confessions in the region, especially Shiites). According to the strategy of the "Islamic State", the distant enemy will be drawn into a regional conflict anyway, as Osama bin Laden wanted, but only as a result of an attack on the near enemy. This scenario, by the way, worked after ISIS fighters captured the city of Mosul in northern Iraq in June 2014 - over 60 countries entered the fight against this group (Chitadze, 2022).

The 2003 war in Iraq gave al-Zarqawi an opportunity to spread his sectarian ideas. Prior to this, Iraqi society was quite resistant to manifestations of religious enmity, including due to the fact that marriages were often concluded in the country between people from different confessional groups. However, al-Zarqawi's followers nevertheless managed to ignite a civil war after suicide bombers carried out several bombings at the Al-Askari mosque in the city of Samarra in 2006. The extremist ideas that infiltrated Iraq with al-Qaeda after 2003 took root in the country as the al-Zarqawi jihadist group developed into a local movement led by Abu Umar al-Baghdadi, who led the Islamic State in Iraq in the period 2006-2010, and his successor, Abu Bakr al-Baghdadi, who leads the group now (Chitadze, 2022).

For al-Qaeda, this focus on fighting the Shiites distracts the Islamists from fighting the West. In addition, most Sunni spiritual leaders oppose the Shiite genocide. The central leadership of al-Qaeda condemned the attacks by ISIS (and its ideological predecessors) on the peaceful Shiite population. Osama bin Laden reportedly advocated the creation of an alliance between Shiites and Sunnis, which would allow them to join forces in the fight against the West.

Al-Zarqawi's letter, published by the US Department of State, calls on Osama bin Laden to focus on the Shiites. Al-Zarqawi wrote that if the one agree with us [on the persecution of Shiites], they should become their loyal soldiers, but if one holds a different perspective, they will still remain brothers and disagreements should not destroy friendship. He thought al-Qaeda with its new leaders and their perspectives became too soft in their activities and in their attitude as a whole.

Leader of al-Qaeda during 2005 Ayman al-Zawahiri had outlined the position on the Shiite issue in a letter that was published in 2015.In the letter he wrote the reasons why the Islamic State should refrain from attacking Shiite communities and mosques. Such acts can lead to the death or injury of women and children, as well as the civilian population of the Shiite communities, which are under protection, since they are forgiven for their ignorance through ignorance [of the true religious doctrine, in contrast to the Shiite religious leaders]. This is the position of the Sunnis on the issue of Shiite communities and ignorant followers of Shiism.

In February 2014, al-Qaeda officially disassociated itself from the Islamic State. In general, it can be noted that outside of the territories held by the Islamic State, its leadership was unable to enlist the support of any well-known ideologues of jihad, with a few exceptions. Most jihadist ideologues criticize ISIS's indiscriminate violence and sectarianism. Abu Muhammad al-Maqdisi, who was once al-Zarqawi's mentor, calls ISIS's actions "a deviation from the norm." He condemns the public executions and alienation of local Muslim communities and armed groups in Syria.

Ideological differences between ISIS and al-Qaeda are also evident in the attitude of the Islamic State towards spiritual and secular leaders and actions based on it. The rigidity and ossification of ISIS ideology stands out against the background of all existing jihadist religious movements. ISIS's refusal to compromise creates a "culture of takfirism within takfirism" in which there is no room for tolerance.

In a video interview posted online in October 2013, Sami al-Aridi, the spiritual leader of Al-Nusra Front, a group linked to al-Qaeda, highlighted several points in ISIS ideology that distinguish it from other jihadist groups, including Al-Qaeda. Unlike representatives of the Islamic State, al-Aridi cites leading Wahhabi theologians who adhere to the mainstream in Islam, such as the Grand Mufti of Saudi Arabia Sheikh Abdul Aziz al-Sheikh and the famous theologian Abdul Aziz ibn Baz. Al-Aridi emphasized in an interview that al-Qaeda members are supporters of four Sunni schools of jurisprudence and are tolerant of the Islamic clergy and often come into contact with them.

On the contrary, the Islamic State holds the clergy responsible for the fact that tyranny and lawlessness still dominate the Muslim world. The Islamic State believes that it is sometimes necessary to resort to tabayun[19] to identify true Muslims. According to al-Aridi, ISIS can declare a Muslim a kafir[20] based on intuitive suspicions, logical constructions and vague doubts.

ISIS believes that ordinary Muslims receive religious knowledge from the clergy, who act in concert with the corrupt rulers who support Western hegemony. Accordingly, ISIS views the fight against mainstream Islamists and corrupt rulers as more important than fighting the West.

The Islamic State is also characterized by the emphasis on the Sunnah (the traditions of the Prophet) as an integral part of the Muslim faith - in the mainstream of Islam, the Sunnah are considered optional and secondary elements of religious practice, designed to strengthen the faith of a Muslim. Accordingly,

ISIS believes that those believers who honor the Sunnah show respect for the Prophet, and those who departed from them are disrespectful to his covenants. Abu Maria al-Qahtani, who was the spiritual leader of the Al-Nusra Front prior to al-Aridi's appointment, said in February 2014 that ISIS has frankly incorporated these traditions into Islamic jurisprudence, replacing the words "discretion" and "in the order of recommendation "to others -" must "and" obligatory ".

Another interesting figure is Juhayman al-Oteibi, who was a former Saudi extremist and was more than a very popular person with his views and goals. His idea was that according to legend, the religious followers of al-Oteibi constantly were praying in mosques in shoes, and after leaving the mosque they took them off, as the Prophet Muhammad sometimes was doing. ISIS wanted to restore the old because they thought that the revival of ancient rituals proves adherence to true Sunni traditions.

As for the next beliefs, the violation of the requirements of Islam and Sharia law was another direction where IS toot a radical position. If we go in to the depth accordingly to Salafism we will find a number of other rule that, must have to followed by all Muslims. The list of the violations was reduced by the founder himself to the number of ten actions:

1. Heresy (adherence to polytheism).
2. Recognition of intermediaries in the administration of religious rites.
3. Inability to recognize the unbelievers as such, or doubt or justification of their unbelief.
4. Mockery of religious rites.
5. Belief that there are more perfect instructions or rules than those given by the Prophet.
6. Neglect of the rituals bequeathed by the Prophet.
7. Performance of rituals of black magic or belief in them.
8. Joining the infidels in the fight against Muslims.
9. The belief that some people can do without Sharia law.
10. Deliberate refusal to study or practice religion (Paravicini, 2017).

There are some people who believe into the varying degrees of unbelief and that the sinner does not necessarily become unfaithful by committing certain acts, but in the case of ISIS the situation is different, as they totally deny any kind of gradation of sinfulness and assume that all acts of unbelief are equally serious in any case.

The Islamic State believes that if one does not declare a person who deserves it to be unfaithful, he himself should be declared unfaithful. This is the reason why after al-Qaeda leader al-Zawahiri expressed sympathy for ousted Egyptian President Mohammed Morsi IS were not very happy with that.

Hazmiya is a movement among which this kind of views are very popular. SO the conclusion is that many of the Islamic State followers believe in the Hazmiyah doctrine because they think that it gives them a right to murder Muslims who are falling under that category, in other words they see it as a charge that can be brought against most Muslims under their control.

THE DEFEAT OF ISIS?

The fact that the United States defeated the Islamic State was announced by US President Donald Trump back in 2018. Immediately after that, he ordered the withdrawal of American troops from Syria. And recently, speaking to reporters in Florida, Trump said that the IS group was "100% defeated" (Chitadze, 2022).

In support of his words, the owner of the White House showed reporters two geographical maps of Syria. On the first, the red dotted line marked the areas captured by the militants at the time of his election as President of the United States, and on the second, these lines were erased, which, obviously, should indicate the complete defeat of IS.

In this strategy closely combines the tactics of lightning war, terrorist attacks, demonstrative cruelty, hostage-taking, deception, the spread of incredible all sorts of rumors designed to cause the audience has horror, emotional shock.

M.F. Ilminskaya, says that the uniqueness of the IS really lies within the truth that, the group was trying to solidify Islamists and Baathists. It seems that Ba'athism in the beginning may indeed have a big introduction to the east with its ideological understandings with the main point to try recreate nationality of the region. It looks like an ordinary ancient east patriotism, to which we have such examples as are: G. Nasser, S. Hussein, H. Assad, but this kind of patriotism always appears ineffective (Chitadze, 2022).

Islam presupposes the existence of a caliphate. The period without a caliphate is seen as a time of humiliation of Islam. Such an understanding of the place and role of Islam means the desire to redraw the political map of the world, in in any case, the Arab-Islamic world.

However, after major defeats as a result of the loss of Aleppo, Mosul and other key territories in both Syria and Iraq, the leadership ISIS and Al-Baghdadi himself were forced to admit defeat. The leader of the organization called on its members to take refuge in hard-to-reach terrain on the territory of the two countries and "to continue resistance from the existing there or newly created bases ".

As was mention before the fall of this king of group and other maybe other terrorist organizations cannot be thought as the finale battle or as the solution.

Talking simply there will always be something, some source or a factor that once have built up such groups and organizations as are al-Qaeda or ISIS, or any other terrorist groups. But in case of ISIS we should take into consideration the huge significance of the geopolitical interests of extra-regional actors, who use the Shiite-Sunni confrontation in the global political game.

Once ISIS controlled over110 thousand km of Syria and Iraq, and if we count their population together it will make around already 8 million which actually was the top of what ISIS conquered, but thankfully these territories were later given back (Chitadze, 2022).

As for today, Islamic State has lost its power, including its territories and bases in Syria and Iraq as well, but more than that, they have lost their face and their influence that one was on the top. But even though, they have lost everything, it is still too early to announce their defeat. Religion and Ideology are the best tools of the influence and in bad hand they can play a crucial role.

Most probably ISIS will just go dark, sitting and waiting for the good moment to start gathering the strength that the group one had, and maybe rethinking their values and making new laws and believes.

There is another danger ahead. As some rumors state, several members of the group are planning to continue their criminal and terrorist activities inside the other terrorist organizations. So the phenomenon of ISIS, a terrorist group that has created a semblance of statehood, alas, can become contagious.

So with the disappearance of ISIS, Islamist terrorism has not disappeared anywhere.

Unfortunately, no one or at least no one yet has any kind of answers to the question. The AID for the forces that very fighting against ISIS became the knowledge of their ability to manipulate and recruit the younger generation of Muslims who were feeling left out of their own states. Considering this information, it seems even more possible that ISIS will maybe find a new place to make their goals and believes come true.

IS No Longer Exists, but Terrorists Still Remain

Bente Scheller, head of the Heinrich-Böll-Stiftung (Heinrich-Böll-Stiftung) in Beirut, points out that although most of Syria has been liberated from terrorists, IS fighters still remain on the territory of the state: held captive by the Syrian Kurds, but this is a small figure compared to how many IS members fought in Syria. "

According to him, there are still small territories on the territory of Syria, in which scattered gangs of terrorists from IS are operating. In particular, these are desert lands in the southeast of the province of Homs near the city of As-Sukhna, which connects the ancient city of Palmyra with the "capital" of eastern Syria - the city of Deir az-Zor. This enclave emerged after the Syrian army's large-scale offensive operation "Great Dawn", which liberated most of eastern and central Syria from IS terrorists. In addition, numerous cells of IS militants exist underground in the provinces of Aleppo, Idlib, Deir az-Zor, Homs and Daraa (Chitadze, 2022).

IS Ideology Being Not Dead and May Be Revived

Bente Scheller notes the absolute importance of the physical destruction of the ISIS was that terrorist movement saw itself precisely as a state. Following her idea, the attractiveness and ideology of ISIS are just lost with the absence of territory once controlled by the militants.

However, the physical destruction of the "Islamic State" does not mean that the terrorist group has been defeated. Still lots of people also suggest that the material which terrorists have left in such sources as is internet with its social networks and lots of different websites as well as forgotten by youth but still the media. All those sources still carry on the information about and from the terrorists, which can lead to huge problems concerning this issue, so it really is too early to think about the defeat of the ideological platform of IS.

Considering all the information given above, it is of an importance to make sure that those who were fighting against ISIS and those who are thinking for the future will be directed and take actions against the return of ISIS or any other terrorist group. The work should start first of all from the normalization of the situation in the Middle East. Any possible measures should be taken to stop the radicalization of the relatives of militants and more than that it is necessary to find funds for an education system for the population in order to reduce the social base for terrorists.

What Awaits Syria After the Destruction of IS

The liberation of most of Syria from IS does not mean that peace will finally come to the country. Bente Scheller recalls that the main conflict in Syria is the confrontation between the state regime and the Syrian opposition, and therefore the destruction of IS by itself will not end the war in the country.

The political future of Syria, in turn, should be determined by the Syrian Constitutional Commission, consisting of the Syrian government, opposition and UN representatives. She should write a new constitution for Syria, which will outline the fate of President Bashar al-Assad, the position of the Syrian Kurds and the procedure for holding new elections. According to Kusa, around this document "political battles will be no less fierce than battles on the ground" (Chitadze, 2022).

ANALYSIS AND DISCUSSION

Researchers disagree about the reasons for the formation of such an aggressive nature of ISIS. Some believe that the Islamic State is following traditions rooted in the distant past, while others associate the rapid spread and atrocities of ISIS with the aftermath of the US invasion of Iraq in 2003, as well as with Iran's growing role in supporting Shiite self-defense forces in region. A number of commentators explicitly call political Islam a harbinger of ISIS intolerance and brutality, while others relegate ISIS to the level of an organization where sectarian hatred is based on opportunism charged by regional political players.

In fact, the ideology of ISIS is a much more multifaceted phenomenon, its appearance cannot be explained by the influence of any one personality, or movement, or even time. At the same time, we note that you should not trust the names of books and other publications of ISIS, since they do not provide reliable information and can form a false idea of the ideology of the "Islamic State". On the contrary, it is important to carefully analyze how this group chooses its ideas and concepts, interprets and disseminates them.

By themselves, Salafism and political Islam do not lead to an increase in the number of ISIS supporters and are not a catalyst for extremism. On the contrary, there are limitations in both Salafism and political Islam that can deter the type of extremism that Islamic State follows. Likewise, political grievances or morale alone cannot push people to join ISIS. The optimal environment for the prosperity of this group is political oppression, inaction of state power, as well as interfaith disagreements. But this same political context can lead people - and often does - to join moderate insurgent groups rather than ISIS.

This work analyzes the ideology of the "Islamic State" and the interfaith enmity associated with it, based on sources and direct evidence of Islamic religious leaders and ISIS members in Syria and Iraq. The study also explores broader topics to explain the origins of the concept of violence and exclusivity of ISIS. Until the myth that the group's ideology goes back directly to Salafism is debunked, the world community will not be able to understand the reasons for the attractiveness and popularity of ISIS and will not be able to defeat the Islamic State.

The initial goal of IS was to create a theocratic Sunni Islamic state within the borders of Syria, Lebanon, Israel, Palestine, Jordan, Turkey, Cyprus and Egypt. However, after the group was renamed the Islamic State, its territorial claims spread to the entire Islamic world and even to territories that previously belonged to the Ottoman Empire in Europe (the Balkans and even southern Ukraine). In the future, IS plans to "liberate" the peoples of the Caucasus from the rule of Russia, including Chechnya from the dictator Ramzan Kadyrov.

In addition, the Islamic State was seeking to destroy traces of all cultures that have ever existed in the lands of Syria, Iraq, Iran, Turkey before the advent of Islam. To this end, the militants looted the historical museums of Mosul, demonstratively destroying a number of exhibits, blew up the city's oldest library and burned more than 10,000 ancient books from it (Chitadze, 2022). They also destroyed the artifacts of the ancient cities of Nimrud and Dur-Sharrukin - which were the capital of Assyria in the 1st millennium BC - the ancient Christian monastery of Behnama and Sarah.

However, according to a number of analysts, many of the allegedly destroyed objects of art and artifacts were illegally sold to wealthy collectors from around the world through intermediaries.

CONCLUSION

It is important to understand that this a terrorist organization entered into a political struggle before everything, using the religious factor. Its ideological basis activity is an extremist interpretation of Islam, and, in particular, the Salafi concept of jihad used by ISIS leaders to the justification for the terrorist attacks, violence and murders carried out by it.

Due to the fact that religious fanatics-terrorists use for their own purposes one of the directions in Islam - Wahhabism, today in the everyday consciousness of people terrorism is associated with Islamic fundamentalism and radicalism. This leads to colossal social tension in society, since many terrorists are associated with Islam only in everyday life and purely ceremonially, without the slightest idea of the culture, values and great aspirations of the religion of which they formally represent.

Terrorists, often posing as "freedom fighters", make it difficult to objectively assess their criminal actions, since ideological attitudes and religious landmarks used by terrorists are one of the most powerful means of manipulating people's minds and distracting society's attention from the true goals of the organizers of terrorist acts.

The emergence of the Islamic State is a consequence of geopolitical realities in the rapidly changing Middle East. But this is a symptom, not a disease. The most obvious reason for the emergence of IS after conducting the research for me became is the exacerbation of identity politics. In Iraq, the Sunnis, who have long controlled the state apparatus, found themselves dominated by a Shiite majority and a powerful Kurdish bloc. Sunnis in Iraq felt overwhelmed. In addition, the policy of former Iraqi Prime Minister Nuri al-Maliki of hyper-centralization of power forced the Sunnis to look for an alternative, which became the best social basis for IS. Similar events took place in Syria, where Assad's dictatorship ruled out a democratic option for the realization of interests for the Sunnis.

As for another triggers that were standing behind of the conflict are that, from the beginning they did not have Khalifat and territory it was easy to start the development of ISIS as a cause of the weakening institutions of the country and power loose, while al-Qaeda was on its top and was able to use its position. If we look at the criminal index, corruption index, the index of human development as well as democracy index of Iraq at that time we will see how desperate the country was. These made a push for such organizations to take control and concentrate the flow of money and weapons on the territory.

Then very handy comes fundamentalism and radicalism, younger generation who were tired of the life they were living of course were searching for any kind of get away from there which in many cases they found in religion and radicalism, beautifully put on the plate for them.

Its ideological basis activity is an extremist interpretation of Islam, and, in particular, the Salafi concept of jihad used by ISIS leaders to the justification for the terrorist attacks, violence and murders carried out by it.

It is also necessary to add that Shiites and Sunnis cannot be compared in terms of radicalism. And if we compare, then the Sunnis will be more radical, because almost all terrorist organizations are Sunni, and Salafism and Wahhabism are precisely Sunni movements. Among the Shiite extremists, only Hezbollah is remembered, and they, of course, are not at all such extremists as some Sunni apostates (now Hezbollah is fighting against IS, and protects the Christians of Syria).

For Shiites, Salafis are far more conservative. For example, in Shiism, the veneration of graves and shrines in general is practiced, which arose over time, and which was not widespread at all and was prohibited at the time of the Prophet:

The question is not about radicalism: ISIS appeared as a result of the persecution of the Sunnis by the Shiites in Iraq after the 2003 war and by the Alawite Assad regime in Syria. The Alawites are a branch of the Shiites. The Assad clan are Alawites. The Alawites are a religious and political minority in Syria that usurped power in the country since 1970, when Assad Sr. became the head of state as a result of a military coup.

The Shiites in Iraq are the majority of the population, which has been suppressed - often with a lot of blood - by the Sunni regime of Saddam Hussein for several decades. With the defeat of Saddam as a result of the second war (2003), the ruling Ba'ath party, the army and law enforcement agencies were dispersed. The top and middle echelons of these structures, finding themselves out of work and forced to seek "food" for themselves, went over to the armed opposition and formed the backbone of the current ISIS. Failure to assimilate these groups into the structures of the new Iraq and the lack of civil accord are the biggest mistakes of the Americans and the new, Sunni Iraqi government.

REFERENCES

Al-Shishani, M. B. (2010). *Saudi Arabia's Jihadi Jailbird: A Portrait of al-Shu'aybi Ideologue Nasir al-Fahd*. Intelligence Quarterly.

Arango, T. (2014). Escaping Death in Northern Iraq. *New York Times*.

Arango, T. (2015). Key Iraqi City Falls to ISIS as Last of Security Forces Flee. *The New York Times*.

Bergen, P. (2010). *Strange Bedfellows Iran and al Qaeda*. CNN.

Calvert, J. (2010). *Sayyid Qutb and the Origins of Radical Islam*. Columbia University Press.

Chitadze, N. (2022). Global Security and Political Problems of the 21st Century. IGI Global.

Cochrane, J., & Fuller, T. (2016). Jakarta Attack Raises Fears of ISIS' Spread in Southeast Asia. *The New York Times*.

Crooke, A. (2014). *You Can't Understand ISIS If You Don't Know the History of Wahhabism in Saudi Arabia. Huffington Post*.

Dearden, L. (2019). ISIS Claims Responsibility for Sri Lanka Easter Massacre. *The Independent*.

Freeman, C. (2015). *Chief Foreign Correspondent. Islamic State mints its own 'Islamic Dinar' coins*. The Telegraph.

Fuller, J. (2015). ISIS or ISIL? The debate over what to call Iraq's terror group. *The Washington Post*.

Hassan, H. (2014). *New Syrian Islamic Council Repeats the Patterns of Old*. National.

Hudson Teslik, L. (2015). *Interview with Arabic Interviewer*. Marifah.

Jumuah, A. (2012). *Wasila, Circumambulating Graves and Accusing Others of Shirk and Kufr* (M. Lock, Trans.). Marifah.

Kesling, M. S. (2014). Jordan Releases Zarqawi's Spiritual Mentor From Prison. *Wall Street Journal*.

Kuznetsova, A. (2015). *Islamic State in the context of political changes in the Middle East.* Vestnik MGIMO. doi:10.24833/2071-8160-2015-2-41-221-229

McKernan, B. (2015). Tehran attacks: ISIS claims responsibility for 'first major attack on Iran. *The Independent.*

Nour, Y. (2017). Motives in Egypt's Deadliest Terrorist Attack: Religion and Revenge. *New York Times.*

Paravicini, G. (2017). Brussels ISIL cell 'initially' planned to 'strike France again. *Politico.*

Ramey, C. R. (2007). *Mass media unleashed: How Washington policymakers shortchanged the American public.* Rowman & Littlefield.

Roggero, B. (2014). *ISIS announces formation of Caliphate, rebrands as "Islamic State".* Long War Journal.

Schmitt, E. (2014). In Battle to Defang ISIS, U.S. Targets Its Psychology. *New York Times.*

Sly, L. (2014). Syrian Tribal Revolt Against Islamic State Ignored, Fueling Resentment. *Washington Post.*

Stout, D. (2014). ISIS Massacres Sunni Tribe in Iraq. *Time.*

Taylor, L. (2013). *Islamic State Seeks to Justify Enslaving Yazidi Women and Girls in Iraq.* Reuters.

Weiss, H. (2015). *ISIS: Inside the Army of Terror.* Regan Arts.

White, J. (2014). *Military Implications of the Syrian Regime's Defeat in Raqqa.* The Washington Institute for Near East Policy.

ENDNOTES

1 Daesh - according to the first letters of the group's Arabic name - "adDaula al-Islamiyya f'il-Iraq va ash-Sham"

2 The term "Shiite" in translation from Arabic means "adherent of Ali" ("shii at Ali ").

3 The Mahdi armed force, a Shia volunteer army made by pastor Muqtada al-Sadr, was ascending and Sacolick, then a colonel, was summoning an exceptional operations team in Iraq.

4 De-Ba'athification (Arabic: اجتثاث حزب البعث) refers to a policy undertaken in Iraq by the Coalition Provisional Authority (CPA) and subsequent Iraqi governments to remove the Ba'ath Party's influence in the new Iraqi political system after the 2003 invasion.

5 Monotheism and Jihad

6 The Assad government describes itself as secular, while some political scientists have claimed that the government exploits sectarian tensions in the country and relies upon the Alawite minority to remain in power.

7 The capital of Assyria in the 1st millennium BC - the ancient Christian monastery of Behnama and Sarah.

8 The Islamic State – also known as ISIS, ISIL.

9 real name Qasem Rashid al-Jiburi

10 The terrorist organization created in January 2012 by Abu Mohamed al-Golani.

11 translated from Arab. "Accusation of unbelief", "aversion from faith" - approx. author

12 allegiance to Islam and rejection of non-Islamic ideas and rituals

13 also known as Said Imam al-Sharif and Dr. Fadl

14 Calvinists, Presbyterians and Baptists

15 Shiites from the Arabic word "shia" - party

16 Sunnis "Sunna" - an example, tradition

17 literally, the efforts that Muslims must make both to protect their faith and for self-improvement, relentlessly following the precepts of the Prophet

18 the desire to get closer to Allah and earn his favor

19 tabayun - investigation procedure

20 Kafir - an unbeliever, a non-believer

Chapter 7
Victimology of Terrorism

Nika Chitadze
International Black Sea University, Georgia

ABSTRACT

Terrorist acts have become an integral part of modern life. Terror (lat. terror – fear, horror) is aimed at "intimidation." It is this circumstance that defines terror as a special form of political violence, characterized by cruelty, purposefulness, and apparent effectiveness. Terror is horror, that is, an emotional state, the emergence of which terrorists achieve by carrying out certain special actions: terrorist acts. An act of terrorism is a means that brings real or potential victims to a state of horror. The totality of links terrorist-terrorist act-terror constitutes terrorism as an integral phenomenon. Terrorism is the use of violence to intimidate people. This violence is carried out in various forms: it is physical, political, social, economic, informational, etc. violence. Taking into account the degree of mass character and the degree of organization, four types of violence are distinguished: mass organized and mass spontaneous and individual spontaneous and individual organized. Each of them has its own specifics and features.

INTRODUCTION - THE CONCEPT OF "VICTIM OF TERRORISM"

A terrorist act is a special kind of emergency event, and its main goal is to spread a feeling of horror and fear among the population. The loss of security in the mass consciousness becomes chronic and leads to a violation of mental and physical health. The characteristic features of a terrorist act include suddenness (carrying a life threat that breaks all the basic values of a person, Which leads to the disorientation of a person in the psychological and social space) and the violent nature of the event. The psychological consequences of terrorism include a negative impact on the psycho-emotional health of a person. A victim of a terrorist act is a person (or a group of persons) who has directly suffered an infringement on his fundamental rights by another person (or a group of persons) acting consciously (UN, 2022). Victims of terrorism tend to consistently experience the following feelings: fear, which develops into horror, causing apathy, or panic, which can turn into aggression. There is also an opinion about the existence of differences in the behavior of the victim depending on gender, education level, intellectual abilities, and the level of human well-being. One of the main consequences of a terrorist act is the psychopathological symptoms of its victims and witnesses. The meaning of psychic trauma is that people who have

DOI: 10.4018/978-1-6684-5311-7.ch007

experienced a stressful event may find after a while that they cannot live and interact in society, coping with the life problems that arise as before. Post-traumatic stress affects both the victims themselves and the "spectators" who witnessed the traumatic event or learned about it through the media. Acute Stress Disorder (ASD) and Post Traumatic Stress Disorder (PTSD) are among the most serious psychiatric disorders from exposure to psychic trauma. Such diseases seriously impair the quality of life of people and can cause a person's permanent mental inability to function normally.

Psychology of Interaction Between Terrorists and Hostages

The interaction of terrorists with detained hostages can be identified as a socio-psychological phenomenon (UN, 2022), which has several specific phenomena. The first stage is hostage-taking, characterized by lightning-fast actions of terrorists and a complete surprise for the hostages. The second stage is the submission to the terrorists of the will of the hostages of subsequent intimidation. The third stage is to prevent open panic among the hostages. The means of this may be beating or even shooting the alarmist. The fourth stage is the introduction of strict norms for the behavior of hostages, the dictates of what can and cannot be done. The fifth stage is the notification of the outside world about hostage-taking. For example, there were some cases, when the terrorists allowed the hostages to talk on the phone with their relatives and friends. Mobile phones have been affected. The sixth stage is the sorting of hostages to destroy the established interpersonal ties. The terrorists separated men from women, children from adults, and local citizens from foreigners. The seventh stage is the organization of the hostages, providing food, sleep, life, etc. The eighth stage is the adaptation of the hostages to an extreme situation, the onset of fatigue, and dulling of feelings. The ninth stage is the identification of depression in the hostages; emotional breakdowns are possible both on the part of the hostages and on the part of the terrorists. The tenth stage is the release of hostages and the destruction of terrorists.

Psychology of Hostages

In the work of N. Pukhovsky (2000), based on a study conducted in the city of Budyonnovsk (during the first Chechen war) immediately after the hostage-taking in the summer of 1995, the general psychological traits of various types of victims of terror have been presented (hostages directly affected by terrorist actions, their relatives, as well as unwitting witnesses - city dwellers) (Chitadze, 2011). The first group of people involved in terror - close relatives of the hostages and the "missing" (presumed hostages) - suddenly found themselves in a situation of "psychological swaying": they rushed from hope to despair. All these people showed acute reactions to stress with a characteristic combination of a whole complex of affective-shock disorders (grief, depression, anxiety), paranoia (hostile distrust, alertness, manic persistence), and somatoform reactions (fainting, heart attacks, skin-allergic rashes). The state of the representatives of the second group - the newly released hostages - was determined by the residual effects of the acute affective-shock reactions they experienced. In clinical and psychological terms, this was a fairly typical picture of the so-called adynamic depression with its usual "masks" of asthenia, apathy, and anhedonia. Characteristic features were unwillingness to remember the experience. Let us especially note the obsessive desire to "cleanse" as soon as possible, in particular, "to take a bath" - it was especially symptomatic and was expressed by many of the released hostages. According to the stories of the released hostages, three types of behavior were observed in this extreme situation. - the first type is a regression with "exemplary" infantilism and automated submission, a depressive experience of fear, horror, and an immediate threat to life. This is apathy in its direct and immediate form; - the second type is demonstrative obedience, the desire of the hostage to "get ahead of the order and earn praise" from the terrorists. This is rather not a depressive, but a sthenic active-adaptive reaction. This type is typical for women with children or pregnant women. - the third type of behavior - is chaotic protest actions, demonstrations of discontent and anger, constant refusal to obey, and provoking conflicts with terrorists. This type is typical for single men and women with a low level of education and a reduced ability to reflect. In addition to these behavioral differences, two types of specific psychopathological phenomena have been noted separately. The first type of phenomenon is situational phobias. In the focus of the emergency, the hostages experienced situationally determined agoraphobic phenomena. This is the fear of going to the window, standing up to his full height, the desire to walk crouching, "short dashes", the fear of attracting the attention of terrorists, etc. Naturally, all this was determined by the desire to survive in what was happening around. However, already in the next few days after their release, the hostages with pronounced effect complained about the appearance of obsessive agoraphobia (fear of open spaces) and a tendency to restrictive behavior. They again had symptoms such as fear of going to windows - already at home; fear of going to bed and desire to sleep on the floor under the bed, etc. Such complaints were most typical for young women, pregnant women, or mothers of young children. The second type of phenomenon is various distortions of perception. In the structure of the "hostage syndrome", even after the release, the victims sometimes spoke about the correctness of the actions of the terrorists; the validity of their cold cruelty and ruthlessness, in particular, the "injustice of the authorities"; about the justification of the actions of terrorists by the "lofty goals of the struggle for social justice" facing them; about the "guilty of the authorities in the victims" in the case of active opposition to terrorists, etc. Such statements corresponding to the "Stockholm syndrome", are typical for middle-aged, single men and women with a low level of education and low incomes. These statements were permeated with the effect of hostile distrust and did not yield to criticism. Such judgments arose only after liberation - during the period of hostage, it was these people who demonstrated the behavior of the third type described above, they were distinguished by chaotic protest actions that provoked conflicts and aggression on the part of terrorists. When a person finds himself in a hostage situation, the structure of communication between the victims of terrorist changes.

There are several stages in the development of such communication (Lynch, 2018).

The first stage. A person, as it were, freezes, hides, looks closely at others, evaluating the prospect of contact with others. This stage is characterized by a decrease in the activity of communication. Verbal communication stops almost completely, but the person does not "drop out" of communication, he carefully monitors the behavior of others. There is an assessment of the danger on the part of the social environment, a person tries to predict the development of events, and determines for himself the need for any immediate action. In the vast majority, one of the mechanisms of psychological defense works - denial. People simply don't believe (and often don't want to believe) that "it" happened to them. If the conditions of detention are harsh, then after a few hours one of the hostages begins to flare up angrily, swear with neighbors, maybe even with their loved ones. Such aggression helps to "relieve" emotional overstrain, but at the same time exhausts a person. This stage of communication can last up to several hours, depending on the personality and condition of the person.

Second stage. There is an increase in the intensity of certain manifestations of communication, sometimes there is unusual for a given person's (in ordinary, non-stressful situations) activity in communication. The emergency of the situation cancels the prevailing stereotypical forms of behavior, people behave differently than in everyday life. During this stage, the hostages are divided into roles, leaders, passive observers, "activists", etc. are determined. Some at this stage begin to behave aggressively, not only toward other hostages but also toward criminals.

Third stage. If there is a hostage nearby who has a bodily ailment, then there is a closer communication associated with caring for this sick person. At the same time, the zonal division of the interpersonal territory of people is destroyed. This situation of assisting (albeit forced) is a powerful anti-stress factor, both for the one who assists (he feels his need for others) and for the one to whom it is provided (he also feels like a cementing link). At this stage, the role status of the hostages is specified, and informal micro-groups are created.

Fourth stage. If the situation is not resolved, the following communication changes occur. In some cases, interaction components predominate, consolidating the group, in others - disorganizing it, i.e. in each informal group (which was formed earlier) an opponent may appear to the leader who does not agree with his opinion and actions in everything. This opponent uses any excuse to prove the failure of the leader. At this stage, depending on individual characteristics (someone earlier, some later), asthenic syndrome begins to develop, that is, apathy. It is characterized by a combination of increased fatigue, exhaustion of neuropsychic processes, autonomic symptoms, and sleep disturbances. In this case, the mood drops sharply, there is constant tearfulness, increased sensitivity to bright light, loud sounds, and pungent odors. At this point, people cannot bear any touch with them. In the psychology of victims of terrorism, there is a phenomenological symptom, the so-called "Stockholm syndrome" (or "traumatic connection"), characterized by the manifestation of an inexplicable sympathy of the victim for his "tormentor". The term belongs to the criminologist Niels Biggeroth, who analyzed the situation that occurred in a bank in Sweden. The robbers barricaded themselves on the territory of the bank with the hostages. Subsequently, four of the hostages were imbued with understanding for the robbers and, when they surrendered to the police, defended them. One of the women later divorced her husband and married one of the criminals. Psychologically, the victims of terrorists, under the influence of fear, to avoid violence and to save their own lives, try to please their tormentors. Subsequently, aggression is replaced by complete humility, the hostage understands that his life is completely subordinate to the invader, who could kill him, but did not carry out the threat. Therefore, the victims may develop a strong emotional attachment and sincere sympathy for the terrorist. For the "Stockholm syndrome" to form, several circumstances are necessary:

- the factor of surprise and the psychological shock from understanding the situation of lack of freedom and dependence on terrorists;
- the duration of being in a state of hostage. The more time a person is under pressure, the more the feeling of humility and submission to the invader grows;
- psychological protection in the form of a state of depression. Many psychologists associate "Stockholm Syndrome" with a psychological defense mechanism (Chitadze, 2016).

A person regresses into the state of a child who is offended, and, not finding protection, he begins to adapt to the offender and tries to negotiate with him.

Law enforcement officials need to be careful with victims of "Stockholm Syndrome", as they may give false information in an attempt to justify the captor; interfere with the investigation and the search for evidence of the guilt of the offender. "Stockholm Syndrome" is a condition of the victim (as a result of hostage-taking) in which the victim shows an unreasonably good attitude towards the hostage-taker, as a result of which he may deliberately distort information about the crime and the offender. The highest degree of manifestation of this is the complete approval, support, and understanding of the activities of terrorists, the provision of assistance and support to them, up to the complete "transition" to their side (i.e., the victim becomes complicit in the crime) (Turkovic, 2018).

Basic Mental Reactions of Victims of Terrorism

Common signs for released hostages. The first phase - the "phase of psychological shock" - contains two main components: inhibition of activity, disorientation in the environment, disorganization of activity; denial of what happened. This phase is usually short-lived. The second phase - "impact" - is characterized by pronounced emotional reactions to the event and its consequences. It can be anxiety, fear, horror, or anger, i.e. emotions that are extremely intense. Gradually, these emotions are replaced by a reaction of self-criticism or self-doubt. This phase is critical. After it, either the process of recovery occurs in the form of adequate adaptation to newly arisen circumstances - the phase of "normal response", our fixation on the injury with the subsequent development of the post-stress disorder. In the latter case, mental personality changes can be represented in the following sequence:

- traumatic stress (during a critical incident and immediately after it - up to 2 days);
- acute stress disorder (within 1 month after a critical incident - from 2 days to 4 weeks);
- post-traumatic stress disorder (more than 1 month after the critical incident
- more than 4 weeks);
- post-traumatic personality disorder (throughout the subsequent life of a person who has experienced trauma) (UN, 2022).

The result of a person being in a traumatic situation with mass casualties is the development of the following clinical manifestations: PTSD (Post-traumatic stress disorder), acute stress disorder, psychological burnout or exhaustion syndrome, depressive disorder, anxiety, sleep disturbance, and alcohol and drug abuse. Many researchers note the potential effect of a terrorist act on the psyche of people who have experienced a tragic event - the experience of traumatic grief. These symptoms of distress can be defined as a constellation of several manifestations: focus on dead loved ones, loss of faith in oneself and life prospects; inability to accept the death of loved ones, a state of bitterness or anger towards death; avoidance of people. The cause of post-traumatic stress disorder (PTSD) may be exposure to some traumatic stressor, for example, a person becomes a witness to a situation with a fatal outcome for the victim or is himself in danger of death (physical harm). In such a situation, the individual turns on a reaction of intense fear and/or horror. Symptoms of re-experiencing the event, avoidance, numbness, and increased arousal should appear within a month, are considered acute if they appear for up to three months, and become chronic from three months or more. Acute stress disorder (ASD) is symptomatic similar to PTSD, but its symptoms are shorter in duration and focus more on dissociative symptoms than PTSD. ASD is considered "…is the development of characteristic restlessness, dissociative and other symptoms within one month of exposure to an extreme stressor" (DSM-IV). Symptoms must have been present for at least two days before a diagnosis is made. As in the case of PTSD, the individual must be a direct witness/participant in an event in which his life or physical condition was threatened, resulting in affective reactions such as fear, horror, and helplessness. A diagnosis of this disorder requires three or more dissociative symptoms, marked avoidance, anxiety, or symptoms of arousal. Depression is diagnosed two or more weeks after the traumatic event, during which the individual reports his depressive state or lack of will to live in most areas of his life activity. Depression is generally associated with symptoms such as insomnia and lethargy. Often there are feelings about their uselessness, worthlessness, and suicidal thoughts. In a mass casualty situation, the symptoms associated with deprivation should be considered separately from the potential diagnosis, and treatment should be related to the problem of grief if the individual has lost close relatives and friends.

Anxiety/anxiety syndrome. Subclinical symptoms of anxiety may be common in the setting of a massive catastrophic event with human casualties. Evidence suggests that feelings of fright or anxiety immediately after a large-scale disaster may increase the risk of PTSD. However, the clinical diagnosis of Generalized Anxiety Disorder (GAD) requires that the symptoms be present (manifest) consistently over six months. People with GAD find it difficult to control their anxiety. They show the following symptoms: fussiness, fatigue, weakening of concentration, irritability, muscle tightness, and sleep disturbances. One of these symptoms is enough to make a diagnosis in children.

Insomnia. Insomnia is diagnosed when an individual has difficulty falling asleep, with interruption or lack of restorative sleep for one or more months. Insomnia causes severe debilitation of vital functions and is not due to biological sleep problems such as respiratory arrest or heart rhythm disturbances. In traumatized people, nightmares may occur as a specific sleep disorder. This is usually accompanied by frequent interruption of sleep with a detailed recollection of a nightmare or extended frightening fantasies involving safety, life, and death, or loss of self-worth. To meet the clinical criteria for a diagnosis of the disorder, nightmares must cause several significant difficulties in the person's life functioning and not be present in the presence of another disorder, such as PTSD. Psychotherapists, clinicians, and social workers who have identified traumatized victims of terrorist attacks as having a specific form of addiction should refer to the DSM-IV for more information. We will confine ourselves to describing general criteria for identifying these abuses: inability to fully perform their functional duties at work, at school, or home; repetitive alcohol abuse that puts the individual at risk of physical injury; Difficulties with the law due to alcohol abuse; continued use despite social or personal problems associated with intoxication. These criteria must be met within six months. As with depression, addiction to cigarette, alcohol, or drug abuse appears to be particularly likely when subsequent terrorist attacks increase. Multiple Unexplained Symptom Syndrome (OMUS). The OMUS syndrome is not included in the DSM-IV taxonomy. Unlike the classic mass panic, it happens quite often and is periodically observed as a reaction to specific environmental factors. The manifestation of this syndrome is often reinforced by the media, rumors, and visual response of the emergency and special services to a catastrophic situation. As already noted, the OMUS phenomenon is referred to as "mass anxiety", or "mass hysteria" in the early formulations. OMUS can generate real psychosomatic symptoms, including gag reflexes, diarrhea, skin allergies, and breathing difficulties, which are difficult to separate from symptoms caused by exposure to chemical, radiological and biological components in terrorist attacks. This phenomenon is often referred to as "psychic contagion" or "social transmission" of symptoms. This phenomenon is seen as a social and psychological reaction to potential agents of infection, often in the absence of an actual threat, causing somatic symptoms that spread rapidly through the population and are usually transient.

CLASSIFICATION OF VICTIMS OF TERRORIST ACTS

After any catastrophic event (in our case, a terrorist act), the people involved in it, two groups of needs must be taken into account by emergency response services. Most important are the needs of survivors of a terrorist attack. The definition of who should be counted among the victims can be greatly expanded.

For example, these are not only those people who physically managed to survive and leave the disaster site but also their family members, acquaintances, and other representatives of the local community that was subjected to a terrorist act. Another group of needs refers to the employees of the emergency services themselves, involved in the elimination of the consequences of a terrorist act and providing various types of assistance to the direct victims.

The experience of emergency services specialists in dealing with the consequences of terrorist attacks and other catastrophic events (including representatives of psychological services) made it possible to identify a working classification scheme for victims of terrorist attacks. At the same time, "victims" refers to people whose lives were at great risk from the impact of a catastrophic event. This classification scheme contains several categories.

- People who were seriously injured at the epicenter of a catastrophic event.
- Their families, close friends, and acquaintances.
- Employees of emergency services and organizations whose work obliges them to directly participate in dangerous operations to eliminate the consequences of terrorist attacks.
- Members of the local community experiencing grief and identifying with the suffering victims.
- People with deviant psychological and mental behavioral reactions; are so-called troublemakers who are inclined to use the situation in their interests.
- Other people who have been shocked. The selected categories are rather conditional, so some people may fall into more than one category. Also, not all people who fall into one category or another will need the same kind of help. This is because their needs may depend on several factors: personal perception of the traumatic event, the current state of mental and physical health, their mental tolerance for stressful events, etc. But this classification provides a "starting position" for psychologists and psychotherapists. seeking to assess the diversity of perceptions and psychological problems of affected people.

Rescue Recommendations for People Who Are Held Hostage

This is especially true for the first minutes of the action when the criminals are extremely excited. It is necessary to try to correct your mental balance. To this end, you can concentrate on your breathing, and focus on the environment (count the number of light bulbs in the room, determine the number of "comrades in misfortune", etc.) (UN, 2022). Many different methods make it possible to manage your condition. Usually, it takes months and years of hard training to master them, but there are several equally effective methods that do not require much effort and a long time:

- managing emotions by regulating their external manifestation (in an extreme situation, you need to force yourself to look calm outwardly by concentrating internally);
- the method of "sobering" pain effect, which consists in mobilizing activity with the help of pain: prick yourself with something sharp (needle, badge, etc.);
- self-hypnosis, carried out by repeated repetition of words or verbal formulations, which should be brief, extremely clear, simple and clear, realistically feasible in a particular situation, not containing negation. Having calmed down yourself, you should try to help others do it, paying special attention to children whose psyche is not yet very stable and who find it difficult to stay in one place for a long time. If there are a lot of strangers nearby, try to get to know them. In the process

of this exchange of information, it will be clear who is unable to cope with their condition on their own, who needs help, etc., i.e., to determine "who is who" from among your environment (one of the options: accomplice of terrorists). If you notice unusual behavior behind you that you did not expect, incomprehensible sensations, do not be afraid - you have not gone crazy, this is the natural reaction of your body to the circumstances that have arisen. This will pass (about two weeks after release). Relationships with criminals. Do not offer aggressive resistance, do not make sudden and threatening movements do not provoke terrorists to rash actions. Avoid direct eye contact with criminals whenever possible. From the very beginning (especially the first half hour), follow all their orders and instructions. Take a position of passive cooperation. Speak in a calm voice.

Avoid expressions of contempt, provoking a hostile tone, and behavior that may provoke the ire of invaders. Be calm, while maintaining self-esteem. Don't be blunt about refusing, but don't be afraid to make calm requests for what you need most. Try to become aware of your role as a hostage. Remember "Stockholm Syndrome". Just as weaker people become dependent on stronger personalities, helpless hostages become dependent on their captors, may take their point of view, or begin to perceive authorities as something antagonistic not only to their captors but also to themselves. Be aware of this fact and that kidnapping makes you addicted. Your life depends on the whim of the terrorists. Be aware of these feelings of dependency and empathy for the terrorists and resist them. Talk to your comrades in misfortune, if you are not alone, be united. They are your comrades, not terrorists. Be alert to the manifestation of "Stockholm Syndrome" in other hostages and help them free themselves from these feelings. Keep them upbeat. Remind them that you have a high chance of staying alive. Insist that they remain cool and dignified. Do not think that you will be able to stop the terrorists. Avoid political discussions, you can only irritate with these conversations. But at the same time try to be an attentive listener. One of the hostages in Latin America was able to defeat one of his most evil captors by listening to his ordinary poems for hours. Don't give advice. If your captors follow your advice and things don't work out, only you will be to blame. Act as if you are being watched all the time. Most likely, that is exactly what will happen. Accept the lack of personal privacy and learn to live in such conditions. In addition, the kidnappers can record all your conversations and interrogations on tape to use this information against you in the future. Keep your dignity. After your freedom, dignity is the most important thing that your captors might try to take away from you. Perhaps you will be kept in the mud. Your clothes may be confiscated, and it is not unusual for the situation to be forced to walk around in your underwear. Food may also be inedible and you may be required to eat it with your fingers.

There is no reason to think that you will not be bullied or humiliated. Don't give up and don't beg them. Behave naturally, do not rush to fulfill the requirements, but do not show defiant defiance either. Eat whatever is given to you, even if the food is stale and inedible. It is very important to keep your strength, and therefore you need to eat. If you have digestive problems, drink plenty of fluids to avoid dehydration. Find the safest position in the place where you are being held. If shooting starts while trying to get free, you should quickly find a place where you can take cover from bullets. Think about it ahead of time. If there is no such cover, fall to the floor as soon as you hear gunfire or some kind of noise. Exercise regularly. Try to stay in shape as usual. Do your best to download it yourself. Isometric exercises and running in place, for example. If you are dressed in uncomfortable oversized clothing, consider jumping exercises. Pushing, squeezing, and knee bending doesn't require much space.

Fight loneliness. Ask your kidnappers for reading material. Read as much as possible to avoid the longing of loneliness. If you have read everything and nothing else, memorize the magazines and books that you have. Come up with thought games. Whatever you do, do not stop the brain, because it is at such moments that depression can seize you. Adapt to your surroundings. No matter how bad you feel, be thankful you're still alive. Never lose sight of this fact. Inform your kidnappers about health problems. If you need regular medication or have other health problems, let your kidnappers know as soon as possible. In the same way, if your health is deteriorating as a result of captivity, do not be silent about it. Keeping hostages is always a heavy burden, and keeping a healthy hostage is always easier than keeping a sick one. Moreover, a dead hostage has no value at all. Therefore, it is more likely that you will receive the necessary medicine or medical care if you need it. With a long stay in the position of a hostage. Do not allow feelings of pity, confusion, and confusion to arise. Mentally prepare yourself for future challenges. Keep mentally active. Avoid the feeling of despair, and use the internal resources of self-persuasion for this. Think and remember pleasant things. Remember that the chances of being released increase over time. Rest assured that every effort is being made to ensure your speedy release. Always find something to do. Set a daily schedule of physical and intellectual activity, and do things in a strict methodical order. behavior during interrogation. Answer questions briefly. Talk more freely and at length on unimportant general topics, but be careful when important public or personal issues are raised. Carefully monitor your behavior and responses. Do not make statements that, now or in the future, may harm you or others. Remain polite, and tactful under any circumstances. Control your mood. If you are forced to express support for the terrorists' demands (in writing, audio, or video), indicate that they come from the kidnappers. Avoid appeals and statements in your name. Gather information about your kidnappers. You will feel that you can repay them in full and thus be satisfied. Since the kidnappers will most likely hide their faces, you may hear snippets of some conversations. Try to remember their names, information about their families, higher and school education, where they come from, and their life path. Try to memorize their physical characteristics, including height, weight, conspicuous features (tattoos, scars, birthmarks), speech style, accent, or physical inconsistencies. Leave your fingerprints somewhere in the cell. Later, this may serve as proof that you were kept here. It's usually best not to try to run. It is most likely that you will not succeed, and you will be subjected to severe punishment. The chance to stay alive is given rather by your exchange or release by the authorities. Moreover, your captors have probably already evaluated all possible escape routes and did everything to prevent this. Don't try to be a hero. Think of escape only as a last resort. Only if you are sure that your captors are going to kill you, does it makes sense to try to flee. If, for example, they take off your bandage or their bandages that hide their faces, this usually means that they have decided to end you and it makes no sense for them to hide their faces anymore. Successful escapes in most cases involve a very careful thoughtful plan and preparation for it. During the storming of the building by special forces. If possible, stay away from windows, doors, and the thieves themselves, that is, in places of greater security, in case the special forces take active measures (storming the premises, sniper fire to defeat criminals, etc.). In the event of an assault on a building, it is recommended to lie face down on the floor with your hands clasped behind your head. Do not be indignant if, during the assault and capture, you may at first (before establishing your identity) be treated incorrectly, as with a probable criminal. You may be searched, handcuffed, tied up, emotionally or physically hurt, or interrogated. Be sympathetic to the fact that in such situations, such actions of the Stormers (until the final identification of all persons and the identification of true criminals) are justified. After release, do not make hasty statements until the moment when you are in complete control of yourself, restore your thoughts, and familiarize yourself with information from official and other sources.

The Needs of Terrorist Victims

Need for support. The exact nature of such support is sometimes quite obvious, and sometimes it is not, both for the victims waiting for help and the "helpers". Nevertheless, a wide range of people feels the need for some form of assistance. Emotional support is considered to be important, although other types of support are often paramount in the initial stages and should be provided immediately, both directly and indirectly.

The need for connections. During catastrophic events, relief services can meet the victims' needs for connections between the families of the survivors and the community. On the one hand, there is a group of people who are in despair that they have lost their loved ones, who could have died in a disaster. Many are trying to get to the crash site to establish contact with loved ones. On the other hand, bereaved victims need to connect with other family members and friends. Family members living abroad also seek to establish ties with loved ones.

The need for information. Information is often the most needed type of support. People living in the zone of the terrorist act, and in other regions, need objective information about the catastrophe.

First, they want to know the situation "based on facts" and turn to help services and government agencies to get it. Secondly, it is necessary information for the availability of emergency services, representatives of which people seek to find even before these services are formed and begin to function at the crash site. Thirdly, information assistance is teaching people what will happen over time. The need for medical assistance for the victims of a terrorist attack needs no special description.

Need for emergency services and support structures. Services dealing with the liquidation of the consequences of a terrorist act also have their own needs to ensure an effective response and their survival.

The need to assess the situation. With the urgent need to provide emergency assistance to the victims of a terrorist attack, the helping structures should simultaneously strive to understand and evaluate: what is happening? What will happen shortly? What will be required in a rapidly changing environment? etc. Therefore, they must plan and predict the requirements to respond to the emerging development of the situation and be ready to carry out a comprehensive multifaceted assessment of the situation. To assess their real possibilities, helping structures must determine their staff resources. Such self-assessment is also necessary for interaction with other structures.

The need for coordination and information exchange when interacting with the public. This group of needs does not need a special explanation. In the initial period of an emergency, chaos and confusion reign everywhere, and emergency services often receive mismatched and conflicting information. This fact hurts the entire subsequent process of liquidating the consequences of a terrorist act.

The need to take into account the cultural specifics of the community that survived the catastrophe. This problem requires emergency personnel working in the disaster zone to take into account ethnocultural factors when interacting with the local population. These questions concern whether they work in their cultural region or a region with different cultural traditions, where attitudes, beliefs, traditions, customs, and communication patterns differ significantly from their own.

Psychological workers must be convinced that their psychotherapeutic concepts, assessment, and treatment methods are appropriate for the ethnic groups and settings in which they will be applied.

So, the material of this topic is devoted to the consideration of the concept of "victims of terrorism", which include not only those who directly suffered as a result of a terrorist attack, their relatives, people living in the region of the event, but also employees who take measures to eliminate the consequences of terrorist activities.

The main reactions of the victims as a result of a terrorist act are considered in detail, recommendations are given that are necessary for self-defense in a hostage situation.

Questions for self-examination

1. Expand the essence of the concept of "victim of a terrorist act."
2. Describe the stages of interaction between terrorists and hostages.
3. List the psychological traits of different types of victims of terror.
4. Describe the specific psychopathological phenomena of the hostages.
5. Describe the structure of communication between terrorist hostages.
6. "Stockholm syndrome": reveal the main characteristics of the phenomenon.
7. List the main features characteristic of the released hostages.
8. List and describe the main syndromes characteristic of persons who have suffered the consequences of a terrorist act.
9. Describe rescue recommendations for people who are held, hostage.
10. List the basic needs of victims of a terrorist attack.

CONCLUSION

Modern society has to overcome a large number of various threats, among which terrorist acts occupy a special place. The fight against terrorism is an important element in ensuring the security of the entire world community. Terrorism is on the rise in the 21st century. The most large-scale terrorist acts in the history of mankind can be called the events that unfolded in the United States on September 11, 2001. The terrorists hijacked civilian planes that were used as weapons of mass destruction. The result is more than 3 thousand direct victims. The increase in the number of terrorist acts in different regions of the world over the past 15-20 years is associated with the deterioration of the socio-economic and political situation in specific countries. The explosions of residential buildings and the actions of terrorists in different places where people gather were unprecedented in their scale and cruelty.

Victimology is the science of the victim of a crime, which provides for a comprehensive study of the victim in all its manifestations. Recently, the assumption has become known that not every person can become a victim of terrorism. There is a certain mysterious predisposition, a special "sacrifice". There are cases in the world when one person was among the victims of terrorist attacks that took place at different times. For example, American lawyer Mark Sokolov. His office was located on the 38th floor of one of the US Twin Towers. At the last minute on September 11, 2001, before a plane hijacked by terrorists crashed into it, he left the tower. Then Mark Sokolov and his whole family came to Jerusalem. And on the day his family was doing their last shopping before heading to the airport and returning to the United States, there was a terrorist attack, as a result of which he and his loved ones ended up in the hospital. Another case is Shoshana Anzhel, a resident of Jerusalem, who was the victim of terrorist attacks 12 times and was wounded in all of them. The next incident occurred with the Arab M. Auatt, the baker of the Sbarro restaurant, in which the attack was carried out. The young man was wounded, and even then the doctors stated that he had a nervous breakdown. After that, he was wounded in 2 more terrorist attacks. Terror is horror. This is precisely the emotional state that the terrorists seek to create. An act of terrorism is only a means that brings real or potential victims into a state of horror. The well-known victimologist E. A. Fattakhov in the late 70s of the twentieth century drew attention to the need to form an independent direction of victimology - the victimology of terrorism. But until now, criminological science has not developed the theoretical foundations of the victimology of terrorism. The most important element of the victimology of terrorism is the victim, which, following international practice, is defined as an individual and (or) legal entity who has suffered physical, material, moral, or reputational harm by a terrorist act or terrorist activity. Victims of terrorism can be classified according to the degree of interaction between the perpetrator and the victim and according to the role of the victim in the crime committed. According to the degree of interaction between the perpetrator and the victim, there are, firstly, direct victims. These include individuals and legal entities who, as a result of a terrorist act, suffered physical, material, moral or reputational harm, or their constitutional rights and freedoms are violated. Secondly, these are indirect victims, that is, persons who are not personally harmed, but suffer indirectly, as well as international and state institutions, political parties, public associations, and political or public figures associated with the implementation of the functions of state power.

Demonstration of violence creates in him a feeling of fear and insecurity. Another equally common basis for the victimological classification of victims is their role in the commission of the crime. These include victims with neutral, complicit (positive), wrongful (provoking), and lawful behavior. The first category includes persons who become victims as a result of a random combination of circumstances. For example, when hostages were taken by terrorists and demanded by state authorities their release, as was the case in Beslan (North Ossetia, Russian Federation) in September 2004, when terrorists held 1,128 hostages in the school gym, 334 people died as a result of the terrorist attack, which 186 were children, over 800 wounded; terrorist acts in crowded places (markets, shops, concert halls).

Within this category, individual citizens and groups of individuals are distinguished, united according to various random characteristics of criminals (airplane passengers, students of the same class, employees of the same institution). For example, the A321 crash occurred on October 31, 2015, over the Sinai Peninsula. As a result of a bomb planted in the plane, an Airbus A321 crashed. All 217 passengers and 7 crew members died. The second category of victims of terrorism includes those persons who sympathize with criminals, provide them with asylum or hide them on their territory, or assist in their illegal activities. The third group consists of persons who provoke criminal behavior in various ways, from direct incitement of perpetrators to refusing to apply victimological security measures to them. The fourth category is persons who are harmed in connection with the performance of their official or public duty. In addition, victimologists identify a group of "impatient" victims. Usually, they include no more than 0.5% of all hostages. But this figure may increase if the "impatient" push the "hysterical" people with their recklessness. As a rule, hysterical women in critical situations cry, and rush about with screams and sobs. Hysteroid men become aggressive and respond with anger to any pressure.

The next group of hostages is people who are unyielding in the face of adversity, reasonable and cautious people. Stress pressure strengthens their resilience. Such persons provide moral support to others. There may be 5-12% of them among the hostages. "Persistent" help to survive the imprisonment of other unfortunates. The rest of the hostages, longer their imprisonment lasts, the closer they become to the terrorists who captured them. Among them are the "obsequious" who approach the criminals to somehow reduce the threat of terror. And sympathizers. For such persons, the longer the traumatic situation lasts, the stronger they feel a family connection with the terrorists who captured them. This psychological reaction is called "Stockholm Syndrome". This concept appeared as a result of studying the psycho-emotional transformations that were observed in persons taken hostage during a failed bank robbery in 1974 in the city of Stockholm. 3 women and 1 man were taken hostage by 2 terrorists who threatened to kill them, but at the same time showed them a kind attitude. Usually, the victims of terrorist acts are innocent civilians. When taking hostages, terrorists are interested not so much in the identity of the victims as in the possibility of using violence against them as a means of pressure on the addressee. During a terrorist act, during the period of exposure to an extraordinary psycho-traumatic factor, a person becomes so scared that he begins to experience horror and a sense of hopelessness. Emotions prevail over the mind, which leads to an effective narrowing of consciousness and, as a result, to inadequate actions. As a result of terrorist attacks, children are the most victimized, since their psychological reactions to a terrorist situation are similar to the reactions of those who have experienced the impact of a military situation. So, for example, about 20% of the children hostages of the Nord-Ost had a lower academic performance after the terrorist attack, although before it they studied more or less satisfactorily. The scientist N. Pukhovsky conducted a study of the hostages, who in 1995 were captured and held by terrorists for 5 days in the maternity hospital of the city of Budennovsk. In the first days after the attack, an atmosphere of confusion and fear reigned in the city, which quickly changed to a dual, internally contradictory atmosphere of powerless susceptibility to someone else's will, the expectation of harm and damage, on the one hand, and offended dignity, alertness and heightened readiness to repel the threat, - with another (Chitadze, 2016). The local population showed a wide prevalence of sleep disorders (insomnia), and complaints of poor health. People worried about the rising guilt in the form of self-reproach for the feeling of joy and relief that they were not in the place of the hostages. The state of the newly released hostages was determined by the residual effects of the acute affective-shock reactions they experienced. They showed a mass unwillingness to remember what they had experienced. They wanted to get home as soon as possible, take a bath, go to bed, and forget everything, returning to their normal lives. After a certain time after the terrorist attack, its victims retain psychopathological symptoms, which manifest themselves in the form of delayed fear, as well as various kinds of phobias and regular nightmares. Thus, the victimology of terrorism, as a private victimological theory, should study the victims of terrorism, terrorist victimization, victimological factors of terrorism, develop mechanisms and technologies for victimological prevention of potential terrorist attacks, and victimological rehabilitation of real victims of terrorism.

REFERENCES

Chitadze, N. (2011). *Geopolitics*. Universal.

Chitadze, N. (2016). *Political Sciences*. International Black Sea University.

Lynch, O., & Argomaniz, J. (2018). Victims and Perpetrators of Terrorism Exploring Identities, Roles, and Narratives. Routledge.

Turkovic, K. (2018). What Victimology has to Offer in the Fight Against Terrorism. *NATO Security through Science Series - E: Human and Societal Dynamics. Volume 13: Large-Scale Victimisation as a Potential Source of Terrorist Activities.*

UN Office on Drugs and Crime. (2022). *Victims of terrorism*. Retrieved from: https://www.unodc.org/unodc/en/terrorism/expertise/victims-of-terrorism.html

KEY TERMS AND DEFINITIONS

Terrorism: Is the calculated use of violence to create a general climate of fear in a population and thereby bring about a particular political objective. Terrorism has been practiced by political organizations with both rightist and leftist objectives, by nationalistic and religious groups, by revolutionaries, and even by state institutions such as armies, intelligence services, and police.

Victims of Terrorism: Most victims of terrorism are innocent citizens who find themselves at the wrong place and at the wrong time, randomly targeted in brutal attacks. The lives of survivors of attacks, and those of victims' families, are irreparably damaged. Many survivors take years to recover physically from their injuries or come to terms with their losses, and many remain deeply traumatized. While states take terrorism very seriously as a security threat, they do not necessarily always ensure adequate support to victims and their families. Victims of terrorism and their families need focused and dedicated mechanisms to ensure that their rights as individuals are upheld and protected.

Chapter 8
State Terrorism and Its Impact on the Global Processes

Valeria Gonitashvili
Ukrainian Youth Organization of Georgia, Georgia

ABSTRACT

The complexity and versatility of modern international relations, the struggle for energy resources, the division of spheres of influence between main geopolitical actors, the presence of problems of the global nature – all these factors greatly complicate the interaction of states in the international arena. Such difficulties give rise to many geopolitical strategies and tactics designed to protect the national interests of a particular state. And one such strategy may be state terrorism. First of all, it must be stated that the concept state terrorism has two aspects: internal political and foreign policy. Under state terrorism, internal political phenomenon is understood as the actions of state bodies' law and order against their own people. Often the state uses for this non-state terrorist structures. It is necessary to note that in world history, domestic terror is not a single occurrence. Most often it has manifested itself in totalitarian societies.

INTRODUCTION

State terrorism is a term used to refer to state violence against civilians. Acts of state terrorism are usually understood as unlawful detentions, murders, abductions, torture, and execution of citizens without trial or investigation, carried out by law enforcement officers (police and other law enforcement agencies). State terrorism is also called terrorist acts committed by employees of special state bodies. State-supported terrorism is also distinguished - the case when the state, without itself participating in terrorism, finances and supports terrorist groups (Aust, 2010).

State support for terrorism is state support for non-state armed groups engaged in terrorism. Because of the varying definitions of terrorism, the list of specific examples is the subject of political debate.

DOI: 10.4018/978-1-6684-5311-7.ch008

Definition

One possible definition is the US State Department's list of State Sponsors of Terrorism. The composition of the list is determined by three US laws: the Export Administration Act of 1979, the Arms Export Control Act, and the Foreign Assistance Act. According to these laws, there are four types of sanctions imposed on the countries included in the list: restrictions on US foreign aid, a ban on the export and sale of defense products, certain controls on the export of dual-use items, and various financial and other restrictions. At the beginning of 2021, there are four countries on the list: North Korea, Iran, Sudan, and Syria (Williamson, 2009).

Geneva Declaration on Terrorism

The Geneva Conference on Terrorism in 1987 adopted the Declaration "The Geneva Declaration on Terrorism", which defines the following phenomena as state terrorism:

- Police state practices against its citizens: surveillance, dispersal of meetings, news control (media), beatings, torture, false arrests, mass arrests, false charges, show trials, and murders.
- Delivery by a state of weapons of mass destruction to the territory of other states, to their territorial waters, or international waters.
- Military maneuvers and exercises carried out near the borders of another state and posing a threat to its independence and territorial integrity.
- An attack by the armed forces of a state on targets that poses a threat to the civilian population living in another state.
- Creation and support of armed groups of mercenaries to destroy the sovereignty of another state.
- Assassinations and attempted assassinations of statesmen of other states or national liberation movements, directed by the state, whether carried out by military strike, special operations, or hiring agents.
- Covert operations by intelligence or other state forces aimed at destabilizing or subjugating another state, a national liberation movement, or an international peace movement.
- disinformation campaigns aimed at destabilizing other states.
- Arms sales that support the continuation of regional wars and delay the political resolution of conflicts.
- Cancellation of civil rights and freedoms, provisions of the constitution, and laws under the pretext of countering terrorism.
- The development, testing, and deployment of nuclear and space weapons increase the likelihood of genocide and ecocide, dooming the poor to continued poverty and all of humanity to constant fear (Nairn, 2005).

SUPPORT TYPES OF STATE TERRORISM

Ideological Support

Ideological support for terrorism is a tactic in which a terrorist organization is used to spread the ideology of the state. Examples of countries that have used this tactic include the Soviet Union and Iran.

The terrorist organizations founded by these two countries contributed to the spread of the ideology of communism and Islamic fundamentalism in different countries. These organizations include Hezbollah and the Palestinian Islamic Jihad. In particular, the "Palestinian Islamic Jihad" enlisted the support of Iran, adopting its ideology in exchange for material assistance. Such organizations receive ideological support from the sponsoring state in various forms: political, religious, or ideological.

Financing of Terrorism

Terrorist financing is the provision of funds or the provision of financial support to terrorists. Most countries have introduced anti-terrorist financing measures often as part of their money-laundering laws. Some countries and multinational organizations have created a list of organizations that they consider terrorists, although there is no consensus on this. The Financial Action Task Force on Money Laundering (FATF) has prepared recommendations for members on countering the financing of terrorism. She created black and gray lists of countries that did not take adequate action in the framework of combating the financing of terrorism. As of October 24, 2019, only two countries, North Korea and Iran are listed on the FATF blacklist (countries calling for action); while the FATF (Other Controlled Jurisdictions) Greylist includes 12 countries: Pakistan, Bahamas, Botswana, Cambodia, Ghana, Iceland, Mongolia, Panama, Syria, Trinidad and Tobago, Yemen and Zimbabwe (Schmid, 2011).

Initial efforts to combat terrorist financing focused on non-profit organizations, unregistered companies providing money services (including so-called underground banking or "hawala"), and criminalizing the act itself.

Methods Used to Finance Terrorism

Several countries and multinational organizations form lists of organizations that they classify as a terrorist, although there is no consensus on which organizations to classify there. In the United States, the Office of Foreign Assets Control of the Department of the Treasury maintains a list of states that the organization believes are associated with terrorists. Financial transactions carried out in the interests of these terrorist organizations are usually prohibited.

Organizations designated as terrorists undertake various strategies to avoid having their funding restricted. For example, they may make multiple money transfers instead of just one, splitting the payment into small amounts to bypass controls, or they may use people with no criminal record to make financial transactions to make transfers more difficult to trace. These transactions can also be disguised as charitable donations or as gifts to family members. Not all countries are in a position to fight terrorism, as corporate entities need to independently verify financial transactions.

If corporate entities are not subordinate to the state, fines or regulatory sanctions may be applied to them.

Terrorists and terrorist organizations often use any source of money they can access to fund them. The sources can vary from the distribution of drugs and oil on the black market to the opening of organizations such as car dealerships, taxi companies, etc. It is known that ISIS uses the distribution of oil on the black market as a means of financing its terrorist activities.

The Internet is a growing modern form of terrorist financing because it can preserve the anonymity of the funder and the funded. Terrorist organizations use propaganda to get financial support from their supporters. They may also raise funds through online criminal activity, such as stealing online banking information from people who are not affiliated with these terrorist organizations. Terrorist organizations also use philanthropic funds to finance themselves. It is known that Al-Qaeda used the Internet to finance their organization since thanks to this platform they can reach a wider audience (Gvimradze, 2014).

Money Laundering

Terrorist financing and money laundering, often linked in law and regulation, are conceptual opposites. Money laundering is the process by which money derived from criminal activity is made legal for reintegration into the financial system, while for terrorist financing the source of the funds is not as important as what the funds will be used for.

The forensic literature has published a detailed study of the symbiotic relationship between organized crime and terrorist organizations found in the United States and other countries, which are called links between crime and terror. The article by Perry, Lichtenwald, and McKenzie highlights the importance of interagency working groups and tools that can be used to identify, infiltrate and eliminate organizations operating at the intersection of crime and terrorism.

Mass smuggling and placement of money through cash-intensive businesses is one typology. Now they are also moving money through new online payment systems. They also use trade-related schemes to launder money. However, the old systems are still relevant. Terrorists also continue to move money through MSB / Hawala and international transactions through ATMs. Charitable organizations also continue to be used in countries where controls are not so strict.

Said and Sheriff Kouachi used money laundering to fund their activities before they orchestrated the Charlie Hebdo terrorist attack in 2015. Examples were the resale of counterfeit goods and drugs.

"This funding chain demonstrates a clear correlation between transaction laundering and terrorism, using legitimate marketplaces to conduct illegal activities (in this case, selling counterfeit shoes) and then using the proceeds to launder money for terrorists" (Blakeley, 2009).

Prevention of Terrorist Financing

In the financial world, there is a non-governmental international organization AML CFT (English AML CFT CWMDF - anti-money laundering and counter-terrorist financing and counter-weapons of mass destruction financing - countering money laundering, countering the financing of terrorism and financing the creation of weapons of mass destruction) and the principle of KYC - (Know Your Customer or Know Your Client - "Know your client") applies. Financial transactions require organizations that perform them to identify an individual or company and respect the legality of transactions. However, this methodology is frowned upon by banks, lawyers, or other offshore professionals, because business and client relationships may suffer in the identification process. This can damage the relationship between long-term clients who need to verify their identity and respected members of the public who do not want to be asked for personal identification every time. In countries where there are legal restrictions on the conduct of financial activities and state control over business entities, the implementation of the KYC principle is usually provided for in contracts (Blakeley, 2009).

Suspicious Activity

Operation Green Quest, a U.S. multi-agency task force created in October 2001 with the official goal of countering terrorist financing, considers the following activities as indicators of the collection and movement of funds that may be related to terrorist financing:

- Account transactions that do not match past deposits or withdrawals, such as cash, checks, wire transfers, etc.
- Transactions involving a large volume of incoming or outgoing wire transfers, without any logical or explicit purpose, that pass through the countries of concern.
- Unexplained clearing or reconciliation of third-party checks and their deposits in foreign bank accounts.
- Structuring in several branches or one branch with several activities.
- Corporate level, transfers between bank accounts of related individuals or charitable organizations for no apparent reason.
- Remittances from charitable organizations to companies located in countries known to be banking or tax-havens.
- No obvious fundraising activity, such as no small checks or typical donations associated with charitable bank deposits.
- Using multiple accounts to raise funds, which are then transferred to the same foreign beneficiaries.
- Transactions without a logical economic purpose, that is, without a link between the entity's activities and other parties involved in the transaction.
- Overlapping corporate officers, bank signatories, or other identifiable similarities related to addresses, references, and financial activities.
- Cash debit schemes where US deposits are directly linked to ATM withdrawals in countries of concern. Reverse transactions of this kind are also suspicious.
- The issuance of checks, money orders, or other financial instruments, often numbered consecutively, to the same person or business, or a person or business with a similar name.

From such activity alone, it would be difficult to determine whether a particular act is linked to terrorism or organized crime. For this reason, these activities must be considered together with other factors to determine the link to terrorist financing. Simple transactions can be considered suspicious, and money laundering from terrorism usually involves cases where simple transactions (retail foreign exchange transactions, international funds transfers) reveal ties to other countries, including countries on the FATF black list. Some of the clients may have police records, especially for drug and arms dealing, and may be associated with foreign terrorist groups. Funds may move through "state sponsors of terrorism" or a country where there is a terrorism problem. The association with a politically exposed person may ultimately be linked to a terrorist financing transaction. Charity can be one of the links in the transaction. Accounts (particularly student accounts) that receive only periodic deposits, and ATM withdrawals for two months and are idle during other periods may indicate that there are active preparations for a terrorist attack (Lind, 2009).

FEATURES IN DIFFERENT COUNTRIES RELATED TO MONEY LAUNDERING

Pakistan

As of October 24, 2019, Pakistan was on the FATF Terrorist Financing Greylist and only complied with 5 out of 27 action items. He was given four months to complete the remaining items of action to prevent the financing of terrorism (US Department of State, 2022).

Bahrain

Bahrain is regularly accused of taking very little action to prevent the flow of funds for terrorist financing in other countries. Bahrain recognizes the Muslim Brotherhood-affiliated Minbar as a legitimate political player.

Qatar

Qatar cooperates with the militants by funding the US-recognized terrorist organization Hamas and allowing several Taliban units to maintain their Qatari offices.

Saudi Arabia

Saudi Arabia is regularly accused of doing very little to prevent the flow of funds to finance terrorism in other countries. Saudi Arabia cooperates with the Yemeni al-Islah party, affiliated with the Muslim Brotherhood.

Saudi Arabia seeks to join the FATF to have easy access to global financial markets. However, a recent FATF report highlighted serious shortcomings in Saudi Arabia's efforts to combat terrorism. Terrorist financing emerging in Saudi Arabia has become an important source of funding for Al-Qaeda and other terrorist organizations.

In a leaked secret memo, Hillary Clinton said that in 2009 the kingdom was a critical source of funds for Sunni terrorist groups, including al-Qaeda, the Taliban, and the Lashkar Taiba.

In 2019, the European Commission added Saudi Arabia, along with several other countries, to its blacklist of states that have failed to control money laundering and terrorist financing. Saudi Arabia has been accused of failing to attempt to control the huge amounts of money being transferred to Islamist extremists and terrorist groups (US Department of State, 2022).

United Arab Emirates

The United Arab Emirates was accused of being a financial hub for terrorist organizations. The UAE banking system was found to be involved in the September 11, 2001 attacks against the United States by al-Qaeda. The 9/11 terrorists had bank accounts in the UAE. The attack cost the terrorist group about $400,000-500,000, of which $300,000 was transferred through one of the hijackers' bank accounts in the United States. The movement of funds was carried out using both state-owned banking systems, and al-Qaeda-created hawala networks (US Department of State, 2022).

According to the 9/11 Commission Report, in response to concerns that the UAE's banking system was being used by 9/11 hijackers to launder funds, the UAE passed a law granting the Central Bank in 2002 the power to freeze suspicious accounts for 7 days without prior legal clearance. The report states that "banks have been advised to closely monitor transactions passing through the UAE from Saudi Arabia and Pakistan and are now subject to stricter transaction and customer reporting requirements." The UAE government has since reaffirmed its stance and policy of zero tolerance for terrorist financing (Permanent Mission of the United Arab Emirates to the United Nations, 2017).

Australia

Australian counterterrorism finance laws include:

- Criminal Code Act 1995:
    - section 102.6 (receiving funds from or from a terrorist organization);
    - section 102.7 (providing support to a terrorist organization);
    - section 103.1 (financing of terrorism);
    - section 103.2 (terrorist financing);
    - section 119.4(5) (providing or receiving goods and services to facilitate the commission of a foreign invasion offense).
- Charter of the UN Act of 1945:
    - section 20 (concerning frozen assets);
    - section 21 (transfer of an asset to a prohibited person or entity) (Aleksidze, 2018).

These offenses are punishable by individuals and entities under Australian and international law. The responsibility for prosecuting these crimes in Australia lies with the Australian Federal Police, the State Police, and the Director of the Commonwealth Attorney's Office.

Germany

In July 2010, Germany banned the International Humanitarian Organization (IHH), saying it used donations to support projects in Gaza linked to Hamas, which the European Union considers a terrorist organization.

According to research conducted by the Abba Eban Institute as part of an initiative called the Janus Initiative, Hezbollah is funded through non-profit organizations such as the Lebanese Orphans Project, a German charity for Lebanese orphans. It turned out that she donated part of her donations to a foundation that finances the families of Hezbollah members who committed suicide attacks. The European Endowment for Democracy has released information that the Lebanese Orphan Project is directing financial donations from Germany to the Al-Shahid Association of Lebanese, which is part of the Hezbollah network and promotes suicide bombings in Lebanon, especially among children. In Germany, financial donations to the Lebanon Orphan Project are tax-free and are thus subsidized by the tax policy of the German state.

In 2018, a US Drug Enforcement Administration investigation called "Operation Cedar" led to the arrest of Hezbollah operatives involved in laundering millions of euros of South American drugs destined for Europe and Lebanon. One of the militants arrested was Hassan Tarabolsi, a German national who runs a money laundering business around the world. Tarabolsi represents a close link between the criminal operation and Hezbollah leaders (Laqueur, 2007).

India

In India, a campaign is underway to link the IMF's macroprudential regulation and lending policy to the FATF's key anti-money laundering and counter-terrorist financing provisions to significantly increase IMF member countries' compliance with these issues that threaten the global economy. India is also seeking to link this IMF policy to secrecy jurisdictions, cyber risks, and tax havens.

Spain

In February 2019, the Spanish Treasury, through the Commission for the Prevention of Money Laundering and Monetary Crimes (SEPBLAC), published its strategy for the prevention of terrorist financing.

Great Britain

The British Prevention of Terrorism Act was passed in 1989. This was done largely to help close funding for the Republican paramilitaries in Northern Ireland. Sources of income for the republic's paramilitaries were slot machines, taxi companies, charitable donations, and other funding (Aleksidze, 2018).

Supranational Organizations

European Union

The European Union has taken several measures to combat money laundering and terrorist financing. These include the preparation of reports and the implementation of recommendations: a report on the assessment of supranational risks, a report on publicly known cases of combating money laundering involving EU banks, a report of the financial intelligence unit, the interconnection of registers of accounts of the Central Bank.

UN

UN Article 2.1 of the 1999 Financing of Terrorism Convention defines the offense of terrorist financing as an offense committed by "any person" who "by any means, directly or indirectly, unlawfully and knowingly, provides or collects funds with the intent that they were used, or in the knowledge that they will be used, in whole or in part, to commit" to "cause the death of any civilian or any other person not taking an active part in hostilities in a situation of armed conflict, or inflict serious bodily harm, when the purpose of such an act, by its nature or context, is to intimidate a population or to compel a government or an international organization to do or refrain from doing any act". The UN Security Council adopted Resolution 1373 after the September 11 attacks. This meant that states were not allowed to provide funding to terrorist organizations, provide them with safe havens, and that information about terrorist groups had to be shared with other governments. A committee was formed in the UN that was responsible for collecting a list of organizations and people who were associated with terrorism or suspected of terrorism, whose financial accounts were to be frozen, and that no financial institution would be able to trade with them (Aleksidze, 2018).

MAIN CONCEPT OF THE POLICE STATE

A police state is a figurative expression used for a social system in which the government strictly (including through repression) seeks to control the social, economic, and political life of citizens.

In a police state, the legislative and executive powers are loosely separated; such a state often has signs of a dictatorship.

The signs of police states are controversial; states themselves do not call themselves that. Usually, the term "police state" is used by internal and external opponents of the existing regime.

History of the Origin of the Term

German term. Polizeistaat was actively used in the German language already at the end of the 18th - beginning of the 19th centuries as an image of strict administrative control, especially regarding religion. At that time, the meaning of the word Polizei differed from the modern one and denoted administrative power in general, while the word Polizeistaat evoked images of the absolute monarchs of the past and was opposed to the rule of law in a constitutional state (Rechtsstaat) proposed by Kant.

Features of a Police State

The hallmarks of a police state are:

- there is no separation of powers;
- there is no top-down structuring of the law (the main law is not the Constitution, but, most often, oral orders and instructions from a local authority representative);
- in the event of a conflict between a citizen and a police representative, in practice the point of view of the latter is prevailing;
- the police have much more rights about the citizen than duties;
- police officers at all levels are appointed from above and answer only to those who appointed them and those who provide the maximum material benefits;
- any actions and demands of a police officer are considered lawful, except those whose criminality, firstly, is obvious, secondly, has attracted public attention, and thirdly, public outrage over which may lead to political consequences.

Possible Examples of Police States

Some critics believe that Russia, since 2000, has been a police state or is rapidly becoming one. For example, already in 2004, prominent Russian sociologists Lev Gudkov and Boris Dubin considered the "seemingly limited capacity or inefficiency of the police, courts, and law enforcement agencies" to be a sign of a "new social state — the emergence of a police state", which they saw, contrary to the government's point of view, not "temporary difficulties", but "a system of bureaucratic-police arbitrariness". Subsequently, Russia was characterized as a police state not only by representatives of the Russian opposition but also by several MEPs, Western media, including Newsweek and the Washington Post, as well as Russian journalists. The reason for this was the virtually uncontrolled, according to critics, the position of law enforcement agencies (the police and the FSB) in the system of the Russian government, the lack of an independent judiciary, as well as several specific measures, laws, and bills that expand the rights and powers of law enforcement agencies at the expense of the rights of citizens (Aleksidze, 2018).

The Image of the Police State in Culture

The country of unknown fathers in the novel "Inhabited Island" was a state in which several anonymous rulers manipulated the public consciousness of the majority of citizens with the help of special towers. The radiation from the towers did not manipulate the consciousness of the so-called "geeks", which were all the unknown fathers (the fiery creators in the censored version) and some of the few citizens who resisted these rulers. However, when the towers were turned on, the geeks experienced a terrible headache. The towers did not affect earthlings. The inhabitants of the planet Suraksha, on which the novel takes place, though they lived on the inner surface of the sphere, and not the outer.

Yevgeny Zamyatin's dystopian novel "We," tells about a society that is under the total control of the state. People live in houses with glass walls, which allow you to control even intimate life, names and surnames are replaced by numbers, and the only way to get information is through a censored government newspaper.

The theme of the police, the totalitarian state was also the main one in the famous works of Sinclair Lewis "It's impossible for us", Alan Moore's "V for Vendetta" (and the film of the same name).

States - Sponsors of Terrorism (US List)

"State Sponsors of Terrorism" is a list of states that, according to the official position of the US State Department, have repeatedly supported acts of international terrorism.

Inclusion on the list entails severe economic and political sanctions from the United States.

The compilation of the list began on December 29, 1979. It included Libya, Iraq, South Yemen, and Syria. Then Cuba, Iran, and North Korea were added (US Department of State, 2022).

Countries on the List

Cuba

Cuba was included in the list of state sponsors of terrorism on March 1, 1982. According to a 2012 US State Department report, Cuba continued to provide asylum to about 2 dozen members of the Basque terrorist group ETA, providing haven and safe movement for members of the Revolutionary Armed Forces of Colombia (FARC) and persons wanted by the United States. At the same time, the US State Department noted in 2013 that "there are no signs that the Cuban authorities provided weapons or provided military training to terrorist groups." The report states that Cuba is a sponsor of the peace talks between the FARC and the Colombian government and has distanced itself from the Basques. The State Department accuses Cuba of harboring and assisting fugitives from US justice. Cuba does not deny this but claims that these people are not connected with terrorism.

On April 15, 2015, Barack Obama proposed to exclude Cuba from this list and sent the proposal to Congress. On May 29, Cuba left the list of state sponsors of terrorism.

On January 12, 2021, in the last days of Donald Trump's presidency, the US State Department relisted Cuba (US Department of State, 2022).

Iran

Iran was included by the US State Department in the list of state sponsors of terrorism on January 19, 1984. According to a 2012 report, Iran continues to increase terrorist activity. According to the American side, he provides financial, material, and logistical support to terrorist militant groups in the Middle East and Central Asia. The Islamic Revolutionary Guard Corps is called the main body and mechanism for supporting terrorists. In 2012, Iran was suspected by the United States of preparing terrorist attacks in India, Thailand, Georgia, and Kenya.

Iran is being blamed for its extensive support of the Syrian government, including with weapons, in the context of the Syrian conflict. Iran provides weapons, training, and funding to Hamas and other Palestinian terrorist groups. After 2006, Iran assisted in the rearmament of Hezbollah, bypassing the direct ban of the UN Security Council (UN Security Council Resolution No. 1701). The State Department believes that Iran supported terrorists in Yemen and provided assistance to al-Qaeda (US Department of State, 2022).

Syria

Syria was included in the list of state sponsors of terrorism on December 29, 1979 (US Department of State, 2022). According to a 2012 US State Department report, despite the internal conflict, Syria continues to support international terrorism and, in particular, the Lebanese Hezbollah and Palestinian terrorist groups. Syria also plays a significant role in illegal terrorist financing schemes (US Department of State, 2022).

Democratic People's Republic of Korea

The DPRK was listed in 1988 and delisted on 11 October 2008. The United States removed the DPRK from the list after an agreement that IAEA experts would be allowed to visit all of North Korea's nuclear facilities declared by the agency.

On November 20, 2017, the DPRK was again included in the list of sponsors of terrorism (US Department of State, 2022).

Countries that have been excluded

Iraq

Iraq was added to the list on December 29, 1979, and removed in 1989 to allow US companies to supply arms to Iraq during the Iran-Iraq War; Iraq was added back to the list due to Iraq's invasion of Kuwait. The US State Department explained the reason for inclusion in the list by the fact that Iraq provided bases for the Organization of the Mujahideen of the Iranian People, the PKK, the Palestinian Liberation Front, and the Abu Nidal Organization. Iraq was again excluded from the list as a result of the invasion of the coalition forces into Iraq and the defeat of the government of Saddam Hussein. Subsequently, US sanctions on Iraq were suspended on May 7, 2003, and US President George W. Bush announced Iraq's delisting on September 25, 2004 (US Department of State, 2022).

Libya

Libya was listed on 29 December 1979 and delisted in 2006 (Aleksidze, 2018).

People's Democratic Republic of Yemen

The NDRY was listed on 29 December 1979 and delisted in May 1990 as it ceased to exist (Aleksidze, 2018).

Sudan

Sudan was included in the list of state sponsors of terrorism on August 12, 1993. Despite some efforts by the government in the fight against terrorism and cooperation with the United States, several terrorist groups continue to operate on the territory of Sudan and carry out terrorist attacks both in Sudan itself and in neighboring countries. Sudan cooperates with Iran, is included in the list of state sponsors of terrorism, and supports the Palestinian terrorist group Hamas. There are suspicions about the involvement of the Sudanese authorities in the escape from the prison of terrorists responsible for the murder of two American diplomats.

The United States began the process of removing Sudan from the list of state sponsors of terrorism after Sudan transferred $ 335 million in compensation to the families of victims of terrorist attacks in the United States. On December 14, 2020, the US officially removed Sudan from the list (US Department of State, 2022).

Countries Discussed for Inclusion

Russia

On April 19, 2018, Republican Senator Corey Gardner, in connection with the Skripal case, planned to pass a law that obliges the Secretary of State to determine whether Russia meets the criteria for recognizing a state as a sponsor of terrorism. In July 2020, Democratic Congressman Max Rose[en] introduced a similar bill in connection with a publication in The New York Times, which alleged that the Russian Federation paid Taliban fighters money for attacks on the US military in Afghanistan. After the poisoning of Alexei Navalny, as well as because Russia supported the DPR and LPR, new demands were voiced to recognize Russia as a sponsor of terrorism. On December 16, 2021, according to a release published on the website of the United States Senate Committee on Foreign Relations, Republican Senator Jim Rish proposed declaring Russia a state sponsor of terrorism. In March 2022, in connection with the full-scale invasion of the Russian Armed Forces into the territory of Ukraine, President of Ukraine Volodymyr Zelensky asked Joe Biden to add Russia to the list of sponsors of terrorism.

In May 2022, Democratic Senator Richard Blumenthal, together with Republican Senator Lindsey Graham, registered a resolution appealing to the Joe Biden administration to recognize Russia as a state sponsor of terrorism (Reuters, 2022).

Venezuela

On November 20, 2018, the Donald Trump administration intended to declare Venezuela a sponsor of terrorism (US Department of State, 2019).

STATE TERRORISM ON THE EXAMPLE OF RED TERROR IN SOVIET RUSSIA AND THE USSR

The Red Terror is a set of punitive measures carried out by the Bolsheviks during the Civil War in Russia (1917-1923) against social groups proclaimed class enemies, as well as against persons accused of counter-revolutionary activities. It served as a deterrent for both anti-Bolshevik forces and the population that did not take part in the Civil War. Terror and violence were widely used by the Bolsheviks against class enemies earlier, even before the official proclamation of the decree of September 5, 1918 "On the Red Terror" (Llewellyn, 2019).

F. E. Dzerzhinsky, one of the ideologists and leaders of this policy, defined the concept of "red terror" as "intimidation, arrests, and destruction of the enemies of the revolution based on their class affiliation" (Jennifer, 2019).

Currently, the term "red terror" has two definitions:

- For some historians, the concept of red terror includes the entire repressive policy of the Soviet government, starting with the lynching of October 1917, and is defined as a logical continuation of the October Revolution; the red terror began earlier than the white terror and was inevitable, since the Bolshevik violence, justified by Marxism as the dictatorship of the proletariat, was directed not against the current resistance, but against the outlawed sections of society: nobles, landowners, officers, priests, kulaks, Cossacks, scientists, industrialists and the like.
- Another part of the historians characterizes the Red Terror as an extreme and forced, defensive and retaliatory measure, as a reaction against the White Terror and international intervention, and considers the beginning of the Red Terror to be the decision of the Council of People's Commissars of the RSFSR of September 5, 1918 "On the Red Terror" (McConnell, 2019).

The Rationale for the Red Terror

K. Marx in November 1848, in a newspaper article about the bloody defeat of the uprising in Vienna as part of the Austrian revolution of 1848-1849, wrote: that there are only one means to reduce, simplify and concentrate the bloodthirsty agony of the old society and the bloody birth pangs of the new society, only one means - revolutionary terrorism " without revealing the essence of this type of terrorism and without further development of this topic.

The Chairman of the Council of People's Commissars of the RSFSR, V. I. Lenin, proposed a method of carrying out terror, declaring morality a "deceit", emphasizing that everything useful to the revolution is moral (Felshtinsky, 2013).

Lenin and the leadership of the Communist Party opposed humanity in response to the actions of the counter-revolutionaries, encouraging mass terror, called "the completely correct revolutionary initiative of the masses", which the Bolshevik leader writes in his letter to G. Zinoviev on June 26, 1918:

Only today we heard in the Central Committee that the workers in St. Petersburg wanted to respond to the assassination of Volodarsky with mass terror and that you ... withheld. I object strongly! We compromise ourselves: even in the resolutions of the Soviet of Deputies we threaten with mass terror, and when it comes down to it, we slow down the revolutionary initiative of the masses, which is quite correct. It's impossible! The terrorists will consider us rags. Archival time. We must encourage the energy and mass character of terror against the counter-revolutionaries (Felshtinsky, 2013).

However, at the same time, in several statements by the Bolsheviks, the need to avoid "unfair, cruel and unmotivated sentences" was noted. In an interview published in the newspaper "Izvestia of the All-Russian Central Executive Committee", the first Chairman of the Revolutionary Military Tribunal of the RSFSR, K. Danishevsky, said the following:

... no matter how merciless each verdict is, it must necessarily be based on a sense of solidary justice, it must awaken this feeling. Given the enormous complexity of the tasks of the military tribunals, their leaders also bear an enormous responsibility. Sentences unfair, cruel, and unmotivated should not take place. In this regard, the leaders of the military tribunals must exercise particular caution.

But at the same time, this interview contains a rather widely known formulation, first voiced by him, about the direction of the activities of the punitive organs of revolutionary power. He stated:

Military tribunals are not and should not be governed by any legal rule. These are punishing organs created in the course of the most intense revolutionary struggle (Felshtinsky, 2013).

At the Fifth All-Russian Congress of Soviets, Ya. M. Sverdlov spoke with a report to the Congress on the activities of the All-Russian Central Executive Committee on July 5, 1918. In the conditions of the deepening crisis of the Bolshevik power, he openly called in the said speech for "mass terror", which must be carried out against the "counter-revolution" as well as "enemies of the Soviet power" and expressed confidence that "the whole of working Russia will react with full approval to such least as the execution of counter-revolutionary generals and other enemies of the working people. Congress officially approved this doctrine (McConnell, 2019).

In September 1919, in his article "How the Bourgeoisie Uses Renegades", V. I. Lenin criticized K. Kautsky's book "Terrorism and Communism", clarifying his point of view on terror in general and on revolutionary violence in particular. In response to the accusation that before the revolution the Bolsheviks were against the use of the death penalty, and when they seized power they used mass executions, Lenin declared that:

Firstly, it is a direct lie that the Bolsheviks were opponents of the death penalty for the era of the revolution ... Not a single revolutionary government can do without the death penalty, and the whole question is only what class the death penalty is directed against by this government.

Such intransigence was not the result of white terror during the civil war, because back in September 1917, in his work "The Threatening Catastrophe and How to Fight It", Lenin said that:

... without the death penalty for the exploiters (that is, the landowners and capitalists), any revolutionary government can hardly manage (Felshtinsky, 2013).

Soon after seizing power in Russia's large cities, the Bolsheviks began to carry out Marxist economic reforms, which amounted to the confiscation of the property available to the population and the mobilization of human resources to build socialism as soon as possible. In his article "How to organize a competition?" (December 1917 - January 1918). Lenin speaks of the need to apply harsh measures about elements that are class alien to the proletariat, which, according to Lenin, needed various forms of re-education:

In one place, a dozen rich people, a dozen crooks, and half a dozen workers who shirk work will be put in prison ... In another, they will be put in jail to clean the toilets. In the third, they will provide them, after the departure of the punishment cell, with yellow tickets, so that all the people, until they are corrected, will supervise them as harmful people. In the fourth, they will shoot on the spot, one of the ten guilty of parasitism.

In his article "Everything to fight against Denikin!", published in Izvestia of the Central Committee of the RCP (b) of July 9, 1919, Lenin wrote:

Let us only note that the petty-bourgeois democrats closest to the Soviet government, who, as usual, call themselves socialists, for example, some of the "Left" Mensheviks, etc., are especially fond of being indignant at the "barbaric", in their opinion, method of taking hostages. Let them be indignant, but wars cannot be waged without this, and when the danger is aggravated, the use of this means must, in every sense, be expanded and increased.

Officially, the Red Terror was announced on September 5, 1918, by the Decree of the Council of People's Commissars of the RSFSR of September 5, 1918 "On the Red Terror", and terminated on November 6, 1918.

In the pamphlet "On the food tax" (April 21, 1921), V. I. Lenin pointed out the need for "red terror":

a terrorist purge is needed: a court on the spot and an unconditional execution. Let the Martov's, Chernovs, and non-Party philistines like them beat their breasts and exclaim, "I praise you, Lord, for not being like 'them', for not recognizing and not recognizing terror." These fools "do not recognize terror", because they have chosen for themselves the role of servile accomplices of the White Guards in terms of fooling the workers and peasants. The Socialist-Revolutionaries and the Mensheviks "do not recognize terror", for they are fulfilling their role of bringing the masses under the flag of "socialism" under the White Guard terror (Felshtinsky, 2013).

Let the servile accomplices of the White Guard terror praise themselves for their denial of all terror. And we will speak the painful but undoubted truth: in countries experiencing an unheard-of crisis, the collapse of old ties, the intensification of the class struggle after the imperialist war of 1914-1918 — such are all the countries of the world — it is impossible to do without terror, despite the hypocrites and phrasemongers. Either the White Guard, the bourgeois terror of the American, English (Ireland), Italian (fascist), German, Hungarian and other styles, or the red, proletarian terror. There is no middle ground, there is no "third" and there cannot be (Felshtinsky, 2013).

Sergei Melgunov uses the term "Red Terror" to describe repression throughout the Russian Civil War, that is, from 1918 to 1923.

The perpetrators of the repressions were the bodies of the Cheka of the Council of People's Commissars of the RSFSR (Extraordinary Commission for Combating Counter-Revolution, Profiteering, and Crime ex officio) and, according to the Decree, "responsible party comrades" (Thompson, 2019).

Number of Victims of Red Terror

According to V. V. Ehrlichman, the number of victims of the Red Terror is at least 1 million 200 thousand people.

At the end of 1919, the Special Investigation Commission to investigate the atrocities of the Bolsheviks determined the number of deaths from the state policy of terror pursued by the Soviet government at 1,766,188 people only in the period 1918-1919, including 260,000 soldiers and 54,650 officers, about 1.5 thousand priests, 815 thousand peasants, 193 thousand workers, 59 thousand policemen, 13 thousand landowners and more than 370 thousand representatives of the intelligentsia and the bourgeoisie (Kamenskaya, 2005).

The historian S. V. Volkov, assessing the red terror as the entire repressive policy of the Bolsheviks during the years of the civil war (1917-1922), pointed out that the number of victims of the red terror is estimated at 2 million people. The historian pointed out that sometimes even larger numbers are given, but in such cases, victims of terror include such victims as death from starvation and disease of family members of those who were shot without a livelihood, and the like (Llewellyn, 2019).

For comparison: in tsarist Russia, from 1825 to 1905, 625 death sentences were pronounced for political crimes, of which only 191 were carried out, and in the revolutionary years - from 1905 to 1910 - 5735 death sentences were pronounced for political crimes, counting sentences of courts-martial, of which 3,741 sentences were carried out (Kamenskaya, 2005).

The Number of Those Executed by the Verdicts of the Cheka

According to Robert Conquest, a total of 140,000 people were shot by the revolutionary tribunals and extrajudicial sessions of the Cheka from 1917-1922.

O. B. Mozokhin, a researcher of the history of the Cheka, criticized this figure based on archival data. According to him, "with all reservations and exaggerations, the number of victims of the organs of the Cheka can be estimated at no more than 50 thousand people." Based on the study of the minutes of meetings of the Extraordinary Commissions, he also noted that sentences to capital punishment were the exception rather than the rule, and most of the executed were executed for ordinary crimes (Felshtinsky, 2013).

Nikolai Zayats, Candidate of Historical Sciences, points out that the number of those executed by the organs of the Cheka in 1918–1922 is approximately 37.3 thousand people; only about 50-55 thousand people (Kamenskaya, 2005).

When assessing the total number of victims of the Red Terror, it should be borne in mind that the Red Terror was carried out not only by the organs of the Cheka.

Ratings

Historians Yu. G. Felshtinsky and G. I. Chernyavsky note that, unlike the Whites, who did not find ideological and practical necessity in mass terror, the terrorist policy of the Bolsheviks was fundamentally different, since, despite all the demagogic statements and assurances of Bolshevik leaders, the Soviet government did not fight for the interests of the people (Felshtinsky and G. I. Chernyavsky, 2013). Therefore, the course of violence by the leaders of the Bolsheviks was carried out on almost the entire peasantry. In these actions, the Soviet government relied on rural outcasts - drunkards, lazybones, and rogues, whom it adorned with the regalia of the "rural proletariat". The Soviet government declared almost the entire stratum of educated and economically active people who bore the burden of the country's economic progress and were the bearers of its culture a mortal enemy.

Felshtinsky and Chernyavsky conclude in the work "Red Terror" that the main reason for the Red Terror was the alienation of Soviet power from the main social structures of society, its hostility to ordinary working people, and people of knowledge and social initiative. The Red Terror, carried out with the "highest blessing" of the leader of the Bolshevik Party and head of government V. I. Lenin, in terms of its scale, depth, and inhumanity, can in no way be likened to the "White Terror", which was secondary, retaliatory and conditioned by circumstances and conjuncture civil war.

Historian P. A. Golub in his work "White Terror in Russia (1918-1920)" argues that the Red Terror was a defensive, retaliatory, and therefore just reaction against the White Terror, against the actions of the Whites and their supporters in the Soviet rear and the armed intervention of foreign states to restore the pre-revolutionary regime (McConnell, 2019).

FASCIST STATE TERROR

Fascist state terror is the policy of destruction by the fascist and militaristic regimes in Germany, Japan, and Italy (the so-called Axis countries) and their allies of both their own and foreign civilian populations in World War II, as well as in some of the conflicts that preceded it. The largest contribution to the number of victims of fascist terror was made by Nazi Germany (19.5 million victims of genocide in the occupied territory of the USSR; 6 million victims of the catastrophe of European Jewry; 2.4 million Poles) and militaristic Japan (between 7.5—16 million victims of genocide in the occupied territory of China) (Mkurnalidze, 2000).

The fascist state's terror against the unarmed civilian population has no other explanation than the motives of racial and social hostility based on the ideology of fascism. Unlike incidental casualties and war crimes against civilians during hostilities, it cannot be blamed on a specific military unit alone and explained as an accidental excess. The massive number of victims of state terror under fascism led to its widespread official ban in the world after the defeat of fascist regimes in World War II.

State Terror of Nazi Germany

Nazism made the largest contribution to the number of victims of genocide in World War II, mainly due to the genocide of the inhabitants of the USSR and the Holocaust.

The central idea of National Socialism was the "Aryan race" and its opposition and confrontation with the hostile "Semitic race" (Jews). This idea served as the basis for radical racial anti-Semitism, covering all spheres of human life, which in turn determined the desire to fight against Marxism, Bolshevism, pacifism, liberalism, and democracy - according to Nazi doctrine, manifestations, and tools for realizing the interests of "world Jewry". History was understood as a continuous racial struggle of biologically perceived peoples for survival, protection, and expansion of the "living space" they needed. The result of this struggle was the establishment of the world domination of the "Aryan race", superior to other races in biological and cultural terms and occupying the highest position in the "racial hierarchy" - the race of natural masters. The ideology included militarism: war was presented as the natural state of mankind, the legitimate and only possible means of asserting the world leadership of the "master people". The key to victory in this struggle should be the consolidation of the German nation under the leadership of a single leader ("Fuhrer"), "racial hygiene" - the cleansing of the nation from "racially alien" and "inferior" elements, as well as strengthening its "physical health" (Chitadze, 2016).

Ethnic and Racial Groups

Slavs

Several historians, including the authors of the specialized Encyclopedia of Genocide, characterize the persecution of the Slavs as genocide. At the same time, several historians deduce the persecution of the

Slavs from the concept of genocide, pointing to significantly higher selectivity of murders compared to those of Jews, Gypsies, and the disabled and the absence of plans to exterminate all Slavs (for example, Slovaks - the First Slovak Republic) and Croats - The Independent State of Croatia, the Nazis considered valuable allies). An additional difficulty is the attempt to separate racially motivated killings from those related to military operations.

According to the "Encyclopedia of Genocide", the total number of victims of the genocide of the Slavs ranged from 19.7 to 23.9 million people (among them residents of the USSR, Poles, Slovenes, Serbs, etc.). According to the American political scientist Rudolf Rummel, the possible number of victims of the genocide of the Slavs is about 10.5 million people (among them Poles, Ukrainians, Belarusians, Russians, as well as Soviet prisoners of war) (Chitadze, 2016).

Poles

According to the US Holocaust Memorial Museum, the Nazis viewed Poles and other Slavs as an "inferior race" that must be subdued, enslaved, and ultimately destroyed. The Poles, whom the Nazis considered ideologically dangerous, including thousands of intellectuals and Catholic priests, became victims of Operation Tannenberg. From 1939 to 1945, at least 1.5 million Polish citizens were deported to Germany for forced labor, according to the Holocaust Memorial Museum. In addition, several hundred thousand were imprisoned in Nazi concentration camps. According to some estimates, during the Second World War, the Nazis killed at least 1.9 million Poles, not counting the dead Polish Jews. According to Rummel, approx. 2.4 million Poles (Mkurnalizde, 2000).

Jews

In the Nazi ideology and public consciousness of the Germans, a specific image of the racial enemy of the "Aryan race" and the "enemy of the nation" was formed - the Jews and the "world Jewry" striving for world domination, achieving its goals with the help of the "capitalist plutocracy" or democratic and Marxist parties.

The authorities of Nazi Germany are the main perpetrators of the genocide of Jews during the Second World War, although all the fascist regimes of the Axis countries and their collaborators, except Italy and militaristic Japan, took a significant part in the genocide of Jews. The victims of the Nazis and their accomplices were about 6 million Jews in Europe (Mkurnalizde, 2000).

Gypsies

Gypsies were also among the ethnic groups that were persecuted by the Nazis under racial laws. According to the German racists, the gypsies were a "racially inferior" group. Under the Nazi regime, Roma was subjected to arbitrary arrests, forced labor, and massacres. Tens of thousands of Roma were killed in the occupied territories of the USSR and Serbia, and thousands in death camps and concentration camps in Poland and other countries. Historians believe that about a quarter of all Roma in Europe, or about 220,000 people, were killed during the Holocaust. After the war, the German government thought that until 1943 the Roma were not persecuted for racial reasons and the measures taken by the state of that time were legal. The racial persecution of the Roma was only recognized at the end of 1979.

Along with the gypsies, the Yenish were persecuted - an ethnographic group leading a lifestyle close to the gypsy, however, unlike them, of purely German origin (Chitadze, 2016).

Black People in Germany

German citizens who had parents - immigrants from Africa, were subjected to forced sterilization. Children were also sterilized. The number of persons subjected to this operation, according to various sources, ranged from 400 to 3,000 (Mkurnalidze, 2000).

Social Groups

As part of the extermination program for persons considered "biologically threatening to the health of the country", which got its name from the address of the main office in Berlin at Tiergartenstrasse 4, over 70 thousand people with mental disorders, mentally retarded, mentally ill, disabled people, as well as children with neurological and somatic diseases. After the official closure of the program, the destruction of patients, however, continued, and by 1945 the number of those killed exceeded 200 thousand people; in addition, between 1942 and 1945, about a million patients were starved to death in German psychiatric hospitals.

The prerequisites for this program were the widespread prevalence in Germany of eugenics, then popular in several countries, the ideas of racial purity, and ideas about degenerative mental illnesses that were passed down from generation to generation. Such scientists-ideologists as Alfred Hohe, and Carl Binding, argued that people with mental disorders are carriers of incurable diseases that weaken the "master race", and to save public funds, they should be eliminated.

Massacres were carried out on the territory of Germany, and later - on the territory of Poland, the USSR, and other occupied countries through the introduction of toxic substances, poisons, gas poisoning, and executions. It was within the framework of the T-4 program for the first time (even before being used in concentration camps) that the Nazis used gas chambers; the first gas chamber was tested in Hadamar (Hesse) at the end of 1939.

From the very beginning, the race was one of the criteria for selecting victims. The systematic murder of Jewish patients in psychiatric clinics was the first decisive step toward the genocide of European Jews. From the summer of 1940, Jewish patients were exiled to certain collection institutions and then exterminated in the gas chambers of the T-4 program solely based on their origin. After August 1941, Jewish patients who lived in the only permitted clinic at that time, Bendorf-Sayn near Neuwied, were sent east to death camps (Chitadze, 2016).

Sexual Minorities

After the entry into force in 1935 of a more stringent, amended version of paragraph 175 of the Criminal Code (1871), homosexuals, mostly males, began to be persecuted. According to scientists from the American Holocaust Memorial Museum, concentration camps contained from 5 to 15 thousand convicted of homosexual activity; in addition, representatives of sexual minorities were sent to prisons and labor camps, as well as to compulsory treatment in psychiatric hospitals. It was supposed to "cure" them and allow them to "correct" with the help of hard physical labor. Castration and medical experiments were carried out on some homosexuals. Concentration camp inmates treated homosexuals as rejected by society. In the camps, homosexuals wore a pink triangle on their clothes. Many of them died after the brutal beatings and tortures of the SS.

How many homosexuals died in concentration camps will probably never be known. Rediger Lautmann, for example, believes that the death rate of convicts under Section 175 in the camps may have been as high as sixty percent. For comparison: 41% of political prisoners and 35% of Jehovah's Witnesses died in concentration camps (Chitadze, 2016).

Social and Political Groups

Masons

In his book Mein Kampf, Hitler wrote that the Masons "fell into the trap" of the Jews: "Freemasonry, which is entirely in the hands of the Jews, serves as an excellent tool for them in the fraudulent struggle for these goals. Through the threads of Freemasonry, the Jews entangle our government circles and the most economically and politically influential sections of the bourgeoisie, doing it so skillfully that those who are entangled do not even notice it. Freemasons were sent to concentration camps as political prisoners and were required to wear an inverted red triangle.

According to the American Holocaust Memorial Museum, "because many of the Masons arrested were Jews and/or members of the political opposition, it is not known how many people were sent to concentration camps and/or killed just because they were Freemasons". However, the Grand Lodge of Scotland estimated that between 80,000 and 200,000 Freemasons were executed (Mkurnalidze, 2000).

German Anti-Fascists

Underground communist and social democratic groups were the main internal target of the repressive apparatus of the Third Reich.

Jehovah Witnesses

Thousands of Jehovah's Witnesses were among the first to be sent to Nazi camps and prisons. They declared their position of neutrality in all matters relating to politics and war.

Jehovah's Witnesses were persecuted primarily for refusing military service in the Wehrmacht, refusing to participate in armaments production, and refusing to pronounce the Nazi salute.

Approximately 2,000 Witnesses died during the Nazi repressions, of which more than 250 were executed (Chitadze, 2016).

Repressions Having Been Committed by the Militarist Japan

Numerous acts of terror (including tests of bacteriological weapons) against the civilian population of China and other countries of Southeast Asia were recorded on the Pacific front of World War II.

Thus, during the Nanjing Massacre alone in 1937, about 300,000 civilians of the former Republic of China were killed, and about 20,000 more women (aged 7-60) were raped.

According to Western historians, China lost 16 million civilians between 1931 and 1945, while according to Chinese estimates, this figure is much higher (Mkurnalizde, 2000).

In February 1945, the plan developed in Tokyo for the destruction of Manila was methodically implemented, accompanied by the massacre of the civilian population.

State Terror Policy of Fascist Italy

A series of deliberate acts of extermination of the local population (including the use of chemical weapons) was allowed by the Italian-fascist troops in several countries in North Africa:

- In 1930, about 20,000 Bedouins were placed in Italian concentration camps in Libya, a fifth of whom died by 1933
- The massacre of the 12th Yekatit (February 1937), was carried out in response to an assassination attempt on Rodolfo Graziani, which killed 30,000 Ethiopians; several thousand more later died in the Italian concentration camps at Danane (Chitadze, 2016).

Mass Massacres in Croatia During World War 2

During World War II, the Ustaše in the Independent State of Croatia established a system of death camps mainly for the Serbian population under the general name "Jasenovac". The degree of bitterness on the part of the Croatian fascists can be indicated by the fact that in the German city of Solingen they ordered special knives for killing Serbs - the so-called "Serboseki". Also, for the rapid destruction of people, such a tool as a hammer was used (see "Serb hammer").

According to various estimates, between 83,000 and more than 700,000 people were killed by the Croatian Ustaše in Jasenovac - hundreds of thousands of Serbs, as well as thousands of Jews and Gypsies (Mkurnalidze, 2000).

Pressure on Population in Francoist Spain

The Francoist regime is regarded by several historians and political scientists as a variety of totalitarianism and fascism. Others characterize it as an authoritarian regime of limited conservative pluralism with features of a military dictatorship. After the fall of the Second Spanish Republic in 1939, the Francoist authorities physically destroyed from 50,000 to 200,000 Republicans (Chitadze, 2016).

CONCLUSION

There is neither an academic nor an international legal consensus regarding the proper definition of the word "terrorism". Some scholars believe the actions of governments can be labeled "terrorism". Using the term 'terrorism' to mean violent action used with the predominant intention of causing terror, Paul James and Jonathan Friedman (2006) distinguish between state terrorism against non-combatants and state terrorism against combatants, including 'shock and awe' tactics:

Shock and Awe" as a subcategory of "rapid dominance" is the name given to massive intervention designed to strike terror into the minds of the enemy. It is a form of state terrorism. The concept was however developed long before the Second Gulf War by Harlan Ullman as chair of a forum of retired military personnel (Chitadze, 2016).

However, others, including governments, international organizations, private institutions, and scholars, believe the term "terrorism" applies only to the actions of violent non-state actors. Historically, the term terrorism was used to refer to actions taken by governments against their citizens whereas now it is more often perceived as targeting non-combatants as part of a strategy directed *against* governments.

Historian Henry Commager wrote that "Even when definitions of terrorism allow for *state terrorism*, state actions in this area tend to be seen through the prism of war or national self-defense, not terror." While states may accuse other states of state-sponsored terrorism when they support insurgencies, individuals who accuse their governments of terrorism are seen as radicals, because actions by legitimate governments are not generally seen as illegitimate. Academic writing tends to follow the definitions accepted by states. Most states use the term "terrorism" for non-state actors only (Mkurnalidze, 2000).

The Encyclopedia Britannica Online defines terrorism generally as "the systematic use of violence to create a general climate of fear in a population and thereby to bring about a particular political objective", and states that "terrorism is not legally defined in all jurisdictions." The encyclopedia adds that "establishment terrorism, often called state or state-sponsored terrorism, is employed by governments—or more often by factions within governments—against that government's citizens, against factions within the government, or foreign governments or groups" (Chitadze, 2016).

While the most common modern usage of the word terrorism refers to political violence by insurgents or conspirators, several scholars make a broader interpretation of the nature of terrorism that encompasses the concepts of state terrorism and state-sponsored terrorism. Michael Stohl argues, "The use of terror tactics is common in international relations and the state has been and remains a more likely employer of terrorism within the international system than insurgents. Stohl clarifies, however, that "not all acts of state violence are terrorism. It is important to understand that in terrorism the violence threatened or perpetrated, has purposes broader than simple physical harm to a victim. The audience of the act or threat of violence is more important than the immediate victim" (Chitadze, 2016).

Scholar Gus Martin describes state terrorism as terrorism "committed by governments and quasi-governmental agencies and personnel against perceived threats", which can be directed against both domestic and foreign targets. Noam Chomsky (2002) defines state terrorism as "terrorism practiced by states (or governments) and their agents and allies" (Chomsky, 2022).

Stohl and George A. Lopez have designated three categories of state terrorism, based on the openness/secrecy with which the alleged terrorist acts are performed, and whether states directly perform the acts, support them, or acquiesce in them (Chitadze, 2016).

REFERENCES

Aleksidze. (2018). *Handbook in International Law*. Tbilisi State University.

Aust, A. (2010). *Handbook of International Law* (2nd ed.). Cambridge University Press. doi:10.1017/CBO9780511841460

Blakeley, R. (2009). *State Terrorism and Neoliberalism: The North in the South*. Routledge. doi:10.4324/9780203876510

Chitadze. (2016). *Political Sciences*. International Black Sea University.

Chomsky, N. (2002). What Anthropologists Should Know about the Concept of Terrorism. *Anthropology Today*.

Felshtinsky & Chernyavsky. (2013). *Red Terror during the Civil War*. Knigovek.

Gvimradze, G. (2014). *The Iraq Crisis*. Georgian Foundation for Strategic and International Studies. Retrieved from: https://gfsis.org.ge/files/library/opinion-papers/24-expert-opinion-eng.pdf

James, P., & Friedman, J. (2006). *Globalizing War and Intervention* (Vol. 3). Globalization and Violence. Sage Publications.

Kamenskaya, A. (2005). *Political Science*. Aspect Press.

Lind, M. (2009). *The Legal Debate is Over: Terrorism is a War Crime*. New America Foundation.

Llewellyn, J., McConnell, M., Llewellyn, J., & Thompson, S. (2019). *The Red Terror*. Russian Revolution. Alpha History.

Mkurnalizde, G., & Khamkhadze, G. (2000). *Political Sciences*. Tsodna.

Nairn, T., & James, P. (2005). *Global Matrix: Nationalism, Globalism and State-Terrorism*. Pluto Press.

Permanent Mission of the United Arab Emirates to the United Nations. (2017). *UAE calls for zero tolerance for all those who support terrorism financing*. Retrieved from: https://www.un.int/uae/news/uae-calls-zero-tolerance-all-those-who-support-terrorism-financing

Primoratz, I. (2007). *Defining "Terrorism"*. Stanford Encyclopedia of Philosophy.

Reuters. (2022). *U.S. senators introduce bill to designate Russia state sponsor of terrorism*. Retrieved from: https://www.reuters.com/world/europe/us-senators-introduce-bill-designate-russia-state-sponsor-terrorism-2022-09-14/

Schmid, A. P. (2011). *The Definition of Terrorism. The Routledge Handbook of Terrorism Research*. Routledge. doi:10.4324/9780203828731

US Department of State. (2022). *States Sponsors of Terrorism*. Retrieved from: https://www.state.gov/state-sponsors-of-terrorism/

Williamson, M. (2009). *Terrorism, war, and international law: the legality of the use of force against Afghanistan in 2001*. Ashgate Publishing.

KEY TERMS AND DEFINITIONS

Crimes Against Humanity: A category of activities, made illegal at the Nuremberg war crime trials, condemning states that abuse human rights.

Ethnic Cleansing: The extermination of an ethnic minority group by a state.

Genocide: The attempt to eliminate in whole or in part, an ethnic, racial religious, or national minority group.

International Terrorism: The threat or use of violence as a tactic of terrorism against targets in other countries.

State Terrorism: Refers to acts of terrorism that a state conducts against another state or its citizens.

State-Sponsored Terrorism: Terrorist violence carried out with the active support of national governments provided to violent non-state actors. States can sponsor terrorist groups in several ways, including but not limited to funding terrorist organizations, providing training, supplying weapons, providing other logistical and intelligence assistance, and hosting groups within their borders. Because of the pejorative nature of the word, the identification of particular examples is often subject to political dispute and different definitions of terrorism.

Terrorism: Premeditated violence perpetrated against non-combat targets by subnational or transnational groups or clandestine agents usually intended to influence an audience.

Chapter 9
Russian Aggression in Georgia and Ukraine as an Example of State Terrorism:
Comparative Analysis

Gurami Jajanidze
Ilia State University, Georgia

ABSTRACT

The chapter overviews Russian aggression in Georgia and Ukraine and provides comparative analyses – demonstrating the differences and similarities between Russia's tactics and policies during Russo-Georgian war (2008), the conflict in Eastern Ukraine (2014), and later during the Russian invasion of Ukraine (2022). It also analyzes Russian war crimes and atrocities committed during those conflicts. The first part was written in Spring 2021 before the war in Ukraine (2022), so initially the comparative analysis was made based on two cases – Russo-Georgian War 2008 and Russian aggression in Eastern Ukraine 2014. The second part of the chapter was written in Spring 2022 after Russia launched a full-scale invasion against Ukraine. The chapter was written based on the qualitative analyses of the existing literature – comparative analyses, researches about Russian hybrid war, independent case studies based on the information from archives of articles from the media outlets from 2008, 2014, and 2022 analyzing different documents, such as NATO summit declarations, Constitution of Russia, etc.

INTRODUCTION

Russian aggression in Georgia in 2008 and in Ukraine in 2014 changed the overall geopolitical and security picture in Europe. Ongoing Russian invasion of Ukraine (2022) impacts the rules of the political game on the world-wide level. On the one hand Russia created significant leverages in terms of presence of its own military on the territory of those countries to influence the decisions of authorities in Tbilisi and Kyiv, on the other hand it demonstrated claims about "exclusive Russian sphere of interests" in post-Soviet space. Analyzes of those conflicts is very important as far as it concerns geopolitical and security

DOI: 10.4018/978-1-6684-5311-7.ch009

architecture in Europe. It is important to know according to what foreign policy principles Moscow carries out its aggressive polices in the neighborhood to achieve its objectives and what is the toolkit that Russia uses against its targets. The paper will overview exactly Russia's foreign policy thought and will provide comparative analyzes of the Kremlin's aggression in Georgia (2008) and in Eastern Ukraine (2014) and finally Russian Invasion of Ukraine (2022) - discussing the differences and similarities.

The structure of the paper is the following. As already pointed out in the abstract, the paper is divided in two parts: The first part written in spring, 2021 and the second part in spring, 2022.

The first part starts with the chapter overviewing what are the theoretical explanations for Russian aggression in a neighborhood, what the points for consensus among the scholars are, which dimension is well-researched and what is lacking in the existing literature. The chapter discusses theoretical basis for Russia's aggression in Georgia and Ukraine. It provides the theories, which can explain the Kremlin's behavior. First of all it discusses Russian geopolitical view in terms of offensive neorealism with the incentives to change the existing status quo in the world - referring to Russian perception of unipolarity, especially in early 2000s with the US in the lead. Later it explains the logic behind Russian motives for direct military aggression as the tool to advance its expansionist interests. Then it overviews another theory about kin-state policies that is often used by Russia to "justify" its intervention in the domestic affairs of other nations. Then the paper goes through chronological development of the conflicts separately in Georgia and Ukraine to create overall understanding of them. This demonstrates the point, that despite the objective of the paper to provide comparative analysis - thus demonstrating both differences and similarities about two cases, still those conflicts are classified as different in their essence - the Russian invasion of Georgia, 2008 is a traditional conventional war with some hybrid war elements, while Russian aggression in Eastern Ukraine, 2014 is a classic example of hybrid war with more significant and essential components other than military as an integral part of it. The last and the biggest chapter of the first part is dedicated to comparative analysis itself. First of all the chapter overviews the differences between the conflicts in Georgia and Ukraine and later discusses the similarities. While discussing the differences, the paper mostly concentrates on the different path to the conflict - distinction in terms of chronological development and the way to the escalation, difference in Russia's preparatory work for aggression, it also discusses the difference in terms of classification of the conflicts and assessing military component of it. Finally the paper draws attention to different response from the west in those cases. When analyzing the similarities from Russian toolkit in those two cases, the paper will concentrate on securitization of national minorities and manipulation with international norms by Russia, Passportization policy, and economic pressure over Georgia and Ukraine, cyber-attacks, disinformation and propaganda campaigns. Despite the fact that in this part the paper discusses those actions as the common weapons from Russian toolkit against Georgia and Ukraine, it also provides analyze of difference in implementation of those tools in case of Georgia and Ukraine. The difference, which can be explained in terms of timing, objectives and some other features of those tools.

The second part of the paper was written in spring, 2022 – so during the War in Ukraine which broke out by the illegitimate Russian invasion on the 24th of February. The second part of the paper starts with the chapter describing the post-Maidan Ukraine, namely the relations of Ukraine with Russia since 2014. Basically there is an overview of deterioration of Russo-Ukrainian relations since Russian-led aggression and hostilities in Eastern Ukraine. The next chapter concerns Ukrainian Presidential elections of 2019. It discusses the reasons of electing Zelenskyi by the population, including his promises related to putting an end to the war via negotiations with Putin. The chapter analyzes how Zelenskyi tried to achieve this objective and how all the things didn't went in the way it was anticipated by him initially.

Then comes the chapter which provides comparative analysis between the Russo-Georgian War 2008 and Russo-Ukrainian War 2022. Basically it's all about "One Playbook, Two Cases". Final chapter concerns the Russian atrocities committed in Georgia (2008) and Ukraine (2022).

THEORETICAL OVERVIEW OF RUSSIAN FOREIGN POLICY - ESSENTIAL FOR UNDERSTANDING KREMLIN'S AGGRESSION IN GEORGIA AND UKRAINE

There are several theories that can explain Russia's foreign policy and namely Kremlin's behavior with regard to Georgia and Ukraine. Russia is practicing neorealist policies with a strong component of frequent practice of kin-state policies.

Neorealist Russia With Its View of Sphere of Exclusive Interests

First of all what makes Russia the actor with neorealist views is two key components of Moscow's foreign policy. First one is emphasize on *a power*, as the key factor in managing international relations and achieving foreign policy goals. Second one is the understanding of the world in terms of poles and perceiving post-Soviet space as its "*exclusive sphere of interests*", or the "backyard" as understood by Russian authorities. So Russia views post-Soviet space as its sphere of influence and this Russia's proclaimed zone of "exclusive interests" also covers territory of Georgia and Ukraine. This is exactly the point that leads to the escalation - Georgia and Ukraine that have quite negative experience of Russian rule both from times of Tsar's Empire and Soviet Union, try their best to escape from Russia's sphere of influence and find their better future within boundaries of Western civilization. At some point, after dissolution of Soviet Union those countries at some level managed to get closer to the West and they still maintain aspirations to integrate in Euro-Atlantic organizations - NATO and the EU. On the other hand Russia uses all the means, including last resort measure - military engagement in order to prevent Georgia and Ukraine from becoming part of the West. This is a typical example of Clash of Civilizations (Huntington, 1993, pp. 22-49). In this case the frontline is the territory of Ukraine and Georgia. In this regard from theoretical perspective Russia can be categorized as *offensive neorealist state* as well with *revisionist* views. This means that Kremlin pursues to change the current status quo. Current status quo is the situation, when both Ukraine and Georgia still maintain pro-Western vector as the primary objective of their foreign affairs. Russia tries its best to forcibly change Georgia's and Ukraine's Western aspirations, because pro-Western Georgia and Ukraine confronts Russia's idea of sphere of exclusive interests. Russia dissatisfaction with the existing reality and willingness to change the existing status quo was explicitly demonstrated in Vladimir Putin's "Munchen Speech" delivered in 2007 (Kushnir, 2017, p. 4). On 12th of February, 2007 Putin, who was President of Russia right then during the 43rd Munich Conference on Security Policy delivered a speech, which is sometimes perceived as declaration of another Cold War against the West (Kushnir, 2017, p. 4). Putin claimed that since dissolution of Soviet Union the world became unipolar with the US in the lead and that "unipolar world is neither acceptable nor possible in modernity" (*Kremlin*, 2007). Putin compared increasing economic potential of BRIC countries that can overcome Western economies and stated, that increasing economic capacity would transform into political influence - leading to multipolarity (*Kremlin*, 2007). He manifestly criticized the West for NATO expansion in the East, claiming that "it didn't have anything to do with modernization" and that it was "provocation" (*Kremlin*, 2007).

Why Military Aggression in Georgia and Ukraine Is a Mean for Russia to Maintain Those Countries in Its Exclusive Sphere of Interests?

Russia aims to stop Georgia's and Ukraine's escape from its sphere of influence and prevent them from integration in the Western civilization. The question is - what does specifically mean integration in Western civilization? First and foremost this means integration of those nations in Euro-Atlantic structures - namely NATO and the EU. Despite the fact that Russia neither adores the idea of post-Soviet countries joining the EU, Georgia and Ukraine becoming members of the NATO is the biggest nightmare for the Kremlin. This is explained by the idea of NATO itself - which is not only political organization, but military alliance as well, which means that Georgia and Ukraine in NATO means more Western military presence near Russia.

How Military Conflicts in Georgia and Ukraine Keep Them Away From Becoming Member of NATO?

According to NATO's criteria for accession together with other prerequisites such as well-functioning democracy, free-market economy and accordance with standards of NATO in terms of army, the key point for North-Atlantic Treaty Organization is future members to have settled the issue of territorial disputes (NATO, 1995). In the other words, the aspirant country should first of all take care of border issues with its neighbors and then it can become the member of NATO in the way it won't pose much threat to alliance's security system. Indeed, there was the case in history, when the country with serious territorial problems, in particular - Germany joined the organization (*Britannica*, n.d.). Back then Germany was divided in two and was partially occupied by the USSR. This means that in case there is a political will, neither territorial problems that in fact are also created to prevent countries to join the Western institutions can stop their accession, still - in today's reality this is a serious issue perceived as essential obstacle in some of the Western countries to accept new members. Presence of break-away regions was already an obstacle for Georgia before the war with Russia in 2008. Still Georgia together with Ukraine was intensively negotiating with Brussels for integration and just before NATO summit of Bucharest in May, 2008 there was expectations in Tbilisi and Kyiv that those countries would receive Membership Action Plan (MAP) - prerequisite for joining NATO. Georgia and Ukraine weren't given MAP in Bucharest, but they were given a pledge - official promise that they would become the members of NATO one day (*NATO*, 2008). On the one hand abstaining from giving MAP to Georgia and Ukraine was a good news for Moscow, on the other hand the summit declaration about those countries becoming members of NATO in future was both threat and signal for Russia that it needed to act as fast as possible in order to at least delay this process of Georgian and Ukrainian integration in Euro-Atlantic structures, not if fully terminate it. The best scenario for increasing Western skepticism in terms of accepting Tbilisi and Kyiv in NATO was escalating the conflict and make those states even more problematic for the Western security system. Just in few months from Bucharest summit Russia waged a full-scale invasion of Georgia, creating its regular military presence in Georgia's break-away regions - Abkhazia and Tskhinvali region, recognizing so called "independence" of separatist regimes and creating totally different reality from the one that existed before the war - postponing Georgia's accession in NATO for a while. Russian authorities neither hide their incentive of aggression in Georgia. Former president of Russia - Dmitry Medvedev later said: "If you had faltered back in 2008, the geopolitical situation would be different now, And a number of countries which (NATO) tried to deliberately drag into the alliance, would have most likely already been part of it now" (Dyomkin, 2011). Medvedev's words explicitly demonstrate Russia's motivation - it obstructed Georgia from becoming member of NATO (at least for a while) and also it was a clear signal to Ukraine, that Kremlin was ready for using military force in order to secure its geopolitical goals. Book written by Ariel Cohen and Robert E. Hamliton - "The Russian Military and the Georgia War: Lessons and Implications" which was published in 2011, states, that Russia not only expelled Georgia from its own regions - creating serious leverage over Tbilisi, but also hit its pro-Western aspirations and moreover, sent a serious signal to Kyiv that Kremlin was ready for any scenario (Ariel Cohen, 2011, p. 1). This message was actually translated into actions in 3 years from publishing this book - in 2014 Russian aggression in Eastern Ukraine made Kyiv end up in a same scenario as Tbilisi - becoming serious security challenge for the West exactly because of disputed territories and Russian military presence on its internationally recognized territory.

So, Russian aggression in Georgia (2008) and Ukraine (2014) was a deliberate attempt to postpone, if not fully eradicate ambitions of Tbilisi and Kyiv of becoming members of Euro-Atlantic family.

Russia's Kin-State Policies

There is one more theory that can explain Russian behavior in separatist regions of Georgia and Ukraine. This is kin-state policy theory. Kin-state policies, that generally refer to the policies targeted at the co-ethnical groups living abroad is widely used by Russia in order to justify its aggression and expansionist policies also on the example of Georgia and Ukraine. But Russia's kin-state policy differs significantly from the analogues of other countries. Generally kin-state policies aim to support and carry out pro-active steps in favor of ethnic groups living on the territory of other countries (Duvold, 2015, pp. 19-32). But on the example of Russia such policies are not limited within frame of "ethnical" component and are broadened in terms of "members of Russian world". In the other words, Russia has ambition to carry out active policies in "support" of every single person all over the world, which can be labeled as "member of Russian world".

What Does Russian World Include and What Role It Has in Justification of Kremlin's Aggressive Policy?

Russian world includes the people from different groups. Russian kin-state policy has a civilizational emphasize. According to Russian view the persons that can be labeled as part of Russian world are the ones who are ethnically Russians, Russian speakers (for instance such claim can be made over ethnical Ukrainians speaking Russian as major language in South-East of Ukraine) or even simply Russian compatriots, or citizens of Russia (for instance Ossetians and Abkhazs that became "citizens of Russia" after artificial "passportization" policy in break-away regions (Matsaberidze, 2015, p. 9)). The latest category is widely-used by Russia to justify its aggression and intervention in Georgia and Ukraine. Especially after adoption of Citizenship Law in Russia, every citizen in the former USSR can become citizen of Russia with a simplified procedure (*State Duma of Russia*, 2002, p. 6). Russia very practically used this point in both Donetsk and Luhansk and Abkhazia and Tkshinvali region. Kremlin carried out aggressive policy of "passportization" - delivering Russian passports to locals living in the break-away regions (Matsaberidze, 2015, p. 9). In the other words, Russia artificially created "components of Russian world" in those territories and then justified its aggression in the name of "protecting its compatriots" and "fulfilling its obligation by constitution", considering Article 61 stating that "the Russian Federation shall guarantee its citizens protection and patronage abroad" (*THE CONSTITUTION OF THE RUSSIAN FEDERATION*, 1993).

OVERVIEW OF RUSSIAN INVASION IN GEORGIA (2008) AND IN UKRAINE (2014) - ARE THOSE SAME TYPE OF CONFLICTS?

First and foremost, despite the fact that the paper provides comparative analyzes, which also includes the objective to demonstrate the similarities in Russian aggressive policy in Georgia and Ukraine - it should be explicitly stated that the conflict in Georgia and the one in Ukraine are in overall of totally different character.

Russian invasion in Georgia, 2008 was a well-prepared traditional military operation with regular troops which was carried out in the peak of escalation between Tbilisi and Moscow. The military confrontation in August, 2008 was preceded by increasing tensions between Georgia and Russia since summer, 2004, which lasted for four years - putting those countries in the conditions of "Cold War". Before the war, conflicting sides experienced almost all kinds of inter-state confrontation - starting with embargo, informational warfare, mass-deportation of citizens, spy scandal, regular small scale military clashes in the break-away regions, exchange of hypercritical and offensive statements - so the conflict was not something which emerged unexpectedly - it was an predictable continuation and actually a peak of long-lasting escalation. The patterns of upcoming large-scale clashes were evident already by Spring, 2008 - when Russians created so called "embassies" in Tskhinvali region and Abkhazia (before only one operating was in Tbilisi), deployed railway forces and later airborne forces on the territory of Georgia and later mobilized tens of thousands of troops in North Caucasus, meanwhile significantly increasing number of provocations in break-away regions, especially from July, 2008 - leading to the whirlpool of escalation - ended up with full-scale war. Moreover, Russian authorities admitted that they were preparing for this invasion for years. Later in 2012 Putin stated that the plan of military invasion in Georgia had been prepared in 2006 and was approved by him later in 2007 (Felgenhauer, 2012). In 2012. Russian invasion in Georgia had some hybrid war features as well, but in difference from developments in Eastern Ukraine in 2014, it can't be classified as a classic example of hybrid war.

On the other hand, Russian aggression in Eastern Ukraine was more like a classic example of Hybrid war. Despite the fact, that as in case of Georgia, Russia had similar incentives in Ukraine - namely creating obstacles for Ukraine's western integration, the scenario was quite different. Despite the fact, that Russian military presence in Ukraine is proved, still it didn't carry out military operations officially with its regular troops and mostly used either local proxies, or informal groups (even though they could be members of Russian regular army) or "green men" as they call it (*Radio Free Europe / Radio Liberty*, 2019). In difference from explicit Russian invasion in Georgia, in Ukraine the Kremlin still tries to deny its presence in Luhansk and Donetsk (Crimea is a difference) Oblasts, despite the fact, that obviously everybody knows that the key actor and aggressor there is Russia. In this sense Russian aggression in Ukraine in 2014 have more similarities with Russia's view of itself in Abkhazia and Tskhinvali region - back in 1990s, when again - everybody knew Russia was a conflict side, but it still was attempting to portray itself as mediator and the party beyond conflict. Moreover, Russian aggression in Ukraine was not a final moment of the long-lasting confrontation as it was in case of Georgia. It was not a logical peak of chain of escalation as it was in case of Russo-Georgian war. Despite the fact, that Ukraine was in a tandem with Georgia aspiring to join Euro-Atlantic family for a while, since 2010 as a result of electing pro-Russian president - Victor Yanukovych from Party of Regions, almost everything in Ukraine's foreign policy interests was going on in accordance with Russia's interests. Ukraine's progress in terms of Euro-Atlantic integration became really suspicious and in the end, Yanukovych almost managed to literally change Ukraine's pro-Western foreign policy vector - giving up on aspirations to join the EU and declaring readiness to become member of Russian-led Eurasian Union (Matsaberidze, 2015, p. 9). But Yanukovych's inefficient governance and betrayal of pro-Western vector angered Ukrainian people so much that by the end of 2013 people went to streets and massive manifestations started - leading to famous Maidan events. In the flares of domestic chaos in Ukraine Russia decided to act rapidly - using its chance to gain control over Crimean peninsula, literally invading and annexing it without shooting a single bullet and later creating separatists movements in Eastern regions - Luhansk and Donetsk oblasts - leading to permanent clashes in Eastern Ukraine and the conflict which is still ongoing.

In the other words, both chronological development of conflict and type of aggression in Georgia and Ukraine is quite different from one another. Still, they share a lot of similarities such as the common incentives and geopolitical calculations of the Kremlin and policy tools that were used by Russia in both cases, which will be discussed later.

Before that, it is still important to go through the details of chronological development of conflicts in Georgia and Ukraine, that was discussed briefly above, because the way those conflicts emerged matters in terms of understanding the key point - what is the main difference between them.

Georgia: The Peak of the Escalation – Cold War (2004-2008) Transforming Into the Military Conflict - Russo-Georgian War

It is important to trace a little bit earlier times of Georgia's modern history to understand the Russo-Georgia War in 2008. Everything starts with the Rose Revolution - establishment of explicitly pro-Western government in Georgia with the ambitions of restoring Georgia's territorial integrity.

Situation Just After Rose Revolution

The new stage in Russo-Georgian relations starts with Rose Revolution in Georgia, in 2003. In 2003 Mikheil Saakashvili - later the 3rd President of Georgia led the revolution against Shevardnadze's regime. Saakashvili's movement was strongly supported by the public, which was exhausted by socio-economic problems and one of the highest rate of corruption in the world. When Saakashvili's government take possession of the power - the interesting point was what type of foreign policy he would have. Saakashvili decided to not only stay loyal to Shevardnadze's pro-Western vector, which Shevardnadze decided to go for especially after declaring willingness to join NATO, but to promote the idea of rapid integration in the Western institutions (Peuch, 2002). Despite the fact, that from the beginning up for 8 months Saakashvili had quite good relations with Putin, since summer 2004 the situation started deteriorating. The key obstacle in Russo-Georgian relations were two of the following points - pursuit of Georgian government to regain effective control over break-away regions, which were led by separatist regimes supported by Russia and aspirations of Georgia to become member of civilized West, which automatically means getting away from Russian sphere of influence.

Situation Gradually Gets Deteriorated

The first patterns of potential Russo-Georgian confrontation were already visible by summer, 2004. In May 2004 Georgia regained control over Adjara region. Adjara Autonomous Republic was controlled by local authority - Aslan Abashidze, who didn't obey the commands of Tbilisi and had quite close ties with the Moscow. Saakashvili's government overcome Abashidze's resistance. As a result of civil protests in Adjara, which were coordinated with Tbilisi's actions, despite the attempts of resistance and threat of military confrontation, in May, 2004 Abashidze had to flee to Russia (*Radio Free Europe / Radio Liberty*, 2004). Adjara returned to efficient control of Georgia. For sure, this was not an acceptable development for the Kremlin, but in this case they didn't try their best to maintain Abashidze's presence in Adjara region.

In summer, 2004 the situation get more complicated. Georgian authorities decided to close Ergneti bazaar (*Civil.ge*, 2004). Ergneti is a village just few hundred matters away from city of Tskhinvali (main city of break-away Tskhinvali region). Ergneti is up to this moment Georgian-controlled administrative unit. Before 2004 there was a marketplace, where people from the territory controlled under Georgian authorities and also persons living in break-away region were capable to trade. Despite the fact that it was a good place for maintaining people-to-people contacts, there was a serious issue of smuggling as well. In order to prevent this issue and mobility of illegal goods from break-away regions, Georgian authorities decided to close the marketplace (*Civil.ge*, 2004). Disclosure of the marketplace was negatively responded by Ossetians. In August, 2004 situation started getting deteriorated - there were clashes between Georgian and Ossetian de-facto police units and soon the troops from Peace-keeping battalions from both sides joined the hostilities. As a result, a small scale-war happened already in August, 2004, where 26 Georgians and unknown number of Ossetians lost their lives (*Radio Liberty*, 2004). Georgian troops took some of the heights near Tskhinvali under their control, but had to withdraw from those positions later after Russian pressure (*Radio Liberty*, 2004). Hostilities ended up with a cease-fire agreement in the second part of the August.

Meanwhile, alongside with attempts of regaining control over separatist regions, Georgia was strengthening its ties with the West. In 2005 the President of the US - George Bush visited Georgia (*CNN*, 2005). The rhetoric between Tbilisi and Moscow was becoming more and more complicated. In 2005 the terrorist act happened in city of Gori, where the explosion of bomb killed Georgian policemen (*Radio Liberty*, 2005). According to Georgian authorities the explosion was organized by Russian intelligence services. In 2005 Russia put Georgian agricultural products under embargo, in 2006 already Georgian wine and mineral waters shared the same fate (*Business Media Georgia*, 2019). In winter, 2006 Russia suspended gas supply to Georgia for a while - that was caused by explosion of pipe-line in North Caucasus (*Business Media Georgia*, 2019). Also in 2006 Russia started massive deportation of Georgian citizens. More than 4000 Georgians were deported from Russia with cargo planes, which even caused death of some Georgian nationals (*BBC*, 2006) (*Radio Free Europe / Radio Liberty*, 2006). The same year was famous also for a "spy scandal". Georgian intelligence services have arrested Russian intelligence officers. One of the officers was also accused of being in connection with explosion in Gori, 2005. The arresting of spies was even more scandalous as far as arrested Russian officers were positioned in front of the TV cameras (*Civil.ge*, 2006). Russia has withdrawn its ambassador for consultations and stated that it was starting "evacuation of staff and their family members due to increased threat" (*Civil.ge*, 2006). In September, 2006 group of Russian attacked Georgian embassy in Moscow as well (*Civil.ge*, 2006). Due to the Spyscandal Russia also suspended withdrawal of military forces, the obligation of which it took earlier in 1999, on OSCE summit in Istanbul (*Civil.ge*, 2006). At the same time, there were organized number of military drills on both sides. Russia was organizing military drills called "Kavkaz", (for instance Kavkaz 2006), while Georgian side was organizing the annual military drills - "Kavkasioni" (for instance Kavkasioni 2006, where more than 8000 Georgian troops participated) (*Civil.ge*, 2006). In 2007 several other incidents happened as well. In August, 2007 Russian aircraft SU-24 crossed Georgian air space and fired a rocked near Georgian village - Tsitelubani, which is located 80 kms away from border of Russia and 60 kms away from Tbilisi (*Civil.ge*, 2007). Later in October, 2007 Russian military group from Peace-keeping battalion went to Georgian controlled territory in Ganmukhuri Youth Camp and took Georgian policemen as prisoners. Georgian and Russian troops at some point opened fire at each other as well and Georgian troops came into defense readiness conditions (*Civil.ge*, 2007). Soon Georgia's president Mikheil Saakashvili went to Ganmukhuri as well. He declared General Chaban, head of Russian peace-keeping forces as persona-non-grata (*Civil.ge*, 2007). The level of the tensions was quite well expressed in the attitudes of the societies too. By 2007, 46% of Russian population was perceiving Georgia as hostile country towards Russia - being the leader of the list together with Estonia (*Levada Center*, 2020). At the same time 93% of Georgian population according to IRI polls was evaluating Georgia's relations with Russia as negative and 70% of Georgians were perceiving Russia as a main economic and political threat (*International Republican Institute*, 2007, pp. 47-48).

2008 - It Seems the War Was Already Inevitable

In early 2008 the war seemed already imminent - increasing number of accidents and mobilization of troops indicated the high probability of military conflict. From February to March there were several explosions in conflict zones - killing 3 persons and 5 wounded, among casualties there were soldier of North Ossetian Peacekeeping battalion and 25 years old woman in Tskhinvali (*Civil.ge*, 2008). In March, 2008 one of the intelligence services of Baltic republics was warning, that Russia was preparing for a war against Georgia in 2008 and that the 58th Army and the 76th Air Assault division would participate in the military campaign (Ariel Cohen, 2011, p. 17). In the same month Moscow left the agreement of Commonwealth of Independent States (CIS) from 1996 that was imposing sanctions on Abkhazia (*Civil.ge*, 2008). In March - Russia's ambassador in NATO - Dimitri Rogozin warned Georgia, that in case "Tbilisi would receive clear signals about NATO membership, the "real separation" of Abkhazia and Tskhinvali region would start" (*Civil.ge*, 2008). Georgia also stated that Russia was deploying heavy AA and Artillery pieces in the region, which for sure couldn't have any peacekeeping purpose. Meanwhile Georgian UAV was also shot down over Abkhazia by Russian aircraft - MIG29 (Ariel Cohen, 2011, p. 17). Surely presence of MIG29 in Abkhazia can be neither explained in terms of "Peacekeeping" mandate - Peacekeeping forces doesn't require attacking aircraft. In April, Russia has opened so called "embassies" in Sokhumi and Tskhinvali (*Civil.ge*, 2008). Earlier in that month Tskhinvali defacto regime also opened "embassy" in Sokhumi (*Civil.ge*, 2008). Now Moscow was not communicating with only Tbilisi on "official" level, but with separatist entities as well. On the 18th of April, separatist regime of Abkhazia accused Georgia of deploying military in Zugdidi district - the claim was denied by Georgian side, stating that "separatist regime was trying to provoke military confrontation with Tbilisi" (*Civil.ge*, 2008). In the end of April, representative of Russian Ministry of Foreign Affairs - Valeryi Kenyakin stated that in case of military confrontation in Georgia's breakaway regions, Russia would intervene with military (*Civil.ge*, 2008). After that statement Russia increased number of "Peacekeeping troops" in Abkhazia and made accusations against Tbilisi about increasing number of military and police units in Kodori Gorge, claiming, that "Georgia was preparing for military operation against Abkhazia" (*Civil.ge*, 2008) (*Civil.ge*, 2008). Russia deployed 500 airborne units, airborne units were within Peacekeeping mandate, but their number and type - Airborne was posing the questions regarding their function (Ariel Cohen, 2011, p. 17). Also it should be mentioned that Russia increased number of peacekeeping troops in the internationally recognized territory of Georgia (by this time neither Russia was recognizing so-called independence of those breakaway entities) without agreeing it with Tbilisi (*Civil.ge*, 2008).

According to Tbilisi increasing number of peacekeeping troops by Russia in Abkhazia was seriously increasing the threat of military escalation (*Civil.ge*, 2008). In the period of March-April two of Georgia's initiatives were ignored by the separatist regimes - one was the proposal of Georgia's President - Saakashvili about creating free economic zone in Abkhazia, second about creation of joint-police forces with Abkhazian de-facto regime (*Radio Liberty*, 2008) (*Civil.ge*, 2008). Meanwhile Saakashvili addressed Abkhazs and Ossetians to counter-act aggressive foreign power, which was trying to cause bloodshed in the region (*Civil.ge*, 2008). Secretary of the State of the US by that time - Condoleezza Rice stated, that she was concerned about increased military presence of Russia in Georgia's break-away region and that there was not necessity for it (*Civil.ge*, 2008). Meanwhile de-facto "foreign minister" of Abkhazia - Shamba stated, that he hoped Medvedev, new president of Russia would continue the policy of Putin, who created the basis for recognition of Abkhazia and added, that he hoped Medvedev would finalize it (*Civil.ge*, 2008). In Mid-May Sokhumi claimed that they shot down two more Georgian UAV's, Tbilisi denied the information (*Civil.ge*, 2008). On the 15th of May, General Assembly of the UN made a resolution about supporting IDP's from Georgia's break-away regions to go back to their houses - the resolution was criticized by Russia, calling it "politically motivated" and "counterproductive" (*Civil.ge*, 2008). In May-June the number of accidents increased. On the 16th of May, after explosion near Tskhinvali, in the village of Eredvi Georgian policeman was wounded (*Civil.ge*, 2008). On the 21th of May, in Abkhazia there was an explosion near the buses that were transporting ethnically Georgians from Gali region to Zugdidi to vote in Georgia's elections - wounding 4 persons (*Civil.ge*, 2008). In late May, the provocations started near Tskhinvali region as well - namely there was a targeted fire on Georgian positions near village of Tamarasheni, close to Tskhinvali (*Civil.ge*, 2008). The following day another explosion happened in Tskhinvali - wounding 4 Ossetian policemen (*Civil.ge*, 2008). Later, in the beginning of June Russia deployed railway forces in Abkhazia as well (Ariel Cohen, 2011, p. 17) . Railway troops were stated to be illegal by Georgian side, but Russia claimed that they were deployed only for "humanitarian purpose" (Ariel Cohen, 2011, p. 17). In June Georgia announced its readiness and willingness to withdraw Russian Peacekeeping forces from the region (it was formally possible by putting an end to their mandate), later in the June Tbilisi stated that it was ready to postpone this process in case the EU and the US would be more involved in the process (*Civil.ge*, 2008) (*Civil.ge,* 2008). In early July, the visit of the US state secretary - Condoleezza Rice, was accompanied by interference of Russian aircraft in Georgian air-space (Ariel Cohen, 2011, pp. 19-20). In the middle of June NATO representatives tried to discuss the case of Georgia with Ministry of Defense of Russia - Anatoly Sedyukov, but he neither talked about Georgia before, nor after he was asked about the situation in the region (*Civil.ge*, 2008). From the middle of June the number of clashes and accidents increased even more. In the period between 15th of June up until 3rd of July up to 6 accidents happened - causing casualties on both sides, including exchange of fire in Tskhinvali region, explosion on the railway in Abkhazia, two of de facto regime's security service members being wounded in Sokhumi, explosion in Gagra, (*Civil.ge*, 2008) (*Civil.ge*, 2008) (*Civil.ge*, 2008), (*Civil.ge*, 2008). On the 3rd of July the line of cars of Dimitry Sanakoev - head of temporary administration of Tskhinvali region - controlled by Tbilisi, was attacked - wounding members of his security service (*Civil.ge*, 2008). There were few more accidents in the first half of the July - causing casualties on both sides, leading to the accusations from both Tbilisi and separatist regimes against each other. On the 8th of July the US called for creation of "international police forces" due to the tensions that were present in the region - the proposal was rejected by de-facto Abkhaz government - accusing the US of being "subjectively" pro-Georgian (*Civil.ge*, 2008). On the 11th of July Lavrov, minister of foreign affairs of Russia stated once more that "giving MAP to Georgia would be an obstacle for solving the conflicts" (*Civil.ge*, 2021). Later de-facto Abkhaz authorities also rejected so called "German Plan" for resolution of the conflict (*Civil.ge,* 2008). In mid-July Russia launched military drills - Kavkaz 2008. The exercise plot officially was a counterterrorist operation, but the scenarios also involved an intervention in a fictional neighboring country. Also the soldiers who participated in the drills received the cards with listed key personnel and equipment data about Georgian army, assessments of strengths and weaknesses of it and the text: "Soldier, Know Your Probable Enemy! (Ariel Cohen, 2011, p. 17)". As the military drills ended, part Russian troops didn't get back to their initial point of dislocation and stayed on their positions in North Caucasus - ready to attack Georgia (Engvall, 2020). Later in July two more negotiation proposals - one in Brussels and another in Berlin was denied by de-facto regimes of Tskhinvali and Sokhumi, which were protesting the format of the negotiations (*Civil.ge*, 2008) (*Civil.ge*, 2008). Despite the fact that earlier in spring the escalation was more predictable in Abkhazia, in late July situation worsened in Tskhinvali region. Ossetians started intensive bombing of villages inhabited by ethnically Georgians (*IDFI*, 2020). At the same time de-facto regime earlier in August started partial evacuation of city of Tskhinvali itself (*Radio Liberty*, 2010). Meanwhile Russians also sent up to 50 reporters to Tskhinvali region several days before the war would broke out - another point proving that the war was almost unavoidable and Russia was actually preparing for it (Ariel Cohen, 2011, p. 47). Since late July up until August, 7 - despite the fact, that there were several attempts to cool down the tensions and settle the situation with diplomatic means, separatist regime backed up by Russia continued intensive shelling of Georgian villages and positions of peace-keeping forces, which throughout the week were both responding with fire and partially ceasing the fire, but without reciprocity from the opposing side (*IDFI*, 2020). As a result, on the 7th of August - late at night Georgian forces started large-scale military operation against separatist forces. Already in the morning of August, 8 it was explicit that Georgia was not dealing with some de-facto regime, but it was facing full scale-invasion by Russia - invading Georgia with its regular forces, bombing all type of military and civilian strategic infrastructure all over the country, not only in the conflict zone and attacking all means to neutralize Georgian resistance - including cyber-attacks and informational warfare - that mainly concentrated on justifying Russian invasion in Georgia in the perspective of world actors. Later in August, after finalizing military operation by 12th of August, Russia recognized so called "independence" of break-away entities of Georgia - Abkhazia da Tskhinvali region (*IDFI*, 2020).

Ukraine: From Euromaidan to Explicit Russian Aggression in Eastern Ukraine

What's different in case of Ukraine is that the conflict there didn't have that much long prelude and the conflict there in a chronological perspective wasn't as evident to predict as in case of Georgia, where the probability of the conflict was significantly increasing from 2004 to 2008. The case of Ukraine is more a situation, where dynamic and also unpredictable radical developments that occurred in a short time perspective created the chaos, for which it seems Kremlin was already well-prepared in order to manage this chaos on its behalf.

Despite the fact, that in the second half of the 2000s, Ukraine was trying to integrate with Euro-Atlantic structures in a tandem with Georgia, which was logically making it another potential victim of Russia, still the situation after 2010 was not developing in the way that it could make Russian aggression predictable in Ukraine anymore. This was mostly because of what happened in 2010. In 2010 the President of Ukraine became Victor Yanukovych from "Party of Regions". Yanukovych was a pro-Russian leader who almost managed to make Ukraine fully change its foreign policy vector. In the other words, in the period between 2010-2013 there was no more necessity of escalation for Moscow, because they were having someone in Kyiv which was capable to carry out the policy that would be acceptable for the Kremlin. Indeed, Yanukovych was ready to carry on playing with Russian rules in order to prolong his presidential reign and this could cost Ukraine even more in case he would manage maintain power. By the end of 2013 Ukraine was facing economic crisis and high prices in the energy sector, causing much dissatisfaction of people. Ukraine was also facing much pressure from Russia both in economic and political terms. As a result, Yanukovych decided not to sign Association Agreement with the EU during Vilnius summit in November and moreover, accept Russian offer related to bailout and later propose the idea of joining Russian led Eurasian Union (Laure Delcour, 2014). In the other words, Yanukovych was at the edge of prolonging its rule in Ukraine with pretty clear authoritarian features with the help of Russia by the way of accepting terms and conditions of the Kremlin - namely giving up pro-Western aspirations, terminating integration process with the EU and joining the Eurasian Union - that in case it happened would mean simply full-scale return of Ukraine on the political orbit of Moscow (Matsaberidze, 2015, P. 5). Yanukovych's decision about refusing signing Association Agreement and strengthening links with Russia angered Ukrainians and made them demonstrate their protest in the streets - leading to Euromaidan events. Protests started in November at some point transformed into large-scale confrontation between police and the protesters - causing more than hundred deaths and more than 2500 injured people (*Radio Liberty*, 2019). The negotiations between the opposition and Yanukovych were mediated by the EU and Russia. In February. Later in the month Ukrainian parliament also removed Yanukovych from the position of the president, as a result - he had to flee to Russia (Bērziņš, 2014, p. 3). Despite the fact that as a result of removing Yanukovych from the office Ukraine managed to avoid the serious threat of getting back to the Russian geopolitical sphere of influence, the Kremlin still managed to use the chaos and destabilization in Ukraine on its behalf - simply saying Russia waged the hybrid war on Ukraine. At the outset, Russia simply annexed Crimea in a matter of days without resistance on a local level and all 190 Ukrainian military basis in Crimean peninsula surrendered soon (Bērziņš, 2014, p. 5). After that, Russia soon organized "referendum", where according to Russia's claims "more than 95,5% of population voted for joining Russia", in reality the referendum was boycotted by Crimean Tatars and other groups loyal to Kyiv (*BBC*, 2016). Russia didn't stop with Crimea and later provoked separatist movements in Eastern regions of Ukraine - namely in Donetsk and Luhansk. Creation of conflict in those regions was possible by Russia with an efficient synthesis of military support to secessionist forces and very precise informational warfare - targeted on the local population - portraying the anti-Yanukovych protesters in Kyiv as "Nazis" and "Russophobes" that were ready to "wipe out Russians and Russian-speaking people from Ukraine". Despite the fact, that Moscow managed to destabilize the situation in Eastern Ukraine and created territorial problems for the country, which similarly to Georgia also drives Ukraine back from its Euro-Atlantic aspirations, it is worth mentioning that Kremlin didn't manage its maximum. Initially Kremlin pursued to destabilize situation in most regions of South-East Ukraine - creating so called "Novorossyia" - which includes Russian speaking population of Ukraine from several regions - including Luhansk and Donetsk oblasts (Laure Delcour, 2014). Russia practiced majority of its Hybrid War toolkit leverages just after the outbreak of the conflict - including economic pressure, cyber-attacks, information warfare and etc. When we compare Russian aggression in Georgia and Ukraine, it should be also mentioned that in difference from Ukraine some of those tools were used against Georgia already before the war - mostly since 2005 during the "Cold War" phase in Russo-Georgian relations.

To sum up - this broader overview of chronological development of conflicts in Georgia and Ukraine demonstrate the following picture: Russian invasion in Georgia was a traditional military campaign with regular forces, which was a final stage of a long-term confrontation between two countries that started in 2004. While Russian aggression in Eastern Ukraine was more like a classic hybrid war example, more like plan B scenario after failure of Yanukovych, which still ended up to be quite well organized and prepared. Still, despite the difference in character, Russian aggression in both cases had common objective - maintain leverage and effective control over foreign policy of Georgia and Ukraine and create the efficient mechanism to indirectly veto accession of those countries in Euro-Atlantic structures.

COMPARATIVE ANALYSES – THE CASES OF 2008 AND 2014

Differences Between Russian Aggression in Georgia (2008) and Ukraine (2014)

Different Path to the Conflict

The chronological overview above have quite well demonstrated the key difference between the conflicts in Georgia and Ukraine. Russian aggression in Georgia was a peak of a long-lasting confrontation and escalation between two states - Georgia and Russia. Confrontation scale was increasing step by step since summer, 2004 and by 2008 there were explicit patterns and preconditions for imminent war.

In case of Ukraine the scenario was a little bit different. After pro-Western policies since Orange Revolution during Yuschenko's times, Ukraine fell into the rule of pro-Russian President Yanukovych back in 2010. Yanukovych's decision to give up aspirations of integration with the Western institutions and join the Russian alternative of it - Eurasian Economic Union angered people so much that it led them to massive protests - which ended up in famous Euromaidan events and impeachment of Yanukovych. The developments in rest of the Ukraine was translated by Russian propaganda as "Russophobic" and "nazi" movement against Russians and Russian-speakers. Russia used the opportunities created by the domestic chaos, annexed Crimean peninsula and created separatist uprising against Ukraine in Donetsk and Luhansk oblasts.

Difference in Russia's Preparation for the Conflict

As mentioned in overview, Russian authorities and namely Putin has admitted that the plan of military operation in Georgia was already being prepared by spring, 2006 (Felgenhauer, 2012). In spring, 2008 intelligence services of Baltic States were already making warnings that Russia was preparing for military invasion, in which Russian the 58th Army and the 76th Air Assault division would participate (Ariel Cohen, 2011, p. 16).

In case of Ukraine, as demonstrated in the paper by Lesia Dorosh, Olha Ivasechko, Jaryna Turchyn "Comparative Analysis of the Hybrid Tactics Application by the Russian Federation in Conflicts with Georgia and Ukraine" - Russia's actions were more simultaneous - there was a clear political goal to demoralize and distract Ukrainian society, but the rest of the actions by Russia were mostly opportunistic, fragmentary and at some points even not in accordance and in a logical chain with one another - leading to some unexpected realities (Lesia Dorosh, 2019, p. 19).

Conflicts of Different Classification and Distinction in Military Component

Russian invasion in Georgia was a classic war with some hybrid warfare elements. Georgia was explicitly invaded by Russia's regular army. Russian occupation forces according to different sources composed of up to 35-40 000 soldiers together with separatist militia and strong air and naval support (Lesia Dorosh, 2019, p. 11). In Georgia during the military campaign Russia deployed its 58th Army, which was based in Vladikavkaz (North Caucasus) and also deployed the troops from the 19th and 42nd Motorized Rifle divisions, Kremlin also airlifted troops from the 76th Air Assault Division from St. Petersburg Military District, also elements from the 98th Airborne Division, the 45th Intelligence regiment from Moscow and battalion from the 33rd Special Mountain Brigade (Ariel Cohen, 2011, p. 11). During the hostilities Russia attacked not only positions of Georgian troops in the conflict zone in Tskhinvali region - but intensively bombed military and civilian strategic infrastructure all over the country (Lesia Dorosh, 2019, pp. 10-11). Russia also opened the second front from Abkhazia and occupied significant part of West Georgia. In the other words, Russia was on its way to destroy full capacity of Georgia's military and political rule. By the end of the war most of Georgian troops were positioned around the capital of Georgia - preparing to defend the city from Russian attack.

In difference - the conflict in Ukraine is a classic hybrid war example, where non-military components are not just addition to military warfare - but are crucial components of Russian hybrid war itself. In case of Ukraine, on the one hand Russia explicitly annexed Crimean peninsula, but actual hostilities and military engagement didn't take place there, on the other hand created separatist uprising in two regions of Eastern Ukraine - Donetsk and Luhansk Oblasts. Russia in difference from Georgia in 2008 didn't use regular units of its army and mostly used either local proxies, or deployed "masked forces", so called "green men" to confront Ukrainians. The Kremlin deployed the soldiers without signs on their uniforms. According to some sources, 6 to 10 thousand Russian servicemen was deployed in Donbass. Another 40 000 was positioned at the borders - sending the clear signal, that in case Ukraine would launch large-scale conventional offensive, Kremlin was ready to use all the means to support its interests (Lesia Dorosh, 2019, pp. 10-11). It can be stated that Russian military operation in Ukraine shares even more similarities with conflicts in Abkhazia and Tskhinvali region back in 1990s - when Russia officially was pretending to be a "mediator" in the conflict, but in reality was supporting separatists. In the other words, Russia used disinformation and hybrid war tactics to create social protest, upon which it based separatism that it has supported with its own military and pretty much supported acts of terrorism and criminal activity as well (Lesia Dorosh, 2019, p. 4). In Ukraine unmarked militants, who were not easily distinguishable from civilians but were well-equipped with Russian arms, started blocking Ukrainian police and military units by the way of setting barricades, making it clear that Ukrainian units would have to use force in order to leave their bases and take the situation under control (Rácz, 2015, p. 60).

Difference in the Response From the West

The response from West towards Russia after the aggression against Georgia and Ukraine was not similar as well. In 2008 the West declared its support towards Georgia's sovereignty and territorial integrity - the leaders of 5 European nations - Poland, Latvia, Lithuania, Estonia and Ukraine arrived in Georgia during the War in order to demonstrate their support (*CNN*, 2008). The US launched a humanitarian mission to help Georgia, which was carried out by the US Navy and Air Forces (John D. McKinnon, 2008). The US also transported Georgian troops from Iraq during the war (*Veterans for Common Sense*,

2008). Although, Russia was not punished for its aggression. In case of Ukraine the situation was a little bit different - the West finally realized that Russia was not a constructive power and they imposed the sanctions on Russia for what it has done in Ukraine (*The Guardian,* 2014).

Similarities of Russian Toolkit in Georgia and Ukraine

Securitization of National Minorities and Manipulation With International Norms

In both cases - in Georgia and Ukraine Kremlin has securitized national minorities in order to advance its own political goals. In case of Georgia those were local ethnic minorities - Abkhazians and Ossetians, in case of Ukraine it was both local ethnic Russians and at some point Russian-speaking people as well (Matsaberidze, 2015, p. 4).

In both cases Kremlin attempts to artificially create two main narratives: "Aggressors are trying to suppress local minorities and Russia doesn't have much choice left - it has to enforce Responsibility to Protect principle" and the second one - that "people under pressure have the right of remedial secession and self-determination" (Burai, 2015). In reality those two narratives are products of Russian propaganda and in both cases it becomes evident that the ones who are victim of aggression are the citizens of attacked states and neither secession happens in accordance with international norms. This is proved by international response and resolutions, which explicitly support territorial integrity of Georgia and Ukraine. In both cases Russia quite often refers to the example of Kosovo, in order to demonstrate the following point: "If the West can support secession of Kosovo from Serbia, I can do the same in Georgia and Ukraine" (Burai, 2015).

Passportization Policy

In order to justify intervention in Georgia and Ukraine, Russia used the similar policy of "passportization" in both cases. Simply saying - Russia artificially created the reality, where it would have the justification related to "protecting" compatriots. In Georgia's breakaway regions - Tskhinvali region and Abkhazia the Kremlin intensively started providing Russian passports and Russia's citizenship to the locals living in de-facto entities (Matsaberidze, 2015, p. 9). Russia did the same in case of Ukraine (Matsaberidze, 2015, p. 9). The scenario is simple - after artificial "Russification" of the regions, once the tensions rise - Russia simply states that "according to its constitution it has obligation of protecting its citizens inside Russia and beyond the borders as well" so in this logic "it is obliged to intervene" (*THE CONSTITUTION OF THE RUSSIAN FEDERATION*, 1993, Art.61).

The idea of "protecting national minorities abroad" became integral part of Russian national security concept already in 1990s and after giving Russian passports to locals in Abkhazia, Tskhinvali region and Crimea - Russia actively used the argument of "defending its citizens (which it created artificially) all over the world by any means necessary" (Matsaberidze, 2015, p. 10).

Economic Pressure Over Georgia and Ukraine

Both Georgia and Ukraine experienced economic pressure from Russia. It can be said that economic dependence is the leverage, which is quite often used by the Kremlin as a political weapon. Despite the fact that this type of pressure was used in both cases, there was difference in timing.

In case of Georgia - as mentioned in the overview of the conflict, embargo on particular products and suspension of gas supply was a part of Russo-Georgian "Cold War" in the period between 2004-2008 - namely 2006 was the year, which was the tensest in this regard.

In case of Ukraine the timing was different - considering the fact, that during Yanukovych's times there was not confrontation between Kyiv and Moscow and the conflict erupted after Euromaidan events, pressure with economic leverages was introduced by Russia also after the escalation. It can be said that Russia waged trade war on Ukraine. It hit exports of Ukraine within Russian market, created serious problems for companies such as Roshen (Peter Pomerantsev, 2014, p. 31). Russia reduced export of Ukrainian goods to its market with 70%, causing 18% decrease in total exports of Ukraine and it also stopped gas supply to Ukraine (Aslund, 2015).

Despite the fact, that Russian economic pressure is the common tool against Georgia and Ukraine, the difference is not only about the timing of using this tool by the Kremlin, but it is about the situation aftermath as well. Namely it is about restoring economic relations with Russia - which was done by Tbilisi, but not by Kyiv. Since 2012 after change of government in Georgia, Georgian Dream ruling party declared "normalization policy" with Russia. In fact, it didn't have any significant outcomes in terms of de-occupation of Georgian territories, moreover - Russia made particular steps to de-facto annexation of Georgia's break-away regions in terms of the "strategic agreements" with Tskhinvali and Sokhumi that were made in 2014-2015 (*Civil.ge*, 2014). Still, Georgian Dreams "normalization" or "non-irritation policy" created the reality, where economic relations with hostile northern neighbor advanced and by this moment, there is a paradoxical reality when Russia, key security threat and foreign policy challenge, explicit enemy of Georgia is again one of the largest economic partners of it. It is worth adding that increased economic relations with Russia creates more political threat and risks than economic profit. Both Georgia and Ukraine knew from their experience quite well that economic dependence on Moscow is a political leverage for the Kremlin. This point was proved once again in 2019, when following the famous events of "Gavrilov's Night" on the 19th of June, Putin decided to punish Georgians with suspending direct flights from Russia and this was because of massive protests in the streets of Tbilisi following Gavrilov's visit and kicking out of communist MP of Russian legislative body from Georgia (*BBC*, 2019). Georgians were especially angered with Gavrilov's visit and his act of sitting in the seat of chairman of the parliament of Georgia, considering that he has broken the law about occupation several times, recognizes illegal so-called "independence" of Georgia's break-away regions and also fought against Georgia back in 1990s (Radio Liberty, 2019). In difference from Georgia, Ukraine isn't that motivated to restore economic ties with Russia following the conflict and this is more a type of logical behavior, because giving Russia economic influence in the country means creating political leverages for the Kremlin to impact.

Cyber Attacks

Another common weapon from Russian toolkit during the aggression in Georgia and Eastern Ukraine was cyber-attacks. It is worth mentioning that during those attacks not only local web-pages were the target, but the ones belonging to embassies and international organizations - such as NATO as well (Schwartz, 2014).

In case of Georgia first wave of cyber-offensive on Georgian web occurred just before the war - in July. During the attack in July among the list of the targets were governmental web-pages, also banking system - causing temporary shut down and telecommunications (Corbin, 2009). It can be said that the cyber-attack in July was kind of rehearsal for the next attack which took place already during the war. As mentioned - second attack by Russian hackers, mainly RBN (Russian Business Network) was launched during the war in August. This was the first time in history, when military conventional attack was supported by cyber and informational means as well (Ariel Cohen, 2011, p. 44). The motivation of this offensive was to paralyze the country - creating obstacles for communication both on local level and also to separate Georgia from rest of the world. Moreover, as David Hollis states in "Cyberwar Case Study: Georgia" Russian cyber-offensive was coordinated with conventional attacks and bombardment of Georgian positions, for instance official sites in Gori and local media platforms were hit hard and shut down by denial-of-service attacks (DDOS) just before Russian planes bombed the city of Gori itself (Hollis, 2010, p. 5). So the timing and location of cyber-attack and bombardment was coincided - making logical impression that it was coordinated. Total number of 38 web-pages were hit, including the US and UK embassies (Ariel Cohen, 2011, p. 44).

In case of Ukraine Russia also used cyber-attacks - namely with the involvement of Cyber Berkut groups, which also launched DDOS (denial of service) attacks on governmental web-pages, Ukrainian and NATO media websites and also hit UKRTELECOM, mobile phones of members of Ukrainian Rada (Pavel Polityuk, 2014). But in case of Ukraine there was no necessity to fully shut down Ukraine's cyber and especially information space, because of the reason, that Russian and Ukrainian web-space are already pretty much integrated and Russia already enjoyed domination there, taking into consideration the tele-communication companies and infrastructure that Russia has there (Giles, 2015, p. 8). In the other words, there was no reason for Russia to disrupt Ukrainian cyberspace, where it had already enjoyed domination. It is also worth mentioning that Cyber Berkut's attack included the warning for NATO member countries as well, stating that "If NATO cannot protect their resources, the protection of personal data of ordinary European cannot be considered" (Schwartz, 2014).

Disinformation and Propaganda Campaign

Disinformation and propaganda had one of the key roles during Russian invasion of Georgia and later even more significance during Russian aggression in Eastern Ukraine. But, despite the fact that on overall perspective this component can be perceived as similarity in Russian toolkit against Georgia and Ukraine, some of the objectives and character of Russian disinformation and propaganda campaign was quite distinctive in those cases.

Propaganda - Justifying Russian Invasion in Georgia, but Used as Weapon of Domestic Destabilization in Ukraine

It can be stated that in case of Georgia Russian disinformation and propaganda campaign had relatively "modest" objective than in case of Ukraine. In case of August War, 2008 the key objective of Russian propaganda was to create justification for Russian invasion in the perspective of Russian citizens and international community. In the other words, its efforts were directed at the creation of the vision, where "Georgia was aggressor, labeling its military operation in Tskhinvali region as "genocide", while according to this view Russia was "peacekeeper" and "protector" of "victims", "not infiltrator" (Lesia Dorosh, 2019, pp. 13-14). As mentioned, target audience of this narratives were Russians themselves and international community, but such narratives couldn't be efficiently directed at Georgians themselves, because for Georgians everything was crystal clear - their country was facing full-scale invasion from the aggressor state, that was shelling all regions of Georgia and was pushing its armed forces from several dimension, being on its way of full occupation.

In case of Ukraine the situation was a little bit different. Of course, like in case of Georgia Russian propaganda in 2014 also targeted its own citizens and international community as well, but here another key target group of it was Ukrainian society itself. Russian propaganda network was making a lot of efforts to portray the events in Maidan as "Nazi", "Russophobic" and "radical" movement that was ready to "wipe out everything and everyone that had something in common with Russia". Kremlin's propaganda aimed to create social dissatisfaction in Ukraine, demoralize and destabilize the society in order to artificially create a crisis, the chaos that would be managed by Kremlin on its behalf, attempting to position Ukrainians, especially those living in South-Eastern regions against their own authorities (Lesia Dorosh, 2019, pp. 13-14). The key objective of Russian propaganda was to create the situation, where the citizens of Ukraine would have sympathies towards the aggressor - Russia and would be vulnerable for Kremlin's softpower tools (Lesia Dorosh, 2019, p. 19). The efforts of Russian propaganda were especially challenging taking into consideration that in Eastern Ukraine quite significant proportion of the population is at least bilingual and Russia media there is quite popular, making the people living there vulnerable target for Kremlin's disinformation. Still, as indicated in some of the sources, Russian disinformation campaign didn't fully accomplish its objectives in Eastern Ukraine, meaning that Russian-speaking Ukrainian population didn't end up being that much enthusiastic joining separatist movement against Kyiv as it was predicted by Kremlin (Michael Kofman, 2015, p. 5).

"Ethnic Cleansing" and "Genocide" - Useless Cornerstones of Russian Propaganda

Both in case of Georgia and Ukraine Russian propaganda made a lot of efforts in order to somehow convince their target groups that attacked states - Georgia and Ukraine were the ones "which carried out massive atrocities, ethnic cleansing and genocide against national minorities". Due to lack of any evidence, in both cases it was quite challenging for Russian media to convince even the people living in Russia believe in those fake claims. In case of August War, Russian media during the early days of the war was claiming that after "Georgian artillery's massive shelling, up to 2000 civilians were killed in Tskhinvali region", but in reality the official number of civilian casualties in Tskhinvali were 133 persons, including those militias, which were fighting in civilian uniforms (Ariel Cohen, 2011, p. 48). The claim was so absurd, that even Russian journalists in the upcoming days of the war were mostly referring to information from international agencies such as Radio Free Europe / Radio Liberty in terms of information from the conflict zone (Ariel Cohen, 2011, p. 48).

Similarly there were the attempts to claim that Ukraine's central government was attempting to carry out "ethnic cleansing" against those, who were Russians or Russian-speakers. For instance on the 3rd of July, the document that supposedly belonged to "RAND Corporation" was "leaked online", "demonstrating" that think tank was giving advices to President Poroshenko about carrying out "ethnic cleansing" in Eastern Ukraine, "suggesting heavy bombardment and creation of internment camps for locals" (Peter Pomerantsev, 2014, p. 31). On the 15th of October, 2014 Sergei Ivanov (Kosmolskaya Pravda) secretary of the Presidential Administration stated, that there was no Russian military involvement in Donbas and that the region experienced "ethnic cleansing" and "genocide" against those, who didn't want to speak Ukrainian and rather speak in their "native language" (Darczewska, 2014, pp. 8-9).

AFTERMATH: WHAT HAPPENED IN UKRAINE AFTER 2014

Russo-Ukrainian Relations in Post-Maidan Reality (2014-2019)

Breakdown of Economic Ties

In post-Maidan reality the economic relations between Russia and Ukraine have significantly deteriorated. Similarly to the situation with regard to Georgia in 2006-2007, import of Ukrainian agricultural products were banned in Russia since 2016 (Gordiienko, 2015). It was preceded by the decision of Ukraine to stop the supply of military components to Russia that was necessary for production of military equipment (Gordiienko, 2015). Following the decision of ban on Ukrainian goods, Ukraine also decided to place a trade embargo on Russia (Deutsche Welle, 2015). The mobility of people between two countries was also limited. In October 2015 all direct flights between Ukraine and Russia were banned by Ukraine (Rainsford, 2015). In the following month Ukraine also closed its airspace for Russia's civil and military aircraft (BBC, 2015).

The political crises in 2013-2014 and the Russian aggression in Eastern Ukraine significantly deteriorated Ukraine's economic situation. The total trade was deteriorated with majority of external actors (including the EU). But the hostilities between Ukraine and Russia and the tough economic measures against one-another decreased economic ties between those countries even more than the economic relations of Ukraine with other external actors. For example, in 2011 total trade value between Russia and Ukraine was $49 billion, by 2016 this number was decreased 6 times – making total value of $8,7 billion (Bhutia, 2019). In comparison, the trade value with the EU of Ukraine in 2011 was $43,8 billion. Even though following the crises by 2015 it was reduced to 28,3 billion (the lowest rate), after recovery in 2018 it reached almost the same rate as in 2013 (in 2018 – $43,3 billion, in 2013 - $43,8 billion), meanwhile with regard to Russia this number in 2018 was no more than $11,7 billion (in 2011 it was $48,9 billion, in 2013 – $38,2 billion) (Bhutia, 2019).

Warfare in Informational Sphere and Culture

Several decisions were made in terms of informational sphere and culture as well. In March 2014, following the decision of the Kremlin to suspend broadcasting of Ukraine-based channels in Crimea, Kyiv also made a decision to ban Russian TV channels spreading disinformation about Ukraine, respectively – more than 15 Russian TV channels were banned by spring, 2016 (Dziadul, 2016). In 2015 Ukraine started banning Russian artists from entering the country (Deutsche Welle, 2015). In 2017 Poroshenko's government also banned commercial importation of books from Russia (Gerden, 2017). Another decision which was criticized by the Kremlin was related to making Ukrainian the only language of education in the primary schools (Council of Europe, 2017). This decision became the point of tough discussions both within Ukraine and beyond its boundaries.

Deterioration of Security Situation

Apart from confrontation in different areas, in post-Maidan reality there were several occasions, when the tensions within the security area also significantly increased. Apart from regular hostilities in Eastern Ukraine with constant different scale combat clashes in Luhansk and Donetsk regions between Ukrainian army and Russian-backed up separatists, there were several incidents between Ukrainian and formal-Russian sides as well. In March 2018, Russia-flagged vessel Nord was detained by Ukrainian border guards in the Azov Sea. The vessel was accused of entering the territory which was under a temporary occupation by Russia (Uawire, 2018). In November, 2018 situation became even more fragile following the detainment of 24 Ukrainian sailors in Kerch Strait. Russian FSB fired upon and later captured three Ukrainian vessels and kept the crew members in the captivity (Roth, Kerch strait confrontation: what happened and why does it matter?, 2018). Ukrainian vessels were captured after the incident when they were blocked by Russian side on their way to Azov Sea, once they tried to go back – they were captured in International waters (Roth, Kerch strait confrontation: what happened and why does it matter?, 2018). Following this case, Petro Poroshenko imposed Martial Law in 10 Oblasts – stating, that there was an evident threat of full-scale war with Russia (Roth, Kerch strait confrontation: what happened and why does it matter?, 2018).

Ukraine's Presidential Elections of 2019 and the Impact on Russo-Ukrainian Relations

Putting an End to the War in Eastern Ukraine – Demand of the Society, Promise of Zelenskiy

The polls demonstrate, that in the post-Maidan reality putting an end to the hostilities in Eastern Ukraine was among the key priorities of Ukrainian citizens during those years. International Republican Institute organized Opinion Surveys in Ukraine on a regular basis and among the questions in each of those surveys there was the one with the following formulation: "Which three of the following issues are the most important for Ukraine?" and all the time since 2014 "Military Conflict in Donbass" was either the first or the second issue for the population (with the exception in November, 2021) (IRI, 2014-2021). Moreover, in December 2018 – IRI arranged another opinion poll, where there was the question – "When making your decision on whom to vote for in the upcoming presidential elections, currently scheduled for March 31, 2019, which issues influence your vote the most?" the leading issue was once again "Military Conflict in the Donbass" with 39% of total respondents selecting it as the first choice option. Respectively, it is logical to state, that the stance of Zelenskyi (before he would become the President) on the conflict and relations with Russia was one of the key determinants of the success in Presidential elections. As stated in the article by Radio Free Europe / Radio Liberty – "One of Zelenskiy's two main promises was to bring the war to an end, a goal that polls have shown Ukrainians want to see accomplished more than anything (Miller, 2020)." And indeed, once observing the support rate of Zelenskiy according to the Oblasts, it also becomes quite explicit that he was mostly supported in the regions with relatively softer stance on Russia (Central, Southern and Eastern Oblasts) rather than in Northern and Western ones (with more tougher position on relations with Russia). Moreover, Zelenskiy not only promised people to put an end to the war in Donbass and normalize relations with Russia, but he also attempted to do so. Zelenskiy met with Vladimir Putin in Paris, in 2019, there were also prisoner exchanges, troop withdrawals from three locations at the line between the government-controlled and separatist-held lands and also the civilian bridge near Stanytsya Luhanska was completed (Miller, 2020). But in the end the Russian and Ukrainian perspectives on putting an end to the hostilities in Donbass remained quite distant. Nevertheless, the final outcomes demonstrate, that his willingness of negotiating with Russia was quite naïve. According to the same article from Radio Free Europe / Radio Liberty – "Alyona Hetmanchuk, director of the new Europe Center, a Kyiv think tank, says that "the main thing" is not what Zelenskiy managed to do on the war issue but what he did not do: "He did not achieve peace on Russian terms," which would be unacceptable for most Ukrainians (Miller, 2020)."

To sum up, Zelenskiy is the president, whose success on electoral polls was significantly determined by his promise and willingness of putting an end to the conflict in a very constructive way via negotiations with Russia, but on the contrary ended up to being the one facing the greatest challenge – most destructive type of Russian aggression in the XXI century – full scale invasion and terror.

SIMILARITIES: WAR IN 2008 AND WAR IN 2022

One Playbook – Two Scenarios

The prelude of the war and the toolkit of the Kremlin of the invasion in Georgia and Ukraine was almost identical. If the pre-war scenario in Georgia (2008) was quite different from the reality in Eastern Ukraine (2014), the pre-war scenario in Ukraine (2022) was simply a copy-paste version of the one from Russian aggression in Georgia's with minor adjustments.

Massive Mobilization of Troops Justified as "Regular Military Drills"

In July, 2008 – 2-3 weeks before the invasion in Georgia Russia started military drills called "Kavkaz 2008". As mentioned beforehand in this paper, the exercise plot included the elements related to intervention in a fictional neighboring country and also the military personnel received the cards with the listed characteristics of Georgian army and the text: "Soldier, Know Your Probable Enemy!" (Ariel Cohen, 2011). After finalizing the exercises, Russian troops didn't return back to their initial locations of dislocation and later they participated in the assault on Georgia (Engvall, 2020).

Similarly – in case of Ukraine the invasion by the Kremlin was also preceded by massive mobilization troops quite often justified as "regular military drills". During the last months of 2021, there were significant reports, including the ones provided by the US intelligence highlighting the massive mobilization of Russian troops near Ukrainian borders and explicit threat of the invasion in the early part of 2022. "Russia planning massive military offensive against Ukraine involving 175,000 troops, U.S. intelligence warns" – that is the title from one of many articles in prominent Western media agencies. The article was published on December 3, 2021 and stressed out the real threat of upcoming Russian invasion (Shane Harris, 2021). Even though the Western agencies were warning about highly-likeable Russian invasion, Vladimir Putin was still denying that he was planning to invade Ukraine. Although, he was very assertive with regard to demanding official guarantees that Ukraine wouldn't join NATO (Ben Fox, 2022). Just few days before the invasion Russia launched another joint military drills together with Belarus. The response by the Kremlin related to the accusations of escalation was that "it has a right to move its troops wherever it likes on its own territory." Russia also stated, that its "security concerns were ignored". Kremlin spokesperson Dmitry Peskov noted, that "Both Russia and Belarus are confronted with unprecedented threats and their nature and, perhaps, concentration are, unfortunately, far more considerable and far more dangerous now than before (Ellyatt, 2022)."

Partial Withdrawal Trick

In both cases few days preceding the war Kremlin organized partial withdrawal of the troops claiming that it was all part of their regular rotation or military drills, attempting to assure, that mobilization was not related to some other incentives.

In case of Georgia Russia announced about the withdrawal of Railway troops on the 30th of July, 2008 - just a week before the war. The troops were deployed in July in Abkhazia and the formal justification was "rehabilitation of railway infrastructure in Abkhazia" (Civil.ge, 2008). It is worth mentioning that rehabilitation of railway infrastructure in Abkhazia few days just before the war can be also the explicit sign of Russian preparations for ensuring proper functioning of logistics at the outset of the invasion.

Similarly, just few days before the war in case of Ukraine Kremlin partially withdrawn troops from the borders on the 15th of February, 2022, 9 days preceding the war. Even though there could be a hope that this step would be related to de-escalation of the situation, most of the Western leaders were quite skeptical about the willingness of Kremlin to cool down the tensions. "The size of the withdrawal remains unclear and it may involve only a fraction of Russia's forces at the border, which western officials estimate at more than 130,000 troops, at least 60% of the country's ground forces." – notes The Guardian in the article (Roth, Russia confirms 'partial' withdrawal of troops from Ukraine border, 2022).

Evacuation of the Civilians Few Days Before the War

In both cases Kremlin organized partial evacuation of the civilians from the conflict zones few days before the war. On the 5th of August, 2008, Ministry of Emergency Situations of the Russian Federation stated, that more than 800 persons were taken to North Ossetia, most of them – children and women (Civil.ge, 2008). Although, this step was justified by Ermak Dzansolov (the authority from North Ossetia) as "hosting children from "South Ossetia" by them likewise during previous years", stressing, that it was not "evacuation" (Civil.ge, 2008).

Just a week before the war, international media agencies noted, that tens of thousands of civilians were being evacuated from partially-occupied Ukrainian Oblasts of Donetsk and Luhansk to the territory of Russia (AlJazeera, 2022).

According to Aljazeera, based on the information provided by the authorities from Donetsk, up to 700 000 people were meant to leave. The massive evacuation from occupied lands of Ukraine as in case of Russian invasion of Georgia was another important point of pretext of upcoming Russian aggression.

Disinformation Hysteria

In both cases intensive Russian informational warfare preceded the actual full-scale invasion. The reason was simple – to justify upcoming Russian aggression in advance. The article on Foreignpolicy – "Russia Is Reenacting Its Georgia Playbook in Ukraine", which was published on the 22nd of February, 2022 - 2 days prior to Russian invasion in Ukraine – precisely describes the mechanism of Russian informational warfare and claims about non-existent "ethnic cleansing" or "genocide". In both cases Kremlin decided to blame both Georgia and Ukraine and accuse them of "suppressing Russian speakers, ethnically Russians", simply people, who are perceived by Russia as "part of Russian world" (Seskuria, 2022). None of those claims were proved by any international human rights mechanisms. Moreover, Russian narratives and accusations related to "genocide" or "ethnic cleansing" have been barely believed by any prominent international actors. Mostly the disinformation campaign was productive for domestic audience of

Putin, Russian society, which actively supports Kremlin's aggressive actions in neighboring countries. For instance after invasion in Ukraine Putin's approval rating increased to 83% from 71%, like in 2014, when after annexing Ukraine his approval rating jumped up from 6% to 83% (Evan Gershkovich, 2022).

Even Though Kremlin Tried to Make Up Casus Belli, in Both Cases Preceding the War Its Authorities Manifestly Pointed at Real Incentive of Upcoming Aggression – To Destroy Pro-Western Vector of Georgia and Ukraine

Russia organized massive disinformation campaigns both before the Russo-Georgian and Russo-Ukrainian wars. In both cases it intended to make up *casus belli* or justify its actions both in the perspective of international and domestic audience. In both cases Kremlin tried to justify its aggression, trying to argue that it was not the one that "initiated", but the one "responding". Still, despite those justifications, Kremlin authorities pretty often either hinted or manifestly highlighted the real motive of war for them – ensuring that neither Georgia, nor Ukraine join NATO. In the other words, the real motive of Kremlin is to burst pro-Western foreign policy ambitions of those countries, which are perceived by the Kremlin as the "zone of exclusive interests".

The minor difference is that Kremlin was not that straightforward in case of Invasion of Georgia. Meanwhile in case of Ukraine, the invasion was preceded by very manifest demands from Putin regarding "guarantees that Ukraine will not become the member of NATO". Although, Kremlin hinted and meant the same about Georgia before the war and it was admitted by Medvedev later after the war, stating: "If you had faltered back in 2008, the geopolitical situation would be different now, And a number of countries which (NATO) tried to deliberately drag into the alliance, would have most likely already been part of it now" (Dyomkin, 2011).

In 2008, on the 6th of July - Sergei Prikhodko, representative of the administration of the President of Russia – Medvedev stated, that expansion of NATO and namely membership of Georgia and Ukraine was "red line" in the framework of Russo-American relations (Civil.ge, 2008). Prikhodko stated, that this issue would be highlighted by Medvedev during the meeting with George Bush in Japan, at the Summit of Group of Eight. Later during that month, on the 12th of July, 2008 Medvedev affirmed Foreign Policy Conception of Russia, where there was stressed out strong opposition to expansion of NATO, namely membership of Ukraine and Georgia (Civil.ge, 2008).

As noted above, apart from those pre-war announcements, just after the war Medvedev already highlighted, that in case there was no war in Georgia, Georgia itself and some other countries would have been "dragged into NATO" as claimed by Medvedev (Dyomkin, 2011).

Despite the fact that incentive of aggression was quite similar in both cases (preventing Georgia and Ukraine from joining NATO), preceding the invasion of Ukraine Putin was far more aggressive and assertive. Putin manifestly threatened Ukraine. The West and Ukraine were given an ultimatum by Kremlin. Among the list there were the demands such as promise about not never accepting Ukraine in NATO, Putin also had demands related to "demilitarization" of Ukraine. Putin also stressed on the importance of "pulling back" NATO from "frontline" countries, such as Bulgaria, Romania and Poland (Tisdall, 2022) (TASS, 2022).

Recognition of Separatist Entities: Different Timing

Another similarity in Russia's playbook about Georgia and Ukraine is playing with the status and "recognition tool" of Kremlin backed up separatist entities from Georgia and Ukraine. In the context of both wars Russia used the "Recognition tool", but the difference was in terms of timing.

President of Russian Federation, Medvedev officially recognized "independence" of Georgia's breakaway regions on the 26th of August, 2008 – exactly two weeks after the active phase of Russo-Georgian war. The decision made by Kremlin was condemned by Western countries and organizations (CNN, 2008). Apart from Kremlin, so-called "independence" of separatist entities is recognized by few Russia's allies, including Venezuela, Nauru, Nicaragua and Syria.

In case of Ukraine this tool was used by Putin in advance. He decided to recognize so-called "independence" of Donetsk and Luhansk regions on the 22nd of February, two days prior to invasion in Ukraine (Reuters, 2022). It is worth mentioning that by that moment Russian-backed up separatist forces controlled only 35% of those territories that were recognized by Putin as "independent states". Thus, in the upcoming war seizing control over whole territories would have become one of the arguments from aggressor state.

In both cases recognition of separatist entities create a significant challenge for Georgia and Ukraine in long-run with regard to their potential NATO membership. One of the key arguments of those who are skeptical towards Georgia's and Ukraine's NATO membership in the West is exactly related to issues of territorial integrity. Even though there could be the ways to deal with current circumstances to find a way around this issue, this argument remains as one of the key narratives for those who oppose accession of those nations in North Atlantic Treaty Organization.

RUSSIA AS A TERRORIST STATE – WAR CRIMES COMMITTED BY RUSSIA AND RUSSIAN BACKED-UP SEPARATISTS

One of the key similarity between Russian aggression in Georgia and in Ukraine is that Russian forces and the separatist units backed up by Kremlin regularly committed atrocities and crimes against the humanity. Some of the crimes committed in Georgia have been already formally acknowledged by the international courts such as International Criminal Court and European Court for Human Rights. The processes have continued for more than a decade. Many investigations are being proceeded and the verdicts will be made in following years. Even though the investigations will continue for years, the scale and brutality of the atrocities committed by Russians and Russian backed-up forces in Ukraine are already explicit. The intensive media coverage, proved facts of massive execution, torture and rape of civilians and the human rights reports being made on ad-hoc basis make it explicit, that the evaluation of the atrocities committed against Ukrainians will be very strict by all means. Some state actors already recognized the atrocities committed by Russians as genocide. On 21st of April Estonian Parliament was the first recognizing the mass-crimes by Russian Federation as "genocide against Ukrainians" (Askew, 2022). Latvian Parliament did the same on the same day (Reuters, 2022). Later legislative body of Canada also did the same on the 28th of April, 2022 (Treisman, Canada's House backs a motion recognizing Russia's actions in Ukraine as genocide, 2022).

Atrocities Committed Against Georgia

Ethnic Cleansing in 1990s

In 1990s Georgia faced two conflicts. In 1991-1992 the conflict broke out in Tskhinvali region. In 1992-1993 the country experienced the war in Abkhazia – leaving tens of thousands dead and hundreds of thousands displaced inside the country. Even though Russia was not official "party of the conflict" and was portraying itself as mediator, there are significant evidences of Russian support of separatist regimes. In Abkhazia ethnically Georgian population experienced ethnic cleansing and this is recognized by the OSCE Budapest, Lisbon and Istanbul summits. "They [participating states] expressed their deep concern over "ethnic cleansing", the massive expulsion of people, predominantly Georgian, from their living areas and the deaths of large numbers of innocent civilians." – notes the Budapest Document from 1994 (CSCE, 1994). As mentioned above, according to the position of international community by this moment most of the responsibility burden was upon separatist regime. Lisbon Summit Document of the OSCE also highlights the ethnic cleansing of Georgian population in Abkhazia, but perceives Russian Federation as "facilitator". "We are convinced that the international community, in particular the United Nations and the OSCE with participation of the Russian Federation as a facilitator, should continue to contribute actively to the search for a peaceful settlement." – notes the Document of Lisbon Summit from 1996 (OSCE, 1996). Even though back then Russian Federation was perceived as "facilitator" and "mediator", based on the following events and active role of Russia in terms of supporting separatists and ensuring their victory through different means (including diplomatic and military) leaves quite logical ground for sharing part of the responsibility on Russian Federation itself as well already in 1990s.

HRW Report About 2008

Human Rights Watch published 200-page report where it provides information about the findings regarding the international law in Russo-Georgian War of August, 2008. At the outset the report blames both sides for using indiscriminate fire which caused collateral damage, including civilian sufferings. Both conflict sides are also accused of using cluster munitions as well (Lokshina, 2009). Other parts of the report mostly writes about the breach of human rights against ethnically Georgian population. Namely it's about opening fire on civilian vehicles by Russia's occupying forces, killing or wounding civilians (Lokshina, 2009). The report writes about South Ossetian forces deliberately and systematically destroying ethnic Georgian villages. Beating, looting or threatening ethnic Georgians and unlawfully detaining them (Lokshina, 2009). According to the report no fewer than 159 ethnic Georgians were detained, killing at least one of them and subjecting nearly all of them to inhuman treatment (Lokshina, 2009). The report also writes that Ossetian separatists tortured at least four Georgian Prisoners of War and executed three of them. According to the report, the responsibility is upon Russian occupying forces as well, as they were having effective control over the territory. "Russian forces were at times involved in the looting and destruction, as passive bystanders or active participants, or by providing militias with transport into villages." – notes the report (Lokshina, 2009).

ICC and ECHR Decisions

Number of cases have been under investigation in International Criminal Court and European Court of Human Rights. Most of the decisions were made recently considering that the investigations and court procedures last for a while, sometimes for more than a decade.

ECHR Verdict About Georgia vs. Russia Case Over the War in 2008, March 21, 2021

On the 21st of January, 2021 European Court of Human Rights made verdict about Georgia vs Russia Case over the war in 2008. The court decided, that Russia was responsible over breach of six articles from European Convention of Human Rights. Russia was also held responsible for failure concerning conduct of effective investigation in the aftermath of the war. The court ruled, that Russia experienced effective control over both separatist regions and also so-called "buffer zones" since the 12th of August. (In case of "buffer zone" till 10th of October). ECHR accused Russia over the breach of following articles:

- Articles 2, 3, and 8 of the Convention, involving the right to life, prohibition of torture and respect for private and family life, Article 1 – the protection of the property. This concerned 160 civilians detained by Ossetian forces, but where under Russian jurisdiction (16 votes to 1)
- Article 1, Article 3, related to the prohibition of torture against those 160 civilians who were detained by Ossetian forces, but where under Russian jurisdiction (unanimously)
- Article 5 related to the right to liberty and security (unanimously)
- Unanimously ruling, that Georgian PoWs were under Russian Jurisdiction and 16 votes to 1 ruling that there was breach of Article 3 – prohibition of torture – concerning Georgian Prisoners of War
- Russia failed to meet its obligations under Article 38, by failing to examine the case (16 votes to 1)

The final verdict was that even though "the Russian forces' direct involvement had not been clearly demonstrated, the fact that the Georgian civilians fell within the Russian jurisdiction meant that the latter had also been responsible for the actions of the S. Ossetian authorities (ECHR, 2021)."

ECHR Finds War Crime Claims Against Georgia Inadmissible, October 22, 2021

Later that year ECHR announced, that it found war crime claims against Georgia as inadmissible. Complains were made by Russian citizens resided in Tskhinvali region. Claims were related to "disproportionate use of military force by the Georgian armed units.", "putting people under real and immediate danger," "causing anxiety and fear" and etc. The court asserted that "country cannot be considered accountable merely because the territory in which the hostilities took place was formally Georgian," and that "the Russian and Georgian armed forces resorted to massive bombing and shelling of the territories within the same period of time," making it "impossible to track" and single out the party responsible for the applicants' distress and suffering (Civil.ge, 2021)."

ICC Filed Arrest Warrants for Ossetian Officials, March 10, 2022

Earlier in the Spring, 2022 another international judiciary institution – International Criminal Court made a decision against Russian backed-up separatists. Lt.-Gen. Mikhail Mindzaev, de facto interior minister in 2005-2008; Hamlet Guchmazov, Head of the Preliminary Detention facility of the de facto interior ministry at the time of events; and David Sanakoev, de facto presidential representative for human rights in S. Ossetia were accused of war crimes, namely unlawful confinement, torture, inhuman treatment, outrages upon personal dignity, hostage taking, and unlawful transfer (Civil.ge, 2022).

ECHR Finds War Crime Claims Against Georgia Inadmissible, March 24, 2022

Likewise in 2021, ECHR found another wave of claims against Georgia inadmissible. This time ECHR threw out 370 Applications against Georgia, stating, that those applications were "identical" as the previous ones found inadmissible before, so there was no reason to provide a different approach other than during the previous findings (Civil.ge, 2022).

Atrocities Committed Against Ukraine

The scale of the devastation and atrocities committed by Russian forces in Ukraine is horrifying. Even though the international courts will require significant time for making final verdicts for all the cases, photo / video content and the reports made from Ukrainian territories about the crimes committed by Russian forces make the responsibility of Kremlin's forces crystal clear.

Human Rights Watch Report

Human Rights Watch report from the 3rd of April provides brief summary of the atrocities committed by Russian forces in Ukraine in the period between February 27 and March 14 (Human Rights Watch, 2022). The war-time crimes include cases of repeated rape, summary execution and unlawful violence and threats against civilians. Among the crimes there are also pillaging and looting civilians. ""Rape, murder, and other violent acts against people in the Russian forces' custody should be investigated as war crimes." – notes Hugh Williamson, Europe and Central Asia director at Human Rights Watch. The summary includes execution of men from Bucha, the village of Staryi Bykv (Chernihiv region), killing woman and 14-year old child in the village of Vorzel and repeated rape from Kharkiv region (Human Rights Watch, 2022). It is worth mentioning that this report doesn't include the facts from the late part of March, the period, when the Bucha massacre outcomes became explicit.

Deliberate Bombardment of Civilian Areas

The footage of Russian invasion in Ukraine includes numerous cases of deliberate bombardment of civilian areas. One of the most significant examples were seen in Kharkiv, the second biggest city of Ukraine. The city is under heavy bombardment regularly after the outbreak of the war. The footage from the 28th of February is one of many proofs of Russian forces heavily bombarding civilian areas with rocket launchers (Harding, 2022). On the 1st of March the footage presenting bombardment of Kharkiv center with ballistic missile also was aired on the net. Accordingly at least 10 people were killed as a result of the missile attack in that moment (BBC, 2022).

Bombardment of Hospitals and Shelters of Children: Maternity Hospital From Mariupol and the Theater

Later in the March Maternity and Children's hospital from Mariupol became another target of Russian artillery. The bombardment of hospital killed at least three people, including a child (BBC, 2022). The besieged port of Mariupol experienced the war in the most horrifying way. One of the most well-known war-crime committed by the Russian forces was bombardment of the Theater in Mariupol which was a shelter for 600 civilians, mostly children. The satellite images of upper view of the theater shows the giant letters in front of the theater written in Russian – Дети (Children). Those who found the shelter in the theater made those writings explicitly visible, hoping that Russians wouldn't bombard the shelter of hundreds of children. But the theater experienced the heavy bombardment, causing estimated death of 300 people (BBC, 2022).

Bucha Massacre

Bucha Massacre is one of the most evident proofs of Russian war-crimes in Ukraine so far. Bucha is a town north-west of capital – Kyiv. Bucha was occupied by Russian forces from late February up until the end of March. The video and photo footage, also the reports and interviews provide evidence of dozens of war-crimes and atrocities, such as rape, summary execution, torturing, beheading and other types of inhuman treatment carried out by Russian forces (Human Rights Watch, 2022). On the 21st of April Human Rights Watch published a report "Ukraine: Russian Forces' Trail of Death in Bucha" writing about the atrocities committed by Russian forces in Bucha (Human Rights Watch, 2022). "Nearly every corner in Bucha is now a crime scene, and it felt like death was everywhere," – noted Richard Weir, crisis and conflict researcher at Human Rights Watch (Human Rights Watch, 2022). According to regional prosecutor - Ruslan Kravchenko, by the 15th of April 278 bodies were found in the town, most of them – civilians. Many of the bodies were found in communal graves. Funeral home worker – Serhii Matiuk, who was helping in terms of collecting bodies stated, that most of the bodies were shot with bullets, 50 of them with hands tied and bodies with the signs of torture (Human Rights Watch, 2022). "Human Rights Watch documented the details of 16 apparently unlawful killings in Bucha, including nine summary executions and seven indiscriminate killings of civilians – 15 men and a woman." – notes the report. There are also the reports of victim-activated booby traps placed on at least two dead bodies (Human Rights Watch, 2022). The report provides details from all the documented cases.

Some Countries Start to Recognize the Actions of Russia in Ukraine as Genocide

By the second part of April Latvian and Estonian parliaments announced that they recognized the actions of Russia in Ukraine as genocide. "evidence of mass brutal crimes committed by the army of the Russian Federation, including the murder, torture, sexual abuse and desecration of Ukrainian civilians, including women and children, in Bucha, Irpin, Mariupol and elsewhere" – stated Latvia's Parliament. "murders, enforced disappearances, deportations, imprisonment, torture, rape, and desecration of corpses" – cites the legislative body of Estonia (Reuters, 2022). Later the parliament of Canada did the same and recognize the war crimes committed by Russia in Ukraine as genocide (Treisman, 2022). Earlier in April the President of the US – Joe Biden also assessed Russia's actions in Ukraine as genocide (Shannon Pettypiece, 2022).

CONCLUSION

Russian invasion in Georgia (2008) and aggression in Eastern Ukraine (2014) changed the overall picture of security frame in Europe. Russian invasion in Ukraine (2022) with its far more enormous scale is going to impact the world-wide security architecture in following decades and the role of Russia there as well, which so far seems to be totally isolated by most of democratic nations. Russia's offensive neorealist policies - ambition to change the current status quo and the view of having its exclusive zone of interests in post-Soviet space came into contradiction with the free will of Georgia and Ukraine to find their different path in Euro and Euro-Atlantic institutions. As a result, in order to counter Georgian and Ukrainian pro-Western aspirations the Kremlin decided to carry out military aggression against those states - postponing their integration with the West and creating serious leverages over Tbilisi and

Kyiv to influence their foreign policies and decisions. But ongoing war in Ukraine also seems counter-effective for Russia as well. Following Russia's invasion in Ukraine (2022) the EU decided to work on the candidate status of Ukraine, Moldova and Georgia as soon as possible. Before Russian-led war that broke out in 2022, this was not the perspective in a foreseeable near future. Despite the fact that there is a similarity in terms of incentives of Russia for carrying out military operation against those countries, there are several distinctive aspects that should be discussed. August, 2008 and Russian aggression in Eastern Ukraine, 2014 are different types of conflict. Meanwhile, even though Russo-Georgian War 2008 and Russo-Ukrainian War 2022 are both examples of conventional warfare (with significant hybrid elements), the case of Ukraine is far more large-scale one.

When there is a comparison between the cases of 2008 and 2014, there can be said that Russo-Georgian war was the traditional conventional war with some hybrid war elements, where Russia without much attempt to cover its troops manifestly invaded the country from different dimensions and bombed all types of strategic architecture - both military and civilian, including the targets far away from the conflict zone as well. The case of Ukraine was more like a classic hybrid war, where Russia created separatist uprising and supported it by "masked" forces without any signs indicating their belonging to Russian Federation (despite the fact, that everybody knows they belong to Russian Federation). Despite the fact that in Georgia some hybrid war elements were present as well, in case of Ukraine their value and significance was far more essential and they were no less important than military component. There was a difference in terms of prelude of the conflicts in Georgia and Ukraine as well. In case of Georgia the conflict was the peak of the long-lasting escalation between Georgia and Russia since summer, 2004. In case of Ukraine, despite the fact that those countries also had different foreign policy view especially during Yuschenko's rule, who was explicitly pro-Western, still during the rule of Yanukovych, who in contrast was pro-Russian, there were no indications that the conflict between Russia and Ukraine would emerge in that short period of time - because Yanukovych was acting in accordance with Russian interests. Russian aggression emerged exactly after Yanukovych was removed from the office following famous Euromaidan events. So the path to the conflict was quite different in case of Georgia and Ukraine. So both the pre-phase of the conflict and Russian preparation for it was different in those two cases. In terms of difference there can be stated one more thing - the response from the West in those cases was not identical as well. In case of Russo-Georgian War the West was still more reluctant to punish Russia properly for aggression in Georgia, while in case of Ukraine, the West finally realized that Russia was an aggressive revisionist power and decided to impose sanctions on it. What can be said about the similarities is that Russia used number of common tools during its aggression in Georgia and Ukraine. This concerns securitization of national minorities in both cases and then using their name in terms of justifying the intervention, carrying out "passportization" policies, organizing cyber-attacks on the digital architecture of Georgia and Ukraine, using economic leverages as a tool of pressure and organizing massive disinformation campaign against Tbilisi and Kyiv. Despite the fact, that those policies were part of the common toolkit, implementation of them was sometimes different in terms of timing and objectives, for instance disinformation campaign in case of Georgia was mostly aiming to justify Russian invasion, while the same type of campaign in Ukraine was not only tool for justification, but also the weapon to demoralize and divide local Ukrainian society as well.

Once it comes to comparison of the cases of 2008 and 2022, even though the scale of the conflict is far more extensive in case of Ukraine, the similarities are even more explicit than in comparison of cases of 2008 and 2014. The Kremlin simply copy-pasted its playbook of Georgia (2008) in Ukraine (2022) with identical steps preceding the invasion. The pretext of the conflict had also similarities. In the pretext in this case there is meant the deterioration of the relations for years before the extensive military warfare. In case of Georgia the deterioration of relations with Russia started in summer, 2004. Meanwhile for Ukraine it all significantly started since Russian aggression in Eastern Ukraine, 2014. The deviation here from the "common storyline" is that in Ukraine in 2019 the Presidential elections was won by the President, which promised normalization of relations with Russia and putting an end to the hostilities via negotiating with Putin. But the recent history demonstrates, that his expectations were excessive, attempts – failed and Zelenksyi ended up exactly the one, who is currently leading Ukraine in the large-scale warfare defending its sovereignty and independence from Russian imperial ambitions. There were many similarities in terms of breach of international humanitarian law principles by Kremlin's regime as well – committing explicit crimes and atrocities during the hostilities. In case of Russo-Georgian War, taking into account that already more than a decade has passed this was already concluded by judgements by ICC or ECHR. In case of Russian invasion in Ukraine (2022) the number of atrocities and the scale is far more enormous. Some of the countries, their leaders or parliaments have already evaluated the actions of Russian Federation in Ukraine as genocide. In following years after all the cases will be investigated it's almost inevitable that Russia will face similar judgements by ECHR and ICC as it have already faced in the context of the August War, 2008. But taking into account the scale and character of those atrocities in Ukraine, this time the judgements will cover far more cases and it can be anticipated, that they will be even stricter than previous ones.

To sum up - it can be said that Russia had common incentive in both cases and the overall objective was same - keep Georgia and Ukraine away from the West. The manifest demands preceding Russian invasion in Ukraine (2022) were even more ambitious and assertive. In order to achieve those objectives Russia used the common tool - military aggression. Within frame of this aggression it used different tools, some of them similar in those cases, some - different according to unique context of each country. It is important to analyze both cases and Russian toolkit that it has used against Georgia and Ukraine, because that's the way the Kremlin makes its foreign policy and it is quite logical to state, that Georgia and Ukraine maybe are not the last targets of it.

REFERENCES

AlJazeera. (2022, February 18). *Russian-backed separatists evacuate residents from east Ukraine*. Retrieved March 19, 2022, from AlJazeera: https://www.aljazeera.com/news/2022/2/18/russian-backed-separatists-announce-evacuation-from-east-ukraine

Ariel Cohen, R. E. (2011). *The Russian Military and the Georgia War: Lessons and Implications*. Strategic Studies Institute. doi:10.21236/ADA545578

Askew, J. (2022, April 21). *'Massive war crimes': Estonia accuses Russia of genocide in Ukraine*. Retrieved April 25, 2022, from Euronews: https://www.euronews.com/my-europe/2022/04/21/massive-war-crimes-estonia-accuses-russia-of-genocide-in-ukraine

Aslund, A. (2015, July 5). *Russia's war on Ukraine's economy*. Retrieved May 17, 2021, from The Japan Times: http://www.japantimes.co.jp/opinion/2015/07/13/commentary/worldcommentary/russias-war-on-ukraines-economy/#.WFmsAhGg-1t

BBC. (2006, October 6). *Georgians deported as row deepens*. Retrieved May 19, 2021, from BBC: http://news.bbc.co.uk/2/hi/europe/5412672.stm

BBC. (2015, November 25). *Ukraine closes airspace to all Russian planes*. Retrieved March 16, 2022, from BBC: https://www.bbc.com/news/world-europe-34920207

BBC. (2016, March 16). *Crimea referendum: Voters 'back Russia union*. Retrieved May 21, 2021, from BBC: https://www.bbc.com/news/world-europe-26606097

BBC. (2019, June 21). *Georgia protests: Thousands storm parliament over Russian MP's speech*. Retrieved June 5, 2021, from BBC: https://www.bbc.com/news/world-europe-48710042

BBC. (2022a, March 1). *Building hit by missile in Kharkiv's Freedom Square*. Retrieved April 10, 2022, from BBC: https://www.bbc.com/news/av/world-europe-60568298

BBC. (2022b, March 10). *Ukraine war: Three dead as maternity hospital hit by Russian air strike*. Retrieved April 10, 2022, from BBC: https://www.bbc.com/news/world-europe-60675599

BBC. (2022c, March 25). *War in Ukraine: Estimated 300 dead in Mariupol theatre strike*. Retrieved April 10, 2022, from BBC: https://www.bbc.com/news/world-europe-60873435#:~:text=An%20estimated%20300%20people%20were,building%20when%20it%20was%20hit

Ben Fox, V. I. (2022, January 29). *Russia denies it plans to invade Ukraine. Putin's remaining options are still risky*. Retrieved March 19, 2022, from Globalnews: https://globalnews.ca/news/8580055/russia-ukraine-putin-tensions/

Bērziņš, J. (2014). Russia's new generation warfare in Ukraine: Implications for Latvian defense policy. National Defence Academy of Latvia, Center for Security and Strategic Research.

Bhutia, S. (2019, November 25). *How has conflict with Russia affected Ukraine's trade?* Retrieved March 16, 2022, from Eurasianet: https://eurasianet.org/how-has-conflict-with-russia-affected-ukraines-trade

Blank, S. (2017). *Cyber War and Information War à la Russe*. Georgetown University Press.

Britannica. (n.d.). *North Atlantic Treaty Organization*. Retrieved June 4, 2021, from Britannica: https://www.britannica.com/topic/North-Atlantic-Treaty-Organization/The-role-of-Germany#:~:text=In%20May%201955%20West%20Germany,eastern%20Europe%20the%20same%20year

Burai, E. (2015, November 5). *Parody as Norm Contestation: Russian Normative Justifications in Georgia and Ukraine and Their Implications for Global Norms*. Retrieved May 20, 2021, from Taylor Francis Online: https://www.tandfonline.com/doi/full/10.1080/13600826.2015.1092424

Business Media Georgia. (2019, June 23). რუსული ემბარგოს ქრონოლოგია საქართველოში. Retrieved May 15, 2021, from Business Media Georgia: https://www.bm.ge/ka/article/rusuli-embargos-qronologia-saqartveloshi/35815

Carolina Vendil Pallin, F. W. (2009, June 2). Russia's war in Georgia: Lessons and consequences. *Small Wars & Insurgencies, 20*(2), 400–424. doi:10.1080/09592310902975539

Civil.ge. (2004, September 2). *Closure of Ergneti Black Market Boosted Customs Revenues*. Retrieved June 4, 2021, from Civil.ge: https://civil.ge/archives/115946

Civil.ge. (2006a, September 28). მოსკოვმა თბილისიდან ელჩი გაიწვია. Retrieved May 23, 2021, from Civil.ge: https://civil.ge/ka/archives/139150

Civil.ge. (2006b, September 30). რუსეთი წყვეტს საქართველოდან ჯარების გაყვანას. Retrieved May 23, 2021, from Civil.ge: https://civil.ge/ka/archives/139186

Civil.ge. (2006c, September 29). საგარეო უწყება რუსეთში საქართველოს საელჩოზე თავდასხმას გმობს. Retrieved May 23, 2021, from Civil.ge: https://civil.ge/ka/archives/139173

Civil.ge. (2006d, June 28). ქართული არმია ფართომასშტაბიან წვრთნებს ატარებს. Retrieved May 23, 2021, from Civil.ge: https://civil.ge/ka/archives/138378

Civil.ge. (2006e, September 27). შსს–მ ჯაშუშობის ბრალდებით 4 რუსი ოფიცერი დააკავა. Retrieved May 23, 2021, from Civil.ge: https://civil.ge/ka/archives/139137

Civil.ge. (2007a, October 30). განმუხურის ბანაკთან მომხდარი ინციდენტის გამო ქართულმა მხარემ საბრძოლო მზადყოფნა გამოაცხადა. Retrieved May 23, 2021, from Civil.ge: https://civil.ge/ka/archives/141769

Civil.ge. (2007b, October 30). განმუხურში ქართულ ძალებსა და რუს სამშვიდობოებს შორის დაპირისპირება მოხდა. Retrieved May 23, 2021, from Civil.ge: https://old.civil.ge/geo/article.php?id=16477

Civil.ge. (2007c, August 9). მოხსენება დაბომბვის ზოგიერთ დეტალზე საუბრობს. Retrieved May 23, 2021, from Civil.ge: https://civil.ge/ka/archives/141175

Civil.ge. (2008a, July 15). აფხაზეთის ლიდერი "გერმანულ გეგმას" უარყოფს. Retrieved June 3, 2021, from Civil.ge: https://old.civil.ge/geo/article.php?id=18798&search=

Civil.ge. (2008aa, July 8). სოხუმმა ამერიკელების წინადადება უარყო. Retrieved June 2, 2021, from Civil.ge: https://old.civil.ge/geo/article.php?id=18737&search=

Civil.ge. (2008ab, May 7). სოხუმს მედვედევის "გადამწყვეტი ნაბიჯის" იმედი აქვს. Retrieved May 29, 2021, from Civil.ge: https://old.civil.ge/geo/article.php?id=18211&search=

Civil.ge. (2008ac, June 19). სოხუმში რკინიგზაზე ორი აფეთქება მოხდა. Retrieved June 1, 2021, from Civil.ge: https://old.civil.ge/geo/article.php?id=18588&search=

Civil.ge. (2008ad, June 21). სოხუმში უსაფრთხოების ორი თანამშრომელი დაჭრეს. Retrieved June 1, 2021, from Civil.ge: https://old.civil.ge/geo/article.php?id=18608&search=

Civil.ge. (2008ae, June 25). ქართული მხარე სამშვიდობო პროცესის დასაწყებად ორი წინაპირობის შესრულებას მოითხოვს. Retrieved May 30, 2021, from Civil.ge: https://old.civil.ge/geo/article.php?id=18632&search=

Civil.ge. (2008af, August 5). ჩრდილოეთ ოსეთში ცხინვალიდან 800-ზე მეტი ადამიანი ჩავიდა. Retrieved March 19, 2022, from Civil.ge: https://civil.ge/ka/archives/144198

Civil.ge. (2008ag, May 16). ცხინვალის რეგიონში მომხდარი აფეთქების შედეგად პოლიციელი დაიჭრა. Retrieved May 30, 2021, from Civil.ge: https://old.civil.ge/geo/article.php?id=18279&search=

Civil.ge. (2008ah, June 16). ცხინვალის რეგიონში მომხდარი სროლის შედეგად ერთი ადამიანი დაღუპა, ოთხი კი დაშავდა. Retrieved June 1, 2021, from Civil.ge: https://old.civil.ge/geo/article.php?id=18566&search=

Civil.ge. (2008ai, April 15). ცხინვალმა სოხუმში "საელჩო" გახსნა. Retrieved May 25, 2021, from Civil.ge: https://old.civil.ge/geo/article.php?id=18008&search=

Civil.ge. (2008aj, July 19). ცხინვალმა უარყო ევროკავშირის წინადადება ბრიუსელში მოლაპარაკებების გამართვის თაობაზე. Retrieved June 3, 2021, from Civil.ge: https://old.civil.ge/geo/article.php?id=18837&search=

Civil.ge. (2008ak, May 29). ცხინვალში აფეთქება მოხდა. Retrieved May 30, 2008, from Civil.ge: https://old.civil.ge/geo/article.php?id=18429&search=

Civil.ge. (2008b, May 21). აფხაზეთში მომხდარი აფეთქების შედეგად "ოთხი ადამიანი" დაშავდა. Retrieved May 30, 2021, from Civil.ge: https://old.civil.ge/geo/article.php?id=18328&search=

Civil.ge. (2008c, June 29). გაგრაში აფეთქებამ ექვსი ადამიანი დაჭრა. Retrieved June 1, 2021, from Civil.ge: https://old.civil.ge/geo/article.php?id=18666&search=

Civil.ge. (2008d, July 3). დიმიტრი სანაკოევის კორტეჟს თავს დაესხნენ. Retrieved June 2, 2021, from Civil.ge: https://old.civil.ge/geo/article.php?id=18692&search=

Civil.ge. (2008e, March 28). ეუთოს თავმჯდომარე ცხინვალში მომხდარი აფეთქების გამო შეშფოთებულია. Retrieved May 26, 2021, from Civil.ge: https://old.civil.ge/geo/article.php?id=17889&search=

Civil.ge. (2008f, May 28). თამარაშენში სროლების შედეგად არავინ დაშავებულა. Retrieved May 30, 2021, from Civil.ge: https://old.civil.ge/geo/article.php?id=18423&search=

Civil.ge. (2008g, April 29). თბილისი აფხაზეთის წინააღმდეგ "სამხედრო ოპერაციას" გეგმავს - აცხადებს რუსეთი. Retrieved May 27, 2021, from Civil.ge: https://old.civil.ge/geo/article.php?id=18137&search=

Civil.ge. (2008h, June 24). თბილისი სამშვიდობოების გაყვანის მოთხოვნამდე ევროკავშირის და აშშ-ს ჩარევას ელის. Retrieved May 30, 2021, from Civil.ge: https://old.civil.ge/geo/article.php?id=18622&search=

Civil.ge. (2008i, April 12). თბილისი სოხუმს ერთობლივი პოლიციის შექმნას სთავაზობს. Retrieved May 25, 2021, from Civil.ge: https://old.civil.ge/geo/article.php?id=17992&search=

Civil.ge. (2008j, April 18). თბილისი უარყოფს ძალების განთავსებას აფხაზეთის კონფლიქტის ზონაში. Retrieved May 26, 2021, from Civil.ge: https://old.civil.ge/geo/article.php?id=18041&search=

Civil.ge. (2008k, May 16). მოსკოვი აფხაზეთზე გაეროს გენასამბლეის რეზოლუციას "კონტრპროდუქტიულს" უწოდებს. Retrieved May 30, 2021, from Civil.ge: https://old.civil.ge/geo/article.php?id=18276&search=

Civil.ge. (2008l, June 14). ნატომ საქართველოს საკითხი რუსეთთან შეხვედრაზე დააყენა. Retrieved May 30, 2021, from Civil.ge: https://old.civil.ge/geo/article.php?id=18563&search=

Civil.ge. (2008m, July 6). ნატოს გაფართოება "წითელი ხაზია" რუსეთ-ამერიკის ურთიერთობებში – კრემლის წარმომადგენელი. Retrieved March 20, 2022, from Civil.ge: https://civil.ge/ka/archives/143999

Civil.ge. (2008n, May 2). რაისი აფხაზეთში დამატებითი რუსული ძალების შეყვანის გამო შეშფოთებულია. Retrieved May 28, 2021, from Civil.ge: https://old.civil.ge/geo/article.php?id=18167&search=

Civil.ge. (2008o, March 11). როგოზინი თბილისს აფხაზეთის და სამხრეთ ოსეთის გამოყოფაზე აფრთხილებს. Retrieved May 26, 2021, from Civil.ge: https://old.civil.ge/geo/article.php?id=17678&search=

Civil.ge. (2008p, April 16). რუსეთი აფხაზეთთან და სამხრეთ ოსეთთან ურთიერთობების ლეგალიზებას იწყებს. Retrieved May 5, 2021, from Civil.ge: https://old.civil.ge/geo/article.php?id=18014&search=

Civil.ge. (2008q, March 6). რუსეთი აფხაზეთისთვის სანქციების დაწესების შესახებ შეთანხმებას ტოვებს. Retrieved May 25, 2021, from Civil.ge: https://old.civil.ge/geo/article.php?id=17678&search=

Civil.ge. (2008r, April 29). რუსეთი აფხაზეთში სამშვიდობოთა რაოდენობას ზრდის. Retrieved May 26, 2021, from Civil.ge: https://old.civil.ge/geo/article.php?id=18140&search=

Civil.ge. (2008s, July 15). რუსეთის საგარეო პოლიტიკური კონცეფცია: მოსკოვი საქართველოს ნატოს წევრობის წინააღმდეგია. Retrieved March 20, 2022, from Civil.ge: https://civil.ge/ka/archives/144081

Civil.ge. (2008t, April 26). რუსეთის სამხედრო ქმედება აფხაზეთში შესაძლებელია - რუსი დიპლომატი. Retrieved May 26, 2021, from Civil.ge: https://old.civil.ge/geo/article.php?id=18117&search=

Civil.ge. (2008u, May 1). რუსეთმა აფხაზეთში დამატებითი ძალები შეიყვანა. Retrieved May 27, 2021, from Civil.ge: https://old.civil.ge/geo/article.php?id=18158&search=

Civil.ge. (2008v, July 30). რუსეთს აფხაზეთიდან სარკინიგზო ძალები გაყავს. Retrieved March 19, 2022, from Civil.ge: https://civil.ge/ka/archives/144165

Civil.ge. (2008w, April 30). სააკაშვილი მოუწოდებს აფხაზებს და ოსებს ერთად დაუპირისპირდნენ გარეშე ძალას. Retrieved May 27, 2021, from Civil.ge: https://old.civil.ge/geo/article.php?id=18148&search=

Civil.ge. (2008x, June 10). სააკაშვილი: თბილისი მზადაა მოითხოვოს რუსი სამშვიდობოების გაყვანა. Retrieved May 30, 2021, from Civil.ge: https://old.civil.ge/geo/article.php?id=18529&search=

Civil.ge. (2008y, July 25). სოხუმი ბერლინის შეხვედრაზე უარს აცხადებს. Retrieved June 3, 2021, from Civil.ge: https://old.civil.ge/geo/article.php?id=18868&search=

Civil.ge. (2008z, May 12). სოხუმი კიდევ ორი უპილოტო თვითმფრინავის ჩამოგდებას იტყობინება. Retrieved May 29, 2021, from Civil.ge: https://old.civil.ge/geo/article.php?id=18242&search=

Civil.ge. (2014, November 22). მოსკოვმა და სოხუმმა "მოკავშირეობისა და სტრატეგიული პარტნიორობის" ხელშეკრულების საბოლოო პროექტი მოამზადეს. Retrieved June 4, 2021, from Civil.ge: https://old.civil.ge/geo/article.php?id=28877

Civil.ge. (2021a, October 22). *ECHR Finds Wartime Crimes Claims Against Georgia Inadmissible*. Retrieved March 22, 2022, from Civil.ge: https://civil.ge/archives/449488

Civil.ge. (2021b, January 21). *European Court Verdict into Georgia vs. Russia Case over 2008 War*. Retrieved March 22, 2022, from Civil.ge: https://civil.ge/archives/392226

Civil.ge. (2021c, July 10). საქართველოსთვის *MAP*-ის მინიჭება შეაფერხებს კონფლიქტების მოგვარებას - ლავროვი. Retrieved June 2, 2021, from Civil.ge: https://old.civil.ge/geo/article.php?id=18770&search=

Civil.ge. (2022d, March 24). *2008 War: ECHR Throws Out 370 Applications Against Georgia*. Retrieved March 25, 2022, from Civil.ge: https://civil.ge/archives/481227

Civil.ge. (2022e, March 10). *2008 War: ICC Files Arrest Warrant for S. Ossetian Officials*. Retrieved March 23, 2022, from Civil.ge: https://civil.ge/archives/478448

CNN. (2005, May 11). *Bush: Georgia 'beacon of liberty'*. Retrieved June 4, 2021, from CNN: https://edition.cnn.com/2005/WORLD/europe/05/10/bush.tuesday/

CNN. (2008, August 12). *Leaders of ex-Soviet republics support Georgia at rally*. Retrieved June 4, 2021, from CNN: http://edition.cnn.com/2008/WORLD/europe/08/12/georgia.rally/

CNN. (2008, August 26). *Russia condemned for recognizing rebel regions*. Retrieved March 22, 2022, from CNN: https://edition.cnn.com/2008/WORLD/europe/08/26/russia.vote.georgia/

Constitution of the Russian Federation. (1993). Retrieved from https://publicofficialsfinancialdisclosure.worldbank.org/sites/fdl/files/assets/law-library-files/Russian%20Federation_Constitution_1993_EN.pdf

Corbin, K. (2009, March 12). *Lessons From the Russia-Georgia Cyberwar*. Retrieved from Internet News: https://www.internetnews.com/government/article.php/3810011/Lessons+From+the+RussiaGeorgia+Cyberwar.htm

Council of Europe. (2017, October 10). *The new Ukrainian law on education: a major impediment to the teaching of national minorities' mother tongues*. Retrieved March 18, 2022, from Council of Europe: https://assembly.coe.int/nw/xml/XRef/Xref-XML2HTML-en.asp?fileid=24125&lang=en

CSCE. (1994, December 21). *Budapest document 1994 towards a genuine partnership in a new era*. Retrieved March 23, 2022, from CSCE: https://www.osce.org/files/f/documents/5/1/39554.pdf

Darczewska, J. (2014). *The information war on Ukraine*. Centre for Eastern Studies.

Darczewska, J. (2016). *Russia's armed forces on the information war front*. OSW Studies.

Deutsche Welle. (2015a, August 9). *Ukraine blacklists Depardieu and 13 other Russian artists*. Retrieved March 18, 2022, from Deutsche Welle: https://www.dw.com/en/ukraine-blacklists-depardieu-and-13-other-russian-artists/a-18636568

Deutsche Welle. (2015b, December 24). *Ukraine to impose tit-for-tat trade embargo on Russia*. Retrieved March 16, 2022, from Deutsche Welle: https://www.dw.com/en/ukraine-to-impose-tit-for-tat-trade-embargo-on-russia/a-18940722

Duvold, K. (2015). *Beyond Borders: The return of kin-state politics in Europe.* Retrieved from https://www.semanticscholar.org/paper/Beyond-Borders-%3A-The-Return-of-Kin-state-Politics-Duvold/9db5a4655f97bf9936aa8d505115e9fe91206817

Dyomkin, D. (2011, December 21). *Russia says Georgia war stopped NATO expansion*. Retrieved May 10, 2021, from Reuters: https://www.reuters.com/article/idINIndia-60645720111121

Dziadul, C. (2016, February 12). *Ukraine bans 15 Russian channels*. Retrieved March 18, 2022, from Broadbandtvnews: https://www.broadbandtvnews.com/2016/02/12/ukraine-bans-15-russian-channels/

ECHR. (2021, January 21). *Georgia v. Russia (II) [GC] - 38263/08*. Retrieved from ECHR: https://hudoc.echr.coe.int/eng#{%22appno%22:[%22\%2238263/08\%22%22],%22itemid%22:[%22002-13102%22]}

Ellyatt, H. (2022, February 10). *Russia begins massive military drills with Belarus; U.S. slams 'escalatory' action*. Retrieved March 19, 2022, from CNBC: https://www.cnbc.com/2022/02/10/russia-set-to-begin-massive-military-drills-with-belarus.html

Engvall, J. (2020, January 8). *Military confidence-building in crises: lessons from Georgia and Ukraine*. Retrieved May 19, 2021, from Taylor & Francis Online: https://www.tandfonline.com/doi/full/10.1080/14702436.2020.1776615

Felgenhauer, P. (2012, August 9). *Putin Confirms the Invasion of Georgia Was Preplanned*. Retrieved May 5, 2021, from The Jamestown Foundation: https://jamestown.org/program/putin-confirms-the-invasion-of-georgia-was-preplanned/

Gerden, E. (2017, February 10). *Ukraine Enacts a Winter Ban on Book Imports From Russia*. Retrieved March 18, 2022, from Publishing Perspectives: https://publishingperspectives.com/2017/02/ukraine-ban-book-imports-from-russia/

Gershkovich. (2022, Mar 30). *Putin's Approval Rating Jumps After Invasion, Poll Shows*. Retrieved April 3, 2022, from Wall Street Journal: https://www.wsj.com/livecoverage/russia-ukraine-latest-news-2022-03-30/card/putin-s-approval-rating-jumps-after-invasion-poll-shows-fm8f4uSdiVfTxORQOE0v

Giles, K. (2015). *Russia and Its Neighbours: Old Attitudes, New Capabilities*. Conflict Studies Research Centre.

Gordiienko, O. (2015, August 23). *Trade war with Russia hurts Ukraine less*. Retrieved March 15, 2022, from Kyiv Post: https://www.kyivpost.com/article/content/business/trade-war-with-russia-hurts-ukraine-ever-less-396266.html

Harding, L. (2022, March 1). *'Horrendous' rocket attack kills civilians in Kharkiv as Moscow 'adapts its tactics'*. Retrieved April 10, 2022, from The Guardian: https://www.theguardian.com/world/2022/feb/28/ukraine-several-killed-by-russian-rocket-strikes-in-civilian-areas-of-kharkiv

Hollis, D. (2010). *Cyberwar Case Study: Georgia 2008.* Small Wars Journal.

Human Rights Watch. (2022a, April 3). *Ukraine: Apparent War Crimes in Russia-Controlled Areas.* Retrieved April 10, 2022, from Human Rights Watch: https://www.hrw.org/news/2022/04/03/ukraine-apparent-war-crimes-russia-controlled-areas

Human Rights Watch. (2022b, April 21). *Ukraine: Russian Forces' Trail of Death in Bucha.* Retrieved April 23, 2022, from Human Rights Watch: https://web.archive.org/web/20220421062141/https://www.hrw.org/news/2022/04/21/ukraine-russian-forces-trail-death-bucha

Huntington, S. P. (1993). The Clash of Civilizations? *Foreign Affairs*, 22-49.

IDFI. (2020, August 7). *12 წელი 2008 წლის აგვისტოს ომიდან: რუსული დეზინფორმაცია და რეალური ფაქტები.* Retrieved June 4, 2021, from IDFI: https://idfi.ge/ge/august_war_russian_desinformation

International Republican Institute. (2007). *Georgian National Voter Study.* International Republican Institute.

IRI. (2014-2021). *IRI Polls and Qualitative Research.* Retrieved March 18, 2022, from IRI: https://www.iri.org/polls/

John, D., & McKinnon, N. K. (2008, August 14). *U.S. Launches Airlift to Aid Georgia.* Retrieved June 4, 2021, from The Wall Street Journal: https://www.wsj.com/articles/SB121866388366238327

Kofman, M. R. (2015). *A Closer look at Russia's "Hybrid War".* Wilson Centre.

Kremlin. (2007, February 10). *Speech and the Following Discussion at the Munich Conference on Security Policy.* Retrieved from President of Russia: http://en.kremlin.ru/events/president/transcripts/24034

Kushnir, O. (2017). *Russian geopolitical advancements in the black sea region: The annexation of Crimea.* Polish Political Science Studies.

Laure Delcour, K. W. (2014, August 9). *Spoiler or facilitator of democratization?: Russia's role in Georgia and Ukraine" by Laure Delcour and Kataryna Wolczuk.* Retrieved May 19, 2021, from Taylor & Francis Online: https://www.tandfonline.com/doi/full/10.1080/13510347.2014.996135

Lesia Dorosh, O. I. (2019). Comparative Analysis of the Hybrid Tactics Application by the Russian Federation in Conflicts with Georgia and Ukraine. *Central European Journal of International and Security Studies.*

Levada Center. (2020, September 30). *Attitudes toward countries.* Retrieved May 23, 2021, from Levada Center: https://www.levada.ru/en/2020/09/30/attitudes-toward-countries-4/

Lokshina, T. (2009, January 30). *Georgia war: auditing the damage.* Retrieved March 22, 2022, from Human Rights Watch: https://www.hrw.org/news/2009/01/30/georgia-war-auditing-damage

Matsaberidze, D. (2015). *Russia vs. EU/US through Georgia and Ukraine.* CONNECTIONS The Quarterly Journal. doi:10.11610/Connections.14.2.06

Miller, C. (2020, April 25). *Zelenskiy's First Year: He Promised Sweeping Changes. How's He Doing?* Retrieved March 18, 2022, from Radio Free Europe / Radio Liberty: https://www.rferl.org/a/zelenskiys-first-year-he-promised-sweeping-changes-how-s-he-doing-/30576329.html

NATO. (1995, September 3). *Study on NATO Enlargement*. Retrieved May 25, 2021, from NATO: https://www.nato.int/cps/en/natohq/official_texts_24733.htm

NATO. (2008, April 3). *Bucharest Summit Declaration*. Retrieved May 5, 2021, from NATO: https://www.nato.int/cps/en/natolive/official_texts_8443.htm

OSCE. (1996, December 3). *LISBON DOCUMENT 1996*. Retrieved March 22, 2022, from OSCE: https://www.osce.org/files/f/documents/1/0/39539.pdf

Pavel Polityuk, J. F. (2014, March 4). *Ukraine says communications hit, MPs phones blocked*. Retrieved June 4, 2021, from Reuters: https://www.reuters.com/article/ukraine-crisis-cybersecurity-idUSL6N0M12CF20140304

Peter Pomerantsev, M. W. (2014). *The Menace of Unreality: How the Kremlin Weaponizes Information, Culture and Money*. Institute of Modern Russia. Retrieved from https://lccn.loc.gov/2015433465

Peuch, J.-C. (2002, November 22). *Georgia: Shevardnadze Officially Requests Invitation To Join NATO*. Retrieved June 4, 2021, from Radio Free Europe / Radio Liberty: https://www.rferl.org/a/1101463.html

Pomerantsev, P. (2014, September 9). *How Russia Is Revolutionizing Information Warfare*. Retrieved May 23, 2021, from Defense One: https://www.defenseone.com/threats/2014/09/how-russia-revolutionizing-information-warfare/93635/

Rácz, A. (2015). *Russia's Hybrid War in Ukraine*. The Finnish Institute of International Affairs.

Radio Free Europe / Radio Liberty. (2004, May 6). *Georgian President In Adjaria After Abashidze Flees*. Retrieved June 4, 2021, from Radio Free Europe / Radio Liberty: https://www.rferl.org/a/1052653.html

Radio Free Europe / Radio Liberty. (2006, October 17). *Georgia: Hundreds Left Stranded After Deportations From Russia*. Retrieved June 4, 2021, from Radio Free Europe / Radio Liberty: https://www.rferl.org/a/1072088.html

Radio Free Europe / Radio Liberty. (2019, February 25). *The Changing Story Of Russia's 'Little Green Men' Invasion*. Retrieved June 4, 2021, from Radio Free Europe / Radio Liberty: https://www.rferl.org/a/russia-ukraine-crimea/29790037.html

Radio Liberty. (2004, August 21). რა მოხდა ცხინვალის რეგიონში და რისთვის გაიღო იქ საქართველომ ახალი მსხვერპლი. Retrieved June 4, 2021, from Radio Liberty: https://www.radiotavisupleba.ge/a/1536767.html

Radio Liberty. (2005, July 26). გორის ტერაქტი გახსნილია, გამოძიებამ ამ დანაშაულში რუსეთის აგენტურის კვალს მიაგნო. Retrieved April 30, 2021, from Radio Liberty: https://www.radiotavisupleba.ge/a/1542418.html

Radio Liberty. (2008, April 7). როგორ უნდა მოგვარდეს აფხაზეთის კონფლიქტი? რუსი და ქართველი ექსპერტები მიხეილ სააკაშვილის ინიციატივის თაობაზე. Retrieved May 25, 2021, from Radio Libertya: https://www.radiotavisupleba.ge/a/1557203.html

Radio Liberty. (2010, August 7). ომის მეორე წლისთავი გორში. Retrieved June 3, 2021, from Radio Liberty: https://www.radiotavisupleba.ge/a/2121443.html

Radio Liberty. (2019a, February 19). *Amnesty International: Five Years After Euromaidan, Justice For The Victims 'Still Not Even In Sight'*. Retrieved May 25, 2021, from Radio Liberty: https://www.rferl.org/a/ukraine-maidan-justice-victims-amnesty-fifth-anniversary/29779358.html

Radio Liberty. (2019b, June 20). სერგეი გავრილოვის ბიოგრაფია. Retrieved May 25, 2021, from Radio Liberty: https://www.radiotavisupleba.ge/a/%E1%83%A1%E1%83%94%E1%83%A0%E1%83%92%E1%83%94%E1%83%98-%E1%83%92%E1%83%90%E1%83%95%E1%83%A0%E1%83%98%E1%83%9A%E1%83%9D%E1%83%95%E1%83%98%E1%83%A1-%E1%83%91%E1%83%98%E1%83%9D%E1%83%92%E1%83%A0%E1%83%90%E1%83%A4%E1%83%98%E1

Rainsford, S. (2015, October 24). *Ban due on direct flights between Russia and Ukraine*. Retrieved March 15, 2022, from BBC: https://www.bbc.com/news/world-europe-34622665

Reuters. (2022a, April 21). *Latvian and Estonian parliaments say Russia committed genocide in Ukraine*. Retrieved April 25, 2022, from Reuters: https://www.reuters.com/world/europe/latvian-estonian-parliaments-say-russia-committed-genocide-ukraine-2022-04-21/

Reuters. (2022b, April 21). *Latvian and Estonian parliaments say Russia committed genocide in Ukraine*. Retrieved April 23, 2022, from Reuters: https://www.reuters.com/world/europe/latvian-estonian-parliaments-say-russia-committed-genocide-ukraine-2022-04-21/

Reuters. (2022c, February 21). *What does Russian recognition of breakaway Ukraine territories mean?* Retrieved March 22, 2022, from The Guardian: https://www.theguardian.com/world/2022/feb/21/what-would-russian-recognition-of-breakaway-ukraine-regions-mean

Roth, A. (2018, Nov 27). *Kerch strait confrontation: what happened and why does it matter?* Retrieved March 18, 2022, from The Guardian: https://www.theguardian.com/world/2018/nov/27/kerch-strait-confrontation-what-happened-ukrainian-russia-crimea

Roth, A. (2022, February 15). *Russia confirms 'partial' withdrawal of troops from Ukraine border*. Retrieved March 19, 2022, from The Guardian: https://www.theguardian.com/world/2022/feb/15/russia-ukraine-border-troops-withdrawal

Schwartz, M. J. (2014, March 17). *DDoS Attacks Hit NATO, Ukrainian Media Outlets*. Retrieved May 5, 2021, from DARKReading: https://www.darkreading.com/attacks-and-breaches/ddos-attacks-hit-nato-ukrainian-media-outlets/d/d-id/1127742

Seskuria, N. (2022, February 22). *Russia Is Reenacting Its Georgia Playbook in Ukraine*. Retrieved from Foreign Policy: https://foreignpolicy.com/2022/02/22/russia-ukraine-invasion-georgia-2008-south-ossetia-tskhinvali/

Shane Harris, P. S. (2021, December 3). *Russia planning massive military offensive against Ukraine involving 175,000 troops, U.S. intelligence warns*. Retrieved March 19, 2022, from Washington Post: https://www.washingtonpost.com/national-security/russia-ukraine-invasion/2021/12/03/98a3760e-546b-11ec-8769-2f4ecdf7a2ad_story.html

Shannon Pettypiece, Z. R. (2022, April 13). *Biden says Russia is committing 'genocide' in Ukraine*. Retrieved April 14, 2022, from NBCNews: https://www.nbcnews.com/politics/white-house/biden-calls-putin-actions-ukraine-genocide-rcna24131

State Duma of Russia. (2002, May 31). *Russian Federation federal law on citizenship of the Russian Federation.* Retrieved May 29, 2021, from https://www.refworld.org/cgi-bin/texis/vtx/rwmain/opendocpdf.pdf?reldoc=y&docid=5a9d48314

TASS. (2022, February 23). *Putin: Russia stands for demilitarization of Ukraine*. Retrieved March 22, 2022, from Russian News Agency: https://tass.com/russia/1408629?utm_source=google.com&utm_medium=organic&utm_campaign=google.com&utm_referrer=google.com

The Guardian. (2014, July 29). *EU and US impose sweeping economic sanctions on Russia*. Retrieved June 4, 2021, from The Guardian: https://www.theguardian.com/world/2014/jul/29/economic-sanctions-russia-eu-governments

Thiele, R. D. (2015). *Crisis in Ukraine – The Emergence of Hybrid Warfare.* The Institute for Strategic, Political, Security and Economic Consultancy (ISPSW).

Tisdall, S. (2022, February 12). *The edge of war: what, exactly, does Putin want in Ukraine?* Retrieved March 22, 2022, from The Guardian: https://www.theguardian.com/world/2022/feb/12/russia-ukraine-what-does-putin-want

Treisman, R. (2022a, April 28). *Canada's House backs a motion recognizing Russia's actions in Ukraine as genocide*. Retrieved April 29, 2022, from NPR: https://www.npr.org/2022/04/28/1095272683/canada-russia-genocide-ukraine

Treisman, R. (2022b, April 28). *Canada's House backs a motion recognizing Russia's actions in Ukraine as genocide*. Retrieved April 29, 2022, from NPR: https://www.npr.org/2022/04/28/1095272683/canada-russia-genocide-ukraine

Uawire. (2018, March 27). *Ukrainian border guards detain a Russian fishing boat in the Sea of Azov.* Retrieved March 18, 2022, from Uawire: https://www.uawire.org/border-guards-detain-a-russian-fishing-boat-in-the-sea-of-azov

Veterans for Common Sense. (2008, August 12). *US Takes Georgian Troops Home from Iraq*. Retrieved June 4, 2021, from Veterans for Common Sense: http://veteransforcommonsense.org/2008/08/12/us-takes-georgian-troops-home-from-iraq-2/

APPENDIX: ABBREVIATIONS

AA - anti-aircraft systems
BBC - British media channel
BRIC - grouping acronym which refers to the countries of Brazil, Russia, India and China
CIS - Commonwealth of Independent States
CNN - American media channel
CSCE – Conference of Security and Cooperation in Europe
EU - European Union
ECHR – European Court of Human Rights
HRW – Human Rights Watch
IRI - International Republican Institute
ICC – International Criminal Court
MAP - Membership Action Plan
NATO - North-Atlantic Treaty Organization
OSCE - Organization of Security and Cooperation in Europe
RBN - Russian Business Network
UAV - unmanned aerial vehicle
UN - United Nations
US - United States
USSR - Union of Soviet Socialist Republic

Chapter 10
Psychological Aspects of Negotiation With Terrorists

Irakli Kervalishvili
Georgian Technical University, Georgia

ABSTRACT

Negotiation can be defined as a type of interaction with a partner, which is aimed at solving a specific problem. There are two opposite negotiation strategies: "hard" and "soft." The American researchers S. Sigel and L. Fureker were among the first authors of the "tough" strategy. They argued that a concession by one of the parties in the negotiation process would lead to a toughening of the other. In their opinion, for a successful outcome of negotiations, one should start with exaggerated demands and demonstrate intransigence. In contrast to them, Charles Osgood spoke out with a "soft" line of conduct in the negotiations, according to which the greatest benefit can be obtained only through mutual concessions. It should also be borne in mind that the first impression of the partner and his vision of the problem are very important, influencing the subsequent interaction. One of the types of stereotypes of behavior is prejudice. (Any information that contradicts the established views is ignored.)

INTRODUCTION

Hostage negotiation is one type of extreme negotiation. These negotiations are resorted to in the event of hostage taking in order to reduce the threat and save people's lives. It is used as one of the ways to resolve a conflict situation with the taking of hostages along with the forceful solution of the problem (the use of armed forces), the use of chemicals, and the satisfaction of the requirements of criminals.

The following components can be distinguished in the structure of negotiations with capture:

- a special criminal situation that requires such negotiations (without them it is impossible to achieve goals);
- dialogue between the parties - the subjects of negotiations - to achieve a result;
- solving various problems regarding the crime and related issues by reaching an agreement;
- execution of obligations

DOI: 10.4018/978-1-6684-5311-7.ch010

Goals that are set for the negotiator:

1. Saving the life and health of the hostages;
2. Deceleration of the offender to stop illegal actions;
3. Obtaining additional information about the identity of criminals and hostages;
4. Ensuring that the demands of criminals are reduced and counter conditions are put forward to them for the release of hostages;
5. Providing other structures with temporary resources.

The challenge of crisis negotiation is to use verbal strategies to gain time and intervene in such a way that the perpetrator's emotionality can be reduced and rational thinking increased.

The subjects of negotiations can be: parties to the conflict, part of the public, self-government bodies, representatives of different groups (for example, the media, relatives and friends of criminals) (Siedel, 2014).

One of the main points in organizing negotiations with terrorists is the selection and training of negotiators. Selection should be based on a voluntary basis, taking into account the personal characteristics of candidates, the ability to act in stressful situations, quick response, self-control, emotional stability, the presence of the necessary intellectual abilities, etc. Potential negotiators must have the necessary knowledge in the field of psychology and pedagogy, as well as receive special training in the field of extreme negotiations.

FEATURES OF NEGOTIATING IN SITUATIONS OF HOSTAGE-TAKING

Many experts identify the following features of negotiations in a situation of hostage-taking:

- Forced nature of negotiations. The parties enter into negotiations with terrorists out of necessity, and not to find a compromise solution, as is often the case in other types of negotiations;
- Surprise of actions of criminals;
- Use of manipulative techniques by the opposite party. Criminals make demands on the terms of the negotiations, for example, they personify the negotiator;
- Involvement of third parties to solve the problem (additional mediators, representatives of self-government bodies, etc.);
- Diametrically opposed interests;
- The need for a constant mix of "positional negotiations" and "substantive" negotiations. An analysis of cases of successful negotiations with criminals shows that negotiators in the course of extreme negotiations, depending on the specific situation, must combine the opportunities that both of these varieties provide. This makes the tactics of law enforcement agencies more flexible (International Center for Counter terrorism, 2022).

Stages of Negotiation

The negotiation process in terms of hostage-taking consists of several stages, at each of which certain tasks are solved.

There Are 4 Stages in Total

1. The first stage: generalization of initial information about a crisis situation that requires negotiations, making a decision on the need for them, identifying negotiators, collecting additional data on the conflict that has arisen, developing negotiating tactics, establishing contact with criminals, achieving a stable situation.
2. The second stage ("seizure of positions"): the organization of involvement in the resolution of the issue of forces and means that ensure public safety, through psychological and pedagogical influence, criminals are persuaded to abandon illegal behavior. The possibility of resolving the conflict by force is being considered.
3. The third stage: putting forward conditions and discussing their acceptability, searching for compromise options, bargaining, psychological struggle, active dialogue to develop mutually acceptable solutions.
4. Fourth stage: reaching a full or partial agreement, determining ways to implement it, analyzing the work done (Research Gate, 2011).

At any stage of the negotiations, there is the possibility of reducing the number of hostages, primarily women, children, the sick and the elderly, using every opportunity to raise this issue. This possibility must always be kept in mind by the negotiator. Each released hostage is a success achieved during the negotiation process.

Negotiation Success Criteria

Negotiations in a hostage-taking situation are assessed positively if:

- the categoricalness, sharpness of the demands put forward are reduced;
- the number of threats, aggressive actions by criminals decreases;
- the positive coloring of the dialogue between the parties intensifies;
- since the start of negotiations, there has been no violence or killing of any of the participants in the negotiations, hostages, police officers;
- hostages are released;
- the offender refuses to implement the original intentions and surrenders (Chitadze, 2022).

Often the concessions that the negotiator makes are explained precisely by the desire to achieve these positions.

Who Is a Hostage?

Hostage - a person held by force in order to force someone (relatives of the hostage, representatives of the authorities, or the like) to perform certain actions, fulfill certain obligations, or refrain from committing undesirable actions in order to free the hostage, prevent his murder or harm to his health.

The practice of taking hostages has been widespread since ancient times, where hostages from among the relatives of the rulers of certain territories were a guarantee of their loyalty to the hostage-holding rulers of other territories. There are also known cases of "horizontal" hostage-taking, when the parties' exchanged hostages in the form of guarantees of fulfillment of obligations. During wars, hostages were often taken for additional pressure on the enemy or used as a "human shield".

Currently international agreements (the Geneva Convention, the UN Convention against the Taking of Hostages, etc.) and the national laws of the countries of the world, taking hostages is prohibited and is a serious crime (Aleksidze, 2018). However, the practice of taking hostages has remained widespread in terrorist actions, and is also sometimes used by states to put pressure on each other or political opponents within the country.

TYPES OF HOSTAGE-TAKING

Hostage-taking can be expressed in various forms and pursue various goals. The simplest and most ancient case is "vertical" hostage-taking for the purpose of extorting something, that is, creating new obligations to the invader; cases of hostage-taking with the aim of forcing the fulfillment of existing obligations are less common, and cases of "horizontal" voluntary decision of one of the parties, remained only in history. Recently, in terrorist attacks, hostage-taking has become an end in itself (Bock, 2010).

Stockholm Syndrome

Stockholm Syndrome is a term popular in psychology that describes the defensive-unconscious traumatic connection, mutual or one-sided sympathy that occurs between the victim and the aggressor in the process of capture, abduction and / or the use of threat or violence. Under the influence of a strong experience, the hostages begin to sympathize with their captors, justify their actions and ultimately identify with them, adopting their ideas and considering their victim necessary to achieve a "common" goal.

Due to the apparent paradoxical nature of the psychological phenomenon, the term "Stockholm syndrome" has become widely popular and has acquired many synonyms: such names as Hostage Identification Syndrome, Common Sense Syndrome, Stockholm Factor, Hostage Survival Syndrome, etc. are known, who introduced it during an analysis of the situation that arose in Stockholm during the hostage-taking in August 1973. The hostages defended their captors after their release and did not agree to testify against them in court. The psychological defense mechanism underlying the Stockholm syndrome was first described by Anna Freud in 1936, when it was called "identification with the aggressor" (Beruashvili, 2022).

Researchers believe that Stockholm Syndrome is not a psychological paradox, disorder or syndrome, but rather a normal human response to a severely traumatic event. So, Stockholm syndrome is not included in any classification of mental disorders.

According to the FBI data on more than 1200 cases of hostage-taking with the barricading of the hostage-takers in the building, Stockholm syndrome was noted in only 8% of cases (US Department of Justice, 2022).

Hostage-Taking in Stockholm in 1973

On August 23, 1973, Jan-Erik Olsson, released from prison, single-handedly seized the Kreditbanken bank (Stockholm, Sweden), injuring one policeman and taking hostage four bank employees: three women (Birgitta Lundblad, Kristin Enmark, Elisabet Oldgren) and a man (Sven Sefström). At Olsson's request, the police brought his cellmate Clark Olofsson to the bank. The hostages called Prime Minister Olof Palme and demanded that all the conditions of the criminals be met (Siedel, 2014).

On August 26, the police drilled a hole in the ceiling and took pictures of the hostages and Olofsson, but Olsson noticed the preparations, started shooting and promised to kill the hostages in the event of a gas attack. On August 28, the gas attack did take place. Half an hour later, the invaders surrendered, and the hostages were taken out safe and sound. Former hostages said that they were not afraid of the invaders, who did nothing wrong to them, but of the police. According to some reports, they hired lawyers Olsson and Olofsson at their own expense.

The psychiatrist Niels Beyeruth, who advised the police during the incident and whose decisions were criticized by the hostages, coined the term Norrmalmstorgssyndromet (Norrmalmstorg Syndrome) to explain their behavior, later transformed into the concept of "Stockholm Syndrome"

During the trial, Olofsson managed to prove that he did not help Olsson, but, on the contrary, tried to save the hostages. He was cleared of all charges and released. In freedom, he met with Christine Enmark, and they became friends with families. Olsson was sentenced to 10 years in prison, where he subsequently received many admiring letters from women (Siedel, 2014).

The Danger of the Syndrome

The danger of Stockholm Syndrome lies in the actions of the hostage against their own interests, such as preventing their release. There are cases when, during an anti-terrorist operation, hostages warned terrorists about the appearance of a commando and even shielded the terrorist with their body. In other cases, the terrorist hid among the hostages and no one exposed him. As a rule, the Stockholm syndrome passes after the terrorists kill the first hostage (Siedel, 2014).

Factors Affecting the Formation of Stockholm Syndrome

Stockholm syndrome can develop when:

- political and criminal acts of terrorism (hostage-taking);
- military punitive operations (for example, when taking prisoners of war);
- imprisonment in concentration camps and prisons;
- administration of judicial procedures;
- development of authoritarian interpersonal relations within political groups and religious sects;
- implementation of some national rituals (for example, when kidnapping a bride);
- kidnapping for the purpose of enslavement, blackmail or ransom;
- outbreaks of domestic, domestic and sexual violence.

The mechanism of psychological defense is based on the hope of the victim that the aggressor will show indulgence, provided that all his requirements are unconditionally met. Therefore, the captive tries to demonstrate obedience, to logically justify the actions of the invader, to arouse his approval and patronage.

The humanization of the relationship between the invader and the victim is key in the formation of the Stockholm syndrome and is determined by the following factors:

- possibility and quality of social interaction. To hinder the development of emotional relationships, captives may be blindfolded or gagged. For the same purpose, the guards can often change places;
- the possibility of a rational explanation for the cruelty shown. Inexplicable, irrational cruelty kills the development of sympathy between the parties. Otherwise, if, for example, one of the hostages dies as a result of resistance to terrorists, then the survivors try to justify the outburst of cruelty by the provocative (dangerous for the rest) behavior of the deceased himself;
- language barrier. The prohibition to speak and (or) ignorance of the language greatly complicates the formation of sympathy between the hostages and the terrorists;
- psychological literacy, knowledge of survival techniques. A psychologically literate hostage and/or terrorist are more likely to influence each other;
- personal qualities of both sides, their ability to communicate diplomatically. A hostage with diplomatic qualities is able to convince the enemy, to shift his point of view;
- a system of cultural stereotypes. Racial, ethnic, religious and ideological differences have a severe negative impact on the development of sympathy between the invader and his victim. They are difficult to change in such a short period of time and can provoke hostility, an outbreak of cruelty, and even death of the hostages;
- length of stay in captivity. Stockholm syndrome is formed after 1-4 days of imprisonment and intensifies in the case of isolation of captives. With a long stay in captivity, the hostage communicates with the captor, recognizes him as a person, understands the reasons for the capture, what the captor wants to achieve and in what way; This is especially evident in terrorist attacks that have political overtones - the hostage recognizes the captor's claims to power, is imbued with them and can convince himself that the position of the captor is the only correct one (Chitadze, 2022).

Knowing that the terrorists are well aware that as long as the hostages are alive, the terrorists themselves are alive, the hostages take a passive position, they have no means of self-defense either against the terrorists or in the event of an assault. The only protection for them can be a tolerant attitude on the part of terrorists. As a result, the hostages become psychologically attached to the terrorists and begin to interpret their actions in their favor. There are cases when the victims and the invaders were together for months, waiting for the demands of the terrorist to be fulfilled.

In cases of particularly ill-treatment, the hostages psychologically distance themselves from the situation; convince themselves that this is not happening to them, that this could not happen to them, and they displace the traumatic event from memory by engaging in specific activities.

If no harm is done to the victim, some people, being less susceptible to the syndrome in the process of adapting to the situation and sensing the potential inability of the invaders to harm them, begin to provoke them.

After being released, the surviving hostages can actively support the ideas of the captors, petition for a commutation of the sentence, visit them in places of detention, etc.

Varieties of Stockholm Syndrome

Household Stockholm syndrome, which occurs in dominant family relationships, is the second most well-known variety of Stockholm syndrome. Actions and attitudes similar to those experiencing Stockholm Syndrome have also been found in victims of sexual abuse, human trafficking, terror, and political and religious oppression.

There is evidence that some victims of childhood sexual abuse feel connected to their abuser. They often feel flattered by the attention of adults or fear that disclosure will lead to the destruction of the family. In adulthood, they resist disclosure for emotional and personal reasons.

There is an unusual variety of Stockholm Syndrome called "corporate". It manifests itself during the dictatorship at work and the subordination of a person to his "leader"(Chitadze, 2022).

NEGOTIATION PREVENTION AND DEBRIEFING

In hostage negotiation, one of the psychological tasks of the mediator is to encourage the development of mutual sympathy (Stockholm syndrome) between the hostages and the hostage-takers in order to increase the chances of the hostages to survive. Director of Research Programs at the Center for the Prevention of International Crimes, Dr. Adam Dolnik said this in an interview with Novaya Gazeta:

The negotiator is simply obliged to provoke, encourage the formation of this syndrome by any means. Because if the terrorists and the hostages like each other, then there is less chance that the hostages will do something stupid that would lead to violent terrorist actions. And it will be extremely difficult for terrorists, in turn, to decide to kill the hostages for whom they feel sympathy.

Methods for debriefing (psychological consultation) of surviving hostages in the event of their successful release vary depending on the nature of the situation that formed the Stockholm syndrome. For example, the debriefing of released prisoners of war differs in its structure from the debriefing of hostages of political terrorist attacks (International Center for Counter Terrorism, 2022).

Negotiation Strategies in Conflict Situations

Negotiation can be defined as a type of interaction with a partner that is aimed at solving a specific problem. There are two opposite negotiating strategies: "hard" and "soft". One of the first authors of the "hard" strategy were American researchers S. Siedel and L. Fureker. They argued that the concession of one of the parties in the negotiation process leads to a toughening of the other. In their opinion, for a successful outcome of negotiations, one should start with excessive demands and demonstrate intransigence (Siedel, 2014). In contrast to them, Ch. Osgood spoke with a "soft" line of conduct in negotiations, according to which the greatest benefit can be obtained only through mutual concessions. It should also be borne in mind that the first impression of the partner, his vision of the problem is of great importance, influencing subsequent interaction (Research Gate, 2011). One of the varieties of stereotypes of behavior is prejudice (any information that contradicts established views is ignored). In order to avoid the negative aspects associated with the phenomenon of perception during negotiations, one should try to accept the partner's point of view in order to understand the possible logic of the partner's argumentation without bringing down one's counter argumentation on his position.

In conflict situations, the method of "bargaining" or "arguing" is often used. The essence of bargaining is to get the maximum benefit in the negotiations, while making minimal concessions. The main task in implementing the concept of bargaining is to "bargain" from the opposite side as much as possible. For this purpose, weak points in the partner's position are searched for, means of pressure, threats, blackmail, etc. are used. Positional bickering is most often resorted to in the following cases:

- when the means of negotiation are limited (time, money, psychological resources);
- when the participant (s) of the negotiations want to receive the maximum amount that appears as a payment;
- when the interests of the parties are not interdependent, but opposite or mutually exclusive;
- when the existing or future relationship is less significant for the parties than the immediate gain (International Center for Counter terrorism. 2022).

Stages of Negotiation and Some Manipulative Negotiation Techniques

In the most general terms, we can talk about 4 main stages of negotiation:

1. creating a climate of relations favorable for negotiations;
2. clarification of interests, concepts, points of view and positions of the participants in the negotiations;
3. joint discussion (both parties put forward arguments in support of their views, make suggestions, justify them);
4. coordination of positions and development of agreements (Chakhava, 2022).

Before starting negotiations, it is necessary to pay attention to establishing contact with a partner. At this stage, you need to internally answer the following questions:
What is the person in front of me?
What condition is he in?
How can we adjust it to the topic we are going to talk about?
You need to tune yourself to this person:

- move away from all your beliefs and attitudes regarding appearance;
- internally settle down to a partner;
- Show goodwill and patience throughout the negotiations.

The microclimate that has been achieved for negotiations must be maintained throughout the course of the negotiations.

- A tactic that can be used at any stage of a negotiation to emphasize commonality with an opponent is to "agree" with the negotiating partners' views. The following statements can serve as an example of it: "I agree with you", "I fully share your point of view".
- The opposite of this technique is the technique of emphasizing differences - "expressing disagreement" with a partner.
- The next tactic is called "salami". It represents a gradual, unhurried disclosure of one's own position (the analogy of cutting salami sausage into thin slices). This technique contributes to delaying negotiations in order to obtain more information about the partner and identify the "weak points" of the enemy.
- "Packaging" is a technique when several proposals or questions are used at once for consideration by a partner in the form of a "package", that is, individual proposals or questions are subject to discussion only as a whole. The use of a "package" within the framework of the auction involves linking attractive and unacceptable offers for the partner into one "package". At the same time,

the author of the "package" proceeds from the fact that the partners, being extremely interested in several proposals from this "package", will accept the rest.

- The "gradual increase in complexity" of the issues discussed. The meaning of this technique is to start negotiations with easy questions, gradually moving on to complex ones. A positive resolution of such issues has a positive psychological impact on the parties and contributes to reaching an agreement on other issues.
- Another technique is to "break the problem down", which means it's easier to break the problem down into its components than to try to solve the problem as a whole. In this case, these components are identified in the first two stages.
- "Overestimation of requirements". The main point is that it is necessary to include questions that have no value in your points before starting negotiations, and subsequently refuse them, thus showing the opponent that you are making concessions, and this will allow you to demand similar actions from him.
- "Placing false accents in one's own position." Using this technique, demonstrate interest in any issue that is secondary. This is done in order to get the necessary decisions on a more important issue.
- Creation of uncertainty at the first stage of negotiations due to "silence". This technique, which to some extent paralyzes the activity of the opposite side, can be an important element of tactics. Closing positions includes giving deliberately false information (bluff).
- "Don't ignore your opponent's emotions." His attacks are often driven by anger; "stone wall" often hides fear; until you dissipate these emotions, the arguments of the mind will not be heard (Chakhava, 2022).

Psychology of Negotiating With Terrorists

Negotiations with criminals should be considered as a type of persuasive communication between a specialist negotiator and a person (persons) committing a criminal act, aimed at suppressing a crime, preventing the commission of criminal intentions and saving human lives. The purpose of the negotiations is to suppress the crime (terrorist act) with the least losses. The following tasks follow from this goal:

- assessment of the situation;
- Gaining time to make a decision;
- saving the life and health of citizens;
- suppression of criminal intent;
- Detention of criminals (Research Gate, 2011).

As a rule, the subject of negotiations is often the release of hostages, the provision of food for the hostages, the conditions imposed by the captors, etc. Negotiations with criminals are psychologically specific compared to other types of negotiations. The main features are:

- forced nature;
- Negotiations are conducted with a clear enemy who does not hide his hostility;
- participants in the negotiation process are often determined by opponents;
- the presence of danger to the life of the negotiators;

- the impossibility of abandoning their conduct without taking other measures to achieve the planned goals, etc.

Group of experts described the main personality types of terrorists and how to negotiate with them:

1. paranoid personality;
2. depressive personality;
3. antisocial personality;
4. inadequate personality (International Center for Counter terrorism. 2022).

The paranoid has such an agitated psyche that in fact he is out of contact with reality. He captures people in order to carry out some outstanding plan. At the same time, he can receive orders from someone. Paranoids tend to be of above average intelligence. Therefore, you should not try to deceive them. It is better to accept their statements as if they are true for you. In this case, the rule is introduced: to avoid arguing with this person about his ideas, since it is impossible to rationally convince him that his fantasies are wrong. Instead, you should discuss other topics with him in order to establish a connection, and based on this, look for an alternative solution to meet his requirements. For example, in 1982 in Arkansas, a bus was hijacked by people who believed that they were the ones the Bible was talking about: the hour of death had come, and in three and a half days they would be resurrected. The hostages were released, but the invaders could not be persuaded to surrender. They committed suicide. The depressed person may also be out of touch with reality. There is a very high potential for suicide and murder of hostages, since such a person can consider himself, for example, responsible for all the sins of the world. The hostages are often family members of the depressed person, who may believe that by killing, he is taking them away from this terrible world. This type of terrorist speaks slowly, takes 15-30 seconds longer to answer a question, all his thoughts are centered around his uselessness. Therefore, evidence of its value must be woven into the negotiation process here. This is done in the following way. If you just say "things are not so bad", he will think that he is not understood. Instead, the conversation is transferred to the area of his interests, hobbies, something positive. An inadequate person always loses, and so throughout his life. Taking hostages becomes for her an attempt to prove to someone (wife, friends, parents, girlfriend) that she can do something. This type of symbolic world can be deciphered by phrases like "I'll show them I can do something" or "I'll prove I'm not a scapegoat" (International Center for Counter Terrorism, 2022). The most familiar image of a terrorist for us is an antisocial person who has no morals and values of society, who has no sense of guilt. He is very impulsive, requires an immediate reaction. It should be remembered that you cannot promise him things that he knows you will not fulfill. It is necessary to constantly maintain contact with him so that he does not switch to hostages for his excitement. In the case of hostage-taking, the so-called "Stockholm syndrome" occurs. An important consequence follows from this: you cannot trust the information coming from the victims. The problem of communicative contact, the establishment of the necessary level of trust among terrorists requires a rather complex work. Establishing contact consists in the desire to speak with the terrorist in his own language. Questions should be structured in such a way as to receive detailed answers, and not just "yes" or "no". You should avoid negative responses on your part by at least pretending that you are trying to solve the problem exactly the way the terrorist wants it. You should not use the words "captor", "hostage", so as not to increase tension. As well as the words "surrender", which for him means failure. You should always bargain. Even if his demand is small, you should still ask for something from him in return for fulfilling it (International Center for Counter terrorism. 2022).

Rules for Physical Interaction with Terrorists

1. Don't underestimate the terrorist.
2. It is necessary to approach the terrorist, foreseeing danger and threat to life in any situation, therefore it is necessary to agree that you will not be harmed.
3. Carefully evaluate whether it is possible to approach the terrorist.
4. Keep a safe spatial distance: at close range, you can only talk when contact is established and there is trust.
5. It is necessary to negotiate with only one terrorist.
6. Keep an eye on the terrorist's hands and maintain eye contact.
7. Don't negotiate if you're being held under a gun, insist that the terrorist lower his weapon.
8. Make full use of legal measures to curb resisters or attackers.
9. Tackle, reduce tension in incidents and conflicts with terrorists.
10. At the scene, try to keep everyone in sight.
11. Don't let strangers surround you.
12. Don't turn your back on the terrorist.
13. Try to choose a comfortable place for a conversation with a terrorist, so that the light fell on his face and he was constantly in the light.
14. Plan ahead for a rescue plan. Terrorists use a wide arsenal of methods of communicative pressure: ultimatum demands, exaggerated demands, urgency to fulfill them, avoiding specific proposals, false emphasis in presenting their position, belittling and insulting the personality of negotiating partners, threats, rejection of agreements reached, their double interpretation (International Center for Counter terrorism. 2022).

The skill of negotiators lies in the ability to detect and eliminate the communicative tricks of terrorists, to outplay them in verbal combat. Negotiators can use the following methods:

1. Cover talks are used to delay the violent actions of armed criminals. During such negotiations, search, reconnaissance, and operational activities are carried out;
2. imitation of negotiations is carried out in the case when you have to deal with a mentally ill person. There is no subject of negotiations here, reacting to the logical component of the dialogue and giving an account of what he has done. Imitation of negotiations is aimed at removing aggressive behavior;
3. negotiations in a situation of interethnic conflicts are carried out by involving the warring parties. It is effective to use an intermediary negotiator (mediator) as a neutral party. The task of the mediator is to organize the negotiation process, but not to conduct the negotiations themselves (International Center for Counter terrorism. 2022).

Four Basic Rules Can Be Formulated in the work of Negotiators With Terrorists

- "Never say never"". It is necessary to communicate with a terrorist with the help of positively colored words and sentences. You shouldn't say to a terrorist: "No", "I can't", "It's impossible, it's impossible".

- "Talk constantly. When people are talking, guns don't fire." It is necessary to talk with terrorists all the time, without using long pauses. It is desirable to maintain contact with terrorists constantly.
- "Do not evaluate or belittle the individual." Psychological assessment of the identity of terrorists during negotiations is unacceptable. The reaction to the demands of the terrorists must be as correct as possible. The negotiator should try to use such turns of speech as "I believe you", "I will try to help", "I am ready to listen to you", "I am ready to talk to you". It should be remembered that the terrorists who have taken hostages are primarily interested in reaching an agreement.
- "Don't make me wait too long." A long wait for the fulfillment of their demands embitters the terrorists. At the same time, no forceful actions can be used if the hostage-takers have proved that they are ready to kill them. Therefore, the strategy and tactics of the negotiator's work is extremely complex and responsible. To establish contact and win the confidence of the terrorist, the negotiator switches to his symbolic system. The purpose of the negotiation is to make the terrorist feel that you really want to help him find a way out of his difficult situation. Criminals often lower their guards when they feel they have succeeded in negotiating. When planning a capture, you should give in to some important requirements for a terrorist. And this is also a planned transfer of the criminal to a different emotional state (International Center for Counter terrorism. 2022).

Requirements for the Personality of the Negotiator

The right choice of negotiators is extremely important. Selection is carried out on a voluntary basis, taking into account the individual characteristics of candidates, their ability to speak and think in extreme situations. Of particular importance are such personality traits as observation, quick reaction, the ability to maintain self-control in any situation, and emotional stability. It is also important to have intellectual and communication skills. It is terrorists themselves who often choose those with whom they want to negotiate. In the most general form, the main components of the training system for "extreme negotiators" include the following:

- selection of candidates with the necessary professional qualities;
- teaching them methods of express diagnostics of both their own and others' actual mental states and personal characteristics;
- formation of negotiation skills and psychological impact; - practical development of skills and abilities in model and real conditions.

An indicative list of mental characteristics, properties and states necessary for a negotiator can be represented as follows: high intelligence (general - above average, communicative - high) and pace of thinking; significant flexibility and switch ability of thinking; quick orientation in a new situation; good intelligibility and emotional expressiveness of speech; significant volume, distribution and speed of switching attention; the ability to mentally observe the situation from the outside; accurate subjective assessment of time; low level of spontaneous aggressiveness and endurance; authenticity, sincerity and ability to inspire confidence. At the same time, the most developed integrative qualities, apparently, should be intelligence, high stress resistance and over-situational activity, as well as intuition (the ability to predict the dynamics of events based on personal and situational express diagnostics). It is important to emphasize that each extreme situation requires, along with the listed "non-specific" (important in any crisis) qualities, the constellation and emphasis of certain "specific" professional qualities, which in another situation may be insufficient (Bock, 2010). The latter presupposes the specialization of negotiators and, accordingly, a variety of forms and methods of their preparation. The ability to quickly navigate the situation, to identify the current mental states and personality traits of terrorists requires the cultivation of observation, the ability to concentrate, see and hear, and correctly interpret information. One of the tasks of the negotiator is to carry out negotiations at the lowest possible emotional level and not provoke negative and unpredictable reactions of terrorists. And only then try to get as much information as possible in order to use it for a possible release of the hostages (or a counter-terrorist operation), although this is already largely the task of the special services, and not the negotiator himself. Thus, the process of negotiations with terrorists is a persuasive type of communication that has specific features, such as: the forced nature of negotiations; danger to the person performing the negotiations; a high degree of responsibility for the outcome of negotiations. Therefore, the personality of the negotiator is subject to increased requirements, also due to psychological skills and abilities.

CONCLUSION

Most Western countries have a declared policy of not negotiating with terrorists. This policy is typically used during hostage crises and is limited to ransom demands and no other forms of negotiation. Motives for such policies include the lack of assurance that terrorists will ensure the safe return of hostages and reducing the incentive for terrorists to take more hostages in the future.

On June 18, 2013, G7 leaders signed an agreement to pay ransom to terrorists. However, most Western states have violated this policy in some cases. An investigation by The New York Times found that al-Qaeda and its affiliates have received at least $125 million in revenue from kidnappings since 2008. These payments were made almost exclusively by European governments, which channeled the money through a network of proxies, sometimes. masquerading it as development aid (Chakhava, 2022).

Some Western countries, such as the United States, Canada, and Britain, do not negotiate or pay ransoms to terrorists. Others, such as France, Germany, Italy and Switzerland, are more open to negotiations. This is a source of tension between governments with opposing policies.

The United States has traditionally had a policy against negotiating with terrorists. However, there have been highly criticized incidents of US government leaders negotiating with terrorists:

Israel does not negotiate with terrorists at all. Examples of counters include:

In 1988, the Spanish government negotiated with ETA six months after the group killed 21 shoppers in the 1987 Hipercor bombing.

The British government maintained a secret channel for the Irish Republican Army even after the 1991 Downing Street mortar attack.

In January 2015, hostages Haruna Yukawa and Kenji Goto were beheaded by ISIL after Japan refused to meet ISIL's demand of $200 million for the hostages' release (Chakhava, 2022).

Working with criminals and terrorists. Negotiations and tactics - The problem of the spread of crimes and terrorism is acute for a modern civilized society, one of the most important tasks of law enforcement agencies in such situations is to preserve the life and safety of citizens who have been attacked.

Hostage-taking is the forcible capture of people and their holding against their will (restriction of freedom), as a rule, posing a danger to their life and health.

Hostage-taking is a dramatic situation, since not only property (a building, an aircraft), but also the life of a person or a group of people is under threat of destruction. It can be spontaneous or planned, which defines: the time and date, the place of capture, the demands put forward, the conditions for the release of the hostages, etc.

There are two options for resolving a terrorist attack with hostage-taking:

1. hard - the destruction of criminals, forceful capture and release of hostages;
2. flexible - organizing and conducting negotiations, observing security measures to preserve the life and health of the hostages.

In order to organize and conduct a negotiation process with terrorists, a negotiating group is involved. Negotiations can be conducted by a single mediator (negotiator) or by a group of negotiators.

Before negotiating with criminals, it is determined:

- type of situation (environment);
- type of offender;
- negotiating tactics;
- available forces and means, as well as powers.

The main objectives of the negotiations:

1. reduce the tension of the situation, reduce the aggression of terrorists;
2. clarify the goals of terrorists, their intentions, plans;
3. create conditions and guarantees for the security of the hostages (International Center for Counter terrorism. 2022).

In the process of negotiations, the negotiator deals with a criminal personality (character traits, temperamental characteristics, level of cognitive and moral qualities, etc.). Therefore, taking into account the personal characteristics of a terrorist is especially important in the work of a negotiator.

There are several types of terrorist invaders.

1. Emotional-affective, impulsive. Such criminals are capable of committing violence at any moment; when making a decision, they are guided by their own experiences, which are difficult to predict and often beyond their control. They are divided into three subspecies:
    a. suicide - ready for the worst-case scenario, either has a clear plan to commit an act of self-destruction, or unknowingly takes the fire upon himself;
    b. inadequate - when committing a crime, he is not aware of his actions, often has a real mental disorder;
    c. avenger - commits a crime out of revenge for the damage caused to him by someone (real or fictional).
2. Offender taken by surprise. Due to surprise, it can capture random hostages (when organizing a chase or encirclement) to use them as a human shield or guarantee of its safety.
3. Extortionist. He tries to achieve the most favorable conditions for himself. At the same time, he is often ready to make sacrifices among the hostages. Coolly performs decisive, carefully thought-out actions, realizing the likely consequences (both successful and unsuccessful for him).

4. Protester. By his ideology, he is a fan, an adherent of any political movement that is fighting: for the rights of individuals, for social equality, for truth, etc. Such a criminal does not understand the consequences of his actions very well, since he often commits a crime as a result of the failure of his other attempts to achieve the intended goal.
5. True terrorist. Such a criminal is a fanatical follower of some criminal organization. His goal is to intimidate civilians, spread specific criminal ideas, force the authorities to comply with the requirements of the terrorist organization in which he is a member (International Center for Counter terrorism. 2022).

There are four main stages of negotiating with criminals. At each stage of the negotiation, certain tasks are solved:

1. Collecting information and determining the requirements of criminals, developing tactics for negotiating, establishing contact with terrorists.
2. Involvement of forces and means of law enforcement agencies, outlines the main tactics of negotiation (hard, flexible), a proposal to terrorists to refrain from illegal actions.
3. Search for optimal solutions: consideration of options, bargaining, psychological pressure, building a dialogue, acceptance of a mutual agreement.
4. Reaching a full or partial agreement with the terrorists, determining ways to implement it, summarizing.

At each stage of work, the goal of the negotiators should be to reduce the number of victims, to free the hostages. First of all, the interests of children, women, the disabled and the elderly are affected. The salvation of each person is an achievement of the negotiation process and personally of the negotiator.

The criteria for the success of the negotiations can be considered:

- reduction of the categoricalness of the demands put forward by the criminals;
- decrease in the number of threats and manifestations of aggression;
- positive dynamics are outlined in building a dialogue with criminals;
- there is no violence against hostages, law enforcement officers;
- the release of all (or most) of the hostages held by the criminals;
- refusal of the offender from his plans and voluntary surrender to law enforcement officers (International Center for Counter terrorism. 2022).

REFERENCES

Aleksidze, L. (2018). *Contemporary International Law*. Tbilisi State University.

Beruashvili, N. (2022). *Psychological Factors during the Foreign Policy Decision-Making Process. World Politics and Challenges for International Security*. IGI Global.

Bock, A. (2010). *Negotiate with Terrorists! or: Why Terrorism Cannot be Deterred*. Retrieved from: https://www.fes.de/ipg/arc_07_d/01_07_d/pdf/12_RE_Bock_GB.pdf

Chakhava, K. (2022). *Terrorists Psychology and their impact on International Security. World Politics and Challenges for International Security*. IGI Global.

Chitadze, N. (2022). *World Politics and Challenges for International Security. Global Security and Political Problems of the 21-st Century. World Politics and Challenges for International Security*. IGI Global.

International Center for Counter Terrorism. (2022). *Negotiating with Terrorists*. Retrieved from: https://icct.nl/event/negotiating-with-terrorists/

Research Gate. (2011). *Being Tough or Being Nice? A Meta-Analysis on the Impact of Hard- and Softline Strategies in Distributive Negotiations*. Retrieved from: https://www.researchgate.net/publication/273653071_Being_Tough_or_Being_Nice_A_Meta-Analysis_on_the_Impact_of_Hard-_and_Softline_Strategies_in_Distributive_Negotiations

Siedel, G. (2014). *Negotiating for Success: Essential Strategies and Skills*. University of Michigan.

Slatkin, A. (2008). The Stockholm Syndrome Revisited. The Police Chief Magazine, 75(12).

US Department of Justice. (2022). *Terrorism and hostage negotiations*. Retrieved from: https://www.ojp.gov/ncjrs/virtual-library/abstracts/terrorism-and-hostage-negotiations

KEY TERMS AND DEFINITIONS

Negotiation: A strategic discussion that resolves an issue in a way that both parties find acceptable. In a negotiation, each party tries to persuade the other to agree with his or her point of view. By negotiating, all involved parties try to avoid arguing but agree to reach some form of compromise.

Psychology: The scientific study of mind and behavior. Psychology includes the study of conscious and unconscious phenomena, including feelings and thoughts. It is an academic discipline of immense scope, crossing the boundaries between the natural and social sciences. Psychologists seek an understanding of the emergent properties of brains, linking the discipline to neuroscience. As social scientists, psychologists aim to understand the behavior of individuals and groups

Terrorism: Premeditated violence perpetrated against non-combat targets by subnational or transnational groups or clandestine agents usually intended to influence an audience.

Chapter 11
A Critical Look at the Cold War Era on the Axis of Moscow and Hollywood

Pelin Pelin
https://orcid.org/0000-0002-7235-4671
University of Dicle, Turkey

ABSTRACT

By the end of the 20th century, significant differentiation occurred in international media. These differentiations left their place in the unipolar system as the bipolar system, which had dominated the world for more than 40 years, lost its currency. However, the acceleration in international relations has led to competition in trade, military, and economy. This study tried to discuss the fail-safe movie about the Cold War period ideologically. This study aims to examine how the social and political events experienced during the Cold War period took place in the cinema and determine how the dominant ideology in this context affects the language of cinema. In the study, the film will be evaluated from a political and ideological point of view. The chapter determines which social positions and ideological reflections they reproduce by analyzing them within the framework of the stated questions and associating them with the political period they are in.

INTRODUCTION

After World War II, a political, ideological and strategic war called the Cold War broke out between the United States and Western European countries, the Union of Soviet Socialist Republics and the remaining communist countries. The period between 1948-1963 was accepted as the years when the effect of this war was seen the most. II. After World War II, socialist, totalitarian systems were established in all Eastern European countries with the influence of the Union of Soviet Socialist Republics, and special efforts were made by the two great powers to include many former colonies in their bloc. These efforts were mostly intended to support the efforts of the newly liberated countries to become a nation-state and secure the national security of those states. During the Cold War, the two superpower democracies

DOI: 10.4018/978-1-6684-5311-7.ch011

continued their existence at two different poles in terms of state-society relations. However, the control mechanism created by the countries that are party to their poles over the societies with the perception of the threat of war is similar. The states that are party to the two superpowers have also increased their national security levels with the perception of enemy threat.

Purpose and Method

This study aims to examine how the social and political events experienced during the Cold War Period took place in the cinema and determine how the dominant ideology in this context affected the language of cinema. For this purpose, an ideological analysis will be applied to the examined film. The ideological analysis assumes that artistic works are made for social groups within specific historical contexts such as film, television, and literature (Özden, 2004, p. 169). As in all cultural representations, social reality in cinema is constructed by the internalization of cultural representations. After the information and positioning process conveyed by the filmic narrative, the cinema audience internalizes the cultural representations given to them and assimilates the value system that belongs to them, and enters under ideological conditioning and positioning. Thus, movies make it possible to create a false consciousness that prevents people from changing the foundations of the social order in which they exist (Özden, 2004, p. 170).

Moreover, it is possible to determine the ideological positions of the films by looking at their attitudes towards the opposite vital institutions and values. The contrasts Gianetti identified are as follows: Democracy vs. Hierarchy, Environment vs. Heredity, Relativity vs. Precision, Future vs. Past, Unity vs. Competition, Outsiders vs. Insiders, Universals vs. Nationalists. The films on the first side of these contracts are on the left of the ideological spectrum, and the second one is on the right (Güçhan, 1999, p. 197). The film, which was taken as a sample of this study, will be analyzed within the framework of the following questions, and it will be tried to determine which social positions and ideological reflections they reproduce by associating them with the political period they are in.

The questions to be answered in the analysis are listed below:

- How does the relationship between people progress in the movie? Are there friendships in relationships, or are relationships in superior-subordinate relationships?
- How is the relationship between the private and state institutions and the characters in the movie progressing?
- What are moral values endorsed or particularly emphasized in the movie?
- Are there any religious values emphasized or especially emphasized in the film?
- Is there an emphasis on class structure in the film?
- What is the class positioning of the protagonists in the movie?
- Where does the film sit on the ideological spectrum?

IDEOLOGY

Ideology is mostly defined as a concept that shows the meanings, thoughts and symbolic codes associated with social life (Serpil, 1997, p.8). The concept of ideology has been studied by various disciplines, from sociology to communication and politics, and has been tried to be interpreted by different disciplines.

While the concept of ideology is being studied by different disciplines, each discipline has attributed its own meaning to ideology, which has led to some difficulties in studies on ideology (Burton, 1995, p.19). In 1797, the French philosopher Antonie Destutt de Tracy used the concept of ideology for the first time. The concept is used to express the science of thought, which is planned to allow all people to think correctly. Various thinkers have widely defined ideologies. However, it is basically conceptualized with three different views. The first is that ideology is a set of thoughts that do not contain any wrong or right and serve as a window for people to make sense of life. Second, ideology is a state of false consciousness. According to this, ideology is accepted as all of the actions, discourses and ideas that force the system to comply with the dominant power and contain the view of the dominant structure. Third, he sees ideology as a mentality that can bring together the members of the society who are outside the hegemonic power and create the opportunity to act together (Başbuğ, 2013, p.28). Althusser states that the dominant powers use ideology to ensure continuity in their domination. According to Althusser, the statement "The state is the (oppression) apparatus of the state" defined by the Marxist view is insufficient. Althusser used the concept of "State Ideological Devices" to eliminate this deficiency. The Marxist view argues that structures such as the army, police, courts, prisons and government act in line with the views of the sovereign power and by applying pressure, the power dictates its thoughts to the people. These structures are "State Press Devices". However, the "State Repression Devices" that Althusser refers to are very different from the structures mentioned.

Although these devices have incredibly different and diverse structures, they have a unity structure that does not physically come to life under the title of "Sovereign ideology", which is the ideology of power (Althusser, 2014) (Althusser, 2014, pp. 50-53). Althusser says that no power can fully provide social order and control without using the Ideological Devices of the State (IMA). He gives cultural ISAs as an example. He states that the cultural ISA is trying to "reform" the "herds" or society by censoring them in some ways. He says that cultural devices serve ideology through activities carried out in fine arts, literature, cinema, and theatre, an ideological surrender (Althusser, 2014, p. 51). Due to the chaotic structure that existed during the First and Second World Wars and the desire of the dominant powers to stay in power, a great propaganda function was attributed to art. The world view of the dominant power was conveyed to the masses by using art, by making ideological orientations in authoritarian regimes with cinema and radio.

CINEMA AS THE STATE'S POLITICAL PROPAGANDA DEVICE

Propaganda refers to communication consciously directed through a reliable source for reflecting ideological messages with high impact. (Burton, 1995, p. 224). In another view, propaganda is defined as "continuous efforts to create or shape existing events to influence the public's relations with an initiative, an idea or a group (Traverse, 1988), p.14). Since cinema is both an audio and visual mass media, its power to influence people is exceptionally high. In the 19th century, states realized the power of cinema and used it to influence their citizens. Ideologies are connected with cinema. Ideologies expand their fields of activity through cinema. Cinema is an essential medium for ideologies constantly trying to find a place for themselves.

For this reason, cinema is an essential field of ideological struggle (Çelik, 2016, p. 99). In this medium, people have tried to give new ideas ideologically. Cinema and television "have been beneficial ideological weapons, as they are well suited to serving the dominant class's need to present the status quo as reality itself." According to Çelik, "Cinema has been able to bring the same society to the desired level by showing itself differently, depending on the capacity of the dominant mass to direct the society. With this aspect, cinema has become a means of imagining a day in the future, not the past or the present, with a meaning and mission beyond reflecting reality." Elites, political groups, administrators and other dominant segments attributed the mission of directing the society to cinema. In this sense, cinema has caused transformations in society self through propaganda following its task (Çelik, 2016, p. 104).

Cinema ranks first in all branches of art in terms of influencing and persuading the masses. As soon as the states realized that cinema had this power of influence, especially after the end of the First World War, they made unique films to persuade society on different issues such as news, economy, and politics and create public opinion. Films made to mobilize the masses, make them believe in a particular ideology and direct them and convey the message directly are called "Propaganda" films (Kıraç, 2012, p. 41). Production companies and states worldwide make films that trigger the nationalist feelings of individuals and give messages to the masses to adopt the ideas of the dominant ideology. When the history of cinema is examined, it is seen that countries such as Germany, Italy, England and France, especially the USA and Russia, are among the countries that make films reflecting the dominant ideology (Kıraç, 2012, p. 42).

Lenin, who came to power in Russia after the October Revolution of 1917, and Hitler, who came to power in Germany, were aware of the power of cinema to influence the masses, so the two leaders gave great importance to cinema. Lenin and Hitler both benefited from the artistic aspect of cinema and used it as a propaganda tool (Clark, 2004, p. 20). Mosfilm, Lenfilm, Gorki Film, and Sverdlovsk film studios were the most effective ideological devices in the cinema industry, in which widespread communist propaganda was made in the USSR during the period. When we look at the period in general, it is seen that the majority of the films made until the collapse of the USSR, starting with Lenin, are productions that support the current ideology.

The United States of America is one of the countries that uses propaganda very strongly. However, the USA's use of cinema as a propaganda tool is different from other countries. While Hollywood cinema uses cinema as a propaganda tool, it does not do this clearly and by showing. Propaganda is made with the stories and icons placed in the movie in Hollywood cinema. Hollywood cinema, which mainly made fictional films during the war and after the war, adopted this style of expression to keep the morale of the people who had a high level of anxiety and constantly felt threatened during the war. Even though society is not ideologically pro-state, fictional films have been used effectively. In this period, musicals and melodrama-style productions came to the fore. In the movies shot, the subjects such as the war being fought for just reasons and what the citizens should do in this process were frequently covered in the movies (Kıraç, 2012, p. 51). After the end of the war in 1945, movements against communism developed in American cinema. Several inspections and restrictions were made within the House of Representatives Hollywood. The Committee questioned 19 artists working in Hollywood, including the German artist Bertolt Brecht, on charges of communism, blacklisted these names and prevented them from making movies. The Committee, which also took control of the studios of film production centres, took measures restricting the activities of filmmakers by creating black lists for ten years.

As a result of the developments after the Second World War, it can be said that American cinema is an area where bourgeois ideology is produced and reproduced, even if there are exceptions. The narrative structure that Griffith initiated is based on the classical continuity style, and the principle of the form is invisible, in other words, not being noticed. In conservative productions, gender roles are determined, and family is given as a sacred value. Monogamy and bourgeois male domination were supported. From the early periods of western movies to today's cinema, female characters have assumed the role of the passive centre of the house and the transmitter of the values of white civilization to children (Yılmaz, 2008, p. 72). The fact that the family is one of the fundamental phenomena that produces patriarchal values has led to this situation (Özkent, 2021, p. 234). On the other hand, in order for all these ideological messages not to be noticed, the form was prevented from being visible, and the audience was prevented from questioning and criticizing (Türten, 2017, p. 70).

COLD WAR PERIOD SOCIAL AND CULTURAL CHANGES

Cold War and Superpowers

"From Stettin in the Baltic to Trieste in the Adriatic, an iron curtain descends across the continent of Europe. On March 5, 1946, when Churchill gave his famous "Iron Curtain" speech in the State of Missouri in the USA, it is accepted as the beginning of the Cold War (Acar, 1991, p. 123). The Cold War is considered to be a period between the USA and the USSR, in which there were no certain rules to control the actions of these blocs and their member states, and only behaviour based on power took place (Sander, 1997, p. 202). The Cold War is a period that lasted for almost half a century, starting with the Berlin blockade in April 1948 and ending with the collapse of the Soviet Union in December 1991. During this period, America and Russia attacked each other with all kinds of means, except nuclear weapons. The struggle that started with Stalin and Harry Truman and ended with Mikhail Gorbachev and Ronald Reagan has an important place in world history. The Cold War lasted longer than any of the world's wars and was waged on every continent, including the space dimension. It has been the most expensive war in terms of human loss and resources spent (Powaski, 1998, p. 9). It is possible to list the following factors that constitute the Cold War period. The international political structure, which was formed after the Second World War and continued its influence for a long time, has changed greatly. After the war ended, two new balances of power emerged in the political arena; these are the USA and the USSR. After the war, the international political structure changed, and a two-pronged structure was formed. Secondly, one of the important events in this process is the liquidation of colonialism. The liberation of the colonies by declaring their independence is thought to be the entry of a new power called the "Third Block, the Non-Aligned Bloc" into the international arena (Armaoğlu, 1999, p. 419). During the Cold War, there was a period when diplomacy, which was the primary method that would allow the establishment of agreement rules between countries and the development of relations by limiting them according to a particular order, almost entirely ended between the two blocs. Diplomacy, which will create and implement the rules, has been replaced by power relations. There are diplomatic relations between the members of the two blocs, and the diplomats of the members of the two blocs are in the opposite bloc, but diplomacy has lost its functional meaning (Sander, 1997, p.182). After the Second World War, the world was divided into two eastern and western blocks, and the Cold War period began between these blocks.

The USSR and the USA played a leading role in constructing the world in this way, and in the subsequent years, sometimes on the brink of nuclear war, in determining the relations of the world states with each other (Uçarol, 2003, p. 817). The Cold War inflicted high economic costs, destruction and many casualties. While the phenomenon of bipolarity dates back to the past, the concept of the Cold War emerged after the Second World War. When the Second World War ended, the USSR—from Western Europe to the Pacific Ocean—became a superpower. II. The emergence of pro-Soviet communist regimes in Western European countries after World War II caused the relations between the USSR and the USA to become tense. The US administration tried to prevent the spread of Soviet influence and leftist ideology to the West, Latin America, Asia and Africa. While these were happening outside of America, anti-communist movements known as the "Witch Hunt" started in the USA (Powaski, 1998), p. 4). During the Cold War, one of the essential elements in the relations between the USA and the USSR was the arms race. Starting from August 1945, the USA began to see itself as a monopoly power possessing nuclear weapons and used its success in nuclear armament as a vital trump card in its repression policy against the USSR. As a result of this pressure, the USSR, which made significant investments in military technology, acquired nuclear weapons in 1949 and later had the technologies to transport these weapons to the territory of the potential enemy. Both countries have invested heavily in the arms industry, and the combined nuclear weapons of the two states have reached the power to destroy the world several times (Powaski, 1998), p. 6). In the early 1960s, the USA and the USSR came to the brink of nuclear war: The deployment of Soviet nuclear weapons in Cuba in response to the planting of American nuclear weapons in Turkey led to the Cuban crisis in 1962. Only the common sense and political will of John Kennedy and Nikita Khrushchev prevented the outbreak of nuclear war. After the 1962 crisis, the period called "Softening" started. Several important agreements have been made to prevent the deposition of nuclear weapons because the arms race may cause economic weakening of countries with the threat of nuclear war. In this context, negotiations on the reduction of strategic weapons took place in the 1970s, resulting in the signing of the ABM (1972) and SALT-1 (1979) agreements.

The West alone was not directly influential in the collapse of the Soviet Union. A single reason cannot explain it. First, the collapse of the Soviets was the result of many simultaneous repressions. Second, if the collapse of the Soviet Union is to be attributed to a single cause, it will be a weak and unsuccessful domestic economic system. Although the West put pressure on this system, the problems of the Soviet economy stemmed from the Stalinist growth model. Third, if we have to talk about a Western influence in the collapse of the Soviet Union, this effect mainly emerged with the availability of the domestic situation. Western governments presented new opportunities by imposing restrictions that would affect Gorbachev's options and the behaviour of political players present in the Soviets in the late 1980s. Although the West did not cause the collapse of the Soviet Union alone, it played a role in this collapse by supporting some limited and unique ways. The USSR played an essential role as an excellent state for 69 years, especially after the early 1930s. In 1945 and the following years, as the leader of one of the two blocs in the world and one of the two superpower states, it directly affected and directed the world balance of power and international relations in the first degree. After Gorbachev came to power in 1985, reform movements began to occur in the USSR. The change in the structure of the Soviets also affected the satellite states, and independence movements began to be seen in the states. There have been system changes in Hungary, Poland, Czechoslovakia, Bulgaria, Romania, Germany, Albania and Mongolia. The system changes in the states that formed the Eastern Bloc and the actions of transition to pluralist democracy and market economy led these states to separate from the bloc they belonged to and to independence. This situation led to the disintegration of the eastern bloc.

The collapse of the USSR, one of the world's two superpowers, and the Eastern Bloc affiliated with it led to the end of the bipolar and bipolar political structure, the balance of power based on it, and the Cold War. In the early 1990s, a new situation emerged, along with new developments and structuring in the balance of power (Uçarol, 2003, p. 825). The disintegration of the Soviet Union; While it shows that the USA, one of the two superpowers, was victorious against another superpower, the Soviet Union, on the other hand, it means that the bipolar system of the Cold War period has come to an end.

THE STRUCTURE OF CINEMA IN SUPERPOWERS IN THE COLD WAR PERIOD

The current ideology of the USA has also influenced the cinema industry, and even the American cinema has become the representative of the American ideology. Political issues such as security issues, war and armed violence are among the subjects that are mostly covered in the cinema. American Hollywood cinema is the cinema that uses propaganda most professionally and skillfully in motion pictures. From the birth of cinema to today, many films were made only for specific political purposes. After the Second World War, propaganda films continued to be made (Özsoy, 1998, p. 358). The biggest challenge for Hollywood, the heart of the American movie industry, has always been what to market and how. Star actors and diversity in films have been the biggest supporters of Hollywood cinema (Abisel, 1999, p. 42). Even in movies made to make money, effective propaganda was made using secret propaganda techniques in a very professional way.

American cinema shapes the audience by operating mechanisms to determine their reaction to specific subjects, plots, places and actors (Abisel, 1999, p, 44). For this reason, Hollywood cinema has not limited it to the political field while making propaganda. He also did it in commercial cinema to support political ideology. The audience strongly identifies with the chosen star actor. He begins to think like him, to perceive life as he describes it in the film. The audience now thinks that everything the star actor does is correct. At this point, the desired message, propaganda, and secret codes directly affect the audience (Bayramoğlu, 2001, p. 21-23).

American Hollywood movies are not only shown in America. These films are watched in many parts of the world. Naturally, the clothes are worn by the star actors in American Hollywood cinema; the mentality, behaviour and attitudes of the star actors also profoundly affect the audience in the country where they are shown. People watching the movie can adopt lifestyles that are not in their own culture in a much simpler way. Hollywood cinema has succeeded in using propaganda in this way in a much softer and much more effective way (Scognamillo, 2004, p. 175). American films are supported in certain areas by the powers that own the country, and for this reason, they are demanded in return (Robb, 2005, p. 129). The threat, which is tried to be kept up to date by the Pentagon in the consciousness of the American people, has become a concept that is constantly studied and tried to be shaped by strategic studies. The threat phenomenon primarily provides a variety of subjects to the cinema industry. Generally, in movies, America successfully eliminates the existing threat; while doing this, new technological systems and defence systems are used so that the new technological systems in the audience's consciousness are reflected to be highly effective and reliable.

Bond films appeal to the audience's expectation of identification (Yenigün, 1996, p. 219). Made under the influence of the political agenda during the Cold War; The Rocky series is about the conflict of two superpowers and shows that the USA is peaceful and superior to the Soviet Union; In the James Bond series, he successfully markets the American political and cultural ideology to other countries. The central theme of Bond films is usually the Soviet Union, which threatens the free world, or how to eliminate a terrorist organization that aims to take over the world. In the films of the Bond series, it is told how a single hero, with the help of the latest technological developments and using his superior abilities, neutralized the mostly eastern attacks that threatened the western culture.

After the end of the cold war, the change in American policy also affected the cinema. The films of main characters such as Rambo, Rocky, and Superman, whose primary purpose is to make propaganda, have been replaced by films that start to confuse philosophically and question life. The movie "The Matrix", shot in 1999, is the best example. The subjects of "information warfare" and "information dominance" are presented in a fabled way. The film is a tale created to manipulate reality norms and criteria, which are designed as one of the primary data for constructing and making sense of reality by power centres in the cyberspace age. The Matrix questions the effect of virtual strategy, which can completely distort the connections between the individual, social world and power, and create the fantastic effects of "unseen" destructiveness in the project of increasing state power in favour of the oligarchy, which manages strategic tools based on space power rather than a terrorist formation. Soviet Cinema primarily aims at educating the masses. Therefore, it seeks ways to provide a political and general education opportunity for them. It is aimed to inform the people who are considered to have low education levels with documentary productions and films containing Soviet political and cultural elements (Akarcalı, 2003, p. 216). Vigilance stands out as an essential theme in the films made. Espionage has become an obsession. In war movies, everyone, including children and older women, strives to unmask spies. The recurring theme in the movies is the struggle against saboteurs and traitors. None of the later contemporary films focused on traitors. As the internal enemy disappeared, it was replaced by foreigners or their agents. The country is preparing to face a foreign enemy. Instead of hunting down the supposed internal enemy, the films told how the nations that made up the Soviet Union should work together for the 'common good. Propaganda movies were made to support the immediate goals of Soviet domestic and foreign policy. In Mihail Çiaureli's film "The Collapse of Berlin", which represents the peak of Stalin's culture, the Soviet leader is depicted as a supernatural figure who can see into the hearts of ordinary people (Akarcalı, 2003, p. 219).

FINDINGS AND COMMENT

The Story of the Movie

The movie begins with a matador attacking a bull in the arena. This scene reflected on the screen is the general's dream. The matador thrusts a spear into the bull repeatedly. The general's face is reflected on the stage in close-ups. From the general's facial features, we can see that he was disturbed by the matador's attack on the bull. The general wakes up in a sweat, realizing it was a dream. Waking up nervously, the character looks at his sleeping children and then comes to his room and talks to his wife. He tells his wife that he has seen the same dream again and that he thinks that these dreams are related to his job and that he knows that if he quits his job, these dreams will end. His wife says to the general that he cannot give up his job, and the general says to his wife that he cannot give up on him and the children; he gets dressed and goes to the meeting. The Political Scientist Professor is at a home meeting and is shouting warmongering. The people who will die in war are insignificant to him. The only thing that matters is the continuation of American culture and its superiority over Russian culture. Every way is permissible to achieve this. The Professor is a civilian adviser to the Pentagon. Visitors visit the military base to see where the technology investments are made. After the devices are introduced, they use the following sentence to explain how well they work and how advanced they are technological, "our satellites are so good that they can distinguish between the water a submarine takes off and the water a whale takes off". While the visitors are at the base, a UFO is attached to the radars and tense moments begin at the base. After a few minutes, it is understood that the object that entered the radar is a commercial plane and everything returns to normal. He is present at the general in a meeting that includes the Professor. While the Professor advocates over-armament and war, the

General advocates the opposite. The general here contradicts his profession as a soldier. Shortly after that, a US plane, which had turned its route to Russia, is noticed. The plane received a false signal due to a mechanical failure and thought it was his mission to bombard Moscow. Although it is known that the signal was given to the aircraft as a result of an error, a connection with the aircraft could not be established. In training given to the pilots, after reaching a certain distance, they were taught not to disregard the radio calls given about the withdrawal of the order in any way. After the aircraft reached a certain distance, radio communication was possible, but the pilots did not accept the withdrawal of the order as a result of their training. Other planes sent to shoot down the planes were not successful. The American President talked to the President of Russia on the phone and tried to explain that this was a mistake and that the planes were getting the wrong signal due to a mechanical failure. They stated that they are open to all kinds of cooperation for the downing of the planes. The President says that if the planes reach their target despite everything, he will bomb Washington to prove it was a mistake and to prevent a war that may arise. He assigns the general who sees a matador in his dream to do this. The general ordered that all necessary information be given to the Russians connected to the base by conference call. All kinds of information about planes and missiles are given to the Russians, but a plane reaches the target, Moscow, and drops its bombs. Buna karşılık Amerikan Başkanı da Washington bir uçak göndertir ve orayı bombalatır. In the final scene, the general realizes that he is the matador, the matador der matador himself. People living in daily life appear on the screen, and after the bomb is dropped, it is understood that those people are no longer alive.

IDEOLOGICAL ANALYSIS OF THE FAIL-SAFE MOVIE

In the film, explicit messages take up more space than hidden messages. In the movie, messages are given clearly, and detailed information about this world is given to the audience.

Relationship Between Characters in Fail-Safe Movie

In the movie, the general is seen as the representative of the good. Although the general is against the policy of excessive armament, he appears to be anti-war, contrary to his profession. The representative of the villains in the film is the Professor. The Professor is in favour of over-arming. He thinks that American culture is more valuable than other cultures and defends American culture against Russian culture. It is observed that he is constantly shouting war. When we look at the relations between the characters, it is seen that the characters' relations with each other are based on the upside-down relationship. No character is a friend of another character.

Relationships Between Institutions and Individuals in the Movie Fail-Safe

Filmde iki kurum bulunmaktadır bunlar, Pentagon ve Beyaz Saraydır. The representative of the White House is the President of the United States. Pentagon's representatives are senior Generals. All the characters were working in the Pentagon work for the military defence of the state. On the other hand, the President is both the leader of the country and the last decision maker against foreign attacks. There is no institutional structure over which the President has a sanction. In addition, although the Parliament and Gordon Knapp's building are not visible in the movie, we see representatives of both institutions.

Moral Values Emphasized/Confirmed in the Fail-Safe Movie

In the movie, loyalty to the state, working for state interests, self-sacrifice, devotion to duty and absolute obedience to orders is emphasized and approved.

Religious Emphasis in Fail-Safe

There is no religious symbol or institution in the film.

Class Structure Emphasis in Fail-Safe Film

There are clear class differences in the movie, but; It is known that there is a separation between the Pentagon, the staff at the base, the Presidential Palace and the public.

Class Structure of Heroes in the Movie Fail-Safe

In the movie, the protagonists are usually in the upper class. The President and the Minister belong to the ruling class. The Generals and the Professor are representatives of the upper class. Although the characters belong to the upper class, they are in the service of the dominant system. The fact that the American President is in a position to decide the death of 5 million people living in Washington is "based on a divine power attributed to him".

The Relationship Between Economic, Political and Social Events of the Period When Fail-Safe Was Filmed

The 1964 film ultimately reflects the political and military policies of the USA at that time. Bringing the Cold War era policies to the stage, the film also reflects the social structure of the period. We can see the excessive armament policies of Russia and the USA and their investment in technology. The Russians are constantly observed through satellites launched into space, and they seem to have almost the same military and technological power in both countries. Significant investments in technology are shown to the public through the film. It is also seen that an attempt is made to create a horror empire in the movie. For the Russians, the USA and the USA, the Russians are always a dangerous element, so both countries are ready for war if a war breaks out. The Russians and Communism are seen as absolute enemies and perceived as targets to be destroyed.

Psychological Structures of the Characters in the Movie Fail-Safe

Although there is no hot war or conflict in the movie, the cold war affects the characters negatively. Waiting for a war that is likely to break out constantly makes the high-ranking soldiers and other soldiers at the military base uneasy; UFOs detected by the radars are considered Russian attack planes, and they are alarmed. This situation puts the soldiers under intense stress, and this tense environment is reflected in their business and social lives. The general, who is dreaming in the movie's opening scene, tells his wife that he has always had the same dream and that he knows that it is related to his job; maybe if he quits his job, these dreams will end. Again, a soldier working at the base attacked another soldier, took the podium, and said that he had taken office from the American President in an imaginary way. It is known that people experience severe traumas during war periods. The possibility of being attacked at any moment and starting a war at any moment affects all people, whether civilian or military.

Film's Place on the Ideological Spectrum

The film is located between the centre and the right of the ideological spectrum created by Gianetti, closer to the right because the film highlights approval and proposes values such as heredity, loyalty to the past, nationalism and traditionalism.

CONCLUSION

II. After World War II, a political, strategic and ideological war called the Cold War started between the United States of America and Western European countries, the Union of Soviet Socialist Republics and the remaining communist countries. With this war, while the influence of the USSR increased in all the countries of Eastern Europe, the influence of the USA began to be seen in the Western European countries. What happened both during and after the war created the beginning of the new world's new world order. The balance of power in Africa, Asia and Europe, where nations are divided, has changed, and new world order has come to life. The most striking change during this time has been in the international order. Increasing social, cultural relations and economic mobility between countries are seen as the most important factor behind the need for such a system. Thus, many countries came together and tried to create a new world order to prevent new wars that may occur. Great expectations were placed on the United Nations organization, which was established in 1945. Beneficial work has been done with the organizations of the United Nations Organization on basic issues such as world culture, health and education. Countries have entered into the great competition and a race for superiority in political, military and economic fields. Destructive and striking functional weapons with high mass destruction power have been developed. Ensuring international integration has been achieved with the development of information technologies. This process was recorded as the period in which the most important was given to scientific and artistic activities. On the other hand, technological developments have made the gap between states even more evident. After the end of the cold war, the change in American policy also affected the cinema. James Bond, who fought against Russian spies in the 1970s, whose main purpose was to make propaganda, met with the audience towards the end of the 90s with topics such as international spies and terrorists. The director or producer chose the subjects for cinema, which is a signification process, consciously or unconsciously revealing an ideological attitude. It can be said that Hollywood cinema and its representational traditions have the function of legitimizing the dominant institutions and traditional values of the dominant system and to instill ideology. States resort to perception management to create an image in the international arena, dominate other states, and direct the citizens of other countries to their ideology in line with the country's interests. At the beginning of the 20th century, states realized the power of cinema to influence the masses and therefore began to take the cinema under control. This effect of cinema has been used to spread the current ideology in both foreign and domestic politics. States have benefited from cinema to make the public believe their thoughts and hide some facts. In Hollywood movies, perception operations are seen too much. In Hollywood movies, the sound of sirens and images of ambulances and fire trucks are given much space. The aim is to show the public that institutions such as security and health are successful and functioning well. In order to show the other world states that America has the most powerful army in the world, the American army allocates large budgets to the film industry and provides great support. For this reason, the heroic stories and achievements of the American military forces come to the fore in the films. Hollywood films contribute to internalizing these issues by erasing the signs of cinematic artificiality informal conventions. Thematic conventions, masculine heroic adventures, seeking romance, female melodrama, saviour stories of violence, racist and criminal stereotypes, etc. It connects reality with social institutions, values and institutions and ensures that these are perceived as natural and obvious indicators of an unchanging world. Cinema has become too complex to be underestimated with the technological development, aesthetic and political level it has reached today. Hollywood cinema was making films about America's sole and absolute power in the world until the September 11 attacks. However, more films about terror and freedom were made after this attack. Hollywood's versatile productions have allowed it to become much more popular than other countries' cinemas. The main criterion for Hollywood to have versatile productions can be explained by the support given by the American state and army to film productions. Hollywood-made films have an audience of all cultures, races, and faiths globally, which is extremely influential on the audience. It has an audience that takes place, which has a huge impact on the audience. This phenomenon is always recurring. People watch these movies when they are stressed and hectic, waiting for hope and peace, experiencing financial difficulties, in war and peace situations, even after natural disasters. This is not an ordinary coincidence. In Hollywood, where many interactions and phenomena intersect, the decisions made by top studio officials and the efforts of distribution and marketing masters intersect. In this context, Fail-Safe is a political production that reflects the American ideology. Throughout the film, it is seen that the American ideology is tried to be dominated, and the technological superiority of the American state is emphasized in the film. Although the official and ideological representations of the state, such as the Presidential Palace and the Pentagon, are not shown as venues, they are felt to the audience in the film. The film reflects the official ideology of the period and expresses unconscious social fears. In this way, they provide psychological escape by calming the fears they express. All of this puts the movie in the typical escape movie category.

FUTURE RESEARCH DIRECTIONS

The limitation of this study was that it was not possible to analyze the movies from the cold war period. Future researchers should conduct progressive-centered field research and cultural studies of the cold war period.

REFERENCES

Abisel, N. (1999). *Popular Cinema and Genres*. Alan Publishing.

Acar, C. (1991). *Superpowers Domination Struggle*. İrfan Publishing House.

Akarcalı, S. (2003). *Communication and Propaganda in the Second World War*. Image Publications.

Althusser, L. (2014). *Ideology and Ideological Devices of the State*. Ithaki Publications.

Armaoğlu, F. (1999). *20th Century Political History*. Alkim Publishing House.

Başbuğ, E. D. (2013). *Official Ideology on the Stage*. İletişim Publications.

Bayramoğlu, M. (2001). The Role and Function of the Star in Hollywood Cinema. *Journal of Universal Culture*.

Burton, G. (1995). *More Than Looks*. Alan Publishing.

Çelik, M. A. (2016). *Political Cinema*. Night Library.

Clark, T. (2004). *Art and Propaganda*. Details Publications.

Güçhan, G. (1999). *Genre Cinema, Image and Ideology*. Anadolu University Press.

Kıraç, R. (2012). *The ABC of cinema*. Say Publications.

Özden, Z. (2004). *Movie Review*. Image Bookstore.

Özkent, Y. (2021). Tracing Gender in Hollywood Cinema: Kramer vs. Marriage Story Forty Years After Kramer. *Culture and Communication*, *24*(1), 227–259.

Özsoy, O. (1998). *Propaganda and Public Opinion*. Alfa Publications.

Powaski, R. (1998). *The Cold War United States And The Soviet Union*. University Press.

Robb, D. (2005). *Hollywood Operations*. Current Publishing.

Sander, O. (1997). *Political history*. Icon Bookstore.

Scognamillo, G. (2004). *Turkish Cinema History*. Kabalci Publications.

Serpil, S. (1997). *The Adventure of Ideology*. Image Publications.

Traverse, T. H. (1988). *Public Relations and Propaganda: Comparative Values*. Route Publications.

Türten, B. (2017). *Making Short Documentary Films: The Example of Social Documentaries*. Doruk Publications.

Uçarol, R. (2003). *Political history*. Der Publications.

Yenigün, H. (1996). *The Language of the Media*. Der Publications.

Yılmaz, E. (2008). *On the Relations of Cinema and Ideology*. Orient Publishing.

ADDITIONAL READING

Ashley, R. (1984). The Poverty of Neorealism. *International Organization*, *38*(2), 225–286. doi:10.1017/S0020818300026709

Burchill, S. (1995). Realism and Neo-realism. In *Theories of International Relations*. St. Martin's Press.

Cox, R. W. (1986). Social Forces, States and World Orders: Beyond International Relations Theory. In *Neorealism and its Critics* (pp. 204–254). Columbia University Press.

Donnelly, J. (2004). *Realism and International Relations*. Cambridge University Press.

Gaddis, J. L. (1997). The Cold War, the Long Peace, and the Future. In *The End of the Cold War: Its Meaning and Implications* (pp. 21–38). Cambridge University Press.

Scott, L. (2001). International History 1945-1990. In *The Globalization Of World Politics: An Introduction to International Relations* (pp. 74–91). Oxford University Press.

Waever, O. (1996). The Rise and Fall of the Inter-paradigm Debate. In *International Theory: Positivism and Beyond* (pp. 149–185). Cambridge University Press. doi:10.1017/CBO9780511660054.009

KEY TERMS AND DEFINITIONS

Cold War: The Cold War is a form of sustained tension and limited conflict between the United States and the Soviet Union after the Second World War. The cold war was a product of the East-West conflict in 1917.

Eastern Bloc: Soviet Bloc or Iron Curtain is a term used during the Cold War to describe the Soviet Union and its allies in Eastern and Central Europe.

Superpower: A superpower is a state in the first place in the international system that can influence events around the world and use force. It is higher than great power status in the international system.

War: States, economic and political disputes between them, etc., armed action with their armies against each other by severing their political ties.

Chapter 12
Combating Terrorism Based on the Principles of International Law

Valeria Gonitashvili
Ukrainian Youth Organization of Georgia, Georgia

ABSTRACT

There is a growing body of international law that is directly relevant to the fight against terrorism. International law provides the framework within which national counterterrorism activities take place and which allows states to cooperate with each other effectively in preventing and combating terrorism. This framework includes instruments addressing specific aspects of counterterrorism alongside other international instruments designed for international cooperation in criminal law, the protection of human rights or refugees, or the establishment of the laws of war, which provide the broader context within which counterterrorism activities take place. International law specifically addressing terrorism exists within the general framework of international law including international criminal law, international humanitarian law, international human rights law, and refugee law.

INTRODUCTION

Definition of "rule of law" The concept of "rule of law" is central to the United Nations system, including concerning its work in countering terrorism. As has been widely recognized by various UN bodies, organizations, and Member States, terrorism threatens both the rule of law and the fundamental freedoms of citizens and society as a whole; Indeed, the General Assembly has reaffirmed in the UN Global Counter-Terrorism Strategy that one of the main goals of terrorism is often the erosion of the rule of law, together with "human rights, fundamental freedoms, and democracy..." (United Nations, General Assembly, 2006, A/RES60 /288). Accordingly, counter-terrorism responses that do not comply with the rule of law may undermine their legitimacy and effectiveness while encouraging such terrorist goals. Although there is no single definition of the concept of "rule of law", its essence was captured by the former UN Secretary-General Kofi Annan in the report "The Rule of Law and Transitional Justice in

DOI: 10.4018/978-1-6684-5311-7.ch012

Conflict and Post-Conflict Societies", when he described the "rule of law" as "a principle of governance, in under which all persons, institutions and entities, public and private, including the State itself, operate under laws that have been publicly enacted, are equally enforced and independently enforced by the judiciary, and are consistent with international law and standards human being" (United Nations, Security Council, 2004, S/2004/616, paragraph 6). In the context of counter-terrorism, UN bodies and organizations regularly express the strong opinion that respect for human rights in the context of counter-terrorism is not only a matter of legal obligation but is critical to the ultimate success of any counter-terrorism strategy. For example, a recent report by the United Nations High Commissioner for Human Rights notes: Effective counter-terrorism measures and the protection of human rights are complementary and mutually reinforcing goals that must be pursued jointly as part of the responsibility of states to protect individuals under their jurisdiction. World experience has shown that the protection of human rights and the rule of law in themselves contribute to countering terrorism, in particular, by creating an atmosphere of trust between the state and persons under their jurisdiction. (UN, General Assembly, Human Rights Council, 2016, A/HRC/34/30, para. 56). This is confirmed by the indivisible relationship between international human rights law and criminal law (both national and international). From a rule of law perspective, the essence of criminal law is to define the parameters of what is acceptable and unacceptable behavior in a given social context. If, for example, definitions of crimes are ambiguous, this can undermine the core function of criminal law, making it easier for others to act contrary to the rule of law. In addition, UN bodies and organizations, including the General Assembly and the Security Council, regularly emphasize the importance of respecting not only international human rights law but also international humanitarian law and international refugee law (UN Security Council Resolution 1373 (2001), especially in the context of the UN Global Counter-Terrorism Strategy.

UN Global Counter-Terrorism Strategy

Overview The United Nations Counter-Terrorism Strategy is the main starting point for examining the framework governing the global counter-terrorism effort. Adopted without a vote by the UN General Assembly in Resolution 60/288 of 8 September 2006, and thus reflecting universal consensus and legitimacy, for the first time UN member states have agreed and adopted a common strategic approach and framework for combating terrorism. The Counter-Terrorism Strategy is reviewed and updated by the UN General Assembly every two years, taking into account changing priorities (see, for example, UN, General Assembly, 2008, A/RES/62/272, 2010, A/RES/64/297, 2012, A/RES/66/272, 2014, A/RES/68/276, 2016 (b), A/RES/70/291). Thus, the Counter-Terrorism Strategy remains a constantly updated document. This is evidenced by the review of the General Assembly dated 1 July 2016 (UN, General Assembly, 2016 (b), A/RES/70/291), which was related to the consideration of the UN Secretary-General's Plan of Action to Prevent Violent Extremism (UN, General Assembly, 2015 (a), A/70/674, 2015 (b), A/70/675) due to growing international concern (Chitadze, 2016). Changing conditions and accompanying priorities are reflected in the biennial reports of the UN Secretary-General "UN system activities to implement the UN Global Counter-Terrorism Strategy" (most recently UN, General Assembly, 2016 (a), A/70/826), which provide information on the progress made and challenges related to the implementation of the Counter-Terrorism Strategy. The Counter-Terrorism Strategy is a unique global tool for intensifying national, regional, and international efforts to counter terrorism, including strengthening cooperation among all key actors. Its adoption demonstrated not only the agreement of all Member States with a common strategic and operational approach to combating terrorism, making it clear that terrorism in all its forms and manifestations is unacceptable, but also their determination to take practical action, individually and collectively. to prevent and combat it. Such practical actions include a wide range of measures, from strengthening the capacity of states to counter the threat of terrorism, to better coordinating the counter-terrorism activities of the UN system.

UN Global Counter-Terrorism Strategy (2006) The Strategy was adopted in the form of a resolution with an attached Action Plan consisting of 4 sections:

- Measures to eliminate conditions conducive to the spread of terrorism;
- Measures to prevent and combat terrorism;
- Measures to strengthen the capacity of states to prevent and combat terrorism and strengthen the role of the UN system in this area;
- Measures to ensure universal respect for human rights and the rule of law as a fundamental basis for the fight against terrorism.

INTERNATIONAL COOPERATION AND THE UN GLOBAL COUNTER-TERRORISM STRATEGY

The need to continuously strengthen existing levels of cooperation is central to international counter-terrorism efforts and, as such, it is included in the goals and framework of the UN Counter-Terrorism Strategy. As already discussed, terrorism is a complex, non-static phenomenon. Associated motives, funding and support mechanisms, methods of attack, and targeting often change, thus complicating the challenges of providing an effective strategy to counter it. Moreover, its increasingly transnational nature calls for increased criminal justice cooperation between states to deny haven to those who commit or attempt to commit terrorist crimes. Terrorism has indeed become a global threat requiring a global, prevention-oriented response. Numerous UN outputs, including Security Council resolutions, have articulated and re-emphasized that such cooperation needs to be strengthened at all levels, including bilaterally, regionally, and internationally, among all relevant actors (UNSCR 2370 (2017), UNSCR 2178 (2014)). A 2004 UN High-Level Panel report notes: Today more than ever, threats are interconnected and a threat to one is a threat to all. The mutual vulnerability of the weak and the strong has never been so obvious…. No state, no matter how strong it may be, can only protect itself from modern threats by its efforts. Each state, to ensure its security, needs other states to cooperate with it. The Counter-Terrorism Strategy outlines the many levels at which such cooperation should take place and highlights the various obligations of Member States to work together to combat terrorism. It expresses the determination of the international community to cooperate fully in this regard, following its obligations under international law, to find, deny asylum and prosecute, based on the principle of extradition or prosecution, any person who supports, contributes, participates, or attempts to participate in the financing, planning, preparation or commission of terrorist acts, or provides a haven to those who do so. In each section of the Strategy, Member States have decided to take different measures to achieve this goal. This is important because while international cooperation, including under the auspices of various international organizations such as the UN, is essential here, states still have the ultimate shared responsibility for effective counter-terrorism responses consistent with the rule of law. rights. Despite numerous achievements and significance, including in reaching a universal consensus, in practice, the potential of the Counter-Terrorism Strategy has not yet been fully realized. For example, work remains to be done on how best to translate some of its objectives into national or regional laws, policies, and practices.

Legal Sources and the United Nations Global Counter-Terrorism Strategy

Having introduced the UN Counter-Terrorism Strategy, we now turn to consider the various types of binding and non-binding legal sources that underlie the Strategy, as well as the 19 counter-terrorism documents and Security Council resolutions that form the basis of the institutional response to terrorism. There are two categories of legal sources. One of them is "material" sources, i.e. an instrument or document that contains obligations, such as contracts and judgments. The other type is the "formal" source, referring to the document's authority, that is, its legal weight and the impact of certain rules. The Counter-Terrorism Strategy is based on both types of sources. Formal sources are of particular interest to the entire university module series as they are relevant to the extent to which states comply with or violate their rule of law obligations in their national, regional and global efforts to effectively counter-terrorism.

FORMALLY BINDING LEGAL SOURCES

Under Article 38(1) of the 1945 Statute of the International Court of Justice, there are two main sources of binding legal sources: international treaties (Article 38(1)(a)) and customary international law (Article 38(1)(b)) (UN, 2005). In addition, national law is binding in the context of the States concerned, and the practice of courts and tribunals is binding on parties involved in specific legal proceedings. Although these last two sources are not discussed in detail here, examples of both are reflected in the series of modules for universities through case studies.

International Treaties

International treaties of particular importance to international counter-terrorism efforts include the 1945 United Nations Charter, the 19 United Nations (sectoral) counter-terrorism instruments (to be discussed in this section), and other key instruments governing international human rights law, international law Refugee Rights, and International Humanitarian Law, which are clearly stated by the UN to be an integral part of any effective response to terrorism by its Member States (UN, 2005).

Charter of the United Nations

About the Charter of the United Nations (Treaty Series, Vol. 1, No. XVI), as stated in Article 1 "Purposes", its main objectives include the maintenance of international peace and security (Article 1(1)). This is important because, as has been reaffirmed by the Security Council in various resolutions, terrorist activity is often seen as a threat not only to specific countries but to regional and global security as a whole (UNSCR 1373 (2001), UNSCR 1540 (2004)) (UN, 2005). It is in the interests of all States to counter the relevant threats in a manner that does not undermine international peace and security in a broader context. Since terrorist threats tend to be transnational, the founding principles of the Organization, as articulated in Article 2, are also important in guiding relevant counter-terrorism efforts. In particular, these principles are that: the Member States will fulfill in good faith the obligations assumed under the Charter (Article 2 (2)); "international disputes [must] be settled by peaceful means in such a manner as not to endanger international peace and security and justice" (Article 2 (3)); there is a presumption against "the threat or use of force against the territorial integrity or political independence of any State"

(Article 2(4)), except in cases of self-defense outlined in Article 51; and the principle of non-intervention by the United Nations "in matters which are essentially within the domestic jurisdiction of any State" (art. 2 (7)). Following these principles, including the doctrine of state sovereignty, a state should not use military force against non-state terrorist actors located in the territory of another sovereign state without its permission, thereby violating its territorial integrity, except for certain, limited exceptions allowed under international law. For example, when the state is unable or unwilling to prevent such entities from planning and committing terrorist attacks against third parties. Of course, after the September 11 attacks, under such circumstances, states more often resorted to military measures (see, for example, Dempsey, 2006; Newman, 2007). While this categorization of a state is not in itself determinative of the legality of engaging military force, it can be an important factor in the perception of the need to use such force in the absence of any alternative means. This is even though terrorist groups can thrive and operate from any state. Also noteworthy is Article 1(3), which aims to achieve international cooperation "in the promotion and development of respect for human rights and fundamental freedoms for all without distinction as to race, sex, language or religion", which is reflected in other provisions of the Charter, in particular in Article 55 (with accompanying Article 56, under which the Member States undertake to take joint and separate action to achieve the objectives of Article 55). These principles are also a common thread in other UN documents related to issues of countering terrorism, including resolutions of the General Assembly and the Security Council, as well as international anti-terrorism conventions discussed below (UN, 2005).

United Nations (Sectoral) Counter-Terrorism Conventions

In addition to the Charter, over the past five decades, the UN has developed 19 special agreements in the field of combating terrorism (Chitadze, 2022). They have largely evolved as a response to specific terrorist incidents or threats and cover crimes related to civil aviation (ie unlawful hijacking of aircraft, aircraft sabotage, use of an aircraft as a weapon); crimes against internationally protected persons (ie kidnapping of diplomats); taking hostages; illegal use or handling of nuclear materials; actions against the safety of maritime navigation and fixed platforms located on the continental shelf; terrorist explosions; financing of terrorism and activities related to the criminal use or handling of chemical, biological, radiological or nuclear materials or weapons. In essence, these instruments do not define terrorism, but rather create obligations for states to criminalize the offenses in question under national law; exercise jurisdiction over criminals in compliance with established requirements; establish an obligation to extradite or prosecute, and establish mechanisms to strengthen international cooperation in criminal matters.

Reservations to International Treaties

An important principle of treaty formation, as set out in the 1969 Vienna Convention on the Law of Treaties (Treaty Series, vol. 1155, p. 331), is that "[a] treaty does not create obligations or rights for a third State without its consent." as provided for in Article 34. A situation may sometimes arise where a State is prepared to agree to comply with most, but not all, obligations arising from an international treaty, including the world counter-terrorism conventions. Since this is in the interests of the international community, including promoting international cooperation in the field of countering terrorism, there is a mechanism for the states that are parties to these important legal instruments - the introduction of a reservation, according to which the state can agree to most, but not all, obligations under the contract.

Under Article 2(d) of the Vienna Convention, a "reservation" is defined as a unilateral declaration, in whatever wording and under whatever name, made by a State when signing, ratifying, accepting, or acceding to a treaty, by which it wishes to exclude or modify the legal effect of certain provisions of the treaty in their application to a given state. However, not all reservations by States are permissible. They are subject to certain restrictions provided for in Article 19, which states: A State may, when signing, ratifying, accepting, approving or acceding to a treaty, formulate a reservation unless: (a) the reservation is prohibited by the treaty; (b) the treaty provides that only certain reservations may be made, which do not include the reservation in question; or (c) in cases not covered by paragraphs (a) and (b), the reservation is incompatible with the object and purpose of the treaty. Regarding universal counter-terrorism instruments, several States rely on such reservations. For example, several states, such as Algeria, China, India, Mexico, etc., expressed reservations about the 1979 International Convention Against the Taking of Hostages (Treaty Series, vol. 1316, p. 205), opposing the enforcement of decisions regarding the interpretation of provisions between participating States (Ignatenko, 2002).

Customary International Law

Another source of binding legal obligation recognized in the 1945 Statute of the International Court of Justice is customary international law (article 38(1)(b)). Customary international law is an important source of law. It includes Rules of law arising from the generally accepted behavior of states acting on the belief that they are required by law to act in such a way. It springs from the general and consistent practice of States, applied for reasons of a legal obligation, to such an extent that it becomes customary law. Customary international law must be based on a clear consensus among States, both as a result of widespread behavior and a palpable sense of duty. (OSCE, ODIHR, 2007, p. 55). Therefore, in the context of human rights law, States parties to a particular treaty will have obligations not only under that treaty but also in respect of those rights and freedoms that have become part of customary international law. It is noteworthy that, in general, these obligations will be binding on States that are not parties to the conventions that articulate such customary rights and obligations, since they are binding on all States, whether or not they are parties to any particular treaty. For example, many of the rights and obligations outlined in the 1948 Universal Declaration of Human Rights (United Nations, General Assembly, 1948) and the 1949 Geneva Conventions (Treaty Series, vol. 75, p. 31, p. 85, p. 135, 287), as well as some of those set out in the 1966 International Covenant on Civil and Political Rights and the 1951 Refugee Convention, reflect customary international law (see later in the module). As recognized by the International Court of Justice in the Case of Military and Paramilitary Actions in and Against the Territory of Nicaragua, there is no hierarchy of rules in international law between international treaties (in this case, Articles 2(4) and 51 of the Charter) and customary international law (1986, paras. 177 -182) (Karumidze, 2005). This means that one legal source is not more important or authoritative than another. As the Court further held, both sources of law exist in parallel but separate from each other, and yet are not interdependent. Rules of customary international law often form the basis of international treaty texts, but may be further developed through the process of codification in the final adopted text. Consequently, there may be some differences between comparable rules in these legal sources. However, from a practical point of view, contractual obligations are easier to define in written text. One issue of particular relevance to counter-terrorism raised by some Member States is whether there is even a partial definition of terrorism under customary international law. This is potentially important in a context where there is still no generally accepted agreed definition in treaty texts.

Jus Cogens (Peremptory Norm of International Law)

Several customary international law obligations are of particular relevance to global efforts to counter terrorism, including under the auspices of the UN Counter-Terrorism Strategy. As a rule, they have the status of jus cogens (mandatory) (Article 53 of the Vienna Convention), which means that they cannot be derogated from and that they have concomitant erga omnes obligations of States to the international community as a whole to respect and enforce them (Belgium v. Spain, 1970, The Prosecutor v. Anto Furundzia, 1998, para. 151) (Aleksidze, 2018). The jus cogens standards are an important exception to the general rule that all rules in the international legal sphere are horizontal. Instead, they are in a vertical relationship, which means that in the event of any conflict between obligations created by peremptory and non-mandatory rules, the former will prevail over the latter. A common starting point for identifying the key qualities for jus cogens (or peremptory norms) is Article 53 of the Vienna Convention on the Law of Treaties: A treaty is void if, at the time of its conclusion, it conflicts with a peremptory norm of general international law. As far as this Convention is concerned, a peremptory norm of general international law is a norm that is accepted and recognized by the international community of States as a whole as a norm from which no derogation is permitted and which can only be modified by a subsequent norm of general international law of the same character. While there is no generally agreed set of such principles, prohibitions on the threat or use of force, torture, genocide, slavery, racial discrimination, and crimes against humanity are widely recognized as peremptory norms (Aleksidze, 2016).

GENERAL PRINCIPLES OF LAW

The current consensus is that a comprehensive global legal regime against terrorism is still in the process of being developed. One important consequence of this is that existing legal regimes may have gaps that are not specific to counter-terrorism when applied in the context of counter-terrorism, both more generally and in response to new or emerging phenomena. associated with terrorism. One important way to bridge such gaps is to use a third source, namely the general principles of law referred to in Article 38(1)(c) of the Charter of the International Court of Justice. The exact nature and role of general principles of law are not entirely clear, as there is disagreement about their precise function, nature, and scope. Also, the distinction between customary and general principles of international law is not always clear, especially because general principles usually take on the qualities of customary law as well. An example is the principle of due diligence, which includes the generally accepted obligation of states to take reasonable and appropriate measures to protect their citizens, for example by preventing terrorist attacks. However, there is agreement that general principles can assist in the interpretation and development of treaty and customary international law rules and, as such, they complement other sources of international law (Bassiouni, 1990).

Resolutions of the UN General Assembly and the Security Council

Over the past five (almost six) decades, the General Assembly and the Security Council have dealt with issues of terrorism to varying degrees. In particular, the General Assembly has been informed of such matters since 1960 since the adoption of the Declaration on the Granting of Independence to Colonial Countries and Peoples (United Nations, General Assembly, 1960, A/RES/15/1514), adopting non-binding, but less having a decisive impact resolution. As regards the division of labor between these two bodies, they have different but complementary functions. The Security Council is primarily concerned with the effectiveness of terrorism-related measures in fulfilling its key role in striving to maintain international peace and security; while the main focus of the General Assembly is to ensure that such measures are just and consistent with the purposes and principles of the Organization as set out in Articles 1 and 2 of the UN Charter. There are three stages in the approaches of both bodies to issues of terrorism, including how the legal norms are formed. The first phase is the period between the adoption of the 1960 Declaration and the late 1980s when the bulk of the terrorism-related discussions in the General Assembly concerned the struggle for self-determination and the move away from colonialism and other forms of foreign subjugation or domination (Karumidze, 2005). This reflected the growth in the number of UN member states as the former colonies sought their independence. A feature of this period was the debate about whether individuals or organizations involved in armed struggle should be classified as non-state terrorist actors. The second phase covers the period from the early 1990s to 2001, when the main focus of the General Assembly was on the criminalization of terrorist acts, regardless of any alleged motive. It is this question that is the leitmotif of the General Assembly resolution on measures to eliminate international terrorism (United Nations, General Assembly, 1995, A/RES/49/60) and remains so to this day. During these two periods, the involvement of the Security Council in matters related to terrorism was less extensive than that of the General Assembly. For example, his statements that any activity related to terrorism poses a threat to international peace and security were very rare. All this changed after the attacks of September 11, 2001, when the Security Council may have become more aware of issues related to terrorism than the General Assembly. This is evidenced by the creation of various bodies such as the United Nations Security Council Counter-Terrorism Committee, supported by the Counter-Terrorism Committee Executive Directorate, and the greatly expanded role, scope, and impact of the Sanctions Committee established under resolution 1267 (1999) against certain non-state terrorist organizations (Resolution 1276 (1999) UNSCR (following the recent UNSCR 2253 (2015) also includes ISIS) while the General Assembly remains actively involved, including through the adoption of resolutions, in the negotiations on the fight against treaty against terrorism within the Sixth Committee, which led to the adoption of the sectoral conventions discussed in Module 4, as well as the biennial review of the UN Counter-Terrorism Strategy. An important feature of this third phase, which is of particular relevance to legal sources, has been the increased willingness of the Security Council to state that then a terrorist act (or a form or manifestation of terrorism more generally) poses a threat to international peace and security (see para. for example, UNSCR 1566 (2004). One consequence of this is that the Council is more likely to rely on Article 39 of the Bylaws, invoking its powers under Chapter VII of the Bylaws, which can lead to non-violent and coercive measures under Articles 41 and 42 of the Bylaws, respectively (Chitadze, 2022).

The Nature of General Assembly and Security Council Resolutions as Legal Sources

As regards the decisions of the General Assembly, they are not legally binding. Under Chapter IV of the Charter, which describes its functions and powers, the General Assembly may make recommendations regarding the exercise of the powers and functions of the United Nations more generally. Since these are non-binding recommendations and not binding decisions, they are referred to as "soft law". Despite this, referring to the ICJ Advisory Opinion on the Legality of the Threat or Use of Nuclear Weapons of 8 July 1996 (ICJ, 1996, p. 25, para (Aleksidze, 2018). legal principles that may subsequently acquire the status of customary international law, and/or inclusion in the process of codification in the texts of binding international treaties. The most authoritative form of decisions of the General Assembly is its "declarations", which usually affirm key legal principles. On the other hand, Security Council resolutions may be non-binding or binding, depending on which of its powers are being exercised at the time the resolution is adopted. Resolutions adopted under Chapter VI of the Charter for the "peaceful settlement of disputes" are not binding, while those adopted under Chapter VII, "action concerning threats to the peace, breaches of the peace and acts of aggression", are more likely to be binding. Of particular relevance to recent counter-terrorism discussions and responses are resolutions that have stemmed from the powers stemming from Chapter VII of the Charter. It is generally accepted that taken together with Article 25 of the Charter, which provides that "the Members of the Organization agree, following this Charter, to abide by and carry out the decisions of the Security Council," this makes them binding on the Member States of the United Nations. The potential law-making value and reach of such resolutions are illustrated by Security Council resolutions 1373 (2001) and 1566 (2004). The first of these was adopted shortly after the September 11 attacks. One feature was that the Security Council relied on its powers under Chapter VII to require states to comply with several specific measures, including legislation at the national level (UNSCR 1373 (2001), para. 2 (e)). This unprecedented call for Chapter VII has sparked much debate, especially among scholars, as to whether or not the Security Council technically had (quasi-)legislative powers under the Charter (Aleksidze, 2018).

In practice, Resolution 1373 has received broad support from the Member States through the required inclusion in legislation (UN, Counter-Terrorism Committee). To be sure, Resolution 1373 had the desired effect in strengthening counter-terrorism efforts, especially at the national level. In terms of legal force, the Resolution has been described as a founding factor in "an emerging legal architecture that, over time, may lead to the crystallization and consolidation of the conventional international crime of terrorism" (Chitadze, 2022). Security Council Resolution 1566 was also adopted under Chapter VII of the Charter. One of its features is that it includes terminology related to terrorism to guide the subsequent practical activities of states in the field of countering terrorism (UN Security Council Resolution 1566 (2004) paragraph 3), but does not imply the existence of a generally accepted definition of terrorism. It was intended to help harmonize the counter-terrorism instruments being developed under the mandate of Security Council Resolution 1373 (Chitadze, 2016). It will be interesting to see if, in the future, Resolution 1566 will play the role of a legal source in informing the possible emergence of a definition of terrorism in customary international law, although this was not its intention. Resolution 1540 (2004) (UNSCR 1540 (2004)) is another example of an important Security Council resolution that provides for the obligations of Member States in the global counter-terrorism effort. Adopted under the provisions of Chapter VII, this resolution commits states, among other things, to refrain from supporting, by any means, non-state actors that attempt to develop, acquire, manufacture, possess, transport, transfer or use nuclear, chemical, or biological weapons and their means of delivery (Karumidze, 2006). To achieve this goal, states are required to establish national controls to prevent the proliferation of nuclear, chemical, and biological weapons and their means of delivery, including by establishing appropriate controls over materials related to them.

Legal Sources That Are Not Officially Binding

In addition to the formally binding legal sources discussed above, the universal framework governing counter-terrorism, including within the framework of the Counter-Terrorism Strategy, includes several documents that are not officially binding (often referred to as "soft law"). Just because they're not formally required doesn't mean they're less important; sometimes such legal instruments can be more influential in practice, especially on issues where broad consensus has not yet been reached. In an environment where states may not want to sign on to the text of an international treaty and the accompanying obligations, they are more likely to be willing to support and at least to some extent follow a non-binding instrument. Indeed, a carefully crafted, detailed soft law instrument can be much more effective in practice than, for example, a weak, poorly drafted, or ratified treaty. This section examines the various types of non-binding sources that are part of the international framework, namely General Assembly and Security Council resolutions, jurisprudence, UN special mandates and procedures, and tools such as codes of practice and guidelines.

Resolutions and Other Documents of the Activities of the UN Bodies and Structures

From a technical point of view, most resolutions adopted within the UN system, except Security Council resolutions, as explained in the previous section, are non-binding. However, they and other influential documents such as the Report of the High-Level Panel for 2004 (United Nations, General Assembly, 2004, A/59/565) can play a key role in developing the legal norms that will ultimately lead to their inclusion in the text of treaties and/or their evolution into customary international law. For example, General Assembly resolution 60/158 (2005) sets out a fundamental framework for the protection of human rights and fundamental freedoms while countering terrorism (United Nations, General Assembly, 2006, Section IV, paragraph 1). The annual resolutions of the General Assembly "Measures to eliminate international terrorism", the latest of which is UNGA Resolution 72/123 (2017) (United Nations, General Assembly, 2017), also play an important role in shaping the legal principles regarding approaches to terrorism, many of which were subsequently included in anti-terrorist instruments. As noted earlier in this Module, both the General Assembly and the Security Council have different but complementary roles in countering terrorism at the political level and in assessing (through the Counter-Terrorism Committee) compliance by states with key resolutions such as UNSCR 1373 (2001). This is equally true of other United Nations bodies and entities involved in upholding the rule of law in counter-terrorism responses, such as the Human Rights Council. Although they are not binding, their documents can be influential, including in strengthening the rule of law. For example, for many years the Human Rights Council has adopted a resolution on the theme "Protection of human rights and fundamental freedoms while countering terrorism" (United Nations, General Assembly, Human Rights Council, 2017 (b), A/HRC/35/L .27, one of the last such resolutions). Of particular relevance to this university module series is that the Human Rights Council regularly expresses and monitors its "concerns about violations of human rights and fundamental freedoms and international refugee law and international humanitarian law in the context of countering terrorism and violent extremism that contribute to terrorism" (United Nations, General Assembly, Human Rights Council, 2017 (b), A/HRC/35/L.27, para. 2). He regularly emphasizes the critical importance of respect for and adherence to the rule of law, including the international legal framework addressed in this module (United Nations, General Assembly, Human Rights Council, 2017 (b), A/HRC/35/L.27); and the importance of enhancing international cooperation to strengthen ongoing efforts to prevent, counter and counter-terrorism (United Nations, General Assembly, Human Rights Council, 2017 (b), A/HRC/35/L.27, para. four).

Judicial Practice of Courts and Tribunals

Another important legal source referred to in Article 38, paragraph 1 (d) of the Charter of the International Court of Justice is "judgments ... ... as an aid to the determination of rules of law". As a rule, such decisions are only legally binding on the parties to the case, as set out in Article 59 (Aleksidze, 2018). However, the case-law of national, regional, and international courts and tribunals can be an important legal source in terms of shaping future decisions, as well as new laws, policies, and practices, including promoting and maintaining the rule of law in counter-terrorism approaches.

United Nations Treaty Body Documents

Another form of jurisprudence considered here concerns the United Nations treaty bodies (committees) that derive their mandate from each of the nine core international human rights treaties, some of which are of particular relevance to counter-terrorism. Each treaty body includes a committee of 18 independent experts who monitor the implementation of the treaty within national legal systems (Karumidze, 2005). By ratifying treaties, Member States assume certain obligations to take steps to ensure that everyone can enjoy the rights outlined in the text of the treaties. Several treaty body documents can be informative to States on how their treaty obligations should be implemented and interpreted. Such documents also, in turn, form part of a wider range of norms in the field of countering terrorism. One of these is the non-binding "concluding observations", which are prepared as a result of consideration of the periodic reports of States Parties on the implementation of treaty obligations. While they are only recommendations to the State under review on how treaty compliance can be improved, the final observations are important. States are expected to make progress in implementing such recommendations, and the concluding observations have a broader meaning in terms of improving understanding of how treaty rules should be applied and respected by all participating States. Another source is the consideration by some of these Committees of individual complaints alleging alleged violations by States of specific treaty obligations if there is an Optional Protocol to the main treaty instrument allowing such complaints. It is through individual complaints that human rights are given concrete meaning. Although the process is quasi-judicial and decisions on complaints are not strictly binding, they are nonetheless an important part of jurisprudence in treaty interpretation. The other documents considered here are general comments adopted by committees regarding the interpretation, as well as difficulties associated with the implementation of the provisions of the treaties. Unlike concluding observations, general comments do not refer to any particular State party. They highlight and explain key issues such as interpretation and compliance with treaty principles. In preparing them, the treaty bodies draw on all their experience to identify common priority themes. Such documents are quite weighty, despite their technically non-binding nature. This series of modules for HEIs presents several such treaty body documents.

SPECIAL PROCEDURES OF THE HUMAN RIGHTS COUNCIL

Another important non-mandatory source is the output of the special procedures of the Human Rights Council. These procedures are carried out by independent human rights experts authorized to inform and advise on specific human rights issues or human rights situations in certain countries. The Special Procedures system is the centerpiece of the UN human rights machinery and covers all human rights. As of August 1, 2017, there were 44 thematic and 12 country mandates (Aleksidze, 2018). With the support of the Office of the United Nations High Commissioner for Human Rights (OHCHR), special procedures country visits are undertaken; they respond to individual cases of human rights violations and broader and structural issues, and contribute to the development of international human rights standards, participate in advocacy activities, and provide technical co-operation advice. Their tasks are defined in resolutions establishing or extending their mandates. Of particular relevance here is the Special Rapporteur on the promotion and protection of human rights while countering terrorism, the position currently held by Fionnuala Nia Ayoline (since 1 August 2017). Like other special procedures mandate holders, he submits regular reports (usually annually) to the General Assembly and the Human Rights Council (United Nations, General Assembly, 2016(c), United Nations, General Assembly, Human Rights Council, 2017(a)). These reports can cover a wide range of human rights issues, such as violations of key international human rights treaties about arrest, detention, fair trial, prohibition of torture, and violation of democratic freedoms; they may contain examples of good practices that can be transferred to other countries; contain recommendations on how to strengthen the existing legal framework to counter-terrorism. Although these reports, their conclusions, and recommendations are also not binding on States, they are nonetheless significant, including how States apply and should apply the relevant legal framework. In addition, the work of several other special rapporteurs and working groups is relevant to this series of university modules, such as the Working Group on Arbitrary Detention, the Special Rapporteur on Extrajudicial, Summary and Arbitrary Executions, and the Special Rapporteur on Torture and other cruel, inhuman or degrading treatment or punishment.

Codes of Practice, Declarations, and Guidelines

Guiding principles, codes of practice, and standards are another important source of soft law that informs and facilitates the implementation of the goals of the UN Counter-Terrorism Strategy. A fairly large number of such non-binding instruments have been developed to complement the binding obligations. Although they are not legally binding, they are agreed on principles that all states must adhere to and can provide important guidance to legislators and policymakers, as well as practitioners, including the courts. Documents relevant to counter-terrorism, some of which are discussed in subsequent thematic modules, include the Declaration of Basic Principles of Justice for Victims of Crime and Abuse of Power (United Nations, General Assembly, 1985 (a), A/RES/40/43); Principles for the Effective Prevention and Investigation of Extra-legal, Arbitrary and Summary Executions (United Nations, General Assembly, 1989, A/RES/1989/65); Declaration on the Protection of All Persons from Enforced Disappearance (1992) (United Nations, General Assembly, 1993, A/RES/47/133) and Principles for the Effective Investigation and Documentation of Torture and Other Cruel, Inhuman or Degrading Treatment or Punishment (Istanbul Protocol) (1999) (United Nations, OHCHR, 2004, HR/P/PT/8/Rev.1).

Regional and National Approaches

Regional organizations also play an integral role in multilateral efforts to counter terrorism (United Nations, General Assembly, 2006, A/RES/60/288, para. 3(d)), including the implementation of the UN strategy. Such regional instruments and outputs can take the form of binding regional anti-terrorism conventions (and in some cases regional customary international law) as well as (non-)binding resolutions, codes of practice, guidelines, and jurisprudence. Ultimately, while regional and international organizations and their respective legal frameworks play an important role in counter-terrorism efforts, it is the States that remain the main actors, including in terms of implementing and enforcing these principles. It is on their territories that terrorist activities take place, against which retaliatory measures must be taken, and decisions are made on the issue of compliance with internationally agreed standards and principles. In addition to national constitutional rights guaranteeing fundamental human rights, democracy, and the rule of law, many States have ratified and are therefore party to at least some of the international treaties relevant to counter-terrorism measures, including the universal conventions against terrorism, and also international human rights treaties, international humanitarian law, and international refugee law. The effect of ratification is to create obligations for States requiring them to be incorporated into their national legal frameworks.

The Principle of Legislative Consolidation

An issue worthy of attention here, which has created serious challenges for the effective implementation and enforcement of the international legal framework that underpins the UN Counter-Terrorism Strategy, concerns the "principle of legislating". It concerns how international treaty instruments are anchored in the national legal systems of the participating States. Monistic and dualistic systems After ratifying international treaties, States are obliged to start incorporating their norms into their national legislation based on a comprehensive review of existing legislation to ensure the effective implementation of treaty obligations. For example, Article 4 of the International Convention for the Suppression of the Financing of Terrorism, 1999 (Treaty Collection, Vol. 2178, p. 197) provides: Each State Party shall take such measures as may be necessary to: a) the law of the crimes referred to in Article 2; (b) to impose proportionate penalties for these crimes, taking into account the gravity of these crimes (Aleksidze, 2018). The process of becoming a party to an international treaty or convention includes both an international and a national component. The international component consists of a formal procedure dictated by the terms of the agreement and governed by the principles of international law. As a rule, the analysis of legislation is the first step to becoming a party to an international treaty. This allows the state and the legislature to anticipate changes in the national legal system that will be required as a result of participation in an international treaty or compliance with international standards. Some States, due to domestic law or considerations of principle, will not accept a treaty until legislation is in place to comply with all international obligations. The treaty does not apply in a country until it is implemented in national law. This is often referred to as a "dualistic system", whereby international law and national law are treated as two separate systems. To introduce an international obligation into the domestic legal regime, it is necessary to adopt a legislative act. In other countries that adhere to the "monist tradition", once the treaty is ratified, it is automatically incorporated into domestic law. Under this system, some, if not most, of the provisions of the treaty are directly applicable. Even in these countries, however, legislation is often required to provide for the non-direct elements that are necessary to implement the treaty. The clearest example of this concerns the criminalization of various forms of behavior, as required by the global counter-terrorism instruments. None of these instruments provides for penalties for the offenses in question. Thus, domestic legislation is required. Many legal systems take a mixed approach. For example, in the legal systems of the customary law traditions, rules of customary international law are generally treated as part of the common law. On the other hand, international treaties must be incorporated into domestic legislation by a normative act adopted by Parliament. Since all the elements of various crimes provided for by the treaties are introduced into the criminal legislation of the participating States, there is no single correct approach to comply with the requirements of the universal instruments for countering terrorism on criminalization; the criminal policy and legal traditions of each state dictate how and in what documents to make the necessary changes. Likewise, the drafting style of the document may vary depending on the choice of each State. The classic division is between civil law countries and common law countries. The following is a non-exhaustive list of issues that different countries may approach differently without compromising overall international compliance: • Special anti-terrorism laws or criminal codes: some countries adopt special laws, while others prefer to amend their criminal code to close any gaps between existing laws and the requirements of specific treaties. • Place of definitions: some countries need to explicitly include all definitions contained in treaties. Other countries take a less rigid approach, and once the necessary offenses have been introduced into law, criminal justice officials may revert to the text of the convention when there is doubt about the meaning of a particular term. • "Thematic" headings: each general convention or protocol covers several criminal acts that do not automatically fall under one chapter or section of a State's penal code. This applies to the offenses outlined in the International Convention for the Suppression of Acts of Nuclear Terrorism, 2005 (Treaty Collection No. 2445, p. 89); Because of the complex nature of the issues covered, a State may find it convenient to include them under the section dealing with weapons of mass destruction in general, while another State may decide that some of the acts described in the Convention fall under the section dealing with environmental crimes. Regardless of the style of writing and the position of the various offenses, these offenses must be linked to other requirements of international treaties, such as provisions on the jurisdiction, including in particular the principle of aut dedere aut judicare.

National Constitutions

Particular difficulties arise with national constitutions when the requirements of such conflict with obligations under international treaties. Traditionally, national constitutions are considered the "custodian" in terms of fulfilling other obligations, including those arising following international law. They often provide a lens through which treaty obligations are interpreted, for example by national courts. Since the requirements of national constitutions, which vary from State to State, are generally considered to take precedence over any incompatible obligations, even those arising from an international treaty to which that State is a party, this may weaken the nature and scope of treaty obligations compared to what was originally envisaged at the time of the adoption of the contract. As a rule, when an alleged conflict arises, the approach taken by the courts is not to invalidate it, but to interpret it as best as possible through the lens of the constitution. A related problem is that it can be difficult for states to implement United Nations resolutions such as Security Council resolution 1373 (2001), which requires states to criminalize terrorist financing within their national legal systems (Aleksidze, 2018). There may be other issues and differences between common law and civil/continental law systems regarding the legislating of certain terrorist offenses.

Effective Legislation

Each State must choose what it considers the most appropriate mechanism for the implementation of treaty obligations. Concerning universal instruments against terrorism, the legal framework can be established in one of the following ways: (1) a comprehensive review of national criminal law and its relevant provisions, followed by additions and amendments to the legislation; (2) the inclusion in national criminal law of a special section of the criminal code, which may be more appropriate for states intending to undertake broader reforms in criminal law; or (3) the adoption of an autonomous law containing all the elements required by the general conventions. The resulting national legislation is also an integral part of the overall international legal framework governing counter-terrorism responses. The effective criminalization of various terrorist acts is a prerequisite for intervention by the criminal justice system. Criminalization is not only a legal obligation for state parties to various counter-terrorism treaties but also a necessary condition for effective international cooperation. In practice, there are usually several problems, some of which are discussed in more detail in other modules. Such problems can range from inconsistent national definitions of terrorism that hinder rather than facilitate international cooperation; to partial fulfillment of contractual obligations within the framework of national legislation, which leads to gaps in the rights and procedures provided for by international treaties; and, as with any international obligation, lack of effective implementation of treaty obligations, even if provided for by national law (Aleksidze, 2018).

Challenges in Implementation and Enforcement

Another issue that should be briefly noted here, and which is not specific to counter-terrorism measures, is related to the current challenges to the effective implementation and subsequent implementation of international obligations by States. Notwithstanding that States must voluntarily agree to be bound by the specific treaties to which they are parties and under which they are bound by the principle of pacta sunt servanda to fulfill their treaty obligations in good faith following article 24 of the 1969 Vienna Convention on the Law of Treaties, State practice may sometimes fall short of such obligations (Kolosov, 1996). The same applies to obligations arising under customary international law. One reason for this is that there are limited enforcement mechanisms within regional and international legal systems that often rely on political and diplomatic approaches to encourage rather than enforce compliance. One consequential consequence of particular concern is the creation of impunity for States for any violations committed in the context of counter-terrorism measures, or the deprivation of legitimate remedies for victims of terrorist acts.

INTERNATIONAL LEGAL FRAMEWORK

The legal regimes addressed in this series of modules for HEIs are those that have been agreed within the international community to form the fundamental basis of the international framework under which counter-terrorism efforts and measures should be carried out, such as reflected in the UN Counter-Terrorism Strategy itself, as discussed earlier. These include the Charter of the United Nations; national/international criminal law; international human rights law; international humanitarian law and international refugee law. Other applicable legal regimes include, for example, the law governing the use of force (jus ad bellum). They are not the subject of a series of university modules that focus on criminal justice responses to terrorism, as such responses should be the normal societal response to terrorism. At the same time, the use of military force remains an exceptional measure.

International Human Rights Law

The UN Counter-Terrorism Strategy and the related legal framework are based on the understanding that effective counter-terrorism while respecting human rights and fundamental freedoms, is not only possible but necessary. While outside the scope of this university module series, reference should be made to the numerous criticisms, complaints, and litigation against the Security Council's practice, especially concerning the sanctions regime under Security Council Resolution 1267 (1999) (Aleksidze, 2018). They demonstrate that not only States but also international organizations, including the United Nations, must uphold fundamental human rights standards regarding their institutional responses to terrorism (see United Nations, Security Council Committee). The scope of international human rights norms is vast, and human rights norms and obligations underlie national, regional, and international responses to terrorism. However, there are often conflicts between the fulfillment of national security objectives and the observance of human rights, these issues will be explored in subsequent modules. Respect for and observance of human rights principles in the context of countering terrorism is of particular importance since the overall goal of terrorist activities is to attempt to undermine these very rights and fundamental freedoms. Because terrorism hurts human rights, any counter-terrorism measure that ignores or harms human rights is doomed to failure and unacceptable in a society governed by the rule of law and democratic values. Human rights are universal values and legal guarantees that protect individuals and groups from acts and omissions, driven primarily by State action, that interfere with fundamental freedoms, rights, and human dignity. As such, they are universal, interdependent, and indivisible. This section focuses on international human rights instruments.

1948 Universal Declaration of Human Rights

As regards the main legal instruments, the starting point is the 1948 Universal Declaration of Human Rights (UDHR). The text was adopted as a "common standard of achievement for all peoples and nations", which set out common goals that states should strive to achieve. The UDHR is notable for several reasons. First, it represents the first human rights instrument of worldwide relevance, despite some ongoing debate about the principle of cultural relativism. Even though at the time of the adoption of the UDHR by the General Assembly there were only 48 UN member states, at the World Conference on Human Rights in Vienna in 1993, 171 states reaffirmed the universality, indivisibility, and interdependence of human rights and reaffirmed their commitment to the UDHR.

First of all, the UDHR combines civil and political rights with economic, social, and cultural rights, although subsequent negotiations did not reflect this, resulting in the adoption of two treaty instruments - the International Covenant on Civil and Political Rights of 1966 (ICCPR) (Collection of Treaties vol. 999, p. 171 and vol. 1057, p. 407) and the 1966 International Covenant on Economic, Social and Cultural Rights (ICESCR) (Treaty Collection vol. 993, p. 3) (Karumidze, 2005). This is due to factors such as disagreement about the nature of the associated obligations, the relative importance of these rights, and so on. (which also emerged during the negotiations on the text of the UDHR). Furthermore, while it is not in itself a legally binding document as a declaration (i.e. resolution) of the General Assembly, the text of the Declaration is nonetheless a source of inspiration for hundreds of other binding and non-binding documents, such as national constitutions and law (she is often mentioned in their preambles) and more than 60 regional and international human rights treaties. The Declaration has also been translated into at least 439 languages (UN, 2005). The founding principles of the UDHR include: "All human beings are born free and equal in dignity and rights" (Article 1); and the basic principles of equality and non-discrimination on grounds such as "race, color, sex, language, religion, political or another opinion, national or social origin, birth status, property, birth or another status" (Article 2). Of particular relevance to counter-terrorism efforts are Articles 4-21, which deal in detail with civil and political rights (eg the right to life, liberty, and security of person, the prohibition of torture). Articles 22-27 then focus on economic, social, and cultural rights. Some argue that the UDHR itself has acquired the status of customary international law (Continued Presence of South Africa in Namibia, 1971, p. 16; United States of America v. Iran, 1981, p. 45). While certainly some of its provisions have such status, such as the prohibition of torture, it is doubtful that the entire document has entered customary international law, despite subsequent state practice. See, for example, the vague and general language in Articles 10 and 19 (UN, 2005).

International Human Rights Instruments

Within the United Nations human rights system, there are nine major international human rights instruments, some of which have optional protocols, which should inform the laws, policies, and practices of States in the field of countering terrorism, as well as allow for the consideration of individual complaints of violations of human rights of participating States about their treaty obligations. A number of these treaties are of particular importance for countering terrorism.

International Human Rights Conventions Relevant to Counter-Terrorism

- International Convention on the Elimination of All Forms of Racial Discrimination (adopted 21 December 1965, entered into force 4 January 1969)
- International Covenant on Civil and Political Rights (adopted 16 December 1966, entered into force 23 March 1976) o Optional Protocol (adopted 16 December 1966, entered into force 23 March 1976) o Second Optional Protocol to the International Covenant on Civil and Political Rights Aiming at the Abolition of the Death Penalty (adopted 15 December 1989, entered into force 11 July 1991)
- International Covenant on Economic, Social and Cultural Rights (adopted 16 December 1966, entered into force 3 January 1976)
- Convention against Torture and Other Cruel, Inhuman or Degrading Treatment or Punishment (adopted 10 December 1984, entered into force 26 June 1987) o Optional Protocol to the Convention against Torture and Other Cruel, Inhuman or Degrading Treatment or Punishment (adopted on December 18, 2002, entered into force on June 22, 2006)
- Convention on the Rights of the Child (adopted 20 November 1989, entered into force 2 September 1990)
- International Convention for the Protection of All Persons from Enforced Disappearance (adopted 20 December 2006, entered into force 23 December 2006) (Aleksidze, 2018).

Fulfillment of these obligations requires States to develop national counter-terrorism policies, laws, and practices aimed at preventing terrorism and prosecuting and punishing those responsible for terrorist acts in a manner consistent with the promotion and observance of human rights. These activities should also include measures to prevent the spread of terrorism, including measures to strengthen human rights, prevent ethnic, national, or religious discrimination, political exclusion, and socioeconomic marginalization, as well as measures to eliminate impunity for human rights violations. In terms of approach, the starting point for counter-terrorism responses and any related allegations of breach of treaty obligations is the ICCPR, both in terms of articulated basic human rights principles (Parts I-III) and monitoring mechanisms (Part IV) (Aleksidze, 2018).

Its key principles include:

- the right to live;
- prohibition of torture, cruel, inhuman, or degrading treatment or punishment;
- the right to liberty and freedom of movement;
- the right to equality before the law;
- the right to be presumed innocent until proven guilty;
- the right to legal personality;
  the right to privacy and the protection of such privacy by law;
- the right to apply to the court in case of violation of rights;
- freedom of thought, conscience, and religion or belief;
- freedom of opinion and expression;
- freedom of assembly and association;
- non-discrimination on any grounds such as race, sex, color, national origin, or language (Chitadze, 2022).

Documents of International Humanitarian Law

There are about 100 treaties aimed at alleviating human suffering during times of war, which form the body of law known as IHL. These include the 1899 and 1907 Hague Conventions, as well as thematic international treaties such as the 1997 Convention on the Prohibition of the Use, Stockpiling, Production, and Transfer of Anti-Personnel Mines and Their Destruction. For this module, the most significant international treaties are the four Geneva Conventions of 1949 and their two additional protocols of 1977.

Documents of International Humanitarian Law There are four Geneva Conventions of 1949: • Convention (I) for the Amelioration of the Condition of the Wounded and Sick in Armed Forces in the Field (adopted 12 August 1949, entered into force 21 October 1950). • Convention (II) for the Amelioration of the Condition of the Wounded, Sick, and Shipwrecked Members of Armed Forces at Sea (adopted 12 August 1949, entered into force 21 October 1950). • Convention (III) concerning the Treatment of Prisoners of War (adopted 12 August 1949, entered into force 21 October 1950). • Convention (IV) concerning the Protection of Civilian Persons in Time of War (adopted 12 August 1949, entered into force 21 October 1950). In addition, there are Additional Protocols to the 1949 Geneva Conventions: • Protocol Additional to the Geneva Conventions of 12 August 1949, Relating to the Protection of Victims of International Armed Conflicts (Protocol I) (adopted 8 June 1977, entered into force 7 December 1978). • Protocol Additional to the Geneva Conventions of 12 August 1949, Relating to the Protection of Victims of Non-International Armed Conflicts (Protocol II) (adopted 8 June 1977, entered into force 7 December 1978) (Kolosov, 1996).

The commentaries accompanying these treaty documents, as tools for their interpretation and application, are currently being updated by the International Committee of the Red Cross (ICRC), the primary custodian of these treaty documents, to reflect 21st-century interpretations and issues. This includes changes in law and practice since the Geneva Conventions were adopted in 1949 when some of the current problems associated with the war did not yet exist. It is hoped that this will contribute to a better application of the conventions in contemporary situations of armed conflict. Customary IHL is also important as a source of law. In an extensive decade-long study by the ICRC on which IHL rules have become customary IHL, findings published in 2005 reflected 161 rules (Aleksidze, 2018). This source of law is particularly important for states that are not parties to all six core IHL treaties since they are nonetheless bound by parallel obligations that exist under customary IHL. Most of these treaty provisions are widely accepted by States as having now acquired the status of customary IHL. This source of law is of particular relevance in situations of internal armed conflict, which is currently the predominant form of armed conflict and a common setting in which military counter-terrorism operations take place, for which the treaty framework is less developed and detailed than for international armed conflicts. Customary international law also has several advantages over treaty law in that it is constantly evolving in parallel with State practice and opinio juris.

It can more easily and quickly adapt to new challenges and legal changes than contract law since no lengthy negotiation process is required to agree on changes. Documents of International Humanitarian Law There are four Geneva Conventions of 1949: • Convention (I) for the Amelioration of the Condition of the Wounded and Sick in Armed Forces in the Field (adopted 12 August 1949, entered into force 21 October 1950). • Convention (II) for the Amelioration of the Condition of the Wounded, Sick, and Shipwrecked Members of Armed Forces at Sea (adopted 12 August 1949, entered into force 21 October 1950). • Convention (III) concerning the Treatment of Prisoners of War (adopted 12 August 1949, entered into force 21 October 1950). • Convention (IV) concerning the Protection of Civilian Persons in Time of War (adopted 12 August 1949, entered into force 21 October 1950). In addition, there are Additional Protocols to the 1949 Geneva Conventions: • Protocol Additional to the Geneva Conventions of 12 August 1949, Relating to the Protection of Victims of International Armed Conflicts (Protocol I) (adopted 8 June 1977, entered into force 7 December 1978). • Protocol Additional to the Geneva Conventions of 12 August 1949, Relating to the Protection of Victims of Non-International Armed Conflicts (Protocol II) (adopted 8 June 1977, entered into force 7 December 1978). Another important issue concerns violations of IHL, including grave violations of the Geneva Conventions, which are governed both by treaty instruments, in particular, the 1998 Rome Statute of the International Criminal Court, and by customary international law (Aleksidze, 2018).

CONCLUSION

Current Challenges in the International Legal Framework

On the one hand, the strengthening of the relationship between the principles of asylum and refugee recognition and other legal regimes, which form the key international legal framework in which counter-terrorism responses must take place, is a positive development, however, and not least in terms of promoting the principles of each of the identified legal regimes, it is also associated with certain difficulties. One important problem is that international refugee law was not originally intended as a tool for counter-terrorism. In this regard, its designation as a key legal regime within the international counter-terrorism legal framework may adversely affect the protection of asylum-seekers and refugees by providing such persons with less rather than more or equivalent protection. This view was echoed by the UNHCR in response to increased counter-terrorism measures following the September 11 attacks: Equating a haven with a haven for terrorists is not only legally wrong and still unsupported by facts, but also contributes to stigmatizing refugees in the public mind and singling out faces specific races or religions for discrimination and hate-motivated harassment. Since 9/11, several immigrants and refugee communities have been attacked and persecuted based on ethnicity or religion, leading to increased social tensions. While there are indeed some asylum seekers and refugees who have been or will be associated with a serious crime, this does not mean that the rest of the majority should be damned for being associated with these few. (United Nations High Commissioner for Refugees, 2015). Another problem has been that some states have applied the "terrorist" saving clause on a collective basis, relying on lists of banned terrorists and terrorist organizations such as those of the UN and the European Union, rather than making individual assessments. From a rule of law perspective, such approaches are not always accompanied by a basic level of due process and can be difficult to challenge, including in court. Another related problem is that this approach does not address the underlying issues, instead shifting the problem from one State to another. However, a number of these challenges and risks can be considered at least partially offset by the benefits of integrating international refugee law into the international legal framework. It can be argued that reconciling national security interests with the right to be protected from refoulement is best served by bringing together different areas of law. The application of refugee law, along with criminal law, extradition law, and human rights law, can play an important role in properly ensuring that anyone involved in terrorist activities is not afforded refugee protection. On the contrary, protecting national security interests by prosecuting individuals following due process, guaranteeing the rights and protection of the most vulnerable, and taking other appropriate measures to protect fundamental human rights puts the rule of law at the forefront of counter-terrorism.

REFERENCES

Aleksidze. (2018). *Contemporary International Law*. Tbilisi State University.

Basic Facts about the United Nations. (2005). Charter of the United Nations. UN Department of Public Information.

Bassiouni. (1990). *A Functional Approach to General Principles of International Law*. Retrieved from: https://via.library.depaul.edu/lawfacpubs/317/

Chitadze, N. (2022). *World Politics and The Challenges for International Security*. IGI Global. doi:10.4018/978-1-7998-9586-2

Chitadze. (2016). *Political Sciences*. International Black Sea University.

Ignatenko, A. (2022). *International Law*. Aspect Press.

Ignatenko, A. (2022). *International Law*. Aspect Press.

Karumidze. (2005). *International Organizations*. Tbilisi State University.

Kolosov. (1996). *International Law*. Aspect Press.

UN. (1960). *United Nations, General Assembly Resolution, 1960, A/RES/15/1514*. Retrieved from: http://www.un-documents.net/a15r1514.htm

UN. (1985). UN Resolution, (a), A/RES/40/43. United Nations, General Assembly.

UN. (1989). UN Resolution A/RES/1989/65. United Nations, General Assembly.

UN. (1993). *UN Resolution A/RES/47/133*. United Nations, General Assembly.

UN. (1995). *United Nations, General Assembly, Resolution, A/RES/49/60*. Retrieved from: https://www.un.org/en/ga/sixth/69/int_terrorism.shtml

UN. (1999). International Convention for the Suppression of the Financing of Terrorism. *Treaty Collection, 2178*.

UN. (2001). *UN Security Council Resolution 1373*. Retrieved from: https://digitallibrary.un.org/record/449020?ln=en

UN. (2004). *OHCHR Resolution. 2004, HR/P/PT/8/Rev.1*. United Nations General Assembly.

UN. (2004). *Security Council Report A/59/565*. Retrieved from: https://www.securitycouncilreport.org/un-documents/document/cpr-a-59-565.php

UN. (2005). International Convention for the Suppression of Acts of Nuclear Terrorism. *Treaty Collection, 2445*, 89.

UN. (2006). *United Nations, General Assembly, 2006, Section IV, paragraph 1*. Retrieved from: https://treaties.un.org/doc/source/docs/a_61_611_e.pdf

UN. (2006). *General Assembly Resolution A/RES/60/288, para. 3(d)*. UN General Assembly.

UN. (2016). *General Assembly, Human Rights Council. The resolution, A/HRC/34/30, para. 56*. Retrieved from: https://www.unodc.org/e4j/zh/terrorism/module-3/key-issues/defining-rule-of-law.html

UN. (2016). *UN Global Counter-Terrorism Strategy. (a), A/70/826*. Retrieved from: https://www.un.org/counterterrorism/un-global-counter-terrorism-strategy

UN. (2017). *UNGA Resolution 72/123*. Retrieved from: https://www.un.org/en/ga/72/resolutions.shtml

UN. (2017). *United Nations, General Assembly, Human Rights Council, 2017 (b), A/HRC/35/L. 27*. Retrieved from: https://www.ohchr.org/en/hr-bodies/hrc/regular-sessions/session35/list-reports

UN Security Council. (2014). *UNSCR 2178*. Retrieved from: https://documents-dds-ny.un.org/doc/UNDOC/GEN/N14/547/98/PDF/N1454798.pdf?OpenElement

UNHCR. (2016). *United Nations High Commissioner for Refugees, 2015*. Report. Retrieved from: https://www.unhcr.org/statistics/unhcrstats/576408cd7/unhcr-global-trends-2015.html

United Nations. (2004). *Security Council Resolution S/2004/616, paragraph 6*. Retrieved from: https://digitallibrary.un.org/record/527647?ln=en

United Nations. (2006). *General Assembly Resolution: A/RES60/288*. Retrieved from: https://documents-dds-ny.un.org/doc/UNDOC/GEN/N05/504/88/PDF/N0550488.pdf?OpenElement

United Nations. General Assembly, 2016(c), United Nations, General Assembly, Human Rights Council, 2017. Retrieved from: https://research.un.org/en/docs/ga/quick/regular/71

United Nations Digital Library. (2022). *UNSCR 2370*. https://digitallibrary.un.org/record/1298311/usage?ln=en

KEY TERMS AND DEFINITIONS

International Law: Also known as public international law, the law of nations, and international ethics, is the set of rules, norms, and standards generally recognized as binding between nations.

International Terrorism: The threat or use of violence as a tactic of terrorism against targets in other countries.

Terrorism: Premeditated violence perpetrated against non-combat targets by subnational or trans-national groups or clandestine agents usually intended to influence an audience.

Chapter 13
Cyberterrorism and Its Reflection on International Security

Mary Tseruashvili
Ilia State University, Georgia

ABSTRACT

The purpose of this chapter is to analyze cyberterrorism and its reflection on international security. More specifically, it focuses on the analysis of the challenges facing the modern world arising from the urgency of cyber threats. While the development of information technology and the availability of information, in general, make the life of the world community easier in some respects, there are also threats, the elimination of which require the full mobilization of states. Hence, the chapter is based on the analysis of the various articles, reports, analytical papers, and case studies, depending on which it becomes possible to answer the main research question and identify the cyber threats facing the modern states.

INTRODUCTION

With globalization, the concept of security in international relations has become quite complex and has shown that the protection of national borders only in traditional ways can no longer cope with the impending threats. The development of information technology and systems has generated a great deal of prosperity, but at the same time, various types of hybrid threats, such as cybercrime and cyberterrorism, have emerged. Terrorism is one of the major challenges of globalization, although cyber-terrorism is one of the most dangerous of its many manifestations today. Technological advancement is considered to be the main source of information in the modern world for states, organizations within the state, companies, or other private or public entities located in digital spaces. Therefore, the main target of terrorism is to penetrate these spaces and obtain information, destroy, process, and so on. It should be noted that a large number of countries and international organizations are involved in the fight against it, as the fight against cyber threats is a major global security challenge. Nevertheless, the effectiveness of the steps taken by countries around the world against cyber threats needs to be addressed.

DOI: 10.4018/978-1-6684-5311-7.ch013

The sources of cyber threats, cybersecurity aspects, and strategies are the major topics of this chapter and aim to answer the main research question: „Whether cyberterrorism presents an unsolved problem in the world “. The chapter offers qualitative research and it is based on the analysis of various articles, reports, analytical papers, and case studies.

To answer the research question, the chapter begins by analyzing the concept of cyberterrorism and the sources of cyber threats. It then focuses on access to information and the related problems. After that, the research analyzes the Paris Terrorist Attack and the new challenges in cyberspace. Moreover, the Post-Soviet space and cybersecurity aspects are also discussed and the chapter explains the European Union and NATO cybersecurity strategies. Furthermore, in order to outline the effectiveness of steps taken by the countries against cyber threats, the cyber capabilities of the US, Russia, and Iran are analyzed accordingly as case studies. Finally, the chapter focuses on the role of cybersecurity in International Relations to demonstrate its influence on International Security.

CYBERTERRORISM AND THE SOURCES OF CYBER THREATS

The term "cyberterrorism" was first used in the 1980s by Barry Collin, a senior fellow at the California Institute of Security and Intelligence, to combine cyberspace and terrorism. And the first working definition belongs to a special agent - Mark Pollitt, according to which cyberterrorism is politically motivated violence premeditated by subnational or covert agents against a "peaceful" (non-combatant) target. The issue of cybersecurity concerns technologies, ongoing processes, and practices designed to protect the network, technological devices, applications, and data during an attack that would be vulnerable to unauthorized access (Pollitt, 1998).

It must be noted the detrimental consequences that hacking action can have. Deliberate destruction of information in cyberspace is an integral part of a terrorist act, depending on its purpose and outcome (Pollitt, 1998). Given the fact that any state can be a victim of cyberterrorism, addressing this problem requires joint action by states.

With the development of new technologies, there are growing threats that cause great harm to cyberspace and its users. "Cyberspace" is a complex interconnected information and technology infrastructure, which includes global Internet and telecommunications networks, computer systems, as well as embedded processors, servers, and control devices used in various industries. It is obvious that the state and government agencies are primarily interested in ensuring national security, protecting critical information and information infrastructure from encroachment by both foreign state and non-governmental entities and groups to prevent information theft or transmission, network damage, and total destruction (Grove, 2000).

There is no doubt that the real threat to the security of the state is cyber-attacks aimed at destroying such vital infrastructure as telecommunication networks, power generation, and oil refining systems, as well as electricity supply, finance, and healthcare systems. One of the main problems in the fight against cybercrime is the fact that it is often very difficult to pinpoint not only the direct perpetrators but also their location or the country from which the attack took place. Therefore, an offender or a group of criminals can easily hide not only their involvement in organizing a cyber-attack, but also identify themselves as other users of the network or remain anonymous altogether (Grove, 2000).

The sources of cyber threats are representatives of the public and private sectors, as well as organizations and individuals created under different types and brands. When considering the sources of origin of cyber threats, it is possible to classify them as follows: States, corporations, hackers, hacktivists, terrorists, and so on (Singer & Friedman, 2014).

The state is a source of cyber threats when foreign intelligence services use computer technology to gather information and spy. Such actions may be directed at both friendly and adversary countries, or against non-state actors by the intelligence services. The state, using its intelligence services, carries out cyber-attacks against potential adversaries to disinform, destabilize, intimidate, or produce large-scale cybercrime. Also noteworthy is the fact that violations of the safety and rights of the individual often occur. In particular, the special services of the state may resort to actions that are used to capture, steal and use citizens' personal data. Such actions often take place without the sanction and proper democratic control of the relevant bodies of the judiciary (Singer & Friedman, 2014).

Corporations engage in corporate espionage or subversive activities, often used by hackers and organized crime groups. It should be noted that companies, corporations, and others in the private sector may violate human rights by collecting and analyzing personal data, or in some cases by exchanging that data with government agencies or other stakeholders (Singer & Friedman, 2014).

As for hackers, there was a time when their unauthorized hacking or hacking of programs was linked to gaining authority in the hacker community or petty hooliganism. Nowadays the picture is drastically changed, in particular, the actions of most hackers are criminal in nature. In the past, if hackers needed to have special skills in computer technology to break into a network, now it is enough to download the relevant instructions and protocols from the Internet and use them to organize a cyber attack on a selected site. As a result, the implementation of the cyberattack has become more accessible to the user. It is also noteworthy that hacker services are used not only by corporations and companies but also by intelligence or other special services (Singer & Friedman, 2014).

The term "hacktivism" comes from the combination of the words "Hack" and "Activism" and refers to a new phenomenon of social protest, which is a synthesis of social activism and hacking of certain websites or postal services. In order to achieve their political goals, hacktivists seek to damage or shut down some websites altogether (Singer & Friedman, 2014).

In contrast, terrorists try to dismantle important infrastructure facilities, destroy them altogether, or use them for their own purposes. Their actions seriously endanger the national security of countries, cause massive human casualties, weaken the economy, as well as damage the moral condition of society, and reduce their credibility with the government. Despite the fact that not all terrorist organizations and gangs have sufficient knowledge and technical means to carry out an effective cyber-attack, there is a theoretical assumption that they will acquire similar knowledge and capabilities, or seek the help of organized crime services (Singer & Friedman, 2014).

Various hacking methods can be used during cyber-attacks to destroy or distort the data integrity and make changes. One of them is propaganda and misinformation, which involves arranging destabilizing regimes in the territories of foreign states, influencing political processes or the results of commercial activities, spreading incorrect data, or making changes to existing data (Hatamleh, 2012).

In addition, common methods are data destruction, espionage, and personality theft. The first involves the permanent and deliberate destruction of data to cause harm to foreign states or competitors. In particular, similar attacks may be carried out in parallel with other actions in the event of a larger conflict. Espionage is about obtaining information from corporations, companies, and firms about the current and future activities of their competitors. As for stealing a person, it involves stealing the user's personal details. Trojans and similar programs are used to steal personal data (Hatamleh, 2012).

ACCESS TO INFORMATION AND RELATED PROBLEMS

Advances in technology have led to a rapid spread of information, thus leading to the activation of the internet media, which has made it a significant competitor to the method of disseminating information through television, radio, and especially newspapers. It is noteworthy that information through online media is obtained not only by young people who are relatively better adapted to technology but also by older people (Copeland, 2000).

While there is widespread agreement that information sharing is essential to enhance security, the recent expansion of information sharing has raised a number of potential problems that require careful management and oversight. For instance, law enforcement may impose enforcement actions based on general information that is unreliable and therefore there is a high risk that information shared by intelligence services will be disclosed in subsequent trials (Copeland, 2000). As a result, the protection of the rights of individuals, especially the inviolability of their personal lives, is at great risk.

In many countries, intelligence services have traditionally been reluctant to share classified information with the police and other law enforcement agencies. The Canadian Commission of Inquiry found that such an attitude facilitated the successful investigation after the 1985 Indian Airlines bombing. Intelligence services tend to protect information because they fear that sharing information will lead to its eventual disclosure, which in turn could lead to the possible disclosure of important sources and methods and jeopardize the service's ability to collect intelligence data in the future. In addition, if the information was obtained in a way that would be unacceptable to the trial, sharing it with law enforcement could become more problematic. Police authorities, who are more willing to share information with intelligence services, are also concerned that information sharing will undermine their ability to investigate security threats and act accordingly (Eriksson & Giacomello, 2006).

Worth bearing in mind that, structures tasked with overseeing the intelligence service face the greatest difficulty. They need to be constantly aware of a large amount of information being shared, the volume of which is so large that they are forced to systematically rely on an audit that verifies only selected information. In addition to that, intelligence services face difficulties in gaining access to and traceability of shared classified information. For example, a supervisory body whose jurisdiction extends to the police may not have the authority to investigate how information obtained by the police has been collected from the intelligence service. This is especially true when the information is provided by a foreign agency (Eriksson & Giacomello, 2006).

In many jurisdictions, intelligence and security services networks are designed to gather information on security threats provided by multiple internal and external sources. Some of these networks even allow foreign agencies to exchange information with each other. Agencies within the country need to have access to information gathered and disseminated by similar networks to fully understand the operations of the agency under their supervision, especially if the agency provides or receives information from such regional, national, and supranational institutions. Intelligence services clearly need to exchange information with internal and external partners. A service that simply collects intelligence data without sharing will not be able to warn others of detected threats. It is obvious that the transnational nature of many modern threats requires the need to increase information sharing at both national and international levels (Eriksson & Giacomello, 2006).

Despite the above mentioned, the increase in information sharing is accompanied by its shortcomings. It may lead to violations of privacy and other rights in a way that is neither permitted by law nor ethically justified. It also jeopardizes the disclosure of classified information obtained from sensitive sources (Aghaie & Rasooli Sani Abadi, 2011).

Sharing information through national and unified centers may lead to scattering and distortion of accountability. Parliamentary oversight bodies and experts, whose mandate extends their authority to a single agency, often do not have access to the records of networks involving intelligence services - and a lack of access to them can seriously hamper their oversight activities (Aghaie & Rasooli Sani Abadi, 2011).

Sharing information across national borders can also lead to a conflict of policy principles, for example, when countries with credible human rights records are forced to exchange information with countries with scarce records in this regard. Moreover, sharing information in a similar way may make one state an accomplice to human rights abuses, such as torture perpetrated by an information-sharing partner (Aghaie & Rasooli Sani Abadi, 2011).

Proceeding from all the above mentioned, intelligence services will not be able to do their job if they jointly refuse to exchange information, although increasing information sharing is associated with many risks. Concerning individuals, it includes human rights violations, especially the right to privacy. As for intelligence services, the risks are related to the dissemination of information obtained through the unreliable and incorrect information, which can damage the reputation of the service and lead to inefficient use of scarce resources.

The Paris Terrorist Attack and the New Challenges in Cyberspace

In Paris, the January 7 terrorist attack on the French satirical weekly Charlie Hebdo was preceded by a series of rather massive hacker cyber-attacks on French cyberspace. The hackers attacked the websites of both the public and private sectors, as well as the websites of foreign companies whose activities were linked in various ways to France and French companies. It is noteworthy that the number of cyber-attacks increased even more after the terrorist attack. In particular, since January 7, a hacking attack had been carried out on 19,000 French websites, which had never happened and was the first time in French history (Sedrati, 2016).

It should be noted that, in recent years, especially after the war in Syria and the emergence of the Islamic State (ISIS), the number of cyber-attacks has increased significantly. Hacker groups, such as the Middle Eastern Cyber Army – MECA, Fallaga Hackers Team, and Cyber Caliphate are particularly active in this area (Sedrati, 2016).

The Syrian Electronic Army (SEA), also often referred to as the Syrian Cyber Army, enjoys the support of Syrian President Bashar al-Assad. It is the first virtual public army in the Arab world to target members of the country's political opposition and Western websites. The targets of the Syrian Electronic Army (SEA) are BBC News, the Associated Press, National Public Radio, CBC News, Al Jazeera, Financial Times, The Daily Telegraph, The Washington Post, Orient TV, and al-Arabia TV. It is noteworthy that the "Army" carried out a number of cyberattacks on the websites of US President Barack Obama and the White House, as well as Human Rights Watch (Sedrati, 2016).

Another hacker group is the Middle Eastern Cyber Army - MECA, which appeared on the scene on September 23, 2014, when it carried out hacking attacks on US cyberspace. There is no information on who might be behind the MECA. However, it can be either a terrorist group or a state, as well as an individual (Sedrati, 2016).

Recent developments in cyberspace clearly show that hacker groups are being used more and more by terrorist organizations and individuals associated with them, producing unauthorized intrusions and hacking attacks on public or private sector websites. This poses a direct threat to individual organizations and consumers, as well as to international, regional, or national security as a whole. In addition to that, the situation is further complicated by the fact that the latest computer and software technologies are used in criminal activities.

Post-Soviet Space and Cybersecurity Aspects

Analyzing the ongoing conflicts in the post-Soviet space with the participation of Russia, it becomes clear that the Kremlin views the conflict zones as a kind of testing ground for both kinetic types of weapons and cyber-attack potential. A clear example of this is the "progress" made in Ukraine by Russia, even during the period of the cyberattack on Georgia, and the sharp increase in the area of use of the cyber element (Lilly & Cheravitch, 2020).

The cyber element is now an important part of all wars and conflicts. It is extremely important to consider the recent trends in the use of cyber elements in war or crises and the specifics of the use of cyberattacks in the ongoing conflicts in the post-Soviet space with the participation of Russia. Based on this, it is essential to develop the cyber defense potential in these countries, to integrate the cyber element with the military capabilities, which makes them reliable partners and reliable players in the global security architecture (Lilly & Cheravitch, 2020).

Cyberspace as an area of confrontation between the parties is gaining more and more importance daily. The number of units involved in cyber security in developed countries is growing daily, with budgets amounting to billions of dollars. The growing interest of countries in the cyber domain is also confirmed by the fact that despite the economic crisis or financial difficulties, no state has yet reduced this cost (Lilly & Cheravitch, 2020).

In terms of offensive cyber potential, Russia is one of the leaders. Its appearance is evident in the events of the "Arab Spring", in Syria and Iraq, Ukraine, and around it. At the same time, the shift of military threats to the information space was highlighted. However, it should be noted that the shift from specialized cyber- and information security conferences to public policy is not the only Russian trend. It is also noteworthy that Russia and China have signed an agreement on international information security. The reasons for this agreement are the subject of a separate discussion, but it should not be overlooked that from the three biggest players in the field of cyber defense (USA, Russia, China), accusations of cyber-attacks are constantly heard against Russia and China. This is happening at a time when no cyber-threatening incident has taken place between the two countries, which in itself makes sense for their alliance. It should also be noted that while the target of Chinese cyberattacks is mainly commercial classified information, Russia is actively using the cyber element to solve state goals and objectives, including military or geopolitical advantage (Hakala & Melnychuk, 2021).

Based on all of the above mentioned, the objective reality is that creating reliable protection in cyberspace is an extremely difficult task, and preventing a large-scale cyber-attack and an adequate response is almost impossible. States try to focus on offensive operations to use cyberspace effectively and to achieve their goals. Moreover, there are examples of interstate cooperation in controlling or banning the use of cyber weapons, but cooperation is complicated by the fact that cyber-attacks in this area will always remain cheaper and have devastating consequences, while protection will be expensive and extremely difficult process.

EU AND NATO CYBERSECURITY STRATEGIES

At the Prague Summit in 2002, NATO leaders recognized cyber-terrorism as a significant threat and developed the NATO Cyber Defense Program, which included three phases of the Action Plan. In the first phase, the NATO Computer Incident Response Capability (NCIRC) was established, which entered full operation in the second phase. The third phase involves putting into practice the experience gained from the first two phases and the use of modern defense tools in the fight against cyber-terrorism. It should be noted that on June 14, 2007, when a massive cyber-attack was carried out on Estonia, the defense ministers of NATO member states agreed that an active fight against cyber-terrorism was necessary. As a result, NATO has established a cyber-defense center in Estonia (Štitilis, 2017).

The United States first developed a cybersecurity strategy in 2000 to prevent cyber security breaches. After that, Europe soon became convinced of the extent to which cyberterrorism could harm the world and began to work collectively against the impending threat. Since 2007, Europe has become more active in strengthening its cyberspace, as it has become apparent how vulnerable it was when Russia attacked Estonia's cyberspace. Estonia has begun to enact legal regulations on cyberspace protection, and EU or NATO member states have agreed to work together more effectively against cyber-terrorism than separately. It should be noted that the common vision of all countries is different, but on several issues, their principles coincide (Štitilis, 2017).

In order to show the steps taken by the EU in terms of cyber security, it is necessary to outline the efforts of individual countries based on development in this area. For instance, the Cyber Security Strategy was adopted by Finland in 2008 and it is based on the understanding of cyber security as an economic problem that is closely linked to the development of the country's information systems and society. In Slovakia, ensuring information security is considered a necessary condition for the normal functioning and development of society. Therefore, the purpose of the strategy is to provide a solid foundation for information protection. The strategy developed in 2008 is aimed at mitigating the threat, as well as preparing and strengthening the necessary means for it (Europol, 2016).

2011 was marked by the fact that several EU countries simultaneously developed strategies to ensure their cyber security. For example, the main direction of the cyber security strategy of the Czech Republic includes the protection of vulnerable areas of information and communication systems, as well as the maximum reduction of risks and imminent threats. The strategy mainly focuses on the problems of free access to information systems, as well as the integrity of the country's cyberspace and the protection of data privacy. France focuses its strategy on protecting information through technical means, combating cybercrime, and strengthening cyber defense. The strategy focuses on the capabilities of information systems and it must anticipate cyber events that negatively affect access to information, integrity, and privacy (Europol, 2016).

The German cybersecurity strategy is based on ensuring the security of critical information systems. The country is mainly focused on the timely detection, neutralization, and prosecution of cyber-attacks, as well as the disabling of information and communication technology (ICT) equipment malfunctions caused by accidental factors. The strategy also provides an analysis that allows for additional measures to be taken to protect information and communication technology (ICT) systems. In addition to that, security measures for small and medium-sized businesses are also defined (Europol, 2016).

On the one hand, the Netherlands strives for the safe and reliable operation of information and communication systems, and on the other hand, recognizes the need for freedom and transparency of the internet space. It is noteworthy and important to define cyber security in the strategy, according to which cyber security is the protection of information and communication systems from improper operation, which can have a negative impact on access and reliability of information and communication systems (Europol, 2016).

It should be noted that there is no agreement on the definition of cyber security at the international level. Definitions of cybersecurity, cyberspace, cybercrime, and related keywords in each country may differ significantly. Moreover, each country's approach to developing a cyber-security strategy differs as well. Although the importance of international cooperation is recognized by all countries, at least common key terms and the absence of a common "language" greatly complicates cooperation at the international level. As a rule, each country's cybersecurity strategies still have common principles related to the development of the state model and policy, the definition of the appropriate mechanism based on the state partnership, and the planning of the necessary policy and mechanism regulations. Besides that, the principles include cooperation at the international level on the exchange of information on cybercrime and the existence of the necessary legal framework for this purpose, the definition of the objectives of information programs, the conduct of complex research, and the need for new education programs (Europol, 2016).

It is obvious that, in an environment where cyber threats are constantly evolving and evolving, EU member states, which are constantly facing new challenges and global threats in cyberspace, will benefit greatly from a flexible and operational cybersecurity strategy. The transboundary nature of cybercrime forces member states to work closely with each other and at the international level in general. Such co-operation is necessary not only for effective preparation for cyber-attacks but also for timely response to them. Hence, the approach of the state strategy toward cyber security should be complex (Europol, 2016).

Close cooperation of the private and public sectors is essential for the implementation of the cyber security strategy. This cooperation should take place at the state and EU level in general through the exchange of information, the sharing of technology and practical knowledge, and scientific collaboration (Europol, 2016).

Proceeding from all the above mentioned, The European Union does not have a unified cyber security strategy, and it is limited to issuing separate recommendations to member states. Member states individually implement and take care of their own cyberspace. Nevertheless, it should be noted that the cyber security strategies of each member state still have common principles.

The Cyber Capabilities of The United States

The United States is a leader in cybersecurity and one of the major players in the world. At the same time, most cyberattacks take place in the United States cyberspace and its infrastructure. The United States originally began working on cybersecurity after the September 11, 2001, terrorist attacks. Before that, in 1991, the Air Force used the latest information technology in the "Desert Storm" in Iraq, and was protected by a specially created unit (Trautman, 2015).

In May 2011, the United States announced its cybersecurity strategy. The strategy is based on a model of cooperation between the government, international partners, and the private sector, which describes a number of measures that need to be taken in different directions. These directions include economics, national network protection, legal protection, military sector, government internet network, international development, and internet freedom (Trautman, 2015).

2015 was a year of significant change for the United States in cybersecurity. In particular, in February 2015, the US Presidential Administration decided to create a new special service-Cyber Threat Intelligence Integration Center, under the direct supervision of the Director of National Intelligence (DNI). Allocating military aspects of cybersecurity to Pentagon priorities began during George W. Bush's presidency. At the same time, there was fierce competition between US special services for powers in this area. In addition, there was the issue of creating a unified joint cyber command that would facilitate military action in cyberspace, although at the time the Pentagon was not ready for that and the issue remained open again. Therefore, the overall responsibility for cyber issues was assigned to the Strategic Command of the Armed Forces, while the actual implementation of combat operations in cyberspace was entrusted to the Air Force. The leadership of the United States Armed Forces has brought cybersecurity under one structural unit, otherwise, the degree of coordination and efficiency would have been very low (Pernik, Wojtkowiak, & Verschoor-Kirss, 2016).

The experience of the United States shows that from an organizational-structural point of view, it is necessary to separate the functions of the Armed Forces and the civil sector, including special services. Cyber command carries out its tasks in parallel or jointly with the Central Intelligence Agency, the Ministry of Internal Security, the National Security Agency, and other structural units of the state. It is therefore essential to fight cyber threats (Pernik, Wojtkowiak, & Verschoor-Kirss, 2016).

The Cyber-Capabilities of Russia

The main organizations in the field of information security in Russia are the Security Council, the Federal Security Service, the Federal Service for Technical and Expert Control, the Ministries of Defense and Information Technology and Communications. Each named organizational body has its scope of competence and responsibilities. In particular, the Security Council identifies Russia's national interests in the field of information, objects, entities, and other resources that must be protected, as well as coordinates the development of an information security strategy. The Federal Security Service is responsible for ensuring the security of the Russian Federation and the protection of critical information infrastructure. The Counterintelligence Service has a Computer and Information Security Division that also oversees hacker groups (Hakala & Melnychuk, 2021).

It should be noted that in January 2014, the Russian Federal Council presented for wide discussion the "Concept of the Cyber Security Strategy of the Russian Federation", which is aimed at identifying new threats in the modern information world. The concept has led to differences of opinion among industry experts, although they have developed common recommendations related to existing information security terminology, the development of complex cybersecurity systems, intelligent methods of ensuring cybersecurity, and so on. The goal of the strategy itself was to ensure the cyber security of individuals, organizations, and the state based on the definition of systems of priorities, principles, and measures in foreign and domestic policy (Hakala & Melnychuk, 2021).

The defense capabilities of the Russian Armed Forces in modern conditions significantly depend on their effective action in the information space. The Armed Forces plan to solve the tasks in the field of defense and security, using the basic principles and rights of the Armed Forces in the information space. Russia is one of the main players in the information space of the world, which is constantly developing its capabilities. The country has constant interests and goals, for the achievement of which it is increasingly using the information space in parallel with its military and political capabilities (Hakala & Melnychuk, 2021).

In Russia, the field of information security is under the control of special services, in parallel with which begins the development of the field in the Armed Forces, where there are already semi-secret units that work not only to deter and prevent but also carry out cyber-attacks themselves (Hakala & Melnychuk, 2021).

The Cyber-Capabilities of Iran

Iran is one of the major players in cyberspace and related issues, and its cyber capabilities are one of the strongest in the world. Iranian hackers have been able to launch a series of cyberattacks on Western banking and financial institutions, as well as the energy sector of Israel and Saudi Arabia. Most similar attacks have been able to do some damage and make it impossible for other groups of hackers to detect them (Farwell & Arakelian, 2013).

Iran's cyber doctrine is mainly based on asymmetric warfare tactics, which are defined as a conflict where the resources, tactics, and essence of the two opposing sides differ qualitatively and substantially from each other. At the same time, the parties try to use the weak and easily vulnerable areas characteristic of the opposing party. Such an approach incorporates non-standard war production tactics and strategies. This implies the use of a strategy that will compensate for both the existing quantitative and qualitative deficits. The active use and encouragement of hacker groups create a certain balance of insufficient military force, which is a major determinant of the asymmetry of Iran's strategy (Farwell & Arakelian, 2013).

In addition to that, the use of psychological aspects in cyber operations is also an asymmetric combat tactic actively used by the Iranian government. It is noteworthy the activity of hacker groups supporting the regime which is related to the statement of the government on the weakening of control over the Internet in order to reduce international tensions. This is the essence of Iran's cyber doctrine and strategy, which includes eliminating Western influence, protecting the country's infrastructure, curbing internal opposition, and developing offensive capabilities against Western cyber assets and capabilities (Farwell & Arakelian, 2013).

The structure of Iran's cyber forces is sophisticated and difficult to comprehend. The level of control over security and communication between members and rings within the structure and the links is so high that most hackers do not even know that they are working for the Iranian government. The creativity, talent, and skills of Iranian hackers are so high that experts have compared them to their counterparts from the United States, Russia, and Israel (Farwell & Arakelian, 2013).

Interesting and important is the General Staff of the Iranian Armed Forces, which structurally unites the organizations responsible for protecting cyberspace and also carrying out cyberattacks themselves. The General Staff of the Armed Forces includes cyber units of the Passive Civil Defense Organization and the Pasdaran. The Passive Civil Defense Organization plays a defensive role in protecting Iran's network, and it includes the Cyber Defense Command and the Gerdab, which was responsible for identifying and intimidating supporters of political unrest in Iran in 2009. The Pasdaran is the mainstay of the regime in Iran, its cyber capabilities are quite strong and contain various cyber units. Moreover, there are also various independent hacker groups in Iran, operating under the indirect leadership of the Pasdaran (Farwell & Arakelian, 2013).

THE ROLE OF CYBERSECURITY IN INTERNATIONAL RELATIONS

The concept of international security includes the most important indicators of international relations, including development stability, overcoming external threats, ensuring sovereignty and independence, and all aspects that are of vital interest to the state at the international level. The scale of international security is divided into three levels: national, regional, and global (Tsakanyan, 2017).

Security at the national level means ensuring the conduct of the state's foreign or domestic policy and the normal life of the country's population. The regional level is the level of international security, which includes the specific geopolitical region and the security of the states within the region. In addition, it covers a set of national security indicators at the regional level. When comes to ensuring global security, involves tackling issues that pose a threat to the planet's population. Global security issues include: international terrorism, drug trafficking, maintaining global economic stability, arms control, ethnopolitical conflicts, inviolability of religious and cultural heritage, and environmental issues (Tsakanyan, 2017).

The development factors of the modern world significantly depend on the process of globalization. In this case, the process of globalization involves the existence of a single tight financial-information space that includes society, as well as international and economic relations. With this in mind, a condition has been created in which the information technology component acquires special importance (Tsakanyan, 2017).

Elements of cyber security are a relatively new component in international security. It should be noted that in the conditions of multipolar world order and information-technological advances, it is difficult to identify or predict the interests of any actor in International Relations. This is especially the case when actors are considered to be separate groups, influential individuals, or corporations. Therefore, it can be said that the conditions of transformation include international security levels, as well as the actors in international relations and poles of interest (Duić, Cvrtila, & Ivanjko, 2017).

The problem of cyber security is relatively new in the world of security settings. It originated when the first computing equipment, computer, and communication networks were put into operation. Back then, the motive for the crime was a simple human factor, to strengthen one's own knowledge and capabilities. As a result of technological development and intensive integration, threats have taken on a much larger scale, and technologies have been made available for use in financial machinations as well as in planning terrorist acts and carrying out attacks against state infrastructure (Duić, Cvrtila, & Ivanjko, 2017).

One of the major challenges to international security is international terrorism. In the 21st century, an element of cyber security has been added to the combat mechanisms of international extremist groups. The term "cyber-terrorism" was coined in international security in the United States in the 1980s. Then, as today, the term was used in a virtual dimension to describe terrorist acts. The main problem is that the exact concept of cyber-terrorism is quite difficult to explain, given that there is no precise definition and characterization of cybercrime in the world (White, 2017).

The effectiveness of the use of cyber methods for terrorist organizations depends on several factors. First of all, this resource does not require a large financial investment. On the other hand, the Internet itself provides global access, which makes it easy to use propaganda levers anywhere in the world and quickly disseminate information among terrorist affiliates. The threat posed by cyberterrorism varies in scale. Based on the classification of illegal acts committed with extremist motives, it is possible to determine how important a virtual tool plays in the combat methods of a terrorist organization (White, 2017).

Along with non-state actors in international relations, attention is paid to state actors and their role in global cybersecurity policy. Another term used to describe the use of cyberspace for aggressive actions is Cyberwar. "It is a destructive action by one state to pursue its own political and strategic interests in another state's virtual infrastructure and network system" (Alazab & Broadhurst, 2017).

Cyberwar is one of the components of information warfare and is a complex confrontation between several actors in the virtual space. The main priority of information warfare is not only to attack, but also to ensure the inviolability of its own critical infrastructure and information, and that is why the issue of cyber security is a dominant subject of cyber warfare for the state strategy. Like any other cyber-attack, the target is the basic governing structures and systems of the state on which the financial, energy, and transport infrastructure of the country is built (Alazab & Broadhurst, 2017).

Nowadays, cybersecurity is an integral part of the security strategies of international organizations and various countries. The practical application of cyber security does not only involve the development of a legal framework. Information warfare involves the use of the same methods between two countries, which involves having sufficiently qualified personnel, building relevant infrastructure and software at the national level. In this case, the main challenge is to draw the exact line between defense and attack (Alazab & Broadhurst, 2017).

Cyber threat settings are directly proportional to virtual technological integration. It is obvious that the more critical infrastructure depends on network support, the greater the potential for this facility to become a target for cyberattacks. To avoid cyber threats, it is necessary to accurately predict risks and respond on time, which requires constant monitoring and control of the situation. Technological advances have already made it possible to use automated techniques for 24-hour monitoring of data inviolability, although it is also important to note that behind each cyberattack is a professional hacker acting with a different motive. Another problem is social awareness. A society in which people are active users of cyberspace and pay less attention to the protection of personal information (Alazab & Broadhurst, 2017).

Based on all of the mentioned, in today's world, a high percentage of virtual-technological integration is evident, as evidenced by the use of technology in various fields, systemic work, and the life of an individual. Therefore, protecting critical infrastructure is vital to the state, and the element of cybersecurity is paramount in this case.

CONCLUSION

The main purpose of this chapter was to determine the influence of cyberterrorism on International Security. Based on this, the aim was to answer the main research question regarding the emergence of cyberterrorism as an unresolved problem facing countries in today's world. The research revealed that although the states around the world are actively trying to develop the right strategy and legal approaches to address the threats of cyber-terrorism, much more work needs to be done in this area. In particular, it is necessary to refine the relevant legislation, which will regulate the already existing activities of each entity - mutually coordinated activities, define the scope of each entity and additional obligations. Moreover, International relations are of great importance in the field of cyber security, especially the need to work closely with strategic partners and organizations.

The arguments were based on the analysis of various articles, reports, analytical papers, and Case Studies as a result of the use of a qualitative research method. The analysis of the concept of cyberterrorism and cyber-threats revealed the fact that there is no universal definition of cyber-terrorism, which significantly hinders the cooperation of states in the fight against it. Besides that, it is difficult to determine the location of the people behind the cyber-attacks, which presents also one of the major challenges.

Globalization, the development of the Internet, and modern information technologies have created many opportunities, but at the same time posed a new challenge to the world. Access to information that could be sensitive not only to national structures but also to members of the public has been made possible, which has put states in a dilemma. In order to fight against cyber threats, joint efforts and information sharing are the major aspects, however, lack of trust and consequently delays in access to information between state structures and states in general offer this approach another serious challenge.

Cyber threats offer serious challenges to international security. States are trying to develop cyber security strategies that will protect them from cyber-attacks. Furthermore, it should be noted that cyber methods of warfare have significantly replaced traditional means of combat in our time. Terrorist organizations are actively using various methods of cyber attacks to attract the attention of the world community, harm Western structures, and promote the spread of their ideology. The reason for this new trend is that cyberattacks are usually affordable for terrorist organizations and can be carried out from any location. As a result, the development of technology makes this new manifestation of terrorism even more popular and highlights the need for state mobilization and joint action.

Despite the fact that there are examples of interstate cooperation, it is clear that some states are developing cyber security not only for defense but also for attack. A clear example of this is Russia, which is actively trying to use cyber elements to spread its influence and ideology in the post-Soviet space. Therefore, as long as the elements of cyber-attack remain popular methods of combat not only for terrorist organizations but also for individual states, the problem of combating cybercrime remains unresolved and reflects a lack of cooperation and general trust.

REFERENCES

Aghaie, S., & Rasooli Sani Abadi, E. (2011). Information revolution and its effect on national security from the perspective of international relations theories. *The Political Quarterly*, *41*(3), 23–37.

Alazab, M., & Broadhurst, R. (2017). An Analysis of the Nature of Spam as Cybercrime. In S. Hakim, E. A. Blackstone, & R. M. Clark (Eds.), Cyber-Physical Security. Protecting Critical Infrastructure at the State and Local Level (pp. 251-267). Springer International Publishing Switzerland. doi:10.1007/978-3-319-32824-9_13

Copeland, T. (2000). *The Information Revolution and National Security*. doi:10.21236/ADA382498

Duić, I., Cvrtila, V., & Ivanjko, T. (2017). International cyber security challenges. *40th International Convention on Information and Communication Technology, Electronics and Microelectronics (MIPRO)*, 1309-1313. 10.23919/MIPRO.2017.7973625

Eriksson, J., & Giacomello, G. (2006). The Information Revolution, Security, and International Relations. *International Political Science Review*, *27*(3), 221–244. doi:10.1177/0192512106064462

Europol. (2016). *European Union Terrorism Situation and Trend Report*. European Police Office.

Farwell, J. P., & Arakelian, D. (2013). What Does Iran's Cyber Capability Mean For Future Conflict? *The Whitehead Journal of Diplomacy and International Relations*, 49-65.

Grove, G. D., Goodman, S., & Lukasik, S. (2000). Cyber-attacks and International Law. *Survival*, *42*(3), 89–103. doi:10.1093urvival/42.3.89

Hakala, J., & Melnychuk, J. (2021). *Russia's Strategy in Cyberspace*. NATO StratCom COE and NATO Cooperative Cyber Defence COE.

Hatamleh, H. (2012). A Review and Comparing of all Hacking Techniques and Domain Name System Method. *Contemporary Engineering Sciences*, *5*(2), 239–250.

Lilly, B., & Cheravitch, J. (2020). The Past, Present, and Future of Russia's Cyber Strategy and Forces. In *12th International Conference on Cyber Conflict* (pp. 129-155). Tallin: NATO CCDCOE Publications. 10.23919/CyCon49761.2020.9131723

Pernik, P., Wojtkowiak, J., & Verschoor-Kirss, A. (2016). *National Cyber Security Organisation: United States*. NATO Cooperative Cyber Defence Centre of Excellence.

Pollitt, M. (1998). Cyberterrorism—Fact or fancy? *Computer Fraud & Security*, *1998*(2), 8–10. doi:10.1016/S1361-3723(00)87009-8

Sedrati, A. (2016). *"Sorry, you are not as important!" A study about the unequal media treatment of different terrorist attacks in the world in 2015 –Aftonbladet*. Stockholms Universitet.

Singer, P., & Friedman, A. (2014). *Cybersecurity and Cyberwar: What Everyone Needs to Know*. Oxford University Press. doi:10.1093/wentk/9780199918096.001.0001

Štitilis, D., Pakutinskas, P., & Malinauskaitė, I. (2017). EU and NATO cybersecurity strategies and national cyber security strategies: A comparative analysis. *Security Journal*, *30*(4), 1151–1168. doi:10.105741284-016-0083-9

Trautman, L. (2015). Cybersecurity: What About U.S. Policy? SSRN *Electronic Journal*, 341-387. doi:10.2139/ssrn.2548561

Tsakanyan, V. (2017). The role of cybersecurity in world politics. *Vestnik RUDN International Relations*, *17*(2), 339–348.

White, S. J. (2017). Assessing Cyber Threats and Solutions for Municipalities. In S. Hakim, E. A. Blackstone, & R. M. Clark (Eds.), Cyber-Physical Security. Protecting Critical Infrastructure at the State and Local Level (pp. 49-67). Springer International Publishing. doi:10.1007/978-3-319-32824-9_3

Chapter 14
Female Radicalization:
Why and How Women Join ISIS

Tinatin Gigauri
International Black Sea University, Georgia

ABSTRACT

This chapter discusses the phenomenon of female radicalization based on a case study of the Islamic State. The goal of this chapter is to explore the connection and, possibly, the correlation between the uneven and inconsistent security context and the transformation of gender norms and deeply-rooted gendered segregation inside a jihadist organization through qualitative desk research. Using aspects of securitization theory and a human security paradigm, the research elaborates on the changing politico-military tendencies targeting the Islamic State since the declaration of the War on Terror, the dynamics of changing the strictly domestic role of women inside ISIS, the roles performed by female recruits in the organization, the threat they pose as participants of military jihad, and the propensity of existing counterterrorism measures to ignore the significance of female terrorists. Finally, with proper arguments, the chapter argues that there is a need for implementing a gendered approach to designing case-appropriate counterterrorism strategies.

INTRODUCTION

This study aims to explore the phenomenon of female radicalization. Commonly, a radical is somebody whose beliefs and views differ from that of generally accepted social norms and who thrives to change those norms (Merriam-Webster, n.d.), however, there is not a generally agreed-upon definition for the term "radicalization". Depending on the context, radicalization can have a positive and a negative meaning. In this paper, the term radicalization will refer to 'a gradual process whereby individuals are socialized into extreme beliefs that are articulated in nonviolent and/or violent acts' (Shapiro & Maras, 2018, p. 1). Radicalization itself is not the same as violent extremism or terrorism but the process of radicalization can be understood as a precondition of and evolution toward both. Borum (2003, pp. 7-10) further elaborates on this by suggesting a Four-Stage Model of the Terrorist Mindset to explain that it is a systematic and intentional process of change directed by facilitators (recruiters).

DOI: 10.4018/978-1-6684-5311-7.ch014

The female radicalization phenomenon has not emerged recently, nevertheless examining a gendered dimension of radicalization remains a sensitive topic to this day. The widely accepted gender stereotypes of women describe females as weak sex, nurturing, and gentle creatures who are seen as victims "lured" by terrorist organizations. Consequently, in many of the academic works describing, exploring, and explaining a phenomenon of female radicalization, the motivational factors of female fighters of radical groups and organizations are mostly that of a personal, private character, and seldom political. However, whether or not we accept violence as a resource that can be used by women does not change the fact that female radicalization stands firmly on the international policy agenda. The increasing number of women being socialized into the ideology of the Islamic State (ISIS) has become an alarming concern and threat to international security since the emergence of the organization from Al-Qaeda in 2013.

Islamic State (ISIS) did not follow in the footsteps of its predecessor organization immediately. In the early stages of its existence, ISIS stood strong on gender segregation and traditional domestic roles of female Muslims. Women's engagement in armed conflicts was brought up later, in a 10,000-word manifesto released by ISIS's all-female al-Khansa Brigade, where among other roles that female Muslims were permitted to play in Islamic State, under strictly defined circumstances and a certain defensive context, women could engage in military jihad (Winter C., 2018). Following the manifesto, messages of encouragement to take up arms and join combat when Daesh is facing a lack of manpower against its enemies echoed and was further elaborated in other IS documents and publications, and already in 2017, Islamic State, at the edge of collapsing, decided that women's participation in jihad was obligatory (Khalil, 2019, pp. 9-10). The 2015 ICCT Background Note, focused on the European Union geographical area, states that females compromise 18% of the total number of IS fighters (Bakker & Leede, 2015, p. 1). According to the ICSR 2018 report, the total number of foreign affiliates in Iraq and Syria is between 37,497-41,490, out of which 13% are women (Cook & Vale, 2018, p. 1). The 2021 United Nations article states that among almost 62,000 residents of the Al-Hol camp for displaced people in Syria, more than 80% are women and children (UN News, 2021).

This chapter starts with exploring the international and regional security agenda under which Daesh is securitized by international actors. Then, it analyzes how the uneven security context exposed the Islamic State to extreme pressure from its opponents and created incentives for the transformation of deeply-rooted gender segregation inside the jihadist terrorist organization. Next, the study observes the conversion of the existing norms and roles of women inside ISIS in the face of female radicalization. And last but not least, the paper argues that there is a lack of gender-oriented approaches to implementing counter-terrorism strategies.

PROBLEM STATEMENT AND SIGNIFICANCE OF THE PROBLEM

The research objective of this chapter is to explore the phenomenon of female radicalization based on a case study of ISIS. The gendered recruitment approach has been particularly important for contemporary IR scholars and political actors worldwide for more than a decade now. The reason for the intensified interest is the rapid utilization of female forces by violent extremist organizations for a range of activities, including propaganda, recruitment, logistics, planning and participating in operations, joining combat, and being suicide bombers.

Several scholars have worked on analyzing the reasons, causes, and consequences of recruitment of women into military jihad; how IS propaganda is spread throughout the world and who are participants in this process; the platforms used for the radicalization of future recruits; why do women choose to join Islamic State and how are they migrating from their home-countries inside the borders of ISIS-controlled territories; what are the roles played by those recruits and how are they treated inside Daesh; how are the gender norms transforming inside the terrorist organization; what are the countermeasures adopted by the international political actors and is it important to incorporate gendered perspective into developing the new counter-terrorism strategies to reflect the evolving inner-working of Daesh.

What needs to be emphasized here is that many of these scholarly articles tend to oversee the impact of the security environment on the dynamics of the internal ideological and philosophical transformation of Daesh, its effect on the organization's day-to-day functioning, and the security threats posed by the transformed military roles and responsibilities carried out by female recruits. In addition, earlier academic papers are analyzing the motivations of women who joined the terrorist group from social and psychological perspectives and back up the idea that these incentives for the commitment to a radical organization are mostly rooted in a gendered private sphere.

In this regard, this paper is a valuable input for instead of overlooking women as perpetrators of violence and death (as we often see in the literature on terrorism) it focuses on explaining the importance of fully understanding them as actors who are involved in violent extremism and terrorism, and argues that to establish case-appropriate, inclusive and effective counterterrorism strategies that can respond and prevent the threats posed to the international security by female radicalization and female terrorists, it is essential to incorporate gendered-oriented approaches into designing those measures and tactics in the future.

GOAL STATEMENT

The main aim of the paper is to (i) analyze the changing politico-military tendencies targeting extremist groups and the Islamic State since the declaration of the War on Terror after 9/11, (ii) explore the dynamics of transforming gender segregation and strictly domestic roles of women inside ISIS (causes and consequences), (iii) discuss the roles female radicals play inside the Islamic State as participants of military jihad, and lastly, (iv) emphasize that the existing counter-terrorism strategies overlook the threat posed to human security by the female recruits of ISIS.

For attaining the final goal of the study, we establish a theoretical framework by combining the aspects of a securitization theory and a human security paradigm. Through the securitization theory, we try to explore and explain how the declaration of the War on Terror and the changing security context influenced and transformed the ideological basis of the Islamic State and reiterated the jihadi convention throughout the years. Next, the chapter aims to discuss the roles played by the ISIS female recruits in military jihad and, according to the human security paradigm, highlights the need to refer to the potential threats originated by female terrorists.

The above-mentioned objectives are accomplished through the study of secondary sources and peer-reviewed articles of field experts and renowned scholars, policy briefs issued by the international political actors, and the already implemented counter-terrorism strategies. This chapter was not designed to offer a conclusive, resolute response to the research question and its subtypes; instead, it provides a further incentive for more detailed and empirical-based studies on the female radicalization phenomenon in the future.

THEORETICAL FRAMEWORK

There is not a prevailing theoretical framework that is applied to the study of radicalization processes of women in academic circles but there are identifiable dominant narratives that are often used for the study of female terrorism. As observed, in scholarly literature there is an inclination to explain why and how women join terrorist organizations such as the Islamic State from behavioral and psycho-social perspectives. In this paper, however, we use a different approach to setting up a theoretical framework for the study of female radicalization.

This research implements the securitization theory along a human security paradigm to explore the reasons, motivations, environmental enablers, and consequences of the transforming gender norms and segregation inside Daesh that allows females to carry out roles and responsibilities that defy the strictly domestic image of women in jihadist society.

The securitization theory was developed by the Copenhagen School at the Copenhagen Peace Research Institution (COPRI) in the 1990s. The theory suggests that understanding the security concept is not universal or objective, rather it's driven by the interests of those who are in charge of defining the security threats. In this sense, securitization appears as a political act rather than neutral, which indicates that security issues are dealt with urgency when they are identified as alarming and dangerous by actors who possess institutional power to do so. 'By uttering "security," a state-representative moves a particular development into a specific area, and thereby claims a special right to use whatever means are necessary to block it' (Wæver, 1993, pp. 6-7). The securitization actor triggers certain responses from the target audience by drawing attention and amplifying the level of the threat at the right times, which then leads to a shared public understanding and approval of implementing urgent measures (often in military terms) for eliminating and eradicating the declared security issue. The global counter-terrorism campaign led by the United States after the terrorist attacks of September 11, 2001, is a clear demonstration of this process. The declaration of War on Terror by George W. Bush had a momentous impact on international relations and signified a new stage in global political relations.

Exploring the uneven security environment characterized by highly pressuring politico-military discourse since the 9/11 terrorist attack, in which terrorist organizations, and specifically the Islamic States operate today and which affects the structural and ideological basis of the jihadist organization requires a complex approach. The reason for choosing securitization as the theoretical framework for this research resonates with the main objective of this study and enables us access to the deeper and systemic analysis of the unclear security context by incorporating the positioning of the securitizing actor, features of the threat originated from ISIS, the timing of securitization of Daesh by the international political actors and acceptance of justification of intervention by the general public.

While the Pre-Cold War idea of security fixated more on states by analyzing political and military stability, the post-Cold War period witnessed the widening of the security agenda by including aspects of human security, notions of culture, identity, and gender into the definition of security context (Buzan, Wæver, & Wilde, 1998, pp. 21-47). The human security paradigm that emerged in the wake of the end of the Cold War challenges a state's place as the subject of security and focuses on individuals, thereby moving from state-based notions to broadening what constitutes a security issue by including the security of people (Shepherd, 2013, pp. 24-35). The human-centric approach considers the individual as a referent and evaluates security issues on the supposition that when an individual faces a threat, so does the international security (Burgess, 2012, pp. 85-105).

Radicalization, violent extremism, and terrorism are direct hazards to the concept of human security. Subsequently, the threat posed by female radicalization and female recruits of Daesh should not be ignored or denied. Islamic State, along with other radical groups, has successfully used females as perpetrators of violence for achieving their objectives due to the characterization of violent women as innocent victims of ISIS propaganda and coercion, and that on its own feeds the widespread stereotype of females as vulnerable caring motherly figures. Even though, in many of the violent extremist and radical organizations women remain in a traditional, strictly domestic environment, the responsibilities and acts carried out by radical females go beyond being mothers or "jihadi brides". Their evolving roles inside terrorist groups as planners, propagandists, recruiters, perpetrators of violence, and death need to be addressed and discussed in the framework of the human security paradigm as a way of designing a relevant gendered-oriented counter-terrorism strategy.

RESEARCH METHODOLOGY AND METHODS

This study is essentially exploratory desk research. The main goal of this paper is to analyze the constantly changing security context in which the Islamic State has been operating and which predisposed the change and transformation of deeply-rooted gender norms and segregation inside the organization. This is done based on the case study of the Islamic State and its gendered recruitment strategy. The reason for choosing ISIS as the unit of analysis for the case study is connected with the relevance and acknowledgment of the terrorist organization as one of the main security threats in international relations nowadays. The main research question about the causal factors of female radicalization is answered through thorough studies and analysis of secondary sources and peer-reviewed articles and publications of renowned field experts and researchers who have been observing and studying the phenomenon of gendered recruitment in terrorist organizations, especially ISIS, for years. We try to explore and shed the light on the uneven security agenda which has been preconditioned by international actors that are actively involved in framing and implementing the counter-terrorism measures against the Islamic State. This deductive character of the qualitative research is revealed via exploration of the feasibility of the above-stated argument. The additional sources used for exploration of the research topic include observation of media outlets capturing former ISIS female fighters and careful examinations of United Nations Security Council resolutions, United Nations Counter-Terrorism Center (UNCCT) reports, and International Centre for Counter-Terrorism – The Hague policy brief, etc.

One of the major limitations of this chapter is the lack of credible primary sources as a representation of personal motives for female radicalization. Due to the scarcity and incomprehensiveness of the materials found in the face of interviews with former female recruits of ISIS and also due to the lack of the ability to interview knowledgeable figures who may be related to the subject of the research, the study is mostly based on the secondary sources. In addition, the lack of transparency and publicity of the Islamic State contributes to the difficulty of obtaining data for conducting the Critical Discourse Analysis (CDA), which would help us better understand the mindset and underlining ambitions of the organizational leadership of the terrorist group.

To sum up, the final goal of collecting and analyzing the non-numerical data in this paper is not to provide a resolute conclusion or response for the research question and its subcategories but to provide further incentives for deeper, more detailed-oriented, and empirical, evidence-based studies in the future.

Securitization of the Islamic State

We start this paper by exploring the security environment that preconditioned the exposure of the Islamic State to heightened external pressure which pushed the Islamic organization into reconsidering the strictly defined roles of ISIS women in military jihad. First, we start by discussing how the security threats posed by terrorism were conceptualized and amplified after the 9/11 attacks and then observe how the US-led Global Coalition weakened the strength and strategic advantage of Daesh in the Middle East.

Redefining the Security Threats and Objectives After 9/11

'Our war on terror begins with Al Qaeda, but it does not end there. It will not end until every terrorist group of global reach has been found, stopped, and defeated... This is not, however, just America's fight… This is the world's fight. This is civilization's fight (President Bush Addresses the Nation, 2001).'

'And the world has come together to fight a new and different war... A war against all those who seek to export terror, and a war against those governments that support or shelter them (Bush on State of War, 2001).'

Those are the words George W. Bush used to address the Nation after the September 11 terrorist attacks in 2001. The attacks resulted in mass casualties with more than 3000 people dying and many more injured. The nationals of 80 countries suffered from the September attacks (The Global War on Terrorism: The First 100 Days, n.d.). 9/11 became the incentive for the redefinition of the American and international security agenda and policy objectives in the long run.

The attack on US interests by terrorist organizations was not a new phenomenon, however, those terrorist acts took place outside American borders, in third world countries with a majority of Muslim population where the United States had diplomatic and military installations (Rajaee B. M., 2007, p. 71). September 11, 2001, was precedential in the sense that the United States was attacked by a non-state actor, a violent extremist terrorist group with political objectives, inside its territory. With the initial support of the majority of the States, United Nations, and NATO, The President of the United States called for joint action against terrorist organizations and regimes, which marked the launching of a US-led global military campaign already in the first 100 days of the War on Terror (Aaronson, 2014, p. 124).

The chain of responses to the September attacks emerged as a part of the Bush Doctrine and United Nations 2002 and 2006 national security strategies devised for the confrontation of raising terrorist threats. And despite the rotation of presidential powers, the goal of the international military campaign against extremist groups has remained consistent and revolved around the prevention of further escalation of terrorist threats and future terrorist attacks, spreading and promoting democratic values, and undermining the conditions that fuel international terrorism (Goepner, 2016, pp. 107-108; Rajaee B. M., 2007, p. 69). Subsequently, countries continually extended their directives of counter-terrorism legislature and authorizations.

According to these policy objectives of the United States, three sequential strategic approaches can be identified that have been used for the prosecution of the War on Terror in the global campaign – the traditional counter-terrorism strategy directed at terrorists themselves and leading to the intervention in Afghanistan, "the Pre-emption and Pre-eminence" strategy that marked changes in the conceptualization of the War on Terror and actions that can be taken under it, and the third strategy for the democratization of the Middle East that aimed to undermine and replace the old terrorist regimes with democratic values and governments. Coordination of these three strategic approaches is what has kept the international military campaign dynamic for years to come (Dunn, 2005, pp. 11-33). Since then, United States foreign policy objectives regarding counter-terrorism initiatives (eliminating the state-sponsored terrorism, socio-economic and political liberation of the Islamic world) have remained consistent over time (Miller & Stefanova, 2007, pp. 90-93; Goepner, 2016, pp. 107-108; Rajaee B. M., 2007, p. 69).

What needs to be emphasized is how those strategic objectives demonstrate the way terrorist threats were conceptualized by the United States and its allies after 9/11. The Bush administration and the allies participating in the international campaign could not justify accentuating the threats emerging from the Islamic world and military interventions in the Middle East without the much-needed public support. For this, triggering certain responses from the general public was needed, and this is where conceptualizing the objectives of the War on Terror comes to the frontlines. The goal was to achieve such a robust response to September 11, 2001 attacks that went beyond seeing those events as simply criminal activities committed by terrorists, and it was supported by the idea of 'ultimate security costs as illustrated by 9/11' (Rajaee B., The Bush and US policy after 9/11, 2007, p. 159).

Subsequently, The questions asked after the September terrorist attacks revolved around identifying the mutual enemy ('a radical network of terrorists'), their motivation for attacking the "civilized world" ('They stand against us because we stand in their way'), and ways to counter threats posed by this exact mutual enemy – Al-Qaida, and other already existing or newly emerging extremist organizations and regimes (President Bush Addresses the Nation, 2001; Dunn, 2005, pp. 11-33). This language of the War on Terror became an organic part of American political discourse and has remained a dominant narrative on the international and regional security agenda for a long time. The public support was further fueled by the continuous dehumanizing and demonizing of terrorist groups and regimes, the sustained idea of the worldwide battle against terrorism for the protection of international peace and security, and the spread of democratic values.

ISIS Under Extreme Military Pressure

The Islamic State emerged as an alarming threat to international peace and security in 2014, when the insurgent group gained control over the vast territories of Syria and Iran, terrorized local ethnic and religious minorities, performed mass executions, beheadings of foreign citizens, and declared reestablishment of Caliphate with Abu Bakr al Baghdadi as the leader. At first, the responses of international and regional actors were not immediate, but as ISIS's strategic ambitions, extremist ideology, and implementation of transnational terrorism became clear, the international community, the US with its NATO allies, and regional powers actively assembled a multilateral coalition against the terrorist group, engaged in a debate about abrupt preventive measures and designing future counter-extremism strategies to fight against the capabilities and aims of Daesh (Banai, 2018, pp. 152-157; Blanchard & Humud, 2018, p. 1).

According to President Obama, the central goal of the coalition was to 'degrade, and ultimately destroy ISIL/ISIS through a comprehensive and sustained counter-terrorism strategy' (Hudson, 2014) This encompassed military action (airstrikes, artillery, ground units), military assistance and funding for forces fighting against the Islamic State in the region, preventing financial support of the organization, countering its jihadist ideology and improving defense capabilities of the coalition together with regional partners (including partner forces in Syria and Iraq, namely the SDF and the Iraqi Security Forces), working on intelligence, stopping the recruitment of new members and foreign fighters and countering Islamic State propaganda (In the Middle East, as well as, outside the war-torn regions, i.e. North Africa and in the West), ensuring humanitarian aid for innocent civilians without discrimination and achieving a stable security environment on affected territories. These military operations and policy initiatives were pioneered by the United States in the international military campaign against ISIS (Banai, 2018, pp. 152-157; Hudson, 2014).

Although there were some modifications, the Trump Administration maintained the general principle of partnership-based tactics against the Islamic State. Mainly, the changes were directed toward the U.S. military operations (i.e., provisional disposition of supplementary military personnel in Syria and Iraq), assistance programs, and financial support. Operating under the command of Combined Joint Task Force – Operation Inherent Resolve, together with local Syrian and Iraqi partner forces, the international campaign cooperated around the following 'lines of an effort': coordinated military operations, elimination of ISIS leaders, preventing recruitment of foreigners into Daesh, eliminating financial support of the organization, working on resolving the humanitarian crisis in the region, and exposing the true nature of the Islamic State as a way of countering ISIS propaganda (State, n.d.).

In 2017, the U.S.-led coalition and its local partner forces, based on mutual partnership, were able to recapture the territories formerly controlled by the jihadist terrorist organization, including Mosul and Raqqah, which was a huge blow for Daesh, however, this does not mean that the Islamic State or its affiliated groups stopped functioning inside and outside of Syria and Iraq. The loss of important territories by Daesh provided incentives for the rising threat of insurgence campaign, resulting in upcoming politico-military and socio-economic challenges and expanding ISIS's proficiency in regional destabilization (Blanchard & Humud, 2018, pp. 1-11).

Since the recapturing of the majority of the ISIS-controlled lands in Syria and Iraq by the Global Coalition, it is clear that the military strength, financial resources and human capital, territorial assets, and networking capabilities of Daesh have diminished, however, in the face of fundamental environmental enables that facilitated the rise of the Islamic State in the first place, the success of US-led coalition against the organization cannot be maintained in a long-run without appropriate strategies and systemically executed good practices directed at the stabilization and reconstruction of the liberated territories. Upholding the regional peace and stability in the Middle East is especially challenging if we take into account that there are competing interests of coalition members that are at odds with the core mission of the global campaign. These competing interests, result in insufficiencies and drawbacks of the U.S. policy against ISIS transnational terrorism and hamper strategic responses and regional dynamics of the international alliance (Al-Istrabadi, 2018, pp. 173-174; Banai, 2018, pp. 152-157). Even though mostly Daesh is not as active as before in North Africa, the organization continues to be an 'entrenched insurgency' with low-level uprisings and revolts on the territories of Sinai, Syria, and Iraq.

Additionally, according to a Quarterly Report of the Lead Inspector General for Operation Inherent Resolve (2021) ISIS actively pursues 'recruitment and indoctrination activities' in the al-Hol camp and the group's latest insurgencies reflect its 'higher level of operational maturity'. Besides, despite the organization's reduced financial support from state sponsors, according to the Analytical Support and Sanctions Monitoring Team (UNSC, 2021, p. 17), Islamic State still possesses a significant number of monetary resources in the face of $25-50 million available funds. Taking into account the active radicalization, recruitment, training of group members, and the financial resources that Daesh owns right now, it is not entirely wrong to assume that the extremist group could be able to plan, perform and withstand high-risk military operations and terrorist attacks in the near future.

1. Breaking With Jihadi Convention

As it was mentioned in a previous chapter, the September 11 attacks resulted in the redefinition of security threats on regional, international, and national levels. Subsequently, the actions and counter-terrorism efforts undertaken by the United Nations, NATO, regional powers, and other political actors were largely focused on identifying, preventing, and countering potential terrorist threats. Stereotypically enough, for the international community and general public, those threats were generated by Muslim males. What they failed to comprehend and what puts the policymakers at disadvantage in their efforts to prevent the global spread of terrorism and radicalization is that despite their differences in aspirations and ideological foundation, violent extremist and terrorist groups are characterized by a highly adaptive nature. Seeing the need, potential, and strategic advantage of employing women as facilitators and perpetrators of radical ideas, propaganda, violence, and death, these organizations looked further into recruiting female volunteers, despite their philosophical, ideological, and religious fundamentals (CUNNINGHAM, 2010, pp. 171-173). Islamic State is not an exception. Although, as was briefly discussed in the introduction of this chapter, ISIS did not start radicalization of females from the beginning of the declaration of the Caliphate. In this chapter, we will explore how Daesh slowly, step-by-step broke from the jihadi convention and modified the vision of the roles and responsibilities women were permitted to play in military jihad.

ISIS Female Recruitment and Contemporary Military Jihad

There are essentially two ways of understanding the meaning of Jihad. First, jihad can be interpreted as a struggle within one's self against enticement; second, it is a fight, holy war against oppression, injustice, and the enemies of Islam. In this chapter, we will address the latter – violent Jihad – an ideology that plays a fundamental role in defining the politico-military objectives of Daesh (LEEDE & et.al, 2017, pp. 6-7).

We can trace the origins of modern jihadist ideology back to USSR when the Union occupied Afghanistan and the supporters of jihadist fighters began to migrate to Afghanistan to join them on the battlefield. Later, influenced by Abu Musab al-Zarqawi, Osama Bin Laden, and Abdullah Azzam, the defensive jihad acquired a transnational character with amplified anti-Western sentiments. Of course, with years to come and with the numerous extremist organizations in the Middle East, with their different aspirations, aims, and philosophical and ideological foundations, contemporary Islam is not a singular, defined, unchangeable movement, rather it is a complex system of different contours (Leede S. d., 2018, pp. 13-16; Winter & Margolim, 2017, pp. 23-27).

According to the Islamic State's radical interpretation of Islam, specifically Salafism, the Muslim community under the reestablished Caliphate should be governed by the Sharia law with its strict, puritanical understanding. This non-Western society would be based on traditional Islam and would be offering an alternative way of life and divine salvation to those young Muslims who feel marginalized, estranged, and isolated in the West. Naturally, this authentic Islamic ideology rejects the idea of gender equality and liberation of women, and entails deeply-rooted gender segregation under restrictive hierarchical patriarchal order, precisely assigning only strictly domestic roles to women, glorifying the sedentary way of life (without political and social spheres), and thus, repressing their freedom of action, as well as, freedom of choice (MORENO, 2020, pp. 155-174).

It is almost paradoxical how the women defending the ways of Islam and the Prophet Muhammed throughout history are seen as heroic and are praised and honored for their courage, dedication, and sacrifice by Jihadist organizations and their leading circles but at the same time, they are never called for action or encouraged to take up arms and join male combatants of military jihad. Instead, the assigned roles of Muslim females in ISIS, as well as, other Islamist groups (For example, Al-Qaida, and Boko Haram) were predominantly supportive, those of sisters, mothers, and wives. The principal duty of those women was to raise new generations of Muslims according to the ideology of the Islamic State. With the existing severe gender demarcation, it took extreme pressure from the international and regional political and military opponents and growing competition with other jihadist groups for Daesh to realize the strategic advantages of ascribing women operational roles (Leede S. d., 2018, pp. 2-10; MORENO, 2020, pp. 155-174).

The Global military offensive against ISIS started soon after the organization declared the establishment of the Caliphate, in 2014. Initially, ISIS did not differentiate between sexes in its propaganda model and was addressing women as part of the general Muslim population, however gradually we see the rhetoric change in newly released editions of Dabiq – an online newspaper that conveyed the official view and stance of the organization. In the 7th edition of Dabiq, there are articles specifically designed to target women under the name 'To Our Sister' and 'From Our Sisters' and discuss themes like marriage and family life, religious duties, state-building, female migration, sense of belonging, etc. (Tarras-Wahlberg, 2016, p. 7) Already in 2015, the so-called moral police, all-female al-Khansa Brigade of Daesh published a 10-thousand-word manifesto, which alongside the traditional domestic occupations of women mentioned exceptions of carrying out professional roles, and that under certain circumstances, they were permitted to take up arms and participate in battles. The manifesto served as a 'legal authority for women to commit violence within the framework of defensive jihad' (Margolin, 2019, pp. 45-46). Similar messages resonated in Dabiq and al-Zawra Foundation throughout the following years, going as far as stressing that women too had an obligation and right to participate in military jihad in the al-Naba weekly newspaper in 2017. Another 2017 article, this time in Rumiyah 11th edition followed the loss of territorial control over Mosul and other strategically important lands by Daesh. This time, Islamic State was calling women to rise and join combat to sacrifice themselves for the Prophet Muhammed and Allah if it was required by defensive conditions (Winter & Margolim, 2017, pp. 23-27). The encouragement was echoed in the al-Naba publication under the name 'The obligation on women to engage in jihad against the enemies.' The article praised historic warrior women from the early 7th century naming them as examples to be followed by Muslim women. This rhetorical alteration of gender norms and roles in the jihadist extremist organization reflected the struggle of ISIS to compete with the US-led international military campaign. In early 2018, Islamic State went further and released a video recording called 'inside the Caliphate' capturing armed mujahid women in niqabs side by side with men as battlefield fighters. This footage served as conclusive evidence of the permissibility of female engagement in military actions and the breaking of ISIS with the jihadi convention (Margolin, 2019, pp. 45-46; Winter C., 2018).

Thousands of women have migrated into Syria and Iraq to join the Islamic State since the reestablishment of the Caliphate in 2014 (UN News, 2021; Cook & Vale, 2018, p. 3). These waves of migration demonstrated that women are just as willing and capable of participating in violent extremism as their male counterparts. The ideological and operational transformations of the roles and responsibilities of women inside the Islamist terrorist organizations resulted in the widespread partaking of radical females in global jihad (Winter C., 2018).

Roles and Responsibilities of ISIS Women

People migrating to a different country or a region to join a battlefield is not a new phenomenon, however, the high numbers of individuals who volunteered to move to Syria and Iraq and join the Islamic State in the conflict are unprecedented. This is conditioned by the Islamic State propaganda model as well. ISIS has been using numerous social and news media platforms and magazines for spreading its messages, speeches, images, and video footage as a part of its communication strategy directed at potential recruits and supporters of the group's ideology (Cook & Vale, 2018, pp. 7-10; Tarras-Wahlberg, 2016, pp. 5-19).

The percentage of women among those foreign fighters has been extraordinarily high. Already in 2015, only on the European Union territory, females compromised 18% of the total number of Daesh fighters (Bakker & Leede, 2015, p. 1). The ICSR 2018 report further supports earlier statistics declaring that out of the total number of foreign affiliates in Iraq and Syria 13% are women (Cook & Vale, 2018, p. 1). The United Nations 2021 article informs that among the residents of the al-Hol camp, more than 80% are women and children (UN News, 2021). Looking at the numbers, we can confidently state that Islamic State has been the most successful out of the jihadist extremist groups at managing the propaganda apparatus directed at potential members of Daesh, and indoctrinating, recruiting, and incorporating females into the organization.

What are the roles played by those female migrants once they join Islamic State? Of course, as in any other jihadist organization, first and foremost, they are designated to be seen as mothers and wives and carry out mostly domestic roles of supporting their husbands, raising their children, and taking care of the household. Therefore, the majority of the ISIS female recruits are confined to the strictly private sphere. The unmarried women who join ISIS are taken to live in the so-called 'Maqar'. The main function of 'Maqar' is to prepare female recruits for their future roles in the organization. Most of them are wedded to their male counterparts, others are organized and trained to serve the group objectives as supporters, facilitators, propagandists, recruiters, doctors, teachers, and so on (Affairs, 2017, pp. 25-29; Spencer A. N., 2016, pp. 74-98).

The professional roles of women are very important for the state-building efforts of the organization. That's why female recruits often run law-enforcement and administrative offices, are involved in fundraising, logistics, welfare activities, transportation of goods and weapons across borders, ensuring the information flow between local and foreign representatives and members of ISIS, etc. Although, even here, the private sphere is given priority over the public one. The al-Khansa manifesto, which permitted female recruits to take up professional roles and partake in state-building also mentions that their independent duties should not prevail over their domestic responsibilities as mothers and wives (Affairs, 2017, pp. 25-29; Spencer A. N., 2016, pp. 74-98).

Besides professional roles, ISIS female supporters in Syria, Iraq, and outside of their controlled territories, including the West have a great propaganda value. First of all, these women advocate for the Islamic State ideology on social media platforms, facilitate the female-centered propaganda, reach out to potential supporters and recruits, spread misinformation and amplify the stigmatization of Muslims within Western societies, glorify the use of violence as a tool of obtaining the victory over the enemies of Islamic ideology, and spread anti-Western narrative. These efforts are specifically directed at Western women, which makes this whole network a powerful tool in the hands of Daesh. On the one hand, the Islamic State as an organization with an ambition of establishing a legitimate state needs to create an illusion of a utopian state society with all the essential state-building assets present; this includes women, children, and family-building. On the other hand, Women abandoning their lives in the Western countries, committing themselves to Sharia law, going as far as expressing willingness to enlist together with Muslim males on the battlefield and declaring a readiness to perform acts of violence and death in the name of Jihad is used to show the West ISIS transnational terrorist ambitions and capabilities, as well as, shame men into taking up arms instead of violent women (Affairs, 2017, pp. 25-29).

What concerns operational roles and responsibilities, ISIS female recruits have long expressed enthusiasm to carry out military operations in a similar manner to men. Daesh was reluctant about using female combatants, however, under coordinated military pressure from the coalition forces, the organization started assigning operational roles to women inside and outside its controlled territory. The organization started deploying female combatants and suicide bombers on the territory of Libya already in 2016 (Stoter, 2016). Women suicide bombers were also actively participating in the military battle for Mosul in 2017 (News, 2017). The 2017 ICSVE publication (Almohammad & Speckhard) mentions three ISIS-affiliated women-only battalions – al-Khansa, Khadiha Bintu kwalid, and Aumahat al-Moaminin. The data on those military units show around 800 women who were professionally trained. Another women-only military component is al-Zarqawi Battalion with at least 480 female fighters. Those armed units are responsible for educating, training, and preparing ISIS women recruits to serve the organization as operatives, militants, moles and spies, killers, morality police, and suicide terrorists (2017, pp. 6-16).

Even though ISIS actively uses female recruits in operational roles for its ideological and strategic objectives, it should be mentioned that there is no guarantee that this ongoing transformation of gender norms, roles, and responsibilities inside the organization will continue after the extreme pressures from its political and military opponents weakens and Islamic State regains its influence and power positions in the region.

2. The Threat Posed by ISIS Women

Strategic Advantages of Invisibility

Using female recruits as perpetrators of violence and death is advantageous for extremist organizations because women are the least-likely suspects of terrorism. The misperception of terrorist women is preconditioned by a widespread stereotype of females as peaceful, gentle, nurturing creatures to the point where it is seen as deviant and abnormal if a woman chooses to perform an act of violence. The notion of femininity is actively supported by media outlets that use specific language narratives in news, describing female terrorists as vulnerable, naïve, lured, and brainwashed by extremist organizations. Due to this misconception, the motivations of women who engage in violent actions are often perceived as preconditioned by personal tragedies, familiar connections, and grievances, instead of a commitment to a radical ideology, wanting to deliver a powerful political message or express protest against something (EAGER, 2008, pp. 3-4).

The invisibility of violent women gives the jihadist organization number of tactical advantages. A terrorist attack carried out by a female is stealthier. They can easily evade being searched by the representatives of law enforcement and airport security even. That is preconditioned by the fact that women don't stimulate suspicion to the level men do, thus having a natural camouflage and finding it way simpler to effectively blend in masses. This, on the one hand, creates an element of surprise and, on the other hand, plays a role of a shock factor, causing panic, psychological effects, and intimidation in the general public. The shock factor itself guarantees the growth of group publicity (as the organization sends a powerful message through its female terrorists) and results in a higher level of combatants as a catalyst for Muslim males to partake in military actions, and an upsurge of recruits from inside and outside of ISIS-controlled territories (Zedalis, 2004, p. 7; LEEDE & et.al, 2017, pp. 26-28).

Female terrorists erode a sense of safety in societies. If previously the deployment of women for different terrorist acts was unimaginable, now when female terrorists (precisely, female suicide bombers) became a widely used practice for Islamist groups, it creates a fear factor in the population by demonstrating that women are also capable of and willing to commit acts of terror and death. Further, the use of female recruits benefits the group by attracting more female supporters (LEEDE & et.al, 2017, pp. 26-28). Women who may not engage in military actions or acts of terror instead might play important operational roles online and contribute to the organization by spreading its ideology and propaganda messages and indoctrinating new members and supporters through well-designed online networks and direct targeting (Bigio & Vogelstein, 2019, pp. 3-5)

It needs to be emphasized that the invisibility of ISIS female recruits on the frontlines and leadership circles of the organization does not necessarily mean they are passive participants. Even nowadays, with the limited data researchers and field experts rely on, there is little information about the influences and power positions Daesh female fighters possess. There is also a factor of deception playing an important role. We cannot exclude the possibility of ISIS keeping its female fighters hidden to mislead the public. The organizational leadership may want to gain an upper hand over its opponents and competitors in the region and worldwide by keeping the operational proficiency and strategic advantages hidden until the need arises for their employment on the battlefield (CUNNINGHAM, 2010, p. 187).

A Lack of Gender Lens in Designing Counter-Terrorism Strategies

There is a tendency to neglect the threat posed by radicalized women, ISIS, and other jihadist organizations female recruits, and terrorists on the level of policymakers and state institutions responsible for designing effective counter-terrorism strategies and initiatives. The misconception and misinterpretation of female terrorism allow extremist organizations to fully utilize the tactical advantages and propaganda value of recruited women. Therefore, a need has long emerged to implement a gender lens in preventive measures against violent extremism (CUNNINGHAM, 2010, pp. 185-187).

The United Nations Security Council Resolution 2242 (2015) became a benchmark document that advocated and called for gender mainstreaming and alteration of female involvement in devising and implementing CVE programs. Since then, despite the slow process, women-centered initiatives have been adopted by numerous states all around the world. The main mission of those gender-oriented initiatives should be protecting and empowering women worldwide. Still, considering the evolving operational roles and responsibilities of radical females in extremist organizations, there is a clear need for more in-depth research and cooperation among governments, civil societies, and field experts for developing all-inclusive, case-appropriate de-radicalization and counter-terrorism approaches. This entails the correct assessment of threats posed by violent women, as well as, female supporters, propagandists, facilitators, and female returnees (Patel & Westermann, 2018, pp. 73-76).

Currently, policies countering violent extremism and radicalization are characterized by relative ineffectiveness due to their limited scope and impracticality. Patel and Westermann (2018, pp. 76-80) identify prevailing gender stereotypes, securitization, and marginalization of women as the three main causal factors for this. The media perceptions of women as non-violent, nurturing, domestic creatures resonate within the counter-violent extremism programs as well. The denial of radical females as goal-oriented, independent parties who are active decision-makers contributed to the centralization of the "sisters, mothers, wives" narrative by governments and civil societies and again, assigned women to a private sphere and domestic roles. Therefore, what we see is invalidating the importance of women's contribution to violent extremism, society, and state-building. Moreover, Women with familial ties with men connected to Islamic State often become victims of ostracism and alienation in their communities. These women are often approached by state authorities for intelligence determinations, which provides only short-term results at eliminating the security risks. Instead, what needs to be put forward is the development of long-term solutions, including inclusive, well-designed initiatives directed at safeguarding the integration of those women into their societies and ensuring their access to all kinds of resources their communities have to offer, including emotional, financial and healthcare support, educational and occupational opportunities, community engagement, etc. Furthermore, specific community-based legislative and policy initiatives, in this case for Muslim communities, often end up targeting and marginalizing them. Similarly, CVE policies tend to marginalize women from the public sphere, specifically, social and political lives. This provides incentives for the emergence of the "us versus them" attitude among the society members, which may expose Muslim women to hate crimes, xenophobia, and islamophobia within their communities. And this plays as an advantage for the widespread terrorist propaganda (Patel & Westermann, 2018, pp. 76-80).

Several recommendations and considerations have been issued for the future development of counter-terrorism strategies (Saltman & smith, 2015, pp. 70-71; Zeiger & Bhulai, 2016, pp. 181-183; Davis, 2020, pp. 7-10; affairs, 2017, pp. 39-42). It is crucial for the states and policymakers to increase gender awareness and orientation while designing CVE programs. Precisely, those initiatives should be directed at women and identify the push and pull factors that make them vulnerable to ISIS propaganda. Daesh uses a highly-gendered approach to designing radicalization tactics, elaborating on the cultural isolation and identity crisis of young Muslim women in the West by amplifying the "us versus them" narrative and portraying western feminism as exclusively "white" while also offering an alternative in the face of the utopian Islamic society where they can reunite with their true persona according to the will of Allah (affairs, 2017, pp. 39-42).

Reducing the information vacuum and effectiveness of the radicalization approaches is achievable based on promoting critical thinking and increasing youth awareness of extremist narrative and propaganda via comprehensive and all-inclusive educational agendas and good practices (Saltman & smith, 2015, pp. 70-71). Researching and analyzing the gender dimension of CVE policies and programs is crucial, as well as, strengthening partnerships between governments, international and regional organizations, civil societies, and the private sector to promote female empowerment and enhance the capacity of female participants in counter-terrorism initiatives (Zeiger & Bhulai, 2016, pp. 181-183; affairs, 2017, pp. 39-42).

CONCLUSION

In this paper, we discussed the complex phenomenon of female radicalization based on a case study of ISIS.

Islamic State emerged as an essential regional and international security threat in 2014 after the organization declared the re-establishment of the Caliphate with Abu Bakr al Baghdadi in a leading position. Even though the response of international political actors was not immediate, soon enough, after assessing the ambitions and capabilities of ISIS, a U.S.-led global military campaign was evoked.

The extreme pressure from the external forces and regional competitors resulted in big territorial losses for the organization, which provided incentives for the transformation and evolution of gender roles inside the Islamic State. The gender norms, roles, and responsibilities in military jihad started gradually changing according to the present needs of human capital and resources of the organization and soon we witnessed the breaking of Daesh with the jihadi convention, which was demonstrated by developing and enhancing operational roles of female recruits, by intensified training and preparing women for the battlefield and by establishing all-female elite brigades and military units. However, still, the deployment of female fighters by ISIS in times of heightened security struggle does not guarantee a continued change in the organization's perception of gender norms in the near future.

The paper also highlighted the common pattern of invisibility of the vision and perception of radical women as active decision-makers capable of being perpetrators of violence and death, and rational beings dedicated to extremist ideologies among the general public, media outlets describing terrorist acts performed by women, and contemporary counter-terrorism strategies and initiatives. The widespread stereotype of non-violent women is misleading, hinders the potential of designing practical and operative de-radicalization approaches and programs, and prevents us from understanding the full face and potential of feminine violence.

Therefore, the research concluded that to ensure effective prevention and elimination of security threats posed by the continuous radicalization, indoctrination, and recruitment of women by ISIS, devising all-inclusive, comprehensive, gender-oriented, case-appropriated counter-terrorism strategies, tactics, tools, and measures is highly required.

REFERENCES

Aaronson, M. (2014). Intervention in Us foreign policy from Bush to Obama. In M. Bentley & J. Holland (Eds.), Obama's Foreign Policy: Ending the War on Terror (p. 124). Routledge Studies in US Foreign Policy.

Affairs, P. D. (2017). *Radicalisation and violent extremism – focus on women: How women become radicalised, and how to empower them to prevent radicalization.* European Union. Retrieved from https://www.europarl.europa.eu/supporting-analyses

Al-Istrabadi, F. (2018). Regional Constraints on the U.S. Confrontation of ISIS. In *The Future of ISIS: Regional and International Implications* (pp. 173–174). The Brookings Institution.

Almohammad, A. H., & Speckhard, A. (2017). *The Operational Ranks and Roles of Female ISIS Operatives: From Assassins and Morality Police to Spies and Suicide Bombers.* ICSVE Research Reports. Retrieved January 9, 2022, from http://www.icsve.org/research-reports/the-operational-ranks-and-roles-of-female-isis-operatives-from-assassins-and-morality-police-to-spies-and-suicide-bombers/

Anonymous. (2001, October 11). *Bush on State of War.* Retrieved January 4, 2022, from https://www.washingtonpost.com/wp-srv/nation/specials/attacked/transcripts/bush_text101101.html

Anonymous. (2001, September 20). *President Bush Addresses the Nation.* Retrieved January 4, 2022, from https://www.washingtonpost.com/wp-srv/nation/specials/attacked/transcripts/bushaddress_092001.html

Antunez Moreno, J. C. (2020, November 12). Western DAESH Women: Ideology. *Profile and Motivation.*, *6*(2), 155–174. doi:10.18847/1.12.9

Archive. (n.d.). *The Global War on Terrorism: The First 100 Days*. Retrieved January 4, 2022, from https://2001-2009.state.gov/s/ct/rls/wh/6947.htm

Auchter, J. (2012). Gendering terror: Discourses of terrorism and writing woman-as-agent. *International Feminist Journal of Politics*, *14*(1), 125. doi:10.1080/14616742.2011.619780

Auer, M., Sutcliffe, J., & Lee, M. (2018). White Widow': Using Intersectionality to Uncover Complex Representations of Female Terrorism in News Media. *Media, War & Conflict*.

Bakker, E., & Leede, S. D. (2015). European Female Jihadists in Syria: Exploring and Under-Researched Topic. Hague: The International Centre for Counter-Terrorism.

Banai, H. (2018). U.S.-Led International Response to ISIS. In *The Future of Isis: Regional and International Implications* (pp. 152–157). Brookings Institution Press.

Berko, A., & Erez, E. (2007). Gender, Palestinian Women, and Terrorism: Women's Liberation or Oppression? *Studies in Conflict and Terrorism*, *30*(6), 493–519. doi:10.1080/10576100701329550

Bigio, J., & Vogelstein, R. (2019). *Women and Terrorism: Hidden Threats, Forgotten Patterns*. The Council on Foreign Relations.

Blanchard, C. M., & Humud, C. E. (2018). *The Islamic State and U.S. Policy*. Congressional Research Service.

Bloom, M. (2011). Bombshells: Women and Terror. *Gender Issues*, *28*(1-2), 1–21. doi:10.100712147-011-9098-z

Bloom, M. (2016). The changing nature of women in extremism and political violence. *Freedom from Fear*, 40-54.

Borum, R. (2003). *Understanding the Terrorist Mindset*. Academic Press.

Brown, K. E., & Saeed, T. (2017). Radicalization and counter-radicalization at British universities: Muslim encounters and alternatives. *Ethnic and Racial Studies*, 152–168.

Burgess, P. a. (2012). Human security. *Contemporary Security and Strategy*, 89-105.

Buzan, B., Wæver, O., & Wilde, J. D. (1998). *Security: A new framework for analysis*. Lynne Rienner Publishers.

Cook, J., & Vale, G. (2018). *From Daesh to 'Diaspora': Tracing the Women and Minors of Islamic State*. International Center for the Study of Radicalization.

Cunningham, K. J. (2010). Cross-Regional Trends in Female Terrorism. *Studies in Conflict and Terrorism*, *26*, 171–195.

Cunningham, K. J. (2007). Countering Female Terrorism. *Studies in Conflict and Terrorism*, 123.

Dalton, A., & Asal, V. (2011). Is It Ideology or Desperation: Why Do Organizations Deploy Women in Violent Terrorist Attacks? *Studies in Conflict & Terrorism*, 802-819.

Davis, J. (2013). Evolution of the Global Jihad: Female Suicide Bombers in Iraq. *Studies in Conflict and Terrorism*, *36*(4), 279–291. doi:10.1080/1057610X.2013.763598

Davis, J. (2017). *Women in Modern Terrorism: From Liberation Wars to global jihad and the islamic state*. Rowman & Littlefield.

Davis, J. (2020). The future of the Islamic State's Women: assessing their potential threat. ICCT Policy Brief.

Davis, J., West, L., & Amarasingam, A. (2020). Measuring Impact, Uncovering Bias? Citation Analysis of Literature on Women in Terrorism. *Perspectives on Terrorism*, 9.

Deylami, S. S. (2012). Saving the Enemy. *International Feminist Journal of Politics*, 1–18.

Dunn, D. H. (2005). Bush, 11 September and the Conflicting Strategies of the 'War on Terrorism'. *Irish Studies in International Affairs*, *16*, 11–33. Retrieved January 4, 2022, from http://www.jstor.org/stable/30001932

Eager, P. W. (2008). Women and Political Violence. In From Freedom Fighters to Terrorists (pp. 3-4). Ashgate.

Eager, P. W. (2008). From Freedom Fighters to Terrorists: Women and Political Violence. *Journal of Peace Research*.

Galica, N. (2020). *Lifting the Veil: The Impact of Framing on Sentencing Disparities Between Males and Females Convicted of Terrorism since the Rise of ISIS*. The John Marshall Law School.

Gentry, C. (2010). The relationship between new social movement theory and terrorism studies: The role of leadership, membership, ideology and gender. *Terrorism and Political Violence*.

Goepner, E. W. (2016, March 1). Measuring the Effectiveness of America eness of America's War on T ar on Terror. *The US Army War College Quarterly Parameters*, *46*, 107–108. doi:10.55540/0031-1723.2828

Huckerby, J. (2015). When Women Become Terrorists. *The New York Times*.

Hudson, D. (2014, September 10). *President Obama: "We Will Degrade and Ultimately Destroy ISIL"*. Retrieved from https://obamawhitehouse.archives.gov/blog/2014/09/10/president-Obama-we-will-degrade-and-ultimately-destroy-isil

Jacques, K., & Taylor, P. J. (2009). Female Terrorism: A Review. *Terrorism and Political Violence*, *21*(3), 499–515. doi:10.1080/09546550902984042

Khalil, L. (2019). *Behind the veil: Women in jihad after the caliphate*. Lowy Institute.

Lax, F. (2020). *Female terrorists and extremists: An exploratory study*. Johns Hopkins University.

Lead Inspector General for Operation Inherent Resolve Quarterly Report to the United States Congress | July 1, 2021 – September 30, 2021. (2021, November 4). Retrieved January 8, 2022, from www.dodig.mil: https://www.dodig.mil/Reports/Lead-Inspector-General-Reports/Article/2833944/lead-inspector-general-for-operation-inherent-resolve-quarterly-report-to-the-u/

Leede, S. D. (2017). *Radicalisation and violent extremism –focus on women: How women become radicalised, and how to empower them to prevent radicalisation.* European Union; the Policy Department of the Citizen's Rigths and Constitutional Affairs. Retrieved January 5, 2022, from https://www.europarl.europa.eu/supporting-analyses

Leede, S. d. (2018). *Women in Jihad: A Historical Perspective*. ICCT Policy Brief.

Leede, S. d. (2018). *Women in Jihad: A Historical Perspective*. ICCT Policy Brief. doi:10.19165/2018.2.06

Leede, S., & Bakker, E. (2015). *European female jihadists in Syria: exploring an under-researched topic*. ICCT.

Loken, M., & Zelenz, A. (2017). Explaining extremism: Western women in Daesh. *European Journal of International Security*, 3.

Lughod, L. A. (2002). Do Muslim Women Really Need Saving? Anthropological Reflections on Cultural Relativism and Its Others. *American Anthropologist, 104*(3), 783–790. doi:10.1525/aa.2002.104.3.783

MacKenzie, M. (2009). Securitization and Desecuritization: Female Soldiers and the Reconstruction of Women in Post-Conflict Sierra Leone. *Security Studies: Feminist Contributions*, 241-261.

Margolin, D. (2019). The Changing Roles of Women in Violent Islamist Groups. In *Perspectives on the future of women, gender, & violent extremism* (pp. 45–46). The George Washington University.

Merriam-Webster. (n.d.). *Radical*. Retrieved November 20, 2021, from Merriam-Webster.com dictionary: https://www.merriam-webster.com/dictionary/radical

Miller, M. J., & Stefanova, B. (2007). The War on Terror: The second Bush Administration. In B. M. Rajaee (Ed.), *The War on Terror in Comparative Perspective: US Security and Foreign Policy after 9/11* (pp. 90–93). Palgrave Macmillan.

Mironova, V. (2019). Is the Future of ISIS Female? *The New York Times*.

Nacos, B. L. (2005). The Portrayal of Female Terrorists in the Media: Similar Framing Patterns in the News Coverage of Women in Politics and in Terrorism. *Studies in Conflict and Terrorism, 28*(5), 435–451. doi:10.1080/10576100500180352

Ndung'u, I., Sigsworth, R., & Yenwong-Fai, U. (2017). *Violent extremism in Kenya: Why women are a priority*. Academic Press.

News, B. (2017, July 4). *Battle for Mosul: Fierce clashes as IS uses suicide bombers*. Retrieved January 9, 2022, from bbc.com: https://www.bbc.com/news/world-middle-east-40489816

News, U. N. (2021, February 28). *UNICEF urges repatriation of all children in Syria's Al-Hol camp following deadly fire*. Retrieved November 20, 2021, from https://news.un.org/en/story/2021/02/1085982

O'Rourke, L. A. (2009). What's Special about Female Suicide Terrorism? *Security Studies, 18*(4), 681–682. doi:10.1080/09636410903369084

Parashar, S. (2011). Gender, Jihad, and Jingoism: Women as perpetrators, planners, and patrons of militancy in Kashmir. *Studies in Conflict and Terrorism, 34*(4), 295–317. doi:10.1080/1057610X.2011.551719

Patel, S., & Westermann, J. (2018). Women and Islamic-State Terrorism: An Assessment of How Gender Perspectives Are Integrated in Countering Violent Extremism Policy and Practices. *Security Challenges, 14*(2), 73-83. Retrieved from https://www.jstor.org/stable/26558022

Patkin, T. (2004). *Explosive Baggage: Female Palestinian Suicide Bombers and the Rhetoric of Emotion*. Woman and Language.

Rajaee, B. (2007). The Bush and US policy after 9/11. In M. J. Miller & B. Stefanova (Eds.), *The War on Terror in Comparative Perspective: US Security and Foreign Policy after 9/11* (p. 159). Palgrave Macmillan.

Rajaee, B. (2007). The Bush Doctrine and US policy after 9/11. In M. J. Miller & B. Stefano (Eds.), *The War on Terror in Comparative Perspective: US Security and Foreign Policy after 9/11* (pp. 159–160). Palgram Macmillan.

Rajaee, B. M. (2007). US Foreign Policy and Radical Islam. In M. J. Miller & B. Stefanova (Eds.), *US Security and Foreign Policy after 9/11* (p. 69). Palgrave Macmillan.

Saltman, E. M., & Smith, M. (2015). Key Recommendations. In *Till Martyrdom Do Us Part* (pp. 70-71). Institute for Strategic Dialogue .

Saltman, E. M., & Smith, M. (2015). *'Till Martyrdom Do Us Part': Gender and the ISIS Phenomenon*. Institute for Strategic Dialogue.

Shapiro, L. R., & Maras, M.-H. (2018). Women's Radicalization to Religious Terrorism: An Examination of ISIS Cases in the United States. *Studies in Conflict and Terrorism*, 1.

Shepherd, L. J. (2013). *Critical Approaches to Security: an introduction to theories and methods*. Routledge. doi:10.4324/9780203076873

Shepherd, L. J. (2017). *The Role of the WPS Agenda in Countering Violent Extremism*. The Strategist.

Sjoberg, L., & Gentry, C. E. (2007). *Mothers, Monsters, Whores: Women's Violence in Global Politics*. Zed Books.

Sjoberg, L., & Gentry, C. E. (2008). Reduced to Bad Sex: Narratives of Violent Women from the Bible to the War on Terror. *International Relations, 22*(1), 5–23. doi:10.1177/0047117807087240

Sjoberg, L., & Gentry, C. E. (2016). It's complicated: Looking closely at women in violent extremism. *Georgetown Journal of International Affairs*, 23-30.

Speckhard, A., & Shajkovci, A. (2017). *Beware the Women of ISIS: There Are Many, and They May Be More Dangerous Than the Men*. The Daily Beast.

Spencer, A. (2015). European female jihadists in Syria: Exploring an under-researched. *Journal of Strategic Security, 9*(3), 79–87.

Spencer, A. N. (2016). The Hidden Face of Terrorism: An Analysis of the Women in Islamic State. *Journal of Strategic Security, 9*(3), 74–98. doi:10.5038/1944-0472.9.3.1549

State, U. D. (n.d.). *The Global Coalition To Defeat ISIS*. Retrieved January 9, 2022, from www.state.gov: https://www.state.gov/about-us-the-global-coalition-to-defeat-isis/

Stoter, B. (2016, November 16). *As IS loses power, will group tap women jihadis to fight?* Retrieved January 9, 2022, from al-Monitor.com: https://www.al-monitor.com/originals/2016/11/islamic-state-women-role-fighting-syria-iraq.html

Talbot, R. (2000). Myths in the Representation of Women Terrorists. *Eire-Ireland, 35*(3-4), 165–186. doi:10.1353/eir.2000.0032

Tarras-Wahlberg, L. (2016). *Seven Promises of ISIS to its Female Recruits.* ICSVE Research Report. Retrieved from http://www.icsve.org/research-reports/seven-promises-of-isis-to-its-female-recruits/

UNSC. (2015, October 13). *Security Council Unanimously Adopts Resolution 2242 (2015) to Improve Implementation of Landmark Text on Women, Peace, Security Agenda.* Retrieved January 10, 2022, from un.org: https://www.un.org/press/en/2015/sc12076.doc.htm

UNSC. (2021). *Twenty-eighth report of the Analytical Support and Sanctions Monitoring Team submitted pursuant to resolution 2368 (2017) concerning ISIL (Da'esh), Al-Qaida and associated individuals and entities*. United Nations Security Coincil.

Wæver, O. (1993). *Securitization and desecuritization*. Centre for Peace and Conflict Research.

West, J. (2005). Feminist IR and the Case of the "Black Widows": Reproducing Gendered Divisions. *Innovations: Journal of Politics*.

Winter, C. (2018). *ISIS, Women and Jihad: Breaking With Convention*. Tony Blair Institute for Global Change.

Winter, C., & Margolim, D. (2017, August). The Mujahidat Dilemma: Female Combatants and the Islamic State. *The Mujahidat Dilemma: Female Combatants and the Islamic State, 10*(7), 23–27.

Zedalis, D. D. (2004). *Female Suicide Bombers*. The Strutegic Studies Institute. doi:10.21236/ADA424180

Zeiger, N. C., & Bhulai, R. (2016). Conclusion: Program and Policy Recommendations. In A Man's World? Exploring the Roles of Women in Counter Terrorism and Violent Extremism (pp. 181-183). Hedayah and The Global Center on Cooperative Security.

KEY TERMS AND DEFINITIONS

Radicalization: The process by which an individual or a group comes to adopt increasingly radical views in opposition to a political, social, or religious status quo.

Terrorism: the deliberate killing of innocent people, at random, to spread fear through a whole population and force the hand of its political leaders.

Violent Extremism: A form of extremism that condones and enacts violence with ideological or deliberate intent, such as religious or political violence.

Women, Gender, and Terrorism: Explores women's relationship with terrorism, with a keen eye on the political, gender, racial, and cultural dynamics of the contemporary world.

Chapter 15
Organized Crime as One of the Main Reflections of Terrorism in the Modern World

Irakli Kervalishvili
Georgian Technical University, Georgia

ABSTRACT

At the end of the 20th century, security concern went beyond interstate cooperation and disarmament issues. With the development of the globalization process, organized crime became a bigger topic. According to several estimates, since the 1980s, the number of criminal acts, having been carried out within organized crime, has increased by 5% annually. Members of organized criminal groups gain huge income. By estimates, which were presented in 1999, the total amount of so-called dirty money in the world was from 500 to 1500 billion dollars per year, which was equal to 5% of the world GDP during this period. In 2009 it was estimated to generate $870 billion – an amount equal to 1.5% of global GDP for this period. As of 2016, transnational crime was a $1.6 trillion to $2.2 trillion annual "business."

INTRODUCTION

It is recognized that organized crime is one of the most complex and dangerous types of criminal activity that affects the economic, political, legal and moral spheres of society. It poses one of the main threats to the modern international society, which is facilitated by the development of transport and information communications, the simplified movement of capital, the transparency of state borders, the growth of labor migration and other processes related to globalization. Organized crime in the modern world is becoming more and more transnational in nature, in particular, the spheres of activity of various criminal organizations go beyond the borders of any one state. In the last quarter of the last century, the global economy created favorable conditions for the further development of organized crime. The unprecedented ease of international trade, financing, communications, and movement, along with economic development and an increase in the quality of life, have provided ample opportunities for criminals to conduct illegal businesses. Simply put, illegal goods can be produced on one continent and

DOI: 10.4018/978-1-6684-5311-7.ch015

distributed through another to a third. One of the main tasks of all international organizations related to this field is to fight organized crime, because taking into account the global scale of this type of crime, the measures taken by individual countries are insufficient and ineffective. The United Nations is actively involved in measures against organized crime. In terms of international cooperation, the International Criminal Police Organization - INTERPOL plays a special role (Chitadze, 2016). It has a large data base and is the main body for information retrieval, processing and analysis of processes related to organized crime. Interpol conducts global monitoring of organized crime and coordinates international investigations. In relation to this type of crime, Interpol's function is to lead cooperation between member countries, to ensure the exchange of information about organized crime and related corruption between all national and international agencies operating in this field. As for the second, important police organization - Europol, the main purpose of its creation is the fight against organized crime (Chitadze, 2016). Despite the magnitude of the struggle, the phenomenon of organized crime is understudied. Information on transnational criminal markets and trends is rather scarce. With rare exceptions, the majority of research on the subject focuses on one specific country or geographic unit and does not reflect the global picture. Considering all these circumstances, the phenomenon of organized crime is a subject of constant discussion in both scientific and law enforcement fields. At the same time, discussion is taking place both on the institution in general, and on its individual form or directions of activity. Considering these circumstances, it is particularly important to study the concept, origin and development of organized crime, the existing experience of combating it based on legislative and practical methods.

One of the fields of activity of organized crime is caused by the fact that several goods are not taxed. The illegal transfer of these goods from one country to another brings considerable revenue to the members of the groups of organized crime. Other areas of organized crime are connected with illegal arms supplies, illegal activity in the conflict zones, including recruitment of mercenaries, etc. Processes of privatization in the countries of Central and Eastern Europe have also drawn attention.

This problem already holds a specific place because of the scales but has received an additional boost in connection with globalization and the openness of borders generated by it. Considerable streams of drugs go via post-soviet space from Asia, the USA faces the same problem from Colombia and some other countries in Latin America. In general drug trafficking within the second decade of the XXI Century, by different estimates, has increased tens of times, giving more than 500% of profit (Chitadze, 2016).

Fighting against drug distribution has become one of the global problems of the contemporary period. At the same time, their main production is arranged in countries with badly developed economies and a set of internal conflicts, with the military and quasi-military regime. The chief suppliers of opium poppy on the market today are Afghanistan and Burma today. By the estimates given by J. Goldstein, the production of opium from 1998 to 1999 has increased in Afghanistan twice and has made three-quarters of the world's production. More and more synthetic drugs which don't demand vegetable raw materials are widely adopted (Goldstein, 2011).

The Concept of Transnational Organized Crime

Organized crime is taking on a transnational character all over the world. At the threshold of the 21st century, transnational organized crime, with its scale and destructive impact, has become a real threat to the entire humanity with its destructive impact, as well as its scale.

1. Transnational organized crime creates great problems for the state and society, prevents the provision of human security and the protection of law and order by the state, the resolution of internal conflicts and their prevention, as well as the prevention of terrorism, the spread of weapons and the criminal exploitation of people.
2. Transnational organized crime is a phenomenon that hinders the socio-economic development of any state, while its scale is constantly expanding. It can not only seize new markets, but also undermine the economic security of the state, especially if this state is a developing country with a transition economy. In addition, transnational crime has a global character and no country or region is immune from its influence.
3. Criminologists strive to adequately assess the extent and quality of the threat posed by rapidly growing transnational organized crime. For this, they consider this phenomenon not as a modification of "traditional" forms of organized crime, but as a fundamentally new type of activity that allows organized criminal structures to quickly increase criminal income, thereby threatening the economic stability of the state and the development of democratic institutions. At the same time, transnational groups demonstratively present their capabilities and relative immunity from law enforcement structures.
4. It is possible to single out common and optional characteristics that are similar to all organized formations of criminals and special features that characterize transnational organized criminal activity.

Common Signs of Organized Crime

- the stability of a specific criminal organization, which is manifested in its long-term activity and in the repeated commission of similar crimes;
- redistribution of roles among the members of the organization according to the vertical (with separation of the leadership ring) and horizontal (criminal specialization) principles;
- a hierarchical structure, the highest link of which is represented by at least one person who directs the activities of the organization;
- directing efforts to specific types of criminal activity (the bigger the organization, the wider the circle of the mentioned types);
- Existence of the goal of obtaining the maximum income in the minimum time frame;
- functioning of the social mutual aid system among the members of the group (for example, the money collecting system);
- Active opposition to law enforcement bodies, including the use of corruption mechanisms;
- strict internal discipline, the existence of a defined code of conduct, the violators of which are subject to punitive measures.

Optional Features

- Isolation of the head of the organization from specific criminal activity: he does not participate in the commission of the crime, often does not have a direct connection with its perpetrators, and remains the ideological inspirer of the activity;
- use of mechanisms of legalization ("laundering") of criminal income;
- Selection of members according to national and clan signs;

- Use of new technical means in criminal activity.

Features that are characteristic only of transnational organized crime:

- Conduct of organized criminal activities in more than one state;
- Carrying out organized criminal activity in one state, but carrying out its preparation, planning or control in another state;
- Conducting organized criminal activity in one state, but with the participation of an organized group that carries out criminal activity in more than one state;
- Organized criminal activity will be carried out in one state by presenting its main results in another state.

According to the UN Convention on Transnational Organized Crime, transnational organized crime includes crimes related to the criminal exploitation of human beings, such as: human trafficking, organized prostitution, trafficking in human organs and illegal migration. The development of transnational organized crime is based on the following three factors:

- globalization of the economy;
- improvement of global communication systems;
- Increase in immigration processes (Chitidze, 2020).

To operate with the concept of transnational organized crime, first of all, we need to define its essence and main characteristics. The right approach to the definition allows us to really assess the scale of the threat, to determine the ways of transnational organized crime formation, the reasons for its emergence and existence. This, in turn, helps the international community to unite the efforts of all states and develop a complex of adequate measures to counter transnational crime. Unfortunately, the awareness of the global threat caused by the mentioned event and the need for coordinated action against it emerged only recently - at the turn of the XXI century. Therefore, in spite of separate attempts to describe and classify transnational organized crime, until recently, they did not develop a clear definition and comprehensive characterization of it. Transnational organized crime has a hypertrophic growth tendency and is a force that threatens the socio-economic development of any state. It not only expands its activities, but also destroys the economic infrastructure of the society and threatens the state security, the implementation of democratic reforms, first of all in the developed and transition economy countries, which belong to Georgia. The global and aggressive nature of transnational organized crime forced the international community to devote all its efforts to the development of mechanisms for the prevention of this negative event and the fight against it, because not a single state or region is immune from it.

ORGANIZED CRIMINAL FORMATIONS

The organized criminal formations differ from each other, they have both geographical and national specific character and they are distinguished according to the degree of globalization: they can act within the limits of one city, country and even exceed the borders of individual states, becoming transnational.

It should be mentioned, that under the common name "organized criminal formations" in the literature are united two types of collective criminal subjects:

- Criminal organization—all forms of the associations of the persons, directly directed toward to the committing of a crime, conducting the criminal activity: the organized criminal groups, gangs, Illegal Armed Formations and so forth;
- Criminal community (association)—forming, which unites the first type of organizations, which organizes, coordinates, and guides their activity, ensures the interests of the criminal association; also it can fulfill the functions of "criminal trade union", ensuring the social protection of its members. As a rule, such associations are not directly involved in criminal activities, turning these functions to smaller organizations, which are under their influence.

PREVALENCE OF THE ORGANIZED CRIMINALITY

The scale of the activity of organized criminality is extremely high and damage from it is enormous. In the report of national reconnaissance Intelligence Council of USA "Global trend of development of humanity until 2015" is mentioned: "Accessible to us data show, that they early incomes from the organized criminal activity comprise: 100-300 billion of dollars from the trade-in narcotics; 10-12 billion of dollars from the flood of toxic and other dangerous withdrawals; 9 billion of dollars from the embezzlements of vehicles in the USA and Europe; 7 billion of dollars from the displacement through the boundaries of illegal migrants; about Billions of dollars from the violation of rights to intellectual property by the illegal copying of video films, computer programs, and other goods"(Intelligence Council of USA, 2015). Harm from corruption is approximately 500 billion dollars, which is about 1% of the world GNP. This damage is the consequence of retarding economic growth, a decrease in foreign investments, and a reduction in profits. For example, according to the data of the European Bank for Reconstruction and the Developments, firms, which carry out business in Russia, spend from 4 to 8 percent of their annual earnings on bribes (Dolgovaya, 2005).

TRANSNATIONAL CRIMINAL ORGANIZATIONS

The organized criminality sufficiently frequently established international contacts; however, during the centuries these connections were irregular and usually short-term till the middle of XX. Their bloom began only after the internationalization of the economy and the propagation of trade by the illegal goods (narcotics, weapons, etc.) led to significant income growth from the trans-border criminal operations.

Following Basic Transnational Criminal Organizations Can Be Listed

- Italian Mafia, which is the union of several criminal organizations: "Ndrangheta" from Calabria. In the article "Move over, Cosa Nostra", published by *The Guardian*, on 8 June 2006, within this period this group included approximately 100 families, totaling between 4,000 and 5,000 members in Reggio Calabria. Other estimates mention 6,000-7,000 men; worldwide there might be some 10,000 members. In the FBI report under the name "Italian Organized Crime", there are the following dates about other criminal groups in Italy: "*Kamorra*" from Naples Consists of 111 families and totals more than 6 700 members. "*Nuova* Sacra Corona Unita" from Puglia consists of about 50 clans with approximately 2,000 members and finally the Mafia "Cosa *Nostra*" *of Sicily* 25,000 members total, with 250,000 affiliates worldwide. There are more than 3,000 members and affiliates in the U.S., scattered mostly throughout the major cities in the Northeast, the Midwest, California, and the South. Their largest presence centers around New York, southern New Jersey, and Philadelphia (Chitadze, 2016).

The basic source of income for the Italian Mafia is the trade of narcotics; however, it is occupied by other illegal operations too. Particularly: Smuggling of weapons, alcohol, tobacco, taking hostages, and so forth. In the '90s of the XX century, the influence of the Italian Mafia because of the matched efforts of the law-enforcement agencies of Italy was somewhat reduced, however, it continues to preserve one of the leading places in the list of the criminal organizations in the World.

In the article of the journal LE MONDE: "Atlas der Globalisierung - Die Welt von morgen": Kriminalitätohne Grenzen is pointed out about number and activities of the Chinese, Japanese, Columbian and Nigerian criminal groups, particularly:

- Chinese "triads" mostly operate in the territory of Hong Kong and Taiwan; there are about 50 different organizations, which relate to this group, whose number counts according to the different estimations from 160 to 300 thousand people. Despite the rigid hierarchical structure, the components of triads, which directly accomplish the criminal operations, are part of the flexible net system, capable of changing their structure, being adjusted slightly under the ambient conditions. Triads are occupied by extortion, drug trafficking, prostitution, gambling, are the important suppliers of heroin in the USA.
- Japanese" *yakuza*" also known as **gokudō,** are members of transnational organized crime syndicates originating in Japan. The Japanese police, and media by request of the police, call them **bōryokudan** ("violent groups"), while the yakuza call themselves "**ninkyōdantai**" ("chivalrous organizations"). It also consists of several self-contained organizations, from which the largest is Yamaguchi -Gumi, which counts more than 26000 members, then comes Inagava-kay (8600members) and Sumiesi-kay (more than 7000 members). These organizations conduct fights between themselves; however, it is also implemented as a matched activity for the involvement in corruption of the government officials and criminalization of the economy. Besides, the interference in the internal economic processes (by yakuza is controlled the film industry, entertainment industry, professional sport, lottery, the financial sphere, and the sphere of the real estate), it achieves the smuggling of sea products and stealing the motor transport, narcotics (including methamphetamine) and weapon (Le Monde, 2007).
- Colombian drug cartels are occupied practically exclusively by the drug trafficking business, being basic suppliers on the World Market of cocaine (to 80%). The two most known cartels existed in the cities of Medellín and Cali. The Medellin cartel was founded by the families of Pablo Eskobar and Ochoa, and Cali`s - by families of Santacruz and Rodriguez Orikhuella. The leading level of the cartels is built according to a rigid hierarchical diagram, and various cells are separated at the lower level, each of which is occupied by the specific form of criminal activity and it is not informed about the other operations of a cartel. At the end of the 1990's years, the operation of the Colombian police and law-enforcement agencies of other countries led to a significant decrease in the volume of the operations which were carried out by cartels; however, the liberated places have been taken by the smaller criminal organizations.

- Nigerian criminal organizations appeared at the beginning of the 1980's years as a result of the crisis of the economy of Nigeria, connected with a drop in the prices of oil. These criminal organizations specialize in drug trafficking, and also in the knavish operations including the use of new financial instruments and extortion. As a rule, the majority of operations are small, but this is compensated by their large number (Chitadze, 2016).

Criminal Organizations in Europe

In the report of the European Union about the situation in the sphere of organized criminality in 2004 (European Union Organized Crime Report 2004) and the subsequent years ((European Organized Crime Threat Assessment (OCTA) 2007)) are listed the basic international criminal organizations, which act in the territory of Europe. To this number most dangerous of them are referred Albanian (occupying by trade in narcotics and by people, and also being approached the establishment of control of the criminal markets, including by forced methods) and Russian (economic crimes, extortion, illegal immigration).

Furthermore, it is indicated the action of other ethnic groups: Turkish (trade in narcotics and weapon, money laundering, racket), Nigerian (trade in narcotics and by people, swindle), Moroccan (trade by narcotics and smuggling), Colombian (trade-in cocaine), Chinese (illegal migration), Vietnamese (smuggling, illegal migration, other criminal services).

According to the article, presented by the journal LE MONDE: "Atlas der Globalisierung - Die Welt von morgen": Kriminalitätohne Grenzen, one of the most dangerous criminal activities in Europe, fulfills the Russian Mafia. It includes about 160 000 members and 12 000 groups.

Based on the research, prepared by Chris Matthews under the name: "The biggest organized crime groups in the world" on the first place was located the Russian Organized Criminal Organization "Solntsevskaya Bratva" (Solntsevo is the district in Moscow), the revenue of which was estimated $8,5 billion in 2014 (Matthews, 2014).

The International Experience of Fighting Against the Transnational Organized Crime

Understanding with the International community of the seriousness of threats, which emanate from narcotics trafficking, Money laundering, corruption, and other crimes began only in the XX century as the result of the understanding of the increasing of the scales of these challenges, which emerge beyond the framework of individual state and in connection with their negative influence on sociopolitical, economic spheres, National Security and person. The leading role in the legal regulation of the efforts of states and the International Community for the combating transnational organized crime belongs to the UN; in the recent decades, when it became obvious, that the ability of states to separately resist the spreading of international criminality does not correspond to the scales of crimes, under the aegis of the UN many universal documents on the resistance to Transnational Organized Crime (TOC) were adopted, and the work of the world community in this direction acquire sever more system nature. The first international experience of the fighting with the criminal challenges of the international nature was connected with the signing of intergovernmental agreements, including against the slave trade (Viennese convention of 1815), the propagation of pornography (Parisian convention of 1910), forgery of monetary terms (convention of 1929) (UN, 2005).

At the beginning of the XX century, the international nature of several crimes did not make it possible to carry them exclusively to the scope of one state, and an appropriate situation was emerging, when international collaboration in this field became necessary. In 1927, in Warsaw took place the first international conference on the unification of the criminal legislation, where the number of crimes of international nature was related to piracy, slave trade, narcotics trafficking, trade of pornography materials, the forgery of monetary terms. A number of the legal norms in the sphere of combating international criminality, which was reflected in the international-legal documents were worked out, particularly: The international convention about the fight with the acts of nuclear terrorism (2005), Convention of the UN against the transnational organized criminality (2000), convention of the United Nations against corruption (2003), convention of the UN in the fight against the illegal circulation of narcotic drugs and psychotropic substances (1988), Convention of the Council of Europe about washing up, revealing, withdrawal and confiscation of incomes from criminal activity (1990) (Chitadze, 2016).

In the framework of the Council of Europe were adopted 9 conventions in the field of the fight against international criminality. Among them –the European convention about compensation to the victims of crimes (1998), protocol to the convention about cyber terrorism (2003), and others (UN, 2005). Furthermore, as a rule, many international agreements contain positions about the collaboration in the fight with one or another form of international criminality.

About the European Union, it is important to discuss the EU's 'solidarity clause', Article 222 of the Lisbon Treaty (TFEU), which means the mutual assistance and common fighting of the EU member states against terrorism, including the terrorism prevention by EU member states (Parkes, 2015).

The UN since the beginning of its existence was involved with the problems of warning and suppression of the crimes: under the aegis of the UN is adopted several international conventions, the General Assembly of UN regularly considers resolutions with the recommendations regarding the combating of separate types of crimes of the international nature. Since 1955, every five years the congress of the UN for warning of criminality and rotation with the lawbreakers is organized. XI Congress of the UN on warning of criminality and criminal justice took place in Bangkok in April 2005. Based on the results, the Bangkok declaration "Synergies and Responses: Strategic Alliances in Crime Prevention and Criminal Justice" was adopted (UN Congress on Crime Prevention, 2005).

At the beginning of the 1990s, within the framework of the UN was undertaken several major steps, directed toward an increase the effectiveness of the coordination of member states in the fight with the TOC. In 1990, the General Assembly of the UN approved the model standard agreements (in the spheres of criminal justice, extradition, etc.) and the program of the UN in the field of warning of criminality and criminal justice was adopted in 1991. The basic purpose of the program—organize assistance to member nations in a matter of warning crimes and criminal justice.

A Ministerial conference on the fight with transnational organized criminality took place in Naples in November 1994. In the work conference were the representatives of 142 countries; Based on the results, the General Assembly of the UN adopted the Global Action Plan against Transnational organized crime. In 1997, at the sixth session of the commission for warning of crime and criminal justice, a working group was created on the performance of the Naples Declaration (Chitadze, 2016). The working over the determination of the organized crime became a central question in the framework of the working group: as the compromise version was designated the key elements, which characterize the phenomenon of the organized crime—the presence of organization, a constant nature, division of labor inside the group, violence, and deference, the hierarchy, tendency toward obtaining the profit, influence on the society, media means and political structures. In 1998, for developing the text of convention-related the resistance to transnational crime, the commission created the intergovernmental committee of ad hoc, which was opened for the participation of all states, including the states, which were not the members of the UN (Chitadze, 2016). In the operation of the committee, important role-played individual states, which focused attention on the problems, which they directly encountered as most closely. In particular, Austria and Italy raised a question about the illegal migration, Argentina—to trade by children, Japan and Canada offered the inclusion in the text of the future convention a new tool on the fight with the illegal production and trade of firearms.

The signing in 2000 of the convention of the United Nations against transnational organized crime and also three protocols to it became a watershed in the fight with a transnational crime within the framework of the UN. The convention of the UN against transnational organized crime adapts concerning the crimes of transnational nature, perfected with the participation of the organized criminal group. Organized crime is understood through characteristics of the organized criminal groups, the seriousness of the violence accomplished by them (UN, 2005). The convention defines the organized criminal group as "the structurally designed group in the composition of three or more persons, that exists during the specific period and acting in concord to commit of one or several serious crime or crimes, acknowledged as the same following the present convention, to obtain, directly or indirectly, financial or another material benefit" (article.2).

So, fighting against organized crime is a much more complex problem, than fighting with the different types of individual criminality. Effective fighting with organized crime is impossible without the measures, directed toward the sanitation of society as a whole, called to give the legal alternative" to the social services" of the criminal society: the state must ensure to population the availability for the necessary goods and services, employment of the population, normal functioning of ideological and educational institutes, availability of the lawful means of the resolution the social conflicts.

Which of the enumerated measures will prove to be more effective—it depends on the model, on which is built the activity of the organized criminality under the specific social conditions.

The specialist on organized crime issues, Jay Albanese, in his report "The Use of Models in the Study of Organized Crime" presented at the 2003 conference of the European Consortium for Political Research (ECPR), (Marburg, Germany, 19 September 2003), separated three types of these models:

- Traditional model of the large-scale criminal conspiracy, controlled by a small group of leaders. In that case, the most effective will be the measures, directed toward the neutralization of the leaders via their arrest or by another method, which will lead to the collapse of the Arrangement.
- Model of the local organized ethnic groups. In this case, since no centralized organization has existed, the neutralization of leaders will not give the desired result, since they will be replaced by new ones. In this case, the basic directions of the fight can become the measures of financial, social, and other control, and also other steps, directed toward the removal of financial flows from the shady ("black") sector of the economy.
- The model of enterprise, according to which organized crime is characterized by the informal decentralized structure and appears under the specified social and economic conditions when the legal mechanisms of the guarantee of needs of the population are ineffective. To deal with this type it is necessary to, first of all, eliminate the reasons, which created the results of crime, stabilizing and after making transparent social and economic processes.

Furthermore, the law-enforcement agencies could reach significant results in the fighting with organized crime, were necessary the special normative-legal and material and technical base of their activity, allowing taking the necessary measures for the prevention of commission of the crime as the organized groups, to disorganize their activity, not to allow members of the organized criminal associations the fallen in the field of the sight of the organs of the protection of law to leave from the criminal responsibility.

CONCLUSION

Transnational organized crime has a long history. Although many countries started fighting it late, the whole world has been fighting it for a long time. Along with the development of the world, the number of crimes also increases. Obviously, the scale of the world is changing, people are making great strides in science, such that it would have seemed impossible to think about it a few years ago. This is how the development of the world has increased the number of crimes. Transnational organized crime is no longer the struggle and problem of one state. This is a problem of the whole world. Criminal groups communicate with each other easily, regardless of borders and restrictions. This communication allows them to become more powerful, to find more followers in different states and to enrich their criminal ranks and groups with new individuals. The main objective of transnational organized crime is to obtain illegal income, and in the past they have had political objectives. They also wanted to take over the influence of the government. Organized crime is taking the form of transnational crime day by day. This is because they do not commit crimes in one state. Many of these crimes are illegal, of course, and it can be arms, drug trafficking, which is comprehensively shown in this paper with its statistics. as well as trafficking, etc. These criminal groups want to make a lot of money illegally. All groups have different methods of committing crimes. They study the state well in advance, at first they do not come under the attention of law enforcement officers, at this time they study the entire state, after that they organize everything well, strategically, imperceptibly and then commit a crime. If there are corrupt persons at the head of the state, then these groups have a free hand. There are organized crime groups that manage to bribe officials, cross borders, and then both parties receive illegal income.

The fight against transnational organized crime is extremely difficult. For this, it is necessary to have high qualifications of law enforcement officers, to raise the morals of people, and to implement such laws by the state that will be flexible and effective. Transnational organized crime does not have a mass character in many countries so far, so it is good if the state destroys this crime at its root so that it does not spread and involve young people. The state should understand that they cannot do anything without informing the public. Everyone knows that only a well-written law is useless if this law does not solve the problem for which it was created. The recommendations given should be followed as much as possible. In this work, it is well conveyed what the personal formation of a person is. It is necessary for the state to take care of those persons who may become the rulers of this state in the future. The background that is today should be corrected. He should not be satisfied with the results achieved with minors and try his best to bring everything to an ideal level. Most of all, he should fight against crime in the country. The criminal world should not be allowed to return to many countries. There are cases when minors are encouraged by certain groups to engage in crime, and they should work accordingly and punish those persons strictly. Transnational organized crime is a living organism, which along with world development can change several times, develop, strengthen, gather forces, and increase its influence. Refinement of those mechanisms will be used, which will make people and society imagine that this is dangerous not only for the state but also for this society itself. In order for public distrust not to return to law enforcement agencies, frequent and most importantly mass trainings should be conducted so that examples of corruption by specific individuals do not occur. Society and law enforcement agencies must fight transnational organized crime together, and if society again feels that the law enforcement officer is corrupt again, then everything will be over, only the state can do nothing with this crime without people. As part of the fight against transnational organized crime, more international trips should be made. Law enforcement bodies should undergo training in neighboring countries in order to absorb the recommendations they give. Nothing can be solved without cooperation with other countries, because we know that this specific crime does not pose a threat to one country, it is a crime that threatens everyone. Today a country may think that nothing is in danger for them, but tomorrow the same thing may happen to them as happened to their neighboring country. Therefore, international cooperation is necessary. Juveniles must understand that membership in the world of thieves kills them and not only them, but also the state. There should be frequent communication with minors, on the streets, in school yards, to prevent them from entering the criminal world. The population should be frequently informed about the results of law enforcement agencies in the fight against crime and how much assistance the public has provided to law enforcement. The Ministry of Internal Affairs and other police force agencies of many countries, have very good initiatives, but there is still a lot to be done. Based on the above, everyone should do their best against this criminal world. Organized crime is always trying to take different forms in order to fool both law enforcement officers and the part of society that easily believes everything. Therefore, everything should be done to prevent this, the legal base should be changed often and most importantly appropriately. Considering all this, it is possible to fight transnational organized crime.

REFERENCES

Chitadze, N. (2016). *Political Science*. International Black Sea University.

Chitidze, G. (2021). *Transnational Organized Crime. Comparative Legal Analysis*. Tavartkiladze University. Retrieved from: https://openscience.ge/bitstream/1/2518/1/Irakli%20Chitidze%20Samagistro.pdf

Dolgovaya. (2005). *Criminology: University Textbook*. Partnership for Peace Consortium of Defense Academies and Security Studies Institute.

EUROPOL. (2004). *European Union Organized Crime Report 2004*. Retrieved from: https://www.europol.europa.eu/publications-events/main-reports/european-union-organised-crime-report-2004

Goldstein, J. S., & Pevehouse, J. C. (2011). *International Relations*. Pearson.

Intelligence Council of USA. (2015). *Global Trends*. Retrieved from: https://www.dni.gov/files/documents/Global%20Trends_2015%20Report.pdf

Le Monde. (2007). *Atlas der Globalisierung: Die Welt von morgen Paperback*. Retrieved from: https://www.amazon.de/Atlas-Globalisierung-Die-Welt-morgen/dp/3937683380

Matthews. (2014). *Realist Criminology*. Palgrave Macmillan.

Parkes. (2015). The Trafficking Protocol has Advanced the Global Movement against Human Exploitation: The case of the United Kingdom. *Anti-Trafficking Review*.

UN Congress on Crime Prevention. (2005). *Eleventh United Nations congress on crime prevention and criminal justice*. Retrieved from: https://www.unodc.org/congress/en/previous/previous-11.html

United Nations. (2005). *Basic Facts about the United Nations*. UN Department of Public Information.

KEY TERMS AND DEFINITIONS

Chinese "Triads": A Chinese transnational organized crime syndicate based in Greater China and has outposts in various countries with significant overseas Chinese diaspora populations. The Hong Kong triad is distinct from mainland Chinese criminal organizations. In ancient China, the triad was one of three major secret societies. It established branches in Macau, Hong Kong, Taiwan, and Chinese communities overseas. Known as "mainland Chinese criminal organizations", they are of two major types: "dark forces" (loosely organized groups) and "Black Societies" (more-mature criminal organizations). Two features which distinguish a black society from ordinary "dark forces" or low level criminal gangs are the extent to which the organisation is able to control local markets and the degree of police protection able to be obtained. The Hong Kong triad refers to traditional criminal organizations operating in (or originating from) Hong Kong, Macau, Taiwan and south-east Asian countries and regions, while organized-crime groups in mainland China are known as "mainland Chinese criminal groups".

Colombian Drug Cartels: The illegal drug trade in Colombia has, since the 1970s, centered successively on four major drug trafficking cartels: Medellín, Cali, Norte del Valle, and North Coast, as well as several bandas criminales, or BACRIMs. The trade eventually created a new social class and influenced several aspects of Colombian culture and politics.

Italian Mafia: Hierarchically structured society of criminals of primarily Italian or Sicilian birth or extraction. The term applies to the traditional criminal organization in Sicily and also to a criminal organization in the United States.

Japanese "Yakuza": Also known as gokudō are members of transnational organized crime syndicates originating in Japan. The Japanese police and media, by request of the police, call them bōryokudan (violent organization) while the yakuza call themselves ninkyō dantai (chivalrous organizations). The English equivalent for the term yakuza is gangster, meaning an individual involved in a Mafia-like criminal organization. The yakuza are known for their strict codes of conduct, their organized fiefdom nature and several unconventional ritual practices such as yubitsume or amputation of the left little finger. Members are often portrayed as males, wearing "sharp suits" with heavily tattooed bodies and slicked hair. This group is still regarded as being among "the most sophisticated and wealthiest criminal organizations".

Organized Crime: A category of transnational, national, or local groupings of highly centralized enterprises run by criminals to engage in illegal activity, most commonly for profit. While organized crime is generally thought of as a form of illegal business, some criminal organizations, such as terrorist groups, rebel forces, and separatists, are politically motivated. Sometimes criminal organizations force people to do business with them, such as when a gang extorts money from shopkeepers for "protection."

Transnational Organized Crime (TOC): Organized crime coordinated across national borders, involving groups or markets of individuals working in more than one country to plan and execute illegal business ventures. In order to achieve their goals, these criminal groups use systematic violence and corruption. Common transnational organized crimes include conveying drugs, conveying arms, trafficking for sex, toxic waste disposal, materials theft and poaching.

Compilation of References

Aaronson, M. (2014). Intervention in Us foreign policy from Bush to Obama. In M. Bentley & J. Holland (Eds.), Obama's Foreign Policy: Ending the War on Terror (p. 124). Routledge Studies in US Foreign Policy.

Abisel, N. (1999). *Popular Cinema and Genres*. Alan Publishing.

Abrahms, M. (2006). Why Terrorism Does Not Work. *International Security*, *31*(2), 42–78. doi:10.1162/isec.2006.31.2.42

Abrahms, M. (2008). What Terrorists Really Want: Terrorist Motives and Counterterrorism Strategy. *International Security*, *32*(4), 78–105. doi:10.1162/isec.2008.32.4.78

Acar, C. (1991). *Superpowers Domination Struggle*. İrfan Publishing House.

Affairs, P. D. (2017). *Radicalisation and violent extremism – focus on women: How women become radicalised, and how to empower them to prevent radicalization.* European Union. Retrieved from https://www.europarl.europa.eu/supporting-analyses

Aghaie, S., & Rasooli Sani Abadi, E. (2011). Information revolution and its effect on national security from the perspective of international relations theories. *The Political Quarterly*, *41*(3), 23–37.

Akarcalı, S. (2003). *Communication and Propaganda in the Second World War*. Image Publications.

Alazab, M., & Broadhurst, R. (2017). An Analysis of the Nature of Spam as Cybercrime. In S. Hakim, E. A. Blackstone, & R. M. Clark (Eds.), Cyber-Physical Security. Protecting Critical Infrastructure at the State and Local Level (pp. 251-267). Springer International Publishing Switzerland. doi:10.1007/978-3-319-32824-9_13

Aleksidze. (2018). *Contemporary International Law*. Tbilisi State University.

Aleksidze. (2018). *Handbook in International Law*. Tbilisi State University.

Aleksidze, L. (2018). *Contemporary International Law*. Tbilisi State University.

Al-Istrabadi, F. (2018). Regional Constraints on the U.S. Confrontation of ISIS. In *The Future of ISIS: Regional and International Implications* (pp. 173–174). The Brookings Institution.

AlJazeera. (2022, February 18). *Russian-backed separatists evacuate residents from east Ukraine*. Retrieved March 19, 2022, from AlJazeera: https://www.aljazeera.com/news/2022/2/18/russian-backed-separatists-announce-evacuation-from-east-ukraine

Almohammad, A. H., & Speckhard, A. (2017). *The Operational Ranks and Roles of Female ISIS Operatives: From Assassins and Morality Police to Spies and Suicide Bombers*. ICSVE Research Reports. Retrieved January 9, 2022, from http://www.icsve.org/research-reports/the-operational-ranks-and-roles-of-female-isis-operatives-from-assassins-and-morality-police-to-spies-and-suicide-bombers/

Al-Shishani, M. B. (2010). *Saudi Arabia's Jihadi Jailbird: A Portrait of al-Shu'aybi Ideologue Nasir al-Fahd.* Intelligence Quarterly.

Althusser, L. (2014). *Ideology and Ideological Devices of the State*. Ithaki Publications.

Anonymous. (2001, October 11). *Bush on State of War*. Retrieved January 4, 2022, from https://www.washingtonpost.com/wp-srv/nation/specials/attacked/transcripts/bush_text101101.html

Anonymous. (2001, September 20). *President Bush Addresses the Nation*. Retrieved January 4, 2022, from https://www.washingtonpost.com/wp-srv/nation/specials/attacked/transcripts/bushaddress_092001.html

Antunez Moreno, J. C. (2020, November 12). Western DAESH Women: Ideology. *Profile and Motivation.*, *6*(2), 155–174. doi:10.18847/1.12.9

Arango, T. (2014). Escaping Death in Northern Iraq. *New York Times.*

Arango, T. (2015). Key Iraqi City Falls to ISIS as Last of Security Forces Flee. *The New York Times.*

Arce, D., & Sandler, T. (2007). Terrorist Signaling and the Value of Intelligence. *British Journal of Political Science*, *37*(4), 576–586. doi:10.1017/S0007123407000324

Arce, D., & Sandler, T. (2010). Terrorist Spectaculars: Backlash Attacks and the Focus of Intelligence. *The Journal of Conflict Resolution*, *54*(2), 354–373. doi:10.1177/0022002709355414

Archive. (n.d.). *The Global War on Terrorism: The First 100 Days*. Retrieved January 4, 2022, from https://2001-2009.state.gov/s/ct/rls/wh/6947.htm

Ariel Cohen, R. E. (2011). *The Russian Military and the Georgia War: Lessons and Implications*. Strategic Studies Institute. doi:10.21236/ADA545578

Armaoğlu, F. (1999). *20th Century Political History*. Alkim Publishing House.

Arowolo, D. E. (2013). Terrorism, democracy and global security. *European Scientific Journal*, *9*(2), 100–111.

Askew, J. (2022, April 21). *'Massive war crimes': Estonia accuses Russia of genocide in Ukraine*. Retrieved April 25, 2022, from Euronews: https://www.euronews.com/my-europe/2022/04/21/massive-war-crimes-estonia-accuses-russia-of-genocide-in-ukraine

Aslund, A. (2015, July 5). *Russia's war on Ukraine's economy*. Retrieved May 17, 2021, from The Japan Times: http://www.japantimes.co.jp/opinion/2015/07/13/commentary/worldcommentary/russias-war-on-ukraines-economy/#.WFmsAhGg-1t

Asongu, S. A., Joseph, N., Nicholas, B., & Paul, N. (2019). Contemporary drivers of global tourism: Evidence from terrorism and peace factors. *Journal of Travel & Tourism Marketing*, *36*(3), 345–357. doi:10.1080/10548408.2018.1541778

Atran, S. (2004, August). *Trends in Suicide Terrorism: Sense and Nonsense.* Paper Presented to World Federation of Scientists Permanent Monitoring Panel on Terrorism, Erice, Sicily.

Auchter, J. (2012). Gendering terror: Discourses of terrorism and writing woman-as-agent. *International Feminist Journal of Politics*, *14*(1), 125. doi:10.1080/14616742.2011.619780

Auer, M., Sutcliffe, J., & Lee, M. (2018). White Widow': Using Intersectionality to Uncover Complex Representations of Female Terrorism in News Media. *Media, War & Conflict.*

Aust, A. (2010). *Handbook of International Law* (2nd ed.). Cambridge University Press. doi:10.1017/CBO9780511841460

Bakker, E., & Leede, S. D. (2015). European Female Jihadists in Syria: Exploring and Under-Researched Topic. Hague: The International Centre for Counter-Terrorism.

Baldwin, D. A. (2000). The Sanctions Debate and the Logic of Choice. *International Security*, *24*(3), 80–107. doi:10.1162/016228899560248

Banai, H. (2018). U.S.-Led International Response to ISIS. In *The Future of Isis: Regional and International Implications* (pp. 152–157). Brookings Institution Press.

Başbuğ, E. D. (2013). *Official Ideology on the Stage*. İletişim Publications.

Basic Facts about the United Nations. (2005). Charter of the United Nations. UN Department of Public Information.

Basit, A. (2020). The COVID-19 Pandemic: An Opportunity for Terrorist Groups? *Counter Terrorist Trends and Analyses*, *12*(3), 7–12.

Bassey, M. E. (2017). Impact of terrorism on international peace and security in the age of technological advancement. *International Journal of Scientific and Research Publications*, *7*(8), 526–533.

Bassiouni. (1990). *A Functional Approach to General Principles of International Law*. Retrieved from: https://via.library.depaul.edu/lawfacpubs/317/

Bayramoğlu, M. (2001). The Role and Function of the Star in Hollywood Cinema. *Journal of Universal Culture*.

BBC. (2006, October 6). *Georgians deported as row deepens*. Retrieved May 19, 2021, from BBC: http://news.bbc.co.uk/2/hi/europe/5412672.stm

BBC. (2015, November 25). *Ukraine closes airspace to all Russian planes*. Retrieved March 16, 2022, from BBC: https://www.bbc.com/news/world-europe-34920207

BBC. (2016, March 16). *Crimea referendum: Voters 'back Russia union*. Retrieved May 21, 2021, from BBC: https://www.bbc.com/news/world-europe-26606097

BBC. (2019, June 21). *Georgia protests: Thousands storm parliament over Russian MP's speech*. Retrieved June 5, 2021, from BBC: https://www.bbc.com/news/world-europe-48710042

BBC. (2022a, March 1). *Building hit by missile in Kharkiv's Freedom Square*. Retrieved April 10, 2022, from BBC: https://www.bbc.com/news/av/world-europe-60568298

BBC. (2022b, March 10). *Ukraine war: Three dead as maternity hospital hit by Russian air strike*. Retrieved April 10, 2022, from BBC: https://www.bbc.com/news/world-europe-60675599

BBC. (2022c, March 25). *War in Ukraine: Estimated 300 dead in Mariupol theatre strike*. Retrieved April 10, 2022, from BBC: https://www.bbc.com/news/world-europe-60873435#:~:text=An%20estimated%20300%20people%20were,building%20when%20it%20was%20hit

Ben Fox, V. I. (2022, January 29). *Russia denies it plans to invade Ukraine. Putin's remaining options are still risky*. Retrieved March 19, 2022, from Globalnews: https://globalnews.ca/news/8580055/russia-ukraine-putin-tensions/

Bergen, P. (2010). *Strange Bedfellows Iran and al Qaeda*. CNN.

Berko, A., & Erez, E. (2007). Gender, Palestinian Women, and Terrorism: Women's Liberation or Oppression? *Studies in Conflict and Terrorism*, *30*(6), 493–519. doi:10.1080/10576100701329550

Berman, E., & Laitin, D. D. (2008). Religion, terrorism and public goods: Testing the club model. *Journal of Public Economics*, *92*(10–11), 1942–1967. doi:10.1016/j.jpubeco.2008.03.007

Berrebi, C. (2009). The Economics of Terrorism and Counterterrorism: What Matters and Is Rational-Choice Theory Helpful? In P. K. Davis & K. Cragin (Eds.), *Social Science for Counterterrorism: Putting the Pieces Together*. RAND.

Beruashvili, N. (2022). *Psychological Factors during the Foreign Policy Decision-Making Process. World Politics and Challenges for International Security*. IGI Global.

Bērziņš, J. (2014). Russia's new generation warfare in Ukraine: Implications for Latvian defense policy. National Defence Academy of Latvia, Center for Security and Strategic Research.

Bhutia, S. (2019, November 25). *How has conflict with Russia affected Ukraine's trade?* Retrieved March 16, 2022, from Eurasianet: https://eurasianet.org/how-has-conflict-with-russia-affected-ukraines-trade

Bigio, J., & Vogelstein, R. (2019). *Women and Terrorism: Hidden Threats, Forgotten Patterns*. The Council on Foreign Relations.

Blakeley, R. (2009). *State Terrorism and Neoliberalism: The North in the South*. Routledge. doi:10.4324/9780203876510

Blanchard, C. M., & Humud, C. E. (2018). *The Islamic State and U.S. Policy*. Congressional Research Service.

Blank, S. (2017). *Cyber War and Information War à la Russe*. Georgetown University Press.

Bloom, M. (2016). The changing nature of women in extremism and political violence. *Freedom from Fear*, 40-54.

Bloom, M. (2011). Bombshells: Women and Terror. *Gender Issues*, *28*(1-2), 1–21. doi:10.100712147-011-9098-z

Bloom, M. M. (2004). Palestinian Suicide Bombing: Public Support, Market Share, and Outbidding. *Political Science Quarterly*, *119*(1), 61–88. doi:10.2307/20202305

Bock, A. (2010). *Negotiate with Terrorists! or: Why Terrorism Cannot be Deterred*. Retrieved from: https://www.fes.de/ipg/arc_07_d/01_07_d/pdf/12_RE_Bock_GB.pdf

Bockstette, C. (2008). *Jihadist Terrorist Use of Strategic Communication Management Techniques*. George C. Marshall Center Occasional Paper Series (20).

Borum, R. (2003). *Understanding the Terrorist Mindset*. Academic Press.

Borum, R. (2004). *Psychology of Terrorism*. University of South Florida.

Britannica. (n.d.). *North Atlantic Treaty Organization*. Retrieved June 4, 2021, from Britannica: https://www.britannica.com/topic/North-Atlantic-Treaty-Organization/The-role-of-Germany#:~:text=In%20May%201955%20West%20Germany,eastern%20Europe%20the%20same%20year

Brown, K. E., & Saeed, T. (2017). Radicalization and counter-radicalization at British universities: Muslim encounters and alternatives. *Ethnic and Racial Studies*, 152–168.

Burai, E. (2015, November 5). *Parody as Norm Contestation: Russian Normative Justifications in Georgia and Ukraine and Their Implications for Global Norms*. Retrieved May 20, 2021, from Taylor Francis Online: https://www.tandfonline.com/doi/full/10.1080/13600826.2015.1092424

Burgess, P. a. (2012). Human security. *Contemporary Security and Strategy*, 89-105.

Burton, G. (1995). *More Than Looks*. Alan Publishing.

Business Media Georgia. (2019, June 23). რუსული ემბარგოს ქრონოლოგია საქართველოში. Retrieved May 15, 2021, from Business Media Georgia: https://www.bm.ge/ka/article/rusuli-embargos-qronologia-saqartveloshi/35815

Buzan, B., Wæver, O., & Wilde, J. D. (1998). *Security: A new framework for analysis*. Lynne Rienner Publishers.

Byman, D., & Waxman, M. (2002). *The Dynamics of Coercion: American Foreign Policy and the Limits of Military Might*. Cambridge University Press.

Calvert, J. (2010). *Sayyid Qutb and the Origins of Radical Islam*. Columbia University Press.

Campion, K., Ferrill, J., & Milligan, K. (2021). Extremist Exploitation of the Context Created by COVID-19 and the Implications for Australian Security. *Perspectives on Terrorism*, *15*(6).

Carolina Vendil Pallin, F. W. (2009, June 2). Russia's war in Georgia: Lessons and consequences. *Small Wars & Insurgencies*, *20*(2), 400–424. doi:10.1080/09592310902975539

Çelik, M. A. (2016). *Political Cinema*. Night Library.

Chakhava, K. (2022). *Terrorists Psychology and their impact on International Security. World Politics and Challenges for International Security*. IGI Global.

Chitadze, N. (2022). Global Security and Political Problems of the 21st Century. IGI Global.

Chitadze, N. (2022). Global Security and Political Problems of the 21st Century. In *World Politics and Challenges for International Security*. IGI Global. https://www.igi-global.com/chapter/global-security-and-political-problems-of-the-21st-century/298954

Chitadze, N. (2022). World Politics and Challenges for International Security. IGI Global. doi:10.4018/978-1-7998-9586-2

Chitadze. (2016). *Political Sciences*. International Black Sea University.

Chitadze, N. (2011). *Geopolitics*. Universal.

Chitadze, N. (2016). *Political Science*. International Black Sea University.

Chitadze, N. (2016). *Political Sciences*. International Black Sea University.

Chitadze, N. (2022). *World Politics and Challenges for International Security. Global Security and Political Problems of the 21-st Century. World Politics and Challenges for International Security*. IGI Global.

Chitidze, G. (2021). *Transnational Organized Crime. Comparative Legal Analysis*. Tavartkiladze University. Retrieved from: https://openscience.ge/bitstream/1/2518/1/Irakli%20Chitidze%20Samagistro.pdf

Chomsky, N. (2002). What Anthropologists Should Know about the Concept of Terrorism. *Anthropology Today*.

Chowanietz, C. (2010). Rallying Around the Flag or Railing Against the Government? Political Parties' Reactions to Terrorist Acts. *Party Politics*, *2*(1), 111–142.

Civil.ge. (2004, September 2). *Closure of Ergneti Black Market Boosted Customs Revenues*. Retrieved June 4, 2021, from Civil.ge: https://civil.ge/archives/115946

Civil.ge. (2006a, September 28). მოსკოვმა თბილისიდან ელჩი გაიწვია. Retrieved May 23, 2021, from Civil.ge: https://civil.ge/ka/archives/139150

Civil.ge. (2006b, September 30). რუსეთი წყვეტს საქართველოდან ჯარების გაყვანას. Retrieved May 23, 2021, from Civil.ge: https://civil.ge/ka/archives/139186

Civil.ge. (2006c, September 29). საგარეო უწყება რუსეთში საქართველოს საელჩოზე თავდასხმას გმობს. Retrieved May 23, 2021, from Civil.ge: https://civil.ge/ka/archives/139173

Civil.ge. (2006d, June 28). ქართული არმია ფართომასშტაბიან წვრთნებს ატარებს. Retrieved May 23, 2021, from Civil.ge: https://civil.ge/ka/archives/138378

Civil.ge. (2006e, September 27). შსს–მ ჯაშუშობის ბრალდებით 4 რუსი ოფიცერი დააკავა. Retrieved May 23, 2021, from Civil.ge: https://civil.ge/ka/archives/139137

Civil.ge. (2007a, October 30). განმუხურის ზანაკთან მომხდარი ინციდენტის გამო ქართულმა მხარემ საბრძოლო მზადყოფნა გამოაცხადა. Retrieved May 23, 2021, from Civil.ge: https://civil.ge/ka/archives/141769

Civil.ge. (2007b, October 30). განმუხურში ქართულ ძალებსა და რუს სამშვიდობოებს შორის დაპირისპირება მოხდა. Retrieved May 23, 2021, from Civil.ge: https://old.civil.ge/geo/article.php?id=16477

Civil.ge. (2007c, August 9). მოხსენება დაბომბვის ზოგიერთ დეტალზე საუბრობს. Retrieved May 23, 2021, from Civil.ge: https://civil.ge/ka/archives/141175

Civil.ge. (2008a, July 15). აფხაზეთის ლიდერი ”გერმანულ გეგმას” უარყოფს. Retrieved June 3, 2021, from Civil.ge: https://old.civil.ge/geo/article.php?id=18798&search=

Civil.ge. (2008aa, July 8). სოხუმმა ამერიკელების წინადადება უარყო. Retrieved June 2, 2021, from Civil.ge: https://old.civil.ge/geo/article.php?id=18737&search=

Civil.ge. (2008ab, May 7). სოხუმს მედვედევის ”გადამწყვეტი ნაბიჯის” იმედი აქვს. Retrieved May 29, 2021, from Civil.ge: https://old.civil.ge/geo/article.php?id=18211&search=

Civil.ge. (2008ac, June 19). სოხუმში რკინიგზაზე ორი აფეთქება მოხდა. Retrieved June 1, 2021, from Civil.ge: https://old.civil.ge/geo/article.php?id=18588&search=

Civil.ge. (2008ad, June 21). სოხუმში უსაფრთხოების ორი თანამშრომელი დაჭრეს. Retrieved June 1, 2021, from Civil.ge: https://old.civil.ge/geo/article.php?id=18608&search=

Civil.ge. (2008ae, June 25). ქართული მხარე სამშვიდობო პროცესის დასაწყებად ორი წინაპირობის შესრულებას მოითხოვს. Retrieved May 30, 2021, from Civil.ge: https://old.civil.ge/geo/article.php?id=18632&search=

Civil.ge. (2008af, August 5). ჩრდილოეთ ოსეთში ცხინვალიდან 800-ზე მეტი ადამიანი ჩავიდა. Retrieved March 19, 2022, from Civil.ge: https://civil.ge/ka/archives/144198

Civil.ge. (2008ag, May 16). ცხინვალის რეგიონში მომხდარი აფეთქების შედეგად პოლიციელი დაიჭრა. Retrieved May 30, 2021, from Civil.ge: https://old.civil.ge/geo/article.php?id=18279&search=

Civil.ge. (2008ah, June 16). ცხინვალის რეგიონში მომხდარი სროლის შედეგად ერთი ადამიანი დაღუპა, ოთხი კი დაშავდა. Retrieved June 1, 2021, from Civil.ge: https://old.civil.ge/geo/article.php?id=18566&search=

Civil.ge. (2008ai, April 15). ცხინვალმა სოხუმში ”საელჩო” გახსნა. Retrieved May 25, 2021, from Civil.ge: https://old.civil.ge/geo/article.php?id=18008&search=

Civil.ge. (2008aj, July 19). ცხინვალმა უარყო ევროკავშირის წინადადება ბრიუსელში მოლაპარაკებების გამართვის თაობაზე. Retrieved June 3, 2021, from Civil.ge: https://old.civil.ge/geo/article.php?id=18837&search=

Civil.ge. (2008ak, May 29). ცხინვალში აფეთქება მოხდა. Retrieved May 30, 2008, from Civil.ge: https://old.civil.ge/geo/article.php?id=18429&search=

Civil.ge. (2008b, May 21). აფხაზეთში მომხდარი აფეთქების შედეგად ”ოთხი ადამიანი” დაშავდა. Retrieved May 30, 2021, from Civil.ge: https://old.civil.ge/geo/article.php?id=18328&search=

Civil.ge. (2008c, June 29). გაგრაში აფეთქებამ ექვსი ადამიანი დაჭრა. Retrieved June 1, 2021, from Civil.ge: https://old.civil.ge/geo/article.php?id=18666&search=

Civil.ge. (2008d, July 3). დიმიტრი სანაკოევის კორტეჟს თავს დაესხნენ. Retrieved June 2, 2021, from Civil.ge: https://old.civil.ge/geo/article.php?id=18692&search=

Civil.ge. (2008e, March 28). ეუთოს თავმჯდომარე ცხინვალში მომხდარი აფეთქების გამო შეშფოთებულია. Retrieved May 26, 2021, from Civil.ge: https://old.civil.ge/geo/article.php?id=17889&search=

Civil.ge. (2008f, May 28). თამარაშენში სროლების შედეგად არავინ დაშავებულა. Retrieved May 30, 2021, from Civil.ge: https://old.civil.ge/geo/article.php?id=18423&search=

Civil.ge. (2008g, April 29). თბილისი აფხაზეთის წინააღმდეგ "სამხედრო ოპერაციას" გეგმავს - აცხადებს რუსეთი. Retrieved May 27, 2021, from Civil.ge: https://old.civil.ge/geo/article.php?id=18137&search=

Civil.ge. (2008h, June 24). თბილისი სამშვიდობოების გაყვანის მოთხოვნამდე ევროკავშირის და აშშ-ს ჩარევას ელის. Retrieved May 30, 2021, from Civil.ge: https://old.civil.ge/geo/article.php?id=18622&search=

Civil.ge. (2008i, April 12). თბილისი სოხუმს ერთობლივი პოლიციის შექმნას სთავაზობს. Retrieved May 25, 2021, from Civil.ge: https://old.civil.ge/geo/article.php?id=17992&search=

Civil.ge. (2008j, April 18). თბილისი უარყოფს ძალების განთავსებას აფხაზეთის კონფლიქტის ზონაში. Retrieved May 26, 2021, from Civil.ge: https://old.civil.ge/geo/article.php?id=18041&search=

Civil.ge. (2008k, May 16). მოსკოვი აფხაზეთზე გაეროს გენასამბლეის რეზოლუციას "კონტრპროდუქტიულს" უწოდებს. Retrieved May 30, 2021, from Civil.ge: https://old.civil.ge/geo/article.php?id=18276&search=

Civil.ge. (2008l, June 14). ნატომ საქართველოს საკითხი რუსეთთან შეხვედრაზე დააყენა. Retrieved May 30, 2021, from Civil.ge: https://old.civil.ge/geo/article.php?id=18563&search=

Civil.ge. (2008m, July 6). ნატოს გაფართოება "წითელი ხაზია" რუსეთ-ამერიკის ურთიერთობებში – კრემლის წარმომადგენელი. Retrieved March 20, 2022, from Civil.ge: https://civil.ge/ka/archives/143999

Civil.ge. (2008n, May 2). რაისი აფხაზეთში დამატებითი რუსული ძალების შეყვანის გამო შეშფოთებულია. Retrieved May 28, 2021, from Civil.ge: https://old.civil.ge/geo/article.php?id=18167&search=

Civil.ge. (2008o, March 11). როგოზინი თბილისს აფხაზეთის და სამხრეთ ოსეთის გამოყოფაზე აფრთხილებს. Retrieved May 26, 2021, from Civil.ge: https://old.civil.ge/geo/article.php?id=17678&search=

Civil.ge. (2008p, April 16). რუსეთი აფხაზეთთან და სამხრეთ ოსეთთან ურთიერთობების ლეგალიზებას იწყებს. Retrieved May 5, 2021, from Civil.ge: https://old.civil.ge/geo/article.php?id=18014&search=

Civil.ge. (2008q, March 6). რუსეთი აფხაზეთისთვის სანქციების დაწესების შესახებ შეთანხმებას ტოვებს. Retrieved May 25, 2021, from Civil.ge: https://old.civil.ge/geo/article.php?id=17678&search=

Civil.ge. (2008r, April 29). რუსეთი აფხაზეთში სამშვიდობოთა რაოდენობას ზრდის. Retrieved May 26, 2021, from Civil.ge: https://old.civil.ge/geo/article.php?id=18140&search=

Civil.ge. (2008s, July 15). რუსეთის საგარეო პოლიტიკური კონცეფცია: მოსკოვი საქართველოს ნატოს წევრობის წინააღმდეგია. Retrieved March 20, 2022, from Civil.ge: https://civil.ge/ka/archives/144081

Civil.ge. (2008t, April 26). რუსეთის სამხედრო ქმედება აფხაზეთში შესაძლებელია - რუსი დიპლომატი. Retrieved May 26, 2021, from Civil.ge: https://old.civil.ge/geo/article.php?id=18117&search=

Civil.ge. (2008u, May 1). რუსეთმა აფხაზეთში დამატებითი ძალები შეიყვანა. Retrieved May 27, 2021, from Civil.ge: https://old.civil.ge/geo/article.php?id=18158&search=

Civil.ge. (2008v, July 30). რუსეთს აფხაზეთიდან სარკინიგზო ძალები გაყავს. Retrieved March 19, 2022, from Civil.ge: https://civil.ge/ka/archives/144165

Civil.ge. (2008w, April 30). სააკაშვილი მოუწოდებს აფხაზებს და ოსებს ერთად დაუპირისპირდნენ გარეშე ძალას. Retrieved May 27, 2021, from Civil.ge: https://old.civil.ge/geo/article.php?id=18148&search=

Civil.ge. (2008x, June 10). სააკაშვილი: თბილისი მზადაა მოითხოვოს რუსი სამშვიდობოების გაყვანა. Retrieved May 30, 2021, from Civil.ge: https://old.civil.ge/geo/article.php?id=18529&search=

Civil.ge. (2008y, July 25). სოხუმი ბერლინის შეხვედრაზე უარს აცხადებს. Retrieved June 3, 2021, from Civil.ge: https://old.civil.ge/geo/article.php?id=18868&search=

Civil.ge. (2008z, May 12). სოხუმი კიდევ ორი უპილოტო თვითმფრინავის ჩამოგდებას იტყობინება. Retrieved May 29, 2021, from Civil.ge: https://old.civil.ge/geo/article.php?id=18242&search=

Civil.ge. (2014, November 22). მოსკოვმა და სოხუმმა "მოკავშირეობისა და სტრატეგიული პარტნიორობის" ხელშეკრულების საბოლოო პროექტი მოამზადეს. Retrieved June 4, 2021, from Civil.ge: https://old.civil.ge/geo/article.php?id=28877

Civil.ge. (2021a, October 22). *ECHR Finds Wartime Crimes Claims Against Georgia Inadmissible*. Retrieved March 22, 2022, from Civil.ge: https://civil.ge/archives/449488

Civil.ge. (2021b, January 21). *European Court Verdict into Georgia vs. Russia Case over 2008 War*. Retrieved March 22, 2022, from Civil.ge: https://civil.ge/archives/392226

Civil.ge. (2021c, July 10). საქართველოსთვის *MAP*-ის მინიჭება შეაფერხებს კონფლიქტების მოგვარებას - ლავროვი. Retrieved June 2, 2021, from Civil.ge: https://old.civil.ge/geo/article.php?id=18770&search=

Civil.ge. (2022d, March 24). *2008 War: ECHR Throws Out 370 Applications Against Georgia*. Retrieved March 25, 2022, from Civil.ge: https://civil.ge/archives/481227

Civil.ge. (2022e, March 10). *2008 War: ICC Files Arrest Warrant for S. Ossetian Officials*. Retrieved March 23, 2022, from Civil.ge: https://civil.ge/archives/478448

Clark, T. (2004). *Art and Propaganda*. Details Publications.

CNN. (2005, May 11). *Bush: Georgia 'beacon of liberty'*. Retrieved June 4, 2021, from CNN: https://edition.cnn.com/2005/WORLD/europe/05/10/bush.tuesday/

CNN. (2008, August 12). *Leaders of ex-Soviet republics support Georgia at rally*. Retrieved June 4, 2021, from CNN: http://edition.cnn.com/2008/WORLD/europe/08/12/georgia.rally/

CNN. (2008, August 26). *Russia condemned for recognizing rebel regions*. Retrieved March 22, 2022, from CNN: https://edition.cnn.com/2008/WORLD/europe/08/26/russia.vote.georgia/

Cochrane, J., & Fuller, T. (2016). Jakarta Attack Raises Fears of ISIS' Spread in Southeast Asia. *The New York Times*.

COE. (2013). *Profiles on counter-terrorist capacity-France*. Council of Europe.

Constitution of the Russian Federation. (1993). Retrieved from https://publicofficialsfinancialdisclosure.worldbank.org/sites/fdl/files/assets/law-library-files/Russian%20Federation_Constitution_1993_EN.pdf

Cook, J., & Vale, G. (2018). *From Daesh to 'Diaspora': Tracing the Women and Minors of Islamic State*. International Center for the Study of Radicalization.

Copeland, T. (2000). *The Information Revolution and National Security*. doi:10.21236/ADA382498

Corbin, K. (2009, March 12). *Lessons From the Russia-Georgia Cyberwar*. Retrieved from Internet News: https://www.internetnews.com/government/article.php/3810011/Lessons+From+the+RussiaGeorgia+Cyberwar.htm

Council of Europe. (2005). *Media and Terrorism*. Retrieved from: https://assembly.coe.int/nw/xml/XRef/X2H-Xref-ViewHTML.asp?FileID=10914&lang=EN

Council of Europe. (2017, October 10). *The new Ukrainian law on education: a major impediment to the teaching of national minorities' mother tongues*. Retrieved March 18, 2022, from Council of Europe: https://assembly.coe.int/nw/xml/XRef/Xref-XML2HTML-en.asp?fileid=24125&lang=en

Crelinsten, R., & Schmid, A. (2007). Western responses to terrorism: A twenty-five year balance sheet. *Terrorism and Political Violence*, 307–340.

Crenshaw, M. (1981). *The Causes of Terrorism. Comparative Politics, Ph.D. Programs in Political Science*. City University of New York.

Crenshaw, M. (2001). The psychology of terrorism: An agenda for the 21st century. *Political Psychology, 21*(2), 405–420. doi:10.1111/0162-895X.00195

Crooke, A. (2014). *You Can't Understand ISIS If You Don't Know the History of Wahhabism in Saudi Arabia. Huffington Post.*

CSCE. (1994, December 21). *Budapest document 1994 towards a genuine partnership in a new era*. Retrieved March 23, 2022, from CSCE: https://www.osce.org/files/f/documents/5/1/39554.pdf

CTED. (2021). *Update on the impact of the COVID-19 pandemic on Terrorism, counter-terrorism and countering violent extremism.* CTED.

Cunningham, K. J. (2010). Cross-Regional Trends in Female Terrorism. *Studies in Conflict and Terrorism, 26*, 171–195.

Cunningham, K. J. (2007). Countering Female Terrorism. *Studies in Conflict and Terrorism*, 123.

Dalton, A., & Asal, V. (2011). Is It Ideology or Desperation: Why Do Organizations Deploy Women in Violent Terrorist Attacks? *Studies in Conflict & Terrorism*, 802-819.

Darczewska, J. (2014). *The information war on Ukraine*. Centre for Eastern Studies.

Darczewska, J. (2016). *Russia's armed forces on the information war front*. OSW Studies.

Davis, J. (2020). The future of the Islamic State's Women: assessing their potential threat. ICCT Policy Brief.

Davis, J. (2013). Evolution of the Global Jihad: Female Suicide Bombers in Iraq. *Studies in Conflict and Terrorism, 36*(4), 279–291. doi:10.1080/1057610X.2013.763598

Davis, J. (2017). *Women in Modern Terrorism: From Liberation Wars to global jihad and the islamic state*. Rowman & Littlefield.

Davis, J., West, L., & Amarasingam, A. (2020). Measuring Impact, Uncovering Bias? Citation Analysis of Literature on Women in Terrorism. *Perspectives on Terrorism*, 9.

Davitashvili, Z., & Elizbarashvili, N. (2012). *Global Geography*. Tbilisi State University.

Dearden, L. (2019). ISIS Claims Responsibility for Sri Lanka Easter Massacre. *The Independent.*

Dechesne, M. (2009). Explorations in the experimental social psychology of terrorism: The struggle-violence link and its predictors. *Revue Internationale de Psychologie Sociale*, *22*(3), 87–102.

Deutsche Welle. (2015a, August 9). *Ukraine blacklists Depardieu and 13 other Russian artists.* Retrieved March 18, 2022, from Deutsche Welle: https://www.dw.com/en/ukraine-blacklists-depardieu-and-13-other-russian-artists/a-18636568

Deutsche Welle. (2015b, December 24). *Ukraine to impose tit-for-tat trade embargo on Russia.* Retrieved March 16, 2022, from Deutsche Welle: https://www.dw.com/en/ukraine-to-impose-tit-for-tat-trade-embargo-on-russia/a-18940722

Deylami, S. S. (2012). Saving the Enemy. *International Feminist Journal of Politics*, 1–18.

Dolgovaya. (2005). *Criminology: University Textbook.* Partnership for Peace Consortium of Defense Academies and Security Studies Institute.

Drakos, K., & Kutan, A. M. (2003). Regional effects of terrorism on tourism in three Mediterranean countries. *The Journal of Conflict Resolution*, *47*(5), 621–641. doi:10.1177/0022002703258198

Drezner, D. W. (2003). The Hidden Hand of Economic Coercion. *International Organization*, *57*(3), 643–659. doi:10.1017/S0020818303573052

Duić, I., Cvrtila, V., & Ivanjko, T. (2017). International cyber security challenges. *40th International Convention on Information and Communication Technology, Electronics and Microelectronics (MIPRO)*, 1309-1313. 10.23919/MIPRO.2017.7973625

Dunn, D. H. (2005). Bush, 11 September and the Conflicting Strategies of the 'War on Terrorism'. *Irish Studies in International Affairs*, *16*, 11–33. Retrieved January 4, 2022, from http://www.jstor.org/stable/30001932

Duvold, K. (2015). *Beyond Borders: The return of kin-state politics in Europe.* Retrieved from https://www.semanticscholar.org/paper/Beyond-Borders-%3A-The-Return-of-Kin-state-Politics-Duvold/9db5a4655f97bf9936aa8d505115e9fe91206817

Dyomkin, D. (2011, December 21). *Russia says Georgia war stopped NATO expansion.* Retrieved May 10, 2021, from Reuters: https://www.reuters.com/article/idINIndia-60645720111121

Dziadul, C. (2016, February 12). *Ukraine bans 15 Russian channels.* Retrieved March 18, 2022, from Broadbandtvnews: https://www.broadbandtvnews.com/2016/02/12/ukraine-bans-15-russian-channels/

Eager, P. W. (2008). Women and Political Violence. In From Freedom Fighters to Terrorists (pp. 3-4). Ashgate.

Eager, P. W. (2008). From Freedom Fighters to Terrorists: Women and Political Violence. *Journal of Peace Research.*

ECHR. (2021, January 21). *Georgia v. Russia (II) [GC] - 38263/08.* Retrieved from ECHR: https://hudoc.echr.coe.int/eng#{%22appno%22:[%22\%2238263/08\%22%22],%22itemid%22:[%22002-13102%22]}

Eilstrup, S. M., & Jones, C. (2008). Assessing the Dangers of Illicit Networks: Why al-Qaida May Be Less Threatening Than Many Think. *International Security*, *33*(2), 7–44. doi:10.1162/isec.2008.33.2.7

Ellyatt, H. (2022, February 10). *Russia begins massive military drills with Belarus; U.S. slams 'escalatory' action.* Retrieved March 19, 2022, from CNBC: https://www.cnbc.com/2022/02/10/russia-set-to-begin-massive-military-drills-with-belarus.html

Engvall, J. (2020, January 8). *Military confidence-building in crises: lessons from Georgia and Ukraine.* Retrieved May 19, 2021, from Taylor & Francis Online: https://www.tandfonline.com/doi/full/10.1080/14702436.2020.1776615

Eriksson, J., & Giacomello, G. (2006). The Information Revolution, Security, and International Relations. *International Political Science Review*, *27*(3), 221–244. doi:10.1177/0192512106064462

Euben, R. L. (2007). Review Symposium: Understanding Suicide Terror. *Perspectives on Politics*, *5*, 118–140.

EUROPOL. (2004). *European Union Organized Crime Report 2004*. Retrieved from: https://www.europol.europa.eu/publications-events/main-reports/european-union-organised-crime-report-2004

Europol. (2016). *European Union Terrorism Situation and Trend Report*. European Police Office.

Farwell, J. P., & Arakelian, D. (2013). What Does Iran's Cyber Capability Mean For Future Conflict? *The Whitehead Journal of Diplomacy and International Relations*, 49-65.

FATF. (2010). *An introduction to the FATF and its work*. Retrieved from Fatf-gafi: https://www.fatf-gafi.org/media/fatf/documents/brochuresannualreports/Introduction%20to%20the%20FATF.pdf

FBI. (2005). *Terrorism 2002/2005*. Retrieved from: https://www.fbi.gov/stats-services/publications/terrorism-2002-2005

FBI. (2022). *East African Embassy Bombings*. Retrieved from: https://www.fbi.gov/history/famous-cases/east-african-embassy-bombings

Felgenhauer, P. (2012, August 9). *Putin Confirms the Invasion of Georgia Was Preplanned*. Retrieved May 5, 2021, from The Jamestown Foundation: https://jamestown.org/program/putin-confirms-the-invasion-of-georgia-was-preplanned/

Felshtinsky & Chernyavsky. (2013). *Red Terror during the Civil War*. Knigovek.

Freeman, C. (2015). *Chief Foreign Correspondent. Islamic State mints its own 'Islamic Dinar' coins*. The Telegraph.

Fuller, J. (2015). ISIS or ISIL? The debate over what to call Iraq's terror group. *The Washington Post*.

Galica, N. (2020). *Lifting the Veil: The Impact of Framing on Sentencing Disparities Between Males and Females Convicted of Terrorism since the Rise of ISIS*. The John Marshall Law School.

Ganor, B. (2002). Defining terrorism: Is one man's terrorist another man's freedom fighter? *Police Practice and Research*, *3*(4), 287–304. doi:10.1080/1561426022000032060

Gentry, C. (2010). The relationship between new social movement theory and terrorism studies: The role of leadership, membership, ideology and gender. *Terrorism and Political Violence*.

George, A. (1993). *Forceful Persuasion: Coercive Diplomacy as an Alternative to War*. United States Institute of Peace.

Gerden, E. (2017, February 10). *Ukraine Enacts a Winter Ban on Book Imports From Russia*. Retrieved March 18, 2022, from Publishing Perspectives: https://publishingperspectives.com/2017/02/ukraine-ban-book-imports-from-russia/

Gershkovich. (2022, Mar 30). *Putin's Approval Rating Jumps After Invasion, Poll Shows*. Retrieved April 3, 2022, from Wall Street Journal: https://www.wsj.com/livecoverage/russia-ukraine-latest-news-2022-03-30/card/putin-s-approval-rating-jumps-after-invasion-poll-shows-fm8f4uSdiVfTxORQOE0v

Giles, K. (2015). *Russia and Its Neighbours: Old Attitudes, New Capabilities*. Conflict Studies Research Centre.

Gill, P., Horgan, J., & Deckert, M. (2014). Bombing Alone: Tracing the Motivations and Antecedent Behaviors of Lone-Actor Terrorists. *Journal of Forensic Sciences*. Retrieved from: https://onlinelibrary.wiley.com/doi/pdf/10.1111/1556-4029.12312

Gill, P., & Corner, E. (2017). There and back again: The study of mental disorder and terrorist involvement. *The American Psychologist*, *72*(3), 231–241. doi:10.1037/amp0000090 PMID:28383976

Goepner, E. W. (2016, March 1). Measuring the Effectiveness of America eness of America's War on T ar on Terror. *The US Army War College Quarterly Parameters*, *46*, 107–108. doi:10.55540/0031-1723.2828

Goldstein, J. S., & Pevehouse, J. C. (2011). *International Relations*. Pearson.

Goldstein, J., & Pevehouse, C. (2011). *International relations. International Relations: 2010-2011 Update* (9th ed.). Pearson Longman.

Goodin, R. (2006). *What's wrong with terrorism?* SAGE Journals.

Goodwin, J. (2006). A Theory of Categorical Terrorism. *Social Forces*, *84*(4), 2027–2046. doi:10.1353of.2006.0090

Gordiienko, O. (2015, August 23). *Trade war with Russia hurts Ukraine less*. Retrieved March 15, 2022, from Kyiv Post: https://www.kyivpost.com/article/content/business/trade-war-with-russia-hurts-ukraine-ever-less-396266.html

Gould, R. v. (1995). *Insurgent Identities: Class, Community, and Protest in Paris from 1848 to the Commune*. University of Chicago.

Gozman, L. (1996). *Terrorism. Socio-Psychological Research*. Omsk State University.

Greset, P., & Mahan, S. (2008). *Terrorism in perspective: What is terrorism*. Sage Publication.

Grove, G. D., Goodman, S., & Lukasik, S. (2000). Cyber-attacks and International Law. *Survival*, *42*(3), 89–103. doi:10.1093urvival/42.3.89

Güçhan, G. (1999). *Genre Cinema, Image and Ideology*. Anadolu University Press.

Gurr, T. R. (2015). *Why men rebel*. Routledge. doi:10.4324/9781315631073

Gvimradze, G. (2014). *The Iraq Crisis*. Georgian Foundation for Strategic and International Studies. Retrieved from: https://gfsis.org.ge/files/library/opinion-papers/24-expert-opinion-eng.pdf

Hakala, J., & Melnychuk, J. (2021). *Russia's Strategy in Cyberspace*. NATO StratCom COE and NATO Cooperative Cyber Defence COE.

Harding, L. (2022, March 1). *'Horrendous' rocket attack kills civilians in Kharkiv as Moscow 'adapts its tactics'*. Retrieved April 10, 2022, from The Guardian: https://www.theguardian.com/world/2022/feb/28/ukraine-several-killed-by-russian-rocket-strikes-in-civilian-areas-of-kharkiv

Hassan, H. (2014). *New Syrian Islamic Council Repeats the Patterns of Old*. National.

Hatamleh, H. (2012). A Review and Comparing of all Hacking Techniques and Domain Name System Method. *Contemporary Engineering Sciences*, *5*(2), 239–250.

Hirschmann, K. (2003). *The Changing Face of Terrorism*. Retrieved from SemanticScholar: https://library.fes.de/pdf-files/ipg/ipg-2000-3/arthirschmann.pdf

Hoffman, B. (2006). *Inside terrorism, revised and expanded edition*. Columbia University Press.

Hoffman, B. (2017). *Inside Terrorism*. Columbia University Press. doi:10.7312/hoff17476

Hoffman, B. (2018). *Inside terrorism*. Columbia university press.

Hoffman, B., & McCormick, G. H. (2004). Terrorism, Signaling and Suicide Attack. *Studies in Conflict and Terrorism*, *27*(4), 243–281. doi:10.1080/10576100490466498

Hollis, D. (2010). *Cyberwar Case Study: Georgia 2008*. Small Wars Journal.

Horgan, J. (2005). The Social and Psychological Characteristics of Terrorism and Terrorists. In T. Bjorgo (Ed.), *Root Causes of Terrorism: Myths, Realities and Ways Forward.* Taylor and Francis. doi:10.4324/9780203337653_chapter_4

Horgan, J. G. (2017). Psychology of terrorism: Introduction to the special issue. *The American Psychologist, 72*(3), 199–204. doi:10.1037/amp0000148 PMID:28383973

Hor, M. Y. M. (2005). *Global anti-terrorism law and policy.* Cambridge University Press.

Huckerby, J. (2015). When Women Become Terrorists. *The New York Times.*

Hudson Teslik, L. (2015). *Interview with Arabic Interviewer.* Marifah.

Hudson, D. (2014, September 10). *President Obama: "We Will Degrade and Ultimately Destroy ISIL".* Retrieved from https://obamawhitehouse.archives.gov/blog/2014/09/10/president-Obama-we-will-degrade-and-ultimately-destroy-isil

Hultman, L. (2005, September 3). Killing Civilians to Signal Resolve: Rebel Strategies in Intrastate Conflicts. Paper Presented at the *Annual Meeting of the American Political Science Association*, Washington, DC.

Human Rights Watch. (2022a, April 3). *Ukraine: Apparent War Crimes in Russia-Controlled Areas.* Retrieved April 10, 2022, from Human Rights Watch: https://www.hrw.org/news/2022/04/03/ukraine-apparent-war-crimes-russia-controlled-areas

Human Rights Watch. (2022b, April 21). *Ukraine: Russian Forces' Trail of Death in Bucha.* Retrieved April 23, 2022, from Human Rights Watch: https://web.archive.org/web/20220421062141/https://www.hrw.org/news/2022/04/21/ukraine-russian-forces-trail-death-bucha

Huntington, S. P. (1993). The Clash of Civilizations? *Foreign Affairs*, 22-49.

IDFI. (2020, August 7). *12 წელი 2008 წლის აგვისტოს ომიდან: რუსული დეზინფორმაცია და რეალური ფაქტები.* Retrieved June 4, 2021, from IDFI: https://idfi.ge/ge/august_war_russian_desinformation

IEP. (2022). *Global Terrorism Index 2022-Measuring the Impact of Terrorism.* Institute for Economics & Peace.

Ignatenko, A. (2022). *International Law.* Aspect Press.

Institute for Economics and Peace. (2016). *Global Terrorism Index 2015.* Retrieved from: https://privacyinternational.org/sites/default/files/2018-02/Global%20Terrorism%20Index%202015%2C%20Institute%20for%20Economics%20%26%20Peace.pdf

Intelligence Council of USA. (2015). *Global Trends.* Retrieved from: https://www.dni.gov/files/documents/Global%20Trends_2015%20Report.pdf

International Center for Counter Terrorism. (2022). *Negotiating with Terrorists.* Retrieved from: https://icct.nl/event/negotiating-with-terrorists/

International Republican Institute. (2007). *Georgian National Voter Study.* International Republican Institute.

IRI. (2014-2021). *IRI Polls and Qualitative Research.* Retrieved March 18, 2022, from IRI: https://www.iri.org/polls/

Jacques, K., & Taylor, P. J. (2009). Female Terrorism: A Review. *Terrorism and Political Violence, 21*(3), 499–515. doi:10.1080/09546550902984042

James, P., & Friedman, J. (2006). *Globalizing War and Intervention* (Vol. 3). Globalization and Violence. Sage Publications.

John, D., & McKinnon, N. K. (2008, August 14). *U.S. Launches Airlift to Aid Georgia.* Retrieved June 4, 2021, from The Wall Street Journal: https://www.wsj.com/articles/SB121866388366238327

Jumuah, A. (2012). *Wasila, Circumambulating Graves and Accusing Others of Shirk and Kufr* (M. Lock, Trans.). Marifah.

Kapuściński, G., & Richards, B. (2016). News framing effects on destination risk perception. *Tourism Management, 57*(4), 234–244. doi:10.1016/j.tourman.2016.06.017

Karlsrud, J. (2015). The UN at war: Examining the consequences of peace-enforcement mandates for the UN peacekeeping operations in the CAR, the DRC and Mali. *Third World Quarterly, 36*(1), 40–54. doi:10.1080/01436597.2015.976016

Karlsrud, J. (2017). Towards UN counter-terrorism operations? *Third World Quarterly, 38*(6), 1215–1231. doi:10.1080/01436597.2016.1268907

Karumidze. (2005). *International Organizations*. Tbilisi State University.

Kesling, M. S. (2014). Jordan Releases Zarqawi's Spiritual Mentor From Prison. *Wall Street Journal.*

Khalil, L. (2019). *Behind the veil: Women in jihad after the caliphate*. Lowy Institute.

Khan, A. (2006). A Theory of International Terrorism. *Connecticut Law Review.*

Kıraç, R. (2012). *The ABC of cinema*. Say Publications.

Kiser, S. (2005). *Financing Terror. An Analysis and Simulation to Affect Al Qaeda's Financial Infrastructures*. RAND.

Kofman, M. R. (2015). *A Closer look at Russia's "Hybrid War"*. Wilson Centre.

Kolosov. (1996). *International Law*. Aspect Press.

Koops, J. A., & Tercovich, G. (2016). A European Return to UN Peacekeeping? *International Peacekeeping, 23*(5), 597–609. doi:10.1080/13533312.2016.1236430

Kremlin. (2007, February 10). *Speech and the Following Discussion at the Munich Conference on Security Policy.* Retrieved from President of Russia: http://en.kremlin.ru/events/president/transcripts/24034

Kruglanski, A. W., Jasko, K., Chernikova, M., Dugas, M., & Webber, D. (2018). To the fringe and back: Violent extremism and the psychology of deviance. In *The motivated mind* (pp. 344–366). Routledge. doi:10.4324/9781315175867-9

Kushnir, O. (2017). *Russian geopolitical advancements in the black sea region: The annexation of Crimea.* Polish Political Science Studies.

Kuznetsova, A. (2015). *Islamic State in the context of political changes in the Middle East.* Vestnik MGIMO. doi:10.24833/2071-8160-2015-2-41-221-229

Kydd, A. H., & Barbara, F. (2006). The strategies of terrorism. *International Security, 31*(1), 49–80. doi:10.1162/isec.2006.31.1.49

Kydd, A. H., & Walter, B. F. (2002). Sabotaging the peace: The politics of extremist violence. *International Organization, 56*(2), 263–296. doi:10.1162/002081802320005487

Laitin, D. D., & Shapiro, J. N. (2008). The Sources of Terrorism: An Ecological and Organizational Perspective. In P. Keefer & N. Loayza (Eds.), *Terrorism, Economic Development, and Political Openness.* Cambridge University Press. doi:10.1017/CBO9780511754388.008

Laqueur, W. (2007). *History of Terrorism.* Transaction Publishers, Emerald Group Publishing Limited.

Laure Delcour, K. W. (2014, August 9). *Spoiler or facilitator of democratization?: Russia's role in Georgia and Ukraine" by Laure Delcour and Kataryna Wolczuk*. Retrieved May 19, 2021, from Taylor & Francis Online: https://www.tandfonline.com/doi/full/10.1080/13510347.2014.996135

Lax, F. (2020). *Female terrorists and extremists: An exploratory study*. Johns Hopkins University.

Le Monde. (2007). *Atlas der Globalisierung: Die Welt von morgen Paperback*. Retrieved from: https://www.amazon.de/Atlas-Globalisierung-Die-Welt-morgen/dp/3937683380

Lead Inspector General for Operation Inherent Resolve Quarterly Report to the United States Congress | July 1, 2021 – September 30, 2021. (2021, November 4). Retrieved January 8, 2022, from www.dodig.mil: https://www.dodig.mil/Reports/Lead-Inspector-General-Reports/Article/2833944/lead-inspector-general-for-operation-inherent-resolve-quarterly-report-to-the-u/

Lebedeva, M. M. (2011). *World Politics*. Aspect Press.

Leede, S. D. (2017). *Radicalisation and violent extremism –focus on women: How women become radicalised, and how to empower them to prevent radicalisation.* European Union; the Policy Department of the Citizen's Rigths and Constitutional Affairs. Retrieved January 5, 2022, from https://www.europarl.europa.eu/supporting-analyses

Leede, S. d. (2018). *Women in Jihad: A Historical Perspective.* ICCT Policy Brief. doi:10.19165/2018.2.06

Leede, S. d. (2018). *Women in Jihad: A Historical Perspective*. ICCT Policy Brief.

Leede, S., & Bakker, E. (2015). *European female jihadists in Syria: exploring an under-researched topic.* ICCT.

Lemieux, A. F. (2006). Social psychological approaches to understanding and preventing terrorism: Toward an interdisciplinary perspective. *Journal of Security Education*, *1*(4), 75–83. doi:10.1300/J460v01n04_07

Lesia Dorosh, O. I. (2019). Comparative Analysis of the Hybrid Tactics Application by the Russian Federation in Conflicts with Georgia and Ukraine. *Central European Journal of International and Security Studies.*

Levada Center. (2020, September 30). *Attitudes toward countries*. Retrieved May 23, 2021, from Levada Center: https://www.levada.ru/en/2020/09/30/attitudes-toward-countries-4/

Lilly, B., & Cheravitch, J. (2020). The Past, Present, and Future of Russia's Cyber Strategy and Forces. In *12th International Conference on Cyber Conflict* (pp. 129-155). Tallin: NATO CCDCOE Publications. 10.23919/CyCon49761.2020.9131723

Lind, M. (2009). *The Legal Debate is Over: Terrorism is a War Crime*. New America Foundation.

Llewellyn, J., McConnell, M., Llewellyn, J., & Thompson, S. (2019). *The Red Terror*. Russian Revolution. Alpha History.

Loken, M., & Zelenz, A. (2017). Explaining extremism: Western women in Daesh. *European Journal of International Security*, 3.

Lokshina, T. (2009, January 30). *Georgia war: auditing the damage*. Retrieved March 22, 2022, from Human Rights Watch: https://www.hrw.org/news/2009/01/30/georgia-war-auditing-damage

Longo, M. (2022). *Blood in the Sand: Shiite Assassins*. Warfare History Network. Retrieved from: https://warfarehistorynetwork.com/blood-in-the-sand-shiite-assassins/

Lughod, L. A. (2002). Do Muslim Women Really Need Saving? Anthropological Reflections on Cultural Relativism and Its Others. *American Anthropologist*, *104*(3), 783–790. doi:10.1525/aa.2002.104.3.783

Lynch, O., & Argomaniz, J. (2018). Victims and Perpetrators of Terrorism Exploring Identities, Roles, and Narratives. Routledge.

MacKenzie, M. (2009). Securitization and Desecuritization: Female Soldiers and the Reconstruction of Women in Post-Conflict Sierra Leone. *Security Studies: Feminist Contributions*, 241-261.

Mansfield, H. (2001). *Those Hell-Hounds Called Terrorists*. Claremont Review of Books. Retrieved from: https://claremontreviewofbooks.com/those-hell-hounds-called-terrorists/

Margolin, D. (2019). The Changing Roles of Women in Violent Islamist Groups. In *Perspectives on the future of women, gender, & violent extremism* (pp. 45–46). The George Washington University.

Martin, G. (2006). Understanding terrorism: Challenges, perspectives, and issues. *Sage (Atlanta, Ga.)*.

Matsaberidze, D. (2015). *Russia vs. EU/US through Georgia and Ukraine*. CONNECTIONS The Quarterly Journal. doi:10.11610/Connections.14.2.06

Matseketsa, B., & Mapolisa, T. (2013). The effects of terrorism on international peace and security and educational systems in Africa and beyond-a new millennium perspective. *International Journal of Advanced Research*, *1*(8), 694–710.

Matthews. (2014). *Realist Criminology*. Palgrave Macmillan.

McCauley, C. (2001). *Group Identification under Conditions of Threat: College Students' Attachment to Country, Family, Ethnicity, Religion, and University Before and After September 11, 2001*. Wiley Online Library.

McCauley, C., & Moskalenko, S. (2017). Understanding political radicalization: The two-pyramids model. *The American Psychologist*, *72*(3), 205–216. doi:10.1037/amp0000062 PMID:28383974

McKernan, B. (2015). Tehran attacks: ISIS claims responsibility for 'first major attack on Iran. *The Independent*.

Medero, G. (2011). Les sources de financement légal et illégal des groupes terroristes d´aujourd´hui. *Revista de Paz, 4*.

Merari, A. (2006). Psychological Aspects of Suicide Terrorism. In *Psychology of Terrorism*. Oxford University Press. doi:10.1093/med:psych/9780195172492.003.0008

Merari, A. (2010). *Driven to Death: Psychological and Social Aspects of Suicide Terrorism*. Oxford University Press. Retrieved from https://journals.openedition.org/ress/1241

Merriam-Webster. (n.d.). *Radical*. Retrieved November 20, 2021, from Merriam-Webster.com dictionary: https://www.merriam-webster.com/dictionary/radical

Meskhidze, R. (2018). *Terrorism and its Basics*. Retrieved from: http://yata.ge/ge/?p=1585

Miller, C. (2020, April 25). *Zelenskiy's First Year: He Promised Sweeping Changes. How's He Doing?* Retrieved March 18, 2022, from Radio Free Europe / Radio Liberty: https://www.rferl.org/a/zelenskiys-first-year-he-promised-sweeping-changes-how-s-he-doing-/30576329.html

Miller, M. J., & Stefanova, B. (2007). The War on Terror: The second Bush Administration. In B. M. Rajaee (Ed.), *The War on Terror in Comparative Perspective: US Security and Foreign Policy after 9/11* (pp. 90–93). Palgrave Macmillan.

Ministry for Europe and Foreign Affairs. (n.d.). *Terrorism: France's International Action - Ministry for Europe and Foreign Affairs*. Retrieved March 19, 2022, from https://www.diplomatie.gouv.fr/en/french-foreign-policy/security-disarmament-and-non-proliferation/terrorism-france-s-international-action/

Mironova, V. (2019). Is the Future of ISIS Female? *The New York Times*.

Modebadze, V. (2016). *Two Wars in Chechnya*. Universal Press.

Moghaddam, F. (2006). *From the terrorists' point of view: What they experience and why they come to destroy*. Praeger Security International.

Nacos, B. L. (2005). The Portrayal of Female Terrorists in the Media: Similar Framing Patterns in the News Coverage of Women in Politics and in Terrorism. *Studies in Conflict and Terrorism*, *28*(5), 435–451. doi:10.1080/10576100500180352

Nairn, T., & James, P. (2005). *Global matrix: Nationalism, globalism and state-terrorism*. Academic Press.

Nairn, T., & James, P. (2005). *Global Matrix: Nationalism, Globalism and State-Terrorism*. Pluto Press.

Napoleoni, L. (2005, January). Money and Terrorism. *Economist*.

NATO Handbook, . (2007). *NATO Public Diplomacy Division. NATO.*

NATO. (1995, September 3). *Study on NATO Enlargement*. Retrieved May 25, 2021, from NATO: https://www.nato.int/cps/en/natohq/official_texts_24733.htm

NATO. (2008, April 3). *Bucharest Summit Declaration*. Retrieved May 5, 2021, from NATO: https://www.nato.int/cps/en/natolive/official_texts_8443.htm

Ndung'u, I., Sigsworth, R., & Yenwong-Fai, U. (2017). *Violent extremism in Kenya: Why women are a priority*. Academic Press.

News, B. (2017, July 4). *Battle for Mosul: Fierce clashes as IS uses suicide bombers*. Retrieved January 9, 2022, from bbc.com: https://www.bbc.com/news/world-middle-east-40489816

News, U. N. (2021, February 28). *UNICEF urges repatriation of all children in Syria's Al-Hol camp following deadly fire*. Retrieved November 20, 2021, from https://news.un.org/en/story/2021/02/1085982

Ní Aoláin, F. (2016). The "war on terror" and extremism: Assessing the relevance of the Women, Peace and Security agenda. *International Affairs*, *92*(2), 275–291. doi:10.1111/1468-2346.12552

Norlen, T. C. (2020). The Impact of COVID-19 on Salafi-Jihadi Terrorism. *Connections: The Quarterly Journal, 19*(2), 11-23.

North Atlantic Treaty Organisation. (2021, September 14). *Countering terrorism*. https://www.nato.int/cps/en/natohq/topics_77646.htm

Nour, Y. (2017). Motives in Egypt's Deadliest Terrorist Attack: Religion and Revenge. *New York Times*.

O'Rourke, L. A. (2009). What's Special about Female Suicide Terrorism? *Security Studies*, *18*(4), 681–682. doi:10.1080/09636410903369084

Olshansky, D. (2002). *Terrorism Psychology*. Piter.

OSCE. (1996, December 3). *LISBON DOCUMENT 1996*. Retrieved March 22, 2022, from OSCE: https://www.osce.org/files/f/documents/1/0/39539.pdf

OSCE. (2018). *Preventing Terrorism and Countering Violent Extremism and Radicalization that Lead to Terrorism: A Community-Policing Approach*. Retrieved from: https://www.osce.org/files/f/documents/1/d/111438.pdf

Oxford English Dictionary (2nd ed.). (2002). Oxford University Press.

Özden, Z. (2004). *Movie Review*. Image Bookstore.

Özkent, Y. (2021). Tracing Gender in Hollywood Cinema: Kramer vs. Marriage Story Forty Years After Kramer. *Culture and Communication, 24*(1), 227–259.

Özsoy, O. (1998). *Propaganda and Public Opinion.* Alfa Publications.

Pape, R. A. (2003). The strategic logic of suicide terrorism. *The American Political Science Review, 93*(3), 343–361.

Parashar, S. (2011). Gender, Jihad, and Jingoism: Women as perpetrators, planners, and patrons of militancy in Kashmir. *Studies in Conflict and Terrorism, 34*(4), 295–317. doi:10.1080/1057610X.2011.551719

Paravicini, G. (2017). Brussels ISIL cell 'initially' planned to 'strike France again. *Politico.*

Parkes. (2015). The Trafficking Protocol has Advanced the Global Movement against Human Exploitation: The case of the United Kingdom. *Anti-Trafficking Review.*

Patel, S., & Westermann, J. (2018). Women and Islamic-State Terrorism: An Assessment of How Gender Perspectives Are Integrated in Countering Violent Extremism Policy and Practices. *Security Challenges, 14*(2), 73-83. Retrieved from https://www.jstor.org/stable/26558022

Patkin, T. (2004). *Explosive Baggage: Female Palestinian Suicide Bombers and the Rhetoric of Emotion.* Woman and Language.

Pavel Polityuk, J. F. (2014, March 4). *Ukraine says communications hit, MPs phones blocked.* Retrieved June 4, 2021, from Reuters: https://www.reuters.com/article/ukraine-crisis-cybersecurity-idUSL6N0M12CF20140304

Permanent Mission of the United Arab Emirates to the United Nations. (2017). *UAE calls for zero tolerance for all those who support terrorism financing.* Retrieved from: https://www.un.int/uae/news/uae-calls-zero-tolerance-all-those-who-support-terrorism-financing

Pernik, P., Wojtkowiak, J., & Verschoor-Kirss, A. (2016). *National Cyber Security Organisation: United States.* NATO Cooperative Cyber Defence Centre of Excellence.

Peter Pomerantsev, M. W. (2014). *The Menace of Unreality: How the Kremlin Weaponizes Information, Culture and Money.* Institute of Modern Russia. Retrieved from https://lccn.loc.gov/2015433465

Peuch, J.-C. (2002, November 22). *Georgia: Shevardnadze Officially Requests Invitation To Join NATO.* Retrieved June 4, 2021, from Radio Free Europe / Radio Liberty: https://www.rferl.org/a/1101463.html

Pollitt, M. (1998). Cyberterrorism—Fact or fancy? *Computer Fraud & Security, 1998*(2), 8–10. doi:10.1016/S1361-3723(00)87009-8

Pomerantsev, P. (2014, September 9). *How Russia Is Revolutionizing Information Warfare.* Retrieved May 23, 2021, from Defense One: https://www.defenseone.com/threats/2014/09/how-russia-revolutionizing-information-warfare/93635/

Powaski, R. (1998). *The Cold War United States And The Soviet Union.* University Press.

Primoratz, I. (2007). *Defining "Terrorism".* Stanford Encyclopedia of Philosophy.

Primoratz, I. (2007). *Terrorism. Stanford Encyclopedia of Philosophy.*

Purkitt, H. (1984). *Dealing with Terrorism.* Conflict in World Society.

Rácz, A. (2015). *Russia's Hybrid War in Ukraine.* The Finnish Institute of International Affairs.

Radio Free Europe / Radio Liberty. (2004, May 6). *Georgian President In Adjaria After Abashidze Flees.* Retrieved June 4, 2021, from Radio Free Europe / Radio Liberty: https://www.rferl.org/a/1052653.html

Radio Free Europe / Radio Liberty. (2006, October 17). *Georgia: Hundreds Left Stranded After Deportations From Russia*. Retrieved June 4, 2021, from Radio Free Europe / Radio Liberty: https://www.rferl.org/a/1072088.html

Radio Free Europe / Radio Liberty. (2019, February 25). *The Changing Story Of Russia's 'Little Green Men' Invasion*. Retrieved June 4, 2021, from Radio Free Europe / Radio Liberty: https://www.rferl.org/a/russia-ukraine-crimea/29790037.html

Radio Liberty. (2004, August 21). რა მოხდა ცხინვალის რეგიონში და რისთვის გაიღო იქ საქართველომ ახალი მსხვერპლი. Retrieved June 4, 2021, from Radio Liberty: https://www.radiotavisupleba.ge/a/1536767.html

Radio Liberty. (2005, July 26). გორის ტერაქტი გახსნილია, გამოძიებამ ამ დანაშაულში რუსეთის აგენტურის კვალს მიაგნო. Retrieved April 30, 2021, from Radio Liberty: https://www.radiotavisupleba.ge/a/1542418.html

Radio Liberty. (2008, April 7). როგორ უნდა მოგვარდეს აფხაზეთის კონფლიქტი? რუსი და ქართველი ექსპერტები მიხეილ სააკაშვილის ინიციატივის თაობაზე. Retrieved May 25, 2021, from Radio Libertya: https://www.radiotavisupleba.ge/a/1557203.html

Radio Liberty. (2010, August 7). ომის მეორე წლისთავი გორში. Retrieved June 3, 2021, from Radio Liberty: https://www.radiotavisupleba.ge/a/2121443.html

Radio Liberty. (2019a, February 19). Amnesty International: Five Years After Euromaidan, Justice For The Victims 'Still Not Even In Sight'. Retrieved May 25, 2021, from Radio Liberty: https://www.rferl.org/a/ukraine-maidan-justice-victims-amnesty-fifth-anniversary/29779358.html

Radio Liberty. (2019b, June 20). სერგეი გავრილოვის ბიოგრაფია. Retrieved May 25, 2021, from Radio Liberty: https://www.radiotavisupleba.ge/a/%E1%83%A1%E1%83%94%E1%83%A0%E1%83%92%E1%83%94%E1%83%98-%E1%83%92%E1%83%90%E1%83%95%E1%83%A0%E1%83%98%E1%83%9A%E1%83%9D%E1%83%95%E1%83%98%E1%83%A1-%E1%83%91%E1%83%98%E1%83%9D%E1%83%92%E1%83%A0%E1%83%90%E1%83%A4%E1%83%98%E1

Rainsford, S. (2015, October 24). *Ban due on direct flights between Russia and Ukraine*. Retrieved March 15, 2022, from BBC: https://www.bbc.com/news/world-europe-34622665

Rajaee, B. (2007). The Bush and US policy after 9/11. In M. J. Miller & B. Stefanova (Eds.), *The War on Terror in Comparative Perspective: US Security and Foreign Policy after 9/11* (p. 159). Palgrave Macmillan.

Rajaee, B. (2007). The Bush Doctrine and US policy after 9/11. In M. J. Miller & B. Stefano (Eds.), *The War on Terror in Comparative Perspective: US Security and Foreign Policy after 9/11* (pp. 159–160). Palgram Macmillan.

Rajaee, B. M. (2007). US Foreign Policy and Radical Islam. In M. J. Miller & B. Stefanova (Eds.), *US Security and Foreign Policy after 9/11* (p. 69). Palgrave Macmillan.

Ramey, C. R. (2007). *Mass media unleashed: How Washington policymakers shortchanged the American public*. Rowman & Littlefield.

Rapoport, D. C. (2002). The Four Waves of Rebel Terror and September 11. *Anthropoetics*, *8*(1).

Research Gate. (2011). *Being Tough or Being Nice? A Meta-Analysis on the Impact of Hard- and Softline Strategies in Distributive Negotiations*. Retrieved from: https://www.researchgate.net/publication/273653071_Being_Tough_or_Being_Nice_A_Meta-Analysis_on_the_Impact_of_Hard-_and_Softline_Strategies_in_Distributive_Negotiations

Reuters. (2022). *U.S. senators introduce bill to designate Russia state sponsor of terrorism*. Retrieved from: https://www.reuters.com/world/europe/us-senators-introduce-bill-designate-russia-state-sponsor-terrorism-2022-09-14/

Reuters. (2022a, April 21). *Latvian and Estonian parliaments say Russia committed genocide in Ukraine*. Retrieved April 25, 2022, from Reuters: https://www.reuters.com/world/europe/latvian-estonian-parliaments-say-russia-committed-genocide-ukraine-2022-04-21/

Reuters. (2022b, April 21). *Latvian and Estonian parliaments say Russia committed genocide in Ukraine*. Retrieved April 23, 2022, from Reuters: https://www.reuters.com/world/europe/latvian-estonian-parliaments-say-russia-committed-genocide-ukraine-2022-04-21/

Reuters. (2022c, February 21). *What does Russian recognition of breakaway Ukraine territories mean?* Retrieved March 22, 2022, from The Guardian: https://www.theguardian.com/world/2022/feb/21/what-would-russian-recognition-of-breakaway-ukraine-regions-mean

Robb, D. (2005). *Hollywood Operations*. Current Publishing.

Roggero, B. (2014). *ISIS announces formation of Caliphate, rebrands as "Islamic State"*. Long War Journal.

Roth, A. (2018, Nov 27). *Kerch strait confrontation: what happened and why does it matter?* Retrieved March 18, 2022, from The Guardian: https://www.theguardian.com/world/2018/nov/27/kerch-strait-confrontation-what-happened-ukrainian-russia-crimea

Roth, A. (2022, February 15). *Russia confirms 'partial' withdrawal of troops from Ukraine border*. Retrieved March 19, 2022, from The Guardian: https://www.theguardian.com/world/2022/feb/15/russia-ukraine-border-troops-withdrawal

Sageman, M. (2004). Understanding Terror Networks. *International Journal of Emergency Mental Health*, 7. PMID:15869076

Saltman, E. M., & Smith, M. (2015). Key Recommendations. In *Till Martyrdom Do Us Part* (pp. 70-71). Institute for Strategic Dialogue .

Saltman, E. M., & Smith, M. (2015). *'Till Martyrdom Do Us Part': Gender and the ISIS Phenomenon*. Institute for Strategic Dialogue.

Sander, O. (1997). *Political history*. Icon Bookstore.

Saul, B. (2005). Attempts to define "terrorism" in international law. *Netherlands International Law Review*, *52*(1), 57–83. doi:10.1017/S0165070X05000574

Schelling, T. C. (1960). *The Strategy of Conflict*. Harvard.

Schelling, T. C. (1966). *Arms and Influence*. Yale.

Schmid, A. (2004). *Terrorism - The Definitional Problem*. Retrieved from: https://scholarlycommons.law.case.edu/cgi/viewcontent.cgi?article=1400&context=jil

Schmid, A. P. (1983). Political terrorism: A research guide to concepts, theories, data, bases and literature. Academic Press.

Schmid, A. (2011). *Routledge Handbook of Terrorism Research*. Routledge. doi:10.4324/9780203828731

Schmid, A. P., & Jongman, A. J. (2005). *Political terrorism: A new guide to actors, authors, concepts, data bases, theories and literature*. Transaction Books.

Schmitt, E. (2014). In Battle to Defang ISIS, U.S. Targets Its Psychology. *New York Times*.

Schwartz, M. J. (2014, March 17). *DDoS Attacks Hit NATO, Ukrainian Media Outlets*. Retrieved May 5, 2021, from DARKReading: https://www.darkreading.com/attacks-and-breaches/ddos-attacks-hit-nato-ukrainian-media-outlets/d/d-id/1127742

Scognamillo, G. (2004). *Turkish Cinema History*. Kabalci Publications.

Sedrati, A. (2016). *"Sorry, you are not as important!" A study about the unequal media treatment of different terrorist attacks in the world in 2015 –Aftonbladet*. Stockholms Universitet.

Serpil, S. (1997). *The Adventure of Ideology*. Image Publications.

Seskuria, N. (2022, February 22). *Russia Is Reenacting Its Georgia Playbook in Ukraine*. Retrieved from Foreign Policy: https://foreignpolicy.com/2022/02/22/russia-ukraine-invasion-georgia-2008-south-ossetia-tskhinvali/

Setty, S. (2014). Country Report on Counterterrorism. *The American Journal of Comparative Law*, *62*(1), 643–672. doi:10.5131/AJCL.2013.0039

Shane Harris, P. S. (2021, December 3). *Russia planning massive military offensive against Ukraine involving 175,000 troops, U.S. intelligence warns*. Retrieved March 19, 2022, from Washington Post: https://www.washingtonpost.com/national-security/russia-ukraine-invasion/2021/12/03/98a3760e-546b-11ec-8769-2f4ecdf7a2ad_story.html

Shannon Pettypiece, Z. R. (2022, April 13). *Biden says Russia is committing 'genocide' in Ukraine*. Retrieved April 14, 2022, from NBCNews: https://www.nbcnews.com/politics/white-house/biden-calls-putin-actions-ukraine-genocide-rcna24131

Shapiro, L. R., & Maras, M.-H. (2018). Women's Radicalization to Religious Terrorism: An Examination of ISIS Cases in the United States. *Studies in Conflict and Terrorism*, 1.

Shepherd, L. J. (2013). *Critical Approaches to Security: an introduction to theories and methods*. Routledge. doi:10.4324/9780203076873

Shepherd, L. J. (2017). *The Role of the WPS Agenda in Countering Violent Extremism*. The Strategist.

Siedel, G. (2014). *Negotiating for Success: Essential Strategies and Skills*. University of Michigan.

Singer, P., & Friedman, A. (2014). *Cybersecurity and Cyberwar: What Everyone Needs to Know*. Oxford University Press. doi:10.1093/wentk/9780199918096.001.0001

Sjoberg, L., & Gentry, C. E. (2016). It's complicated: Looking closely at women in violent extremism. *Georgetown Journal of International Affairs*, 23-30.

Sjoberg, L., & Gentry, C. E. (2007). *Mothers, Monsters, Whores: Women's Violence in Global Politics*. Zed Books.

Sjoberg, L., & Gentry, C. E. (2008). Reduced to Bad Sex: Narratives of Violent Women from the Bible to the War on Terror. *International Relations*, *22*(1), 5–23. doi:10.1177/0047117807087240

Slatkin, A. (2008). The Stockholm Syndrome Revisited. The Police Chief Magazine, 75(12).

Sly, L. (2014). Syrian Tribal Revolt Against Islamic State Ignored, Fueling Resentment. *Washington Post*.

Smith, M. (1971). Zealots and Sicarii, Their Origins and Relation. *The Harvard Theological Review*, *64*(1), 1–19. doi:10.1017/S0017816000018009

Speckhard, A., & Shajkovci, A. (2017). *Beware the Women of ISIS: There Are Many, and They May Be More Dangerous Than the Men*. The Daily Beast.

Spencer, A. (2015). European female jihadists in Syria: Exploring an under-researched. *Journal of Strategic Security*, *9*(3), 79–87.

Spencer, A. N. (2016). The Hidden Face of Terrorism: An Analysis of the Women in Islamic State. *Journal of Strategic Security*, *9*(3), 74–98. doi:10.5038/1944-0472.9.3.1549

State Duma of Russia. (2002, May 31). *Russian Federation federal law on citizenship of the Russian Federation.* Retrieved May 29, 2021, from https://www.refworld.org/cgi-bin/texis/vtx/rwmain/opendocpdf.pdf?reldoc=y&docid=5a9d48314

State Sponsorship: An Impediment to the Global Fight against Terrorism. (2020). *International Law, 7*(2).

State, U. D. (n.d.). *The Global Coalition To Defeat ISIS*. Retrieved January 9, 2022, from www.state.gov: https://www.state.gov/about-us-the-global-coalition-to-defeat-isis/

Štitilis, D., Pakutinskas, P., & Malinauskaitė, I. (2017). EU and NATO cybersecurity strategies and national cyber security strategies: A comparative analysis. *Security Journal*, *30*(4), 1151–1168. doi:10.105741284-016-0083-9

Stohl, M. (1984). *The Superpowers and International Terror*. Paper presented at the Annual Meeting of the International Studies Association, Atlanta, GA.

Stohl, M. (1988). *States, Terrorism and State Terrorism: The Role of the Superpowers*. https://link.springer.com/chapter/10.1007/978-1-349-18989-2_6

Stohl, M. (1988). *National Interests and State Terrorism, The Politics of Terrorism.* Marcel Dekker.

Stoter, B. (2016, November 16). *As IS loses power, will group tap women jihadis to fight?* Retrieved January 9, 2022, from al-Monitor.com: https://www.al-monitor.com/originals/2016/11/islamic-state-women-role-fighting-syria-iraq.html

Stout, D. (2014). ISIS Massacres Sunni Tribe in Iraq. *Time*.

Talbot, R. (2000). Myths in the Representation of Women Terrorists. *Eire-Ireland*, *35*(3-4), 165–186. doi:10.1353/eir.2000.0032

Tarras-Wahlberg, L. (2016). *Seven Promises of ISIS to its Female Recruits.* ICSVE Research Report. Retrieved from http://www.icsve.org/research-reports/seven-promises-of-isis-to-its-female-recruits/

TASS. (2022, February 23). *Putin: Russia stands for demilitarization of Ukraine*. Retrieved March 22, 2022, from Russian News Agency: https://tass.com/russia/1408629?utm_source=google.com&utm_medium=organic&utm_campaign=google.com&utm_referrer=google.com

Taylor, L. (2013). *Islamic State Seeks to Justify Enslaving Yazidi Women and Girls in Iraq*. Reuters.

The Guardian. (2014, July 29). *EU and US impose sweeping economic sanctions on Russia*. Retrieved June 4, 2021, from The Guardian: https://www.theguardian.com/world/2014/jul/29/economic-sanctions-russia-eu-governments

Thiele, R. D. (2015). *Crisis in Ukraine – The Emergence of Hybrid Warfare.* The Institute for Strategic, Political, Security and Economic Consultancy (ISPSW).

Tisdall, S. (2022, February 12). *The edge of war: what, exactly, does Putin want in Ukraine?* Retrieved March 22, 2022, from The Guardian: https://www.theguardian.com/world/2022/feb/12/russia-ukraine-what-does-putin-want

Tome, L. (2015). *The "Islamic state": Trajectory and reach a year after its self-proclamation as a "caliphate"*. Retrieved from: https://www.redalyc.org/pdf/4135/413541154008.pdf

Trautman, L. (2015). Cybersecurity: What About U.S. Policy? SSRN *Electronic Journal*, 341-387. doi:10.2139/ssrn.2548561

Traverse, T. H. (1988). *Public Relations and Propaganda: Comparative Values*. Route Publications.

Treisman, R. (2022a, April 28). *Canada's House backs a motion recognizing Russia's actions in Ukraine as genocide.* Retrieved April 29, 2022, from NPR: https://www.npr.org/2022/04/28/1095272683/canada-russia-genocide-ukraine

Treisman, R. (2022b, April 28). *Canada's House backs a motion recognizing Russia's actions in Ukraine as genocide.* Retrieved April 29, 2022, from NPR: https://www.npr.org/2022/04/28/1095272683/canada-russia-genocide-ukraine

Tsakanyan, V. (2017). The role of cybersecurity in world politics. *Vestnik RUDN International Relations*, *17*(2), 339–348.

Turkovic, K. (2018). What Victimology has to Offer in the Fight Against Terrorism. *NATO Security through Science Series - E: Human and Societal Dynamics. Volume 13: Large-Scale Victimisation as a Potential Source of Terrorist Activities.*

Türten, B. (2017). *Making Short Documentary Films: The Example of Social Documentaries.* Doruk Publications.

Uawire. (2018, March 27). *Ukrainian border guards detain a Russian fishing boat in the Sea of Azov.* Retrieved March 18, 2022, from Uawire: https://www.uawire.org/border-guards-detain-a-russian-fishing-boat-in-the-sea-of-azov

Ullman, R. (1983). *Redefining Security. International Security.* The MIT Press. Retrieved from: https://muse.jhu.edu/article/446023/summary

UN Congress on Crime Prevention. (2005). *Eleventh United Nations congress on crime prevention and criminal justice.* Retrieved from: https://www.unodc.org/congress/en/previous/previous-11.html

UN Office on Drugs and Crime. (2022). *Victims of terrorism.* Retrieved from: https://www.unodc.org/unodc/en/terrorism/expertise/victims-of-terrorism.html

UN Security Council. (2014). *UNSCR 2178.* Retrieved from: https://documents-dds-ny.un.org/doc/UNDOC/GEN/N14/547/98/PDF/N1454798.pdf?OpenElement

UN. (1960). *United Nations, General Assembly Resolution, 1960, A/RES/15/1514.* Retrieved from: http://www.un-documents.net/a15r1514.htm

UN. (1963). *Convention on Offences and Certain Other Acts Committed on Board Aircraft.* International Civil Aviation Organization.

UN. (1970). Convention for the suppression of unlawful seizure of aircraft. United Nations.

UN. (1971). *Montreal Convention for the Suppression of Unlawful Acts against the Safety of Civil Aviation.* United Nations.

UN. (1977). Ad-Hoc Committee on International Terrorism. United Nations General Assembly.

UN. (1985). UN Resolution, (a), A/RES/40/43. United Nations, General Assembly.

UN. (1989). UN Resolution A/RES/1989/65. United Nations, General Assembly.

UN. (1993). *UN Resolution A/RES/47/133.* United Nations, General Assembly.

UN. (1995). *United Nations, General Assembly, Resolution, A/RES/49/60.* Retrieved from: https://www.un.org/en/ga/sixth/69/int_terrorism.shtml

UN. (1997). *International Convention for the Suppression of Terrorist Bombing.* New York: United Nations.

UN. (1999). International Convention for the Suppression of the Financing of Terrorism. *Treaty Collection, 2178.*

UN. (1999a). *International Convention for the Suppression of the Financing of Terrorism.* Retrieved from United Nations: https://www.un.org/law/cod/finterr.htm

UN. (1999b). *International Convention for the Suppression of the Financing of Terrorism.* New York: United Nations.

UN. (2001). *UN Security Council Resolution 1373*. Retrieved from: https://digitallibrary.un.org/record/449020?ln=en

UN. (2004). *OHCHR Resolution. 2004, HR/P/PT/8/Rev.1*. United Nations General Assembly.

UN. (2004). *Security Council Report A/59/565*. Retrieved from: https://www.securitycouncilreport.org/un-documents/document/cpr-a-59-565.php

UN. (2005). *International Convention for the Suppression of Acts of Nuclear Terrorism*. New York: United Nations.

UN. (2005). International Convention for the Suppression of Acts of Nuclear Terrorism. *Treaty Collection, 2445*, 89.

UN. (2006). *General Assembly Resolution A/RES/60/288, para. 3(d)*. UN General Assembly.

UN. (2006). *United Nations, General Assembly, 2006, Section IV, paragraph 1*. Retrieved from: https://treaties.un.org/doc/source/docs/a_61_611_e.pdf

UN. (2016). *General Assembly, Human Rights Council. The resolution, A/HRC/34/30, para. 56*. Retrieved from: https://www.unodc.org/e4j/zh/terrorism/module-3/key-issues/defining-rule-of-law.html

UN. (2016). *UN Global Counter-Terrorism Strategy. (a), A/70/826*. Retrieved from: https://www.un.org/counterterrorism/un-global-counter-terrorism-strategy

UN. (2017). *UNGA Resolution 72/123*. Retrieved from: https://www.un.org/en/ga/72/resolutions.shtml

UN. (2017*). United Nations, General Assembly, Human Rights Council, 2017 (b), A/HRC/35/L. 27*. Retrieved from: https://www.ohchr.org/en/hr-bodies/hrc/regular-sessions/session35/list-reports

UN. (2018). *Introduction to International Terrorism*. United Nations Office at Vienna.

UNHCR. (2016). *United Nations High Commissioner for Refugees, 2015*. Report. Retrieved from: https://www.unhcr.org/statistics/unhcrstats/576408cd7/unhcr-global-trends-2015.html

United Nations Digital Library. (2022). *UNSCR 2370*. https://digitallibrary.un.org/record/1298311/usage?ln=en

United Nations Office on Drugs and Crime. (2018). *Education for Justice University Module Series. Counter-Terrorism Module 1. Introduction to International Terrorism*. Retrieved from: https://www.unodc.org/documents/e4j/18-04932_CT_Mod_01_ebook_FINALpdf.pdf

United Nations. (2004). *Security Council Resolution S/2004/616, paragraph 6*. Retrieved from: https://digitallibrary.un.org/record/527647?ln=en

United Nations. (2005). *Basic Facts about the United Nations*. UN Department of Public Information.

United Nations. (2006). *General Assembly Resolution: A/RES60 /288*. Retrieved from: https://documents-dds-ny.un.org/doc/UNDOC/GEN/N05/504/88/PDF/N0550488.pdf?OpenElement

United Nations. (2009, December 9). *Threats to international peace and security caused by terrorist acts - SecCo meeting - Verbatim record (excerpts) - Question of Palestine*. https://www.un.org/unispal/document/auto-insert-184742/

United Nations. General Assembly, 2016(c), United Nations, General Assembly, Human Rights Council, 2017. Retrieved from: https://research.un.org/en/docs/ga/quick/regular/71

United States Mission to the United Nations. (2022, March 14). *Remarks at a UN Security Council Briefing by the Chair of the 1540 Committee on Nonproliferation and Weapons of Mass Destruction United States Mission to the United Nations*. https://usun.usmission.gov/remarks-at-a-un-security-council-briefing-by-the-chair-of-the-1540-committee-on-nonproliferation-and-weapons-of-mass-destruction/

UNSC. (2015, October 13). *Security Council Unanimously Adopts Resolution 2242 (2015) to Improve Implementation of Landmark Text on Women, Peace, Security Agenda.* Retrieved January 10, 2022, from un.org: https://www.un.org/press/en/2015/sc12076.doc.htm

UNSC. (2021). *Twenty-eighth report of the Analytical Support and Sanctions Monitoring Team submitted pursuant to resolution 2368 (2017) concerning ISIL (Da'esh), Al-Qaida and associated individuals and entities.* United Nations Security Coincil.

US Department of Justice. (2022). *Terrorism and hostage negotiations.* Retrieved from: https://www.ojp.gov/ncjrs/virtual-library/abstracts/terrorism-and-hostage-negotiations

US Department of State. (2007). *Office of Coordinator for Counterterrorism.* Retrieved from: https://2001-2009.state.gov/s/ct/info/c16718.htm

US Department of State. (2022). *States Sponsors of Terrorism.* Retrieved from: https://www.state.gov/state-sponsors-of-terrorism/

Veterans for Common Sense. (2008, August 12). *US Takes Georgian Troops Home from Iraq.* Retrieved June 4, 2021, from Veterans for Common Sense: http://veteransforcommonsense.org/2008/08/12/us-takes-georgian-troops-home-from-iraq-2/

Victoroff, J. (2005). The Mind of the Terrorist: A Review and Critique of Psychological Approaches. *The Journal of Conflict Resolution, 49*(1), 3–42. doi:10.1177/0022002704272040

Wæver, O. (1993). *Securitization and desecuritization.* Centre for Peace and Conflict Research.

Walter, B. F. (2009). Bargaining failures and civil war. *Annual Review of Political Science, 12*(1), 243–261. doi:10.1146/annurev.polisci.10.101405.135301

Weinstein, J. (2007). *Inside Rebellion: The Politics of Insurgent Violence.* Cambridge University Press.

Weiss, H. (2015). *ISIS: Inside the Army of Terror.* Regan Arts.

West, J. (2005). Feminist IR and the Case of the "Black Widows": Reproducing Gendered Divisions. *Innovations: Journal of Politics.*

White, S. J. (2017). Assessing Cyber Threats and Solutions for Municipalities. In S. Hakim, E. A. Blackstone, & R. M. Clark (Eds.), Cyber-Physical Security. Protecting Critical Infrastructure at the State and Local Level (pp. 49-67). Springer International Publishing. doi:10.1007/978-3-319-32824-9_3

White, J. (2014). *Military Implications of the Syrian Regime's Defeat in Raqqa.* The Washington Institute for Near East Policy.

Williamson, M. (2009). *Terrorism, war, and international law: the legality of the use of force against Afghanistan in 2001.* Ashgate Publishing.

Williamson, M. (2009). *Terrorism, war, and international law: The legality of the use of force against Afghanistan in 2001.* Ashgate Publishing.

Winter, C. (2018). *ISIS, Women and Jihad: Breaking With Convention.* Tony Blair Institute for Global Change.

Winter, C., & Margolim, D. (2017, August). The Mujahidat Dilemma: Female Combatants and the Islamic State. *The Mujahidat Dilemma: Female Combatants and the Islamic State, 10*(7), 23–27.

Wood, D. (2003). Foucault and Panopticism Revisited Editorial. *Surveillance & Society, 1*(3), 243–239.

World History Encyclopedia. (2022). *Zealots.* Retrieved from: https://www.worldhistory.org/Zealots/

Yablonsky, L. (1996). *Terrorism Psychology*. North-Caucasus State University.

Yamamoto, M. M. (2018). *Terrorism Against Democracy*. Center for International and Security Studies at Maryland.

Yenigün, H. (1996). *The Language of the Media*. Der Publications.

Yılmaz, E. (2008). *On the Relations of Cinema and Ideology*. Orient Publishing.

Zedalis, D. D. (2004). *Female Suicide Bombers*. The Strutegic Studies Institute. doi:10.21236/ADA424180

Zeiger, N. C., & Bhulai, R. (2016). Conclusion: Program and Policy Recommendations. In A Man's World? Exploring the Roles of Women in Counter Terrorism and Violent Extremism (pp. 181-183). Hedayah and The Global Center on Cooperative Security.

About the Contributors

Nika Chitadze is a specialist in Caucasus geopolitics, World Politics and strategic affairs. He is currently the Professor at the Faculty of Social Sciences at the International Black Sea University and visited Professor at the European University and Caucasus International University in Tbilisi, Georgia. He is Director of the Center of International Studies at the International Black Sea University, also President of the George C. Marshall Alumni Union, Georgia – International and Security Research Center. Dr. Chitadze previously served as senior advisor on the National Security Council of Georgia and was Head of the Public Relations Division of the State Agency for Regulation of Oil and Gas Resources of Georgia. He has also held senior positions in the Department of Strategic and Military Policy at the Georgian Ministry of Defense and foreign policy research and analysis center of the Ministry of Foreign Affairs. Dr. Chitadze has received his educational credentials in Georgia (Tbilisi State University and Diplomatic Academy of Georgia) as well as several international higher educational institutions, including Oxford University in the UK, George C. Marshall European College for Security Studies (Germany) and several other well-known European educational institutions. He is the author of about 230 researches and articles and six books on Geopolitics, World Geography and International Relations.

* * *

Mukesh Shankar Bharti is a research scholar with a research background in foreign policy analysis and social science research. The author holds a PhD degree in International Relations with a specialization in East and Central Europe. His research area includes democracy, political institutions, European Union, and South Asia.

Valeria Gonitashvili studied at the Yalta Educational and Auxiliary Complex No. 1 "SchoolCollegium" of the Yalta City Council of the Autonomous Republic of Crimea, Ukraine. She is graduated from International Black Sea University in Tbilisi, Georgia. Later She continued her study at the University of Lodz, Poland. Now she is involved at the MA Program of Eurasian and Caucasus Studies (English-language program) at the Ivane Javakhishvili Tbilisi State University. She works at the Ukrainian Youth Organization of Georgia. "Svitanok" - a member of the diaspora of Ukrainians in Tbilisi, regional manager, in charge of the organization of forums. Valeria is the author of several articles in the field of political sciences and international relations.

Gurami Jajanidze is a Project Coordinator at Europe-Georgia Institute and a founding member at Association of European Initiators.

Irakli Kervalishvili got his Bachelor's Degree in Economics and Business (Business Administration) at the Ivane Javakhishvili Tbilisi State University (Georgia). Master Degree in the field: Exact and Natural Sciences (Information Technologies) at the Ivane Javakhishvili Tbilisi State University (Gerogia) and Master Degree at Computing Engineering (Applied Information Systems) at the University of West Attica (Greece) He is Ph.D. Candidate at Informatics and Control Systems (Control Systems, Automation and Test Engineering) | at the Georgian Technical University.

Mary Tseruashvili graduated from International Black Sea University in 2020. Bachelor's degree in Social Sciences, majoring in International Relations. In 2019, studied Social Sciences at Vilnius SA University, Lithuania as an Exchange Program student. Currently, working as an Invited Specialist at Ilia State University, Foreign Relations Office. In addition, a research fellow at George C. Marshall Alumni Union, Georgia-International and Security Research Center and the Center for International Studies. Tbilisi, Georgia.

Pelin Yolcu graduated from the Faculty of Communication at Selcuk University in 2006. In 2010, the scientist received the title of doctor in 2020. Communication studies, digital communication, social media, cinema, new communication technologies, cinema, filmmakers, film analysis are among the author's fields of work. The author still works at Dicle University in Turkey.

Index

A

Act of Terrorism 8, 18, 28, 32, 52, 57, 59, 62-64, 122, 132
Armed Attacks and Assassinations 15, 24
Asymmetric Warfare 36, 262
Atrocities 2, 94, 117, 150, 160, 162, 177, 183, 186-187, 189
August 23, 30, 63, 65, 147, 154, 160, 165, 167, 170, 176-177, 181, 183-185, 188-189, 191, 194-197, 199, 204-205, 222, 242, 248-249, 286

B

Bombings 15, 23, 25, 28, 32, 34, 57, 59, 112, 142

C

Chinese "Triads" 293, 299
Cinema 217-220, 223-224, 227-229
Civil Wars 36
Cold War 6, 22, 33, 162, 165-166, 171, 175, 217-218, 221-223, 226-230, 270
Colombian Drug Cartels 293, 299
Combating Terrorism 11, 19, 29, 69, 76, 83, 231-232, 235
Conflict 19-21, 31, 35-36, 42-43, 53, 65-67, 71-72, 74, 79, 82, 91, 96, 98, 100, 110, 112, 116, 118, 143-144, 146, 160-161, 163, 165-166, 168, 170-173, 175, 177, 179-181, 183-184, 187-188, 190, 195, 201-203, 207, 223, 226, 230, 232, 237, 244, 249, 255, 257-258, 262, 265-266, 277, 282-286, 289
Counter Terrorism 69, 77, 202, 207-208, 210-212, 214-216, 232, 237, 243, 286
Counter-Terrorism Strategies 268-269, 279-281
Crimes 10-11, 36, 41-42, 46, 57, 76, 83-84, 86, 142-143, 151-152, 159-160, 183, 185-187, 189, 194, 196, 207, 213, 232-233, 235, 237, 243-244, 280, 290-291, 294-297, 299
Crimes Against Humanity 36, 57, 159, 237
Criminal Organization 215, 288, 290, 292, 294, 299
Crisis 4, 8, 12, 30, 34, 36, 38, 41, 48, 52, 90, 108, 149-150, 158, 171, 177, 187, 199, 202-203, 212, 222, 258, 274, 280, 294
Cyber Attack 1, 253, 255
Cyber Security 1, 253, 258-261, 263-266
Cyber Terrorism 26, 253, 295
Cyber Warfare 1, 253, 263
Cyberspace 36, 176, 224, 254, 257-265

D

Donetsk 160, 164-166, 171-173, 178, 181, 183

E

Eastern Bloc 217, 222, 230
Ethnic Cleansing 28, 36, 159, 177, 181, 183-184

F

Fascism 136, 152, 156
February 93, 113-114, 143, 156, 161-162, 168, 171, 181, 183, 186-187, 189, 195-199, 260, 284

G

Gender Norms 267, 269-271, 276, 278, 281
Genocide 36, 38, 113, 137, 152-154, 159-160, 176-177, 181, 183, 187, 189, 198-199, 237
Georgia 1, 15, 28, 37, 69, 89, 122, 136, 146, 160-178, 180-185, 187-190, 194-198, 201, 231, 253, 258, 267, 288, 291
Global Security 37, 64-65, 119, 216, 234, 253, 258, 263

H

Hostages 4, 18, 24-26, 59, 69-70, 73, 77, 89, 94, 97, 123-126, 129-130, 132-134, 150, 201-207, 209-

210, 212-215, 235-236, 288, 293

I

Ideology 5, 21, 23, 33, 40-41, 43, 48, 52, 71, 73, 76-77, 80, 82-83, 85-86, 94-95, 98, 100, 102-105, 110, 112-113, 115-117, 137-138, 152-153, 215, 217-220, 222-223, 227-229, 265, 268, 273, 275-279, 282-283
Info War-Tactics 36
Information Warfare 36, 171, 197, 223, 263-264
International Aggression 36
International Law 7, 10, 13, 27, 35, 44, 81, 142, 157-158, 184, 215, 231-237, 239-240, 243-245, 247, 249-252, 265
International Terrorism 2, 5, 8, 11, 14, 17-18, 29, 33, 36, 39-40, 43-44, 55, 76, 78-79, 145-146, 159, 238, 240, 252, 263, 272
ISIS 30, 33, 62, 89-91, 93-106, 111-120, 138, 238, 257, 267-286
ISIS Female Recruits 269, 277-279
Islamic State 16, 30-31, 35, 38, 43, 89-90, 92-99, 101-105, 111-120, 257, 267-278, 280-283, 285-286
Islamic State of IRAQ and Syria 89
Italian Mafia 292-293, 299

J

Japanese "Yakuza" 299

K

Kidnappings and Hostage-Takings 15, 23

L

Luhansk 160, 164-166, 171-173, 178, 181, 183

M

Militarism 136, 152
Military Jihad 267-269, 272, 275-276, 281
Murder 26, 43, 59, 89, 106, 114, 136, 147, 154, 186-187, 203, 210

N

National and International Community 57
National Security 37, 44, 55, 174, 217-218, 246, 250, 254-255, 257, 261, 263, 265, 272, 294
Negotiation 36, 60, 170, 201-203, 207-216, 249

O

Organized Crime 41, 139-140, 255, 288-299

P

Peace and Security 9, 11, 38, 57-65, 67, 234, 238, 273
Peace Settlements 57
Police State 28, 136-137, 144-145
Political Terrorism 5, 13, 15, 21, 26, 33, 40, 67, 77, 81
Politics and Policy 57
Proliferation 36, 239
Propaganda 7-8, 10, 12, 21, 30, 32, 75-76, 83, 86, 96, 138, 161, 172, 174, 176-177, 217, 219-220, 223-224, 227-229, 255, 263, 268, 271, 273-277, 279-280
Psycho Types 69, 72
Psychology 4-5, 15, 37-39, 44-46, 48, 52-53, 55-56, 65, 67, 69-71, 80-81, 87-88, 120, 123, 125, 201-202, 204, 209, 216

R

Radicalization 2, 37, 87-88, 107-110, 116, 267-271, 274-275, 279-282, 285, 287
Red Terror 136, 148, 150-152, 158
Russia 3, 16, 21, 28, 46, 55, 90, 95, 117, 144, 147-149, 151-152, 158, 160-185, 187-190, 194-200, 220-221, 225-226, 254, 258-259, 261-262, 265-266, 292

S

Security Environment 267, 269-270, 272, 274
Smart Bombs 36
Social Psychological Factors 88
Social Psychology of Terrorism 69, 87-88
Sociology 38, 69, 218
State Terrorism 16-17, 26-28, 35, 43, 77, 79, 136-137, 148, 156-157, 159-160
State-Sponsored Terrorism 27, 29, 157, 159, 273
Stockholm Syndrome 124-125, 129, 132-133, 201, 204-207, 210, 216
Superpowers 16, 22, 35, 217-218, 221-223, 228
Syndrome 69, 72, 124-127, 129, 132-133, 201, 204-207, 210, 216

T

Terror 2-3, 5-6, 13, 15, 19-23, 26-29, 32-33, 35, 37-39, 42-43, 47-49, 51, 56, 59, 61-62, 64, 66-67, 70, 73,

78-79, 99-100, 110, 119-120, 122-123, 132-133, 136, 139, 148-152, 155-158, 180, 206, 228, 267, 269-270, 272-273, 279, 281-285, 288
Terrorism 1-30, 32-50, 52-53, 55-67, 69-90, 92, 106-107, 110, 115, 118, 122, 125-126, 131-143, 145-149, 156-160, 173, 202, 205, 207-208, 210-216, 231-248, 251-254, 263, 265, 267, 269-275, 278-279, 282-288, 290, 295
Terrorist Activity 7, 10, 39-40, 44, 52-54, 75, 85-86, 122, 133, 146, 234
Terrorist Groups 3-6, 10-13, 15-18, 20, 22-23, 25, 29-30, 33, 37, 39, 42-43, 46, 48, 52-54, 59-64, 70-71, 78, 115, 136, 140-141, 143, 145-147, 159, 235, 271, 273, 275, 299
Terrorists 4-6, 8, 11-12, 15-21, 23-25, 27, 29-30, 32-35, 37, 40-56, 59-61, 63-66, 69-73, 78-82, 85, 87-89, 96, 101, 103, 111, 116, 118, 122-126, 129-130, 132-134, 138-139, 141, 146-148, 201-202, 205-207, 209-216, 227, 250, 255, 267, 269, 272-273, 278-279, 283-284, 286
Transnational Organized Crime (TOC) 294, 299
Types of Terrorism 4-6, 12, 26, 33, 37-38, 40-41, 56, 76-78, 80

U

Ukraine 16, 28, 95, 117, 147, 160-166, 170-183, 186-190, 194-199, 258
UN Resolutions 231

V

Victims 11, 15, 17, 19-20, 24-25, 28, 32, 48, 51, 55, 62, 70, 72, 77-79, 122-128, 131-135, 147, 150-154, 176, 198, 206-207, 210, 215, 242, 245, 248-249, 268, 271, 280, 288, 295
Victims of Terrorism 62, 122, 125-126, 131, 133-135
Violence 2-3, 5, 9, 11, 13, 19-23, 25, 27, 32-34, 36-39, 41-43, 45, 48, 51-52, 54, 56-57, 59-61, 67-68, 70, 73-75, 77-78, 81-83, 86, 88-89, 95, 98, 110, 112-113, 117-118, 122, 125, 133-136, 148-149, 151, 157-159, 186, 203-205, 214-216, 223, 228, 252, 254, 268-269, 271, 275-278, 281-283, 285, 287-288, 295-296, 299
Violent Extremism 13, 62, 87, 108, 232, 240, 267, 269, 271, 276, 279-281, 284-287

W

War 4, 6, 20, 22, 27-30, 32-36, 63, 66-68, 72, 74, 79, 81, 91-93, 96, 98, 100-104, 106, 110, 112, 115-116, 119-120, 123, 146, 148-153, 155-166, 168, 170-173, 175-177, 179-190, 194-197, 199, 205, 207, 217-218, 220-231, 248-249, 257-258, 262, 267, 269-270, 272-273, 275, 281-285
Women, Gender, and Terrorism 287
Worldview Terrorism 26, 40

X

Xenophobia 36, 280

www.ingramcontent.com/pod-product-compliance
Lightning Source LLC
LaVergne TN
LVHW060419300926
849162LV00006B/1471